Business & Company Resource Center (BCRC) Exercises

Boone & Kurtz keep you up to date and continually interacting with the business world by providing online exercises that point you to current articles located in our BCRC. These exercises ask you to read the articles and answer questions, encouraging you to apply your knowledge of concepts to the ideas discussed in the article. When you purchase *ThomsonNOW* for the Boone & Kurtz text, you will automatically receive access to the BCRC database. View a guided tour of the Business & Company Resource Center at **http://www.gale.com/BusinessRC.**

Introducing – *The Second City* – Boone & Kurtz's New Integrated Video Case

It is no wonder why Boone & Kurtz chose *The Second City* to show how business works in the real world. Throughout the text, the new video cases combine the entrepreneurial and creative spirit with which *The Second City* was founded with the reality of a successful working business model. In these videos, you will examine the history of the theater company as well as the successful business practices that have allowed for expansion and growth.

© 2006. THE SECOND CITY, INC. USED WITH PERMISSION.

MOVING FORWARD FASTER

Contemporary Business

12th Edition

David L. Kurtz
Distinguished Professor and
R.A. and Vivian Young Chair
of Business Administration
University of Arkansas

THOMSON
SOUTH-WESTERN

Australia · Brazil · Canada · Mexico · Singapore · Spain · United Kingdom · United States

THOMSON

SOUTH-WESTERN

Contemporary Business, Twelfth Edition

Louis E. Boone and David L. Kurtz

VP/Editorial Director:
Jack W. Calhoun

Publisher:
Neil Marquardt

Acquisitions Editor:
Erin Joyner

Senior Developmental Editor:
Rebecca von Gillern

Marketing Manager:
Kimberly Kanakes

Marketing Communications Manager:
Sarah Greber

Content Project Manager:
Amy Hackett

Manager of Technology, Editorial:
Vicky True

Technology Project Manager:
Kristen Meere

Senior Manufacturing Coordinator:
Diane Gibbons

Production House:
Lachina Publishing Services, Inc.

Printer:
RR Donnelley
Willard Manufacturing Division

Art Director:
Stacy Jenkins Shirley

Internal and Cover Designer:
Mike Stratton

Cover Image:
© Getty Images/Michael Stratton

Photography Manager:
John Hill

Photo Researcher:
Seidel Associates

Library of Congress Control Number:
2006934271

For more information about our products, contact us at:
Thomson Learning Academic Resource Center
1–800–423–0563

Thomson Higher Education
5191 Natorp Boulevard
Mason, OH 45040
USA

Moving Business Forward...*Faster*

MOVING

FORWARD

FASTER

Contemporary Business is moving forward faster, making Boone &

Kurtz still the most current and comprehensive text and package on the

market! This edition is packed with resources that will help YOU move

forward into the world of business! The authors have incorporated a new

business case throughout the text, focusing on *The Second City*, a world-

renowned comedy troupe that launched such stars as Bill Murray, Chris

Farley, Tina Fey, Stephen Colbert, and Steve Carell. Not only that, this

edition offers you more ways to learn about the different aspects of business

through a variety of study materials including *ThomsonNOW*™ and the

Business & Company Resource Center (BCRC)!

For YOU, the Student – You will benefit from using *ThomsonNOW* as you determine how you learn material most efficiently and study the concepts you have not mastered through a personalized learning path. And, with the Business & Company Resource Center, you can read relevant and exciting articles that will keep you interested in important business concepts.

For YOUR Instructor – Boone & Kurtz can help your instructor move forward faster while he or she prepares for and teaches your course. Our new *ThomsonNOW* integrated homework system helps instructors plan, manage, teach, and grade assignments faster than ever before!

Moving Forward Faster in the Business World
Throughout the 12th edition, you will find this small icon of a businessperson. This icon moves through the book with you, representing today's businessperson on the move in our fast-paced business world, just as you will be better prepared to move forward faster into the business world after using Boone & Kurtz.

New Features to Keep YOU Moving Forward... Faster

ThomsonNOW™ for Contemporary Business 12e

ThomsonNOW is a completely online product that is comprised of *prepopulated* homework, assessments with a personalized learning path, an *eBook*, and other learning resources. When you purchase *ThomsonNOW* for the 12th edition, you automatically receive access to the Business & Company Resource Center (BCRC) database. In addition to questions about articles in the BCRC, *ThomsonNOW* includes a set of comprehensive questions that help you test your knowledge of chapter concepts.

Business & Company Resource Center (BCRC)

Included with your purchase of *ThomsonNOW* for *Contemporary Business 12e* is access to the BCRC. BCRC allows you to research company histories, articles, industry data, company financials, and much more. Boone & Kurtz keep you up to date and continually interacting with the business world by providing online exercises in *ThomsonNOW* that point you to current articles located in the BCRC.

The Second City – Continuing Video Cases

It's no wonder why Boone & Kurtz chose *The Second City* to show how business works in the real world. "The modern purveyors of sketch and improvisational comedy, including SNL, SCTV, and MADTV, all owe a debt to *The Second City*. After 45 years of being one of Chicago's most enduring comedy institutions their members have grown up to be some of the top names in American Comedy." Throughout the text, new video cases illustrate how the entrepreneurial and creative spirit of *The Second City* exemplifies the best of modern business practices.

Assessment Checks – Found at the end of each section, these quick questions allow you to check your knowledge of the chapter material before continuing on to the next topic.

Project and Teamwork Applications – Designed to be a more in-depth learning experience, many of these exercises can be used to promote team building.

Launching Your Business Career – This brand-new feature, which can be found at the end of each Part, gives you an understanding of all the many different jobs that are a part of each function in a business – and the job path that you may take from entry-level positions to high-level management positions in each of these functional areas. At the end of each of these features are Career Assessment Exercises and projects that help you gauge your interest in and natural predisposition for certain careers.

Audio CDs – Included with every purchase of a new copy of the 12th edition are the ever-popular audio chapter review CDs. These CDs give you a quick overview of the main chapter concepts, allowing you to review in the car, on foot, at the gym—anywhere! These audio chapter reviews will also be available for download within the *ThomsonNOW* product.

Introducing – *The Second City* **– Boone/Kurtz's New Integrated Company**

"The modern purveyors of sketch and improvisational comedy, including SNL, SCTV, and MADTV, all owe a debt to *The Second City*. After 45 years of being one of Chicago's most enduring comedy institutions their members have grown up to be some of the top names in American Comedy: John Belushi, Bill Murray, Betty Thomas, Alan Arkin, Tina Fey, Chris Farley, Bonnie Hunt, Steve Carell, and Stephen Colbert, just to name a few."

"*The Second City* also has touring troupes that take our shows on the road, a Training Center that teaches improvisation, acting, writing, and other skills, and a corporate communications division that services the business world."

It is no wonder why Boone & Kurtz chose *The Second City* to show how business works in the real world. Throughout the text, the new video cases combine the entrepreneurial and creative spirit with which *The Second City* was founded with the reality of a successful working business model. In these videos you will examine the history of the theater company as well as the successful business practices that have allowed for expansion and growth.

The Second City

ThomsonNOW™ for Boone/Kurtz's Contemporary Business 12e

Designed BY instructors and students FOR instructors and students, *ThomsonNOW* for Boone & Kurtz's *Contemporary Business 12e* gives you what you want to do, how you want to do it. From extra practice questions to a personalized learning path that helps you study the way you learn best... *ThomsonNOW* delivers!

Access to a Unique Database – When you purchase *ThomsonNOW* for the Boone & Kurtz text, you will automatically receive access to the BCRC database. This access allows you to apply concepts to real business articles while also opening up a database in which you can research company histories, articles, industry data, company financials, and more!

Efficient Paths to Success – *ThomsonNOW* gives you a personalized learning path that helps you focus on what you still need to learn, as well as the opportunity to select activities, videos, animations, web links, text pages, and audio lectures that best match your learning style.

Delivering the Results You Deserve – Students like you report that they do better on exams and come to class better prepared when using *ThomsonNOW*. They also feel they are studying more efficiently and feel more confident taking exams. And both instructors and students report that *ThomsonNOW* gets them the results they want FAST.

To get started with *ThomsonNOW*, log in at **www.thomsonedu.com/login** or if you need to purchase access, go to **www.ichapters.com**.

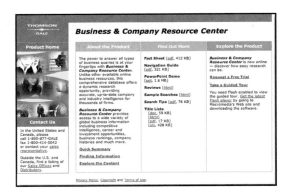

Business & Company Resource Center (BCRC) Exercises

Boone & Kurtz keep you up to date and continually interacting with the business world by providing online exercises that point to current articles located in our BCRC. These exercises ask you to read the articles and answer questions, encouraging you to apply your knowledge of concepts to the ideas discussed in the article. When you purchase *ThomsonNOW* for the Boone & Kurtz text, you will automatically receive access to the BCRC database. This access allows you to apply concepts to real business articles while also opening up a database in which you can research a wide variety of global business information, including competitive intelligence, career and investment opportunities, business rankings, company histories, and much more. View a guided tour of the Business & Company Resource Center at **http://www.gale.com/BusinessRC**.

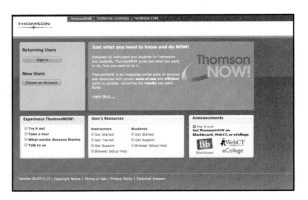

Preface

Boone & Kurtz . . . continuing a legacy of excellence and MOVING BUSINESS FORWARD FASTER!

A part of every business is change; now more than ever, business moves at a pace that is unparalleled. Just like the ever-changing business world, so are there changes in the process of writing a textbook. This 12th edition of *Contemporary Business* is the first edition written without the collaboration of my longtime co-author, Louis E. (Gene) Boone. As with every good business, though, the patterns of innovation and excellence established at the beginning remain steadfast. The goals and standards of Boone & Kurtz, *Contemporary Business,* remain intact and focused on excellence, as always. I present to you a text and supplement package that will not only move your COURSE FORWARD FASTER but also move your STUDENTS FORWARD FASTER into the new business era.

Moving instructors forward . . . faster. This new edition's supplement package is designed to propel the instructor into the classroom with all the materials needed to engage students and help them understand text concepts. All the major teaching materials have been combined into one resource—the Instructor's Manual. While this might not sound revolutionary, good businesses know that the heart of the business is in its ability to keep track of all of its units. In the same way, our new Instructor's Manual combines all of the most important teaching materials into one stellar item. We've included collaborative learning exercises directly in the lecture outlines, so you'll know best where to use them. We've also included references to the Power-Point slides throughout the lecture notes for your convenience. The Second City Theater, Inc., our brand-new continuing case, is highlighted in all-new part videos, while chapter videos showcase a stellar list of companies, including standard-bearers such as BP Oil Company and companies doing business with a brand new set of ideals such as American Apparel. We've heard your appreciation for our PowerPoint presentations and have gone one step further: the PowerPoint presentations for this edition are tailored to meet the needs of all instructors, offering three versions: our Expanded collection, the Basic collection, and a student version available on our Web site. In addition, our new certified test bank, verified separately by two different sources, gives instructors that extra edge needed to drive home key concepts and ignite critical thinking, as well as confidence and assurance when creating and issuing tests. We also listened to your feedback and have incorporated more material on the business plan within the ThomsonNOW product. Past users will note that the new edition is less theme driven and designed to emphasize the very best concepts in the business world today.

Moving students forward . . . faster. With *contemporary* being the operative word, we've showcased a new, exciting company, The Second City Theater, Inc., a comedy corporation that has produced stars of *Saturday Night Live* and other comedy venues, such as John Belushi and Tina Fey—a company that students can really finding interesting! As always, every chapter is loaded with up-to-the-minute business issues and examples to enliven classroom discussion and debate, such as how Jones Soda is rebuilding and reorganizing its business as well as a completely new discussion on the Central American Free Trade Agreement (CAFTA), which President Bush signed in 2005. Processes, strategies, and procedures are brought to life through videos highlighting real companies and employees, an inventive business model, and collaborative learning exercises. And to further enhance the student learning process, we've developed an Introduction to Business–focused technology product, ThomsonNOW, that integrates personalized learning along with a research database of articles.

HOW BOONE & KURTZ BECAME THE LEADING BRAND IN THE MARKET

For more than three decades, *Contemporary Business* has provided the latest in content and pedagogy. Our *current* editions have long been the model for our competitors' *next* editions. Consider Boone & Kurtz's proven record of providing instructors and students with pedagogical firsts:

- *Contemporary Business* was the first introductory business text written specifically for the student—rather than the instructor—featuring a motivational style students readily understood and enjoyed.
- *Contemporary Business* has always been based on marketing research, written the way instructors actually teach the course.
- *Contemporary Business* was the first text to integrate computer applications—and later, Internet assignments—into each chapter.
- *Contemporary Business* has always employed extensive pedagogy—such as opening vignettes and boxed features—to breathe life into the exciting concepts and issues facing contemporary business.
- *Contemporary Business* was the first business text to offer end-of-chapter video cases as well as end-of-part cases filmed by professional producers.
- *Contemporary Business* was the first to use multimedia technology to integrate all components of the Introduction to Business ancillary program, videos, and PowerPoint CD-ROMs for both instructors and students—enabling instructors to custom-create lively lecture presentations.

Pedagogy

The 12th edition is packed with new pedagogical features to keep students interested and bring the text topics to life:

- Business Etiquette: The 12th edition contains a new box feature focusing on business etiquette, addressing the trend of more and more schools to add business etiquette to the curriculum.
- Assessment Checks: In every business department in the country, assessment and assurance of learning among students has become increasingly important. As a result, we've provided you with assessment checks after every main head in every chapter.
- New End-of-Chapter Self-Quizzes: In addition to ensuring that students are learning throughout the chapter, we've taken assessment one step further by incorporating new end-of-chapter self-quizzes called Review Questions. These questions are designed to quickly assess whether students understand the basic concepts in the chapter.
- Teamwork: Teamwork is at the core of every modern business's success, and today's student needs to be well trained on working in a team. To further prepare students to enter business and MOVE FORWARD FASTER, we've incorporated new teamwork exercises at the end of each chapter.
- NEW Launching Your Career: While students often have an amazing ability to understand chapter concepts and intellectually understand business and what a business career entails, they are very often unprepared to take the next step and understand in a real-life sense what a career in each aspect of business may involve. We've added a brand-new feature at the end of each part of the book that helps students understand how to launch a real business career for themselves.

Continuing to Build the Boone & Kurtz Brand

Because the business world is constantly MOVING FORWARD FASTER, the Introduction to Business course must keep pace. Trends, strategies, and practices are constantly changing, and students must understand how to perform business in today's world.

You've come to trust *Contemporary Business* to cover every aspect of the business world with a critical but fair eye. Let's face it: there are best business practices and those we'd never want to repeat. However, both provide learning opportunities and we've always chosen to take a critical look at the way business is being done in the world and help students understand what they need to know in order to have a long and illustrious business career. Keeping this in mind, here are just a few of the important business trends and practices we've focused on for this new edition to help move students forward into a great business career:

- Launching Your Business Career (section preceding Chapter 1): This popular Boone & Kurtz feature has been revised to rely less on annual salary data than in the past, and instead concentrate on the lifetime value of education. Students in Introduction to Business courses must keep up with the newest trends and shifts in career fields. The 12th edition of *Contemporary Business* helps them answer the question, "Where do I fit in the business world?"
- Chapter 1 now includes information on outsourcing, offshoring, and nearshoring as a part of the discussion on the framework of business today.
- The discussion on business ethics in Chapter 2 has been completely reworked to provide a more relevant explanation of how businesses and individuals incorporate their beliefs and standards into everyday business as well as how the Sarbanes-Oxley Act is changing the very essence of reporting.
- International fiscal policy is a new concept for Chapter 3, which also explains the core inflation rate.
- CAFTA and the so-called Doha Round of trade negotiations are now discussed in Chapter 4.
- A discussion of college-based entrepreneurship programs has been added in Chapter 6.
- Given that today's students have grown up with the Internet, Chapter 7 has been substantially revised and now focuses on the business function of the Internet.
- Chapter 9 includes new coverage of cognitive ability tests, family-friendly benefits, and dependent-care spending as well as a new section on goal-setting theory and new information on the federal government's Pension Benefit Guaranty Corporation.
- Chapter 10 now covers problem-solving teams, action learning teams, team level, team diversity, cognitive conflict, and affective conflict and has a new section on crisis management, including the steps companies and managers should take when dealing with a public crisis regarding their organization.
- Chapter 11 now includes an explanation of the six-sigma concept.
- Chapter 12 includes the American Marketing Association's new definition of *marketing* and a short discussion of why the definition was changed.
- More in-depth coverage of the importance of good credit management, including the pros and cons of student loan consolidation, has been included in the personal finance appendix.

The Second City Theater, Inc. Continuing Video Case

Almost no business started in 1959 can still say today that it moves business forward in a new and different way each day. You've come to expect only the best from us in choosing our continuing video case company, and we've taken it one step further with our new choice. No other company combines Second City Theater's unique brand of social and political satire with successful and proven business practices in the same way that has helped The Second City grow from a small but successful comedy troupe into a large international business. With several theaters in two countries, troupes performing every day all over the world, and performances on international cruise lines, The Second City has found a way to turn comedy into business—and in the process they've had fun! Students and instructors alike know and love many of the famous faces that started performing at Second City—John Belushi, Dan Aykroyd, John Candy, Gilda Radner, Chris Farley, Tina Fey, and the list goes on and on. But how many students realize just how important good business practices are in keeping a comedy business that started in 1959 thriving and growing all the way into 2007 and beyond? We've focused on all the aspects of The Second City Theater's business that students need to know in a way that's interesting and fun for them to learn. So sit back, get some popcorn, and enjoy the show!

Written case segments at the end of each part of the text contain critical-thinking questions designed to provoke discussion and interaction in the classroom setting. Answers to the questions can be found in the Instructor's Manual, as can a complete video synopsis, a list of text concepts covered in the videos, and even more critical-thinking exercises.

End-of-Chapter Video Cases

In addition to a stellar new continuing video case, we've also produced a whole new batch of video cases for each and every chapter, designed to exceed your every expectation. Students need to know the basics about life in the real world of business and how businesses succeed and grow, but they don't need a bunch of talking heads putting them to sleep. So while we admit that you will indeed see a few talking heads—they're just there because they really do know what they're talking about—they have something important for students to hear. But do trust us . . . the videos we've created for this new edition of *Contemporary Business* contain so much more!

A complete set of written cases accompanies these chapter videos and can be found in the end-of-book video case appendix. The written segments contain discussion questions. As with the Second City cases, answers to the questions can be found in the Instructor's Manual, as can a complete video synopsis, a list of text concepts covered in the videos, and even more critical-thinking exercises. The video cases are as follows:

Chapter 1: Peet's Coffee & Tea Brews Good Business
Chapter 2: Ford Turns Green with Clean Energy
Chapter 3: BP Meets Global Energy Challenges Head-On
Chapter 4: Cold Stone Creamery Cools off Consumers around the World
Chapter 5: The UL Mark of Approval
Chapter 6: Culver's: Great Food from a Good Business
Chapter 7: Manifest Digital: Putting the User First
Chapter 8: Made in the USA: American Apparel
Chapter 9: Allstate Employees Are in Good Hands
Chapter 10: Meet the People of BP
Chapter 11: Washburn Guitars: Sound Since 1883
Chapter 12: Harley-Davidson: An American Icon Cruises into Its Second Century
Chapter 13: High Sierra Climbs to New Heights
Chapter 14: Wild Oats Promotes Local Foods
Chapter 15: Peet's Coffee & Tea: Just What the Customer Ordered
Chapter 16: Taking Account: The Little Guys
Chapter 17: JPMorganChase Lends a Hand to Small Business
Chapter 18: A.G. Edwards: Helping Business Grow

THE CONTEMPORARY BUSINESS RESOURCE PACKAGE

Since the first edition of this book was published, Boone & Kurtz has exceeded the expectations of instructors, and it quickly became the benchmark for other texts. With its precedent-setting learning materials, *Contemporary Business* has continued to improve on its signature package features—equipping students and instructors with the most comprehensive collection of learning tools, teaching materials, and innovative resources available. As expected, the 12th edition continues to serve as the industry benchmark by delivering the most extensive, technologically advanced, user-friendly package on the market.

For the Instructor

ThomsonNOW (ISBN: 0–324–53974–6) Designed *by* instructors and students *for* instructors and students, ThomsonNOW gives you what you want to do, how you want to do it. ThomsonNOW is an integrated online suite of services and resources with proven ease of use and efficient paths to success, delivering the results you want—NOW! ThomsonNOW includes pre-populated homework, assessments with a personalized learning path, an e-book, and more. In the new edition of *Contemporary Business,* students will receive access to the Business Company and Resource Center automatically with their ThomsonNOW product, allowing them to answer homework questions and conduct research for their own projects.

Instructor's Manual with Collaborative Learning Exercises and Media Guide (ISBN: 0–324–53664–X) The 12th edition of *Contemporary Business* has a new, extremely easy-to-use Instructor's Manual. This valuable tool completely integrates the various supplements and the text. A detailed lecture outline provides guidance about how to teach the chapter concepts. Collaborative learning exercises are included for each chapter, which give students a completely different way to apply chapter concepts to their own lives. References to the PowerPoint slides are included in the chapter outline. You'll also find answers to all of the end-of-chapter materials and various critical-thinking exercises. Full descriptions of the ThomsonNOW product and BCRC exercises can be found in the Media Guide along with complete video synopses, outlines, and extra questions.

Chapter Video Cases on DVD (ISBN: 0–324–53659–3) New end-of-chapter video cases for every chapter of the text focus on successful real companies' processes, strategies, and procedures. Real employees explain real business situations with which they have been faced, bringing key concepts from the chapter to life.

The Second City Theater, Inc. Continuing Case Video on DVD (ISBN: 0–324–53660–7) This brand-new continuing video case combines the entrepreneurial and creative spirit with which Second City was founded with the reality of a successful working business model. Rarely has a creative enterprise so uniquely brought real business savvy to its success. In these videos, we examine the history of the theater company as well as the successful business practices that have allowed for its expansion and growth. The written and video cases are divided into seven sections and are created to be used at the end of each part of the text.

Test Bank (ISBN: 0–324–53665–8) Containing more than 4,000 questions, this is the most accurate test bank we've had in years. For the first time we've put our test bank through a complete verification process. Every question and answer has been read and reviewed for correctness. Each chapter of the test bank is organized by chapter objective, and each question is categorized by difficulty level, type of question, and text page reference, and has also been tagged for AACSB requirements.

Basic and Expanded PowerPoint Presentations on CD (ISBN: 0–324–53662–3)
After reviewing competitive offerings, we are convinced that our PowerPoint presentations are the best you'll find. We offer two separate collections. The Basic PowerPoint collection contains 10 to 20 slides per chapter. This collection provides a basic outline of the chapter, with Web links that are used to bring chapter concepts to life. The Basic collection includes figures and tables from each chapter as well as teaching notes for instructors in the "Notes" view. The Expanded PowerPoint collection includes 20 to 40 slides per chapter and provides a complete overview of the chapter. The Expanded collection includes figures and tables from each chapter, Web links, video links, and teaching notes for instructors.

Instructor's Resource CD (ISBN: 0–324–53661–5)
The IRCD includes electronic versions of all of the instructor supplements: Instructor's Manual, Collaborative Learning Exercises, Media Guide, Test Bank, and Examview Testing Files and Software.

Examview Testing Software on IRCD (ISBN: 0–324–53663–1)
Examview Testing Software is a Windows-based software program that is both easy to use and attractive. We can say with confidence that this is the most accurate test bank we've had in years because it has been through our certification process and every question and answer has been verified. Each chapter of the test bank is organized by chapter objective, and each question is categorized by difficulty level, type of question, and text page reference, and has also been tagged for AACSB requirements.

Contemporary Business, 12th Edition Web Site
Our text Web site (http://www.thomson edu.com/introbusiness/boone) is filled with a whole set of useful tools. Instructors will find all the key instructor resources in electronic format: Test Bank, Basic PowerPoint Presentations, Instructor's Manual with Collaborative Learning Exercises, Media Guide, and BCRC Exercises. Students will also find a host of valuable resources.

Resource Integration Guide (RIG)
The RIG is written to provide the instructor with a clear and concise layout to all of the ancillaries that accompany the text as well as how best to use these items in teaching an Introduction to Business course. Not only are all of the book's ancillaries organized clearly for you, but we also provide planning suggestions, lecture ideas, and help in creating assignments. This guide will help instructors prepare for teaching the course, execute teaching plans, and evaluate student performance. The RIG can be found on the text Web site (http://www.thomsonedu.com/introbusiness/boone) in the Instructor's Resource section.

For the Student

ThomsonNOW (ISBN: 0–324–53974–6)
Designed *by* instructors and students *for* instructors and students, ThomsonNOW gives you what you want to do, how you want to do it. ThomsonNOW includes pre-populated homework, assessments with a personalized learning path, an e-book, and more. In the new edition of *Contemporary Business,* students will receive access to the Business Company and Resource Center automatically with their ThomsonNOW product, allowing them to answer homework questions and conduct research for their own projects.

Contemporary Business, *12th Edition Web Site* Our text Web site (http://www.thom-sonedu.com/introbusiness/boone) is filled with a whole set of useful tools. Students will find a host of valuable resources, including key terms with definitions, quizzes for each chapter, chapter summaries in both English and Spanish, and recent business news tied directly to chapter concepts.

Chapter Audio Reviews These audio reviews, provided on CD-ROM (and available on the Web site for download) contain short summaries of the chapter objectives and major concepts in each chapter and are a good review of reading assignments. Listen to them before you read the chapter as a preview of what's to come or after you read the chapter as a reinforcement of what you've read. Listen to them on the way to class as a refresher before the lecture or after you've left class as a review of what the instructor just discussed. However you choose to listen to them, these concise summaries will help reinforce all the major concepts for each chapter.

ACKNOWLEDGMENTS

Contemporary Business has long benefited from the instructors who have offered their time as reviewers. Hundreds of people have contributed their suggestions over the years. I am most appreciative of their efforts and thoughts. Previous reviewers have included the following people:

Jamil Ahmad
Los Angeles Trade–Technical College

Sylvia Allen
Los Angeles Valley College

Kenneth F. Anderson
Borough of Manhattan Community College

Andrea Bailey
Moraine Valley Community College

Norman E. Burns
Bergen Community College

Diana Carmel
Golden West College

Barbara Ching
Los Angeles City College

Ron Colley
South Suburban College

Scott Colvin
Naugatuck Community College

Peter Dawson
Collin County Community College

Dr. Richard L. Drury
Northern Virginia Community College

John A. Fawcett
Norwalk Community College

Dr. Barry Freeman
Bergen Community College

Richard Ghidella
Fullerton College

Ross Gittell
University of New Hampshire

Clark Hallpike
Elgin Community College

Carnella Hardin
Glendale College—Arizona

Britt Hastey
Los Angeles City College

Dave Hickman
Frederick Community College

Nathan Himelstein
Essex County College

Scott Homan
Purdue—West Lafayette

Howard L. Irby, Jr.
Bronx Community College

Robert Ironside
North Lake College

Charlotte Jacobsen
Montgomery College

Bruce Johnson
College of the Desert

Judith Jones
Norwalk Community College

Marce Kelly
Santa Monica College

Gregory Kishel
Cypress College—Santa Ana College

Patricia Kishel
Cypress College

Andy Klein
DeVry

Mary Beth Klinger
College of Southern Maryland

John S. Leahy
Palomar College

Delores Linton
Tarrant County College—Northwest Campus

Stacy Martin
Southwestern Illinois College

Theresa Mastrianni
Kingsborough Community College

Bob Matthews
Oakton Community College

Hugh McCabe
Westchester Community College

Tricia McConville
Northeastern University

Rebecca Miles
Delaware Tech

Linda Morable
Richland College

Linda Mosley
Tarrant County College

Carol Murphy
Quinsigamond Community College

Andrew Nelson
Montgomery College

Greg Nesty
Humboldt College

Linda Newell
Saddleback College

Emmanuel Nkwenti
Pennsylvania College of Technology

Paul Okello
Tarrant County College

Lynn D. Pape
Northern Virginia Community College—Alexandria Campus

Charles Pedersen
Quinsigamond Community College

John Pharr
Cedar Valley—Dallas County Community College District

Jeff Podoshen
DeVry

Sally Proffitt
Tarrant County College Northeast

Jude A. Rathburn
University of Wisconsin—Milwaukee

Levi Richard
Citrus College

Joe Ryan
Valley College

Althea Seaborn
Norwalk Community College

John Seilo
Orange Coast Community College

Pat Setlik
Harper College

Richard Sherer
Los Angeles Trade–Technical College

Gerald Silver
Purdue University—Calumet

Leon Singleton
Santa Monica College

Malcolm Skeeter
Norwalk Community College

Robert Smolin
Citrus College

Darrell Thompson
Mountain View College

Sandra Toy
Orange Coast College

Phil Vardiman
Abilene Christian University

Sal Veas
Santa Monica College

Gina Vega
Merrimack College

Michelle Vybiral
Joliet Junior College

Rick Weidmann
Prince George's Community College

S. Martin Welc
Saddleback College

Steve Wong
Rock Valley College

A number of other colleagues at colleges and universities throughout the United States participated in focus group sessions. They provided invaluable recommendations for this new edition. They include the following people:

Greg Akins
Lansing Community College

Ken Anderson
Boro of Manhattan Community College

Nancy Bailey
Middlesex Community College

Mary Barnum
Grand Rapids Community College

Sherry Bell
Ferris State University

Ellen Benowitz
Mercer Community College

Mike Bento
Owens Community College

Pat Bernson
County College of Morris

Trudy Borst
Ferris State University

David Braun
Pierce College

David England
John A. Logan College

Barry Freeman
Bergen Community College

Eric Glohr
Lansing Community College

Karen Hawkins
Miami Dade Community College

Nate Himelstein
Essex Community College

Kim Hurns
Washtenaw Community College

Dmitriy Kalyagin
Chabot College

Elias Konwufine
Keiser College

Carl Kovelowski
Mercer Community College

Pierre Laguerre
Bergen Community College

Stacy Martin
Southwestern Illinois College

Duane Miller
Utah Valley State College

Ed Mitchell
Hillsborough Community College

Frank Novakowski
Davenport University

Tom Passero
Owens Community College

Tom Perkins
Lansing Community College

Robert Reck
Western Michigan University

Paul Ricker
Broward Community College

Jenny Rink
Community College of Philadelphia

Susan Roach
Georgia Southern University

Edith Strickland
Tallahassee Community College

Keith Taylor
Lansing Community College

Joyce Thompson
Lehigh-Carbon Community College

Bob Urell
Irvine Valley College

Richard Warner
Lehigh-Carbon Community College

David Woolgar
Santa Ana College

Chuck Zellerbach
Orange Coast College

Thanks also to all of our colleagues who have assisted us in previous editions in our continuing efforts to make the best business text even better. The new edition continues to reflect so many of their recommendations. Among the hundreds of reviewers and focus group participants who contributed to the book during previous editions, we acknowledge the special contributions of the following people:

Alison Adderly-Pitman
Brevard Community College

David Alexander
Angelo State University

Kenneth Anderson
Mott Community College

Charles Armstrong
Kansas City Kansas Community College

Donald B. Armstrong
Mesa College

Nathaniel Barber
Winthrop University

Alan Bardwick
Community College of Aurora

Keith Batman
Cayuga Community College

Robb Bay
Community College of Southern Nevada

Charles Beem
Bucks County Community College

Carol Bibly
Triton College

Daniel Biddlecom
Erie Community College—North Campus

Joseph Billingere
Oxnard College

Larry Blenke
Sacramento City College

Paula E. Bobrowski
SUNY Oswego

Charlane Bomrad Held
Onandaga Community College

Brenda Bradford
Missouri Baptist College

Steven E. Bradley
Austin Community College

Willie Caldwell
Houston Community College

Barney Carlson
Yuba College

Bonnie Chavez
Santa Barbara City College

Felipe Chia
Harrisburg Area Community College

Rowland Chidomere
Winston-Salem State University

Marie Comstock
Allan Hancock College

Ronald C. Cooley
South Suburban College

Suzanne Counte
Jefferson College

Robert Cox
Salt Lake Community College

Pam Crader
Jefferson College

Norman B. Cregger
Central Michigan University

Dana D'Angelo
Drexel University

Dean Danielson
San Joaquin College

Kathy Daruty
Los Angeles Pierce College

David DeCook
Arapahoe Community College

Richard L. Drury
Northern Virginia Area Community College—Annandale

Linda Durkin
Delaware County Community College

Lance J. Edwards
Otero Junior College

William Ewald
Concordia University

Carol Fasso
Jamestown Community College

Jodson Faurer
Metropolitan State College at Denver

Jan Feldbauer
Austin Community College

Sandie Ferriter
Harford Community College

Steven H. Floyd
Manatee Community College

Nancy M. Fortunato
Bryant and Stratton

John G. Foster Jr.
Montgomery College—Rockville

William D. Foster
Fontbonne College

Blane Franckowiak
Tarrant County Community College

Edward Friese
Okaloosa-Walton Community College

Atlen Gastineau
Valencia Community College—West Campus

Milton Glisson
North Carolina A&T State University

Bob Googins
Shasta Community College

Robert Gora
Catawba Valley Community College

Don Gordon
Illinois Central College

Gary Greene
Manatee Community College

Blaine Greenfield
Bucks County Community College

Stephen W. Griffin
Tarrant County Community College

Maria Carmen Guerrero-Caldero
Oxnard College

Annette L. Halpin
Beaver College

Michael Hamberger
Northern Virginia Area Community College—Annandale

Neal Hannon
Bryant College

Douglas Heeter
Ferris State University

Paul Hegele
Elgin Community College

Chuck Henry
Coastline Community College

Thomas Herbek
Monroe Community College

Tom Heslin
Indiana University, Bloomington

Joseph Ho
College of Alameda

Alice J. Holt
Benedict College

Vince Howe
University of North Carolina, Wilmington

Eva M. Hyatt
Appalachian State University

Kathy Irwin
Catawba Valley Community College

Gloria M. Jackson
San Antonio College

Ralph Jagodka
Mount San Antonio College

Chris Jelepis
Drexel University

Steven R. Jennings
Highland Community College

Geraldine Jolly
Barton College

Dave Jones
LaSalle University

Don Kelley
Francis Marion University

Bill Kindsfather
Tarrant County Community College

Charles C. Kitzmiller
Indian River Community College

B. J. Kohlin
Pasadena City College

Carl Kovelowski
Mercer Community College

Ken Lafave
Mount San Jacinto College

Rex Lambrecht
Northeastern Junior College

Fay D. Lamphear
San Antonio College

Bruce Leppine
Delta College

Thomas Lloyd
Westmoreland County Community College

Jim Locke
Northern Virginia Area Community College—Annandale

Paul Londrigan
Mott Community College

Kathleen J. Lorencz
Oakland County Community College

John Mack
Salem State College

Paul Martin
Aims College

Lori Martynowicz
Bryant and Stratton

Michael Matukonis
SUNY Oneonta

Virginia Mayes
Montgomery College—Germantown

Joseph E. McAloon
Fitchburg State College

James McKee
Champlain College

Michael McLane
University of Texas, San Antonio

Ina Midkiff
Austin Community College

Rebecca Mihelcic
Howard Community College

Richard Miller
Harford Community College

Joseph Mislivec
Central Michigan University

Kimberly K. Montney
Kellogg Community College

Gail Moran
Harper College

Linda S. Munilla
Georgia Southern University

Kenneth R. Nail
Pasco-Hernando Community College

Joe Newton
Buffalo State College

Janet Nichols
Northeastern University

Frank Nickels
Pasco-Hernando Community College

Sharon Nickels
St. Petersburg Junior College

Nnamdi I. Osakwe
Livingstone College

Tibor Osatreicher
Baltimore City Community College

George Otto
Truman College

Thomas Paczkowski
Cayuga Community College

Alton Parish
Tarrant County Community College

Jack Partlow
Northern Virginia Area Community College—Annandale

Jeff Penley
Catawba Valley Community College

Robert Pollero
Anne Arundel Community College

Alton J. Purdy
Solano Community College

Surat P. Puri
Barber Scottia College

Angela Rabatin
Prince George's Community College

Linda Reynolds
Sacramento City College

Brenda Rhodes
Northeastern Junior College

Merle Rhodes
Morgan Community College

Pollis Robertson
Kellogg Community College

Robert Ross
Drexel University

Benjamin Sackmary
Buffalo State College

Catherina A. Sanders
San Antonio College

Lewis Schlossinger
Community College of Aurora

Gene Schneider
Austin Community College

Raymond Shea
Monroe Community College

Nora Jo Sherman
Houston Community College

Leon J. Singleton
Santa Monica College

Jeff Slater
North Shore Community College

Candy Smith
Folsom Lakes College

Solomon A. Solomon
Community College of Rhode Island

R. Southall
Laney College

Martin St. John
Westmoreland County Community College

E. George Stook
Anne Arundel Community College

James B. Stull
San Jose State University

Bill Syverstein
Fresno City College

Thomas Szezurek
Delaware County Community College

Daryl Taylor
Pasadena City College

John H. Teter
St. Petersburg Junior College

Gary Thomas
Anne Arundel Community College

Michael Thomas
Henry Ford Community College

Frank Titlow
St. Petersburg Junior College

Roland Tollefson
Anne Arundel Community College

Sheb True
Loyola Marymount University

Robert Ulbrich
Parkland College

Ariah Ullman
SUNY Binghamton

Sal Veas
Santa Monica College

Steven Wade
Santa Clara University

Dennis Wahler
San Jacinto Evergreen Community College District

W. J. Walters
Central Piedmont Community College

Timothy Weaver
Moorpark College

Richard Wertz
Concordia University

Darcelle D. White
Eastern Michigan University

Jean G. Wicks
Bornie State University

Tom Wiener
Iowa Central Community College

Dave Wiley
Anne Arundel Community College

Richard J. Williams
Santa Clara University

Joyce Wood
Northern Virginia Community College

Gregory Worosz
Schoolcraft College

Martha Zennis
Jamestown Community College

Special Acknowledgment

With Gene Boone's passing, I reached out to two experienced textbook authors for help in getting this edition out on time. I am grateful that Douglas Hearth of the University of Arkansas and Chuck Williams of the University of the Pacific were willing to lend their considerable expertise to this project.

Doug and Chuck have each written their own successful books in finance and management. Their writing and editorial skills blended perfectly with the approach that Gene Boone and I have always employed. I am very appreciative of their efforts.

In Conclusion

I would like to thank Karen Hill of Elm Street Publishing and Katie O'Keeffe-Swank of Lachina Publishing Services. Their unending efforts on behalf of *Contemporary Business* were truly extraordinary.

Let me conclude by noting that this new edition would never have become a reality without the outstanding efforts of the Thomson editorial, production, and marketing teams. My editors Melissa Acuna, Neil Marquardt, Erin Joyner, Rebecca von Gillern, Amy Hackett, and Vicky True produced another *Contemporary Business* winner!

Dave Kurtz

Dave Kurtz

About the Author

During Dave Kurtz's high school days, no one in Salisbury, Maryland, would have mistaken him for a scholar. In fact, he was a mediocre student, so bad that his father steered him toward higher education by finding him a succession of backbreaking summer jobs. Thankfully, most of them have been erased from his memory, but a few linger, including picking peaches, loading watermelons on trucks headed for market, and working as a pipefitter's helper. Unfortunately, these jobs had zero impact on his academic standing. Worse yet for Dave's ego, he was no better than average as a high school athlete in football and track.

But four years at Davis & Elkins College in Elkins, West Virginia, turned him around. Excellent instructors helped get Dave on a sound academic footing. His grade point average soared—enough to get him accepted by the graduate business school at the University of Arkansas, where he met Gene Boone. Gene and Dave became longtime co-authors; together they produced more than 50 books. In addition to writing, Dave and Gene were involved in several entrepreneurial ventures.

Today, Dave is back teaching at the University of Arkansas, after tours of duty in Ypsilanti, Michigan; Seattle, Washington; and Melbourne, Australia. He is the proud grandfather of five "perfect" kids and a sportsman with a golf handicap too high to mention. Dave, his wife, Diane, and four demanding canine companions (Daisy, Lucy, Molly, and Sally) live in Rogers, Arkansas. Dave holds a distinguished professorship at the Sam M. Walton College of Business in nearby Fayetteville, home of the Arkansas Razorbacks.

Brief Contents

Contents

Part 2

Chapter 6

STARTING YOUR OWN BUSINESS: THE ENTREPRENEURSHIP ALTERNATIVE

Part 3

Management: Empowering People to Achieve Business Objectives — 251

Chapter 9

Sidebar (Chapter 8):

Sidebar (Chapter 9):

Chapter 10

IMPROVING PERFORMANCE THROUGH EMPOWERMENT, TEAMWORK, AND COMMUNICATION 318

Chapter 11

PRODUCTION AND OPERATIONS MANAGEMENT 344

Part 4

Marketing Management   377

Chapter 12   CUSTOMER-DRIVEN MARKETING   378

Opening Vignette
Whole Foods Market: A
Whole New Kind of
Grocery Store 379

Hit & Miss
One Company Makes a
Cereal Killing 384

Hit & Miss
Marketers Fall Short
When It Comes to Older
Consumers 395

**Solving an Ethical
Controversy**
Are Gift Cards
Really a Gift? 400

Business Etiquette
Thank-You Notes
Do Count 401

Chapter 13

PRODUCT AND DISTRIBUTION STRATEGIES 408

Chapter 14

PROMOTION AND PRICING STRATEGIES 442

Part 5

Managing Technology and Information
481

Chapter 15

USING TECHNOLOGY TO MANAGE INFORMATION
482

Opening Vignette
Google: How to Succeed
without Really Selling
483

Hit & Miss
How Does Dell
Do It? 490

Hit & Miss
Nobody Does
It Better: Oracle 496

Business Etiquette
When—and How—
to Use Your Computer
at Work 499

Solving an Ethical
Controversy
Does Database
Security Exist? 504

Chapter 1

The Framework of Contemporary Business

Learning Goals

1. Distinguish between business and not-for-profit organizations.

2. Identify and describe the factors of production.

3. Describe the private enterprise system, including basic rights and entrepreneurship.

4. Identify the six eras of business and explain how the relationship era—including alliances and technology—influences contemporary business.

5. Explain how today's business workforce is changing.

6. Describe how the nature of work itself is changing.

7. Identify the skills and attributes that managers need to lead businesses in the 21st century.

8. Outline the characteristics that make a company admired by the business community.

Business in a Global Environment

Part 1

More Career Information on the Contemporary Business Web Site

More career information is available to students using *Contemporary Business* at the following Web site: http://www.swlearning.com/business/boone. The "Management Careers" section on the Web site enables you to learn more about business careers and to locate currently posted job opportunities. The site provides a vast number of career resources such as links to job sites and career guidance sites. Many links include extensive career information and guidance, such as interviewing techniques and tips for résumé writing.

1. Prepare your résumé following the procedures outlined earlier in this section. Ask your instructors, friends, and relatives to critique it. Then revise and proofread it.
2. Talk with someone in your community who is working in a profession that interests you. Write, call, or e-mail to request an appointment. The interview should take no more than 15 to 20 minutes. Come prepared with questions to ask. Report to your class about what you learned.
3. Prepare answers to each of the questions that interviewers most often ask. Discuss your answers in class.
4. Select a partner and take turns interviewing each other for a job in front of the class. Use the interview questions mentioned earlier, and develop two or three of your own. After completing the interviews, ask the class to give you feedback on how you looked and acted during your interview. Would they advise you to do or say anything differently?
5. Pick a Web site dealing with careers. Select an employment field and prepare a report on what you learned from the Web site. What jobs are available? From your perspective, were they in desirable locations? What did these jobs pay? Did the information in the Web site agree or conflict with your initial perceptions of the job?

All of these facts combine to shape a picture of the needs of U.S. society and the workforce available to serve it. As the baby boom generation ages, the United States will need more healthcare services as well as services for the leisure and hospitality industries. We could see the addition of 4.4 million new jobs in healthcare and social assistance fields, along with about 500,000 new positions in leisure and hospitality. Professional and business services are expected to increase nearly 50 percent by 2012, adding 5 million new jobs.[12]

Careers in environmental engineering and science are already hot—and expected to get hotter, as the United States and countries around the world place more emphasis on solving and preventing environmental problems. "We expect the U.S. to start exporting environmental expertise to Europe and Asia, including to emerging markets like India," predicts one industry watcher. Fields that require advanced computer skills such as network systems analysts, personal financial advisors, database administrators, and software engineers are on the rise as well.[13] Registered nurses, postsecondary teachers, retail salespeople, and customer service representatives can expect an increase in opportunities. But farmers and ranchers, word processors, and stock clerks can expect a decline.[14]

As the population changes and technology automates certain tasks or simply alters the way they are accomplished, opportunities will grow or shrink. As you plan your career, it is wise to stay up-to-date on the job market.

A LONG-RANGE VIEW OF YOUR CAREER

As we said earlier, choosing a career is an important life decision. A career is a professional journey—regardless of whether you want to run an art gallery or a branch bank, whether you are fascinated by language or math, whether you prefer to work with animals or people. In the end, you hope to contribute something good to society while enjoying what you do—and make a reasonable living at it.

Dreams. Effort. Opportunity. Passion. Performance. Perserverance. Leadership. Results.

At DuPont, diversity and inclusion are catalysts in science and business growth.

Visit us at dupont.com.

COURTESY OF DUPONT

DUPONT
The miracles of science

©2006. DuPont. All rights reserved. The DuPont Oval Logo, DuPont™, and The miracles of science™ are registered trademarks or trademarks of E. I. duPont deNemours and Company or its affiliates.

Following your dreams can lead you to an exciting career. DuPont looks for a wide variety of people who can contribute to its success while fulfilling theirs.

Throughout your career, it is important to stay flexible and continue learning. Challenging new skills will be required of managers and other businesspeople during these first decades of the 21st century. Remain open to unexpected changes and opportunities that can help you learn and develop new skills. Keep in mind that your first job will not be your last. But tackle that first job with the same enthusiasm you'd have if someone asked you to run the company itself, because everything you learn on that job will be valuable at some point during your career—and someday you may actually run the company.

Finally, if you haven't already started your career search, begin now. Do this by talking with various resources, lining up an internship, looking for a part-time job on or off campus, or volunteering for an organization. Register with the campus career center long before you graduate. Then, when you reach your final semester, you'll be well on your way to beginning the career you want.

We are confident that this textbook will present a panorama of career options for you. Whatever you decide, be sure it is right for you—not your friends, your instructors, or your parents. As the old saying goes, "You pass this way just once." Enjoy the journey!

a phone call, followed by a letter outlining the offer in writing. Whether you receive one offer or several, thank the person making the offer. If you choose to accept immediately, feel free to do so. If you have doubts about the job or need to decide between two, it is appropriate to ask for 24 hours to respond. If you must decline an offer, do so promptly and politely. After all, you may end up working for that firm sometime in the future. If you get a few rejections before you receive an offer, don't give up. Every application and interview adds to your experience.

As you think about an offer, consider the aspects that are most important. You'll want to choose a job that comes closest to your career interests and objectives. But don't rule out the element of surprise—you might wind up with a job you like in an industry you'd never considered before. Don't worry too much about the salary. The point of an entry-level job is to set you on a forward path. And keep in mind that your first job won't be your last. Once you have accepted an offer, you'll be given a start date as well as the name of the person to whom you should report on arrival. Congratulations, you are now a member of the workforce!

NONTRADITIONAL STUDENTS

Take a quick glance around your class. You'll likely see classmates of all ages. Some will fall into the traditional college age group of 18 to 22, but many don't. Perhaps you are a veteran returning from military duty overseas. Maybe you have been engaged in a full-time career but want to broaden your education. Students who fall outside the 18-to-22 age group are often referred to as *nontraditional students*, but these students have become the norm on many campuses. Homemakers returning to school to freshen up their résumés before returning to the workforce and workers who have been laid off due to an economic downturn are other examples of nontraditional students. As diverse as this group is, they share one thing in common: they are older than traditional students. This means that they face different challenges—but also enjoy some advantages over their younger classmates.

One major challenge faced by nontraditional students is scheduling. Often they are juggling the responsibilities of work, school, and family. They may have to study at odd times—during meals, while commuting, or after putting the kids to bed. If they are switching careers, they may be learning an entirely new set of skills as well. But nontraditional students have an important advantage: experience. Even experience in an unrelated field is a plus. Older students know how organizations operate. Often they have developed useful skills in human relations, management, budgeting, and communications. Even a former stay-at-home parent has skills in all of these areas. Through observing other people's successes and failures—as well as living through their own—they have developed an inventory of what to do and what not to do. So in some ways, these students have a head start on their younger counterparts. But they also face the reality that they have fewer years in which to develop a career.

THE JOB MARKET: WHERE DO YOU FIT IN?

The industry you choose, and the career you follow within it, are part of a bigger picture. They reflect the needs of society, changing populations, developing technology, and the overall economy. For instance, the U.S. population is expected to increase at a slower rate of growth than during the previous two decades. The U.S. workforce will continue to become more diverse, with Hispanics accounting for the largest share of jobs among minorities, while Asians represent the fastest-growing group of employees. The number of women in the workforce is still growing at a faster rate than that of men.[11]

In a typical format, the interviewer tries to talk as little as possible, giving you a chance to talk about yourself and your goals. You want to present your thoughts clearly and concisely, in an organized fashion, without rambling on to unrelated topics. The interviewer may wait until you are finished or prompt you to talk about certain subjects by asking questions. Be as specific as possible when answering questions. The questions that interviewers ask often include the following:

- "Why do you want this job?"
- "Why do you want to work in this field?"
- "What are your short-term goals? Long-term objectives?"
- "What are your strengths? What are your weaknesses?"
- "What motivates you?"
- "What problem have you solved recently, and how?"
- "Why should my firm hire you?"
- "Are you considering other jobs or companies?"[10]

At some point, the interviewer will probably ask you whether you have any questions of your own. It's a good idea to come prepared with some questions, but others may arise during the interview. Try to keep your list concise, say three or four of your most important questions. The questions you ask reflect just as much about you as the answers you give to the interviewer's questions. Here is a sample of appropriate questions for the initial interview:

- "Could you clarify a certain aspect of the job responsibilities for me?"
- "Do people who start in entry-level jobs at this company tend to develop their careers here?"
- "In what ways could I perform above and beyond the job requirements?"

At some point during your conversation, the interviewer may give you an idea of the salary range for the job. If not, he or she will do so during a subsequent interview. You may ask about the range, but do not ask exactly how much you will be paid if you get the job. Keep in mind that usually there is little or no negotiation of an entry-level salary. However, you may ask if there is a probationary period with a review at the end of the period. Here are a few other questions *not* to ask:

- "When will I be promoted?"
- "How much time off do I get?"
- "When will I get my first raise?"

A successful first interview often leads to a second. The purpose of this interview is to better determine your specific qualifications and fit with the company. You may be introduced to more people—potential co-workers, people in other divisions, or sales staff. You may have another meeting with human resources staff members in which you'll learn more about salary, employee benefits, the firm's code of ethics, and the like. Depending on the type of job, you might be asked to take some skills tests. If you are entering a training program for a bank, you might be required to take some math-oriented tests. If you are going to work for a publisher, you might be asked to take an editing test or do some proofreading. If you are applying for a job as a sales representative, you may be given a test that assesses your personality traits. Don't be intimidated by these tests; just do your best.

Making the Employment Decision

After receiving your résumé, conducting one or two interviews, and administering a skills test, a potential employer knows a lot about you. You should also know a lot about the company. If the experience has been positive on both sides, you may be offered a job. If you have interviewed at several companies and are offered more than one job, congratulations! You may receive

Although you may feel nervous about the interview, you can control some of its outcome by doing your homework: planning and preparing for this important encounter with your potential employer. Before you meet with an interviewer, learn everything you can about the firm. The simplest way to do this is to visit the company's Web site. You can also check with your school's career center. If you know anyone who works for the company, you may ask the person about the firm. Try to learn the answers to the following questions about the organization:

- What does the firm do—manufacture clothing, market snack foods, produce films, sell cars? If you are applying for a job at a large corporation, zero in on the division for which you would be working.
- What is the company's mission? Many firms include a statement about their purpose in the business world—to supply affordable energy to communities, to serve fresh food, to make communication easier. Understanding why the company exists will help you grasp where it is headed and why.
- Where, when, and by whom was the company founded? Learn a little about the history of the firm.
- What is its position in the marketplace? Is it a leader or is it trying to gain a competitive advantage? Who are its main competitors?
- Where is the firm based? Does it have facilities located around the country and the world, or is it purely local?
- How is the company organized? Are there multiple divisions and products?

Learning about the firm indicates to the interviewer that you have initiative and motivation, as well as an interest in the firm's culture and history. You have taken the time and effort to find out more about the organization, and your enthusiasm shows.

Tips for Successful Interviewing

An interview is your personal introduction to the company. You want to make a good impression, but you also want to find out whether you and the firm make a good fit. Although the interviewer will be asking most of the questions, you will want to ask some, as well. People who conduct interviews say that the most important qualities candidates can exhibit are self-confidence, preparedness, and an ability to communicate clearly.

When you are contacted for an interview, find out the name(s) of the person or people who will be interviewing you. It's also appropriate to ask whether the initial interview will be with a human resources manager, the person to whom you would be reporting on the job, or both. Many people who conduct initial job interviews work in their firms' human resources divisions. These interviewers act as gatekeepers and can make recommendations to managers and supervisors about which individuals to interview further or hire. Managers who head the units in which an applicant will be employed may get involved later in the hiring process. Some hiring decisions come from human resources personnel together with the immediate supervisor of the prospective employee. In other cases, immediate supervisors make the decision alone. At your interview, keep in mind the following:

- **Dress appropriately.** Dress as if it is your first day of work at the firm. Conceal any tattoos or body piercings and wear simple jewelry.
- **Arrive a few minutes early.** This gives you time to relax and take in the surroundings. It also shows that you are punctual and care about other people's time.
- **Introduce yourself with a smile and a handshake.** Be friendly, but not overly familiar.
- **Be yourself—at your best.** Don't suddenly adopt a new personality. But try to be confident, polite, respectful, and interested in the people who are spending time with you. Be sure to thank each person who interviews you.[9]

Figure

4 | Results-Oriented Résumé

ANTONIO PETTWAY
101 Beverly Road
Upper Montclair, NJ 07043
820-555-1234
apettway@sbcglobal.net

OBJECTIVE

To apply my expertise as a construction supervisor to a management role in an organization seeking improvements in overall production, long-term employee relationships, and the ability to attract the best talent in the construction field.

PROFESSIONAL EXPERIENCE

DAL Construction Company, Orange, NJ   2006–Present
   Established automated, on-site recordkeeping system, improving communications and morale between field and office personnel, saving 400 work hours per year, and reducing the number of accounting errors by 20 percent. Developed a crew selected as "first-choice crew" by most workers wanting transfers. Completed five housing projects ahead of deadline and under budget.

NJ State Housing Authority, Trenton, NJ   2004–2006
   Created friendly, productive atmosphere among workers, enabling first on-time job completion in 4 years and one-half of usual materials waste. Initiated pilot materials delivery program with potential savings of 3.5 percent of yearly maintenance budget.

Essex County Housing Authority, Montclair, NJ   2004
   Produced information pamphlets, increasing applications for county housing by 22 percent. Introduced labor-management discussion techniques, saving jobs and over $29,000 in lost time.

Payton, Durnbell & Associates Architects, Glen Ridge, NJ   2003–2004
   Developed and monitored productivity improvements, saving 60 percent on information transfer costs for firm's 12 largest jobs.

EDUCATION

Montclair State University, Business   1999–2003

COMPUTER SKILLS

Familiar with Microsoft Office and Adobe Acrobat

PERSONAL

Highly self-motivated. Willing to relocate. Enjoy tennis and hiking.

- Request an interview.
- Thank the person for his or her time and consideration.
- Make sure all your contact information is in the letter—name, address, home phone number, cell phone number, and e-mail address.
- Proofread your letter carefully.[7]

Submitting through Automated Systems

Many large—and small—organizations have moved to automated (paperless) résumé processing and applicant-tracking systems. As a result, if you write and design a technology-compatible résumé and cover letter, you'll enjoy an edge over an applicant whose résumé and cover letter can't be added to a database. Also, remember that résumés are often transmitted electronically and then placed in a company database with an automated applicant-tracking system. Here are a few rules for submitting your résumé by e-mail:

- Use the words in your "Subject" line carefully. Don't just say "seeking employment." If possible, use the job title or a few words from the job description. If you are responding to a published job advertisement, include the job code from the advertisement.

- Include your cover letter in the e-mail.
- Send your résumé following the directions in the instruction.
- If you are answering an ad, read the instructions for application and follow them to the letter.[8]

THE JOB INTERVIEW

Congratulations! You've prepared an effective résumé, and you've been contacted for an interview. An interview is more than a casual conversation. During an interview, at least one company manager will learn about you, and you'll learn more about the company and the job.

Figure

3

Don't:

- Offer any misleading or inaccurate information.
- Make vague statements, such as "I work well with others," or "I want a position in business."
- Include a salary request.
- Make unreasonable demands.
- Highlight your weaknesses.
- Submit a résumé with typos or grammatical errors.
- Include pictures or graphics, or use fancy type fonts.[6]

Take your time with your résumé; it is one of the most important documents you'll create during your career. If you need help, go to your school's career center. If you are dealing with an employment agency, a counselor there should be able to help as well.

Keep in mind that you will probably have to modify your résumé at times to tailor it to a particular company or job. Again, take the time to do this; it may mean the difference between standing out and being lost in a sea of other applicants.

Preparing Your Cover Letter

In most cases, your résumé will be accompanied by a *cover letter*. This letter should introduce you, explain why you are submitting a résumé (cite the specific job opening if possible), and let the recipient know where you can be reached for an interview. An effective cover letter will make the recipient want to take the next step and read your résumé. Here are a few tips for preparing an outstanding letter:

- Write the letter to a specific person, if possible. A letter addressed "to whom it may concern" may never reach the right person. Call the company or check its Web site for the name of the person to whom you should send your letter. Be sure to spell the person's name correctly.
- Introduce yourself and explain the purpose of your letter—to apply for a job.
- Include a few sentences with information about yourself that is not on your résumé—perhaps describe a project you are currently working on that may be relevant to the job.
- Without boasting, explain why you think you are the right candidate for the job.

Functional Résumé

Enrique Garcia
Five Oceanside Drive, Apt. 6B
Los Angeles, CA 90026
215-555-7092
EGARCIA@hotmail.com

OBJECTIVE

Joining a growth-oriented company that values highly productive employees. Seeking an opportunity that leads to a senior merchandising position.

PROFESSIONAL EXPERIENCE

Administration
Management responsibilities in a major retailing buying office; coordinated vendor-relation efforts. Supervised assistant buyers.

Category Management
Experience in buying home improvement, and sport and recreation categories.

Planning
Chaired a team charged with reviewing the company's annual vendor evaluation program.

Problem Solving
Successfully developed a program to improve margins in the tennis, golf, and fishing lines.

WORK EXPERIENCE

Senior Buyer for Southern California Department Stores	2005–Present
Merchandiser for Pacific Discount Stores, a division of Southern California Department Stores	2003–2005

EDUCATION

Bachelor's Degree California State University—San Bernardino	2001–2003
Associate's Degree Los Angeles City College	1999–2001

Figure

| 2 | Chronological Résumé

FELICIA SMITH-WHITEHEAD
4265 Popular Lane
Cleveland, Ohio 44120
216-555-3296
Felicia_SW@aol.com

OBJECTIVE

Challenging office management position in a results-oriented company where my organizational and people skills can be applied; leading to an operations management position.

WORK EXPERIENCE

ADM Distribution Enterprises, Cleveland, Ohio   2006–Present
Office Manager of leading regional soft-drink bottler. Coordinate all bookkeeping, correspondence, scheduling of 12-truck fleet to serve 300 customers, promotional mailings, and personnel records, including payroll. Install computerized systems.

Merriweather, Hicks & Bradshaw Attorneys, Columbus, Ohio   2004–2006
Office Supervisor and Executive Assistant for Douglas H. Bradshaw, Managing Partner. Supervised four clerical workers and two paraprofessionals, automated legal research and correspondence functions, and assisted in coordinating outside services and relations with other firms and agencies. Promoted three times from Secretary to Office Supervisor.

Conner & Sons Custom Coverings, Cleveland, Ohio   2000–2004
Secretary in father's upholstery and awning company. Performed all office functions over the years, running the office when the owner was on vacation.

EDUCATION

Mill Valley High School, Honors   2000
McBundy Community College, Associate's Degree in Business   2004

COMPUTER SKILLS

Familiar with Microsoft Office and Adobe Acrobat

LANGUAGE SKILLS

Fluent in Spanish (speaking and writing)
Adequate speaking and writing skills in Portuguese

PERSONAL

Member of various community associations; avid reader; enjoy sports such as camping and cycling; enjoy volunteering in community projects.

may use narrative sentences to explain job duties and career goals, or you may present information in outline form. A résumé included as part of your credentials file at the career center on campus should be quite short. Remember to design it around your specific career objectives.

Figures 2, 3, and 4 illustrate different ways to organize your résumé—by *reverse chronology*, or time; by *function*; and by *results*. Regardless of which format you select, you will want to include the following: a clearly stated objective, your work or professional experience, your education, your personal interests such as sports or music, and your volunteer work. While all three formats are acceptable, one study showed that 78 percent of employers preferred the reverse chronological format—with the most recent experience listed first—because it was easiest to follow.

Tips for Creating a Strong Résumé

Your résumé should help you stand out from the crowd, just as your college admissions application did. A company may receive hundreds or even thousands of résumés, so you want yours to be on the top of the stack. Here are some do's and don'ts from the pros:

Do:

- State your objective clearly. If you are applying for a specific job, say so. State why you want the job and why you want to work at this particular company.
- Use terms related to your field, so that an electronic scanner—or busy human resources manager—can locate them quickly.
- Provide facts about previous jobs, internships, or volunteer work, including results or specific achievements. Include any projects or tasks you undertook through your own initiative.
- Highlight your strengths and skills.
- Write clearly and concisely. Keep your résumé to a single page.
- Proofread your résumé carefully.[5]

people view state employment agencies as providing services for semiskilled or unskilled workers. However, these agencies *do* list jobs in many professional categories and are often intimately involved with identifying job finalists for major new facilities moving to your state. In addition, many of the jobs listed at state employment offices may be with state or federal government agencies and may include professionals, such as accountants, attorneys, health-care professionals engineers, and scientists.

Learning More about Job Opportunities

Carefully study the various employment opportunities you have identified. Obviously, you will like some more than others, but you can examine a variety of factors when assessing each job possibility:

- Actual job responsibilities
- Industry characteristics
- Nature of the company
- Geographic location
- Salary and opportunities for advancement
- Contribution of the job to your long-range career objectives

Too many job applicants consider only the most striking features of a job, perhaps its location or the salary offer. However, a comprehensive review of job openings should provide a balanced perspective of the overall employment opportunity, including both long-run and short-run factors.

BUILDING A RÉSUMÉ

Regardless of how you locate job openings, you must learn how to prepare and submit a *résumé*, a written summary of your personal, educational, and professional achievements. The résumé is a personal document covering your educational background, work experience, career preferences and goals, and major interests that may be relevant. It also includes such basic information as your postal address, e-mail address, and telephone number. It should *not* include information on your age, marital status, race, or ethnic background.

Your résumé is usually your formal introduction to an employer, so it should present you in the best light, accentuating your strengths and potential to contribute to a firm as an employee. However, it should *never* contain embellishments or inaccuracies. You don't want to begin your career with unethical behavior, and an employer is bound to discover any discrepancies in fact—either immediately or during the months following your employment. Either event typically results in short-circuiting your career path.

Organizing Your Résumé

The primary purpose of a résumé is to highlight your qualifications for a job, usually on a single page. An attractive layout facilitates the employer's review of your qualifications. You can prepare your résumé in several ways. You

TOM STRICKLAND/BLOOMBERG NEWS/LANDOV

Identifying your skills is an important step to locating a great job. RadioShack notifies prospective job seekers that it is looking for people who value teamwork, pride, trust, and integrity for its Sales Management program in its retail chain.

keep in mind that these sites may receive hundreds of thousands of hits each day from job hunters, which means you have plenty of competition. This doesn't mean you shouldn't use one of these sites as part of your job search; just don't make it your sole source. Savvy job seekers often find that their time is better spent zeroing in on niche boards offering more focused listings. Naturally, if a particular company interests you, go to the firm's Web site, where available positions may be posted. If you are interested in Timberland, visit the firm's site at http://www.timberland.com; if you want a job at energy giant Southern Company, go to http://www.southerncompany.com.

Newspapers, the source for traditional classified want ads, also post their ads on the Web. Job seekers can even visit sites that merge ads from many different newspapers into one searchable database, such as CareerPath (http://www.careerbuilder.com). Some sites go a step further and create separate sections for each career area. For example, entire sections may be devoted to accounting, marketing, and other business professions. Searches can then be narrowed according to geographic location, entry level, company name, job title, job description, and other categories.

As mentioned earlier, you can connect with potential employers by posting your résumé on job sites. Employers search the résumé database for prospects with the right qualifications. One commonly used approach is for an employer to list one or more *keywords* to select candidates for personal interviews—for example, "field sales experience," "network architecture," or "auditing"—and then browse the résumés that contain all the required keywords. Employers also scan résumés into their human resources database, and then when a manager requests, say, ten candidates, the database is searched by keywords that have been specified as part of the request. Job seekers can respond to this computer screening of applicants by making sure that relevant keywords appear on their résumés.

The *Contemporary Business* Web site hosts a comprehensive job and career assistance section. The site is updated frequently to include the best job and career sites for identifying and landing the career you want, as well as current strategies for getting the best results from your Web-based career-search activities.

Finding Employment through Other Sources

We've already mentioned the importance of registering at your college's career planning or placement office. If you have completed formal academic coursework at more than one institution, you may be able to set up a placement file at each. In addition, you may want to contact private and public employment services available in your location or in the area where you would like to live.

Private Employment Agencies
These firms often specialize in certain types of jobs—such as marketing, finance, sales, or engineering—offering services for both employers and job candidates that are not available elsewhere. Many private agencies interview, test, and screen job applicants so that potential employers do not have to do so. Job candidates benefit from the service by being accepted by the agency and because the agency makes the first contact with the potential employer.

A private employment agency usually charges the prospective employer a fee for finding a suitable employee. Other firms charge job seekers a fee for helping find them a job. Be sure that you understand the terms of any agreement you sign with a private employment agency.

State Employment Offices
Don't forget to check the employment office of your state government. Remember that in many states, these public agencies process unemployment compensation applications along with other related work. Because of the mix of duties, some

Preparing Your Job Credentials

Most placement or credential files include the following information:

1. Letters of reference from people who know you well—instructors and employers
2. Transcripts of course work to date
3. Personal data form to report factual information
4. Statement of career goals

The career center will provide you with special forms to help you to develop your file. Often these forms can be completed online. Prepare the forms carefully, because employers are always interested in your written communication skills. Keep a copy of the final file for later use in preparing similar information for other employment sources. Check back with the career center to make sure your file is in order and update it whenever necessary to reflect additional academic accomplishments and work experiences.

Letters of reference are very important, because they give prospective employers both personal and professional insights about you. They can influence a hiring decision. So make a careful list of people who might be willing to write letters of reference. Your references should not be family members or close friends. Instead, choose a coach, an instructor, a former employer, or someone else whose knowledge could contribute to your job application. A soccer coach could vouch for your hard work and determination. A music teacher might be able to detail how well you accept instruction. A former employer might describe your punctuality and ability to get along with others. If possible, include someone from your school's business faculty on your list of references, or at least one of your current instructors.

Always ask people personally for letters of reference. Be prepared to give them brief outlines of your academic preparation, along with information about your job interests and career goals. This information will help them prepare their letters quickly and efficiently. It also shows that you are serious about the task and respect their time. Remember, however, that these people are very busy. Allow them at least a couple of weeks to prepare their reference letters; then follow up politely on missing ones. Always call or write to thank them for writing the letters.

Finding Employment through the Internet

The Internet plays an important role in connecting employers and job seekers. Companies of all sizes post their job opportunities on the Web, both on their own sites and on job sites such as Monster.com and HotJobs.com. Some sites are free to applicants, while others charge a subscription fee. Figure 1 provides a sampling of general and more focused career sites.

Career Web sites typically offer job postings, tips on creating an effective résumés, a place to post your résumé, and advice on interviews and careers. If this sounds easy,

Figure

1

Internet Job Sites

General

Monster.com

HotJobs.com

Industry or Employer Focused

USAJOBS and Federaljobs.com—job listings by the federal government

eFinancialCareers.com—jobs in the financial industry

WomensJobList.com and WomenSportsJobs.com—listings open to both men and women

Recruiting.com and hrcareerpage.com—jobs in human resources

SalesJobs.com—jobs in sales

Msajobs.com and MedZilla.com—sales jobs in the medical and biotechnical industries

Technicalsalesjobsblog.com—jobs in computers and telecommunications

Source: Sarah E. Needleman, "Pounding the Pavement on Wall Street, Virtually," *CollegeJournal*, accessed May 26, 2006, http://www.collegejournal.com.

Find a job—or an industry—that you would love as a start to your career search. Pfizer discusses some of the breakthrough medicines that were developed by people who were passionate about solving health problems.

4. ***List your skills and specific talents.*** Write down your strengths—job skills you already have, as well as skills you have developed in life. For instance, you might know how to operate financial software, and you might be good at negotiating with people. In addition, your school's career development office probably has standardized tests that can help determine your aptitude for specific careers. However, take these only as a guideline. If you really want to pursue a certain career, go for it.

5. ***List your weaknesses.*** This can be tough—it can also be fun. If you are shy about meeting new people, put shyness on your list. If you are quick to argue, admit it. If you aren't the best business letter writer or think you're terrible at math, confess to yourself. This list gives you an opportunity to see where you need improvement—and take steps to turn weaknesses into strengths.

6. ***Briefly sketch out your educational background.*** Write down the schools, colleges, and special training programs you have attended, along with any courses you plan to complete before starting full-time employment. Make a candid assessment of how your background matches up with the current job market. Then make plans to complete any further education you may need.

7. ***List the jobs you have held.*** Include jobs that paid, internships, and volunteer opportunities. They all gave you valuable experience. As you make your list, think about what you liked and disliked about each. Maybe you liked working with the general public as a supermarket cashier. Perhaps you enjoyed caring for animals at a local shelter.

8. ***Consider your hobbies and personal interests.*** Many people have turned hobbies and personal pursuits into rewarding careers. Jake Burton Carpenter earned a bachelor's degree in economics, but he loved winter sports. So he started a snowboard manufacturing company. Bonnie Kelly and Teresa Walsh turned their passion for sterling silver jewelry into a successful direct-sales company featuring the jewelry they love, called Silpada Designs.[4]

JOB SEARCH GUIDELINES

Once you have narrowed your choice of career possibilities to two or three that seem right for you, get your job search under way. Because the characteristics that made these career choices attractive to you are also likely to catch the attention of other job-seekers, you must expect competition. Locate available positions that interest you; then be resourceful! Your success depends on gathering as much information as possible.

Register at Your Career Center

Register at your school's career center. Establish an applicant file, including letters of recommendation and supporting personal information. Most placement offices send out periodic lists of new job vacancies by e-mail, so be sure to get your name and e-mail address on the list. Visit the office regularly and become a familiar face. Find out how the office arranges interviews with company representatives who visit campus. If your school has a career-oriented event, be sure to attend.

Top 100 Internships by Mark Oldman and Samer Hamadeh. New editions are published annually by Villard Books.

In addition to an internship, you can build your résumé with work and life experience through volunteer opportunities, extracurricular activities, and summer or off-campus study programs.

SELF-ASSESSMENT FOR CAREER DEVELOPMENT

You are going to spend a lot of time during your life working, so why not find a job—or at least an industry—that interests you? To choose the line of work that suits you best, you must first understand yourself. Self-assessment involves looking in the mirror and seeing the real you—with all your strengths and weaknesses. It means answering some tough questions. But being honest with yourself pays off because it will help you find a career that is challenging, rewarding, and meaningful to you. As you get to know yourself better, you may discover that helping other people really makes you happy. You may realize that to feel secure, you need to earn enough to put away substantial savings. Or you might learn that you are drawn to risks and the unknown, characteristics that might point you toward owning your own business someday. Each of these discoveries provides you with valuable information in choosing a career.

Many resources are available to help you in selecting a career. They include school libraries, career guidance and placement offices, counseling centers, and online job-search services. They include alumni from your college, as well as friends, family, and neighbors. Don't forget the contacts you make during an internship—they can help you in many ways. Ask questions of anyone you know—a shopkeeper, banker, or restaurant owner. Most people will be happy to speak with you or arrange a time to do so.

If you are interested in a particular industry or company, you might be able to arrange an informational interview—an appointment with someone who can provide you with more knowledge about an industry or career path. This type of interview is different from one that follows your application for a specific job, although it may ultimately lead to that. The informational interview can help you decide whether you want to pursue a particular avenue of employment. It also gives you some added experience in the interview process—without the pressure. To arrange an interview, tap anyone you know—friends of your parents, local businesspeople, or coordinators of not-for-profit organizations. Colleges often have databases of graduates working in various fields who are willing to talk with students on an informational basis, so be sure to start your search right at your own school.

The Self-Assessment Process

For a thorough assessment of your goals and interests, follow these steps:

1. *Outline your career interests.* What field or work activities interest you? What rewards do you want to gain from work?
2. *Outline your career goals.* What do you want to achieve through your career? What type of job can you see yourself doing? Where do you see yourself in a year? In five years? Do you have an ultimate dream job? How long are you willing to work to reach it? Write your goals down so you can refer to them later.
3. *Make plans to reach your goal.* Do you need more education? Does it require an apprenticeship or a certain number of years on the job? Write down the requirements you'll need to meet in order to reach your goal.

path, business skills may prove to be important. Consider the $40 billion biotech industry. "Scientists often underestimate the importance of business skills," notes a professional in the biotech field.[2] That's why *Contemporary Business* begins by discussing the best way to approach career decisions and to prepare for an *entry-level job*—your first permanent employment after leaving school. We then look at a range of business careers and discuss employment opportunities in a variety of fields.

INTERNSHIPS—A GREAT WAY TO ACQUIRE REAL-WORLD EXPERIENCE

Many business students complete one or more *internships* prior to completing their academic careers. Some arrange internships during the summer, while others work at them during a semester away from college. An internship gives you hands-on experience in a real business environment, whether it's in banking, the hotel industry, or retailing. Not only does an internship teach you how a business runs, but it can also help you decide whether you want to pursue a career in a particular industry. You might spend a summer interning in the admissions department of a hospital and then graduate with your job search focused on hospital administration. Or you might decide you'd much rather work for a magazine publisher or a construction company.

When you apply for an internship, don't expect to be paid much, if at all. The true value of an internship lies in its hands-on experience. An internship bridges the theory-practice educational gap. It will help carry you from your academic experience to your professional future. Also keep in mind that, as an intern, you will not be running the company. People may not ask for your input or ideas. You may work in the warehouse or copy center, at least for a while. But it is important to make the most of your internship. Because many companies make permanent job offers—or offers to enter paid training programs—to impressive interns, you'll want to stand out. Start your professional attitude now. Here are some tips for a successful internship experience. These guidelines are also helpful for your first job.

- *Dress like a professional.* Dress appropriately for your future career. During an interview visit, look around to see what employees are wearing. If you have any questions, ask your supervisor.
- *Act like a professional.* Arrive on time to work. Be punctual for any meetings or assignments. Ask questions and listen to the answers carefully. Complete your work thoroughly and on time. Maintain good etiquette on the phone, in meetings, and in all interactions with other people.
- *Stand out.* Work hard and show initiative, but behave appropriately. Don't try to use authority that you do not have. Show that you are willing to learn.
- *Be evaluated.* Even if your internship does not include a formal evaluation, ask your employer how you are doing to learn about your strengths and weaknesses.
- *Keep in touch.* Once you complete your internship, stay in touch periodically with the firm so people know what you are currently doing.

Internships can serve as critical networking and job-hunting tools. In many instances, they lead to future employment opportunities, allowing students to demonstrate technical proficiency while providing cost-effective employee training for the company. According to a survey by the National Association of Colleges and Employers, 80 percent of employers say they hire recent grads with internship or co-op experience.[3] An excellent source of information about the nation's outstanding internships can be found at your local bookstore—*America's*

Launching Your Business Career

You'll be hitting the job market soon—if you haven't already. **Regardless of what industry you** want to work in—financial services, marketing, travel, construction, hospitality, manufacturing, wireless communications—you need an education. Attending college and taking a business course like this one gives you an edge because business skills and knowledge are needed in many different fields. But education comes in many forms. In addition to taking classes, you should try to gain related experience, through either a job or participation in campus organizations. Cooperative-education programs, internships, or work-study programs can also give you hands-on experience while you pursue your education. These work experiences will often set you apart from other job seekers in the eyes of recruiters or human resources professionals—people who hire employees.

Every one of you will be responsible for making a living once you leave school. Education influences that, as well. As a graduate with an associate's or bachelor's degree, over your lifetime of work, you will earn between 40 and 80 percent more than someone with a high school degree. That translates to about $500,000 (for an associate's degree) and $1 million (for a bachelor's degree) in your bank account over a lifetime. If you go on for an advanced degree, the figure could double to $2 million.[1] However, keep in mind that while a degree may help you get in the door for certain job interviews and may put you on a path for advancement, it doesn't guarantee success; you have to achieve that yourself.

Companies plan their hiring strategies carefully in order to attract and keep the most productive, creative employees and avoid the cost of rehiring. So soon-to-be graduates still need to be on their toes. But creativity has never been in short supply among business students, and by the time you finish this class—and college—you will be well equipped to take on the challenge. You'll be able to think of your hunt for employment as a course in itself, at the end of which you will have a job. And you will be on your way toward a rewarding business career.

During the next few months you will be introduced to all the functional areas of business. You will learn how firms are organized and operated. You'll find out who does what in a company. Gradually you will identify industries and disciplines—such as sales, finance, or product design—that interest you. And you'll learn about many organizations, large and small—who founded them, what products they offer, how they serve their customers, and what types of decisions they make.

Choosing a career is an important life decision. It sets you on a path that will influence where you live, how much money you earn, what type of people you encounter, and what you do every day. And whether your goal is to operate an organic farm or to rise high in the ranks of a major corporation, you'll need to understand the principles of business. Even if you think you're headed down a different

No matter what career you choose, you need an education. State Farm Insurance tells students from diverse backgrounds that it values their contribution to its company.

You toss your laundry in the washing machine with a scoop of Tide. You pour Iams dry pet food into your dog's food dish. You use Crest Whitestrips while getting ready for a big date. You are loyal to these product brands, but you might not think about the company behind them: Procter & Gamble. P&G, as it is known throughout the business community, has been around for nearly 170 years. Its products are a part of millions of consumers' daily lives. Items such as Glad Press 'n Seal Wrap, the Swiffer duster, Dawn dish detergent, Pampers diapers, and Olay Daily Facials are put into shopping carts every day. Since P&G's acquisition of Gillette, brand names such as Oral-B, Braun, and Duracell are now included in the firm's shopping cart list.

AP PHOTO/TOM UHLMAN

Procter & Gamble: Innovation Drives Business Success

Procter & Gamble is a huge, U.S.-based corporation headed by chief executive A. G. Lafley. Its size has in the past made the company seem lumbering—unable to change quickly in response to shifting consumer preferences, new technology, and marketplace demands. But the firm has been getting back in shape and is now flexing its innovative muscles regularly. With its stream of unique new products, consumers and competitors alike are taking notice.

Lafley's vision for the future of his company is one of problem solver—he wants his firm to provide consumer products that offer solutions to every problem in the home, from laundry to food storage to personal care. This vision relies on innovation, technology, and alliances—all geared toward building relationships with customers. Several years ago, P&G purchased the high-end pet-food manufacturer Iams. Industry watchers predicted the downfall of Iams's quality and prestige within such a huge corporation. But P&G marketers conducted surveys to find out what Iams customers wanted, then put its vast scientific resources to work. As a result, P&G launched a new line of Iams foods aimed at lengthening the lives of pets—weight control formulas, antioxidant food blends, and foods blended with tartar-fighting ingredients. The result? Iams has

moved from the number 5 pet food brand to number 1. Its worldwide sales have doubled to $1.6 billion, and its profits have tripled. Why are these products so successful? "We're offering consumers peace of mind," explains Lafley, who just happens to own a dog and two Maine Coon cats.

Tide laundry detergent has been a marketplace leader for 40 years, which could lead you to remark, "If it isn't broken, don't fix it." But sales in general of laundry detergent have been somewhat stale, growing at less than 1 percent per year industry-wide. So P&G looked for ways to freshen the brand by offering more choices. Today, consumers have their choice of everything from Tide Coldwater, designed for washing clothes in cold water, to Tide Kick—a combination measuring cup and stain remover. Because P&G is as adept at forming alliances among its own divisions as it is at building relationships through new acquisitions, it can adapt good ideas company-wide. One example of this cross-fertilization is the Tide StainBrush, a new electric brush for removing stains that is based on the same mechanism used for the Crest SpinBrush Pro toothbrush—another P&G brand.

Procter & Gamble employs 7,500 people in research and development, located in 20 technical facilities in 20 countries. The firm depends on these employees—as well as everyone else in the firm—to think critically and creatively. It also encourages employees to communicate ideas—that's how the Tide StainBrush was developed. Diane Dietz, who heads the North American oral care division, notes that the ideas for Crest's new flavors actually came from aroma experts who work on Millstone coffee and Herbal Essences shampoos. Colleagues can post or review new ideas on P&G's internal Web site and attend special internal trade shows to learn more about products in other divisions. And if one division needs a few creative thinkers from another division to develop a new product, it "borrows" them for awhile. A. G. Lafley conducts annual "innovation reviews" of each business unit, evaluating the amount of idea sharing among marketers and scientists. He believes that the future of his company—which is number 6 on *Fortune's* worldwide list of most admired companies—lies in the minds of his own employees. "People get as much credit for giving good ideas as for receiving them," says Lafley.[1]

The U.S. has rebounded from the challenges of terrorism, recession, and war. Consumers have regained confidence and are spending again, particularly in the one of the hottest housing markets in the nation's history. Spurred by mortgage rates that have held steady for several years, more people are jumping into the housing market or taking the opportunity to upgrade to that dream home. Despite high gasoline prices, travelers have taken to the roads and skies in record numbers—during one recent holiday weekend, an estimated 37 million drivers hit the road, while the number of air travelers is now actually challenging the capacity of the skies, creating new challenges for the Federal Aviation Administration (FAA) and airlines. And it's not just vacationers seeking getaways; business travel has experienced a tremendous comeback.[2] American Express's Travel Related Services recently reported a 20 percent increase in its revenues, including a significant boost in charges by business travelers on their travel and expense cards.[3]

Perhaps the best evidence of a new outlook among companies is the rate at which they are investing in students—their future employees—particularly in the areas of technology and service. At several high schools in Massachusetts, biology students now dissect DNA as part of their course work, thanks to funding by local biotech companies such as Genzyme and Serono. "It's very philanthropic, but it's also selfish," explains Una Ryan, chair of the Massachusetts Biotechnology Council and CEO of Boston-area vaccine maker Avant Immunotherapeutics Inc. "We need people who are better trained."[4]

In short, business in many sectors is booming—and *Contemporary Business* is right there with it. This book explores the strategies that allow companies to grow and compete in today's interactive marketplace, along with the skills that you will need to turn ideas into action for your own success in business. This chapter sets the stage for the entire text by defining business and revealing its role in society. The chapter's discussion illustrates how the private enterprise system encourages competition and innovation while preserving business ethics.

WHAT IS BUSINESS?

What comes to mind when you hear the word *business*? Do you think of big corporations like General Electric or Microsoft? Or does the local bakery or shoe store pop into your mind? Maybe you recall your first summer job. The term *business* is a broad, all-inclusive term that can be applied to many kinds of enterprises. Businesses provide the bulk of employment opportunities, as well as the products that people enjoy.

business all profit-seeking activities and enterprises that provide goods and services necessary to an economic system.

Business consists of all profit-seeking activities and enterprises that provide goods and services necessary to an economic system. Some businesses produce tangible goods, such as automobiles, breakfast cereals, and computer chips; others provide services such as insurance, banking, and entertainment ranging from Six Flags theme parks and Broadway plays to rap concerts.

Business drives the economic pulse of a nation. It provides the means through which its citizens' standard of living improves. At the heart of every business endeavor is an exchange between a buyer and a seller. A buyer recognizes a need for a good or service and trades money with a seller to obtain that product. The seller participates in the process in hopes of gaining profits—a main ingredient in accomplishing the goals necessary for continuous improvement in the standard of living.

Profits represent rewards for businesspeople who take the risks involved in blending people, technology, and information to create and market want-satisfying goods and services. In contrast, accountants think of profits as the difference between a firm's revenues and the expenses it incurs in generating these revenues. More generally, however, profits serve as incentives for people to start companies, expand them, and provide consistently high-quality competitive goods and services. Consider the role of profits among companies in the travel industry. During one recent year, the average rate of occupancy in hotels rose nearly 4 percent, as did the average price of a hotel room, representing greater profits for those hotels. In turn, the owners of those hotels might choose to reinvest those profits in expansions and improvements in order to grow.[5]

The quest for profits is a central focus of business because without profits, a company could not survive. But businesspeople also recognize their social and ethical responsibilities. To succeed in the long run, companies must deal responsibly with employees, customers, suppliers, competitors, government, and the general public.

Not-for-Profit Organizations

What do Ohio State's athletic department, the U.S. Postal Service, the American Heart Association, and C-SPAN have in common? They are all classified as **not-for-profit organizations**, businesslike establishments that have primary objectives other than returning profits to their owners. These organizations play important roles in society by placing public service above profits, although it is important to understand that these organizations need to raise money so that they can operate and achieve their social goals. Not-for-profit organizations operate in both the private and public sectors. Private-sector not-for-profits include museums, libraries, trade associations, and charitable and religious organizations. Government agencies, political parties, and labor unions, all of which are part of the public sector, are also classified as not-for-profit organizations.

Not-for-profit organizations are a substantial part of the U.S. economy. Currently, 1.5 million nonprofit organizations are registered with the Internal Revenue Service in the United States, in categories ranging from arts and culture to science and technology.[6] These organizations control more than $1 trillion in assets and employ more people than the entire federal government and all 50 state governments combined. In addition, millions of volunteers work for them in unpaid positions. Not-for-profits secure funding from both private sources, including donations, and government sources. They are commonly exempt from federal, state, and local taxes.

Although they focus on goals other than generating profits, managers of not-for-profit organizations face many of the same challenges as executives of profit-seeking businesses. Without funding, they cannot do research, obtain raw materials, or provide services. Habitat for Humanity cannot build new houses for poor families without lumber and tools. The Children's Miracle Network, illustrated in Figure 1.1, could not help children with life-threatening injuries or diseases without raising nearly $250 million for 170 North American children's hospitals in a recent year through telethons, radiothons, corporate donations, and local fund-raising efforts. Without donations from every corner of the world, organizations such as Save the Children and the World Health Organization could not provide much-needed relief to survivors of the

profits rewards for businesspeople who take the risks involved to offer goods and services to customers.

"They Said It"

"My philosophy of life is that if we make up our mind what we are going to make of our lives, then work hard toward that goal, we never lose—somehow we win out."
—Ronald Reagan
(1911–2004)
40th president
of the United States

Figure

1.1

Children's Miracle Network: Helping Fight
Childhood Injury and Illness

"My Children's Miracle Network
hospital saved my life."

Buy a Miracle Balloon and help children in
your community treated at your Children's
Miracle Network Hospital. Visit one of these
sponsors to help kids in your area:

COURTESY OF CHILDREN'S MIRACLE NETWORK

factors of production
four basic inputs for
effective operation: nat-
ural resources, capital,
human resources, and
entrepreneurship.

Table

1.1

recent deadly tsunami that struck Southeast Asia. In an unprecedented effort to raise money for food, shelter, clothing, medical care,
and ultimately rebuild Indonesia and other hard-hit countries, former
U.S. presidents George H.W. Bush and Bill Clinton traveled together
to the region, made television commercials, and conducted personal
appeals for contributions. Within two months of the disaster, experts
estimated that more than $1 billion had been raised from the U.S.
private sector, in addition to the nearly $1 billion pledged by the U.S.
government.[7]

Some not-for-profits sell merchandise or set up profit-generating
arms to provide goods and services for which people are willing and
able to pay. College bookstores sell everything from sweatshirts to
coffee mugs with school logos imprinted on them, while the Sierra
Club and the Appalachian Mountain Club both have full-fledged
publishing programs. The Lance Armstrong Foundation has sold
more than 40 million yellow Live Strong wristbands in the United
States and abroad, with the money earmarked to fight cancer and
support patients and families.[8] Handling merchandising programs like
these, as well as launching other fund-raising campaigns, requires
managers of not-for-profit organizations to develop effective business
skills and experience. Consequently, many of the concepts discussed
in this book apply to not-for-profit organizations as much as to
profit-oriented firms.

Factors of Production

An economic system requires certain inputs for successful operation. Economists use the term **factors of production** to refer to the four basic inputs:
natural resources, capital, human resources, and entrepreneurship. Table 1.1
identifies each of these inputs and the type of payment received by firms and
individuals who supply them.

Natural resources include all production inputs that are useful in
their natural states, including agricultural land, building sites, forests, and mineral
deposits. The sawmill operated by Willamette Industries in the little town of Dallas, Oregon,
takes 2,500-pound second-growth logs from Oregon's hillsides and cuts them into boards.
Other companies use natural resources after they have been processed by companies like
Willamette. Natural resources are the basic inputs required in any economic system.

Capital, another key resource, includes technology, tools, information, and physical facilities.
Technology is a broad term that refers to such machinery and equipment as computers and

Factors of Production and Their Factor Payments

Factor of Production	Corresponding Factor Payment
Natural resources	Rent
Capital	Interest
Human resources	Wages
Entrepreneurship	Profit

Figure

1.2

software, telecommunications, and inventions designed to improve production. Information, frequently improved by technological innovations, is another critical factor because both managers and operating employees require accurate, timely information for effective performance of their assigned tasks. Technology plays an important role in the success of many businesses. Sometimes technology results in a new product, such as hybrid autos that run on a combination of gasoline and electricity. Both Honda and Toyota are successfully marketing these hybrids. Ford has introduced a hybrid version of its Escape SUV, and General Motors offers Chevy trucks with hybrid engines, as illustrated by Figure 1.2.

Sometimes technology helps a company improve a product. Recently, Microsoft came up with a wireless ergonomic keyboard designed to reduce fatigue on users' wrists and fingers. Its Wireless Comfort Keyboard is curved to allow more natural movement of the fingers and wrist. Logitech claims it has built a better cordless mouse by using lasers. Logitech's MX1000 Laser Cordless Mouse uses a tiny laser instead of a light-emitting diode (LED), making it more precise.[9]

GM's Hybrid Trucks

JOE POLIMENI/EPA/LANDOV

And sometimes technology helps a company operate more smoothly by tracking deliveries, providing more efficient communication, analyzing data, or training employees. Unisys offers software to businesses called 3D Visible Enterprise, which creates three-dimensional "blueprints" of the potential outcomes of business decisions. Xerox helped its business customer Dow Chemical gain better access to its more than 5 million pages of archived research and development documents. The latest generation of high-speed wireless networking technology, called WiMax, will soon help businesses communicate more efficiently. SBC Communications is testing a prototype with two of its major corporate customers, while Nortel Networks and LG Electronics have announced plans to develop WiMax-enabled phones.[10]

To remain competitive, a firm's capital needs to be continually acquired, maintained, and upgraded, so businesses need money for that purpose. A company's funds may come from investments by its owners, profits plowed back into the business, or loans extended by others. Money then goes to work building factories; purchasing raw materials and component parts; and hiring, training, and compensating workers. People and firms that supply capital receive factor payments in the form of interest.

Human resources represent another critical input in every economic system. Human resources include anyone who works, from the chief executive officer (CEO) of a huge corporation to a self-employed auto mechanic. This category encompasses both the physical labor and the intellectual inputs contributed by workers. Companies rely on their employees as a valued source of ideas and innovation, as well as physical effort. Some companies solicit employee ideas through traditional means, such as an online "suggestion box" or in staff meetings. Others encourage creative thinking during company-sponsored hiking or rafting trips or during social gatherings. Effective, well-trained human resources provide a significant competitive edge because competitors cannot easily match another company's talented, motivated employees in the way they can buy the same computer system or purchase the same grade of natural resources. Discount airline JetBlue has a mandatory training program in leadership

1.3 The Importance of Human Resources:
Manpower Staffing Services Helps Businesses

The forward plan says
all of these chairs will be filled
by year's end. Of course,
the forward plan doesn't say
how. Or by whom.

Enter Manpower. The first name in reliable staffing is also the first name in reliable, experienced
DIRECT HIRE RECRUITING. Our knowledgeable staff helps you create a unique hiring plan by selecting
from a suite of exclusive direct-hire services, including:

Recruiting. To connect you with your industry's most qualified active and passive candidates.

Online Candidate Prescreening. To quickly zero in on top talent by rating and ranking their responses
to customized questionnaires.

Behavioral Interviewing. To evaluate the core competencies you require.

Assessments. To assess skills, personality and work style.

Training. Six months of free online training and performance support for each direct hire from Manpower.
Courses include software applications, business skills training and more.

When you need talented people fast, visit **MANPOWER** at www.manpowerdirecthire.com/info
or call us at: **5301 N. Ironwood Rd. Milwaukee 414.906.6627**

COURTESY OF MANPOWER INC.

assessment check

1. Identify the four basic inputs
to an economic system.
2. List four types of capital.

qualities. CEO David Neeleman claims that the results have included happier workers and more satisfied customers. He believes that his managers must earn the respect of their employees, and that all managers should teach by example. "We want people to follow our leaders because they respect us, not because they've been told to," says Neeleman.[11]

Figure 1.3 emphasizes the importance of human resources to organizational goals—that people make the business what it is. Manpower provides staffing services to a wide range of companies, helping firms "staff up with skilled, experienced people, fast."

Entrepreneurship is the willingness to take risks to create and operate a business. An entrepreneur is someone who sees a potentially profitable opportunity and then devises a plan to achieve success in the marketplace and earn those profits. Kathy Ireland used to be a supermodel. Today, she is a super businesswoman, having been named Businesswoman of the Year by the National Association of Women Business Owners. Ireland is the CEO and chief designer of her own company, Kathy Ireland Worldwide, which sells its own lines of home furnishings and clothing targeted mainly to busy women on a budget. Ireland is proud of her company's accomplishments, including its recent licensing agreement that allows the firm to reproduce "The Quilts of Gee's Bend"—museum-quality folk art quilts made by a group of African American women from Alabama. "Real brands require infrastructure, leadership, and a strong, committed sales and distribution force," says Ireland. "We've built our brand from the ground up."[12]

U.S. businesses operate within an economic system called the *private enterprise system*. The next section looks at the private enterprise system, including competition, private property, and the entrepreneurship alternative.

GETTY IMAGES

AP PHOTO/CHITOSE SUZUKI

Kathy Ireland (shown in photo at left) is an entrepreneur who started her business by selling socks and has built it into the $1 billion dollar a year in sales revenue—Kathy Ireland Worldwide. The company recently beat out Donna Karan and Calvin Klein for the right to reproduce the acclaimed "The Quilts of Gee's Bend," based on the fine art folk quilts handmade by Mary Lee Bendolph (shown in photo at right) and her women friends in Gee's Bend, Alabama.

THE PRIVATE ENTERPRISE SYSTEM

No business operates in a vacuum. All operate within a larger economic system that determines how goods and services are produced, distributed, and consumed in a society. The type of economic system employed in a society also determines patterns of resource use. Some economic systems, such as communism, feature strict controls on business ownership, profits, and resources to accomplish government goals.

In the United States, businesses function within the **private enterprise system**, an economic system that rewards firms for their ability to perceive and serve the needs and demands of consumers. The private enterprise system minimizes government interference in economic activity. Businesses that are adept at satisfying customers gain access to necessary factors of production and earn profits.

Another name for the private enterprise system is **capitalism**. Adam Smith, often identified as the father of capitalism, first described the concept in his book *The Wealth of Nations*, published in 1776. Smith believed that an economy is best regulated by the "invisible hand" of **competition**, the battle among businesses for consumer acceptance. Smith thought that competition among firms would lead to consumers' receiving the best possible products and prices because less efficient producers would gradually be driven from the marketplace.

The "invisible hand" concept is a basic premise of the private enterprise system. In the United States, competition regulates much of economic life. To compete successfully, each firm must find a basis for **competitive differentiation**, the unique combination of organizational abilities, products, and approaches that sets a company apart from competitors in the minds of consumers. Businesses operating in a private enterprise system face a critical task of keeping up with changing marketplace conditions. Firms that fail to adjust to shifts in consumer preferences or ignore the actions of competitors leave themselves open to failure. In the very competitive food-manufacturing industry, General Mills and Kellogg have been duking it out for decades. When Kellogg cereals grew soggy in the sales bowl, the firm promoted Carlos Gutierrez to CEO in the hope that he could add a crisp snap, crackle, and pop to Kellogg's revenues. Gutierrez immediately took stock of the cereals that consumers preferred, those that had been copied by other companies, and those that were the most profitable. He created a strategy called Volume to Value, in which Kellogg's allocated more of its resources to products such as Special K, which appeals to weight-conscious women; Kashi, for health food consumers; and Nutri-Grain bars, for those who want breakfast or a snack on the go. These products, priced higher than cereals such as Corn Flakes, would generate more profits, which would then be plowed back into research and development for new competitive products. So far, the plan has been successful. Kellogg's share of sales from new cereal products, now at about 18 percent, has rocketed past that of the industry as a whole. Gutierrez's star also rose: from his CEO post at Kellogg, he was tapped to become the 35th U.S. secretary of commerce.[13]

Throughout this book, our discussion focuses on the tools and methods that 21st-century businesses apply to compete and differentiate their goods and services. We also discuss many of the ways in which market changes will affect business and the private enterprise system in the years ahead.

Basic Rights in the Private Enterprise System

For capitalism to operate effectively, the citizens of a private enterprise economy must have certain rights. As shown in Figure 1.4, these include the rights to private property, profits, freedom of choice, and competition.

The right to **private property** is the most basic freedom under the private enterprise system. Every participant has the right to own, use, buy, sell, and bequeath most forms of property,

private enterprise system economic system that rewards firms for their ability to identify and serve the needs and demands of customers.

competition battle among businesses for consumer acceptance.

"They Said It"

"All strategy depends on competition."
—*Bruce D. Henderson (1915–1992) American educator and founder of the Boston Consulting Group*

Figure

1.4 | Basic Rights within a Private Enterprise System

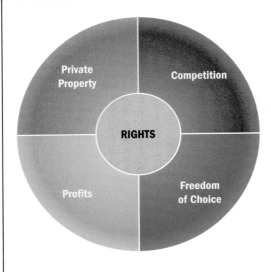

including land, buildings, machinery, equipment, patents on inventions, individual possessions, and intangible properties.

The private enterprise system also guarantees business owners the right to all profits—after taxes—they earn through their activities. Although a business is not assured of earning a profit, its owner is legally and ethically entitled to any income it generates in excess of costs.

Freedom of choice means that a private enterprise system relies on the potential for citizens to choose their own employment, purchases, and investments. They can change jobs, negotiate wages, join labor unions, and choose among many different brands of goods and services. People living in the capitalist nations of North America, Europe, and other parts of the world are so accustomed to this freedom of choice that they sometimes forget its importance. A private enterprise economy maximizes individual prosperity by providing alternatives. Other economic systems sometimes limit freedom of choice to accomplish government goals, such as increasing industrial production or military strength.

The private enterprise system also permits fair competition by allowing the public to set rules for competitive activity. For this reason, the U.S. government has passed laws to prohibit "cutthroat" competition—excessively aggressive competitive practices designed to eliminate competition. It also has established ground rules that outlaw price discrimination, fraud in financial markets, and deceptive advertising and packaging. Not long ago, the Securities and Exchange Commission (SEC), along with internal New York Stock Exchange (NYSE) investigators, discovered that some of the NYSE's in-house floor traders had engaged in "improper proprietary trading" of 2.2 billion shares of stock over a three-year period, resulting in unfair competitive advantage and profits. The subsequent legal charges sparked the reform of certain trading regulations.[14]

The Entrepreneurship Alternative

entrepreneur person who seeks a profitable opportunity and takes the necessary risks to set up and operate a business.

The entrepreneurial spirit beats at the heart of private enterprise. An **entrepreneur** is a risk taker in the private enterprise system. You hear about entrepreneurs all the time—two college students starting a software business in their dorm room or a mom who invents a better baby carrier. Many times their success is modest, but once in a while, the risk pays off in huge profits, as described in the "Hit & Miss" feature. Individuals who recognize marketplace opportunities are free to use their capital, time, and talents to pursue those opportunities for profit. The willingness of individuals to start new ventures drives economic growth and keeps pressure on existing companies to continue to satisfy customers. If no one were willing to take economic risks, the private enterprise system wouldn't exist.

By almost any measure, the entrepreneurial spirit fuels growth in the U.S. economy. Of all the businesses operating in the United States, about one in seven firms started operations during the past year. These newly formed businesses are also the source of many of the nation's new jobs. Every year, they create more than one of every five new jobs in the economy. Most measures of entrepreneurship look at the smallest or youngest businesses on the assumption that they are the enterprises in which entrepreneurship is most significant. These companies are a significant source of employment or self-employment. Of the 20 million U.S. businesses currently in operation, 15 million are self-employed people without any employees. Nearly 12 million U.S. employees currently work for a business with fewer than ten employees.[15] Does starting a business require higher education? Not necessarily, although it can help. Figure 1.5 presents the results of a survey of small-business owners, which shows that about 24 percent of all respondents had graduated from college, and 19 percent had postgraduate degrees.

HIT & MISS

Airborne Takes Off

It's a marketer's dream come true: the cure for the common cold. Airborne may not technically be a cure, but the latest remedy for head colds is nothing to sneeze at. Developed by entrepreneur Victoria Knight-McDowell, the herbal remedy contains many traditional cold-fighting ingredients—vitamins C, E, and A, along with zinc, ginger, and echinacea.

Like many entrepreneurs, Knight-McDowell came up with the idea for Airborne because she needed the product herself. A substitute teacher, she found she was catching too many colds in the classroom. So she headed to her own kitchen to come up with a concoction to help relieve the symptoms. In six months she had come up with a prototype recipe, which she tried on herself, her family, and her friends. It seemed to work. So Knight-McDowell and her husband Rider decided to market the new product directly from their home. The first year, Airborne brought in $25,000—the same as Victoria's teaching salary.

Eight years later, Airborne is making $21 million annually, thanks in part to Knight-McDowell's appearance on *The Oprah Winfrey Show* and endorsements from such celebrities as Kevin Costner and Sarah Jessica Parker. But Knight-McDowell also credits her own and her husband's business sense. "One of the keys to our success is that I'm used to operating on a shoestring budget," she says. "Once a teacher, always a teacher. Now I can be in the classroom and enjoy being with the children, without worrying about money." Airborne's whimsical and humorous packaging is also a factor. Its distinctive yellow box with cartoon-style drawings is pleasing to consumers. And of course, the fact that Knight-McDowell is a teacher is a vital marketing point; everyone trusts a teacher's word.

Questions for Critical Thinking

1. How does Victoria Knight-McDowell embody the entrepreneurial spirit?
2. What might be the next step for Knight-McDowell's company?

Sources: "The Secrets of Success," *The Oprah Winfrey Show,* accessed May 26, 2006, http://www.oprah.com; "Unconventional Cold Remedies Big Sellers," NewsMax.com, May 26, 2006, http://www.newsmax.com; Kerry Fehr-Snyder, "Herbal Cold Remedy Goes Airborne after Oprah Plug," *The Arizona Republic,* May 26, 2006, http://www.azcentral.com.

Besides creating jobs and selling products, entrepreneurship provides the benefits of innovation. In contrast to more established firms, start-up companies tend to innovate most in fields of technology that are new and uncrowded with competitors, making new products available to businesses and consumers. Because small companies are more flexible, they can make changes to products and processes more quickly than larger corporations. Entrepreneurs often find new ways to use natural resources, technology, and other factors of production. Often, they do this because they have to—they may not have enough money to build an expensive prototype or launch a nationwide ad campaign. Sometimes an entrepreneur may innovate by simply tweaking an existing idea. Curves is a chain of no-frills fitness clubs across the nation started by a husband-and-wife team. In the 15 years it has been in existence, the business for single-gender, quick-exercise gyms has shot upward, now accounting for nearly 25 percent of the entire fitness club market in the United States. Enter Scott Smith, a former Curves franchise owner who wanted to give himself and his friends the same kind of deal. So he launched Blitz, a male-only, quick-fitness gym complete

Figure

1.5

Education Levels of Small-Business Owners

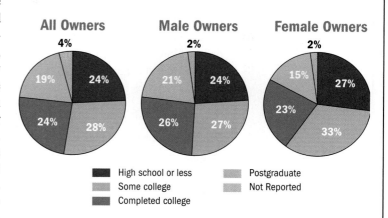

Note: Numbers may not total to 100 percent due to rounding.
Source: Data from "Survey of Business Owners (SBO): Owner's Education Levels at Start-Up, Purchase, or Acquisition of the Business," U.S. Census Bureau, accessed May 26, 2006 http://www.census.gov/csd/sbo/edu.html.

with mock boxing rings and punching bags. Smith, who now has 86 Blitz locations in the United States and Canada, says his customers love the quick pace of the workouts. And he swears by the results. "I don't care what your size or strength is, at the end of two 10-minute circuits, you'll wear yourself out and get blitzed," he promises.[16]

Entrepreneurship is also important to existing companies in a private enterprise system. More and more, large firms are recognizing the value of entrepreneurial thinking among their employees, hoping to benefit from enhanced flexibility, improved innovation, and new market opportunities. Jim Throneburg runs his family's North Carolina sock-manufacturing firm, Thorlo. The company has been around for a long time, and Throneburg makes certain it continually innovates and changes. A few decades ago, he noticed that American consumers had begun buying different athletic shoes for different sports. "If the shoe changed for function, I figured I needed to design a sock that complemented the shoe," he recalls. His figuring resulted in a thick-soled hiking sock and later a padded sock for the military. Since then, Thorlo has created more than 25 varieties of sport socks. Throneburg invests heavily in research—in search of new markets and new technologies. Research helped the firm identify what it calls the "7 Elements of Comfort" for footwear and then develop its Comfort Science program. Thorlo has spent millions on developing new yarns and designs and responded to requests from its customers for new products. Throneburg likes to differentiate his firm from its competitors. "Thorlo does not make socks. There are lots of companies that do that. At Thorlo, all our resources are dedicated to improving the quality of our consumers' lives by providing the most protective sock products in the world."[17]

As the next section explains, entrepreneurs have played a vital role in the history of American business. They have helped create new industries, developed successful new business methods, and improved U.S. standing in global competition.

"They Said It"

"Only do it if you have the passion for it. Only do anything for that reason."
—Francis Ford Coppola (b. 1939)
Film producer, owner of Coppola Companies

assessment check

1. What is an alternative term for private enterprise system?
2. What is the most basic freedom under the private enterprise system?
3. What is an entrepreneur?

SIX ERAS IN THE HISTORY OF BUSINESS

In the roughly 400 years since the first European settlements appeared on the North American continent, amazing changes have occurred in the size, focus, and goals of U.S. businesses. As Figure 1.6 indicates, U.S. business history is divided into six distinct time periods: (1) the Colonial period, (2) the Industrial Revolution, (3) the age of industrial entrepreneurs, (4) the production era, (5) the marketing era, and (6) the relationship era. The next sections describe how events in each of these time periods have influenced U.S. business practices.

The Colonial Period

Before the U.S. Declaration of Independence from England in 1776, Colonial society emphasized rural and agricultural production. Colonial towns were small compared with European cities, and they functioned as marketplaces for farmers and craftspeople. The economic focus of the nation centered on rural areas, because prosperity depended on the output of farms and plantations. The success or failure of crops influenced every aspect of the economy.

Colonists depended on England for manufactured items as well as financial backing for their infant industries. Even after the Revolutionary War (1776–1783), the United States maintained close economic ties with England. British investors continued to provide much of the financing for developing the U.S. business system, and this financial influence continued well into the 19th century.

Figure

1.6

Six Eras in Business History

Era	Main Characteristics	Time Period
Colonial	Primarily agricultural	Prior to 1776
Industrial Revolution	Mass production by semiskilled workers, aided by machines	1760–1850
Industrial entrepreneurs	Advances in technology and increased demand for manufactured goods, leading to enormous entrepreneurial opportunities	Late 1800s
Production	Emphasis on producing more goods faster, leading to production innovations such as assembly lines	Through the 1920s
Marketing	Consumer orientation, seeking to understand and satisfy needs and preferences of customer groups	Since 1950s
Relationship	Benefits derived from deep, ongoing links with individual customers, employees, suppliers, and other businesses	Began in 1990s

The Industrial Revolution

The Industrial Revolution began in England around 1750. It moved business operations from an emphasis on independent, skilled workers who specialized in building products one by one to a factory system that mass-produced items by bringing together large numbers of semi-skilled workers. The factories profited from the savings created by large-scale production, bolstered by increasing support from machines over time. As businesses grew, they could often purchase raw materials more cheaply in larger lots than before. Specialization of labor, limiting each worker to a few specific tasks in the production process, also improved production efficiency.

Influenced by these events in England, business in the United States began a time of rapid industrialization. Agriculture became mechanized, and factories sprang up in cities. During the mid-1800s, the pace of the revolution was increased as newly built railroad systems provided fast, economical transportation. In California, for example, the combination of railroad construction and the gold rush fueled a tremendous demand for construction.

The Age of Industrial Entrepreneurs

Building on the opportunities created by the Industrial Revolution, entrepreneurship increased in the United States. In 1900, Arthur R. Wilson and several partners paid $10,000 in gold coins for a 27-acre parcel of granite-rich land in California. This natural resource was the basis for the Granite Rock Co., which provided the material for roads and buildings in California's booming economy. The company, now called Graniterock, evolved in response to technological, competitive, and marketplace demands and continues to survive in the 21st century. Today the firm, which has stores throughout California, offers consumer products such as granite countertops as well as many "green" products made from recycled materials.[18]

Inventors created a virtually endless array of commercially useful products and new production methods. Many of them are famous today:

- Eli Whitney introduced the concept of interchangeable parts, an idea that would later facilitate mass production on a previously impossible scale.
- Robert McCormick designed a horse-drawn reaper that reduced the labor involved in harvesting wheat. His son, Cyrus McCormick, saw the commercial potential of the reaper and launched a business to build and sell the machine. By 1902, the company was producing 35 percent of the nation's farm machinery.
- Cornelius Vanderbilt (railroads), J. P. Morgan (banking), and Andrew Carnegie (steel), among others, took advantage of the enormous opportunities waiting for anyone willing to take the risk of starting a new business.

The entrepreneurial spirit of this golden age in business did much to advance the U.S. business system and raise the overall standard of living of its citizens. That market transformation, in turn, created new demand for manufactured goods.

The Production Era

As demand for manufactured goods continued to increase through the 1920s, businesses focused even greater attention on the activities involved in producing those goods. Work became increasingly specialized, and huge, labor-intensive factories dominated U.S. business. Assembly lines, introduced by Henry Ford, became commonplace in major industries. Business owners turned over their responsibilities to a new class of managers trained in operating established companies. Their activities emphasized efforts to produce even more goods through quicker methods.

During the production era, business focused attention on internal processes rather than external influences. Marketing was almost an afterthought, designed solely to distribute items generated by production activities. Little attention was paid to consumer wants or needs. Instead, businesses tended to make decisions about what the market would get. If you wanted to buy a Ford Model T automobile, your color choice was black—the only color produced by the factory.

The Marketing Era

The Great Depression of the early 1930s changed the shape of U.S. business yet again. As incomes nose-dived, businesses could no longer automatically count on selling everything they produced. Managers began to pay more attention to the markets for their goods and services, and sales and advertising took on new importance. During this period, selling was often synonymous with marketing.

Demand for all kinds of consumer goods exploded after World War II. After nearly five years of doing without new automobiles, appliances, and other items to contribute to the war effort, consumers were buying again. At the same time, however, competition also heated up. Soon businesses began to think of marketing as more than just selling; they envisioned a process of determining what consumers wanted and needed and then designing products to satisfy those needs. In short, they developed a **consumer orientation**.

Businesses began to analyze consumer desires before beginning actual production. Consumer choice skyrocketed. Today's automobiles no longer come just in black; instead, car buyers can choose from a wide range of colors and accessories.

Businesses also discovered the need to distinguish their goods and services from those of competitors. **Branding**, the process of creating an identity in consumers' minds for a good, service, or company, is an important marketing tool. A **brand** can be a name, term, sign, symbol, design, or some combination that identifies the products of one firm and differentiates them from competitors' offerings.

One of the early masters of branding was Ray Kroc, who was the franchising agent for a small hamburger chain started in San Bernardino, California. Kroc opened his first restaurant in the chain in Des Plaines, Illinois. A few years later, he bought out the owners, the McDonald brothers, and built the franchise into the famous McDonald's restaurant chain. Kroc insisted that every one of his restaurants follow the same operating procedures and offer similar menu items, reinforcing the nationwide image of the growing restaurant franchise in consumer minds across the country. Today, the "golden arches" are among the best-known company symbols in the world.

The marketing era has had a tremendous effect on the way business is conducted today. Even the smallest business owners recognize the importance of understanding what customers want and the reasons they buy.

The McDonald's "golden arches" are one of the most recognizable brand symbols in the world.

The Relationship Era

As business continues in the 21st century, a significant change is taking place in the ways companies interact with customers. Since the Industrial Revolution, most businesses have concentrated on building and promoting products in the hope that enough customers will buy them to cover costs and earn acceptable profits, an approach called **transaction management**.

In contrast, in the **relationship era**, businesses are taking a different, longer-term approach to their interactions with customers. Firms now seek ways to actively nurture customer loyalty by carefully managing every interaction. They earn enormous paybacks for their efforts. A company that retains customers over the long haul reduces its advertising and sales costs. Because customer spending tends to accelerate over time, revenues also grow. Companies with long-term customers often can avoid costly reliance on price discounts to attract new business, and they find that many new customers come from loyal customer referrals.

Business owners gain several advantages by developing ongoing relationships with customers. Because it is much less expensive to serve existing customers than to find new ones, businesses that develop long-term customer relationships can reduce their overall costs. Long-term relationships with customers enable businesses to improve their understanding of what customers want and prefer from the company. As a result, businesses enhance their chances of sustaining real advantages through competitive differentiation. Figure 1.7 illustrates one way that Citibank creates long-term customer relationships—through its Thank You rewards program that offers benefits to Citi credit card users, such as free hotel stays and airline tickets, college savings programs, and electronic gifts.

brand name, term, sign, symbol, design, or some combination that identifies the products of one firm and differentiates them from competitors' offerings.

Figure

1.7

Citibank: Creating Long-Term Customer Relationships

(b)usiness (e)tiquette

Dress for Success

Congratulations—you've got a job interview! You're accustomed to wearing whatever you want to class—jeans, a T-shirt, sneakers. But in the working world, those clothes won't get you very far. In fact, employment experts warn that your appearance can make or break your chances of getting the job you want. While prospective employers care most about your skills, experience, and attitude, they also evaluate the way you present yourself to the world, even if you won't be dealing directly with customers. So an important first step in your career is to assess your wardrobe and make some purchases if necessary. You want to make the best first impression you can.

- Invest in one good-quality suit and wear it with a solid-color shirt or blouse. Men should wear a conservative tie; women might opt for a nice silk scarf or plain gold necklace. Make sure your shoes are clean, simple, and polished—the same goes for your purse or briefcase. If you are interviewing in a cold climate, invest in a good, conservative coat. Don't be tempted to throw on a ski jacket over your nice suit.
- Get a haircut before your interview. Neatly styled hair makes you look pulled together. Don't try giving your hair a radical new color—natural is best. Make sure

the rest of your grooming is meticulous—including teeth and fingernails.

- Avoid any visible body piercings, tattoos, or other decorations. Women may wear simple studs or small hoop earrings; men should leave these at home.
- Leave plenty of time to shower and dress before your interview, then check yourself in a full-length mirror before you head out the door.

Remember that you are dressing for the position you want; an interviewer should be able to visualize you in the job. Although your current budget may be tight, purchasing one good outfit is truly an investment in your career. Retailers are now focusing on post-college consumers for this very reason. Gap and Express are jumping into the career market, as is Abercrombie & Fitch. Department stores and value chains such as Kohl's, Target, and Wal-Mart are always a good bet for career apparel as well.

Sources: "Dress for Interview Success," CollegeGrad.com, accessed May 26, 2006, http://www.collegegrad.com; Randall S. Hansen, "When Job-Hunting: Dress for Success," *Quintessential Careers*, accessed May 26, 2006, http://www.quintcareers.com; Calvin Bruce, "Dress for Success," *Black Collegian*, accessed May 26, 2006, http://www.black-collegian.com; Lorrie Grant, "Trendy Retailers Get Dressed for Work," *USA Today*, May 26, 2006, p. B3.

The relationship era is an age of connections—between businesses and customers, employers and employees, technology and manufacturing, and even separate companies. The world economy is increasingly interconnected, as businesses expand beyond their national boundaries. In this new environment, techniques for managing networks of people, businesses, information, and technology are critically important to contemporary business success. As you begin your own career, you will soon see how important relationships are, beginning with your first job interview, as described in the "Business Etiquette" feature.

Managing Relationships through Technology

Increasingly, businesses focus on **relationship management**, the collection of activities that build and maintain ongoing, mutually beneficial ties with customers and other parties. At its core, relationship management involves gathering knowledge of customer needs and preferences and applying that understanding to get as close to the customer as possible. Many of these activities are based on **technology**, or the business application of knowledge based on scientific discoveries, inventions, and innovations. In managing relationships with customers, technology most often takes the form of communication, particularly via the Internet.

Stonyfield Farm is the largest organic yogurt company in the world, and it relies on technology to help build and maintain relationships with its customers. Using one of the latest forms of Internet communication—Web logs, or blogs, which are online journals that the public can access—Stonyfield reinforces its relationships with consumers. The firm has hired a full-time blogger, Christine Halvorson, to create five different blogs on its Web site, including the Strong Women Daily News, the Bovine Bugle, and Creating Healthy Kids. Halvorson posts various news items, health and fitness tips, and other information on the blogs, to which consumers can respond. Stonyfield CEO Gary Hirshberg believes that giving customers this kind of access to his firm helps develop an emotional connection with them.[19]

relationship management collection of activities that build and maintain ongoing, mutually beneficial ties between a business and its customers and other parties.

THE BUCK STOPS HERE: WHO SHOULD PAY FOR PROFESSIONAL SPORTS STADIUMS?

It sounds great to sports fans: their team gets a new stadium or ballpark, or their city gets a new team. Or both happen at once.

This was the case with baseball's Montreal Expos, as they were trying to move to Washington, D.C., to become the Nationals. Meanwhile, Las Vegas has been attempting to lure a Major League Baseball team. While sports buffs are cheering, fellow taxpayers are moaning—who pays for the new stadium? Often, professional sports team owners negotiate for as much of the cost as possible to be shouldered by the city or state. Mayors and state officials may agree to the terms because they envision long-term benefits to their cities and local businesses. But critics argue that professional sports stadiums should be built with private funds, including those of team owners and leagues.

Should professional sports stadiums be funded with public money?

PRO

1. An updated or new professional sports stadium attracts visitors who spend money at the stadium and surrounding businesses, and enhances the image of the city.
2. Using public money makes the general public feel more like owners and encourages them to attend games and functions.

CON

1. In most cases, public funds are not even necessary. According to one estimate, a team can recoup half the cost of construction within the first 5 years, and all of it within 12 years.
2. A study of the economics of building stadiums concludes that consumers are not spending more money at surrounding businesses. "As sport- and stadium-related activities increase, other spending declines because people substitute spending on sports for other spending," notes the study. So, the surrounding community does not necessarily benefit economically.

Summary

Government officials, team owners, professional leagues, and taxpayer groups continue to haggle over who foots the bill for new stadiums. In recent years, some officials have begun to take a tougher stand against the practice of public funding. A member of the Washington, D.C., city council stood firm against the original financial plan and reduced the public payout to half the cost of construction. In addition, a Boston legislator recently blocked a deal in which Massachusetts taxpayers would have paid for a new ballpark for the Boston Red Sox. "The bottom line is that these new stadiums generate sufficient revenue to pay for themselves," argues one economics professor who has studied the situation. "If the stadium pays for itself internally, that should be sufficient motivation for the owners to build it.

Sources: Eric Fisher, "Stadium Labor Deal Reached," *The Washington Times,* accessed May 26, 2006, http://www.washingtontimes.com; Doug French, "Taxpayer-Financed Sports Stadiums: Deals Benefit Teams, Not Public," *Las Vegas Review-Journal,* accessed May 26, 2006, http://www.reviewjournal.com; Eric Fisher, "District Strikes Stadium Deal," *The Washington Times,* accessed May 26, 2006, http://www.washingtontimes.com; "Public Financing of Stadiums Unnecessary, Study Shows," *CBS SportsLine,* accessed May 26, 2006, http://cbssportsline.com.

solving an **ETHICAL** controversy

Strategic Alliances and Partnerships

Businesses are also finding that they must form partnerships with other organizations to take full advantage of available opportunities. A **partnership** is an affiliation of two or more companies that help each other achieve common goals. One such form of partnership between organizations is a **strategic alliance**, a partnership formed to create a competitive advantage for the businesses involved. While alliances are usually formed to benefit both parties, sometimes the balance appears to be one-sided, as discussed in the "Solving an Ethical Controversy" feature.

E-business has created a whole new type of strategic alliance. A firm whose entire business is conducted online, such as eBay or Amazon, may team up with traditional retailers that

"They Said It"

"It's our customers who have built eBay."
—Meg Whitman (b. 1956) CEO and president, eBay

contribute their expertise in buying the right amount of the right merchandise, as well as their knowledge of distribution. Bloomingdale's, Home Depot, and Motorola all have one thing in common: an arrangement with eBay in which they sell excess or outdated merchandise on its Internet site called eBay Stores. With this agreement between retailers and the Web marketing giant, everyone wins: Consumers get good prices, the retailers get more return on the dollar than they'd earn in a clearance or liquidation sale, and eBay gets a cut.[20] Pepsi and Apple Computer recently joined forces in a short-term promotional effort in which Pepsi agreed to distribute up to 200 million free songs through the Apple iTunes Music Store when consumers bought Pepsi products that contained codes for the free songs. Consumers who participated also had chances to win free Apple iPod minis.[21]

Each new era in U.S. business history has forced managers to reexamine the tools and techniques they formerly used to compete. Tomorrow's managers will need creativity and vision to stay on top of rapidly changing technology and to manage complex relationships in the global business world of the fast-paced 21st century.

assessment check

1. What was the Industrial Revolution?
2. During which era was the idea of branding developed?
3. What is the difference between transaction management and relationship management?

TODAY'S BUSINESS WORKFORCE

A skilled and knowledgeable workforce is an essential resource for keeping pace with the accelerating rate of change in today's business world. Employers need reliable workers who are dedicated to fostering strong ties with customers and partners. They must build workforces capable of efficient, high-quality production needed to compete in global markets. Savvy business leaders also realize that the brainpower of employees plays a vital role in a firm's ability to stay on top of new technologies and innovations. In short, a first-class workforce can be the foundation of a firm's competitive differentiation, providing important advantages over competing businesses.

Changes in the Workforce

Companies now face several trends that challenge their skills for managing and developing human resources: aging of the population, a shrinking labor pool, growing diversity of the workforce, the changing nature of work, and new employer-employee relationships.

Aging of the Population   Members of the baby boom generation, people born between 1946 and 1965, are nearing the peaks of their careers, and the oldest of them have begun to retire. So employers must deal with issues arising from reliance on older workers, such as retirement, disability programs, retraining, and insurance benefits. By 2030, the number of Americans who are age 65 or older will reach 71 million—nearly double what it is today. These seniors will represent nearly 20 percent of the U.S. population. For every five working-age adults in the year 2000, there was one person age 65 or older, but by the year 2030, there will be only three working-age adults for every senior citizen.[22] As Table 1.2 illustrates, the U.S. Census Bureau has even identified the median population age of individual states—Maine has the oldest median population age at 40.6, while Utah has the youngest at 27.9.

A similar trend is occurring on a global scale. The worldwide population of seniors is expected to double by 2030 as well, from 420 million to 973 million. In fact, other countries are aging faster than the United States because of low birth rates and improved healthcare services. The median age in Japan is 42.9; in Europe it is 40.7.[23]

Table

1.2

Twenty States with the Oldest and Youngest Median Ages

Oldest			Youngest		
Rank	State	Median Age	Rank	State	Median Age
1	Maine	40.6	1	Utah	27.9
2, 3	Vermont	40.2	2	Texas	32.8
	West Virginia	40.2	3	Alaska	33.3
4	Montana	39.5	4	Georgia	33.8
5	Florida	39.3	5, 6	Arizona	34.1
6	Pennsylvania	39.2		Idaho	34.1
7	Connecticut	38.8	7	California	34.2
8–10	Iowa	38.0	8	Colorado	34.3
	Rhode Island	38.0	9	Mississippi	34.7
	Wyoming	38.0	10	Louisiana	34.9

Source: Data from U.S. Census Bureau, as cited in Haya El Nasser and Paul Overberg, "Youthquakes Shake Up Gray-Haired States," *USA Today*, March 10, 2005, p. 3A.

Because of these changes, companies are increasingly seeking—and finding—talent at the extreme ends of the working-age spectrum. Teenagers are entering the workforce sooner, and some seniors are staying longer—or seeking new careers after retiring from their primary careers. Companies that once encouraged early retirement are now developing incentives to keep workers on longer. Many older workers work part-time or flexible hours. Monsanto has a program that allows retired workers to return part time without giving up their retiree benefits. Procter & Gamble and Eli Lilly founded YourEncore, a service company that contracts retired scientists, engineers, and product developers out to other firms that need part-time or short-term help.[24]

Shrinking Labor Pool   Today's managers face the opposite problem: a shrinking labor pool. Some economists predict that the U.S. workforce could fall short by as many as 10 million by 2010. More sophisticated technology has intensified the challenge by requiring workers to have more advanced skills. Although the pool of college-educated workers has doubled in the last 20 years, the demand is still greater than the supply of these individuals.

The challenge of a shrinking labor pool is especially great in developed nations, where the birthrate has shrunk to less than the rate of deaths. Particularly in Europe, the population of some countries is expected to decline over the first half of this century. The same forecasts predict continued growth in the U.S. population because immigration more than makes up for the low birthrate. In the future, as in the past, immigrants will provide a significant share of U.S. labor and entrepreneurship. Currently, immigrants represent one of every seven U.S. workers, and one of every two workers who are new to the workforce.[25]

Increasingly Diverse Workforce   Reflecting these immigration trends, the U.S. workforce is growing more diverse. In the last decade, California and Florida received the most immigrants, although Colorado, North Carolina, and Kentucky experienced the greatest *percentage*

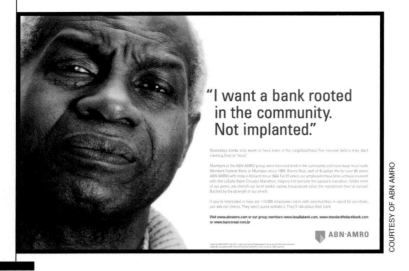

"I want a bank rooted in the community. Not implanted."

COURTESY OF ABN AMRO

assessment check

1. How does the aging workforce affect businesses?

2. How can businesses benefit from a diverse workforce?

outsourcing using outside vendors to produce goods or fulfill services and functions that were previously handled in-country or in-house.

of growth in foreign-born residents. In addition, the two fastest-growing populations in the United States are those of Hispanic and Asian origins. Currently, Hispanics represent about 14 percent of the United States population and Asians represent about 4 percent.[26] Many of these individuals are looking for jobs, and companies are willing to train them. Managers must also learn to work effectively with diverse ethnic groups, cultures, and lifestyles to develop and retain a superior workforce for their company.

Diversity, blending individuals of different genders, ethnic backgrounds, cultures, religions, ages, and physical and mental abilities, can enhance a firm's chances of success. Several studies have shown that diverse employee teams and workforces tend to perform tasks more effectively and develop better solutions to business problems than homogeneous employee groups. This difference is due in part to the varied perspectives and experiences that foster innovation and creativity in multicultural teams.

To benefit from diversity, executives of many companies develop high-profile strategies to encourage and manage multiculturalism. UPS is one such firm. Minorities account for 35 percent of the company's 317,000 employees in the United States. Top leaders at UPS believe that "diversity is a valuable, core component of UPS because it brings a wider range of resources, skills, and ideas to the business." The firm has a UPS Diversity Steering Council that oversees the commitment to diversity, including equal opportunity and promotion programs, team building, and employee stock ownership. UPS has received many awards for its focus on diversity, including being ranked on *Fortune*'s list of "50 Best Companies for Minorities" several years running.[27] The ad for ABN AMRO in Figure 1.8 illustrates the worldwide banking group's commitment to diversity with its 110,000 employees in 60 countries.

Also, practical managers know that attention to diversity issues can help them avoid costly and damaging legal battles. Employee lawsuits alleging discrimination are a major legal issue that employers face. Losing a discrimination lawsuit can be very costly, yet in a recent survey, a majority of executives from racial and cultural minorities said they had seen discrimination in work assignments.

Outsourcing and the Changing Nature of Work Not only is the U.S. workforce changing, but so is the very nature of work. Manufacturing used to account for most of U.S. annual output, but the scale has now shifted to services such as financial management and communications. This means that firms must rely heavily on well-trained service workers with knowledge, technical skills, the ability to communicate and deal with people, and a talent for creative thinking. Different work lifestyles, such as telecommuting, are also becoming common in business life. Many employers allow job flexibility so employees can meet family and personal needs along with job-related needs. Employers are also hiring growing numbers of temporary and part-time employees.

The Internet has made possible another business tool for staffing flexibility—**outsourcing**, using outside vendors to produce goods or fulfill services and functions that were previously handled in-country or in-house. For example, if you dial the call center for America Online, your call most likely will be answered by someone in India. Companies outsource certain functions for several reasons, among them reduction of labor or production costs and improvement in the quality or speed of software maintenance or development. In the best situation, outsourcing allows a firm to concentrate its resources on the things it does best. It also provides access to expertise that may not exist within the firm. But outsourcing also creates its own challenges, such as differences in language or culture. When Dell Computer received numerous complaints from customers who were frustrated by the outsourcing of its help line to a firm in India, Dell began to roll back some of its customer service operations to the United States.

Offshoring is the relocation of business processes to lower-cost locations overseas. This can include both production and services. In recent years, China has emerged as a dominant location for production offshoring for many firms, while India has become the key player in offshoring services. Some U.S. companies are now structured so that entire divisions or functions are developed and staffed overseas—the jobs were never in the United States to start with. According to one survey, nearly 40 percent of start-up companies employ engineers, marketers, and other workers in India and other countries. Google began hiring outside the United States only three years after it opened its virtual doors, and a significant number of its 3,000 employees are located in offices in Toronto, London, Tokyo, Paris, Milan, Sydney, Dublin, and other cities.[28]

Another trend has developed in some industries—**nearshoring,** which involves outsourcing production or services to locations near firm's home base. For example, western European companies have discovered a talented labor pool in the eastern European countries of Bulgaria and Romania. German software giant SAP has a research lab in Bulgaria, where nearly 200 engineers write software for SAP's products. The United States has also benefited from nearshoring by locating offices and factories in Mexico and the Caribbean to tap nearby labor forces.[29]

The New Employer-Employee Partnership The old relationship between employers and employees was pretty simple: workers arrived at a certain hour, did their jobs, and went home every day at the same time. Often the two were tied together for their working lifetime. Companies rarely laid off workers, and employees rarely left for a job at another firm. But all of that—and more—has changed. Employees are no longer likely to remain with a single company throughout their entire careers. In fact, you probably can't imagine working for one company your entire life. On the other hand, you probably expect to work more than the traditional 8-hour workday. You don't necessarily expect lifetime loyalty from the company you work for, but you don't expect to give it either. Instead, you are looking forward to building your own career however and wherever you can.

These changes mean that employers and employees must forge new partnerships. As the nature of work and the workforce are changing, so is the nature of the relationship between employers and employees. Many firms now recognize the value of a partnership with employees that encourages creative thinking, problem solving, and innovation. Managers are being trained to listen to and respect employees. Companies now routinely share financial data and reward employees with benefits such as stock and profit sharing so that they feel more committed to contributing to their firm's success. In addition, employees often receive training geared toward career advancement in the hope that they will remain with the firm that trains them. Microsoft focuses on recruiting employees who are capable of innovative thinking in both business and technology. Founder Bill Gates believes that fostering a culture of creativity among employees has allowed his firm to grow and to take risks on future products.[30]

assessment check

1. Define outsourcing, offshoring, and nearshoring.
2. Describe the new employer-employee partnership.

THE 21ST-CENTURY MANAGER

Today's companies look for managers who are intelligent, highly motivated people with the ability to create and sustain a vision of how an organization can succeed. The 21st-century manager must also apply critical-thinking skills and creativity to business challenges and steer change.

Importance of Vision

To thrive in the 21st century, businesspeople need **vision**, the ability to perceive marketplace needs and what an organization must do to satisfy them. Forty years ago, Amar Bose saw an opportunity in the marketplace when he invented the sound system that still bears his name. He continues to run his firm with the same kind of vision he had when he began: Bose secures his company's place in the future by reinvesting a large portion of its $1.7 billion earnings into the research and development of new products. One of the firm's latest innovations is a super-smooth automobile suspension system. Bose realizes that bringing his firm's products to market involves taking a risk. But he believes in his company. "We just know that we have a technology that's so different and so much better that many people will want it," he says.[31]

It takes vision to turn a tiny handbag shop located in a New York apartment into a $125 million design business that offers shoes, fragrances, china—and, of course, handbags. But Kate Spade and her husband Andy have managed to do exactly that. Once their bags became popular, they decided to take a chance. "We knew we had a window of opportunity, but the point was to get into a category that had a growth prospect, and not for growth to simply be the byproduct," says Kate.[32] Note that the founders of both of these companies understand the importance of following through with sound business and marketing practices.

Importance of Critical Thinking and Creativity

Critical thinking and creativity are essential characteristics of the 21st-century workforce. Today's businesspeople need to look at a wide variety of situations, draw connections between disparate information, and develop future-oriented solutions. This need applies not only to top executives, but to midlevel managers and entry-level workers as well.

Critical thinking is the ability to analyze and assess information to pinpoint problems or opportunities. The critical-thinking process includes activities such as determining the authenticity, accuracy, and worth of information, knowledge, and arguments. It involves looking beneath the surface for deeper meaning and connections that can help identify critical issues and solutions. Without critical thinking, a firm may encounter serious problems, as described in the "Hit & Miss" feature.

Creativity is the capacity to develop novel solutions to perceived organizational problems. Although most people think of it in relation to artists, musicians, and inventors, that is a very limited definition. In business, creativity refers to the ability to see better and different ways of doing business. A computer engineer who solves a glitch in a software program is executing a creative act; so is a shipping clerk who finds a way to speed delivery of the company's overnight packages. Companies must constantly find innovative ways to communicate with and attract new customers, while keeping the interest of established customers. Howard Schultz, founder of Starbucks, looks to all of his employees for new ideas—particularly those who interact with customers in Starbucks stores every day. He loves to tell the story of the Starbucks store manager in West Los Angeles who "was fooling around one day in our store, blending beverages with a blender she bought on her own." The company distributed samples of one of the beverages throughout several southern California stores, and both managers and customers gave it a positive review. "We tested it, named it, and Frappuccino today is a multi-hundred-million dollar business in our stores," says Schultz.[33]

Some practice and mental exercise can cultivate your own ability to think creatively. Here are some exercises and guidelines:

- In a group, brainstorm by listing ideas as they come to mind. Build on other people's ideas, but don't criticize them. Wait until later to evaluate and organize the ideas.
- Think about how to make familiar concepts unfamiliar. A glue that doesn't stick very well? That's the basis for 3M's popular Post-it notes.

How Jones Soda Regained Its Fizz

Entrepreneurs must be willing to take risks—it is part of the job. Often, they make mistakes simply from lack of experience. But the lessons they learn from those mistakes can eventually strengthen their businesses. That's what happened to Peter van Stolk, founder of Jones Soda.

Twenty years ago, van Stolk squeezed fresh fruit juices on the streets of Canada. He was so successful that his company, Urban Juice & Soda, grew to $6 million in sales. Within five years it went public on the Vancouver stock exchange and later began trading in the United States. In 2000, the company's name was changed to Jones Soda. The firm was on a steady climb to fame and fortune. "It all seemed simple," recalls van Stolk, perhaps a bit wistfully.

Then the soft-drink bubble burst. The firm had to recall 1 million bottles because ingredients were breaking down too quickly. That year "was pretty much shot because of that," says van Stolk. He sued the supplier and eventually received a $4 million settlement, but that didn't replace lost sales or confidence in the product. When Jones Soda moved its headquarters to Seattle, few distributors agreed to handle the drinks because they'd never heard of Jones and competition from the larger soft-drink companies was intense. Van Stolk kept spending money on advertising and incentives to distributors until his marketing expenses topped $7.6 million. The company was literally giving away cases of soda. "The only thing that mattered to us was the top line," explains van Stolk. "We were building the company to be sold."

But no one wanted Jones. Meanwhile, Jones botched a potentially lucrative deal with Pepsi by hastily delivering a mislabeled product, resulting in a $400,000 loss, and five of its distributors went bankrupt. "Store shelves were going empty, and our competitors were quick to fill them," notes van Stolk.

Just when Jones couldn't seem to get any flatter, Panera Bread approached the firm and agreed to carry some of its products in their restaurants. Barnes & Noble followed and now carries Jones Naturals juices and teas in all 500 of its cafes. Then Starbucks came through—Jones drinks are now in 4,000 Starbucks shops across the United States. Finally, van Stolk persuaded Target to purchase Jones in concentrated form, then do its own bottling. Target accounts for $1 million of Jones Soda's annual earnings. By selling 22 percent of its beverages directly to retailers instead of dealing with distributors, Jones Soda has returned to profitability with an increase in profits of nearly 300 percent in one year. Van Stolk has learned that haste—as in the case of the Pepsi deal—often makes waste and that business is never simple. But the fizz is back in Jones Soda.

Questions for Critical Thinking

1. Do you think van Stolk had a clear vision when he started his firm? Why or why not?
2. How might critical thinking have helped Jones Soda avoid some of its pitfalls? How might it help the firm in the future?

Sources: Jones Soda Web site, accessed May 26, 2006, http://www.jonessoda.com; Christopher Steiner, "Soda Jerk," *Forbes*, May 26, 2006, pp. 74–75; "Jones Soda Co. Announces Record Fourth Quarter and 2004 Year-End Financial Results," *Yahoo!*, accessed May 26, 2006, http://biz.yahoo .com; "Soda Company Serves Up Feast in a Bottle," *(Danbury, CT) News-Times*, accessed May 26, 2006, http://www .newstimes180.com.

- Plan ways to rearrange your thinking with simple questions such as, "What features can we leave out?" or by imagining what it feels like to be the customer.
- Cultivate curiosity, openness, risk, and energy as you meet people and encounter new situations. View these encounters as opportunities to learn.
- Treat failures as additional opportunities to learn.
- Get regular physical exercise. When you work out, your brain releases endorphins, and these chemicals stimulate creative thinking.
- Pay attention to your dreams and daydreams. You might find that you already know the answer to a problem.

Creativity and critical thinking must go beyond generating new ideas, however. They must lead to action. In addition to creating an environment in which employees can nurture ideas, managers must give them opportunities to take risks and try new solutions.

Figure

1.9

Aetna's Health Fund Insurance Plans: Staying
Ahead through Innovation and Change

COURTESY OF AETNA INC.

Ability to Steer Change

Today's business owners must guide their employees and organizations through the changes brought about by technology, marketplace demands, and global competition. Managers must be skilled at recognizing employee strengths and motivating people to move toward common goals as members of a team. Throughout this book, real-world examples demonstrate how companies have initiated sweeping change initiatives. Most, if not all, have been led by managers comfortable with the tough decisions that today's fluctuating conditions require. For the past decade, managers in the fast-food industry have been searching for ways to create healthier, better-tasting menu offerings that consumers will actually buy and eat. They've had more failures than successes—hardly anyone cared about McDonald's McLean burgers or McSalad Shakers, and Taco Bell's Border Lights didn't light up the cash registers. But they keep trying. "My job has become a lot harder," says the vice president of menu marketing at Jack in the Box.[34]

Factors that require organizational change can come from both external and internal sources; successful managers must be aware of both. External forces might include feedback from customers, developments in the international marketplace, economic trends, and new technologies. Internal factors might arise from new company goals, emerging employee needs, labor union demands, or production problems. Figure 1.9 illustrates health insurance firm Aetna's response to consumer demands for change.

assessment check

1. Why is vision an important managerial quality?
2. What is the difference between creativity and critical thinking?

WHAT MAKES A COMPANY ADMIRED?

Who is your hero? Is it someone who has achieved great feats in sports, government, entertainment, or business? Why do you admire the person—does he or she run a company, earn a lot of money, or give back to the community and society? Every year, business magazines and organizations publish lists of companies that they consider to be "most admired." Companies, like individuals, may be admired for many reasons. Most people would mention solid profits, stable growth, a safe and challenging work environment, high-quality goods and services, and business ethics and social responsibility. *Business ethics* refers to the standards of conduct and moral values involving decisions made in the work environment. *Social responsibility* is a management philosophy that includes contributing resources to the community, preserving the natural environment, and developing or participating in nonprofit programs designed to promote the well-being of the general public. You'll find business ethics and social responsibility examples throughout this book, as well as a deeper exploration of these topics in Chapter 2. Figure 1.10 illustrates medical technology firm Becton, Dickinson's socially responsible commitment to diabetes research.

assessment check

1. Define business ethics and social responsibility.
2. Identify three criteria used to judge whether a company might be considered admirable.

As you read this text, you'll be able to make up your own mind about why companies should—or should not—be admired. *Fortune* publishes two lists of most-admired companies each year, one for U.S.-based firms and one for the world. The list is compiled from surveys and other research conducted by the Hay Group, a global human resources and organizational consulting firm. Criteria for making the list include innovation, financial soundness, use of corporate assets, long-term investment, people management, quality of management, social responsibility,

Table 1.3

Figure 1.10

Fortune's Top Ten Most Admired U.S. Companies

1	General Electric	6	Johnson & Johnson
2	FedEx	7	Berkshire Hathaway
3	Southwest Airlines	8	Dell
4	Procter & Gamble	9	Toyota Motor
5	Starbucks	10	Microsoft

Source: Data from http://www.timeinc.net/fortune/information/Presscenter/ 0,,20060221_mostadmired,00.html, accessed June 13, 2006.

and quality of products and services.[35] Table 1.3 lists the top ten U.S. firms for one recent year.[36]

WHAT'S AHEAD

As business speeds along in the 21st century, new technologies, population shifts, and shrinking global barriers are altering the world at a frantic pace. Businesspeople are catalysts for many of these changes, creating new opportunities for individuals who are prepared to take action. Studying contemporary business will help you prepare for the future.

Throughout this book, you'll be exposed to the real-life stories of many businesspeople. You'll learn about the range of business careers available and the daily decisions, tasks, and challenges that they face. By the end of the course, you'll understand how marketing, accounting, finance, and management work together to provide competitive advantages for firms. This knowledge can help you become a more capable employee and enhance your career potential.

Now that this chapter has introduced some basic terms and issues in the business world of the 21st century, Chapter 2 takes a detailed look at the ethical and social responsibility issues facing contemporary business. Chapter 3 deals with economic challenges, and Chapter 4 focuses on the challenges and opportunities faced by firms competing in global markets.

Becton, Dickinson's Fight to Cure Diabetes: Commitment to Social Responsibility

COURTESY AND © BECTON, DICKINSON AND COMPANY

SUMMARY OF LEARNING GOALS

1 Distinguish between business and not-for-profit organizations.

Business consists of all profit-seeking activities that provide goods and services necessary to an economic system. Not-for-profit organizations are business-like establishments whose primary objectives involve social, political, governmental, educational, or similar functions—instead of profits.

Assessment Check Answers

1.1 What activity lies at the heart of every business endeavor?

At the heart of every business endeavor is an exchange between a buyer and a seller.

1.2 What are the primary objectives of a not-for-profit organization?

Not-for-profit organizations place public service above profits, although they need to raise money in order to operate and achieve their social goals.

2 Identify and describe the factors of production.

The factors of production consist of four basic inputs: natural resources, capital, human resources, and entrepreneurship. Natural resources include all productive inputs that are useful in their natural states. Capital includes technology, tools, information, and physical facilities. Human resources include anyone who works for the firm. Entrepreneurship is the willingness to take risks to create and operate a business.

Assessment Check Answers

2.1 Identify the four basic inputs to an economic system.
The four basic inputs are natural resources, capital, human resources, and entrepreneurship.

2.2 List four types of capital.
Four types of capital are technology, tools, information, and physical facilities.

3 Describe the private enterprise system, including basic rights and entrepreneurship.
The private enterprise system is an economic system that rewards firms for their ability to perceive and serve the needs and demands of consumers. Competition in the private enterprise system ensures success for firms that satisfy consumer demands. Citizens in a private enterprise economy enjoy the rights to private property, profits, freedom of choice, and competition. Entrepreneurship drives economic growth.

Assessment Check Answers

3.1 What is an alternative term for _private enterprise system_?
Capitalism is an alternative word for _private enterprise system_.

3.2 What is the most basic freedom under the private enterprise system?
The most basic freedom is the right to private property.

3.3 What is an entrepreneur?
An entrepreneur is a risk taker who is willing to start, own, and operate a business.

4 Identify the six eras of business and explain how the relationship era—including alliances and technology—influences contemporary business.
The six historical eras are the Colonial period, the Industrial Revolution, the age of industrial entrepreneurs, the production era, the marketing era, and the relationship era. In the Colonial period, businesses were small and rural, emphasizing agricultural production. The Industrial Revolution brought factories and mass production to business. The age of industrial entrepreneurs built on the Industrial Revolution through an expansion in the number and size of firms.

The production era focused on the growth of factory operations through assembly lines and other efficient internal processes. During and following the Great Depression, businesses concentrated on finding markets for their products through advertising and selling, giving rise to the marketing era. In the relationship era, businesspeople focus on developing and sustaining long-term relationships with customers and other businesses. Technology promotes innovation and communication, while alliances create a competitive advantage through partnerships.

Assessment Check Answers

4.1 What was the Industrial Revolution?
The Industrial Revolution began around 1750 in England, and moved business operations from an emphasis on independent, skilled workers to a factory system that mass-produced items.

4.2 During which era was the idea of branding developed?
The idea of branding began in the marketing era.

4.3 What is the difference between transaction management and relationship management?
Transaction management is an approach that focuses on building, promoting, and selling enough products to cover costs and earn profits. Relationship management is the collection of activities that build and maintain ongoing ties with customers and other parties.

5 Explain how today's business workforce is changing.
The workforce is changing in several significant ways: (1) it is aging; (2) the labor pool is shrinking; and (3) it is becoming increasingly diverse.

Assessment Check Answers

5.1 How does the aging workforce affect business?
An aging workforce requires businesses to hire workers at both extreme ends of the working-age spectrum.

5.2 How can businesses benefit from a diverse workforce?
A diverse workforce can enrich a company's chances of success because diverse groups tend to perform tasks more effectively and develop better solutions. They also tend to foster greater innovation.

6 Describe how the nature of work itself is changing.
The nature of work has shifted toward services and a focus on information. More firms now rely on outsourcing, offshoring, and nearshoring to produce goods

or fulfill services and functions that were previously handled in-house or in-country. In addition, new employer-employee partnerships are being forged.

Assessment Check Answers

6.1 Define *outsourcing*, *offshoring*, and *nearshoring*.
Outsourcing involves using outside vendors to produce goods or fulfill services and functions that were once handled in-house or in-country. Offshoring is the relocation of business processes to lower-cost locations overseas. Nearshoring is the outsourcing of production or services to locations near a firm's home base.

6.2 Describe the new employer-employee partnership.
The new employer-employee partnership encourages creative thinking, problem solving, and innovation. Managers are trained to listen to and respect employees. Companies now routinely share financial data and reward employees with certain financial benefits.

7 **Identify the skills and attributes that managers need to lead businesses in the 21st century.**
Managers in the new century need vision, the ability to perceive marketplace needs and how their firm can satisfy them. Critical-thinking skills and creativity allow managers to pinpoint problems and opportunities and plan novel solutions. Finally, managers are dealing with rapid change, and they need skills to help steer their organizations through shifts in external and internal conditions.

Assessment Check Answers

7.1 Why is vision an important managerial quality?
Managerial vision allows a firm to innovate and adapt to meet changes in the marketplace.

7.2 What is the difference between creativity and critical thinking?
Critical thinking is the ability to analyze and assess information to pinpoint problems or opportunities. Creativity is the capacity to develop novel solutions to perceived organizational problems.

Outline the characteristics that make a company admired by the business community.

8 A company is usually admired for its solid profits, stable growth, a safe and challenging work environment, high-quality goods and services, and business ethics and social responsibility.

Assessment Check Answers

8.1 Define *business ethics* and *social responsibility*.
Business ethics refers to the standards of conduct and moral values involving decisions made in the work environment. Social responsibility is a management philosophy that includes contributing resources to the community, preserving the natural environment, and developing or participating in nonprofit programs designed to promote the well-being of the general public.

8.2 Identify three criteria used to judge whether a company might be considered admirable.
Criteria in judging whether companies are admirable include solid profits, stable growth, a safe and challenging work environment, high-quality goods and services, and business ethics and social responsibility.

Business Terms You Need to Know

business 4	private enterprise system 9	brand 15
profits 5	competition 9	relationship management 16
factors of production 6	entrepreneur 10	outsourcing 20

Other Important Business Terms

not-for-profit organizations 5	private property 9	strategic alliance 17
natural resources 6	consumer orientation 14	diversity 20
capital 6	branding 14	offshoring 21
human resources 7	transaction management 15	nearshoring 21
entrepreneurship 8	relationship era 15	vision 22
capitalism 9	technology 16	critical thinking 22
competitive differentiation 9	partnership 17	creativity 22

1. Why is business so important to a country's economy?
2. In what ways are not-for-profit organizations a substantial part of the U.S. economy? What challenges will not-for-profits face in the next decade or two?
3. Identify and describe the four basic inputs that make up factors of production. Give an example of each factor of production that an auto manufacturer might use.
4. What is a private enterprise system? What are the four rights that are critical to the operation of capitalism? Why would capitalism have difficulty functioning in a society that does not assure these rights for its citizens?
5. In what ways is entrepreneurship vital to the private enterprise system?
6. Identify the six eras of business in the United States. How were businesses changed during each era?
7. Describe the focus of the most recent era of U.S. business. How is this different from previous eras?
8. How might a supermarket chain use technology to assist in its relationship management?
9. Define *partnership* and *strategic alliance*. How might a motorcycle dealer and a local radio station benefit from an alliance?
10. Identify the major changes in the workforce that will affect the way managers build a world-class workforce in the 21st century. Why is brainpower so important?
11. Identify four qualities that the "new" managers of the 21st century must have. Why are these qualities important in a competitive business environment?

1. The entrepreneurial spirit fuels growth in the U.S. economy. Choose a company that interests you—one you have worked for or dealt with as a customer—and read about the company in the library or visit its Web site. Learn what you can about the company's early history: Who founded it and why? Is the founder still with the organization? Do you think the founder's original vision is still embraced by the company? If not, how has the vision changed?
2. Brands distinguish one company's goods or services from its competitors. Each company you purchase from hopes that you will become loyal to its brand. Some well-known brands are McDonald's, Coca-Cola, Hilton, and Old Navy. Choose a type of good or service you use regularly and identify the major brands associated with it. Are you loyal to a particular brand? Why or why not?
3. More and more businesses are forming strategic alliances to become more competitive. Sometimes, businesses pair up with not-for-profit organizations in a relationship that is beneficial to both. Choose a company whose goods or services interest you, such as Timberland, Patagonia, General Mills, or Wal-Mart. On your own or with a classmate, research the firm on the Internet to learn about its alliances with not-for-profit organizations. Then describe one of the alliances, including goals and benefits to both parties. Create a presentation for class.
4. This chapter describes how the nature of the workforce is changing: the population is aging, the labor pool is shrinking, the workforce is becoming more diverse, the nature of work is changing, and employers are forging new partnerships with their employees. Form teams of two to three students. Select a company and research how that company is responding to changes in the workforce. When you have completed your research, be prepared to present it to your class. Choose one of the following companies or select your own:

   - Costco
   - Whole Foods Market
   - Nordstrom
   - Marriott
   - Dell Computer

Under Armour: Built with Sweat Equity

You've heard the term *sweat equity*—businesses built with lots of work and little cash. Under Armour, founded by college student Kevin Plank, was built on this concept. Plank, and his college football teammates at the University of Maryland, got tired of wearing soggy, shapeless cotton T-shirts. The clammy shirts made them feel uncomfortable as they played, but Plank couldn't find anything better.

Plank was determined to find an answer to the problem. A natural entrepreneur—he'd already started a floral delivery service from his dorm—Plank began combing fabric stores for something that would give a snug, smooth fit and carry away moisture at the same time. He found a slinky synthetic fabric, bought it, and paid a tailor $400 to sew several prototypes for his teammates to try. They loved it. "They said the shirt was great for football—and baseball and lacrosse, too," recalls Plank. "I realized this wasn't just a shirt but a marketing opportunity."

Once Plank had graduated from college, he pursued his dream full time. Working from the basement of his grandmother's home, he borrowed $40,000 on his credit cards to get started and later received a $250,000 small-business loan. Plank didn't have a sales force, so he took his shirts from school to school, and from pro team to pro team, where some of his college football teammates were now playing. When sports fans started to see Under Armour apparel on pro football players, they wanted the same thing. Then Plank had to find a factory to make more shirts.

Today, Under Armour dominates the market for "tight-fitting compression wear," as it is called, with more than $200 million in sales per year. "When people ask for compression gear, they ask for Under Armour, like Scotch tape or Xerox machines," says Ron Menconi, vice president of the sporting goods

chain G.I. Joe's in Oregon and Washington. Under Armour is currently the official supplier of compression apparel to Major League Baseball and Major League Soccer, and its clothing is worn by players on 30 NFL teams and nearly 100 Division 1-A college football teams, including Plank's alma mater, the University of Maryland. Plank also makes certain that his firm gives something back to the community. As chairman of the Baltimore City Fire Foundation, he uses his firm's popularity to help raise funds for the fire department.

In addition to the original T-shirt, Plank's firm now makes everything from shorts and leggings to knit caps, headbands and wristbands, socks and gloves, and even gym bags. Plank's products are so innovative that competing manufacturer Neal Caplowe of Sport Science calls them "the new mousetrap." Caplowe explains, "Whether it's product innovation, packaging or right-time, right-place or all of the above, they basically were able to light the fuse."

Questions for Critical Thinking

1. Identify specific examples of factors of production that Under Armour requires for effective operation.
2. Explain how innovation, creativity, and critical thinking have all played a role in the development of Under Armour as a company.

Sources: Under Armour Web site, accessed May 26, 2006, http://www.underarmour.com; "ESPN, Under Armour Sign Deal," Brandweek.com, accessed May 26, 2006, http://www.brandweek.com; Jane Bennett Clark and Kimberly Lankford, "How to Make a Million," *Kiplinger's,* February 2005, pp. 69–74; Barbara De Lollis, "No Sweat: Idea for Athletic Gear Takes Him to the Top," *USA Today,* December 13, 2004, pp. B1, B2.

VIDEO Case 1.2

Peet's Coffee & Tea Brews Good Business

This video case appears on page 608. A recently filmed video, designed to expand and highlight the written case, is available for class use by instructors.

Chapter 2

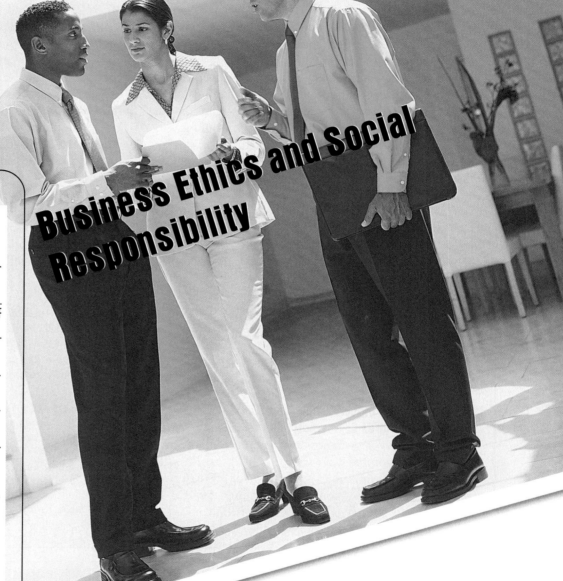

Business Ethics and Social Responsibility

Learning Goals

1. Explain the concepts of business ethics and social responsibility.

2. Describe the factors that influence business ethics.

3. List the stages in the development of ethical standards.

4. Identify common ethical dilemmas in the workplace.

5. Discuss how organizations shape ethical behavior.

6. Describe how businesses' social responsibility is measured.

7. Summarize the responsibilities of business to the general public, customers, and employees.

8. Explain why investors and the financial community are concerned with business ethics and social responsibility.

When a small café in Waitsfield, Vermont, opened for business in 1981, owner Bob Stiller didn't expect that his fresh-roast business would grow into a $137 million firm or become one of the nation's largest specialty-coffee manufacturers. But that's exactly what happened. Thanks to the high quality of Green Mountain's fresh-roasted blends and its commitment to a set of highly ethical guiding principles, the company has more than 7,000 wholesale clients and thousands of mail-order and Internet customers around the country. Its ethical guidelines put the health of the environment second only to passion for coffee—and rank ethics above all. The company's Web site emphasizes Green Mountain's social conscience: "We create the ultimate coffee experience in every life we touch

PHOTODISC/GETTY IMAGES

Green Mountain Cares about More Than Coffee

from tree to cup, transforming the way the world understands business."

As the company has grown, Green Mountain Coffee Roasters has expanded the range of its commitments to include not only making wise use of the world's resources but also safeguarding the welfare of all those it deals with, from customers at home to coffee farmers far away. When it comes to the environment, Green Mountain, now headquartered in Waterbury, Vermont, has three core values:

- to consider the environmental impact of its actions in every decision
- to seek continuous environmental innovation in its products and programs
- to promote employee awareness of and participation in environmental efforts

The company works hard to put these values into practice. For instance, National Wildlife Blend and National Wildlife Decaf are two certified organic blends Green Mountain developed in cooperation with the National Wildlife Federation. These coffees offer consumers an alternative to inexpensive commercial coffees that must be grown in full sun, which means large-scale land clearing for coffee-growing areas and the destruction of bird and other wildlife habitats. The National

Wildlife cobranded coffees are made from shade-grown beans harvested by trusted small-scale farms in Mexico and Peru. Green Mountain is also a staunch supporter of fair trade pricing, which guarantees farmers fair prices for their crops so that "they can afford to feed their families, keep their kids in school and invest in the quality of their coffee."

To contribute to the communities in which it operates, Green Mountain encourages its nearly 600 employees to volunteer their time and expertise. Its Community Action for Employees (CAFÉ) program provides paid time off for community service, including in a recent year nearly 2,000 hours of employee time donated to schools, fire departments, rescue squads, and other community organizations. Employees even volunteer to visit Mexican and Central American coffee farms to help farmers improve their families' and their communities' healthcare and housing.

Green Mountain's corporate-wide efforts to help its communities include financial support for charitable organizations such as the United Way, the Salvation Army, and the Red Cross, as well as for many local organizations such as libraries, schools, and food programs. The company also created two matching funds to supplement the money donated by employees to aid relief of the 2004 tsunami that struck Sumatra, where many coffee growers live and work, and it continues to plan long-term strategies to provide assistance there. In addition to such efforts, the company each year contributes at least 5 percent of its pretax profits to social programs, and it has been frequently recognized for its good works by *Forbes* magazine in its annual list of "200 Best Small Companies" and *Business Ethics* magazine's "100 Best Corporate Citizens."

Within its organization, Green Mountain upholds the values of open dialogue and communication. The firm appreciates employee differences and tries to find opportunity in conflict and continuous learning. Teamwork, shared ownership and use of resources, and a commitment to personal excellence that includes self-awareness and respect all encourage leadership throughout the organization. Last but not least in this company's set of guiding values is to be "a force for good in the world." But good business decisions remain paramount. Says CEO Stiller, "To help the world, we have to be successful. If we help the world and go out of business, we're not going to help anybody."[1]

The values that drive Green Mountain's operations at home and abroad are not unique in the world of business. Many firms are concerned about the environment and their societies. Sometimes that means growing more slowly than they might or reducing short-term profits for longer, sustained benefits. Even Green Mountain faces tough decisions, for example, if one of its small-scale suppliers produces beans the firm must reject for quality reasons or because it has reached its production limit.

But although most organizations strive to combine ethical behavior with profitable operation, some large and prominent organizations have struggled to overcome major ethical lapses in recent years. Ethical failures in a number of large or well-known firms led to lawsuits, indictments, fines, guilty pleas, pleas of ignorance, jail sentences for high-profile executives, the financial failures of several powerful U.S. businesses, job losses for thousands of former employees at these firms, and the loss of billions of dollars in investors' savings that had been held as stock shares in these companies. Troubled firms included Enron, Tyco, MCI (formerly WorldCom), Global Crossing, the investment firm Credit Suisse First Boston, and even the venerable auction house Sotheby's.

The image of the CEO—and of business in general—suffered as the evening news carried dramatic pictures of the so-called perp walk—in which indicted and handcuffed corporate executives were paraded before the media in an exercise previously reserved for local criminals. Following a series of disclosures made in congressional investigations and in civil and criminal investigations conducted by state attorneys general, in 2002 Congress enacted the **Sarbanes-Oxley Act** to correct these abuses by adding oversight for the nation's major companies and a special oversight board to regulate public accounting firms that audit the financial records of these corporations. In 2004 the Federal Sentencing Commission strengthened its guidelines for ethics compliance programs, and more and more firms began to pay attention to formulating more explicit standards and procedures for ethical behavior. Companies were also forced to recognize the enormous impact of a good example, as it became clear that stated ethical values mean little if they are not being strictly followed at the very highest levels of the organization.

As we discussed in Chapter 1, the underlying aim of business is to serve customers at a profit. But most companies try to do more than that, looking for ways to give back to customers, society, and the environment. Sometimes they face difficult questions in the process. When does a company's self-interest conflict with society's and customers' well-being? And must the goal of seeking profits conflict with upholding high principles of right and wrong? In response to the second question, a growing number of businesses of all sizes are answering no.

CONCERN FOR ETHICAL AND SOCIETAL ISSUES

An organization that wants to prosper over the long term cannot do so without considering **business ethics,** the standards of conduct and moral values governing actions and decisions in the work environment. Businesses also must take into account a wide range of social issues, including how a decision will affect the environment, employees, and customers. These issues are at the heart of social responsibility, whose primary objective is the enhancement of society's welfare through philosophies, policies, procedures, and actions. In short, businesses must find the delicate balance between doing what is right and doing what is profitable.

In business, as in life, deciding what is right or wrong in a given situation does not always involve a clear-cut choice. Firms have many responsibilities—to customers, to employees, to investors, and to society as a whole. Sometimes conflicts arise in trying to serve the different needs of these separate constituencies. The ethical values of executives and individual employees at all levels can influence the decisions and actions a business takes. Throughout your own business career, you will encounter many situations in which you will need to weigh right and wrong before making a decision or taking action. So we begin our discussion of business ethics by focusing on individual ethics.

Business ethics are also shaped by the ethical climate within an organization. Codes of conduct and ethical standards play increasingly significant roles in businesses in which doing the right thing is both supported and applauded. This chapter demonstrates how a firm can create a framework to encourage—and even demand—high standards of ethical behavior and social responsibility from its employees. The chapter also considers the complex question of what business owes to society and how societal forces mold the actions of businesses. Finally, it examines the influence of business ethics and social responsibility on global business.

THE NEW ETHICAL ENVIRONMENT

Business ethics are now in the spotlight as never before. High-profile investigations, lawsuits, arrests, and convictions, as well as business failures due to fraud and corruption, have created a long string of headline news. While these events have brought about rapid change in many areas and new laws to prevent them from happening again, they have also obscured for many people the fact that most companies and their leaders are highly ethical. The National Business Ethics Survey found that more than 80 percent of employees believed top management in their organizations kept promises and commitments, and most believed that honesty and respect were more prevalent than a few years ago.[2]

Most business owners and managers have built and maintained enduring companies without breaking the rules. One example of a firm with a longstanding commitment to ethical practice is Johnson & Johnson, the giant multinational manufacturer of healthcare products. The most admired pharmaceutical maker and the ninth-most-admired company in the world, according to *Fortune*, Johnson & Johnson has abided by the same basic code of ethics, its well-known Credo, for more than 50 years. The Credo, reproduced in Figure 2.1, remains the ethical standard against which the company's employees periodically evaluate how well their firm is performing. Management is pledged to address any lapses that are reported.[3]

Many CEOs personify the best in management practices and are highly respected for their integrity, honesty, and business ethics. Jeff Immelt, General Electric's CEO, lists four things needed to keep the company at the top of the "most valuable" and "most admired" lists: Virtue first, followed by execution, growth, and great people. Immelt began by appointing the company's first vice president of corporate citizenship, Bob Corcoran, who started a program for reviewing more than 3,000 of GE's overseas suppliers for compliance with labor, health, and safety standards. In its other workforce programs, the company now offers domestic partner benefits to gay employees and has recently won awards for promoting women and African

Sarbanes-Oxley Act federal legislation designed to deter and punish corporate and accounting fraud and corruption and to protect the interests of workers and shareholders through enhanced financial disclosures, criminal penalties on CEOs and CFOs who defraud investors, safeguards for whistle-blowers, and establishment of a new regulatory body for public accounting firms.

business ethics standards of conduct and moral values involving right and wrong actions arising in the work environment.

assessment check

1. To whom do businesses have responsibilities?
2. If a firm is meeting all its responsibilities to others, why do ethical conflicts arise?

Figure

2.1 Johnson & Johnson Credo

Our Credo

We believe our first responsibility is to the doctors, nurses and patients, to mothers and fathers and all others who use our products and services. In meeting their needs everything we do must be of high quality. We must constantly strive to reduce our costs in order to maintain reasonable prices. Customers' orders must be serviced promptly and accurately. Our suppliers and distributors must have an opportunity to make a fair profit.

We are responsible to our employees, the men and women who work with us throughout the world. Everyone must be considered as an individual. We must respect their dignity and recognize their merit. They must have a sense of security in their jobs. Compensation must be fair and adequate, and working conditions clean, orderly and safe. We must be mindful of ways to help our employees fulfill their family responsibilities. Employees must feel free to make suggestions and complaints. There must be equal opportunity for employment, development and advancement for those qualified. We must provide competent management, and their actions must be just and ethical.

We are responsible to the communities in which we live and work and to the world community as well. We must be good citizens—support good works and charities and bear our fair share of taxes. We must encourage civic improvements and better health and education. We must maintain in good order the property we are privileged to use, protecting the environment and natural resources.

Our final responsibility is to our stockholders. Business must make a sound profit. We must experiment with new ideas. Research must be carried on, innovative programs developed and mistakes paid for. New equipment must be purchased, new facilities provided and new products launched. Reserves must be created to provide for adverse times. When we operate according to these principles, the stockholders should realize a fair return.

Source: "Our Company: Our Credo," Johnson & Johnson Web site, accessed June 7, 2006, http://www.jnj.com.

Americans to executive positions. It began an extensive healthcare project in Ghana and purchased companies that purify water, manufacture solar-energy equipment, and produce wind energy—overall doubling its research budget for investigating environmentally sound technologies. "Good leaders give back," says Immelt. "The era we live in belongs to people who believe in themselves but are focused on the needs of others."[4]

However, not all companies set and meet high ethical standards. A survey by Public Agenda and the Kettering Foundation found that typical Americans, interviewed in focus groups, thought that greed and poor values had led many companies astray from their moral bearings, and that a major ethical priority for business should be preserving jobs. Executives interviewed for the study believed that jobs were a business, rather than an ethical, issue.[5]

With passage of the Sarbanes-Oxley Act of 2002, which establishes new rules and regulations for securities trading and accounting practices, a company is also required to publish its code of ethics, if it has one, and inform the public of any changes made to it. The new law may actually motivate even more firms to develop written codes and guidelines for ethical business behavior. The federal government also created the U.S. Sentencing Commission to institutionalize ethics compliance programs that would establish high ethical standards and end corporate misconduct. The requirements for such programs are shown in Table 2.1.

The current ethical environment of business also includes the appointment of new corporate officers specifically charged with deterring wrongdoing and ensuring that ethical standards are met. Ethics compliance officers, whose numbers are rapidly rising, are responsible for conducting employee training programs that help spot potential fraud and abuse within the firm, investigating sexual harassment and discrimination charges, and monitoring any potential conflicts of interest. In some firms, such as Molson Coors, the ethics training program is closely linked to the audit department and the integrity of the company's financial statements.[6] This last responsibility is more important than ever, now that the Sarbanes-Oxley Act requires financial officers and CEOs to personally certify the validity of companies' financial statements.

Individuals Make a Difference

In today's business environment, individuals can make the difference in ethical expectations and behavior. As executives, managers, and employees demonstrate their personal ethical principles—or lack of ethical principles—the expectations and actions of those who work for and with them can change.

What is the current status of individual business ethics in the United States? Although ethical behavior can be difficult to track or even define in all circumstances, evidence suggests

Table

2.1

Minimum Requirements for Ethics Compliance Programs

- **Compliance standards and procedures.** Establish standards and procedures, such as codes of ethics and identification of areas of risk, capable of reducing misconduct or criminal activities.

- **High-level personnel responsibility.** Assign high-level personnel, such as boards of directors and top executives, the overall responsibility to actively lead and oversee ethics compliance programs.

- **Due care in assignments.** Avoid delegating authority to individuals with a propensity for misconduct or illegal activities.

- **Communication of standards and procedures.** Communicate ethical requirements to high-level officials and other employees through ethics training programs or publications that explain in practical terms what is required.

- **Establishment of monitoring and auditing systems and reporting system.** Monitor and review ethical compliance systems and establish a reporting system employees can use to notify the organization of misconduct without fear of retribution.

- **Enforcement of standards through appropriate mechanisms.** Consistently enforce ethical codes, including employee discipline.

- **Appropriate responses to the offense.** Take reasonable steps to respond to the offense and to prevent and detect further violations.

- **Self-reporting.** Report misconduct to the appropriate government agency.

- **Applicable industry practice or standards.** Follow government regulations and industry standards.

Sources: "An Overview of the United States Sentencing Commission and the Federal Sentencing Guidelines," U.S. Sentencing Commission, accessed June 7, 2006, http://www.ussc.gov; "The Relationship between Law and Ethics, and the Significance of the Federal Sentencing Guidelines for Organizations," Ethics and Policy Integration Center, accessed June 7, 2006, http://www.epic-online.net; U.S. Sentencing Commission, "Sentencing Commission Toughens Requirements for Corporate Compliance and Ethics Programs," USSC news release, April 13, 2004.

that some individuals act unethically or illegally on the job. A survey of British employees found that more than a third admitted to spending up to 30 minutes a day using the Internet and the World Wide Web for personal business when they should have been working. This amount of time may not seem abusive, but it adds up to as much as two weeks a year.[7] In another poll, the main types of unethical behavior observed by employees were lying, withholding information, abusing or intimidating employees, inaccurately reporting the amount of time worked, and discrimination. Related to personal ethics in the workplace is the broader issue of being considerate to co-workers and using common office courtesy. The "Business Etiquette" feature explores these issues.

Technology seems to have expanded the range and impact of unethical behavior. For example, anyone with computer access to data has the potential to steal or manipulate the data or to shut down the system, even from a remote location. Often the people who hack into a company's computers are employees, and some observers consider employee attacks the most expensive. Such attacks often result in the theft of intellectual property, such as patented or copyrighted information.

Nearly every employee, at every level, wrestles with ethical questions at some point or another. Some rationalize questionable behavior by saying, "Everybody's

assessment check

1. What role can an ethics compliance officer play in a firm?
2. What factors influence the ethical environment of a business?

ever, people resort to whistle blowing because they believe the unethical behavior is causing significant damage that outweighs the risk that the company will retaliate against the whistle-blower. Those risks have been real in the past. State and federal laws protect whistle-blowers

HIT & MISS

Under the settlement that the U.S. government made with tobacco companies, the industry must work to avoid targeting young people. Part of that effort also involves smoking prevention programs. This photo of a Los Angeles county youth advocate was taken just prior to a youth rally held in Los Angeles.

Responsibilities to the General Public

The responsibilities of business to the general public include dealing with public health issues, protecting the environment, and developing the quality of the workforce. Many would argue that businesses also have responsibilities to support charitable and social causes and organizations that work toward the greater public good. In other words, they should give back to the communities in which they earn profits. Such efforts are called *corporate philanthropy.*

Public-Health Issues One of the most complex issues facing business as it addresses its ethical and social responsibilities to the general public is public health. Central to the public-health debate is the question of what businesses should do about dangerous products such as tobacco and alcohol. Tobacco products represent a major health risk, contributing to heart disease, stroke, and cancer among smokers. Families and co-workers of smokers share this danger as well, as their exposure to secondhand smoke increases their risks for cancer, asthma, and respiratory infections.

Exposure to viruses is harder to control, although vaccines exist for many diseases. Complications from the flu cause up to 36,000 U.S. deaths each year. However, shortages of flu vaccines can cause unexpected havoc, as happened recently when the U.S. supply fell short of the amounts needed at the height of the flu season. Contamination during vaccine production halted shipment of the supply expected from England and forced the government to appeal to the public to save the remaining vaccine for those most at risk. The vaccine takes months to prepare, so additional quantities could not be manufactured in time. In the wake of the shortage, the three vaccine manufacturers issued production estimates for the following season; the company whose products had been contaminated then lowered its estimates by several million doses due to a lag in increasing its capacity.[21]

Substance abuse is another serious public health problem worldwide. The recent revelations of the use of illegal steroids by many athletes, particularly in professional baseball, highlights the difficulty of devising accurate tests for performance-enhancing and muscle-building drugs and fairly evaluating the results. Many of the drugs in question are so similar to compounds naturally present in the body that identification is extremely difficult. With regard to drug testing, athletes' individual rights to privacy have been questioned, particularly due to their widespread influence on youthful fans. Steroid use is on the rise among high school athletes, despite the wide publicity about the dangers of such drugs. Tougher penalties for professional players who fail drug tests are being formulated but are sure to be controversial for the beleaguered sports industry.[22]

Protecting the Environment Businesses consume huge amounts of energy, which increases the use of fossil fuels such as coal and oil for energy production. This activity introduces carbon dioxide and sulfur into the earth's atmosphere, substances that many scientists believe will result in dramatic climate changes during the 21st century. Meanwhile, the sulfur from fossil fuels combines with water vapor in the air to form sulfuric acid. The acid rain that results can kill fish and trees and pollute groundwater. Wind can carry the sulfur around the entire globe. Sulfur from U.S. factories is damaging Canadian forests, and pollution from London smokestacks has been found in the forests and lakes of Scandinavia. Other production and manufacturing methods leave behind large quantities of waste materials that can further pollute the environment and fill already bulging landfills. Some products themselves, particularly electronics that contain toxins such as lead and mercury, are difficult to reuse or recycle. Few manufacturers are really equipped to deal with recycled materials; some refurbish junked products and sell them abroad—where later recycling is even less likely. Hewlett-Packard, however, is making its scanners with a combination of new and recycled plastics, and lead, mercury, and cadmium will soon be banned from new equipment manufactured in Europe.[23]

For many managers, finding ways to minimize **pollution** and other environmental damage caused by their products or operating processes has become an important economic, legal, and social issue. The solutions can be difficult—and expensive. It costs computer makers up to $20 to recycle each old computer, for instance.[24] Drivers may face high costs, too. Hybrid cars use a combination of gas and electricity to power their engines and promise much better fuel efficiency than conventional autos. As gasoline prices soared, sales of U.S. hybrids reached nearly 7,000 a month. Most of the purchasers chose the Toyota Prius hybrid, followed by the Honda Civic. Hybrid pickups and SUVs are on the market, and many more models are on the way. The fuel saving enjoyed by hybrid owners isn't cheap; experts figure that adding the electric system to the car also adds about $3,000 to $4,000 to the vehicle sticker price.[25]

Despite the difficulty, however, companies such as Green Mountain Coffee Roasters, profiled at the beginning of the chapter, are finding that they can be environmentally friendly and profitable, too. A "totally biodegradable and nontoxic plastic" has been developed for Motorola by a Dutch lab, Pvaxx Research and Development. Although the polymer has many possible uses, Motorola is considering using it first in snap-on cell phone covers. Researchers in Britain have also come up with an unusual method of recycling plastic. They have devised a way to embed a sunflower seed in a phone cover, which would use the polymer's waste products as nutrients to grow after the phone is discarded.[26]

Another solution to the problems of pollutants is **recycling**—reprocessing used materials for reuse. Recycling can sometimes provide much of the raw material that manufacturers need, thereby conserving the world's natural resources and reducing the need for landfills. Several industries are developing ways to use recycled materials, although in many cases getting the public to bring used products in is the first hurdle. A recent drive to collect old cell phones in Westchester County, New York, home to about 900,000 people, yielded only 32 units. And according to the Silicon Valley Toxics Coalition, as much as 60 to 80 percent of material intended for recycling "is being dumped in containers and sent to China." But companies such as Collective Good and ReCellular are taking in tens of thousands of cell phones a day and recycling and refurbishing them. TechCycle, in Colorado, recycles all kinds of used equipment and parts, even shipping old computer monitors to China to be made into televisions.[27]

According to the Environmental Protection Agency, discarded electronic units now make up as much as 40 percent of the lead in landfills in the United States, and the International Association of Electronics Recyclers estimates that consumers and businesses will be disposing of 400 million such units by 2010. Manufacturers and federal agencies are struggling to come up with a way to pay for a voluntary system for managing the problem; one possibility is a surcharge consumers would pay on each electronics purchase. In

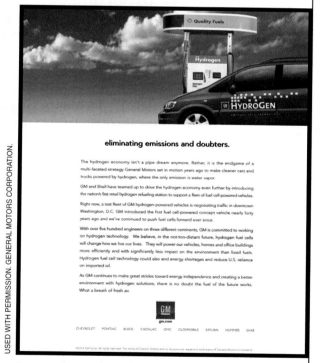

USED WITH PERMISSION. GENERAL MOTORS CORPORATION.

eliminating emissions and doubters.

As part of a research effort to reduce the pollution caused by traditional gasoline vehicles, General Motors is testing hydrogen-powered engines. If you are in Washington, D.C., you may see one of these test cars in downtown traffic. GM has more than 500 engineers on three continents working to make hydrogen power a reality.

recycling reprocessing of used materials for reuse.

Companies often seek to align their marketing efforts with their charitable giving. Many contribute to the Olympics and create advertising that features the company's sponsorship. This is known as *cause-related marketing*. In a recent survey nearly nine out of ten young people said they believed companies had a duty to support social causes, and nearly seven in eight said they would switch brands in order to reward a company that did so. "Writing checks is not enough," says the director for research and policy development at Boston College's Center for Corporate Citizenship.[33]

Another form of corporate philanthropy is volunteerism. In their roles as corporate citizens, thousands of businesses encourage their employees to contribute their efforts to projects as diverse as Habitat for Humanity, the United Way, and Red Cross blood drives. In addition to making tangible contributions to the well-being of fellow citizens, such programs generate considerable public support and goodwill for the companies and their employees. In some cases, the volunteer efforts occur mostly during off-hours for employees. In other instances, the firm permits its workforce to volunteer during regular working hours. Sometimes companies help by contributing resources to promote worthy causes, such as Concern Worldwide's mission to help poverty-stricken people around the world.

Habitat for Humanity is one of many organizations that benefit from corporate philanthropy and partnerships. Organizations like this benefit through a corporation's ability to raise public awareness, volunteer manpower, product donations, and financial support.

Responsibilities to Customers

consumerism public demand that a business consider the wants and needs of its customers in making decisions.

Businesspeople share a social and ethical responsibility to treat their customers fairly and act in a manner that is not harmful to them. They can even encourage harried customers to slow down for a rejuvenating ritual such as a cup of tea, as the "Hit & Miss" feature explains. **Consumerism**—the public demand that a business consider the wants and needs of its customers in making decisions—has gained widespread acceptance. Consumerism is based on the belief that consumers have certain rights. The most frequently quoted statement of consumer rights was made by President John F. Kennedy in 1962. Figure 2.7 summarizes these consumer rights. Numerous state and federal laws have been implemented since then to protect these rights.

The Right to Be Safe Contemporary businesspeople must recognize obligations, both moral and legal, to ensure the safe operation of their products. Consumers should feel assured that the products they purchase will not cause injuries in normal use. **Product liability** refers to the responsibility of manufacturers for injuries and damages caused by their products. Items that lead to injuries, either directly or indirectly, can have disastrous consequences for their makers.

Many companies put their products through rigorous testing to avoid safety problems. Still, testing alone cannot foresee every eventuality. Companies must try to consider all possibilities and provide adequate warning of potential dangers. When a product does pose a threat to customer safety, a responsible manufacturer responds quickly to either correct the problem or recall the dangerous product. For example, General Motors recently recalled more than 300,000 SUVs and trucks to correct problems with a turn signal even though no injuries or damage had been reported.[34]

Figure

2.7 Consumer Rights as Proposed by President Kennedy

Sarbanes-Oxley Act 32
business ethics 32
conflict of interest 37
whistle-blowing 39

code of conduct 40
social responsibility 43
recycling 45
corporate philanthropy 47

consumerism 48
sexual harassment 55

Other Important Business Terms

boycott 37
integrity 39
social audit 43
pollution 45

green marketing 46
product liability 48
family leave 53

**Equal Employment Opportunity
Commission (EEOC) 53**
sexism 55

Review Questions

1. What do the terms *business ethics* and *social responsibility* mean? Cite an example of each. Who are the main constituents that businesses must consider?

2. Identify and describe briefly the three stages in which individuals typically develop ethical standards. What are some of the factors that determine the stage of moral and ethical development an individual occupies at any given time?

3. What are the four most common ethical challenges that businesspeople face? Give a brief example of each.

4. What are the four levels of development of a corporate culture to support business ethics? Describe each briefly.

5. How do organizational goals affect ethical behavior? How might these goals interfere with ethical leadership? Give an example.

6. What basic consumer rights does the consumerism movement try to ensure? How has consumerism improved the contemporary business environment?

7. What are some of the major factors that contribute to the assessment of a company's social performance?

8. Identify the major benefits of corporate philanthropy.

9. What are some of the responsibilities that firms have to their employees?

10. What are quality-of-life issues? How can companies best meet them?

11. What laws protect employees from age discrimination? From sexual harassment?

12. How does a company demonstrate its responsibility to investors and the financial community?

Projects and Teamwork Applications

1. Write your own personal code of ethics, detailing your feelings about ethical challenges such as lying to protect an employer or co-worker, favoring one client over another, misrepresenting credentials to an employer or client, and using the computer for personal purposes while at work. What role will your personal ethics play in deciding your choice of career and acceptance of a job?

2. "Everybody exaggerates when it comes to selling products, and customers ought to take that with a grain of salt," said one advertising executive recently in response to a complaint filed by the Better Business Bureau about misleading advertising. "Don't we all have a brain, and can't we all think a little bit, too?" Do you agree with this statement? Why or why not?

3. Imagine that you work for a company that makes outdoor clothing, such as L.L. Bean, Timberland, or Patagonia. Write a memo describing at least four specific ways in which your company could practice corporate philanthropy. Include the benefits you think the company and the community would realize from such actions.

4. Imagine that you are the human resources director for a company that is trying to establish a written policy to outline its responsibilities to its employees. Choose one of the responsibilities described in the chapter—such as workplace safety—and write a memo describing specific steps your company will take to fulfill that responsibility.

5. Suppose that you own a small firm with twelve employees. One employee tells you in confidence that he has just learned he is HIV positive. You know that healthcare costs for AIDS patients can be disastrously high, and this expense could drastically raise the health insurance premiums that your other employees must pay. What are your responsibilities to this employee? To the rest of your staff? Explain.

Case 2.1

U.S. Federal Sentencing Guidelines: The Carrot and the Stick

The U.S. Federal Sentencing Guidelines were originally designed to help the government find meaningful and consistent ways to sentence organizations—including public and private companies and not-for-profits—convicted of crimes. After discovering that similar cases had been resolved differently by the courts, the Sentencing Commission enacted guidelines that rely on what legislators call the stick-and-carrot approach to corporate ethics: The financial penalties that the courts can impose for wrongdoing are the stick, while the existence of an effective ethics program can reduce the fines the courts can set, which serves as the carrot.

The guidelines make organizations subject to sentencing, fines, and probation if they are convicted of violations of antitrust, securities, bribery, fraud, money laundering, criminal activities, extortion, embezzlement, or conspiracy laws. Because organizations are liable for the offenses committed by their officers, the guidelines were intended to provide for just punishment, deterrence, and the creation of internal company policies to prevent unlawful behavior.

To define what an "effective" ethics program looks like, the guidelines identify seven elements it should include:

1. standards and procedures, such as a code of ethics, to prevent or detect wrongdoing
2. responsibility at all levels and oversight at a high level, such as an ethics officer
3. due care in the delegation of authority

4. communication of the code of ethics, such as training, at all levels
5. auditing, monitoring, and reporting systems, such as an ethics hotline free of internal repercussions
6. enforcement of established ethical standards, including incentives and disciplinary measures
7. appropriate response to any wrongdoing that is found, including prevention of any recurrence

Thousands of U.S. companies have responded by creating new or enhancing existing ethics programs. Even organizations abroad have reacted, such as the CBIC, a bank in Canada, and the Bank of Tokyo, which has adopted the guidelines as the centerpiece of its own compliance program. Surveys of employees find that the changes are making themselves felt in the workplace, and observers believe they are occurring primarily in the areas of ethics training, the establishment of ethics offices and appointment of ethics officers, and the creation of ethics hotlines. Codes of ethics appear to have been affected the least, mostly because according to one survey, about 93 percent of firms already had such a code in place.

After tracking responses for about ten years, the Sentencing Commission strengthened the criteria in order to reflect "best practices" among organizations that had applied them since enactment and the Sarbanes-Oxley Act. These revisions were meant to provide an even clearer model of the "corporate good citizen" and make it easier for organizations both large and small to comply. Some of the changes increase the responsibility of boards of directors and top executives to demonstrate ethical leadership, require the organization to show due diligence in fulfilling the guidelines, and require it to cultivate an organizational culture that encourages ethical conduct and a commitment to compliance with the law. Firms must also periodically assess the risk that criminal behavior might occur in their organizations.

Questions for Critical Thinking

1. Which do you think will be more effective in ensuring that organizations act in ethical ways, the carrot or the stick? Why?
2. Do you think the Sentencing Guidelines provide a sound basis for creating and maintaining a corporate ethics program? Why or why not? If not, how would you modify them?

Sources: "An Overview of the United States Sentencing Commission and the Federal Sentencing Guidelines," U.S. Sentencing Commission, accessed June 7, 2006, http://www.ussc.gov; Dove Izraeli and Mark S. Schwartz, "What Can We Learn from the U.S. Federal Sentencing Guidelines for Organizational Ethics?" European Institute for Business Ethics, accessed June 7, 2006, http://www.itcilo.it/english; Stanley A. Twardy, "Compliance Programs to Detect and Prevent Crime: Amended Federal Sentencing Guidelines," FindLaw, accessed June 7, 2006, http://library.findlaw.com.

 Case 2.2

Ford Turns Green with Clean Energy

This video case appears on page 609. A recently filmed video, designed to expand and highlight the written case, is available for class use by instructors.

Chapter 3

Economic Challenges Facing Global and Domestic Business

DIGITAL VISION/GETTY IMAGES

You probably won't be involved in a police car chase anytime soon. But as a businessperson, you might be interested in the story of the police car itself. For years, Ford Motor Company has dominated the police car market with its special model Crown Victoria Police Interceptor. That souped-up model has accounted for about 85 percent of all police cars sold in the United States. But all that is changing. Police departments now have a choice about what vehicles they purchase, and DaimlerChrysler is in hot pursuit of their dollars.

DaimlerChrysler announced that its Dodge division is unveiling a police model of its classic Dodge Charger. The firm also plans to produce a law enforcement edition of its Magnum, but the Charger is expected to compete directly with

AFP/GETTY IMAGES

version of its Intrepid, but officers did not feel comfortable with front-

Dodge Tries to Dethrone Ford's Crown Victoria

Ford's Crown Victoria. While many police departments claim loyalty to Ford, some are beginning to look at alternatives because of high-profile accidents with the Crown Victoria. According to reports, nearly 20 officers died in fiery explosions that resulted when their cruisers were hit from behind. Some departments have even sued the automaker. The bad publicity has created a window of opportunity for competitors.

While Ford is taking steps to increase the safety of its cars by installing fire suppression devices and gas tank protectors, Dodge is rolling out its new cars. The new Charger has enhanced brakes and a 340-horsepower Hemi engine, features that take direct aim at the Crown Victoria. The Magnum, which is a sport wagon, is expected to attract some interest. But 75 percent of police departments prefer sedans, so the Charger is the flagship model. Dodge developed both cars knowing they will face some tough testing by organizations such as the California Highway Patrol and the Michigan State Police. Both agencies put any prospective police cars through difficult maneuvers and publish the results, which influence the purchase decisions made by many police departments. Dodge has also listened to customers and learned from its previous mistakes. Several years ago, it introduced a police

wheel drive at high speeds or when making tight turns. So it's back to rear-wheel drive for the Charger. "With all of this, we know we'll hit the sweet spot," predicts Eric Ridenour, executive vice president of product development for Chrysler.

Dethroning the Crown Victoria won't be easy, though. Police departments have been comfortable with the auto for years. Officers report that they like the Crown Victoria's roomy interior, which can hold laptop computers, papers, and all the other equipment that they need to haul around on the job. Purchasing managers like to order a single type of vehicle so that officers can swap cars easily, if necessary, and maintenance is more efficient with one type of part to supply. So it is typical for departments to outfit an entire fleet with a single model. But with budgets always in mind, police departments are opening up to the possibility of a new vehicle. "We're excited that there's another competitor out there," says John Alley, fleet administrator for the San Diego Police Department. He manages a fleet of 550 Crown Victorias at about $21,000 to $23,000 each. "We're hoping the new Dodge will be cheaper." DaimlerChrysler marketers hope that when police dispatchers send out the alert, "calling all cars," they'll be talking about the Charger.[1]

When we examine the exchanges that companies and societies make as a whole, we are focusing on the *economic systems* operating in different nations. These systems reflect the combination of policies and choices a nation makes to allocate resources among its citizens. Countries vary in the ways they allocate scarce resources.

Economics, which analyzes the choices people and governments make in allocating scarce resources, affects each of us, because everyone is involved in producing, distributing, or simply consuming goods and services. In fact, your life is affected by economics every day. When you decide what goods to buy, what services to use, or what activities to fit into your schedule, you are making economic choices.

"They Said It"

"Please find me a one-armed economist so we will not always hear 'On the other hand . . .'"
—*Herbert Hoover (1874–1964)*
31st president
of the United States

economics social science that analyzes the choices people and governments make in allocating scarce resources.

The choices you make may often be international in scope. If you are in the market for a new car, you might visit several dealers in a row on the same street—Ford, Chrysler, Honda, Toyota, and Saturn. You might decide on Toyota—a Japanese firm—but your car might very well be manufactured in the United States, using parts from all over the world. Although firms sometimes emphasize the American origin of their goods and services in order to appeal to consumers' desire to support the U.S. economy, many products are made of components from a variety of nations.

Businesses and not-for-profit organizations also make economic decisions when they choose how to use human and natural resources; invest in equipment, machinery, and buildings; and form partnerships with other firms. When a police department decides whether to purchase a Ford or a Dodge for its officers to drive, it is making an economic choice.

microeconomics study of small economic units, such as individual consumers, families, and businesses.

Economists refer to the study of small economic units, such as individual consumers, families, and businesses, as **microeconomics.** On a broader level, government decisions about the operation of the country's economy also affect you, your job, and your financial future. A major feature of the recent Sarbanes-Oxley Act was to limit the consulting services that accounting firms can provide for a company whose financial records they audit. The new law affected the entire accounting profession.

macroeconomics study of a nation's overall economic issues, such as how an economy maintains and allocates resources and how a government's policies affect the standards of living of its citizens.

The study of a country's overall economic issues is called **macroeconomics** (*macro* means "large"). Macroeconomics addresses such issues as how an economy uses its resources and how government policies affect people's standards of living. Macroeconomics examines not just the economic policies of individual nations but the ways in which those individual policies affect the overall world economy. Because so much business is conducted around the world, a law enacted in one country can easily affect a transaction that takes place in another country. Although macroeconomic issues have a broad scope, they help shape the decisions that individuals, families, and businesses make every day.

This chapter introduces economic theory and the economic challenges facing individuals, businesses, and governments in the global marketplace. We begin with the microeconomic concepts of supply and demand and their effect on the prices people pay for goods and services. Next we explain the various types of economic systems, along with tools for comparing and evaluating their performance. Then we examine the ways in which governments seek to manage economies to create stable business environments in their countries. The final section in the chapter looks at some of the driving economic forces currently affecting people's lives.

assessment check

1. Define microeconomics.
2. Define macroeconomics.

MICROECONOMICS: THE FORCES OF DEMAND AND SUPPLY

Think about your own economic activities. You shop for groceries, you subscribe to a cell phone service, you pay college tuition, you fill your car's tank with gas. Now think about your family's economic activities. When you were growing up, your parents might have owned a home or rented an apartment. You might have taken a summer family vacation. Your parents may have shopped at discount clubs or at local stores. Each of these choices relates to the study of microeconomics. They also help determine both the prices of goods and services and the amounts sold. Information about these activities is vital to companies because their survival and ability to grow depends on selling enough products priced high enough to cover costs and earn profits. The same information is important to consumers who must make purchase decisions based on prices and the availability of the goods and services they need.

At the heart of every business endeavor is an exchange between a buyer and a seller. The buyer recognizes that he or she needs or wants a particular good or service—whether it's a hamburger or a haircut—and is willing to pay a seller for it. The seller requires the exchange in order to earn a profit and stay in business. So the exchange process involves both demand and supply. **Demand** refers to the willingness and ability of buyers to purchase goods and services at different prices. The other side of the exchange process is **supply,** the amount of goods and services for sale at different prices. Understanding the factors that determine demand and supply, as well as how the two interact, can help you understand many actions and decisions of individuals, businesses, and government. This section takes a closer look at these concepts.

demand willingness and ability of buyers to purchase goods and services.

supply willingness and ability of sellers to provide goods and services.

Factors Driving Demand

For most us, economics amounts to a balance between what we want and what we can afford. Because of this dilemma, each person must choose how much money to save and how much to spend. We must also decide among all the goods and services competing for our attention. Suppose you wanted to purchase a camera phone. You'd have to choose from a variety of brands and models. You'd also have to decide where you wanted to go to buy one. After shopping around, you might decide you didn't want a camera phone at all. Instead, you might purchase something else, or save your money.

Demand is driven by a number of factors that influence how people decide to spend their money, including price. It may also be driven by outside circumstances or larger economic events. And it can be driven by consumer preferences. Recently, McDonald's decided to introduce a new fruit-and-walnut salad in response to consumer demand for more healthful meal choices. Naturally, McDonald's hopes that people will buy the new salad. But so do the nation's apple growers. If the fruit-and-walnut salad proves popular, McDonald's will order more apples from growers. "Obviously, it's a big boon," says Dave Carlson, president of the Washington Apple Commission. "If we get several other fast-food chains involved as well, it could certainly turn into being a significant factor in the industry."[2]

© SUSAN VAN ETTEN/PHOTOEDIT

Consumers have many choices on how to spend their money. Their choices determine the demand for products, such as high-tech electronics sold at Best Buy.

Figure

3.1 Demand Curves for Gasoline

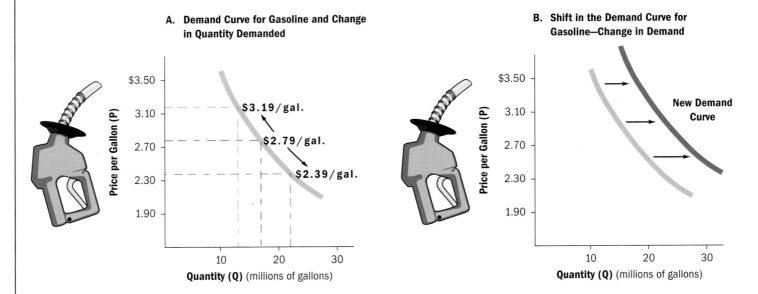

A. Demand Curve for Gasoline and Change in Quantity Demanded

B. Shift in the Demand Curve for Gasoline—Change in Demand

Demand can also increase the availability of certain types of software. As more and more information on consumers is stored in databases, identity theft has been on the rise. Criminals are willing to pay for confidential information about consumers, such as credit history, bank account and credit card numbers, and Social Security numbers. Recently, hackers stole millions of Discover, MasterCard, and American Express numbers from one card-processing company in Atlanta. These numbers were then sold to individuals who wanted to use the information for fraudulent purchases. This situation not only created an uproar among consumers but also increased demand for new information security products to protect against data theft.[3]

In general, as the price of a good or service goes up, people buy smaller amounts. In other words, as price rises, the quantity demanded declines. At lower prices, consumers are generally willing to buy more of a good. A **demand curve** is a graph of the amount of a product that buyers will purchase at different prices. Demand curves typically slope downward, meaning that lower and lower prices attract larger and larger purchases.

Gasoline provides a classic example of how demand curves work. The left side of Figure 3.1 shows a possible demand curve for the total amount of gasoline that people will purchase at different prices. When gasoline is priced at $2.79 a gallon, drivers may fill up their tanks once or twice a week. At $3.19 a gallon, many of them may start economizing. They may combine errands or carpool to work. So the quantity of gasoline demanded at $3.19 a gallon is lower than the amount demanded at $2.79 a gallon. The opposite happens at $2.39 a gallon. More gasoline is sold at $2.39 a gallon than at $2.79 a gallon, as people opt to drive to work or take a weekend trip. However, as mentioned earlier, other factors may cause consumers to accept higher prices anyway. They may have made vacation plans in advance and do not want to cancel them. Or they may be required to drive to work every day.

Economists make a clear distinction between changes in the quantity demanded at various prices and changes in overall demand. A change in quantity demanded, such as the change that occurs at different gasoline prices, is simply movement along the demand curve. A change in overall demand, on the other hand, results in an entirely new demand curve. Businesses are constantly trying to make predictions about both kinds of demand, and a miscalculation can cause problems. In one recent year, experts predicted a 7 percent increase in Chinese demand for oil, when in fact the growth in demand only reaches 5 percent. The overestimation resulted in a drop in investor confidence in the industry.[4]

As American household incomes have risen and lifestyles have changed, many American consumers have chosen to purchase SUVs, which consume large amounts of gasoline. At the same time, in developing countries like India and China, consumers have been able to afford cars for the first time. These changes have increased the demand for gasoline at all prices. The right side of Figure 3.1 shows how the increased demand for gasoline worldwide has created a new demand curve. The new demand curve shifts to the right of the old demand curve, indicating that overall demand has increased at every price. A demand curve can also shift to the left when the demand for a good or service drops. However, the demand curve still has the same shape.

Although price is the underlying cause of movement along a demand curve, many factors can combine to determine the overall demand for a product—that is, the shape and position of the demand curve. These influences include customer preferences and incomes, the prices of substitute and complementary items, the number of buyers in a market, and the strength of their optimism regarding the future. Changes in any of these factors produce a new demand curve. Despite high gasoline prices, soaring airfares, and rising hotel rates, U.S. consumers are traveling more than ever, according to the Travel Industry Association of America. "Usually when prices are high and the dollar is low people stay home," says one travel agent. "But the opposite is true [right now]." Demand for flights to popular locations has been so high that consumers have been forced to travel to other destinations or make plans for another time. Obviously, factors other than price—such as an improved U.S. economy or the urge for adventure—are driving the demand for travel.[5]

Changes in household income also change demand. As consumers have more money to spend, firms can sell more products at every price. This means the demand curve has shifted to the right. The price of related goods and services also can influence demand. As the price of gasoline rose recently, the demand for SUVs fell somewhat, and the demand for hybrid vehicles such as Toyota's Prius increased.[6] Table 3.1 describes how a demand curve is likely to respond to each of these changes.

For a business to succeed, management must carefully monitor the factors that may affect demand for the goods and services it hopes to sell. In setting prices, firms often try to predict how the chosen levels will influence the amounts they sell. The Coca-Cola Company experimented with smart vending machines, adjusting prices to such variables as the weather. If the temperature was hot outside, the machines could automatically raise the price. If the vending machine contained too many cans of root beer and restocking was five days away, the machine

Table 3.1

Expected Shifts in Demand Curves

| Factor | Demand Curve Shifts | |
	to the Right *if*:	to the Left *if*:
Customer preferences	increase	decrease
Number of buyers	increases	decreases
Buyers' Incomes	increase	decrease
Prices of substitute goods	increase	decrease
Prices of complementary goods	decrease	increase
Future expectations become more	optimistic	pessimistic

The Almond Board of California hopes to increase demand for its product by promoting its healthful benefits. Not only do almonds taste great, but they also are packed with vitamins and fiber and may help reduce cholesterol.

could lower the price of root beer. Organizations also try to influence overall demand through advertising, free samples and presentations at retail stores, sales calls, product enhancements, and other marketing techniques.

Factors Driving Supply

Important economic factors also affect supply, the willingness and ability of firms to provide goods and services at different prices. Just as consumers must decide about how to spend their money, businesses must decide what products to sell, and how.

Sellers would prefer to charge higher prices for their products. A **supply curve** shows the relationship between different prices and the quantities that sellers will offer for sale, regardless of demand. Movement along the supply curve is the opposite of movement along the demand curve. So as price rises, the quantity that sellers are willing to supply also rises. At progressively lower prices, the quantity supplied decreases. In Figure 3.2, a possible supply curve for gasoline shows that increasing prices for gasoline should bring increasing supplies to market.

Businesses need certain inputs to operate effectively in producing their output. As discussed in Chapter 1, these *factors of production* include natural resources, capital, human resources, and entrepreneurship. Natural resources include land, building sites, forests, and mineral deposits. Capital refers to resources such as technology, tools, information, physical facilities, and financial capabilities. Human resources include the physical labor and intellectual inputs contributed by employees. Entrepreneurship is the willingness to take risks to create and operate a business.

Factors of production play a central role in determining the overall supply of goods and services. A change in the cost or availability of any of these inputs can shift the entire supply curve, either increasing or decreasing the amount available at every price. If the cost of land increases, a firm might not be able to purchase the site for a more efficient manufacturing plant, which would lower production levels, shifting the supply curve to the left. But if the company finds a way to speed up the production process anyway, allowing it to turn out more products with less labor, the change reduces the overall cost of the finished products, which shifts the supply curve to the right. Table 3.2 summarizes how changes in various factors can affect the supply curve. Sometimes forces of nature can affect the supply curve. When a hurricane swept along the coast of Venezuela, oil exports from the country's ports were halted until the storm passed, reducing the supply of oil for several days.[7] The agriculture industry has often experienced shifts in the supply curve. U.S. apple growers suffered from several years of oversupply and flat prices, losing an estimated $1.7 billion over a period of five years. But the increasing interest in healthful foods and discovery of the health benefits of apples in particular has helped reduce the oversupply.[8] The "Solving an Ethical Controversy" feature describes the debate over the supply of oil and whether the United States should drill for this resource in Alaska.

Figure

3.2 Supply Curve for Gasoline

$3.50

$3.39/gal.

3.10

2.70

$2.69/gal.

2.30

$2.29/gal.

1.90

Price per Gallon (P)

10   20   30

Quantity (Q) (millions of gallons)

TO DRILL—OR NOT TO DRILL—FOR OIL IN ALASKA?

The debate has been raging for decades over whether the United States should begin drilling for oil in the Arctic National Wildlife Refuge in Alaska. It's a complex issue involving many factors, including the impact that drilling would have on the surrounding environment, the potential reduction of American dependence on foreign oil, a possible boost in productivity for the United States, and debate over who would pay for—and benefit from—the drilling activities. Politicians, businesspeople, and average taxpaying citizens all have strong views on the topic.

Should the United States expand oil drilling in Alaska's Arctic National Wildlife Refuge?

PRO

1. "This project will keep our economy growing by creating jobs and ensuring that businesses can expand," noted President George W. Bush in a statement. "And it will make America less dependent on foreign sources of energy, eventually by up to a million barrels of oil a day."
2. Experts argue that today's drilling technology, along with tight environmental restrictions, will dramatically limit the effect on Alaska's tundra, protecting the wildlife habitat.

CON

1. Opponents say that the amount of oil the United States can retrieve from Alaska—and the ten years it will take to reach the market—will have minimal impact on global markets, high gasoline prices, or U.S. dependence on foreign oil.
2. Others argue that the United States should be spending more on developing renewable energy sources such as solar and wind power, as well as producing more fuel-efficient cars, trucks, and other vehicles.

Summary

While legislators, businesspeople, and environmentalists continue the argument, a recent survey revealed that U.S. citizens are split in their views: 42 percent of respondents said that drilling should proceed, while 53 percent said that it should not. Most likely, many people echo the view of Senator Pete Domenici of New Mexico: "Some people say we ought to conserve more. They say we ought to conserve instead of producing this oil. But we need to do everything. We have to conserve and produce where we can."

Sources: "Most Americans Oppose Alaska Oil Drilling," Angus Reid Consultants, accessed June 8, 2006, http://www.angus-reid.com; H. Josef Hebert, "Senate OKs Plan to Allow Oil Wells in Alaska Refuge," *Deseret Morning News*, accessed June 8, 2006, http://www.deseretnews.com; James Kuhnhenn, "Alaska Oil Drilling Gets Boost from Senate," *Detroit Free Press*, accessed June 8, 2006, http://www .freep.com.

solving an ETHICAL controversy

Expected Shifts in Supply Curves

Table 3.2

Factor	Supply Curve Shifts	
	to the Right *if:*	to the Left *if:*
Costs of inputs	decrease	increase
Costs of technologies	decrease	increase
Taxes	decrease	increase
Number of suppliers	increases	decreases

How Demand and Supply Interact

assessment check

1. What is a demand curve?
2. What is a supply curve?
3. How do factors of production influence the overall supply of goods and services?

Separate shifts in demand and supply have obvious effects on prices and the availability of products. In the real world, changes do not alternatively affect demand and supply. Several factors often change at the same time—and they keep changing. Sometimes such changes in multiple factors cause contradictory pressures on prices and quantities. In other cases, the final direction of prices and quantities reflects the factor that has changed the most.

Figure 3.3 shows the interaction of both supply and demand curves for gasoline on a single graph. Notice that the two curves intersect at *P*. The law of supply and demand states that prices (*P*) are set by the intersection of the supply and demand curves. The point where the two curves meet identifies the **equilibrium price,** the prevailing market price at which you can buy an item.

"They Said It"

"You don't make more oil."
—*Sam Shelton (b. 1940) Director, Strategic Energy Initiative at Georgia Tech*

If the actual market price differs from the equilibrium price, buyers and sellers tend to make economic choices that restore the equilibrium level. So how do we explain the shortages of vaccines to protect against such diseases as tetanus, diphtheria, whooping cough, measles, mumps, and chicken pox? Why did many of the 75 million adults seeking flu shots in a recent flu season encounter delays in obtaining flu shots? Part of the answer lies with the federal government, which pays vaccine makers between 38 and 60 percent of the going price for these vaccines in the global marketplace. The result is a reduction in product supply. In recent years, the number of commercial makers of the flu vaccine dropped dramatically, so when one manufacturer's vaccines were discovered to be contaminated and unusable, the supply decreased and consumers could not obtain vaccinations.

In other situations, suppliers react to market forces by reducing prices. To fight off flagging sales and increase demand for its autos, General Motors offered its employee discount to the general public. Sales rebounded. Not surprisingly, Ford and DaimlerChrysler followed suit with similar pricing programs.[9]

As pointed out earlier, the forces of demand and supply can be affected by a variety of factors. One important variable is the larger economic environment. The next section explains how macroeconomics and economic systems influence market forces and, ultimately, demand, supply, and prices.

Figure 3.3 Law of Supply and Demand

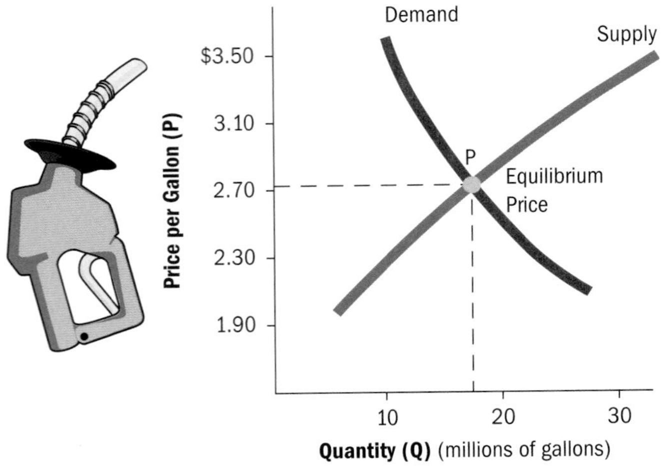

MACROECONOMICS: ISSUES FOR THE ENTIRE ECONOMY

Every country faces decisions about how to best use the four basic factors of production. Each nation's policies and choices help determine its economic system. But the political, social, and legal environments differ in every country. So no two countries have exactly the same economic system. In general, however, these systems can be classified into three categories: private enterprise systems, planned economies, or combinations of the two, referred to as mixed economies. As business becomes an increasingly global undertaking, it is important to understand the primary features of the various economic systems operating around the world.

Capitalism: The Private Enterprise System and Competition

Most industrialized nations operate economies based on the *private enterprise system*, also known as *capitalism* or a *market economy*. A private enterprise system rewards businesses for meeting the needs and demands of consumers. Government tends to favor a hands-off attitude toward controlling business ownership, profits, and resource allocations. Instead, competition regulates economic life, creating opportunities and challenges that businesspeople must handle to succeed. In your career, one area of business that you will encounter in the private enterprise system that is completely unregulated is tipping. Read the "Business Etiquette" feature for hints on how to tip appropriately.

The relative competitiveness of a particular industry is an important consideration for every firm because it determines the ease and cost of doing business within that industry. Four basic degrees of competition take shape in a private enterprise system: pure competition, monopolistic competition, oligopoly, and monopoly. Table 3.3 highlights the main differences among these types of competition.

Pure competition is a market structure, like that of small-scale agriculture or fishing, in which large numbers of buyers and sellers exchange homogeneous products and no single participant has a significant influence on price. Instead, prices are set by the market itself as the forces of supply and demand interact. Firms can easily enter or leave a purely competitive market because no single company dominates. Also, in pure competition, buyers see little difference between the goods and services offered by competitors.

Fishing and agriculture are good examples of pure competition. The wheat grown and sold by one farmer in the Midwest is virtually identical to that sold by others. As rainfall and temperatures affect the crop growth, the price for this commodity rises or falls according to the law of supply and demand. The same concept applies to the fishing industry gathering clams and mussels off the coast of New England. The region's notorious "red tide" of algae sometimes contaminates part of the season's supply of shellfish just when summer tourists want them the most—and prices skyrocket.

(b)usiness (e)tiquette

Tips on Business Tipping

When you eat out, take a cab, or stay in a hotel, you're faced with a dilemma. Whom—and how much—should you tip? If you find tipping a mystery, here are a few guidelines to help you solve the puzzle.

- At a restaurant, it is customary to tip your waiter between 15 and 20 percent of the bill. You may calculate the tip before tax or alcohol, but many people simply base the tip on the total bill. Naturally, if the service is outstanding, you'll want to tip at the upper end of the scale.
- If you check coat(s) at a restaurant or event, tip the person $1 per coat.
- Tip the bellhop $1 to $2 per bag for carrying your luggage.
- Give a valet or parking attendant $1 to $2 for parking or retrieving your car.
- Add a 10 to 15 percent tip to the fare for a taxi ride, or $1 to $2 for a free shuttle.
- If the hotel concierge provides you with special service such as arranging a meeting space or making dinner or theater reservations, tip that person around $5. If he or she has provided an extraordinary service, a tip of $20 is not out of line.

Of course, before you tip, make sure that a service charge has not already been included. Some upscale restaurants and hotels have begun automatically including fees ranging up to 20 percent.

While these guidelines should be helpful, before you make any calculations, remember that service personnel usually try their best to make your experience a good one. "When in doubt, I always operate under the premise that you tip for a service performed with excellence, and you tip more generously for something that exceeds your expectations," advises Amy Ziff of Travelocity Business. "And remember the saying, 'what goes around comes around,' and that in business a little good tipping karma can never hurt."

Sources: "Tipping Etiquette," FindaLink.net, accessed June 8, 2006, http://www.findalink.net; "Proper Tipping Etiquette," Essortment, accessed June 8, 2006, http://msms.essortment.com; "Travelocity Business Makes Travel Easier with Hints on Tipping," *Business Wire*, accessed June 8, 2006, http://www.corporate-ir.net; Laura Bly, "The Tipping Point," *USA Today*, August 26, 2005, p. 1D; "Tipping Etiquette: Travel," AllSands.com, accessed May, 4, 2005, http://www.allsands.com.

Table

3.3 Types of Competition

	Types of Competition			
Characteristics	**Pure Competition**	**Monopolistic Competition**	**Oligopoly**	**Monopoly**
Number of competitors	Many	Few to many	Few	No direct competition
Ease of entry into industry by new firms	Easy	Somewhat difficult	Difficult	Regulated by government
Similarity of goods or services offered by competing firms	Similar	Different	Similar or different	No directly competing products
Control over price by individual firms	None	Some	Some	Considerable in a pure monopoly; little in a regulated monopoly
Examples	Small-scale farmer in Indiana	Local fitness center	Boeing aircraft	Rawlings Sporting Goods, exclusive supplier of major-league baseballs

Monopolistic competition is a market structure, like that for retailing, in which large numbers of buyers and sellers exchange relatively well-differentiated (heterogeneous) products, so each participant has some control over price. Sellers can differentiate their products from competing offerings on the basis of price, quality, or other features. In an industry that features monopolistic competition, it is relatively easy for a firm to begin or stop selling a good or service. The success of one seller often attracts new competitors to such a market. Individual firms also have some control over how their goods and services are priced.

An example of monopolistic competition is the market for pet food. Consumers can choose from private-label (store brands) and brand-name products in bags, boxes, and cans. Producers of pet food and the stores that sell it have wide latitude in setting prices. Consumers can choose the store or brand with the lowest prices, or sellers can convince them that a more expensive offering is worth more because it offers better nutrition, more convenience, more information, or other benefits.

An **oligopoly** is a market situation in which relatively few sellers compete and high start-up costs form barriers to keep out new competitors. In some oligopolistic industries, such as paper and steel, competitors offer similar products. In others, such as aircraft and automobiles, they sell different models and features. The huge investment required to enter an oligopoly market tends to discourage new competitors. The limited number of sellers also enhances the control these firms exercise over price. Competing products in an oligopoly usually sell for very similar prices because substantial price competition would reduce profits for all firms in the industry. So a price cut by one firm in an oligopoly will typically be met by its competitors. However, prices can vary from one market to another, as from one country to another. OPEC, which controls much of the world's supply of crude oil, is considered by many to be a successful oligopoly, as described in the "Hit & Miss" feature.

Farmers produce their crops in a purely competitive market, so the prices of their crops are determined by the laws of supply and demand.

PHOTODISC/GETTY IMAGES

HIT & MISS

OPEC: A Successful Oligopoly

By the time you finish this chapter, you'll know what an oligopoly is; you'll even be able to pronounce it. But can you name successful oligopolies around the world? OPEC—the Organization of Petroleum Exporting Countries—is one. If you aren't sure how OPEC affects you, think of gas prices, which recently have soared. OPEC controls much of the supply of crude oil that is produced in the world, which ultimately affects the cost of heating homes and filling gas tanks in your hometown.

OPEC was founded in 1960 by five nations—Iran, Iraq, Kuwait, Saudi Arabia, and Venezuela. The group was later joined by eight more countries—Qatar, Indonesia, Libya, United Arab Emirates, Algeria, Nigeria, Ecuador, and Gabon. According to the organization's Web site, "OPEC's objective is to coordinate and unify petroleum policies among member countries, in order to secure fair and stable prices for petroleum producers; an efficient, economic and regular supply of petroleum to consuming nations; and a fair return on capital to those investing in the industry."

OPEC nations have worked together to control the supply of their products to the world for nearly 50 years, despite criticism from watchdog agencies such as the International Energy Agency and internal blunders, including exceeding their own production quotas. In what has become a very complex oil market, the cur-rent discussion centers on a simple argument: whether the planet is running out of oil. OPEC insists that, although it is pumping at a high capacity to meet high demand, it still has the capacity to produce more. Some scientists and other experts warn that, in fact, the earth is rapidly being depleted of its total supply of oil. Falling somewhere in the middle of the debate, oil and gas analyst Adam Sieminski of Deutsche Bank AB in London says, "It's not a crisis. If a little more is needed, [OPEC] can bring it on. The market is aware of the fact that demand seems to be rising pretty much in line with OPEC [supply]."

Questions for Critical Thinking

1. Why is OPEC a successful oligopoly?
2. Describe several ways you think this oligopoly affects your daily life.

Sources: OPEC Web site, accessed June 8, 2006, http://www.opec.org; Kevin Morrison, "IEA Says Supply Tightness to Remain," *Financial Times*, accessed June 8, 2006, http://news.ft.com; David Lazarus, "OPEC Still Sings Same Tune," *San Francisco Chronicle*, accessed June 8, 2006, http://www.sfgate.com; Jim Efstathiou, "Attiyah Sees Tough Choices for OPEC," *(Doha, Qatar) Gulf Times*, accessed June 8, 2006, http://www.gulf-times.com.

Cement is another product for which an oligopoly exists. Mexican-based Cemex SA is the third-largest cement manufacturer in the world and the largest seller of cement in both the United States and Mexico. It holds 60 percent of the market share in Mexico. Cement is usually sold in bulk in the United States, like a commodity. However, it is sold as a branded product in Mexico. Cemex's prices are too high for many Mexican families to afford, which often means they must put plans for home building on hold. Because Cemex is also Mexico's largest seller of concrete, which is made with cement, those prices remain high as well. Although large construction companies in the United States can force cement manufacturers to drop their prices, Mexican construction companies are smaller and have little clout, so they end up paying higher prices.[10]

The final type of market structure is a **monopoly,** in which a single seller dominates trade in a good or service for which buyers can find no close substitutes. A pure monopoly occurs when a firm possesses unique characteristics so important to competition in its industry that they serve as barriers to prevent entry by would-be competitors. Microsoft has held a near monopoly in the Internet browser market with its Internet Explorer for quite a while. Recently, its share of the total U.S. market for all operating systems dipped below 90 percent after consumers became alarmed at Internet Explorer's reported security flaws. Another reason for the decrease in market share percentage is the increased competition from Firefox, an open-source

The U.S. Postal Service now offers services at its Web site to help it compete against such firms as UPS, FedEx, and DHL. With its new Click-N-Ship program, customers can calculate rates, print labels, pay postage, and get free delivery confirmation.

assessment check

1. What is the difference between pure competition and monopolistic competition?

2. Distinguish between oligopoly and monopoly.

browser developed by the Mozilla Foundation. Other browsers based on the Mozilla code such as America Online's Netscape and GNOME's Epiphany have also increased market share in the last 2 years.[11]

Many firms create short-term monopolies when research breakthroughs permit them to receive exclusive patents on new products. In the pharmaceuticals industry, drug giants such as Merck and Pfizer invest billions in research and development programs. When the research leads to successful new drugs, the companies can enjoy the benefits of their patents: the ability to set prices without fear of competitors undercutting them. Once the patent expires, generic substitutes enter the market, driving down prices.

Because a monopoly market lacks the benefits of competition, the U.S. government regulates monopolies. Besides issuing patents and limiting their life, the government prohibits most pure monopolies through antitrust legislation such as the Sherman Act and the Clayton Act. The U.S. government has applied these laws against monopoly behavior by Microsoft and by disallowing proposed mergers of large companies in some industries. In other cases, the government permits certain monopolies in exchange for regulating their activities.

With *regulated monopolies*, a local, state, or federal government grants exclusive rights in a certain market to a single firm. Pricing decisions—particularly rate-increase requests—are subject to control by regulatory authorities such as state public service commissions. An example is the delivery of first-class mail, a monopoly held by the U.S. Postal Service (USPS). The USPS is a self-supporting corporation wholly owned by the federal government. Although it is no longer run by Congress, postal rates are set by a Postal Commission and approved by a Board of Governors.

During the 1980s and 1990s, the U.S. government favored a trend away from regulated monopolies and toward **deregulation.** Regulated monopolies that have been deregulated include long-distance and local telephone service, cable television, cellular phones, and electric utilities. Long-distance companies such as MCI are now allowed to offer local service. The idea is to improve customer service and reduce prices for telephone customers through increased competition. Deregulation of electric utilities began when California opened its market in 1998. Several years later, about half the states were on board. In those states, private companies could compete with utilities to sell electricity and natural gas.

Planned Economies: Communism and Socialism

In a **planned economy,** government controls determine business ownership, profits, and resource allocation to accomplish government goals rather than those set by individual businesses. Two forms of planned economies are communism and socialism.

The writings of Karl Marx in the mid-1800s formed the basis of communist theory. Marx believed that private enterprise economies created unfair conditions and led to worker exploitation because business owners controlled most of society's resources and reaped most of the economy's rewards. Instead, he suggested an economic system called **communism,** in which all property would be shared equally by the people of a community under the direction of a strong central government. Marx believed that elimination of private ownership of property and businesses would ensure the emergence of a classless society that would benefit all. Each individual would contribute to the nation's overall economic success, and resources would be distributed according to each person's needs. Under communism, the central government owns the means of production, and the people work for state-owned enterprises. The government determines what people can buy because it dictates what is produced in the nation's factories and farms.

A number of nations adopted communist economic systems during the early 20th century in an effort to correct abuses they believed to be present in their previous systems. In practice, however, communist governments often give people little or no freedom of choice in selecting jobs, purchases, or investments. Communist governments often make mistakes in planning the best uses of resources to compete in the growing global marketplace. Government-owned monopolies often suffer from inefficiency.

Consider the former Soviet Union, where large government bureaucracies controlled nearly every aspect of daily life. Shortages became chronic because producers had little or no incentive to satisfy customers. The quality of goods and services also suffered for the same reason. When Mikhail Gorbachev became the last president of the dying Soviet Union, he tried to improve the quality of Soviet-made products. Effectively shut out of trading in the global marketplace and caught up in a treasury-depleting arms race with the United States, the Soviet Union faced severe financial problems. Eventually, these economic crises led to the collapse of Soviet communism and the breakup of the Soviet Union itself.

Today, communism exists in just a few countries, such as the People's Republic of China, Cuba, and North Korea. Even these nations show signs of growing openness toward some of the benefits of private enterprise as possible solutions to their economic challenges. Since 1978, China has been shifting toward a more market-oriented economy. The national government has given local government and individual plant managers more say in business decisions and has permitted some private businesses. Households now have more control over agriculture, in contrast to the collectivized farms introduced with communism. In addition, Western products such as McDonald's restaurants and Coca-Cola soft drinks are now part of Chinese consumers' lives.

A second type of planned economy, **socialism,** is characterized by government ownership and operation of major industries such as healthcare and communications. Socialists assert that major industries are too important to a society to be left in private hands and that government-owned businesses can serve the public's interest better than can private firms. However, socialism also allows private ownership in industries considered less crucial to social welfare, such as retail shops, restaurants, and certain types of manufacturing facilities. Scandinavian countries such as Sweden and Finland have socialist characteristics in their societies, as do many African nations and India.

Mixed Market Economies

Private enterprise systems and planned economies adopt basically opposite approaches to operating economies. In reality though, many countries operate **mixed market economies,** economic systems that draw from both types of economies, to different degrees. In nations generally considered to have a private enterprise economy, government-owned firms frequently operate alongside private enterprises.

France has blended socialist and free enterprise policies for hundreds of years. The nation's energy production, public transportation, and defense industries are run as nationalized industries, controlled by the government. Meanwhile, a market economy flourishes in other industries. Over the past two decades, the French government has loosened its reins on state-owned companies, inviting both competition and private investment into industries previously operated as government monopolies.

The proportions of private and public enterprise can vary widely in mixed economies, and the mix frequently changes. Dozens of countries have converted government-owned and -operated companies into privately held businesses in a trend known as **privatization.** Even the United States has seen proposals to privatize everything from the postal service to Social Security. Governments may privatize state-owned enterprises in an effort to raise funds and improve their economies. The objective is to cut costs and run the operation more efficiently. For most of its existence, Air Canada was a state-owned airline. But in 1989 the airline became fully privatized, and in 2000 the firm acquired Canadian Airlines International, becoming the world's tenth-largest international air carrier. Recently, Air Canada announced a major agreement with the People's Republic of China to expand passenger and cargo services between the two countries.[12] Table 3.4 compares the alternative economic systems on the basis of ownership and management of enterprises, rights to profits, employee rights, and worker incentives.

assessment check

1. On which economic system is the U.S. economy based?
2. What are the two types of planned economies?
3. What is privatization?

Table 3.4 Comparison of Alternative Economic Systems

| System Features | Capitalism (Private Enterprise) | Planned Economies | | |
		Communism	Socialism	Mixed Economy
Ownership of enterprises	Businesses are owned privately, often by large numbers of people. Minimal government ownership leaves production in private hands.	Government owns the means of production with few exceptions, such as small plots of land.	Government owns basic industries, but private owners operate some small enterprises.	A strong private sector blends with public enterprises.
Management of enterprises	Enterprises are managed by owners or their representatives, with minimal government interference.	Centralized management controls all state enterprises in line with three- to five-year plans. Planning now is being decentralized.	Significant government planning pervades socialist nations. State enterprises are managed directly by government bureaucrats.	Management of the private sector resembles that under capitalism. Professionals may also manage state enterprises.
Rights to profits	Entrepreneurs and investors are entitled to all profits (minus taxes) that their firms earn.	Profits are not allowed under communism.	Only the private sector of a socialist economy generates profits.	Entrepreneurs and investors are entitled to private-sector profits, although they often must pay high taxes. State enterprises are also expected to produce returns.
Rights of employees	The rights to choose one's occupation and to join a labor union have long been recognized.	Employee rights are limited in exchange for promised protection against unemployment.	Workers may choose their occupations and join labor unions, but the government influences career decisions for many people.	Workers may choose jobs and labor union membership. Unions often become quite strong.
Worker incentives	Considerable incentives motivate people to perform at their highest levels.	Incentives are emerging in communist countries.	Incentives usually are limited in state enterprises but do motivate workers in the private sector.	Capitalist-style incentives operate in the private sector. More limited incentives influence public-sector activities.

EVALUATING ECONOMIC PERFORMANCE

Ideally, an economic system should provide two important benefits for its citizens: a stable business environment and sustained growth. In a stable business environment, the overall supply of needed goods and services is aligned with the overall demand for those goods and services. No wild fluctuations in price or availability complicate economic decisions. Consumers and businesses not only have access to ample supplies of desired products at affordable prices but also have money to buy the items they demand.

Growth is another important economic goal. An ideal economy incorporates steady change directed toward continually expanding the amount of goods and services produced from the nation's resources. Growth leads to expanded job opportunities, improved wages, and a rising standard of living.

Flattening the Business Cycle

A nation's economy tends to flow through various stages of a business cycle: prosperity, recession, depression, and recovery. No true economic depressions have occurred in the United States since the 1930s, and most economists believe that society is capable of preventing future depressions through effective economic policies. Consequently, they expect a recession to give way to a period of economic recovery.

Both business decisions and consumer buying patterns differ at each stage of the business cycle. In periods of economic prosperity, unemployment remains low, consumer confidence about the future leads to more purchases, and businesses expand—by hiring more employees, investing in new technology, and making similar purchases—to take advantage of new opportunities.

During a **recession**—a cyclical economic contraction that lasts for six months or longer—consumers frequently postpone major purchases and shift buying patterns toward basic, functional products carrying low prices. Businesses mirror these changes in the marketplace by slowing production, postponing expansion plans, reducing inventories, and often cutting the size of their workforces. During past recessions, people facing layoffs and depletions of household savings have sold cars, jewelry, and stocks to make ends meet. During the most recent recession, they did this as well but with a twist: they turned to eBay. There, they sold everything from old books to kitchen knickknacks, contributing to their own success as well as that of eBay.

If an economic slowdown continues in a downward spiral over an extended period of time, the economy falls into depression. Many Americans have grown up hearing stories about their great-grandparents who lived through the Great Depression of the 1930s, when food and other basic necessities were scarce and jobs were rare and precious.

In the *recovery stage* of the business cycle, the economy emerges from recession and consumer spending picks up steam. Even though businesses often continue to rely on part-time and other temporary workers during the early stages of a recovery, unemployment begins to decline as business activity accelerates and firms seek additional workers to meet growing production demands. Gradually, the concerns of recession begin to disappear, and consumers start eating out at restaurants, booking vacations, and purchasing new cars.

ARKANSAS DEPARTMENT OF ECONOMIC DEVELOPMENT

Arkansas promotes its favorable business climate with this ad featuring the growth and prosperity of its plastics industry.

recession cyclical economic contraction that lasts for six months or longer.

"They Said It"

"It's a recession when your neighbor loses his job; it's a depression when you lose your own."
—Harry S. Truman (1884–1972) 33rd president of the United States

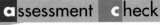

assessment check

1. Which stages of the business cycle indicate a downturn in the economy?
2. Which stages point to an upswing?

Productivity and the Nation's Gross Domestic Product

productivity relationship between the number of units produced and the number of human and other production inputs necessary to produce them.

gross domestic product (GDP) sum of all goods and services produced within a country's boundaries during a specific time period, such as a year.

inflation rising prices caused by a combination of excess consumer demand and increases in the costs of raw materials, component parts, human resources, and other factors of production.

An important concern for every economy is **productivity,** the relationship between the goods and services produced in a nation each year and the inputs needed to produce them. In general, as productivity rises, so does an economy's growth and the wealth of its citizens. In a recession, productivity stalls or even declines.

Productivity describes the relationship between the number of units produced and the number of human and other production inputs necessary to produce them. So productivity is a ratio of output to input. When a constant amount of inputs generates increased outputs, an increase in productivity occurs.

Total productivity considers all inputs necessary to produce a specific amount of outputs. Stated in equation form, it can be written as follows:

$$\text{Total productivity} = \frac{\text{Output (goods or services produced)}}{\text{Input (human/natural resources, capital)}}$$

Many productivity ratios focus on only one of the inputs in the equation: labor productivity or output per labor-hour. An increase in labor productivity means that the same amount of work produces more goods and services than before. Many of the gains in U.S. productivity are attributed to technology, and in recent years the United States alone appears to be enjoying the fruits of technology and productivity. No other industrial nation has experienced the rapid growth of the United States.[13] During the last decade, output per worker has increased at the fastest rate in 40 years. Some analysts believe that the industry that has benefited the most from this increase is healthcare.[14]

Productivity is a widely recognized measure of a company's efficiency. In turn, the total productivity of a nation's businesses has become a measure of its economic strength and standard of living. Economists refer to this measure as a country's **gross domestic product (GDP)**—the sum of all goods and services produced within its boundaries. The GDP is based on the per-capita output of a country—in other words, total national output divided by the number of citizens. As Figure 3.4 shows, the U.S. GDP remains the highest in the world, almost double that of second-ranked China. However, productivity in the United States is suffering in certain areas of the Midwest, where young, educated workers are departing for jobs elsewhere. This situation is described in the "Hit & Miss" feature.

In the United States, GDP is tracked by the Bureau of Economic Analysis (BEA), a division of the U.S. Department of Commerce. Current updates and historical data on the GDP are available at the BEA's Web site (http://www.bea.gov).

Price-Level Changes

Another important indicator of an economy's stability is the general level of prices. For most of the 20th century, economic decision makers concerned themselves with **inflation,** rising prices caused by a combination of excess consumer demand and increases in the costs of raw materials, component parts, human resources, and other factors of production. The **core inflation rate** is the inflation rate of an economy after energy and food prices are removed. This measure is often an accurate prediction of the inflation rate that consumers, businesses, and other organizations can expect to experience during the near future.

Figure 3.4 Nations with Highest Gross Domestic Products

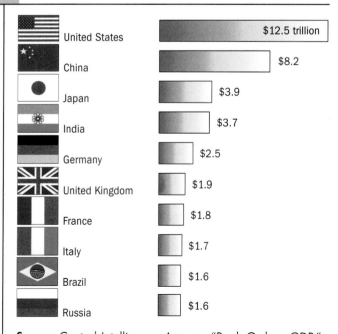

United States	$12.5 trillion
China	$8.2
Japan	$3.9
India	$3.7
Germany	$2.5
United Kingdom	$1.9
France	$1.8
Italy	$1.7
Brazil	$1.6
Russia	$1.6

Source: Central Intelligence Agency, "Rank Order—GDP," *World Factbook,* accessed June 12, 2006, http://www.cia.gov.

HIT & MISS

Is the Midwest Losing Its Brainpower?

Excellent colleges and universities are located in the Midwest, along with beautiful countryside and friendly towns in which to live. Then why have so many Midwestern counties—particularly in rural areas—lost more residents than they have gained in the last half century? According to one survey, Iowa and North Dakota have lost many young, well-educated workers because they want an urban lifestyle and a warmer climate. They are also looking for better pay in professional jobs, which is typically 20 to 50 percent better elsewhere, although this can be offset by a higher cost of living. Colleges and universities in these states are producing highly educated, well-trained workers who leave to find better opportunities in other parts of the country. Experts who study demographics fear that states such as Indiana, Kansas, Iowa, and North Dakota will face a drastic labor shortage within the next 20 years.

Government and business leaders have not ignored the problem, but they haven't yet found a solution. Iowa has abolished its state income tax for workers under age 30. North Dakota has programs to create jobs, increase wages, and keep taxes low. Some towns in Kansas are giving away land to attract new residents. The U.S. Congress is even considering a New Homestead Act, which includes an extensive list of benefits to people who choose to live and work in rural Midwestern areas. Still, the so-called brain drain continues.

But the picture is not entirely bleak. North Dakota has the nation's lowest unemployment rate, which is a huge relief to workers from other regions looking for jobs. And its small cities, Bismarck and Fargo, are actually growing. Technology companies are beginning to invest in the area. Microsoft recently purchased Great Plains Software of Fargo for $1.1 billion, which should attract college graduates who want to stay in the area. Public officials remain optimistic. North Dakota agriculture commissioner Roger Johnson declares, "We're the last undiscovered great place to live."

Questions for Critical Thinking

1. Describe two incentives you think might help recent college graduates stay to work in rural Midwestern areas. Explain why you think these would be successful.
2. How does loss of young, educated workers affect the productivity of these states?

Sources: Tim Swanson, "A Midwestern Brain Drain," Ludwig von Mises Institute, accessed June 8, 2006, http://blog.mises.org; Les Christie, "Stopping the Great Plains Brain Drain," CNN Money, accessed June 8, 2006, http://money.cnn.com; Dennis Cauchon, "Big Cities Lure Away North Dakota Youth," *USA Today*, accessed June 8, 2006, http://www.usatoday.com.

Excess consumer demand generates what is known as *demand-pull inflation*; rises in costs of factors of production generates *cost-push inflation*. America's most severe inflationary period during the last half of the 20th century peaked in 1980, when general price levels jumped almost 14 percent in a single year. In extreme cases, an economy may experience *hyperinflation*—an economic situation characterized by soaring prices. This situation has occurred in South America, as well as in countries that once formed the Soviet Union.

Inflation devalues money as persistent price increases reduce the amount of goods and services people can purchase with a given amount of money. This is bad news for people whose incomes do not keep up with inflation or who have most of their wealth in investments paying a fixed rate of interest. Inflation can be good news to people whose income is rising or those with debts at a fixed rate of interest. A homeowner during inflationary times is paying off a fixed-rate mortgage with money that is worth less and less each year. Over the last decade, inflation helped a strong stock market drive up the number of millionaires to more than 8 million. But because of inflation, being a millionaire does not make a person as rich as it once did. To live like a 1960s millionaire, you would need almost $6 million today.

When increased productivity keeps prices steady, it can have a major positive impact on an economy. In a low-inflation environment, businesses can make long-range plans without the constant worry of sudden inflationary shocks. Low interest rates encourage firms to invest in

If oil and gas prices continue to climb, they may force consumers to look for alternative-fueled vehicles. Some natural-gas-powered cars can already be refueled right in owners' garages through a wall-mounted appliance that taps into a home's natural-gas line.

research and development and capital improvements, both of which are likely to produce productivity gains. Consumers can purchase growing stocks of goods and services with the same amount of money, and low interest rates encourage major acquisitions such as new homes and autos. Despite the recent good news in the U.S. economy, some economists have cautioned that inflation may be "flickering on the horizon." The mounting cost of oil—which is used to produce nearly every product—is a continuing concern. Businesses need to raise prices to cover their costs. Also, smaller firms have gone out of business or have been merged with larger companies, reducing the amount of competition and increasing the purchasing power of the larger corporations. However, other factors signal that inflation will not reach alarming proportions.[15]

The opposite situation—**deflation**—occurs when prices continue to fall. In Japan, where deflation has been a reality for several years, shoppers pay less for a variety of products ranging from Big Macs to apartments. While this situation may sound ideal to consumers, it can weaken the economy.

Measuring Price Level Changes In the United States, the government tracks changes in price levels with the **Consumer Price Index (CPI),** which measures the monthly average change in prices of goods and services. The federal Bureau of Labor Statistics (BLS) calculates the CPI monthly based on prices of a "market basket," a compilation of the goods and services most commonly purchased by urban consumers. Figure 3.5 shows the categories included in the CPI market basket. Each month, BLS representatives visit thousands of stores, service establishments, rental units, and doctors' offices all over the United States to price the multitude of items in the CPI market basket. They compile the data to create the CPI. So the CPI provides a running measurement of changes in consumer prices.

Employment Levels

People need money to buy the goods and services produced in an economy. Because most consumers earn that money by working, the number of people in a nation who currently have jobs is an important indicator of how well the economy is doing. In general, employment has been on the rise in the United States the past few years: the Bureau of Labor Statistics projects a total increase of 21.3 million jobs, or 15 percent.

Economists refer to a nation's **unemployment rate** as an indicator of its economic health. The unemployment rate is usually expressed as a percentage of the total workforce who are actively seeking work but are currently unemployed. The total labor force includes all people who are willing and available to work at the going market wage, whether they currently have jobs or are seeking work. The U.S. Department of Labor, which tracks unemployment rates, also includes so-called discouraged workers in the total labor force. These individuals want to work but have given up looking for jobs, for various reasons. Unemployment can be grouped into the four categories shown in Figure 3.6: frictional, seasonal, cyclical, and structural.

Frictional unemployment applies to members of the workforce who are temporarily not working but are looking for jobs. This pool of potential workers includes new graduates, people who have left jobs for any reason and are looking for other employment, and former workers who have decided to return to the labor force. *Seasonal unemployment* is the joblessness of workers in a seasonal industry. Construction workers, farm laborers, fishery workers, and landscape employees may contend with bouts of seasonal unemployment when wintry conditions make work unavailable.

Figure

3.5

Contents of the CPI Market Basket

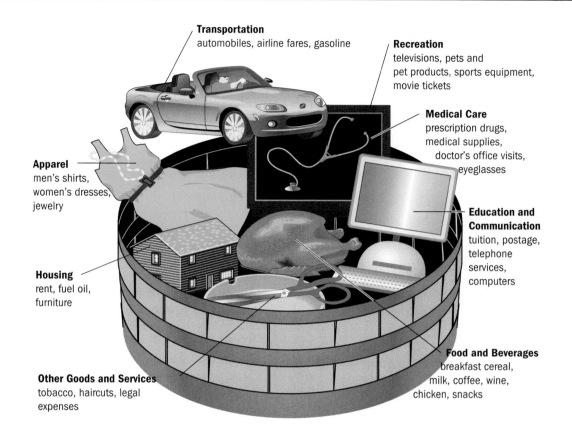

Transportation
automobiles, airline fares, gasoline

Recreation
televisions, pets and
pet products, sports equipment,
movie tickets

Medical Care
prescription drugs,
medical supplies,
doctor's office visits,
eyeglasses

Apparel
men's shirts,
women's dresses,
jewelry

**Education and
Communication**
tuition, postage,
telephone
services,
computers

Housing
rent, fuel oil,
furniture

Other Goods and Services
tobacco, haircuts, legal
expenses

Food and Beverages
breakfast cereal,
milk, coffee, wine,
chicken, snacks

Source: Information from Bureau of Labor Statistics, "Consumer Price Indexes: Frequently Asked Questions," accessed June 8, 2006, http://www.bls.gov/cpi.

Cyclical unemployment includes people who are out of work because of a cyclical contraction in the economy. During periods of economic expansion, overall employment is likely to rise, but as growth slows and a recession begins, unemployment levels commonly rise. At such times, even workers with good job skills may face temporary unemployment. Workers in high-tech industries, air travel, and manufacturing have all faced unemployment during economic contraction.

Structural unemployment applies to people who remain unemployed for long periods of time, often with little hope of finding new jobs like their old ones. This situation may arise because these workers lack the necessary skills for available jobs or because the skills they have are no longer in demand. For instance, technological developments have increased the demand for people with computer-related skills but have created structural unemployment among many types of manual laborers.

MANAGING THE ECONOMY'S PERFORMANCE

As recent years have vividly demonstrated, a national government can use both monetary policy and fiscal policy in its efforts to fight unemployment, increase business and consumer spending, and reduce the length and severity of economic recessions. The Federal Reserve System can

"**They Said It**"

"One American out of work is too many Americans out of work."
—George W. Bush
(b. 1946)
43rd president
of the United States

assessment check

1. What is productivity?
2. How does the U.S. government track changes in price levels?
3. Identify the four categories of unemployment.

increase or reduce interest rates, and the federal government can enact tax cuts or propose other reforms.

Frictional Unemployment
- Temporarily not working
- Looking for a job
Example: New graduates entering the workforce

Seasonal Unemployment
- Not working during some months
- Not looking for a job
Example: Farm laborers needed only when a crop is in season

Structural Unemployment
- Not working due to no demand for skills
- May be retraining for a new job
Example: Assembly line workers whose jobs are now done by robots

Cyclical Unemployment
- Not working due to economic slowdown
- Looking for a job
Example: Executives laid off during corporate downsizing or recessionary periods

Monetary Policy

A common method of influencing economic activity is **monetary policy,** government actions to increase or decrease the money supply and change banking require-ments and interest rates to influence spending by altering bankers' willingness to make loans. An *expansionary monetary policy* increases the money supply in an effort to cut the cost of borrowing, which encourages business decision makers to make new investments, in turn stimu-lating employment and economic growth. By contrast, a *restrictive monetary policy* reduces the money supply to curb rising prices, overexpansion, and concerns about overly rapid economic growth.

In the United States, the Federal Reserve System ("the Fed") is responsible for formulating and implementing the nation's monetary policy. It is headed by a chairman and board of governors, all of whom are nominated by the president. The most well-known chairman, Alan Greenspan, recently retired after heading the Fed for nearly two decades. All national banks must be members of this sys-tem and keep some percentage of their checking and sav-ings funds on deposit at the Fed.

The Fed's board of governors uses a number of tools to regulate the economy. By changing the required percentage of checking and savings accounts that banks must deposit with the Fed, the governors can expand or shrink funds available to lend. The Fed also lends money to member banks, which in turn make loans at higher interest rates to business and individual borrowers. By changing the interest rates charged to commercial banks, the Fed affects the interest rates charged to borrowers and, consequently, their willingness to borrow. That commercial lending rate reached a 46-year low of 1 percent in January 2004, but the Fed later raised rates in a series of quarter-point moves.[16]

Fiscal Policy

Governments also influence economic activities by making decisions about taxes and spend-ing. Through revenues and expenses, the government implements **fiscal policy.** This is the second technique that officials use to control inflation, reduce unemployment, improve the general standard of living, and encourage economic growth. Increased taxes may restrict eco-nomic activities, while lower taxes and increased government spending usually boost spending and profits, cut unemployment rates, and fuel economic expansion.

International Fiscal Policy
Nations in the industrial world, including the United States, are currently struggling to find ways to help developing nations modernize their economies. One proposal is to "forgive" outright the debts of some of these countries, particularly those in Africa, to stimulate their economies to grow. But not all fiscal experts agree with this idea. They suggest that any debt forgiveness should come with certain conditions so that these countries can build their own fiscal policies. Countries should encourage and allow citizens to own property, lower their tax rates, avoid devaluing their currencies, lay a path for new busi-nesses to start up, and reduce trade barriers.[17]

monetary policy govern-ment actions to increase or decrease the money supply and change banking requirements and interest rates to influence bankers' will-ingness to make loans.

The Federal Budget Each year, the president proposes a **budget** for the federal government, a plan for how it will raise and spend money during the coming year, and presents it to Congress for approval. A typical federal budget proposal undergoes months of deliberation and many modifications before receiving approval. The federal budget includes a number of different spending categories, ranging from defense and Social Security to interest payments on the national debt. The decisions about what to include in the budget have a direct effect on various sectors of the economy. During a recession, the federal government may approve increased spending on interstate highway repairs to improve transportation and increase employment in the construction industry. During prosperity, the government may allocate more money for scientific research or the arts.

The primary sources of government funds to cover the costs of the annual budget are taxes, fees, and borrowing. Both the overall amount of these funds and their specific combination have major effects on the economic well-being of the nation. One way governments raise money is to impose taxes on sales and income. But increasing taxes leaves people and businesses with less money to spend. This might reduce inflation, but overly high taxes can also slow economic growth. So governments try to balance taxes to give people necessary services without slowing economic growth.

Taxes don't always generate enough funds to cover every spending project the government hopes to undertake. When the government spends more than the amount of money it raises through taxes, it creates a **budget deficit.** To cover the deficit, the U.S. government borrows money by selling Treasury bills, Treasury notes, and Treasury bonds to investors. All of this borrowing makes up the **national debt.** Currently the Government Accountability Office (GAO) estimates that the national debt is $43 trillion.[18] One of the factors contributing to the budget deficit is the war in Iraq and related military operations. If the government takes in more money than it spends, it is said to have a **budget surplus. A balanced budget** means total revenues raised by taxes equal the total proposed spending for the year.

Achieving a balanced budget—or even a budget surplus—does not erase the national debt, which must be paid off. U.S. legislators continually debate how fast the nation should use revenues to reduce its debt. Most families want to wipe out debt—from credit cards, automobile purchases, and college. But for the federal government, the decision is more complex. When the government raises money by selling Treasury bills, it makes safe investments available to investors worldwide. If foreign investors cannot buy Treasury notes, they might turn to other countries, reducing the amount of money flowing into the United States. U.S. government debt has also been used as a basis for pricing riskier investments. If the government issues less debt, the interest rates it commands are higher, raising the overall cost of debt to private borrowers. In addition, the government uses the funds from borrowing, at least in part, to invest in such public services as education and scientific research. As a society, if we decide our economy needs these services, debt reduction may not always be the best use of government funds. However, it can also be argued that paying down the national debt will free up more money to be invested by individuals and businesses.

fiscal policy government spending and taxation decisions designed to control inflation, reduce unemployment, improve the general welfare of citizens, and encourage economic growth.

budget organization's plan for how it will raise and spend money during a given period of time.

"**They Said It**"

"Three groups spend other people's money: children, thieves, politicians. All three need parental supervision."
—Dick Armey (b. 1940)
Retired American politician

assessment **c**heck

1. What is the difference between an expansionary monetary policy and a restrictive monetary policy?

2. What are the three primary sources of government funds?

3. Does a balanced budget erase the federal debt?

GLOBAL ECONOMIC CHALLENGES OF THE 21ST CENTURY

Businesses face a number of important economic challenges in the 21st century. As the economies of countries around the globe become increasingly interconnected, governments and businesses must compete throughout the world. Although no one can predict the future, both governments and businesses will likely need to meet several challenges to maintain their

Table

3.5 Global Economic Challenges

Challenge	Facts and Examples
International terrorism	Assistance in locating and detaining known terrorists by dozens of nations. Cooperation in modifying banking laws in most nations in an effort to cut off funds to terrorist organizations. Concerns over the safety of mass-transit systems following bombings in London and elsewhere.
Shift to a global information economy	Half of all American workers hold jobs in information technology or in industries that intensively use information technology, products, and services. Software industry in India is growing more than 50 percent each year. Internet users in Asia and western Europe have more than doubled in five years.
Aging of the world's population	Median age of the U.S. population is 35 plus, and by 2025, more than 62 million Americans will be age 65 or older—nearly double today's number. This will increase demands for health-care, retirement benefits, and other support services, putting budgetary pressure on governments. As baby boomers, now beginning to reach their mid- to late 50s, begin to retire, businesses around the globe will need to find ways to replace their workplace skills.
Improving quality and customer service	In today's global marketplace, every company will have to achieve world-class performance in product quality and customer service.
Enhancing competitiveness of every country's workforce	Leaner organizations (with fewer supervisors) require employees with the skills to control, combine, and supervise work operations. Employers must provide training necessary to develop the increased skills they require of their workforce.

global competitiveness. Table 3.5 identifies five key challenges: (1) the economic impact of the continuing threat of international terrorism, (2) the shift to a global information economy, (3) the aging of the world's population, (4) the need to improve quality and customer service, and (5) efforts to enhance the competitiveness of every country's workforce.

No country is an economic island in today's global economy. Not only is an ever-increasing stream of goods and services crossing national borders, but a growing number of businesses have become true multinational firms, operating manufacturing plants and other facilities around the world. As global trade and investments grow, events in one nation can reverberate around the globe.

Despite the risks of world trade, global expansion can offer huge opportunities to U.S. firms. With U.S. residents accounting for less than 1 in every 20 of the world's nearly 7 billion people, growth-oriented American companies cannot afford to ignore the world market. U.S. businesses also benefit from the lower labor costs in other parts of the world, and some are finding successful niches importing goods and even services provided by foreign firms. Still, it is extremely important for U.S. firms to keep track of the foreign firms that supply their products. A recent trend toward the use of overseas service call centers by U.S. firms such as American Express, Sprint, General Electric, and IBM has had mixed results. Despite training in language and other skills, customer service representatives in India often struggle to serve frustrated customers. "Many callers refuse to speak to Indians and ask for an American right away," reports one call center employee.[19]

DHL simplifies global business by offering firms a single source for importing services.

U.S. firms must also develop strategies for competing with each other overseas. In the huge but fragmented snack chip industry, Frito-Lay International currently claims 30 percent of the market outside North America, considerably more than its closest competitor, Procter & Gamble, has captured. Coca-Cola still edges out Pepsi as the top-selling cola worldwide.

WHAT'S AHEAD

Global competition is a key factor in today's economy. In Chapter 4, we focus on the global dimensions of business. We cover basic concepts of doing business internationally and examine how nations can position themselves to benefit from the global economy. Then we describe the specific methods used by individual businesses to expand beyond their national borders and compete successfully in the global marketplace.

assessment check

1. Why is virtually no country an economic island these days?
2. Describe two ways in which global expansion can benefit a U.S. firm.

SUMMARY OF LEARNING GOALS

1 Distinguish between microeconomics and macroeconomics.

Microeconomics is the study of economic behavior among individual consumers, families, and businesses whose collective behavior in the marketplace determines the quantity of goods and services demanded and supplied at different prices. Macroeconomics is the study of the broader economic picture and how an economic system maintains and allocates its resources; it focuses on how a government's monetary and fiscal policies affect the overall operation of an economic system.

Assessment Check Answers

1.1 Define *microeconomics*.
Microeconomics is the study of economic behavior among individual consumers, families, and businesses whose collective behavior in the marketplace determines the quantity of goods and services demanded and supplied at different prices.

1.2 Define *macroeconomics*.
Macroeconomics is the study of the broader economic picture and how an economic system maintains and allocates its resources.

2 Explain the factors that drive demand and supply.

Demand is the willingness and ability of buyers to purchase goods and services at different prices. Factors that drive demand for a good or service include customer preferences, the number of buyers and their incomes, the prices of substitute goods, the prices of complementary goods, and consumer expectations about

the future. Supply is the willingness and ability of businesses to offer products for sale at different prices. Supply is determined by the cost of inputs and technology resources, taxes, and the number of suppliers operating in the market.

Assessment Check Answers

2.1 What is a demand curve?
A demand curve is a graph of the amount of a product that buyers will purchase at different prices.

2.2 What is a supply curve?
A supply curve shows the relationship between different prices and the quantities that sellers will offer for sale, regardless of demand.

2.3 How do factors of production influence the overall supply of goods and services?
A change in the cost or availability of any of the inputs considered to be factors of production can shift the entire supply curve, either increasing or decreasing the amount available at every price.

3 Describe each of the four different types of market structures in a private enterprise system.

Four basic models characterize competition in a private enterprise system: pure competition, monopolistic competition, oligopoly, and monopoly. Pure competition is a market structure, like that in small-scale agriculture, in which large numbers of buyers and sellers exchange homogeneous products and no single participant has a significant influence on price. Monopolistic competition is a market structure, like that of retailing, in which large numbers of buyers and sellers exchange differentiated products, so each participant has some control over price. Oligopolies are market situations, like those in the steel and airline industries, in which relatively few sellers compete and high start-up costs form barriers to keep out new competitors. In a monopoly, one seller dominates trade in a good or service, for which buyers can find no close substitutes. Privately held local water utilities and firms that hold exclusive patent rights on significant product inventions are examples.

Assessment Check Answers

3.1 What is the difference between pure competition and monopolistic competition?
Pure competition is a market structure in which large numbers of buyers and sellers exchange homogeneous products. Monopolistic competition is a market structure in which large numbers of buyers and sellers exchange differentiated products.

3.2 Distinguish between oligopoly and monopoly.
An oligopoly is a market structure in which relatively few sellers compete, and high start-up costs form barriers to new competitors. In a monopoly, one seller dominates trade in a good or service.

4 Compare the three major types of economic systems.
The major economic systems are private enterprise economy, planned economy (such as communism or socialism), and mixed market economy. In a private enterprise system, individuals and private businesses pursue their own interests—including investment decisions and profits—without undue governmental restriction. In a planned economy, the government exerts stronger control over business ownership, profits, and resources to accomplish governmental and societal—rather than individual—goals. Communism is an economic system without private property; goods are owned in common, and factors of production and production decisions are controlled by the state. Socialism, another type of planned economic system, is characterized by government ownership and operation of all major industries. A mixed market economy blends government ownership and private enterprise, combining characteristics of both planned and private enterprise economies.

Assessment Check Answers

4.1 On which economic system is the U.S. economy based?

The U.S. economy is based on the private enterprise system.

4.2 What are the two types of planned economies?
The two types of planned economies are socialism and communism.

4.3 What is privatization?
Privatization is the conversion of government-owned and -operated agencies into privately held businesses.

5 Identify and describe the four stages of the business cycle.
The four stages are prosperity, recession, depression, and recovery. Prosperity is characterized by low unemployment and strong consumer confidence. In a recession, consumers often postpone major purchases, layoffs may occur, and household savings may be depleted. A depression occurs when an economic slowdown continues in a downward spiral over a long period of time. During recovery, consumer spending begins to increase and business activity accelerates, leading to an increased number of jobs.

Assessment Check Answers

5.1 Which stages of the business cycle indicate a downturn in the economy?
Recession and depression indicate a downturn.

5.2 Which stages point to an upswing?
Prosperity and recovery point to an upswing.

6 Explain how productivity, price level changes, and employment levels affect the stability of a nation's economy.
As productivity rises, so do an economy's growth and the wealth of its citizens. In a recession, productivity stalls or possibly declines. Changes in general price levels—inflation or deflation—are important indicators of an economy's general stability. The U.S. government measures price-level changes by the Consumer Price Index. A nation's unemployment rate is an indicator of both overall stability and growth. The unemployment rate shows the number of people actively seeking employment who are unable to find jobs as a percentage of the total labor force.

Assessment Check Answers

6.1 What is productivity?
Productivity is the relationship between the goods and services produced in a nation each year and the inputs that produce them.

6.2 How does the U.S. government track changes in price levels?

The U.S. government tracks changes in price levels with the Consumer Price Index (CPI), which measures the monthly average change in prices of goods and services.

6.3 Identify the four categories of unemployment.
The four categories of unemployment are frictional, seasonal, cyclical, and structural.

7 Discuss how monetary policy and fiscal policy are used to manage an economy's performance.

Monetary policy encompasses a government's efforts to control the size of the nation's money supply. Various methods of increasing or decreasing the overall money supply affect interest rates and therefore affect borrowing and investment decisions. By changing the size of the money supply, government can encourage growth or control inflation. Fiscal policy involves decisions regarding government revenues and expenditures. Changes in government spending affect economic growth and employment levels in the private sector. However, government must also raise money, through taxes or borrowing, to finance its expenditures. Because tax payments represent funds that might otherwise have been spent by individuals and businesses, any taxation changes also affect the overall economy.

Assessment Check Answers

7.1 What is the difference between an expansionary monetary policy and a restrictive monetary policy?
An expansionary monetary policy increases the money supply in an effort to cut the cost of borrowing. A restrictive monetary policy reduces the money supply to curb rising prices, overexpansion, and concerns about overly rapid economic growth.

7.2 What are the three primary sources of government funds?
The U.S. government acquires funds through taxes, fees, and borrowing.

7.3 Does a balanced budget erase the federal debt?
No, a balanced budget does not erase the national debt; it just doesn't increase it. The government must pay off the debt just as consumers pay off their charge accounts.

8 Describe the major global economic challenges of the 21st century.

Businesses face five key challenges in the 21st century: (1) the threat of international terrorism, (2) the shift to a global information economy, (3) the aging of the world's population, (4) the need to improve quality and customer service, and (5) efforts to enhance the competitiveness of every country's workforce.

Assessment Check Answers

8.1 Why is virtually no country an economic island these days?
No business or country is an economic island because many goods and services travel across national borders. Companies now are becoming multinational firms.

8.2 Describe two ways in which global expansion can benefit a U.S. firm.
A firm can benefit from global expansion by attracting more customers and using less expensive labor and production to produce goods and services.

Business Terms You Need to Know

economics 64	supply 65	inflation 78
microeconomics 64	recession 77	monetary policy 82
macroeconomics 64	productivity 78	fiscal policy 82
demand 65	gross domestic product (GDP) 78	budget 83

Other Important Business Terms

demand curve 66	deregulation 74	deflation 80
supply curve 68	planned economy 74	Consumer Price Index (CPI) 80
equilibrium price 70	communism 74	unemployment rate 80
pure competition 71	socialism 75	budget deficit 83
monopolistic competition 72	mixed market economy 75	national debt 83
oligopoly 72	privatization 76	budget surplus 83
monopoly 73	core inflation rate 78	balanced budget 83

1. Distinguish between macroeconomics and micro-economics. Give at least one example of issues addressed by each.
2. Draw supply and demand graphs that estimate what will happen to demand, supply, and the equilibrium price of pizza if these events occur:
   a. A widely reported medical report suggests that eating cheese supplies a significant amount of the calcium needed in a person's daily diet.
   b. The price of flour increases.
   c. The state imposes a new tax on restaurant meals.
   d. The biggest competitor leaves the area.
3. Describe the four different types of competition in the private enterprise system. In which type of competition would each of the following businesses be likely to engage?
   a. a 100-acre Wisconsin dairy farm
   b. Stop & Shop supermarkets
   c. Southwest Airlines
   d. the U.S. Postal Service
   e. Microsoft
4. Describe the two types of planned economies and give an example of each. What is a mixed market economy?
5. What are the four stages of the business cycle? In which stage do you believe the U.S. economy is now? Why?
6. Define *productivity*. Why is it an important concern for every economy?
7. What are the effects of inflation on an economy? How does the Consumer Price Index (CPI) work?
8. Describe the four types of unemployment, and give an example of each. Which type might signify that an economy is in a downturn?
9. Explain the difference between monetary policy and fiscal policy. How does the government raise funds to cover the costs of its annual budget?
10. What are the benefits of paying down the national debt? What might be the negative effects?

1. Describe a situation in which you have had to make an economic choice in an attempt to balance your wants with limited means. What factors influenced your decision?
2. On your own or with a classmate, visit a large general merchandise retailer—such as a Target or Wal-Mart store. (Alternatively, you can visit a retailer online.) List five different goods sold by the retailer. Note also one or two major competitors, if there are any, on the shelves nearby. (If you are online, note one or two brands you think might be competitors.) Classify each good in terms of the competitive environment. Be sure to note the characteristics you used to make each classification. Create a chart illustrating your findings. Include each of the goods, its competitors, its classification of competitive environment, and the characteristics you used to make the classification. Present your chart to the class.
3. Some businesses automatically experience seasonal unemployment—beach or ski resorts, con-struction companies, ice-cream stands. Choose a "business partner" from among your classmates and select a business that interests you that experiences seasonal unemployment. Then develop a plan for increasing demand for your business during the off-season. Present your plan to the class.
4. In the past, many proposals have been made for privatizing certain federal or state-run agencies such as Social Security, Medicare, and the U.S. Postal Service. On your own or with a classmate, select one of these agencies and go online to research more about how it is run. Do you favor privatization of this agency? Why or why not? Discuss your findings with the class.
5. Consider your economic lifetime to date. What stages of the business cycle have you experienced? In what ways have these stages affected your—and your family's—lifestyle? (You might want to talk with your parents, grandparents, siblings, and other relatives about their views.)

General Motors Staggers under the Weight of Healthcare Costs

General Motors is the world's largest auto manufacturer, and it may claim the world's largest healthcare costs to match. GM insures 1.1 million current employees, retirees, and even their widows and widowers as part of the benefits plan it negotiated with the United Auto Workers (UAW) and began implementing over 50 years ago. The plan cost $5.2 billion in a recent year, contributing to losses. Healthcare costs were so significant that GM executives had to search frantically for a solution.

Richard Wagoner, GM's chairman and CEO, charged that U.S. companies and workers pay more for healthcare—and receive less—than their counterparts in other countries. "In the U.S., healthcare costs are rising at an annual rate of 14 percent to 18 percent and already account for 15 percent of our gross domestic product—50 percent higher than the next most expensive country," he argued. Even if he was correct, it didn't solve GM's problem. "Our foreign-based competitors have just a fraction of these costs because they have few retirees in this country and in their own country where the bulk of their people are, their governments pay a much greater proportion of their employee and retiree healthcare costs," Wagoner pointed out. GM was faced with a future cost of $77 billion to cover its current workers and retirees, but had only $20 billion in the bank to cover it. The firm had to come up with a creative answer—and fast.

One possibility was to increase revenues by cutting out discount sales to rental-car agencies and to employees themselves. But the firm recently launched a marketing campaign offering cars to retail consumers at the employee discount to boost lagging sales. To boost revenues, GM could also increase sales, but the firm makes so many models of cars and trucks that its design and engineering teams can't redesign or improve them as often as some of the smaller manufacturers do. This cycle makes GM look sluggish and unresponsive to consumer preferences—and buyers go elsewhere for their cars, reducing demand for GM vehicles. Wagoner began to order the closing of some assembly plants and the retirement of certain brands—such as Oldsmobile—in order to trim down, and convinced the UAW that it had to shoulder more of the healthcare costs to survive. GM succeeded in convincing the UAW that it had to shoulder more of the healthcare costs to survive. After the company reported a staggering $1.6 billion loss in one quarter, the union realized that bankruptcy was a real possibility. So with the cuts to its healthcare coverage, GM estimated it could save $3 billion a year—a significant contribution to its bottom line.

Questions for Critical Thinking

1. How might a positive change in demand for GM's products affect its overall financial picture? What steps might GM take to create that demand?
2. Do you think GM workers and retirees were right to agree to help pay more for their own healthcare costs? Why or why not?

Sources: "GM's $1.1 Billion Loss to Impact UAW," *Washington Times*, accessed June 8, 2006, http://www.washingtontimes.com; Rick Popely and Jim Mateja, "GM, UAW Come to Terms," *Chicago Tribune*, October 18, 2005, section 3, pp. 1, 7; Jonathan Fahey, "Black Hole," *Forbes*, April 11, 2005, p. 54; David Welch, "Running Out of Gas," *BusinessWeek*, March 28, 2005, pp. 28–30.

VIDEO   **Case 3.2**

BP Meets Global Energy Challenges Head-On

This video case appears on page 610. A recently filmed video, designed to expand and highlight the written case, is available for class use by instructors.

Chapter 4

Competing in Global Markets

PHOTODISC/GETTY IMAGES

LON C. DIEHL/PHOTOEDIT

A U.S. shoe manufacturer that can make work boots trendy among young European and Asian consumers must be unusual, and Red Wing Shoe Company certainly is. The 100-year-old firm, which is based in the small Minnesota town that shares its name, has become a standout in its industry, and not just for its growing fashion sense. About 98 percent of the footwear sold in the United States today is imported from somewhere else in the world, which means Red Wing is one of the very few domestic shoe manufacturers still making its products on American soil.

It hasn't always been a smooth ride for the company, which is privately owned and profitable, with annual sales at about $375 million. Competition from lower-priced merchandise has been eating into its market, and Red Wing has worked hard to control costs and expand its product lines in order to remain competitive. Other boot

The company makes about 200 different boot models, some of which are tailored for the needs and hazards of particular jobs and industries. For instance, boots for iron-

These Boots Are Made for Working—Internationally

makers such as Timberland and Doc Martens have pushed ahead on the fashion frontier, while Red Wing has stayed close to the blue-collar workers who have always made up the largest part of its customer base. "Would I say we're the best-looking boot in the world?" asks president and CEO David Murphy. "No, but we're getting better."

Getting better, however, means branching out from the company's classic designs, many of which have remained the same for decades. With new designers on board, the company is now making women's shoes and motorcycle boots. The steel-toed boots needed by young blue-collar workers also come styled like hiking shoes or sneakers. And Red Wing has succeeded in cracking the international market with a new brand of footwear called "Euro Classics," which use special leathers and distinctive stitching to appeal to fashion-conscious youth in Europe and Asia. Says Murphy, "The reason they sell so well in those places is because we're such a genuine American name; you can't create that—it just is or it isn't." About 15 percent of Red Wing's annual sales now come from international markets, and the company recently created a new position—vice president of international and strategic development—to highlight the growing role of international sales in its corporate strategy.

workers have soft soles so that wearers can feel the steel beams under their feet while working on building construction sites. Farmers in the southeastern United States need boots that grip despite slippery floors but don't pick up the sticky clay of the region. But regardless of the industry, one of Red Wing's biggest selling points is the fact that its products come in enough sizes to fit almost anybody—from 4B to 18EE in some models.

Although it's very conscious of the importance its U.S. customer base places on Red Wing's homegrown pedigree, the company also imports some shoes from China that it markets under other brand names, and it imports some of the leather uppers used to make its Red Wing brand products. But Red Wing's managers know that its U.S. customers include many union workers who appreciate products "Made in the U.S.A." The company plans to keep serving them, even though they are, ironically, a customer base that's shrinking as manufacturing jobs continue to move overseas, where labor is cheaper. And, in fact, "the willingness of the American worker to buy American . . . gets less all the time," says Murphy. "In today's world, the young consumer has never worn a shoe made in America." But "we do look beyond pure economics. I think most great companies do."[1]

Consider for a moment how many products you used today that came from outside the United States. Maybe you drank Brazilian coffee with your breakfast, wore clothes manufactured in Honduras or Malaysia, drove to class in a German or Japanese car fueled by gasoline refined from Venezuelan crude oil, and watched a movie on a television set assembled in Mexico for a Japanese company such as Sony. A fellow student in Germany may be wearing Levi's jeans, using a Dell computer, and drinking Coca-Cola.

U.S. and foreign companies alike recognize the importance of international trade to their future success. Economic interdependence is increasing throughout the world as companies seek additional markets for their goods and services and the most cost-effective locations for production facilities. No longer can businesses rely only on domestic sales. Today, foreign sales are essential to U.S. manufacturing, agricultural, and service firms as sources of new markets and profit opportunities. Foreign companies also frequently look to the United States when they seek new markets.

Thousands of products cross national borders every day. The computers that U.S. manufacturers sell in Canada are **exports**, domestically produced goods and services sold in markets in other countries. **Imports** are foreign-made products and services purchased by domestic consumers. Together, U.S. exports and imports make up about a quarter of the U.S. gross domestic product (GDP). U.S. exports recently set a record high of more than $1.1 trillion, and annual imports hit another new high of nearly $1.8 trillion. That total amount is more than double the nation's imports and exports from just a decade ago.[2]

exports domestically produced goods and services sold in other countries.

imports foreign goods and services purchased by domestic customers.

Transactions that cross national boundaries may expose a company to an additional set of environmental factors such as new social and cultural practices, economic and political environments, and legal restrictions. Before venturing into world markets, companies must adapt their domestic business strategies and plans to accommodate these differences.

This chapter travels through the world of international business to see how both large and small companies approach globalization. First, we consider the reasons nations trade, the importance and characteristics of the global marketplace, and the ways nations measure international trade. Then we examine barriers to international trade that arise from cultural and environmental differences. To reduce these barriers, countries turn to organizations that promote global business. Finally, we look at the strategies firms implement for entering foreign markets and how they develop international business strategies.

local   tourist

local   tourist

As the world gets smaller, and flatter, it's increasingly difficult to know who is from where.

And with over 100 million customers on 6 continents, we know for certain that no two people are alike on the outside, or the inside.

Our differences, more than anything else, make the world go round.

Your point of view welcome here.

yourpointofview.com

HSBC ⟨X⟩
The world's local bank

USED WITH PERMISSION. HSBC BANK USA, N.A.

Businesses that are thinking of going global need to understand and appreciate local customs and culture. Banking firm HSBC has offices in 77 countries and territories—in Europe, the Americas, the Middle East, and Africa. The company uses its local knowledge to provide personal service no matter where its banks are.

WHY NATIONS TRADE

As domestic markets mature and sales growth slows, companies in every industry recognize the increasing importance of efforts to develop business in other countries. Wal-Mart operates stores in Mexico, Boeing sells jetliners in Asia, and soccer fans in Britain watch their teams being bought by U.S. billionaires. These are only a few of the thousands of U.S. companies taking advantage of large populations, substantial resources, and rising standards of living abroad that boost foreign interest in their goods and services. Likewise, the U.S. market, with the world's highest purchasing power, attracts thousands of foreign companies to its shores.

International trade is vital to a nation and its businesses because it boosts economic growth by providing a market for its products and access to needed resources. Companies can expand their markets, seek growth opportunities in other nations, and make their production and distribution systems more efficient. They also reduce their dependence on the economies of their home nations.

International Sources of Factors of Production

Business decisions to operate abroad depend on the availability, price, and quality of labor, natural resources, capital, and entrepreneurship—the basic factors of production—in the foreign country. Indian colleges and universities produce thousands of highly qualified computer scientists and engineers each year. To take advantage of this talent, many U.S. computer software and hardware firms have set up operations in India and many others are outsourcing information technology and customer service jobs there, as we'll see later in this chapter.

Trading with other countries also allows a company to spread risk because different nations may be at different stages of the business cycle or in different phases of development. If demand falls off in one country, the company may still enjoy strong demand in other nations. Companies such as Toyota and Sony have long used international sales to offset lower domestic demand.

Size of the International Marketplace

In addition to human and natural resources, entrepreneurship, and capital, companies are attracted to international business by the sheer size of the global marketplace. Only one in five of the world's nearly 7 billion people lives in a relatively well-developed country. The share of the world's population in the less developed countries will increase over the coming years because more developed nations have lower birthrates. But the U.S. Census Bureau says the global birthrate is slowing overall, and the average woman in today's world bears half as many children as her counterpart did 35 years ago.[3]

As developing nations expand their involvement in global business, the potential for reaching new groups of customers dramatically increases. Firms looking for new revenue are inevitably attracted to giant markets such as China and India, with respective populations of nearly 1.3 billion and 1.1 billion each. However, people alone are not enough to create a market. Consumer demand also requires purchasing

REPRINTED WITH THE PERMISSION OF GENERAL MILLS, INC.

Even the French have a taste for Tex-Mex food—chicken fajitas, to be specific. Old El Paso sells its fajita kits there, saying it's "child's play" (*un jeu d'enfant*) to make them.

Table

4.1

The World's Top Ten Nations Based on Population and Wealth

Country	Population (in Millions)	Country	Per-Capita GDP (in U.S. dollars)
China	1,299	Luxembourg	$55,100
India	1,065	United States	$37,800
United States	293	Norway	$37,800
Indonesia	238	Bermuda	$36,000
Brazil	184	Cayman Islands	$35,000
Pakistan	159	San Marino	$34,600
Russia	144	Switzerland	$32,700
Bangladesh	141	Denmark	$31,100
Japan	127	Iceland	$30,900
Nigeria	126	Austria	$30,000

Sources: Data from U.S. Census Bureau, International Database, "Top 50 Countries Ranked by Population," accessed June 11, 2006, http://www.census.gov; Central Intelligence Agency, "GDP—Per Capita," *World Factbook*, accessed June 11, 2006, http://www .cia.gov.

power. As Table 4.1 shows, population size is no guarantee of economic prosperity. Of the ten most populous countries, only the United States appears on the list of those with the highest per-capita GDPs.

Though people in the developing nations have lower per-capita incomes than those in the highly developed economies of North America and Western Europe, their huge populations do represent lucrative markets. Even when the higher-income segments are only a small percentage of the entire country's population, their sheer numbers may still represent significant and growing markets.

Also, many developing countries have posted high growth rates of annual GDP. For instance, over the past few years, U.S. GDP has grown at an annual rate of about 4.4 percent. By contrast, GDP growth in less developed countries is much greater—China's GDP growth rate was 9.1 percent, and Malaysia's was 7.1 percent.[4] These markets represent opportunities for global businesses, even though their per-capita incomes lag behind those in more developed countries. Many firms are establishing operations in these and other developing countries to position themselves to benefit from local sales driven by expanding economies and rising standards of living. Wal-Mart Stores is one of those companies. The retail giant has opened dozens of new stores in developing countries from China to Brazil. It is nearly doubling the number of its stores in China, planning to have more than 90 outlets there by the end of 2006.[5]

The United States trades with many other nations. As Figure 4.1 shows, the top five are Canada, Mexico, China, Japan, and the Federal Republic of Germany. With the United Kingdom, South Korea, France, Taiwan, and Italy, they represent more than two-thirds of U.S. imports and exports every year.[6] Foreign trade is such an important part of the U.S. economy that it makes up a large portion of the business activity in many of the country's individual states as well. Texas exports more than $117 billion of goods annually, and California exports more than $109 billion. Other big exporting states include New York, Michigan, Washington, Ohio, and Illinois.[7]

assessment check

1. Why do nations trade?
2. Cite some measure of the size of the international marketplace.

Figure

4.1

Absolute and Comparative Advantage

Few countries can produce all the goods and services their people need. For centuries, trading has been the way that countries can meet the demand. If a country focuses on producing what it does best, it can export surplus domestic output and buy foreign products that it lacks or cannot efficiently produce. The potential for foreign sales of a particular item depends largely on whether the country has an absolute advantage or a comparative advantage.

A country has an *absolute advantage* in making a product for which it can maintain a monopoly or that it can produce at a lower cost than any competitor. For centuries, China enjoyed an absolute advantage in silk production. The fabric was woven from fibers recovered from silkworm cocoons, making it a prized raw material in high-quality clothing. Demand among Europeans for silk led to establishment of the famous Silk Road, a 5,000-mile link between Rome and the ancient Chinese capital city of Xian.

Absolute advantages are rare these days. But some countries manage to approximate absolute advantages in some products. Climate differences can give some nations or regions an advantage in growing certain plants. Saffron, perhaps the world's most expensive spice at around $40 per ounce, is the stigma of a flowering plant in the crocus family. It is native to the Mediterranean, Asia Minor, and India. Today, however, saffron is cultivated primarily in Spain, where the plant thrives in its soil and climate. Attempts to grow saffron in other parts of the world have generally been unsuccessful.[8]

A nation can develop a *comparative advantage* in a product if it can supply it more efficiently and at a lower price than it can supply other goods, compared with the outputs of other countries. China is profiting from its comparative advantage in producing textiles. On the other hand, ensuring that its people are well educated is another way a nation can develop a comparative advantage in skilled human resources. India, for example, has acquired a comparative advantage in software development with its highly educated workforce and low wage scale. As a result, several companies have moved part or all of their software development to India.

Canon has adopted a strategy for research and development based on various nations' comparative advantage in engineering knowledge. Rather than basing all of its research at its Tokyo headquarters, the company operates regional headquarters in Europe and the Americas, each focused on a different area of expertise. In the United States, engineers concentrate on digital and networking technology, whereas Canon engineers in France focus on telecommunications.

Top Ten Trading Partners with the United States

Source: Data from U.S. Census Bureau, "Top Ten Countries with Which the U.S. Trades," accessed June 11, 2006, http://www.census.gov/foreign-trade/top/dst/current/balance.html.

assessment check

1. Define absolute advantage.
2. How does a nation acquire a comparative advantage?

MEASURING TRADE BETWEEN NATIONS

Clearly, engaging in international trade provides tremendous competitive advantages to both the countries and individual companies involved. Any attempt to measure global business activity requires an understanding of the concepts of balance of trade and balance of payments. Another important factor is currency exchange rates for each country.

Table

4.2

balance of trade difference between a nation's exports and imports.

A nation's **balance of trade** is the difference between its exports and imports. If a country exports more than it imports, it achieves a positive balance of trade, called a *trade surplus*. If it imports more than it exports, it produces a negative balance of trade, called a *trade deficit*. The States has run a trade deficit every year since 1976. Despite being the world's top exporter, the U.S. has an even greater appetite for foreign-made goods, which creates a trade deficit.

balance of payments overall money flows into and out of a country.

A nation's balance of trade plays a central role in determining its **balance of payments**— the overall flow of money into or out of a country. Other factors also affect the balance of payments, including overseas loans and borrowing, international investments, profits from such investments, and foreign aid payments. To calculate a nation's balance of payments, subtract the monetary outflows from the monetary inflows. A positive balance of payments, or a *balance-of-payments surplus*, means more money has moved into a country than out of it. A negative balance of payments, or *balance-of-payments deficit*, means more money has gone out of the country than entered it.

Major U.S. Exports and Imports

The United States, with combined exports and imports of nearly $3 trillion, leads the world in the international trade of goods and services. As listed in Table 4.2, the leading categories of goods exchanged by U.S. exporters and importers range from machinery and vehicles to scientific and telecommunications equipment. Strong U.S. demand for imported goods is partly a reflection of the nation's prosperity and diversity.

Although the United States imports more goods than it exports, the opposite is true for services. U.S. exporters sell more than $338 billion in services annually. Much of that money comes from travel and tourism—money spent by foreign nationals visiting the United States. The increase in that figure is especially significant because the dollar has not been worth as much in terms of foreign currencies in recent years. U.S. service exports also include business and technical services such as engineering, financial services, computing, legal services, and

Top Ten U.S. Exports and Imports

Exports	Amount (in billions)	Imports	Amount (in billions)
Electrical machinery	$86	Motor vehicles	$173
Motor vehicles	$63	Petroleum, petroleum products	$130
Transport equipment	$43	Electrical machinery	$83
Office machines and data-processing equipment	$41	Office machines and data-processing equipment	$81
Miscellaneous manufactured articles	$35	Telecommunications equipment	$71
Power-generating machinery	$34	Apparel and clothing	$68
General industrial machinery	$32	Miscellaneous manufactured articles	$64
Professional scientific instruments	$31	General industrial machinery	$38
Specialized machinery	$25	Organic chemicals	$33
Telecommunications equipment	$24	Power-generating machinery	$32

Sources: Annual data from International Trade Administration, "U.S. Manufacturers Trade: Top Ten Product Exports, Imports, Balances," U.S. Department of Commerce, accessed June 11, 2006, http://www.ita.doc.gov.

entertainment, as well as royalties and licensing fees. Major service exporters include America Online, Citibank, Walt Disney, Allstate Insurance, and Federal Express, as well as retailers such as The Gap and Starbucks.

Businesses in many foreign countries want the expertise of U.S. financial and business professionals. Entertainment is another major growth area for U.S. service exports. Recently Disney, which already operates theme parks in France and Japan, opened a theme park on Hong Kong's Lantau Island. The company invested $318 million for a 43 percent share of the new Magic Kingdom and its three hotels. It also earns fees for managing the theme park and has announced plans to build one in Shanghai as well.

With annual imports far exceeding $1 trillion, the United States is by far the world's leading importer. American tastes for foreign-made goods—which show up as huge trade deficits with the consumer-goods-exporting nations of China and Japan—also extend to European products. The 25 countries of the European Union (EU) ship more than $220 billion of merchandise, including Audi cars, Saeco espresso machines, Norelco electric shavers, to U.S. buyers.[9]

Exchange Rates

A nation's **exchange rate** is the rate at which its currency can be exchanged for the currencies of other nations. It is important to learn how foreign exchange works because we live in a global community and the value of currency is an important economic thermometer for every country. Each currency's exchange rate is usually quoted in terms of another currency, such as the number of Mexican pesos needed to purchase one U.S. dollar. About 11 pesos are needed to exchange for a dollar. A Canadian dollar can be exchanged for approximately 79 cents in the United States. The euro, the currency used in many of the EU countries, has made considerable moves in exchange value during its few years in circulation—ranging from less than 90 cents when it was first issued to around $1.27 in American currency in more recent years. European consumers and businesses now use the euro to pay bills by check, credit card, or bank transfer. Euro coins and notes are also used in many EU-member countries.

exchange rate value of one nation's currency relative to the currencies of other countries.

Foreign exchange rates are influenced by a number of factors, including domestic economic and political conditions, central bank intervention, balance-of-payments position, and speculation over future currency values. Currency values fluctuate, or "float," depending on the supply and demand for each currency in the international market. In this system of *floating exchange rates*, currency traders create a market for the world's currencies based on each country's relative trade and investment prospects. In theory, this market permits exchange rates to vary freely according to supply and demand. In practice, exchange rates do not float in total freedom. National governments often intervene in currency markets to adjust their exchange rates.

Nations influence exchange rates in other ways as well. They may form currency blocs by linking their exchange rates to each other. Many governments practice protectionist policies that seek to guard their economies against trade imbalances. For instance, national governments sometimes take deliberate action to devalue their currencies as a way to increase exports and stimulate foreign investment. **Devaluation** describes a drop in a currency's value relative to other

AP PHOTO/XINHUA, PANG XINGLEI

After nearly a decade of pegging the foreign exchange rate of the yuan to the U.S. dollar, China changed its policy. It now allows its currency to float more flexibly on a mix of foreign currencies. Such a change might make Chinese imports to the United States more expensive, but it might also make U.S. exports to China cheaper.

currencies or to a fixed standard. In Brazil, a recent currency devaluation made investing in that country relatively cheap, so the devaluation was followed by a flood of foreign investment. Pillsbury bought Brazil's Brisco, which makes a local staple, *pao de queijo*, a cheese bread formed into rolls and served with morning coffee. Other foreign companies invested in Brazil's construction, tourism, banking, communications, and other industries. For an individual business, the impact of currency devaluation depends on where that business buys its materials and where it sells its products. St. Paul, Minnesota–based St. Jude Medical, which develops, manufactures, and distributes heart-monitoring and surgical devices, does about a quarter of its business in western Europe. Declines in the dollar-euro exchange rate made its products more competitively priced with those of competing medical suppliers, boosting revenues and profits. When the dollar began to climb again, the growth in value of the euro slowed.[10]

Business transactions are usually conducted in the currency of the particular region in which they take place. When business is conducted in Japan, transactions are likely to be in yen. In the United Kingdom, transactions are in pounds. With the adoption of the euro among the countries of the EU, the number of foreign currencies in that region has been reduced. (The euro is the common currency adopted by some members of the European Union, which include founding members Belgium, Denmark, France, Germany, Greece, Italy, Ireland, Luxembourg, the Netherlands, and the United Kingdom.) Other countries' currencies include the Australian dollar, the Indian rupee, the Italian lira, the Mexican peso, the Taiwanese dollar, and the South African rand.

Exchange rate changes can quickly create—or wipe out—a competitive advantage, so they are important factors in decisions about whether to invest abroad. In Europe, a declining dollar means that a price of ten euros is worth more, so companies are pressured to lower prices. At the same time, the falling dollar makes European vacations less affordable for U.S. tourists because their dollars are worth less relative to the euro.

On the Internet you can find currency converters such as those located at http://beginnersinvest.about.com/cs/currencycalc/index.htm, which can help in your dollar-for-dollar conversions. It also helps you understand how much spending power a U.S. dollar has in other countries.

Currencies that owners can easily convert into other currencies are called *hard currencies*. Examples include the euro, the U.S. dollar, and the Japanese yen. The Russian ruble and many central European currencies are considered soft currencies because they cannot be readily converted. Exporters trading with these countries often prefer to barter, accepting payment in oil, timber, or other commodities that they can resell for hard-currency payments.

The foreign currency market is the largest financial market in the world, with a daily volume in excess of 1.5 trillion U.S. dollars. This is about 50 times the size of the transaction volume of all the equity markets put together, so the foreign exchange market is the most liquid and efficient financial market in the world.

BARRIERS TO INTERNATIONAL TRADE

All businesses encounter barriers in their operations, whether they sell only to local customers or trade in international markets. Countries such as Australia, Germany, and New Zealand regulate the hours and days retailers may be open. Besides complying with a variety of laws and exchanging currencies, international companies may also have to reformulate their products to accommodate different tastes in new locations. Frito-Lay exports cheeseless Cheetos to Asia, and Domino's Pizza offers pickled-ginger pizzas at its Indian fast-food restaurants.

Figure

4.2

Barriers to International Trade

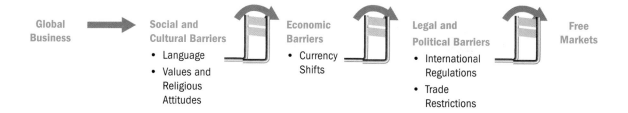

In addition to social and cultural differences, companies engaged in international business face economic barriers as well as legal and political ones. Some of the hurdles shown in Figure 4.2 are easily breached, but others require major changes in a company's business strategy. To successfully compete in global markets, companies and their managers must understand not only how these barriers affect international trade but also how to overcome them.

Social and Cultural Differences

The social and cultural differences among nations range from language and customs to educational background and religious holidays. Understanding and respecting these differences are critical in the process leading to international business success. Businesspeople with knowledge of host countries' cultures, languages, social values, and religious attitudes and practices are well equipped for the marketplace and the negotiating table. Acute sensitivity to such elements as local attitudes, forms of address, and expectations regarding dress, body language, and timeliness also helps them win customers and achieve their business objectives. See the "Business Etiquette" feature for some tips about courtesy in other cultures.

Language English is the second most widely spoken language in the world, followed by Hindustani, Spanish, Russian, and Arabic. Only Mandarin Chinese is more commonly used. It is not uncommon for students abroad for whom English is not their first language to spend eight years of elementary and high school in English language classes. Understanding a business colleague's primary language may prove to be the difference between closing an international business transaction and losing the sale to someone else. Company representatives operating in foreign markets must not only choose correct and appropriate words but also translate words correctly to convey the intended meanings. Firms may also need to rename products or rewrite slogans for foreign markets. See the "Hit & Miss" feature for examples of some spectacular failures in this area.

Potential communication barriers include more than mistranslation. Companies may present messages through inappropriate media, overlook local customs and regulations, or ignore differences in taste. Cultural sensitivity is especially critical in cyberspace. Web site developers must be aware that visitors to a site may come from anywhere in the world. Some icons that seem friendly to U.S. Internet users may shock people from other countries. A person making a high-five hand gesture would be insulting people in Greece; the same is true of making a circle with the thumb and index finger in Brazil and a two-fingered peace sign with the back of the hand facing out in Great Britain. Even colors can pose problems. In the Middle East, people view green as a sacred color, so a green background on a Web page would be inappropriate there.

Gift-giving traditions employ the language of symbolism. For example, in Latin America, knives and scissors should not be given as gifts because they represent the severing of friendship.

> ## "They Said It"
>
> "If you speak three languages, you are trilingual. If you speak two languages, you are bilingual. If you speak one language, you're American."
>
> —*Anonymous*

(b)usiness (e)tiquette

Global Etiquette: Learning about Differences

Committing a social blunder in class or at home is one thing, but committing one in a foreign country may mean the end of your business relationship with your host. Each culture has its own set of rules and customs, and before you head out to dinner with your foreign business associates or venture into their country for a meeting, you'll need to learn all you can about global etiquette and what is and is not appropriate abroad.

For instance, in Iraq you shake hands gently, always with the right hand, and do not use your left hand to eat, gesture, or touch others. If a woman is present, allow her to greet you first. She will shake hands with only her fingertips.

Here are some additional little-known facts about other countries and their customs:

1. In Chile, business gifts should be of good quality but not lavish, and women should not give gifts to men because the gesture can be misunderstood.
2. When in South Africa, dress well in public because your host will expect it.
3. In Iraq, if you must point at something, use your entire hand, not just one finger, which is considered a sign of contempt.
4. The Chinese do not speak with their hands, so do not use large gestures and remember that men should not touch women in public.
5. In Egypt members of the same sex stand much closer to each other than North Americans and Europeans do, but men and women stand farther apart.
6. Avoid casual dress when doing business in Japan and dress to impress, but remember that shoes will be taken off frequently so they should be easy to remove.
7. It is impolite to show the soles of your shoes in Russia.
8. In Germany sudden changes in business transactions are unwelcome even if they are positive, and humor in business settings is not encouraged.

Most important, learn the basic vocabulary and historical background of the country and region, as well as the proper use of greetings and introductions. Pay attention to your physical gestures, facial expressions, dress, and dining and drinking habits. Mastering the details can save you embarrassment and perhaps make or break your career.

Sources: International Business Center Web site, accessed June 11, 2006, http://www.cyborlink.com; Peter Edidin, "How to Shake Hands or Share a Meal with an Iraqi," *The New York Times*, March 6, 2005, p. WK 7; "City Tips," *Worth*, March 2005.

Flowers are generally acceptable, but Mexicans use yellow flowers in their Day of the Dead festivities, so they are associated with death.

Values and Religious Attitudes Even though today's world is shrinking in many ways, people in different countries do not necessarily share the same values or religious attitudes. Marked differences remain in workers' attitudes from country to country, for instance.

U.S. society places a higher value on business efficiency and low unemployment than European society, where employee benefits are more valued. The U.S. government does not regulate vacation time, and employees typically receive no paid vacation during their first year of employment, then two weeks' vacation, and eventually up to three or four weeks if they stay with the same employer for many years. In contrast, the EU mandates a minimum paid vacation of four weeks per year, and most Europeans get five or six weeks. In these countries, a U.S. company that opens a manufacturing plant would not be able to hire any local employees without offering vacations in line with a nation's business practices.

U.S. culture values national unity, with tolerance of regional differences. The United States is viewed as a national market with a single economy. European countries that are part of the 25-member EU are trying to create a similar marketplace. However, many resist the idea of being European citizens first and British, Danish, or Dutch citizens second. British consumers differ from Italians in important ways, and U.S. companies that fail to recognize this variation will run into problems with brand acceptance.

Religion plays an important role in every society, so businesspeople also must cultivate sensitivity to the dominant religions in countries where they operate. Understanding religious cycles and the timing of major holidays can help prevent embarrassing moments when scheduling meetings, trade shows, conferences, or events such as the opening of a new manufacturing plant. People doing business in Saudi Arabia must take into account Islam's monthlong observance of Ramadan, when work ends at noon. Friday is the Muslim Sabbath, so the Saudi workweek runs from Saturday through

HIT & MISS

Lost in Translation

The fact that product names and marketing slogans don't always translate well from one country or culture to another is widely known. But mistakes still happen. Although Chevrolet denies the popular myth about its Nova flopping in Latin America because *no va* means "won't go" in Spanish, most marketers would agree with British business writer Simon Anholt, who says, "Language is in many respects such a silly little thing, but it has the power to bring marketing directors to their knees. That's where the terror lies."

Here are some recent translation errors made—or avoided—by international automakers.

- Toyota's MR2 is known as the MR in France, because in French "MR-deux" sounds too much like merde, another name for manure.
- Mercedes-Benz shortened "Grand Sports Tourer" to GST, but the initials remind Canadians of an unpopular tax on goods and services dubbed the "gouge and screw tax."
- Ford had to change the name of its Pinto in Brazil, where it connotes part of the male anatomy in Portuguese. The car now goes by the name Corcel.
- Although there was no translation problem, Toyota's Canadian division had international naming troubles of its own. The firm announced plans to introduce its new model, the Celica Tsunami. It quickly backpedaled after the disastrous waves hit Southeast Asia, renaming the car the Celica Sport Package.

Car makers are not alone in their naming troubles. Ikea customers are still wondering who chose the names of the Fartfull workbench. The Mexican firm Corona had to rechristen its beer in Spain, because a winemaker there already bore the same name. Corona was fortunate to adopt Coronita, which is easy to associate with its company name. And Sweden's toffee-and-licorice ice cream product known as Nogger Black has come under fire. "We certainly had no intention that the name 'Nogger' would be associated with any negative word," says its maker, GB Glace.

Questions for Critical Thinking

1. Consultants advise against relying solely on non-native translators to help marketing campaigns cross international lines because they lack detailed knowledge of the language and culture. "You can be saved by the right secretary in another country reading [your communications]," says one. Do you agree? Why or why not?
2. One marketing executive says that even perfect literal translations will not ring true to those in other countries. What does he mean, and why is that a potential problem?

Sources: Timothy Noah, "MooLatte, Bested," *Slate,* accessed June 11, 2006, http://slate.msn.com; "What's in a Name? For Cars, Everything," *Detroit News,* accessed June 11, 2006, http://www.detroitnews.com; Sergio Beristain, "Does Your Brand Register Abroad?" Brandchannel.com, accessed June 11, 2006, http://www.brandchannel.com; Ed Garsten and Brett Clanton, "A Tsunami by Any Other Name," *Time,* January 24, 2005, p. 17; Mark Lasswell, "Lost in Translation," *Business 2.0,* August 2004, pp. 68–70.

Thursday. Furthermore, Muslims abstain from alcohol and consider pork unclean, so gifts of pigskin or liquor would be offensive.

Some devout Muslims have raised concern about interest-bearing loans in their nations, such as car loans or home mortgages, which they fear are to be considered usury by the standards of the Qur'an. However, because Muslims have traditionally been traders, and because the Qur'an supports trade, such reservations are slowly being overcome with the help of arguments by Muslim scholars showing that usury implies that the lender is taking unjust advantage of the borrower. Ordinary loans, on the other hand, can help increase the value of the borrowers' assets or property, and they can also help achieve the goal of helping distribute wealth more widely.[11]

Economic Differences

Business opportunities are flourishing in densely populated countries such as China and India, as local consumers eagerly buy Western products. Although such prospects might tempt American

Technology changes. Communication lasts.

Partnership and MORE

In today's fast changing world we all need partners to reach our full potential.

That's why at Huawei we work hand in hand with our customers to develop high quality technology solutions, delivered swiftly and at low cost to satisfy real consumer needs.

As a result of this emphasis on customer-driven R&D and marketing, we have helped build and

develop the industry in China into one of the most advanced telecom networks in the world and we are now helping operators in over 70 countries enjoy greater service and enhanced profits.

Technology is changing faster and faster every day, but at Huawei our pursuit of better communications and better results through partnership and understanding never ceases.

Today, Huawei's products are enjoyed in over 70 countries across the world, including the UK, Germany, France, Spain, Portugal, Russia, Brazil, Singapore, Thailand, Egypt, UAE and South Africa.

Partner for a network world

http://www.huawei.com   (086) 755-28760808

Huawei Technologies

USED WITH PERMISSION. HUAWEI TECHNOLOGIES CO., LTD.

Lack of infrastructure is a concern for global telecommunications. Chinese firm Huawei Technologies helped develop the industry in China, and it now provides network, data communications, and telecommunications products throughout the world through 8 regional headquarters and 55 branch offices outside China.

firms, managers must first consider the economic factors involved in doing business in these markets. A country's size, per-capita income, and stage of economic development are among the economic factors to consider when evaluating it as a candidate for an international business venture.

Infrastructure   Along with other economic measures, businesses should consider a country's **infrastructure.** Infrastructure refers to basic systems of communication (telecommunications, television, radio, and print media), transportation (roads and highways, railroads, and airports), and energy facilities (power plants and gas and electric utilities). The Internet and technology use can also be considered part of infrastructure.

Many consumers in the United States, western Europe, Japan, and Hong Kong own cell phones. Even most of their children have their own phones. So the availability of telecommunications technology creates fertile soil for Internet businesses that use wireless communication. There are about 1.5 billion mobile phone users worldwide, for instance. In rural Kenya, some of the country's 3 million mobile phone users share a phone with several other people, but they enjoy inexpensive text messaging for about a third the cost of sending an e-mail over the country's often unreliable Internet service. A Kenyan firm called OneWorld International has sprung up that puts employers and job seekers in almost instant touch with each other through subscriptions to text messages carried by mobile phone. "The service has an advantage," says a human resource employee for Softa Bottling Company. "It reaches as many people as possible within the shortest time." In fact, about 5,000 people have already signed up for the job search service, which also distributes public health information about AIDS and cancer.[12]

Financial systems also provide a type of infrastructure for businesses. In the United States, buyers have widespread access to checks, credit cards, and debit cards, as well as electronic systems for processing these forms of payment. In many African countries, such as Ethiopia, local businesses do not accept credit cards, so travelers to the capital city, Addis Ababa, are warned to bring plenty of cash and traveler's checks.

Currency Conversion and Shifts   Despite growing similarities in infrastructure, businesses crossing national borders encounter basic economic differences: national currencies. Foreign currency fluctuations may present added problems for global businesses. As explained earlier in the chapter, the values of the world's major currencies fluctuate in relation to each other. Rapid and unexpected currency shifts can make pricing in local currencies difficult. Shifts in exchange rates can also influence the attractiveness of various business decisions. A devalued currency may make a nation less desirable as an export destination because of reduced demand in that market. However, devaluation can make the nation desirable as an investment opportunity because investments there will be a bargain in terms of the investor's currency.

Political and Legal Differences

Like social, cultural, and economic differences, legal and political differences in host countries can pose barriers to international trade. Advocates for children in Britain have long fought to ban television advertising aimed at kids. With concerns for childhood obesity on the rise and blame being laid at the door of fast-food advertising, Turner Broadcasting plans a new cartoon series for British TV that will promote fruit and vegetables to young audiences. The program is offered free to other broadcasters. "We wanted to counter the possible negative effects of advertising on kids' TV," says general manager Richard Kilgariff, "but [the program] quickly developed into a positive project to provide parents and broadcasters with a tool to fight obesity."[13]

To compete in today's world marketplace, managers involved in international business must be well versed in legislation that affects their industries. Some countries impose general trade restrictions. Others have established detailed rules that regulate how foreign companies can operate. The one consistency among all countries is the striking lack of consistent laws and regulations governing the conduct of business.

Political Climate An important factor in any international business investment is the stability of the political climate. The political structures of many nations promote stability similar to that in the United States. Other nations, such as Indonesia, Congo, and Bosnia, feature quite different—and frequently changing—structures. Host nations often pass laws designed to protect their own interests, sometimes at the expense of foreign businesses.

In recent years, the political structures of Russia, Turkey, the former Yugoslavia, Hong Kong, and several central European countries including the Czech Republic and Poland have seen dramatic changes. Such political changes almost always bring changes in the legal environment. Hong Kong's status as part of China makes it an economy where political developments produced changes in the legal and cultural environments. Since the collapse of the Soviet Union, Russia has struggled to develop a new market structure and political processes.

Legal Environment When conducting business internationally, managers must be familiar with three dimensions of the legal environment: U.S. law, international regulations, and the laws of the countries where they plan to trade. Some laws protect the rights of foreign companies to compete in the United States. Others dictate actions allowed for U.S. companies doing business in foreign countries.

The *Foreign Corrupt Practices Act* forbids U.S. companies from bribing foreign officials, political candidates, or government representatives. This act prescribes fines and jail time for U.S. managers who are aware of illegal payoffs. Until recently, many countries, including France and Germany, not only accepted the practice of bribing foreign officials in countries where such practices were customary but allowed tax deductions for these expenses. The United States, France, Germany, and 33 other countries recently signed the Organization for Economic Cooperation and Development Anti-Bribery Convention. This agreement makes offering or paying bribes a criminal offense and ends the deductibility of bribes.[14]

Still, corruption continues to be an international problem. Its pervasiveness, combined with U.S. prohibitions, creates a difficult obstacle for Americans who want to do business in many foreign countries. Chinese pay *huilu*, and Russians rely on *vzyatka*. In the Middle East, palms are greased with *baksheesh*. Figure 4.3 compares 102 countries based on surveys of perceived corruption. This Corruption Perceptions Index is computed by Transparency International, a Berlin-based international organization that rates the degree of corruption observed by businesspeople and the general public.

The growth of online business has introduced new elements to the legal climate of international business. Patents, brand names, trademarks, copyrights, and other intellectual property are difficult to police, given the availability of information on the Internet. However, some countries are adopting laws to protect information obtained by electronic contacts. Malaysia imposes stiff fines and long jail terms on those convicted of illegally accessing computers and using information that passes through them.

International Regulations To regulate international commerce, the United States and many other countries have ratified treaties and signed agreements that dictate the conduct of international business and protect some of its activities. The United States has entered into

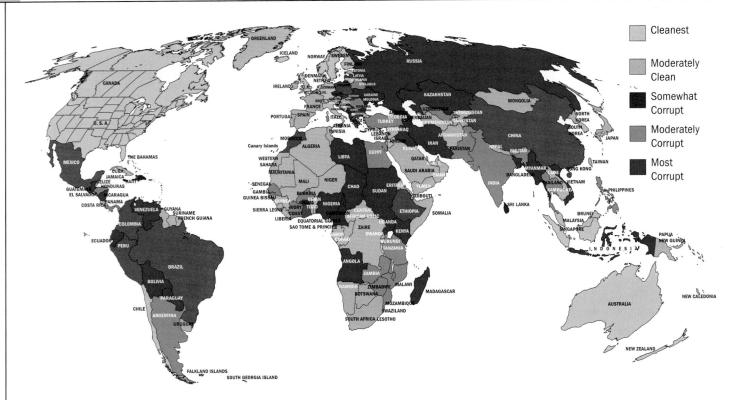

	Cleanest
	Moderately Clean
	Somewhat Corrupt
	Moderately Corrupt
	Most Corrupt

Source: Data from Transparency International, "Transparency International Annual Corruption Perceptions Index," Internet Center for Corruption Research, http://en.wikipedia.org/wiki/Corruption_Perceptions_Index.

many *friendship, commerce, and navigation treaties* with other nations. Such treaties address many aspects of international business relations, including the right to conduct business in the treaty partner's domestic market. Other international business agreements involve product standards, patents, trademarks, reciprocal tax policies, export controls, international air travel, and international communications.

When Congress granted China full trade relations with the United States, China agreed to lower trade barriers, including subsidies that held down the prices of food exports, restrictions on where foreign law firms can open offices, and taxes charged on imported goods. In exchange for China's promise to halve these taxes, called *tariffs*, the United States granted Chinese businesses equal access to U.S. markets enjoyed by most other countries.

Many types of regulations affect the actions of managers doing business in international markets. Not only must worldwide producers and marketers maintain required minimum quality levels for all the countries in which they operate, but they must comply with numerous specific local regulations. Britain prevents advertisers from encouraging children to engage in such unhealthy behavior as overeating or replacing regular meals with candy and snack foods. Malaysia's Censorship Board prohibits nudity and profanity on TV. Germany and France allow publishers to set prices that retailers charge for their books. Because companies such as Amazon.com adhere to the fixed prices, German customers looking for English-language books can get better prices by buying at the U.K. Web site, even with the extra shipping costs.

A lack of international regulations or difficulty in enforcement can generate its own set of problems. Software piracy offers an example, particularly in Asia. More than 90 percent of all software used in Vietnam, for instance, is pirated, making it the biggest offender against intellectual property rights laws and regulations enforced by the World Trade Organization (WTO) worldwide. Close behind Vietnam were Ukraine, China, Zimbabwe, and Indonesia. Translated into dollars, that level of piracy means a loss of about a third of the software industry's annual revenue of $90 billion, according to a regional director for the Business Software Alliance, a worldwide watchdog agency. Contrary to claims that buying software legally is too expensive, the director said, "If you can afford the hardware, you can afford the software." But piracy remains widespread, despite WTO sanctions against offending nations. And with the number of Internet users expected to rise in China alone by about 100 million people over the next few years, enforcement efforts are likely to increase.[15]

Types of Trade Restrictions

Trade restrictions such as taxes on imports and complicated administrative procedures create additional barriers to international business. They may limit consumer choices while increasing the costs of foreign-made products. Trade restrictions are also imposed to protect citizens' security, health, and jobs. A government may limit exports of strategic and defense-related goods to unfriendly countries to protect its security, ban imports of insecticide-contaminated farm products to protect health, and restrict imports to protect domestic jobs in the importing country.

Other restrictions are imposed to promote trade with certain countries. Still others protect countries from unfair competition. Regardless of the political reasons for trade restrictions, most take the form of tariffs. In addition to tariffs, governments impose a number of nontariff—or administrative—barriers. These include quotas, embargoes, and exchange controls.

Tariffs Taxes, surcharges, or duties on foreign products are referred to as **tariffs**. Governments assess two types of tariffs—revenue and protective tariffs—both of which make imports more expensive for domestic buyers. Revenue tariffs generate income for the government. Upon returning home, U.S. leisure travelers who are out of the country more than 48 hours and who bring back goods purchased abroad must pay import taxes on their value in excess of $200 to $1,600, depending on the country of origin. This duty goes directly to the U.S. Treasury. The sole purpose of a protective tariff is to raise the retail price of imported products to match or exceed the prices of similar products manufactured in the home country. In other words, protective tariffs seek to level the playing field for local competitors.

> **tariff** tax imposed on imported goods.

Of course, tariffs create a disadvantage to companies that want to export to the countries imposing the tariffs. In addition, governments do not always agree on the reasons behind protective tariffs. So they do not always have the desired effect. The U.S. imposes a tariff on foreign competitors accused of selling products at lower prices in the United States than U.S. manufacturers charge. The government recently passed a bill giving the money from these tariffs directly to U.S. plaintiff companies, instead of to the Treasury as in the past. In retaliation, U.S. exports of paper, textiles, machinery, farm products, oysters, and other products to Canada, Brazil, Chile, India, South Korea, and Mexico will be subject to punitive tariffs of 15 percent, which may end up costing U.S. exporters as much as $150 million a year, a number some observers say will only grow.[16]

Nontariff Barriers Nontariff, or administrative, trade barriers restrict imports in more subtle ways than tariffs. These measures may take such forms as quotas on imports, restrictive standards for imports, and export subsidies. Because many countries have recently substantially reduced tariffs or eliminated them entirely, they increasingly use nontariff barriers to control flows of imported products.

Quotas limit the amounts of particular products that countries can import during specified time periods. Limits may be set as quantities, such as number of cars or bushels of wheat, or as values, such as dollars' worth of cigarettes. Governments regularly set quotas for agricultural products and sometimes for imported automobiles. Although the U.S. government had previously imposed about 1,000 quotas related to clothing imports from various countries, many of them have now been lifted. Recently, however, quotas on three categories of clothing from China were reinstated, following claims by U.S. manufacturers that the lifting of quotas had created a huge flow of inexpensive cotton garments that might endanger thousands of jobs.[17]

Quotas help prevent **dumping,** a practice that developed during the 1970s. In one form of dumping, a company sells products abroad at prices below its cost of production. In another, a company exports a large quantity of a product at a lower price than the same product in the home market and drives down the price of the domestic product. Dumping benefits domestic consumers in the importing market, but it hurts domestic producers. It also allows companies to gain quick entry to foreign markets.

More severe than a quota, an **embargo** imposes a total ban on importing a specified product or even a total halt to trading with a particular country. Embargo durations can vary to accommodate changes in foreign policy. The U.S. government recently rejected a United Nations resolution opposing the United Sates' long-standing trade embargo on Cuba.

Another form of administrative trade restriction is **exchange controls.** Imposed through a central bank or government agency, exchange controls affect both exporters and importers. Firms that gain foreign currencies through exporting are required to sell them to the central bank or another agency. Importers must buy foreign currencies to pay for their purchases from the same agency. The exchange control authority can then allocate, expand, or restrict foreign exchange in accordance with national policy.

assessment check

1. How might values and attitudes form a barrier to trade, and how can they be overcome?
2. What is a tariff? What is its purpose?
3. Why is dumping a problem for companies marketing goods internationally?

REDUCING BARRIERS TO INTERNATIONAL TRADE

Although tariffs and administrative barriers still restrict trade, overall the world is moving toward free trade. Several types of organizations ease barriers to international trade, including groups that monitor trade policies and practices and institutions that offer monetary assistance. Another type of federation designed to ease trade barriers is the multinational economic community, such as the European Union. This section looks at the roles these organizations play.

Organizations Promoting International Trade

For the 60 years of its existence, the **General Agreement on Tariffs and Trade (GATT),** an international trade accord, sponsored a series of negotiations, called rounds, that substantially reduced worldwide tariffs and other barriers. Major industrialized nations founded the multinational organization in 1947 to work toward reducing tariffs and relaxing import quotas. The last set of negotiations—the Uruguay Round—cut average tariffs by one-third, in excess of $700 billion; reduced farm subsidies; and improved protection for copyright and patent holders. In addition, international trading rules now apply to various service industries. Finally, the new agreement established the **World Trade Organization (WTO)** to succeed GATT. This organization includes representatives from 149 countries.

World Trade Organization Since 1995, the WTO has monitored GATT agreements among the member nations, mediated disputes, and continued the effort to reduce trade barriers through-

World Trade Organization (WTO) 149-member international institution that monitors GATT agreements and mediates international trade disputes.

out the world. Unlike provisions in GATT, the WTO's decisions are binding on parties involved in disputes.

The WTO has grown more controversial in recent years as it issues decisions that have implications for working conditions and the environment in member nations. Concerns have been expressed that the WTO's focus on lowering trade barriers encourages businesses to keep costs down through practices that may increase pollution and human rights abuses. Particularly worrisome is the fact that the organization's member countries must agree on policies, and developing countries tend not to be eager to lose their low-cost advantage by enacting stricter labor and environmental laws. Other critics claim that if well-funded U.S. firms such as fast-food chains, entertainment companies, and Internet retailers can freely enter foreign markets, they will wipe out smaller foreign businesses serving the distinct tastes and practices of other countries' cultures.

Trade unions in developed nations complain that the WTO's support of free trade makes it easier to export manufacturing jobs to low-wage countries. According to the U.S. Department of Commerce, about a million U.S. jobs are lost each year as a result of imports or movement of work to other countries, and the pace of the migration has increased in the last few years. They are not always minimum-wage jobs either. But many small and midsized firms have benefited from the WTO's reduction of trade barriers and lowering of the cost of trade. They currently make up 97 percent of all firms that export goods and services, according to the Department of Commerce. "Trade is now seamless and global," says Randy Tofteland, CEO of SoftBrands, a Minneapolis firm with 500 employees that sells software for the hospitality industry. "Those that take advantage of it are going to be the long-term winners."[18]

The most recent round of WTO talks was called the *Doha Round* after the city in Qatar where it began. After several years of heated disputes and collapsed negotiations, the eight leading industrial nations committed themselves to successful conclusion of the talks. Under discussion were ways to improve global agricultural trade and trade among developing countries. The leaders worked to reduce domestic price supports, eliminate export subsidies, and improve market access for goods. Such changes should help farmers in developing countries compete in the global market.[19]

Although free trade can indeed contribute to economic growth and change, including the creation of new jobs, concerns about WTO policy have led to protest demonstrations—sometimes violent—beginning with the WTO meeting in Seattle a few years ago.

World Bank   Shortly after the end of World War II, industrialized nations formed an organization to lend money to less developed and developing countries. The **World Bank** primarily funds projects that build or expand nations' infrastructure such as transportation, education, and medical systems and facilities. The World Bank and other development banks provide the largest source of advice and assistance to developing nations. Often, in exchange for granting loans, the World Bank imposes requirements intended to build the economies of borrower nations.

The World Bank has been criticized for making loans with conditions that ultimately hurt the borrower nations. When developing nations are required to balance government budgets, they are sometimes forced to cut vital social programs. Critics also say that the World Bank should consider the impact of its loans on the environment and the treatment of workers.

International Monetary Fund   Established a year after the World Bank, the **International Monetary Fund (IMF)** was created to promote trade through financial cooperation and, in the process, eliminate barriers. The IMF makes short-term loans to member nations that are unable to meet their expenses. It operates as a lender of last resort for troubled nations. In exchange for these emergency loans, IMF lenders frequently require significant commitments from the borrowing nations to address the problems that led to the crises. These steps may include curtailing imports or even devaluing currencies. Throughout its existence, the IMF has worked to prevent financial crises by warning the international business community when countries encounter problems meeting their financial obligations. Often, the IMF lends to countries to keep them from defaulting on prior debts and to prevent economic crises in particular countries from spreading to other nations.

However, some countries owe far more money than they can ever hope to repay, and the debt payments make it impossible for their governments to deliver desperately needed services to their citizens. The nations of sub-Saharan Africa are hard-pressed to deal with the ravages of AIDS, yet their debt exceeds their GDP and is three times as high as their total annual exports. The so-called Group of Eight economic powers—the United States, Britain, France, Germany, Japan, Italy, Canada, and Russia—recently agreed to offer full debt relief to African countries that are working toward government reforms on behalf of education and welfare.[20]

International Economic Communities

International economic communities reduce trade barriers and promote regional economic integration. In the simplest approach, countries may establish a *free-trade area* in which they trade freely among themselves without tariffs or trade restrictions. Each maintains its own tariffs for trade outside this area. A *customs union* sets up a free-trade area and specifies a uniform tariff structure for members' trade with nonmember nations. In a *common market*, or economic union, members go beyond a customs union and try to bring all of their trade rules into agreement.

One example of a free-trade area is the **North American Free Trade Agreement (NAFTA)** enacted by the United States, Canada, and Mexico. Other examples of regional trading blocs include the MERCOSUR customs union (joining Brazil, Argentina, Paraguay, Uruguay, Chile, and Bolivia) and the ten-country Association of South East Asian Nations (ASEAN).

NAFTA

NAFTA became effective in 1994, creating the world's largest free-trade zone with the United States, Canada, and Mexico. With a combined population of more than 435 million and a total GDP of nearly $14 trillion, North America represents one of the world's most attractive markets. The United States—the single largest market and one of the world's most stable economies—dominates North America's business environment. Although fewer than 1 person in 20 lives in the United States, the nation's more than $11 trillion GDP represents about one-fifth of total world output.[21]

Canada is far less densely populated but has achieved a similar level of economic development. In fact, Canada's economy is booming and has been growing at a faster rate than the U.S. economy in recent years. More than two-thirds of Canada's GDP is generated in the services sector, and three of every four Canadian workers are engaged in service occupations. The country's per-capita GDP places Canada in the top ten nations in terms of its people's spending power. Canada's economy is fueled by trade with the United States, and its home markets are strong as well. The United States and Canada are each other's biggest trading partners. About 85 percent of Canada's exports and about 60 percent of its imports are to or from the United States.[22] U.S. business is also attracted by Canada's human resources. For instance, all major U.S. automakers have large production facilities in Canada.

North American Free Trade Agreement (NAFTA) agreement among the United States, Canada, and Mexico to break down tariffs and trade restrictions.

ONTARIO
CANADA

If you're looking to expand, put yourself in good company.

More than 1,500 leading multinationals have chosen to locate or expand in Ontario. Why the continuing flow?

If you're looking to expand, make your next move Ontario.

www.2ontario.com
1 800 819-8701

- One of the best educated workforces in the western world.
- A top-rated transportation and telecommunications infrastructure.
- Thanks to North American free trade, ready access to a market of 420 million people.
- A quality of life ranked among the best anywhere.
- The most competitive business costs among the G7 nations.

This message from Ontario, Canada, promotes the province's favorable business climate. The ad states that more than 1,500 multinational companies are located there and highlights the province's low basic business costs and educated workforce.

COURTESY OF ONTARIO MINISTRY OF ECONOMIC DEVELOPMENT AND TRADE.

Mexico is moving from developing nation to industrial nation status, thanks largely to NAFTA. Mexico's trade with the United States and Canada has tripled since the signing of NAFTA, although 40 percent of the country's 106 million people still live below the poverty line and per-capita income is a quarter that of the United States.[23] But Mexico's border with the United States is busy with a nearly endless stream of traffic transporting goods from Mexican factories into the United States. Along its so-called NAFTA Highway between Nuevo Laredo, Mexico, and Laredo, Texas, $52 billion worth of appliances, auto parts, computers, and other goods made the trip in a recent year—amounting to 38 percent of all Mexican exports to the United States.[24]

By eliminating all trade barriers and investment restrictions among the United States, Canada, and Mexico over a fifteen-year period, NAFTA opens more doors for free trade. The agreement also eases regulations governing services, such as banking, and establishes uniform legal requirements for protection of intellectual property. The three nations can now trade with one another without tariffs or other trade barriers, simplifying shipments of goods across the partners' borders. Standardized customs and uniform labeling regulations create economic efficiencies and smooth import and export procedures. Trade among the partners has increased steadily, more than doubling since NAFTA took effect.

CAFTA

Passed by Congress and signed by President Bush in 2005, the **Central American Free Trade Agreement (CAFTA)** created a free-trade area among the United States, Costa Rica, the Dominican Republic, El Salvador, Guatemala, Honduras, and Nicaragua. The agreement ends most tariffs on nearly $33 billion in products traded between the United States and its Latin American neighbors. Agricultural producers such as corn, soybean, and dairy farmers stand to gain under the relaxed trade rules. U.S. sugar producers, which were supported by subsidies keeping their prices higher than the rest of the world's, fought against CAFTA's passage. And labor unions complained that the agreement would lower labor standards and export millions more jobs to lower-wage countries. But overall, CAFTA's effects should be positive, increasing both exports and imports substantially, much as NAFTA did.[25]

Central American Free Trade Agreement (CAFTA) agreement among the United States, Costa Rica, the Dominican Republic, El Salvador, Guatemala, Honduras, and Nicaragua to reduce tariffs and trade restrictions.

European Union (EU) 25-nation European economic alliance.

European Union

Perhaps the best-known example of a common market is the **European Union (EU)**. The EU combines 25 countries, more than 450 million people, and a total GDP exceeding $12 trillion to form a huge common market.[26] As Figure 4.4 shows, ten countries—Cyprus, Malta, Estonia, Latvia, Lithuania, Hungary, Poland, the Czech Republic, Slovakia, and Slovenia—are the latest EU members. Some observers think the EU's efforts to unite Europe suffered a setback after two countries, France and the Netherlands, voted against the proposed constitution intended to make the organization run more smoothly after its recent enlargement from 15 to 25 states. All 25 must ratify the constitution before it can take effect.[27]

The 25 Nations of the European Union

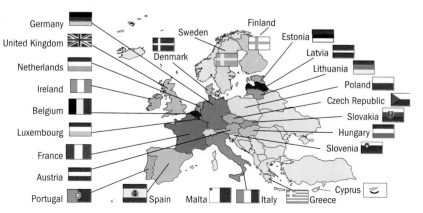

Twelve of the European Union member states use the euro (€) and so quote prices in that currency (left). Denmark, Sweden, and Great Britain (£) still use their traditional currency, the pound note.

The EU's goals include promoting economic and social progress, introducing European citizenship as a complement to national citizenship, and giving the EU a significant role in international affairs. To achieve its goal of a borderless Europe, the EU is removing barriers to free trade among its members. This highly complex process involves standardizing business regulations and requirements, standardizing import duties and taxes, and eliminating customs checks so that companies can transport goods from England to Italy or Poland as easily as from New York to Boston.

Unifying standards and laws can contribute to economic growth. But just as NAFTA sparked fears in the United States about free trade with Mexico, some people in western Europe worried that opening trade with such countries as Poland, Hungary, and the Czech Republic would cause jobs to flow eastward to lower-wage economies.

The EU also introduced the euro to replace currencies such as the French franc and Italian lira. For the twelve member states that have already adopted the euro, potential benefits include eliminating the economic costs of currency exchange and simplifying price comparisons. Businesses and their customers now make check and credit card transactions in euros and use euro notes and coins in making cash purchases.

assessment check

1. What international trade organization succeeded GATT and what is its goal?
2. Compare and contrast the goals of the World Bank and the International Monetary Fund.
3. Identify the members of NAFTA and briefly explain how it works.
4. What are the goals of the European Union and how do they promote international trade?

GOING GLOBAL

While expanding into overseas markets can increase profits and marketing opportunities, it also introduces new complexities to a firm's business operations. Before deciding to go global, a company faces a number of key decisions, beginning with the following:

- Determining which foreign market(s) to enter
- Analyzing the expenditures required to enter a new market
- Deciding the best way to organize the overseas operations

These issues vary in importance depending on the level of involvement a company chooses. Education and employee training in the host country would be much more important for an electronics manufacturer building an Asian factory than for a firm that is simply planning to export American-made products.

The choice of which markets to enter usually follows extensive research focusing on local demand for the firm's products, availability of needed resources, and ability of the local workforce to produce world-class quality. Other factors include existing and potential competition, tariff rates, currency stability, and investment barriers. A variety of government and other sources are available to facilitate this research process. A good starting place is the CIA's *World Factbook*, which contains country-by-country information on geography, population, government, economy, and infrastructure.

U.S. Department of Commerce counselors at the agency's district offices offer a full range of international business advice, including computerized market data and names of business and government contacts in dozens of countries. As Table 4.3 shows, the Internet provides access to many resources for international trade information.

Levels of Involvement

After a firm has completed its research and decided to do business overseas, it can choose one or more strategies:

- Exporting or importing
- Entering into contractual agreements such as franchising, licensing, and subcontracting deals
- Direct investment in the foreign market through acquisitions, joint ventures, or establishment of an overseas division

Although the company's risk increases with the level of its involvement, so does its overall control of all aspects of producing and selling its goods or services.

Companies frequently combine more than one of these strategies. Web portal Yahoo! used joint ventures with local firms to gain a quick presence in Japan, Britain, France, Germany, and South Korea. Only after developing experience as an international company has Yahoo! begun to engage in direct investment by creating foreign subsidiaries. Waiting to develop expertise before moving overseas is risky for online businesses, though, because Web sites are so easy for competitors to copy. Alando, an auction Web site based in Germany, looked remarkably like eBay. Rather than fight the company, eBay entered Germany by acquiring Alando.

Table 4.3

International Trade Research Resources on the Internet

Web Site and Address	General Description
Asia, Inc. http://www.asia-inc.com	Business news in Asia, featuring articles on Asian countries from India to Japan
Europages http://www.europages.com	Directory of and links to Europe's top 500,000 companies in 33 European countries
World Trade Organization http://www.wto.int	Details on the trade policies of various governments
CIA World Factbook http://www.cia.gov/cia/publications/factbook	Basic facts about the world's nations, from geography to economic conditions
STAT-USA http://www.stat-usa.gov	Extensive trade and economic data, information about trends, daily intelligence reports, and background data (access requires paid subscription to the service)
U.S. Commercial Service http://www.export.gov/comm_svc	Information about Commerce Department counseling services, trade events, and U.S. export regulations
U.S. Business Advisor http://www.business.gov	One-stop access to a range of federal government information, services, and transactions
U.S. State Department http://www.travel.state.gov/travel/cis_pa_tw/tw/tw_1764.html	Listing of the State Department's latest travel warnings about conditions that may affect safety abroad, supplemented by the list of consulate addresses and country information

Importers and Exporters   When a firm brings in goods produced abroad to sell domestically, it is an importer. Conversely, companies are exporters when they produce—or purchase—goods at home and sell them in overseas markets. An importing or exporting strategy provides the most basic level of international involvement, with the least risk and control.

Roots, a Canadian clothing manufacturer, has used its success as the chosen outfitter of the U.S. and Canadian Olympic teams to expand its apparel and sportswear brands into the United States and Asia. The company already has 140 stores in Canada and about 70 in Korea, 12 in Taiwan, and 5 in the United States. Roots earns about $200 million in annual sales and now sells eyewear, watches, and fragrance as well.[28]

Exports are frequently handled by special intermediaries called export trading companies. These firms search out competitively priced local merchandise and then resell it abroad at prices high enough to cover expenses and earn profits. When a retail chain such as Dallas-based Pier One Imports wants to purchase West African products for its store shelves, it may contact an export trading company operating in a country such as Ghana. The local firm is responsible for monitoring quality, packaging the order for transatlantic shipment, arranging transportation, and arranging for completion of customs paperwork and other steps required to move the product from Ghana to the United States.

Firms engage in exporting of two types: indirect and direct. A company engages in *indirect exporting* when it manufactures a product, such as an electronic component, that becomes part of another product that is sold in foreign markets. The second method, *direct exporting*, occurs when a company seeks to sell its products in markets outside its own country, as Red Bull does with its energy drink, which is discussed in the "Hit & Miss" feature. Often the first step for companies entering foreign markets, direct exporting is the most common form of international business. Firms that succeed in exporting their products may then move on to other entry strategies.

In addition to reaching foreign markets by dealing with export trading companies, exporters may choose two other alternatives: export management companies and offset agreements. Rather than simply relying on an export trading company to assist in foreign markets, an exporting firm may turn to an *export management company* for advice and expertise. These international specialists help the exporter complete paperwork, make contacts with local buyers, and comply with local laws governing labeling, product safety, and performance testing. At the same time, the exporting firm retains much more control than would be possible with an export trading company.

An *offset agreement* matches a small business with a major international firm. It basically makes the small firm a subcontractor to the larger one. Such an entry strategy helps a new exporter by allowing it to share in the larger company's international expertise. The small firm also benefits in such important areas as international transaction documents and financing, while the larger company benefits from the local expertise and capabilities of its smaller partner.

Countertrade   A sizable share of international trade involves payments made in the form of local products, not currency. This system of international bartering agreements is called **countertrade.**

A common reason for resorting to international barter is inadequate access to needed foreign currency. To complete an international sales agreement, the seller may agree to accept part or all of the purchase cost in merchandise rather than currency. Because the seller may decide to locate a buyer for the bartered goods before completing the transaction, a number of international buyers and sellers frequently join together in a single agreement.

Countertrade may often be a firm's only opportunity to enter a particular market. Many developing countries simply cannot obtain enough credit or financial assistance to afford the

HIT & MISS

Red Bull Charges into Global Markets

Few people would expect a drink with a sour berry taste, an outsized price, and ingredients such as amino acid taurine and a carbohydrate called glucuronolactone to capture half of the U.S. energy drink market. But that's exactly what Austrian-based Red Bull has done.

After successfully branching out across Europe, the drink was introduced in the United States with the slogan "Red Bull Gives You Wings." Red Bull packs 80 milligrams of caffeine per 8.3-ounce can, more than twice as much as found in 12 ounces of Coke, and nearly as many calories—110 to the larger Coke's 140. It owes the ingredients taurine and glucuronolactone to the recipe for a tonic discovered in Asia by CEO Dietrich Mateschitz. But the sugar and caffeine, with carbonation added for Western palates, have helped popularize it. College students, club patrons, fans of extreme sports, and truck drivers all pay $2 a can for Red Bull's jolt.

"When we first started, we said there is no existing market for Red Bull, but Red Bull will create it," says Mateschitz. The drink has benefited from an unusual marketing campaign, funded by 30 percent of annual revenues. The Coca-Cola Company, by comparison, spends less than 10 percent of revenues on marketing. Saturating the market with samples, sponsoring hun-dreds of aspiring athletes, and staging extreme sports events around the world are just a few of the strategies that help increase U.S. sales about 40 percent a year. What could be more appropriate for a hip energy drink than sponsoring a flying contest in which all the flying machines are homemade?

The company is also test-marketing an herbal tea that claims to boost the immune system, and Mateschitz believes many new products lie ahead. "We have the next hundred years in front of us," he says.

Questions for Critical Thinking

1. Do you think it was a smart move to introduce Red Bull throughout Europe before exporting it to the United States? Why or why not?
2. Red Bull sells well in more than 100 countries. What do you think accounts for its success in so many different cultures?

Sources: "Red Bull Founder Rides Wave of Success," 2004 Global Business Influentials, CNN.com, accessed June 11, 2006, http://cnnstudentnews.cnn.com; Christopher Palmeri, "Hansen Natural: Charging at Red Bull with a Brawny Energy Brew," *BusinessWeek*, June 6, 2005, pp. 74–77; Kerry A. Dolan, "The Soda with Buzz," *Forbes*, March 28, 2005, pp. 126–130.

---

imports that their people want. Countries with heavy debt burdens also resort to countertrade. Russian buyers, whose currency is often less acceptable to foreign traders than the stronger currencies of countries such as the United States, Great Britain, Japan, and EU countries, may resort to trading local products ranging from crude oil to diamonds to vodka as payments for purchases from foreign companies unwilling to accept Russian rubles. Still other countries, such as China, may restrict imports. Under such circumstances, countertrade may be the only practical way to win government approval to import needed products.

Contractual Agreements   Once a company, large or small, gains some experience in international sales, it may decide to enter into contractual agreements with local parties. These arrangements can include franchising, foreign licensing, and subcontracting.

Franchising   Common among U.S. companies, franchising can work well for companies seeking to expand into international markets, too. A **franchise,** as described in detail in Chapter 5, is a contractual agreement in which a wholesaler or retailer (the franchisee) gains the right to sell the franchisor's products under that company's brand name if it agrees to the related operating requirements. The franchisee can also receive marketing, management, and

Hello Kitty is a worldwide product-licensing phenomenon. Sanrio, the Japanese company that owns the cartoon character, gets nearly $500 million in revenue each year from the furry feline. Shown here perched on a mobile phone, Hello Kitty has also adorned keychains, screen savers, bracelets, pillows, and tens of thousands of other items in its 30-year-plus history.

business services from the franchisor. While these arrangements are common among leading fast-food brands such as McDonald's and KFC, other kinds of service providers also often look to franchising as an international marketplace option.

Domino's Pizza has expanded by about 1,200 franchised stores over the last few years, and two-thirds of them are outside the United States. The pizza company's largest international market is in Mexico, where it is bigger than McDonald's and Burger King combined, and it is also succeeding in Taiwan and Japan. To entice Chinese consumers, who are more interested in dining out than in having food delivered, the chain is trying larger stores with eating areas.[29]

Foreign Licensing   In a **foreign licensing agreement,** one firm allows another to produce or sell its product, or use its trademark, patent, or manufacturing processes, in a specific geographical area. In return, the firm gets a royalty or other compensation.

Licensing can be advantageous for a small manufacturer eager to launch a well-known product overseas. Not only does it get a proven product from another market, but little or no investment is required to begin operating. The arrangement can also allow entry into a market otherwise closed to imports due to government restrictions. The popular Hello Kitty cartoon character, for instance, appears on about 22,000 different products around the world at any given time, with hundreds of new items appearing every month as old ones are "retired." Sanrio, the Japanese company that owns the character, produces about 6,000 Hello Kitty items itself. It licenses the wide-eyed cat to other manufacturers such as a winery that makes a Hello Kitty Beaujolais and Mitsubishi, which made a pink Hello Kitty minicar for several years. Other license holders have made Hello Kitty laptops, cell phones, thermoses, and even computer USB hubs and a luxury trailer from Airstream.[30]

Subcontracting   The third type of contractual agreement, **subcontracting,** involves hiring local companies to produce, distribute, or sell goods or services. This move allows a foreign firm to take advantage of the subcontractor's expertise in local culture, contacts, and regulations. Subcontracting works equally well for mail-order companies, which can farm out order fulfillment and customer service functions to local businesses. Manufacturers practice subcontracting to save money on import duties and labor costs, and businesses go this route to market products best sold by locals in a given country. Some firms, such as Maryland-based Pacific Bridge Medical, help medical manufacturers find reliable subcontractors and parts suppliers in Asia.[31] Whirlpool, the appliance maker, subcontracts to India and China the manufacture of many of its products, particularly washing machines and refrigerators intended for sale in local markets. These household appliances often require subtle design changes to conform to Asian consumers' needs.[32]

A key disadvantage of subcontracting is that companies cannot always control their subcontractors' business practices. Several major U.S. companies have been embarrassed by reports that their subcontractors used child labor to manufacture clothing.

Offshoring   While it is not generally considered a way of initiating business internationally, *offshoring,* or the relocation of business processes to a lower-cost location overseas, has become a widespread practice. China has emerged as the preferred destination for production off-

ARE MANUFACTURERS TAKING ADVANTAGE OF THE AMERICAN JOBS CREATION ACT?

The American Jobs Creation Act of 2004 was an attempt to keep manufacturing jobs in the United States The act granted tax relief to U.S. manufacturers based on the portion of income derived from domestic production. The income ceiling was limited to 50 percent of wages.

The law also created a 9 percent tax deduction to be phased in over six years, repealed export taxes, imposed a one-year moratorium on foreign profits reinvested in the United States, and gave small business capital investment breaks. But lobbyists for various special interests ensured that about 200,000 different manufacturers got the tax breaks, sometimes by stretching the definition of a manufacturing job. For instance, some of the coffee baristas at Starbucks were counted as manufacturing industry workers, along with employees of movie theaters, shopping malls, and NASCAR. The net result in terms of tax revenue lost and jobs created or saved remains to be seen.

Is it ethical for firms to interpret the American Jobs Creation Act in ways that allow the greatest possible tax break, if the purpose is to save jobs?

PRO

1. U.S. manufacturers pay higher tax rates than in any other industrialized country, and they need tax relief to remain competitive and keep jobs at home.
2. The bill is beneficial because it also closes loopholes that allowed businesses to avoid taxes by sending jobs overseas.

CON

1. It is never ethical to stretch a law for any purpose other than what lawmakers intended.
2. Including industries that are not true manufacturers will deprive the government of revenue it could use to strengthen business and save jobs in other ways such as retraining programs.

Summary

The law's effect, in terms of tax revenue and jobs, is still uncertain at this point. The National Association of Manufacturers (NAM) is very optimistic, however. "Over the next 10 years, this landmark legislation will save U.S. manufacturers billions of dollars and create hundreds of thousands of new jobs," said NAM president and former Michigan governor John Engler.

Sources: "President Bush Signs Important Tax Relief for America's Job Creators," press release, House Committee on Ways and Means, accessed June 11, 2006, http://waysandmeans.house.gov; "NAM Says New Tax Measure Is Great News for American Companies and Workers," National Association of Manufacturers, accessed June 11, 2006, http://www.nam.org; Bill Thomas, "Industry Tax Relief Rewards," *Washington Times*, accessed June 11, 2006, http://www.washtimes.com; "Landmark Business Tax Relief Bill Signed into Law," National Association of Manufacturers, accessed June 11, 2006, http://www.nam.org.

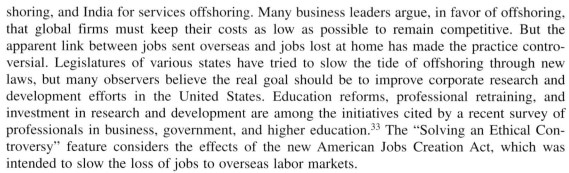

shoring, and India for services offshoring. Many business leaders argue, in favor of offshoring, that global firms must keep their costs as low as possible to remain competitive. But the apparent link between jobs sent overseas and jobs lost at home has made the practice controversial. Legislatures of various states have tried to slow the tide of offshoring through new laws, but many observers believe the real goal should be to improve corporate research and development efforts in the United States. Education reforms, professional retraining, and investment in research and development are among the initiatives cited by a recent survey of professionals in business, government, and higher education.[33] The "Solving an Ethical Controversy" feature considers the effects of the new American Jobs Creation Act, which was intended to slow the loss of jobs to overseas labor markets.

In the meantime, offshoring allows firms such as San Jose–based PortalPlayer, a manufacturer of hardware and software for MP3 media players, to operate almost around the clock. They work with colleagues in India with a twelve-hour time difference. "We keep passing the baton between California and India, and that way, we can cram a lot more work into a 24-hour period," says PortalPlayer's vice president.[34]

"They Said It"

"Outsourcing is just a new way of doing international trade."
—N. Gregory Mankiw (b. 1958)
Former chairman, Council of Economic Advisers

International Direct Investment Investing directly in production and marketing operations in a foreign country is the ultimate level of global involvement. Over time, a firm may become successful at conducting business in other countries through exporting and contractual agreements. Its managers may then decide to establish manufacturing facilities in those countries, open branch offices, or buy ownership interests in local companies.

In an *acquisition*, a company purchases another existing firm in the host country. An acquisition permits a largely domestic business operation to gain an international presence very quickly. This advantage was probably what made the purchase of IBM's ailing Personal Computing Division so attractive to Lenovo Group, the largest PC manufacturer in China. The acquisition boosts Lenovo's share of the Chinese PC market to about a third; in comparison, Dell has about 8 percent. Anchored by a large investment in the company by the Chinese government, which isn't pushing for the quick profits most Western companies must deliver, Lenovo stands poised to make a big impact both at home and abroad. "This is the big experiment," said an information technology consultant. "China is already the factory of the world. Now they're testing whether they can raise the value of that output."[35]

Joint ventures allow companies to share risks, costs, profits, and management responsibilities with one or more host country nationals. H. J. Heinz's European unit recently acquired a majority stake in Petrosoyuz, a top Russian maker of mayonnaise, ketchup, and other condiments and sauces. The two companies formed a new joint venture company to market the products in Russia and its neighbors in Eastern Europe. The CEO of Heinz Europe said of the move, "This joint venture is consistent with our European strategy to build our core businesses in the rapidly emerging markets of eastern Europe. Additionally, it will give Heinz access to local market understanding that will allow us to expand sales of other popular Heinz brands and products throughout Russia."[36]

By setting up an *overseas division*, a company can conduct a significant amount of its business overseas. This strategy differs from that of a multinational company in that a firm with overseas divisions remains primarily a domestic organization with international operations. Panasonic and General Electric, for instance, both rely on overseas divisions. Panasonic's Automotive Systems Company, headquartered in Japan, has overseas divisions in the United States, Mexico, Germany, China, Thailand, Taiwan, and the Czech Republic.[37] General Electric's energy technology company, GE Energy, has headquarters in Atlanta and divisions in Barcelona; Florence, Italy; and Shanghai. Its transportation division has locations in Canada, Italy, and Brazil.[38]

assessment check

1. Name three possible strategies for beginning overseas business operations.
2. What is countertrade?
3. Compare and contrast licensing and subcontracting.
4. Describe joint ventures.

multinational corporation (MNC) firm with significant operations and marketing activities outside its home country.

From Multinational Corporation to Global Business

A **multinational corporation (MNC)** is an organization with significant foreign operations. As Table 4.4 shows, firms headquartered in the United States make up half the list of the world's largest multinationals. The United Kingdom and the Netherlands have two companies each, and Japan's Toyota Motor rounds out the top ten.

Many U.S. multinationals, including Nike and Wal-Mart, have expanded their overseas operations because they believe that domestic markets are peaking and foreign markets offer greater sales and profit potential. Other MNCs are making substantial investments in developing countries in part because these countries provide low-cost labor compared with the United States and western Europe. In addition, many MNCs are locating high-tech facilities in countries with large numbers of technical school graduates, such as India.

Table 4.4

The World's Leading Companies (Based on a Combined Ranking for Sales, Profits, Assets, and Market Value)

Rank and Company	Business	Country of Origin
1. Citigroup	Banking	United States
2. General Electric	Conglomerate	United States
3. Bank of America	Banking	United States
4. American International Group	Insurance	United States
5. HSBC Group	Banking	United Kingdom
6. Exxon Mobil	Oil and gas	United States
7. Royal Dutch/Shell Group	Oil and gas	Netherlands
8. BP (British Petroleum)	Oil and gas	United Kingdom
9. JPMorgan Chase	Financial Services	United States
10. UBS	Financial Services	Switzerland

Source: "The World's Leading Companies," *Forbes*, accessed May 19, 2006, http://www.forbes.com.

DEVELOPING A STRATEGY FOR INTERNATIONAL BUSINESS

In developing a framework in which to conduct international business, managers must first evaluate their corporate objectives, organizational strengths and weaknesses, and strategies for product development and marketing. They can choose to combine these elements in either a global strategy or a multidomestic strategy.

Global Business Strategies

In a **global business** (or *standardization*) **strategy**, a firm sells the same product in essentially the same manner throughout the world. Many companies simply modify their domestic business strategies by translating promotional brochures and product-use instructions into the languages of the host nations. Toyota adapts its marketing not only to international markets but to consumer segments within nations. The company's new Scion model is aimed at U.S. youth.[39]

A global marketing perspective can be appropriate for some goods and services and certain market segments that are common to many nations. The approach works for products with nearly universal appeal and for luxury items such as jewelry. But food retailers such as McDonald's, PepsiCo, and KFC have discovered how much they must adapt their products to consumer tastes in China, for instance. Spinach, egg, and tomato soup is on KFC's menu in China, as are red-bean sundaes at McDonald's. PepsiCo's Frito-Lay chips are lemon-flavored and packaged in pastel colors to accommodate Chinese consumers' love of product flavors and designs that suggest coolness in hot weather. The redesigned chips became Lay's best-selling new product in China.[40] Scientific equipment, on the other hand, is not bound by geographical differences.

global business strategy offering a standardized, worldwide product and selling it in essentially the same manner throughout a firm's domestic and foreign markets.

Multidomestic Business Strategies

Under a **multidomestic business** (or *adaptation*) **strategy,** the firm treats each national market in a different way. It develops products and marketing strategies that appeal to the customs, tastes, and buying habits of particular national markets. Companies that neglect the global nature of the Internet can unwittingly cause problems for potential customers by failing to adapt their strategy. European consumers, for instance, were at first hesitant to adopt online ordering of products ranging from books to railroad tickets. But in recent years, Internet use in western Europe has grown dramatically. Companies as diverse as the European divisions of Amazon.com; Egg PLC of London, an online financial services company; and the French national railroad have seen the numbers of visitors to their Web sites climbing, along with Internet revenues.

assessment check

1. What is a global business strategy? What are its advantages?
2. What is a multidomestic business strategy? What are its advantages?

WHAT'S AHEAD

Examples in this chapter indicate that both large and small businesses are relying on world trade, not just major corporations. Chapter 5 examines the special advantages and challenges that small-business owners encounter. In addition, a critical decision facing any new business is the choice of the most appropriate form of business ownership. Chapter 5 also examines the major ownership structures—sole proprietorship, partnership, and corporation—and assesses the pros and cons of each. The chapter closes with a discussion of recent trends affecting business ownership, such as the growing impact of franchising and business consolidations through mergers and acquisitions.

SUMMARY OF LEARNING GOALS

1 Explain the importance of international business and the primary reasons nations trade.

The United States is both the world's largest importer and the largest exporter, although less than 5 percent of the world's population lives within its borders. With the increasing globalization of the world's economies, the international marketplace offers tremendous opportunities for U.S. and foreign businesses to expand into new markets for their goods and services. Doing business globally provides new sources of materials and labor. Trading with other countries also reduces a company's dependence on economic conditions in its home market. Countries that encourage international trade enjoy higher levels of economic activity, employment, and wages than those that restrict it.

Assessment Check Answers

1.1 Why do nations trade?

Nations trade because trading boosts economic growth by providing a market for products and access to needed resources. This makes production and distribution systems more efficient and reduces dependence on the economy of the domestic market.

1.2 Cite some measure of the size of the international marketplace.

Though developing countries have lower per-capita incomes than developed nations in North America and western Europe, their populations are large and growing. China's population is almost 1.3 billion and India's is roughly 1.1 billion.

2 Discuss the concepts of absolute and comparative advantage in international trade.

Nations usually benefit if they specialize in producing certain goods or services. A country has an absolute advantage if it holds a monopoly or produces a good or service at a lower cost than other nations. It has a comparative advantage if it can supply a particular product more efficiently or at a lower cost than it can produce other items.

Assessment Check Answers

2.1 Define *absolute advantage*.
Absolute advantage means a country can maintain a monopoly in or produce a product at lower cost than any other competitor.

2.2 How does a nation acquire a comparative advantage?
Comparative advantage exists when a nation can supply a product more efficiently and at a lower price than it can supply other goods, compared with the outputs of other countries.

3 Describe how nations measure international trade and the significance of exchange rates.
Countries measure the level of international trade by comparing exports and imports and then calculating whether a trade surplus or a deficit exists. This is the balance of trade, which represents the difference between exports and imports. The term *balance of payments* refers to the overall flow of money into or out of a country, including overseas loans and borrowing, international investments, and profits from such investments. An exchange rate is the value of a nation's currency relative to the currency of another nation. Currency values typically fluctuate, or "float," relative to the supply and demand for specific currencies in the world market. When the value of the dollar falls compared with other currencies, the cost paid by foreign businesses and households for U.S. products declines, and demand for exports may rise. An increase in the value of the dollar raises the prices of U.S. products sold abroad, but it reduces the prices of foreign products sold in the United States.

Assessment Check Answers

3.1 Compare balance of trade and balance of payments.
Balance of trade is the difference between exports and imports; balance of payments is the overall flow of money into or out of a country.

3.2 Explain the function of an exchange rate.
A nation's exchange rate is the rate at which its currency can be exchanged for the currencies of other nations to make it easier for them to trade with one another.

3.3 What happens when a currency is devalued?
Devaluation describes a fall in a currency's value relative to other currencies or to a fixed standard.

4 Identify the major barriers that confront global businesses.
Businesses face several obstacles in the global marketplace. Companies must be sensitive to social and cultural differences, such as languages, values, and religions, when operating in other countries. Economic differences include standard-of-living variations and levels of infrastructure development. Legal and political barriers are among the most difficult to judge. Each country sets its own laws regulating business practices. Trade restrictions such as tariffs and administrative barriers also present obstacles to international business.

Assessment Check Answers

4.1 How might values and attitudes form a barrier to trade, and how can they be overcome?
Marked differences in values and attitudes, such as religious attitudes, can form barriers between traditionally capitalist countries and those adapting new capitalist systems. Many of these can be overcome by learning about and respecting such differences.

4.2 What is a tariff? What is its purpose?
A tariff is a surcharge or duty charged on foreign products. Its purpose is to protect domestic producers of those items.

4.3 Why is dumping a problem for companies marketing goods internationally?
Dumping is selling products abroad at prices below the cost of production or exporting products at a lower price than charged in the home market. It drives the cost of domestic products sharply down.

5 Explain how international trade organizations and economic communities reduce barriers to international trade.
Many international organizations seek to promote international trade by reducing barriers. Examples include the World Trade Organization, the World Bank, and the International Monetary Fund. Multinational economic communities create partnerships to remove barriers to flows of goods, capital, and people across the borders of member nations. Three such economic agreements are the North American Free Trade Agreement, the Central American Free Trade Agreement, and the European Union.

Assessment Check Answers

5.1 What international trade organization succeeded GATT, and what is its goal?

The World Trade Organization (WTO) succeeded GATT with the goal of monitoring GATT agreements, mediating disputes, and continuing the effort to reduce trade barriers throughout the world.

5.2 Compare and contrast the goals of the World Bank and the International Monetary Fund.
The World Bank funds projects that build or expand nations' infrastructure such as transportation, education, and health systems and facilities. The International Monetary Fund makes short-term loans to member nations that are unable to meet their budgets. The fund operates as a lender of last resort.

5.3 Identify the members of NAFTA and briefly explain how it works.
NAFTA created a free-trade zone between the United States, Canada, and Mexico by eliminating trade barriers and investment restrictions among them, as well as easing regulations on services such as banking and establishing uniform rules for protection of intellectual property.

5.4 What are the goals of the European Union and how do they promote international trade?
The European Union's goals include promoting economic and social progress, introducing European citizenship as a complement to national citizenship, and giving the EU a significant role in international affairs. Unifying standards and laws is expected to contribute to international trade and economic growth.

6 **Compare the different levels of involvement used by businesses when entering global markets.**
Exporting and importing, the first level of involvement in international business, involves the lowest degree of both risk and control. Companies may rely on export trading or management companies to help distribute their products. Contractual agreements such as franchising, foreign licensing, and subcontracting offer additional, flexible options. Franchising and licensing are especially appropriate for services. Companies may also choose local subcontractors to produce goods for local sales. International direct investment in production and marketing facilities provides the highest degree of control but also the greatest risk. Firms make direct investments by acquiring foreign companies or facilities, forming joint ventures with local firms, and setting up their own overseas divisions.

Assessment Check Answers

6.1 Name three possible strategies for beginning overseas business operations.
Strategies are exporting or importing; contractual agreements such as franchising, licensing, or subcontracting; and making direct investments in foreign markets through acquisition, joint venture, or establishment of an overseas division.

6.2 What is countertrade?
Countertrade consists of payments made in the form of local products, not currency.

6.3 Compare and contrast licensing and subcontracting.
In a foreign licensing agreement, one firm allows another to produce or sell its product or use its trademark, patent, or manufacturing process in a specific geographical area in return for royalty payments or other compensations. In subcontracting a firm hires local companies abroad to produce, distribute, or sell its goods and services.

6.4 Describe joint ventures.
Joint ventures allow companies to share risks, costs, profits, and management responsibilities with one or more host country nationals.

7 **Distinguish between a global business strategy and a multidomestic business strategy.**
A company that adopts a global (or standardization) strategy develops a single, standardized product and marketing strategy for implementation throughout the world. The firm sells the same product in essentially the same manner in all countries in which it operates. Under a multidomestic (or adaptation) strategy, the firm develops a different treatment for each foreign market. It develops products and marketing strategies that appeal to the customs, tastes, and buying habits of particular nations.

Assessment Check Answers

7.1 What is a global business strategy? What are its advantages?
A global business strategy specifies a standardized competitive strategy in which the firm sells the same product in essentially the same manner throughout the world. It works well for goods and services that are common to many nations and allows the firm to market them without making significant changes.

7.2 What is a multidomestic business strategy? What are its advantages?

A multidomestic business strategy allows the firm to treat each foreign market in a different way to appeal to the customs, tastes, and buying habits of particular national markets. It allows the firm to customize its marketing appeals for individual cultures or areas.

Business Terms You Need to Know

exports 92
imports 92
balance of trade 96
balance of payments 96
exchange rate 97
tariff 105

World Trade Organization (WTO) 106
North American Free Trade Agreement (NAFTA) 108
Central American Free Trade Agreement (CAFTA) 109

European Union (EU) 109
multinational corporation (MNC) 116
global business strategy 117
multidomestic business strategy 118

Other Important Business Terms

devaluation 97
infrastructure 102
quotas 105
dumping 106
embargo 106
exchange control 106

General Agreement on Tariffs and Trade (GATT) 106
World Bank 107
International Monetary Fund (IMF) 107
countertrade 112

franchise 113
foreign licensing agreement 114
subcontracting 114
joint ventures 116

Review Questions

1. How does a business decide whether to trade with a foreign country? What are the key factors for participating in the information economy on a global basis?
2. Why are developing countries such as China and India becoming important international markets?
3. What is the difference between absolute advantage and comparative advantage? Give an example of each.
4. Can a nation have a favorable balance of trade and an unfavorable balance of payments? Why or why not?
5. Identify several potential barriers to communication when a company attempts to conduct business in another country. How might these be overcome?
6. Identify and describe briefly the three dimensions of the legal environment for global business.
7. What are the major nontariff restrictions affecting international business? Describe the difference between tariff and nontariff restrictions.
8. What is NAFTA? How does it work?
9. How has the EU helped trade in European businesses?
10. What are the key choices a company must make before reaching the final decision to go global?

1. When Britain transferred Hong Kong to China in 1997, China agreed to grant Hong Kong a high degree of autonomy as a capitalist economy for 50 years. Do you think this agreement will hold up? Why or why not? Consider China's economy, population, infrastructure, and other factors in your answer.

2. The tremendous growth of online business has introduced new elements to the legal climate of international business. Patents, brand names, copyrights, and trademarks are difficult to monitor because of the boundaryless nature of the Internet. What steps could businesses take to protect their trademarks and brands in this environment? Come up with at least five suggestions and compare your list with your classmates'.

3. The WTO monitors GATT agreements, mediates disputes, and continues the effort to reduce trade barriers throughout the world. However, widespread concerns have been expressed that the WTO's focus on lowering trade barriers may encourage businesses to keep costs down through practices that may lead to pollution and human rights abuses. Others argue that human rights should not be linked to international business. Do you think environmental and human rights issues should be linked to trade? Why or why not?

4. The IMF makes short-term loans to developing countries that may not be able to repay them. Do you agree that the IMF should forgive these debts in some cases? Why or why not?

5. Describe briefly the EU and its goals. What are the pros and cons of the EU? Do you predict that the European alliance will hold up over the next 20 years? Why or why not?

6. Use the most recent edition of "The Fortune Global 500," which is published in *Fortune* magazine normally in late July or early August, or go to *Fortune*'s online version at http://money.cnn .com/magazines/fortune/global500, to answer the following questions.
   a. On what is the Global 500 ranking based (for example, profits, number of employees, revenues)?
   b. Among the world's ten largest corporations, list the countries represented with the number of companies from each nation.
   c. Identify the top-ranked company, along with its Global 500 ranking and country, for the following industry classifications: Food and Drug Stores; Industrial and Farm Equipment; Petroleum Refining; Utilities: Gas and Electric; Telecommunications; Pharmaceuticals.

Exporting to Afghanistan

In the landlocked country of Afghanistan, devastated by a generation of war and repression, efficient transportation is a rarity. There are only 15 miles of railroad in the country's almost 250,000 square miles, and less than 2,000 miles of paved roads. Despite aggressive efforts by the Ministry of Communication, there are only about 12,000 working telephones in the capital city of Kabul, with a population of nearly 2 million people. Though tens of thousands of refugees have returned during the reconstruction efforts of the last several years, more than 4 million people of the country's population of about 29 million still live outside their country.

The United States is at the head of the massive reconstruction of Afghanistan, and experts believe there will be export opportunities in the recovering nation for years to come. But with almost no business infrastructure such as roads, phones, and hotels, no sales and distribution channels, and little available skilled labor to hire, foreign investment will be painfully slow to flourish. Streamlined licensing procedures and tools for international dispute resolution that are now in place should help.

However, local interpreters and drivers are considered essential for those who know enough about the country, its geography, and its culture and language to transact business on Afghan soil.

The U.S. Department of Commerce warns that limited purchasing power in Afghanistan will dictate the pace of export opportunities. But basic industries that can help Afghans in their reconstruction efforts will likely find markets first. The country desperately needs architectural, construction, telecommunications, and engineering services—as well as goods such as construction materials and building equipment, computer hardware, telecommunications equipment, diesel-powered generators, security and safety equipment, and office furniture. Medium- and long-term needs include aircraft, aircraft parts, and airport and ground-support equipment.

Social change is sure to come, though it may be slow. Exporters should not overlook the chance to do business with Afghan women. "There are barriers," says Sara Rahmani, who runs a new and growing clothing business. "We are recovering from war and devastation and Taliban repression. . . . But there's nothing in Shariah [Islamic law] that says women can't do business."

Questions for Critical Thinking

1. A Commerce Department task force on Afghanistan warns that "only the most experienced, well-informed, and open-minded traveler should consider visiting Afghanistan." What difficulties do you think a business traveler to Kabul would need to overcome? How could he or she prepare for such a trip and ensure its success?

2. It is expected that lower-cost and possibly lower-quality goods and services from Pakistan and Iran will compete with U.S. exports to Afghanistan in the coming years. What can U.S. companies wishing to export to Afghanistan do to combat such competition?

Sources: Matthew Pennington, "Women Go into Business in Afghanistan," *Casper (WY) Star Tribune*, accessed June 11, 2006, http://www.casperstartribune .net; U.S. Department of State, "Background Note: Afghanistan," accessed June 11, 2006, http://www.state .gov; Afghanistan Investment and Reconstruction Task Force, "Traveling to and Doing Business in Afghanistan," U.S. Department of Commerce, accessed June 11, 2006, http://www.export.gov/afghanistan.

Cold Stone Creamery Cools off Consumers around the World

This video case appears on page 611. A recently filmed video, designed to expand and highlight the written case, is available for class use by instructors.

The Legal Framework for Business

CLASS-ACTION FAIRNESS

We've all shopped around for the best deal on a car, computer, or sound system. But have you ever heard of lawyers shopping around for clients willing to sue or for the best state courts for their trials? Certain states or counties did seem to reward plaintiffs filing class-action lawsuits with much higher figures than elsewhere. A *class-action suit* groups a number of small plaintiffs, as many as hundreds of thousands of them, to allow for efficient processing under one lawsuit. And the rules for the location of those trials were loose, allowing lawyers to pick locations with juries likely to be favorable to their suits. Certainly, businesses that create defective products that hurt consumers or commit fraud need to be held accountable, and everyone is sympathetic to those who've been harmed. But the mushrooming of frivolous lawsuits was imposing huge fines on businesses and hampering their ability to compete. Critics also said that the lawyers bringing the suits sometimes benefited much more than their clients, receiving percentages of the entire settlement well beyond the work they did. Eventually, the U.S. Chamber of Commerce, legislators, and others called for a change. It came in the form of the **Class-Action Fairness Act of 2005.**

Before the reform, many companies facing such an action, whether it involved a faulty medication or a defective TV, complained that plaintiffs' lawyers shopped around for sympathetic courts. The Class-Action Fairness Act of 2005 imposes certain restrictions on such suits. First, it automatically moves most large, multistate class actions—those with potential damages exceeding $5 million and in which more than two-thirds of the plaintiffs are geographically dispersed—from state courts into federal courts. This restriction prevents "shopping around" in different states for sympathetic courts but lets cases that belong within a particular state remain there. Second, judges must consider the actual monetary value of any damage done so that plaintiffs receive true compensation for injury instead of large—and perhaps arbitrary—awards.

A third major provision of the law affects the way attorneys receive payment for their legal representation. Under the old system, an attorney would usually receive a percentage of the gross settlement amount, regardless of whether all plaintiffs bothered to collect. Now judges can require that any uncollected rewards be given to charities or government organizations, and attorneys may

© MICHAEL NEWMAN/PHOTOEDIT

not include those rewards in calculating their fees. Also, if the attorney's fee was not based on a percentage, then it must be based on time actually spent working on the case. Finally, the act ensures that plaintiffs' interests are protected equally with their lawyers'.

Critics of the Class-Action Fairness Act claim that it will suppress legitimate consumer claims, while supporters believe that it will protect jobs and businesses by exposing them to less risk. If it is successful, both consumers and businesses could experience something new: fairness.[1]

OVERVIEW

The first four chapters of the text show how important the legal environment is to business, government, and the general public and how changes occur to rectify problems. The corporate governance failures discussed in Chapter 2 continue to be addressed throughout the book. In the aftermath of corporate wrongdoing, charges against and convictions of business leaders like Tyco's Dennis Kozlowski and WorldCom's Bernard Ebbers, and the bankruptcies of such firms as Enron and WorldCom, we have seen the passage of new laws designed to end abuses by unethical business executives. In addition, we have seen criminal charges against wayward business leaders end in convictions. Bernard Ebbers, former CEO of WorldCom, was convicted of securities fraud, conspiracy, and filing false documents with regulators.[2] These events have also led to new regulations restricting investment advisors, accountants, and board members in their oversight responsibilities. A business environment of personal greed and excess is being cleaned up to reflect the demands of ethical business leaders, government officials, investors, and the general public.

On a more personal level, you may be frustrated by all the junk e-mail (called *spam*) you receive, in addition to pop-up messages. Also, those annoying telephone solicitations became so pervasive that a Do Not Call law was enacted, making it illegal to call anyone listed on the federal do-not-call roster maintained by the Federal Trade Commission.

Legal issues affect every aspect of business. In fact, most of the remaining chapters will discuss legislation that specifically affects the business functions analyzed in each chapter. Already, an overview of the legal environment was presented in Chapter 2, and legislation affecting international operations was covered in Chapter 4. Chapter 5 discusses laws related to small businesses. Laws regarding human resources management and labor unions are examined in Chapter 9. Laws affecting other business operations, such as environmental regulations and product safety, are one of the topics in Chapter 13, and marketing-related legislation is examined in Chapter 14. Finally, legislation pertaining to banking and the securities markets is discussed in Chapters 17 and 18. In this appendix, we provide an overall perspective of legislation at the federal, state, and local levels, and point out that, while business executives may not be legal experts, they do need to be knowledgeable in their specific area of responsibility. A good dose of common sense also helps avoid potential legal problems.

Despite the best efforts of most businesspeople, legal cases do arise. A dispute may arise over a contract, an employee may protest being passed over for a promotion, or a town may challenge the environmental impact of a new gas station. Unfortunately, the United States has the dubious distinction of being the world's most litigious society. Lawsuits are as common as business deals. Consider Wal-Mart, which is involved in up to 7,000 legal cases at any one time. Even if you are never involved in a lawsuit, the cost still affects you. The average U.S. family pays a hidden "litigation tax" of $2,900 each year because of the costs of lawsuits that force businesses to increase their prices.[3] Small businesses, including doctors' offices, are often the hardest hit and may cut back on their services or close.

On the lighter side, every day there are news reports of proposed new laws intended to protect businesses, consumers, and the general public—but somehow miss the mark. One Texas legislator proposed a law prohibiting weather forecasters from calling themselves "meteorologists" unless they had a certain degree. In Oklahoma, another legislator tried to revive the cockfighting industry—which was banned in his state—by proposing that fighting roosters wear miniature boxing gloves and protective vests. Neither bill was passed.[4]

This appendix looks at the general nature of business law, the court system, basic legal concepts, and finally the changing regulatory environment for U.S. business. Let's start with some initial definitions and related examples.

LEGAL SYSTEM AND ADMINISTRATIVE AGENCIES

judiciary the branch of government charged with settling disputes among parties through the application of laws.

The **judiciary**, or court system, is the branch of government responsible for settling disputes among parties by applying laws. This branch consists of several types and levels of courts, each with a specific jurisdiction. Court systems are organized at the federal, state, and local levels. Administrative agencies also perform some limited judicial functions, but these agencies are more properly regarded as belonging to the executive or legislative branches of government.

At both the federal and state levels, **trial courts**—courts of general jurisdiction—hear a wide range of cases. Unless a case is assigned by law to another court or to an administrative agency, a court of general jurisdiction will hear it. The majority of cases, both criminal and civil, pass through these courts. Within the federal system, trial courts are known as *U.S. district courts*, and at least one such court operates in each state. In the state court systems, the general jurisdiction courts are often called *circuit courts*, and states typically provide one for each county. Other names for general jurisdiction courts are superior courts, common pleas courts, or district courts.

State judiciary systems also include many courts with lower, or more specific, jurisdictions. In most states, parties can appeal the decisions of these lower courts to the general jurisdiction courts. Examples of lower courts are probate courts—which settle the estates of people who have died—and small-claims courts—where people can represent themselves in suits involving limited amounts of money. For example, a landlord might go to small-claims court to settle a dispute with a tenant over a security deposit.

Appeals of decisions made at the general trial court level are heard by **appellate courts.** Both the federal and state systems have appellate courts; for instance, the U.S. Court of Appeals for the Seventh Circuit, located in Chicago, covers Illinois, Indiana, and Wisconsin.[5] The appeals process allows a higher court to review the case and correct any lower court error indicated by the appellant, the party making the appeal.

Appeals from decisions of the U.S. circuit courts of appeals can go all the way to the nation's highest court, the U.S. Supreme Court. Appeals from state courts of appeal are heard by the highest court in each state, usually called the *state supreme court*. In a state without intermediate appellate courts, the state supreme court hears appeals directly from the trial courts. Parties who are not satisfied by the verdict of a state supreme court can appeal to the U.S. Supreme Court and may be granted a hearing if they can cite grounds for such an appeal and if the Supreme Court considers the case significant enough to be heard. In a typical year, the Supreme Court hears roughly 1 percent of the 7,500 cases filed.[6]

While most cases are resolved by the system of courts described here, certain highly specialized cases require particular expertise. Examples of specialized federal courts are the U.S. Tax Court for tax cases and the U.S. Court of Claims, which hears claims against the U.S. government itself. Similar specialized courts operate at the state level.

Administrative agencies, also known as bureaus, commissions, or boards, decide a variety of cases at all levels of government. These agencies usually derive their powers and responsibilities from state or federal statutes. Technically, they conduct hearings or inquiries rather than trials. Examples of federal administrative agencies are the Federal Trade Commission (FTC), the National Labor Relations Board, and the Federal Energy Regulatory Commission. Examples at the state level include public utility commissions and boards that govern the licensing of various trades and professions. Zoning boards, planning commissions, and boards of appeal operate at the city or county level. The FTC has the broadest power of any of the federal regulatory agencies. It enforces laws regulating unfair business practices, and it can stop false and deceptive advertising practices.

TYPES OF LAW

Law consists of the standards set by government and society in the form of either legislation or custom. This broad body of principles, regulations, rules, and customs that govern the actions of all members of society, including businesspeople, is derived from several sources. Common law refers to the body of law arising out of judicial decisions, some of which can be traced back to early England. For example, in some states, an unmarried couple who has lived together for a certain period of time is said to be legally husband and wife by common law.

Statutory law, or written law, includes state and federal constitutions, legislative enactments, treaties of the federal government, and ordinances of local governments. Statutes must be drawn precisely and reasonably to be constitutional, and thus enforceable. Still, courts must frequently interpret their intentions and meanings.

With the growth of the global economy, a knowledge of international law becomes crucial. **International law** refers to the numerous regulations that govern international commerce. Companies must be aware of the domestic laws of trading partners, trade agreements such as NAFTA, and the rulings of such organizations as the World Trade Organization. International law affects trade in all kinds of industries. Recently, the Canadian government announced it would add a 15 percent surtax on such diverse products as oysters, pigs, and cigarettes from the United States. This action is in response to the Continued Dumping and Subsidy Offset Act (commonly called the Byrd Amendment), which distributes proceeds the United States collects to firms, primarily U.S. steel companies. The World Trade Organization declared the Byrd Amendment illegal. "Retaliation is not our preferred option, but it is a necessary action," stated former Canadian trade minister Jim Peterson. "International trade rules must be respected."[7]

In a broad sense, all law is business law because all firms are subject to the entire body of law, just as individuals are. In a narrower sense, however, business law consists of those aspects of law that most directly influence and regulate the management of various types of business activity. Specific laws vary widely in their intent from business to business and from industry to industry. The legal interests of airlines, for example, differ from those of oil companies.

State and local statutes also have varying applications. Some state laws affect all businesses that operate in a particular state. Workers' compensation laws, which govern payments to workers for injuries incurred on the job, are an example. Other state laws apply only to certain firms or business activities. States have specific licensing requirements for businesses, such as law firms, funeral directors, and hair salons. Many local ordinances also deal with specific business activities. Local regulations on the sizes and types of business signs are commonplace. Some communities even restrict the sizes of stores, including height and square footage.

law standards set by government and society in the form of either legislation or custom.

common law body of law arising out of judicial decisions, some of which can be traced back to early England.

statutory law written law, including state and federal constitutions, legislative enactments, treaties of the federal government, and ordinances of local governments.

business law aspects of law that most directly influence and regulate the management of business activity.

REGULATORY ENVIRONMENT FOR BUSINESS

Government regulation of business has changed over time. Depending on public sentiment, the economy, and the political climate, we see the pendulum swing back and forth between increased regulation and deregulation. But the goal of both types of legislation is protection of healthy competition. One industry that has experienced some deregulation in the past is still subject to relatively tight regulations: banking. Despite the relaxation of banking regulations across state lines and the advent of online banking, laws governing everything from stock trading to retirement investing remain strict. Recently, several bills were proposed in Congress to shore up the Pension Benefit Guaranty Corporation, an agency that is running at a $20 billion deficit, particularly after assuming the pensions of some bankrupt companies, including United Airlines. The agency is not funded by tax dollars—instead, it is financed by insurance premiums and investments. But the bills did not pass. When asked later about the agency's ability to continue to absorb such burdens, the chairman of the Federal Reserve noted that the agency's difficulties could be handled within current banking regulations.[8]

Let's look at the issues surrounding regulation and deregulation, and the legislation that has characterized them.

Antitrust and Business Regulation

John D. Rockefeller's Standard Oil monopoly launched antitrust legislation. Breaking up monopolies and restraints of trade was a popular issue in the late 1800s and early 1900s. In fact, President Theodore Roosevelt always promoted himself as a "trust-buster." The highly publicized Microsoft case of the 1990s is an example of antitrust litigation.

During the 1930s, several laws designed to regulate business were passed. The basis for many of these laws was protecting employment. The world was in the midst of the Great Depression during the 1930s, so the government was focused on keeping its citizens employed. Recently, government officials became concerned with the security aspects of international business transactions, Internet usage, the sources of funds, and their effects on U.S. business practices. So, new regulatory legislation in the form of the USA Patriot Act was enacted in 2001. In 2005, Congress voted to extend most provisions of the Patriot Act indefinitely.[9]

The major federal antitrust and business regulation legislation includes the following:

Law	What It Did
Sherman Act (1890)	Set a competitive business system as a national policy goal. The act specifically banned monopolies and restraints of trade.
Clayton Act (1914)	Put restrictions on price discrimination, exclusive dealing, tying contracts, and interlocking boards of directors that lessened competition or might lead to a monopoly.
Federal Trade Commission Act (1914)	Established the FTC with the authority to investigate business practices. The act also prohibited unfair methods of competition.
Robinson-Patman Act (1936)	Outlawed price discrimination in sales to wholesalers, retailers, or other producers. The act also banned pricing designed to eliminate competition.
Wheeler-Lea Act (1938)	Banned deceptive advertising. The act gave the FTC jurisdiction in such cases.
Patriot Act (2001; extended in 2005)	Limited interactions between U.S. and foreign banks to those with "know your customer" policies; allowed the U.S. Treasury Department to freeze assets and bar a country, government, or institution from doing business in the United States; gave federal authorities broad powers to monitor Internet usage and expanded the way data is shared among different agencies.

Business Deregulation

Deregulation was a child of the 1970s whose influence continues today. Many formerly regulated industries were freed to pick the markets they wanted to serve. The deregulated industries, such as utilities and airlines, were also allowed to price their products without the guidance of federal regulations. For the most part, deregulation led to lower consumer prices. In some cases, it also led to a loss of service. Many smaller cities and airports lost airline service for a while because of deregulation. But small and discount airlines such as Southwest and JetBlue began to focus on and serve those locations, with great success.

Following are several major laws related to deregulation:

Law	What It Did
Airline Deregulation Act (1978)	Allowed airlines to set fares and pick their routes.
Motor Carrier Act and Staggers Rail Act (1980)	Permitted the trucking and railroad industries to negotiate rates and services.
Telecommunications Act (1996)	Cut barriers to competition in local and long-distance phone, cable, and television markets.
Gramm-Leach-Bliley Act (1999)	Permitted banks, securities firms, and insurance companies to affiliate within a new financial organizational structure; required them to disclose to customers their policies and practices for protecting the privacy of personal information.

CONSUMER PROTECTION

Many laws designed to protect consumers have been passed in the last 100 years. In many ways, business itself has evolved to reflect this focus on consumer safety and satisfaction. Following some widely publicized problems with brand-name prescription drugs such as Vioxx, the Food and Drug Administration (FDA) is more closely scrutinizing the accuracy of consumer advertisements for such products. However, the FDA does not have the legal authority to ban all consumer advertising for prescription drugs. It is up to the manufacturers and trade associations such as the Pharmaceutical Research and Manufacturers of America to set industry standards for advertising. Some companies have voluntarily opted to avoid advertising for the first year a prescription drug is available.[10]

The major federal laws related to consumer protection include the following:

Law	What It Did
Federal Food and Drug Act (1906)	Banned adulteration and misbranding of foods and drugs involved in interstate commerce.
Consumer Credit Protection Act (1968)	Required disclosure of annual interest rates on loans and credit purchases.
National Environmental Policy Act (1970)	Established the Environmental Protection Agency to deal with various types of pollution and organizations that create pollution.
Public Health Cigarette Smoking Act (1970)	Prohibited tobacco advertising on radio and television.
Consumer Product Safety Act (1972)	Established the Consumer Product Safety Commission with authority to specify safety standards for most products.
Nutrition Labeling and Education Act (1990)	Stipulated detailed information on the labeling of most foods.
Dietary Supplement Health and Education Act (1994)	Established standards with respect to dietary supplements including vitamins, minerals, herbs, and amino acids.

EMPLOYEE PROTECTION

Chapters 2 and 9 cover many of the issues employers face in protecting their employees from injury and harm while on the job. But employees must also be protected from unfair practices by employers. Recently, concerned about the cutbacks on retiree medical benefits at age 65—when they are eligible for Medicare coverage—AARP (the American Association of Retired Persons) won a court decision protecting the health benefits of retired workers. Under the Age Discrimination in Employment Act, employers must provide the same coverage to all their retirees, regardless of their age.[11] Some of the relevant laws related to employee protection include the following:

Law	What It Did
Fair Labor Standards Act (1938)	For hourly workers, provided payment of the minimum wage, overtime pay for time worked more than 40 hours in a workweek, restricted the employment of children, and required employers to keep records of wages and hours.
OSHA Act (1970)	Required employers to provide workers with workplaces free of recognized hazards that could cause serious injury or death and required employees to abide by all safety and health standards that apply to their jobs.
Americans with Disabilities Act (1991)	Banned discrimination against the disabled in public accommodations, transportation, and telecommunications.
Family and Medical Leave Act (1993)	Required covered employers to grant eligible employees up to twelve workweeks of unpaid leave during any twelve-month period for the birth and care of a newborn child of the employee, placement with the employee of a son or daughter for adoption or foster care, care of an immediate family member with a serious health condition, or medical leave for the employee if unable to work because of a serious health condition.
Uniformed Services Employment and Reemployment Rights Act (1994)	Protected the job rights of individuals who voluntarily or involuntarily leave their jobs to perform military service. Also prohibited employment discrimination in such cases.
American Jobs Creation Act (2004)	Reduced taxes for manufacturing in the United States, provided temporary tax breaks for income repatriated to the United States, and encouraged domestic job growth.

INVESTOR PROTECTION

Chapters 16, 17, and 18 describe the institutions subject to investor protection laws and some of the events that brought the Sarbanes-Oxley law into being. (See the entry in the following table for specific provisions of Sarbanes-Oxley.) Following is a summary of legislation to protect investors:

Law	What It Did
Securities Exchange Act (1934)	Created the Securities and Exchange Commission with the authority to register, regulate, and oversee brokerage firms, transfer agents, clearing agencies, and stock exchanges; the SEC also has the power to enforce securities laws and protect investors in public transactions.
Bank Secrecy Act (1970)	Deterred laundering and use of secret foreign bank accounts; created an investigative paper trail for large currency transactions; imposed civil and criminal penalties for noncompliance with reporting requirements; improved detection and investigation of criminal, tax, and regulatory violations.
Sarbanes-Oxley Act (2002)	Required top corporate executives to attest to the validity of the company's financial statements; increased the documentation and monitoring of internal controls; prohibited CPA firms from providing some types of consulting services for their clients; established a five-member accounting oversight board.

CYBERSPACE AND TELECOMMUNICATIONS PROTECTION

Computers and widespread use of the Internet and telecommunications have dramatically expanded the reach of businesses. They have also raised some thorny issues such as computer fraud and abuse, online privacy, and cyberterrorism. Under a recent Supreme Court ruling, Internet file-sharing services are now held accountable if their intention is for consumers to use software to exchange songs and videos illegally. Although lower courts had ruled that file-sharing services such as Grokster and Streamcast couldn't be sued, the Supreme Court unanimously decided that there was enough evidence of unlawful intent on the part of these companies. This ruling also helps protect copyrights, which are covered later in this appendix.[12]

Following are some of the major laws enacted to regulate cyberspace and telecommunications:

Law	What It Did
Computer Fraud and Abuse Act (1986)	Clarified definitions of criminal fraud and abuse for federal computer crimes and removed legal ambiguities and obstacles to prosecuting these crimes; established felony offenses for unauthorized access of "federal interest" computers and made it a misdemeanor to engage in unauthorized trafficking in computer passwords.
Children's Online Privacy Protection Act (1998)	Authorized the FTC to set rules regarding how and when firms must obtain parental permission before asking children marketing research questions.
Identity Theft and Assumption Deterrence Act (1998)	Made it a federal crime to knowingly transfer or use, without lawful authority, a means of identification of another person with intent to commit, aid, or abet any violation of federal, state, or local law.
Anticybersquatting Consumer Protection Act (1999)	Prohibited people from registering Internet domain names similar to company or celebrity names and then offering them for sale to these same parties
Homeland Security Act (2002)	Established the Department of Homeland Security; gave government wide new powers to collect and mine data on individuals and groups, including databases that combine personal, governmental, and corporate records including e-mails and Web sites viewed; limited information citizens can obtain under the Freedom of Information Act; gave government committees more latitude for meeting in secret.
Amendments to the Telemarketing Sales Rule (2003)	Created a national "do not call" registry, which prohibits telemarketing calls to registered telephone numbers; restricted the number and duration of telemarketing calls generating dead air space with use of automatic dialers; cracked down on unauthorized billing; and required telemarketers to transmit their Caller ID information. Telemarketers must check the do-not-call list quarterly, and violators could be fined as much as $11,000 per occurrence. Excluded from the registry's restrictions are charities, opinion pollsters, and political candidates.
Check Clearing for the 21st Century Act (2003)	Created a substitute check, allowing banks to process check information electronically and to deliver substitute checks to banks that want to continue receiving paper checks. A substitute check is the legal equivalent of the original check.

THE CORE OF BUSINESS LAW

Contract law and the law of agency; the Uniform Commercial Code, sales law, and negotiable instruments law; property law and the law of bailment; trademark, patent, and copyright law; tort law; bankruptcy law; and tax law are the cornerstones of U.S. business law. The sections that follow set out the key provisions of each of these legal concepts.

Contract Law and Law of Agency

Contract law is important because it is the legal foundation on which business dealings are conducted. A **contract** is a legally enforceable agreement between two or more parties regarding a specified act or thing.

Contract Requirements   As Figure 1 points out, the four elements of an enforceable contract are agreement, consideration, legal and serious purpose, and capacity. The parties must reach *agreement* about the act or thing specified. For such an agreement, or contract, to be valid and legally enforceable, each party must furnish *consideration*—the value or benefit that a party provides to the others with whom the contract is made. Assume that a builder hires an electrician to install wiring in a new house. The wiring job and the resulting payment are the considerations in this instance. In addition to consideration, an enforceable contract must involve a *legal and serious purpose*. Agreements made as a joke or involving the commission of crimes are not enforceable as legal contracts. An agreement between two competitors to fix the prices for their products is not enforceable as a contract because the subject matter is illegal.

The last element of a legally enforceable contract is *capacity*, the legal ability of a party to enter into agreements. The law does not permit certain people, such as those judged to be insane, to enter into legally enforceable contracts. Contracts govern almost all types of business activities. You might sign a contract to purchase a car, to do a job for someone as a freelancer or outsourcer, or to lease an apartment.

Breach of Contract   A violation of a valid contract is called a **breach of contract.** The injured party can go to court to enforce the contract provisions and, in some cases, collect **damages**—financial payments to compensate for a loss and related suffering.

Law of Agency   All types of firms conduct business affairs through a variety of agents, such as partners, directors, corporate officers, and sales personnel. An **agency** relationship exists when one party, called the *principal*, appoints another party, called the *agent*, to enter into contracts with third parties on the principal's behalf.

The law of agency is based on common-law principles and case law decisions of state and federal courts. Relatively little agency law has been enacted into statute. The law of agency is important because the principal is generally bound by the actions of the agent.

The legal basis for holding the principal liable for acts of the agent is the Latin maxim *respondeat superior* ("let the master answer"). In a case involving agency law, the court must decide the rights and obligations of the various parties. Generally, the principal is held liable if an agency relationship exists and the agent has some type of authority to do the wrongful act. The agent in such cases is liable to the principal for any damages.

Uniform Commercial Code

Most U.S. business law is based on the **Uniform Commercial Code**— usually referred to simply as the UCC. The UCC covers topics such as sales law, warranties, and negotiable instruments. All 50 states have adopted the UCC, although Louisiana also relies on the Napoleonic Code from its French origins. The UCC is actually a "model law" first written by the National Conference of Commissioners on Uniform State Laws, which states can then review and adopt, adopt with amendments, or replace with their own laws. The idea of the UCC is to create at least some degree of uniformity among the states.[13]

Figure 1

Four Elements of an Enforceable Contract

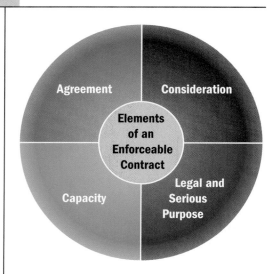

Agreement · Consideration · Capacity · Legal and Serious Purpose · Elements of an Enforceable Contract

Sales law governs sales of goods or services for money or on credit. Article 2 of the UCC specifies the circumstances under which a buyer and a seller enter into a sales contract. Such agreements are based on the express conduct of the parties. The UCC generally requires written agreements for enforceable sales contracts for products worth more than $500. The formation of a sales contract is quite flexible because certain missing terms in a written contract or other ambiguities do not prevent the contract from being legally enforceable. A court will look to past dealings, commercial customs, and other standards of reasonableness to evaluate whether a legal contract exists.[14]

Courts also consider these variables when either the buyer or the seller seeks to enforce his or her rights in cases in which the other party fails to perform as specified in the contract, performs only partially, or performs in a defective or unsatisfactory way. The UCC's remedies in such cases usually involve the award of monetary damages to injured parties. The UCC defines the rights of the parties to have the contract performed, to have it terminated, and to reclaim the goods or place a lien—a legal claim—against them.

Warranties

Warranties   Article 2 of the UCC also sets forth the law of warranties for sales transactions. Products carry two basic types of warranties: an *express warranty* is a specific representation made by the seller regarding the product, and an *implied warranty* is only legally imposed on the seller. Generally, unless implied warranties are disclaimed by the seller in writing, they are automatically in effect. Other provisions govern the rights of acceptance, rejection, and inspection of products by the buyer; the rights of the parties during manufacture, shipment, delivery, and passing of title to products; the legal significance of sales documents; and the placement of the risk of loss in the event of destruction or damage to the products during manufacture, shipment, or delivery.

Negotiable Instruments

Negotiable Instruments   The term **negotiable instrument** refers to commercial paper that is transferable among individuals and businesses. The most common example of a negotiable instrument is a check. Drafts, certificates of deposit, and notes are also sometimes considered negotiable instruments.

Article 3 of the UCC specifies that a negotiable instrument must be written and must meet the following conditions:

1. It must be signed by the maker or drawer.
2. It must contain an unconditional promise or order to pay a certain sum of money.
3. It must be payable on demand or at a definite time.
4. It must be payable to order or to bearer.

Checks and other forms of commercial paper are transferred when the payee signs the back of the instrument, a procedure known as *endorsement*.

Property Law and Law of Bailment

Property law is a key feature of the private enterprise system. *Property* is something for which a person or firm has the unrestricted right of possession or use. Property rights are guaranteed and protected by the U.S. Constitution. However, under certain circumstances property may be legally seized. In a recent ruling by the U.S. Supreme Court, the city of New London, Connecticut, was granted permission to seize a distressed area of real estate—owned by individual citizens—for future economic development by private business. In response, several states are now proposing laws to ban such practices.[15]

As Figure 2 shows, property can be divided into three basic categories. *Tangible personal property* consists of physical items such as equipment, supplies, and delivery vehicles. *Intan-*

Figure

2   Three Basic Types of Property

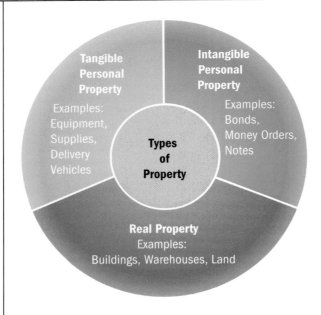

Types of Property

Tangible Personal Property
Examples: Equipment, Supplies, Delivery Vehicles

Intangible Personal Property
Examples: Bonds, Money Orders, Notes

Real Property
Examples: Buildings, Warehouses, Land

gible personal property is nonphysical property such as mortgages, stocks, and checks that are most often represented by a document or other written instrument, although it may be as vague and remote as a computer entry. You are probably familiar with certain types of intangible personal property such as checks or money orders. But other examples include bonds, notes, letters of credit, and warehouse receipts.

A third category of property is *real property*, or real estate. All firms have some interaction with real estate law because of the need to buy or lease the space in which they operate. Some companies are created to serve these real estate needs. Real estate developers, builders, contractors, brokers, appraisers, mortgage companies, escrow companies, title companies, and architects all deal with various aspects of real property law.

The law of bailment deals with the surrender of personal property by one person to another when the property is to be returned at a later date. The person delivering the property is known as the *bailor*, and the person receiving the property is the *bailee*. Some bailments benefit bailees, others benefit bailors, and still others provide mutual benefits. Most courts now require that all parties practice reasonable care in all bailment situations. The degree of benefit received from the bailment is a factor in court decisions about whether parties have met the reasonable-care standards.

Bailment disputes are most likely to arise in business settings such as hotels, restaurants, banks, and parking lots. A series of rules have been established to govern settlement of these disagreements. The law focuses on actual delivery of an item. For instance, a restaurant owner is not liable if a customer's coat or purse is stolen from the back of his or her chair. This is because the customer has not given the item to the restaurant for safekeeping. However, if the customer delivers the coat or purse to the restaurant checkroom, receives a claim check, and the item is stolen, then the restaurant is liable.

TRADEMARKS, PATENTS, AND COPYRIGHTS

Trademarks, patents, and copyrights provide legal protection for key business assets by giving a firm the exclusive right to use those assets. A **trademark** consists of words, symbols, or other designations used by firms to identify their offerings. The Lanham Act (1946) provides for federal registration of trademarks. Trademarks are a valuable commercial property. For instance, Coca-Cola is considered the world's most widely recognized trademark, so it is very valuable to the company.

If a product becomes too well known, its fame can create problems. Once a trademark becomes a part of everyday usage, it loses its protection as a legal trademark. Consider the fate of *aspirin*, *cola*, *nylon*, *kerosene*, and *linoleum*. All these product names were once the exclusive property of their manufacturers, but they have passed into common language, and now anyone can use them. Companies often attempt to counter this threat by advertising that a term is actually a registered trademark. As more firms expand overseas, unintentional overlap between trademarks occurs. Recently, the Indian software firm Wipro, which holds 180 trademarks in India and 3 registered trademarks in Japan, was served notice by the German advertising firm Wipro Werbeagentur, alleging infringement of the German company's trademark. Wipro software denied the allegations.[16] In another international dispute, India's Jet Airways, which was founded in 1993 and plans to begin service between Mumbai and Newark International Airport in New Jersey, has been accused by another Jet Airways (based in Maryland) of trademark infringement.[17]

A **patent** guarantees an inventor exclusive rights to an invention for seventeen years. Copyrights and patents have a constitutional basis; the U.S. Constitution specifies that the federal government has the power "to promote the progress of science and useful arts, by securing for limited times to authors and inventors the exclusive rights to their respective writings or discoveries." Recently, the patent process and patent laws have been under scrutiny. Congress has approved a fee hike in order to hire 900 more staff in an attempt to speed the patent process. In addition, business trade groups have recommended a review that would allow the patent office instead of courts to deal with complaints. A proposal has also been floated to award a patent to the first person to file—instead of trying to prove who came up with the idea for an invention first.[18]

A **copyright** protects written or printed material such as books, designs, cartoon illustrations, photos, computer software, music, and videos. This class of business property is referred to as *intellectual property*. Copyrights are filed with the Library of Congress. Congress recently extended copyright protection for creative material by an additional 20 years, covering artistic works for the lifetime of the creator plus 70 years; for companies the time is 95 years. Not surprisingly, the Internet has opened up a whole new realm of copyright infringement, ranging from downloading music files to illegally sharing video footage. Recently, people suspected of using the popular BitTorrent file-sharing program to obtain versions of the movie *Star Wars Episode III: Revenge of the Sith* were served search warrants for copyright infringement.[19]

As mentioned earlier, the U.S. Supreme Court has ruled that Internet file-sharing services will be held accountable if they intend for their customers to use the software illegally. "We hold that one who distributes a device with the object of promoting it to infringe copyright, as shown by the clear expression or other affirmative steps taken to foster infringement, is liable for the resulting acts of infringement by third parties," wrote Justice David H. Souter.[20] And the U.S. government is becoming stricter about piracy of U.S. property from overseas. "Before Russia enters the [World Trade Organization], many of us will have to be convinced that the Russian government is serious about cracking down on the theft of intellectual property," said Senator Orrin Hatch, who chairs the Senate copyright subcommittee.[21]

Despite publicity about Internet copyright infringement, many people engage in the practice unintentionally. In an effort to educate children, the director of the U.S. Patent and Trademark Office recently gave a commencement speech to a group of elementary school students in Utah about the seriousness of downloading music, movies, and games illegally from the Internet.[22]

Law of Torts

A **tort** (French for "wrong") refers to a civil wrong inflicted on another person or the person's property. The law of torts is closely related to the law of agency because a business entity, or principal, can be held liable for torts committed by its agents in the course of business dealings. Tort law differs from both criminal and contract law. While criminal law is concerned with crimes against the state or society, tort law deals with compensation for injured people who are the victims of noncriminal wrongs.

Tort cases are often extremely complex and may result in large monetary awards. It is typical to read or hear about cases in which patients are awarded millions of dollars in compensation for inadequate medical care. But what about pets? Lawsuits have surged around pets, their owners, and veterinarians. In the last few years, courts in several states have awarded damages to pet owners whose pets were lost or injured while under veterinary care. In Kentucky, a jury awarded $15,000 to the owner of a German shepherd that did not survive surgery. In California, a judge awarded $28,000 in general damages to the owner of a Rottweiler that had to have its teeth capped after improper dental surgery.[23]

Types of Torts   A tort may be intentional, or it may be caused by negligence. Assault, slander, libel, and fraud are all examples of intentional torts. Businesses can become involved in such cases through the actions of both owners and employees. A security guard who uses excessive force to apprehend an alleged shoplifter may have committed a tort. Under agency law, the guard's employers, such as a shopping mall or retailer, can be also held liable for any damages or injury caused by the security guard.

The other major group of torts result from negligence. This type of tort is based on carelessness rather than intentional behavior that causes injury to another person. Under agency law, businesses can also be held liable for the negligence of their employees or agents. A delivery truck driver who kills a pedestrian while delivering goods creates a tort liability for his or her employer if the accident results from negligence.

Product Liability   An area of tort law known as **product liability** has been developed by both statutory and case law to hold businesses liable for negligence in the design, manufacture, sale, or use of products. Some states have extended the theory of tort law to cover injuries caused by products, regardless of whether the manufacturer is proven negligent. This legal concept is known as *strict product liability*.

The business response to product liability has been mixed. To avoid lawsuits and fines, some recall defective products voluntarily; others decide to fight recall mandates if they believe the recall is not justified. Auto manufacturers and toy makers typically issue voluntary recalls, as do drug manufacturers.

Bankruptcy Law

bankruptcy legal non-payment of financial obligations.

Bankruptcy, legal nonpayment of financial obligations, is a common occurrence in contemporary society. The term *bankruptcy* is derived from *banca rotta*, or "broken bench," referring to the medieval Italian practice of creditors breaking up the benches of merchants who did not pay their bills.

Federal legislation passed in 1918 and revised several times since then provides a system for handling bankruptcies. Bankruptcy has two purposes. One is to protect creditors by providing a way to obtain compensation through debtors' assets. The second goal, which is almost unique to the United States, is to also protect debtors, allowing them to get a fresh financial start.

Federal law recognizes two types of bankruptcy. Under voluntary bankruptcy, a person or firm asks to be judged bankrupt because of inability to repay creditors. Under involuntary bankruptcy, creditors may request that a party be judged bankrupt.

Personal Bankruptcies   With a growing number of individuals amassing large personal debt—often through credit cards—Congress recently revised personal bankruptcy law to make it more difficult for people to erase their debt instead of being held accountable for it. Under the revised law, it will be harder for individuals to file Chapter 7 bankruptcy, which traditionally has wiped out most debt. If their earnings exceed their state's median income, they will instead be required to file Chapter 13 bankruptcy, which sets up a repayment plan as designed by the court. Despite criticism by consumer groups that say that banks and credit card companies have caused the problem by encouraging personal debt, many people agree that the revisions are fair. "This practical reform will help ensure that debtors make a good-faith effort to repay as much as they can afford," said President George W. Bush as he signed the legislation into law. "This new law will help make credit more affordable, because when bankruptcy is less common, credit can be extended to more people at better rates."[24]

Business Bankruptcies   Businesses can also go bankrupt for a variety of reasons—mismanagement, plunging sales, an inability to keep up with changes in the marketplace. Under Chapter 11 a firm may reorganize and develop a plan to repay its debts. Chapter 11 also permits prepackaged bankruptcies, in which companies enter bankruptcy proceedings after obtaining approval of most—but not necessarily all—of their creditors. Often companies can emerge from prepackaged bankruptcies sooner than those that opt for conventional Chapter 11 filings. Airlines have managed to accomplish this, as well as large retailers such as Kmart.

Tax Law

A branch of law that affects every business, employee, and consumer in the United States is tax law. A **tax** is an assessment by a governmental unit. Federal, state, and local governments and special taxing authorities all levy taxes. Appendix B, "Personal Financial Planning," also covers tax law.

tax assessment by a governmental unit.

Some taxes are paid by individuals and some by businesses. Both have a decided impact on contemporary business. Business taxes reduce profits, and personal taxes cut the disposable incomes that individuals can spend on the products of industry. Governments spend their revenue from taxes to buy goods and services produced by businesses. Governments also act as transfer agents, moving tax revenue to other consumers and transferring Social Security taxes from the working population to retired or disabled people.

Governments can levy taxes on several different bases: income, sales, business receipts, property, and assets. The type of tax varies from one taxing authority to the other. The individual income tax is the biggest source of revenue for the federal government. Many states also rely heavily on income taxes as well as sales taxes, which vary widely. Cities and towns may collect property taxes in order to operate schools and improve roads. So-called luxury taxes are taxes on items like yachts, and sin taxes are levied on items such as cigarettes and alcohol. During the past decade, the issue of whether to tax different types of Internet services and use has been hotly debated.

"They Said It"

"I am convinced that if most members of Congress did their own taxes, we would have had tax reform long ago."
—Bill Archer (b. 1928)
American politician

Business Terms You Need to Know

judiciary 126	business law 127	negotiable instrument 133
law 127	contract 132	bankruptcy 136
common law 127	agency 132	tax 137
statutory law 127	sales law 133	

Other Important Business Terms

Class-Action Fairness Act of 2005 124	breach of contract 132	copyright 135
trial courts 126	damages 132	tort 135
appellate courts 126	Uniform Commercial Code 132	product liability 136
international law 127	trademark 134	
	patent 135	

Projects and Teamwork Applications

1. Many firms incorporate in Delaware. Such choices are at least partially because Delaware regularly updates its corporate laws. A recent update permits the roughly 500,000 corporations registered in Delaware to hold electronic annual meetings. Delaware also allows annual meetings to be held via Web, e-mail, or fax. What is your opinion of the first state's novel approach to corporate governance? What advantages and disadvantages do you think can result? Discuss your opinions with the class.

2. When a business loses its case in a trial, it may have a chance to appeal to a higher appellate court. That's what the accounting firm Arthur Andersen did after being found guilty of destroying certain documents related to its client Enron as the energy giant fell apart. Specifically, Andersen was convicted of "corruptly persuading its employees to destroy documents." Later, the U.S. Supreme Court overturned the ruling because the jury in the lower court had not been told that, in order to find Andersen guilty, they needed to decide that Andersen had acted "knowingly to subvert an investigation."[25] The court's ruling did little to help Andersen, because its employees left to find other work after the first judgment. Do you agree with the Supreme Court ruling? Do you think that businesses should be able to appeal court decisions based on technicalities such as a person's intent? Why or why not? Discuss your views with the class.

3. On your own or with a classmate, use a Web search engine to select and research a state or federal business-related law enacted during the past year. Why was this legislation passed? What were the arguments for and against it? How do you think the new law will affect businesses? Consumers? Society in general?

4. In place of professional fees—typically billed on an hourly basis—some attorneys accept cases on a contingency basis. The attorney earns nothing if he or she loses the case. If the case results in an award, the attorney collects a contingency fee, which is typically 30 percent or more of the total award. On your own or with a classmate, do online research and construct arguments for and against contingency fees.

5. Because it can copy and distribute material anywhere in the world at lightning speed, the Internet has created a whole new challenge for those who create intellectual property—text, music, videos, software, and the like. Some people argue that old copyright laws are obsolete—they may actually stifle technological creativity. Others claim that creators must be protected at all costs. But some are beginning to think in terms of a new copyright, which preserves some rights but relinquishes others. For instance, music artists might ask for permission and payment for the commercial use of their work, but not for noncommercial use. They might allow a certain amount of sampling before purchase.[26] On your own or with a classmate, use a Web search engine to research examples of companies and cases—such as Napster and Grokster—involving Internet file sharing and copyright. Then write your own opinion about what a "new" copyright should cover.

The Second City

The Second City Theater Continuing Case
Second City: First in Comedy

Writer A. J. Liebling derided the city of Chicago as inferior to what he considered the more appealing cities of Paris, London, and, in particular, New York. Indeed, in his articles for the *New Yorker*, he dubbed Chicago "the second city," after New York, which he considered the country's first city. Chicagoans were understandably offended, but a group of young aspiring performers, including many University of Chicago alumni, embraced Liebling's jab and self-mockingly adopted the name "The Second City" for their new cabaret theater.

Second City opened its doors on December 16, 1959, and the theater's unique brand of social and political satire soon made it a Chicago institution. From the beginning, Second City began building its unique "brand" of theater, reaching larger and larger audiences, and over the years the Second City brand grew to become one of the strongest in comedy. Branding was just getting started at many U.S. businesses in the late 1950s when The Second City was founded. This period would come to be known by business historians as "The Marketing Era," when corporations began to adopt a consumer orientation and to distinguish their brand. The success of Second City in Chicago helped foster the establishment and growth of dozens of theaters in the city.

Almost from the theater's inception, alumni have garnered critical and commercial triumphs. Early troupe members Alan Arkin, Barbara Harris, and Severn Darden enjoyed film and theater success, and in the 1970s, many Second City actors, including John Belushi and Dan Aykroyd, gained fame on the (then) new weekly television show *Saturday Night Live*. This trend of achievement has continued and accelerated through the last 25–30 years. Today, many of the most famous comedic television and film stars have in some way traveled through Second City's doors. For many people, Second City's name has become synonymous with live comedic theater. Patrons enjoy the "up close" and interactive experience at a Second City performance, and the theater labors to maintain and build a strong sense of relationship with its audience.

Success for the theater has also bred expansion. In the United States, Second City currently operates in Chicago, Detroit, Denver, and Las Vegas, with training centers in Los Angeles and New York. The oldest offshoot of the theater is in Toronto, which opened its doors in 1973. Since then Second City has maintained strong ties to its Canadian branch. Canada remains Second City's strongest foreign market, where it is currently involved in a significant amount of television and film production, fueled by government funding available for Canadian productions. Also, Second City's Canadian home base of Toronto is the country's media center. Canada is not the only area of international expansion for the company. In 1962, the theater made its first London appearance with an artistic exchange with the English satirical performing group The Establishment. In 1992, Second City began a long-running relationship with the English Theater in Vienna, Austria, and three years later performed in the Edinburgh Fringe Festival in Edinburgh, Scotland.

Kelly Leonard, vice president of The Second City and president of Second City Theatricals, said, "We aren't focused on international growth. However, it's clear that many of our endeavors can potentially translate internationally. Our focus starts on what our base business is, content creation and talent development, and we look at opportunities that grow out of those two core competencies."

Today, three touring companies travel around the globe, bringing Second City performances to remote audiences worldwide. In 2001, one of Second City's touring companies traveled through Saudi Arabia, Kuwait, and the United Arab Emirates, entertaining U.S. troops stationed abroad. In 2002, Second City toured Tokyo, Singapore, Bangkok, and Hong Kong. Recently, the theater has expanded into the high seas, bringing weekly performances to audiences aboard various international cruise lines. These international performances are often attended by English speakers who live on foreign soil, as well as a growing audience of non-native English speakers.

International growth brings increased revenues and audiences but also potential pitfalls. The biggest potential pitfall is relying on an international audience "getting the jokes" created by a U.S.-based theater company. But as foreign audiences learn what makes Americans laugh, the lesson just may come from The Second City—something that might have disappointed A.J. Liebling and others who see Manhattan as the center of the cultural universe.

QUESTIONS

1. Identify how Second City might use technology to expand its markets. What dangers might it face in its use of technology?
2. What value does a Second City performance bring to its customers?
3. Identify specific factors that might drive demand higher and lower for Second City's products.
4. What unique challenges does Second City face as the company tries to expand internationally?

Part 1: Launching Your Global Business and Economics Career

In Part 1, "Business in a Global Environment," you learned about the background and current issues driving contemporary business. The part includes four chapters and an appendix covering such issues as business ethics and social responsibility, economic challenges facing global and domestic business, competing in global markets, and the legal framework for business. Business has always been an exciting career field, whether you choose to start your own company, work at a local business, or set your sights on a position with a multinational corporation. But today's environment is especially attractive because businesses are expanding their horizons to compete in a global economy—and they need dedicated and talented people to help them accomplish their goals. In fact, professional and business service jobs are found in some of the fastest-growing industries in the U.S. economy and are projected to grow by nearly 28 percent over a decade.[1]

So now is the time to explore several different career options that can lead you to your dream job. Each part in this text profiles the many opportunities available in business. Here are a few related to Chapters 1 through 4.

If you're good at number crunching and are interested in how societies and companies function, then maybe a career as an *economist* is in your future. Economists study how resources are allocated, conduct research by collecting and analyzing data, monitor economic trends, and develop forecasts. They look into such vital areas as the cost of energy, foreign trade and exchange between countries, the effect of taxes, and employment levels—both from a big-picture national or global viewpoint and from the perspective of individual businesses. Economists work for corporations to help them run more efficiently, for consulting firms to offer special expertise, or for government agencies to oversee economic decision making. Typically, advanced degrees are needed to climb to top-level positions. Economists usually earn about $72,780 per year.[2]

Or perhaps you are interested in global business. Companies increasingly search the world for the best employees, supplies, and markets. So you could work in the United States for a foreign-based firm such as Nokia or Toyota; abroad in Africa, Asia, Europe, or Latin America for a U.S.-based firm such as Microsoft or Wal-Mart; or with overseas co-workers via computer networks to develop new products for a firm such as General Electric. With technology and telecommunications, distance is no longer a barrier to conducting business. Global business careers exist in all the areas you'll be reading about in this text—business ownership, management, marketing, technology, and finance.

Global business leaders are not born but made—so how can you start on that career path? Here are the three areas that businesses consider when selecting employees for overseas assignment:

- *Competence*—including technical knowledge, language skills, leadership ability, experience, and past performance.
- *Adaptability*—including interest in overseas work, communication and other personal skills, empathy for other cultures, and appreciation for varied management styles and work environments.
- *Personal characteristics*—level of education, experience, and social compatibility with the host country.[3]

Solid experience in your field or company ranks at the top of the list of needed skills. Firms want to send employees who have expertise in their business and loyalty to the firm to represent them overseas. Those who obtain their master of business administration (MBA) degree are reaping rewards financially: in a recent year, the average starting salary for someone with an MBA reached $88,600 and often included signing bonuses in the tens of thousands of dollars.[4] But companies are reluctant to send new graduates abroad immediately. Instead, they invest in training to orient employees to the new assignment.

Knowledge of and interest in other languages and cultures is the second-highest priority. Businesspeople need to function smoothly in another society, so they are selected based on their familiarity with other languages and cultures. Because China is a business hotspot, some people have become fluent in Mandarin Chinese to boost their career prospects.[5] Also, some elementary school systems are even beginning to offer Chinese language classes in addition to their standard offerings of French, Spanish, German, and Russian.

Finally, employees are evaluated on their personal characteristics to be certain that they will fit well in their new country. More and more diversity is appearing among global managers, and a person's talent is still foremost in making assignments. As IBM's vice president of global workforce diversity puts it, "We have to be in compliance with a country's laws and sensitive to its local customs, but we also want the very best talent."[6]

Career Assessment Exercises in Economics and Global Business

1. With the change in the leadership at the U.S. Federal Reserve (the nation's central bank), economists have been highlighted in the news. Alan Greenspan, who retired after eighteen years as head of the Fed, turned over the reins to Benjamin Bernanke. Both men have backgrounds in economics. To get an idea of the role economists play in a federal government agency, research either Greenspan's or Bernanke's background, qualifications, and abilities. Assess how they performed or are performing at the Fed. Now make a list of your own skills. Where is there a match? What do you need to change?

2. To see the effect of the global economy in your town, go to a major retailer. Take a survey of the number of different countries represented in the products on the shelves. Compare your list with those of your classmates to see who found the most countries and what goods those countries provided. Go online to research the career opportunities at the firm's Web site.

3. To learn more about other countries, do research online for a country in which you are interested. Here are two sources that may be useful:

   - *The World Factbook*, published by the Central Intelligence Agency, http://www.cia.gov/cia/publications/factbook. This publication, updated yearly, contains a wealth of information about countries—geography and climate, population statistics, cultural and political information, transportation and communications methods, and economic data.

- *The Wall Street Journal's CollegeJournal* Web site, http://www.collegejournal.com. This site has a Global Careers link, which contains articles on international news and trends, country profiles, and career tips for several countries.

Write a one-page summary of what you found. Make a list of abilities you would need to function well as a businessperson in that country. Concentrate on the areas of competence, adaptability, and personal characteristics. Now formulate a plan to gain those skills.

Starting and Growing Your Business

Part 2

STOCKBYTE

Chapter 5

Options for Organizing Small and Large Businesses

Learning Goals

1. Distinguish between small and large businesses and identify the industries in which most small firms are established.

2. Discuss the economic and social contributions of small business.

3. Describe the reasons that small businesses fail.

4. Describe how the Small Business Administration assists small-business owners.

5. Explain how franchising can provide opportunities for both franchisors and franchisees.

6. Summarize the three basic forms of business ownership and the advantages and disadvantages of each form.

7. Identify the levels of corporate management.

8. Describe recent trends in mergers and acquisitions.

9. Differentiate among private ownership, public ownership, and collective ownership (cooperatives).

DIGITAL VISION/GETTY IMAGES

More than 30 years ago, Don Dionisio Gutierrez and his father, Don Juan Bautista Gutierrez, opened the first Pollo Campero restaurant in their native Guatemala. The new owners probably never thought it would grow into a hugely popular worldwide chain. Yet today Pollo Campero's quick-serve chicken restaurants have millions of ardent fans who love the authentic recipes and nostalgic atmosphere enough to wait in line to get in. Each new-store opening is a big event in its community; when the first Pollo Campero opened in New York City, the mayor attended the ribbon-cutting ceremony.

An immediate hit at home in Guatemala, Pollo Campero—meaning, roughly, "country chicken"—soon became the centerpiece of many well-remembered special occasions, such as family gatherings and celebrations for blue-collar workers and business executives

AP PHOTO/PAT SULLIVAN

"a brand created and developed in Latin America, featuring the favorite dishes of many Latin American countries and offering top-quality service and product to our loyal customers from home and our new and valued customers in the U.S." Children are always welcome, and

Pollo Campero Feeds Hungry Fans— and Their Nostalgia for Home

alike. "This is something very special," said one U.S. customer who grew up in Guatemala City. "It's part of all of our childhoods. It's a piece of our homelands." Says another native Guatemalan now living in Texas, "Every time we had extra money or it was someone's birthday, we'd head for Pollo Campero." When customers emigrated, they brought their fondness for Pollo Campero with them.

The chain's unique fried chicken specialty, with its spicy secret ingredients, grew popular in other Latin American countries as well, and the chain opened stores in Ecuador, Honduras, El Salvador, Nicaragua, and Mexico. Soon U.S. customers traveling to Latin America became aware of Pollo Campero's unique appeal. After selling about 3 million take-out orders from airports in Central America, which both Americans and nostalgic Guatemalans were taking home on the plane to their family and friends, the company opened its first U.S. restaurant in Los Angeles in 2002.

Today the chain comprises about 200 restaurants. Almost 20 of them are franchises in the United States. "We are very proud to be the first restaurant of our kind in the U.S.," says president and CEO Juan Jose Gutierrez,

the restaurants and service standards are definitely family friendly. Charity events, community involvement, and top employee benefits help strengthen the chain's image wherever it goes.

Although the quick-serve market is nearly saturated, Pollo Campero franchises in the United States are expected to grow. "The number of sites we open next year is limited only by how quickly we can find sites and build restaurants," said Jose Cofiño, CEO of the master franchisor for the western United States. One reason for the high expectations is that black and Asian customers are discovering Pollo Campero, and as one restaurant consultant noted, the public clearly sees the chain as "something different or better" in the crowded fast-food market. Once people taste the menu, they tend to come back, even when advertising and promotion are minimal.

Cofiño defines the competition not just as other chicken outlets but also as all eateries: "Somebody is eating across the street," he says in speaking of competitors. "Why are they eating there and not here?" If Pollo Campero continues to offer the special recipes that have filled countless airplanes with mouth-watering smells, that question won't need to be asked again.[1]

If you have ever thought of operating your own business, you are not alone. In fact, on any given day in the United States, more people are trying to start new businesses than are getting married or having children. However, before entering the world of contemporary business, an entrepreneur needs to understand its framework and choose the form the business will take, as Pollo Campero's owners did when they expanded the business to the United States as a series of franchises.

Several variables affect the choice of the best way to organize your business:

- How easily can you set up this type of organization?
- How much financial liability can you afford to accept?
- What financial resources do you have?
- What strengths and weaknesses do you see in other businesses in the industry?
- What are your own strengths and weaknesses?

This chapter begins by focusing on small-business ownership, including the advantages and disadvantages of small-business ventures, the contributions of small business to the economy, and why small businesses succeed and fail. We also look at the services provided by the U.S. government's Small Business Administration. The role of women and minorities in small business is discussed in detail, as well as franchising and global opportunities for small-business owners. We then provide an overview of the three forms of private business ownership—sole proprietorships, partnerships, and corporations. Next, the structures and operations typical of larger companies are explored, followed by a review of mergers, acquisitions, and joint ventures. The chapter concludes with an explanation of public and collective ownership.

MOST BUSINESSES ARE SMALL BUSINESSES

Although many people associate the term *business* with corporate goliaths such as ExxonMobil, Ford, PepsiCo, Pfizer, Microsoft, and Wal-Mart, 89 percent of firms with employees have fewer than 20 people on staff, and 98 percent have fewer than 100 employees.[2] Many U.S. businesses have no payroll at all: more than 15 million people in the United States earn business income without any employees.[3] Almost half the sales in the United States are made by small businesses.[4]

Small business is also the launching pad for entrepreneurs from every sector of the diverse U.S. economy. Thirty-four percent of the nation's 17 million small businesses are owned by women.[5] Hispanic-owned businesses account for 5.8 percent of all U.S. businesses with fewer than 100 employees. Asian Americans own another 4.4 percent, and African Americans own 4 percent.[6]

What Is a Small Business?

small business firm that is independently owned and operated, is not dominant in its field, and meets industry-specific size standards for income or number of employees.

How do you distinguish a small business from a large one? Are sales the key indicator? What about market share or number of employees? The Small Business Administration (SBA), the federal agency most directly involved with this sector of the economy, considers a **small business** to be a firm that is independently owned and operated and is not dominant in its field. The SBA also considers annual sales and number of employees to identify small businesses for specific industries.

- Most manufacturing businesses are considered small if they employ fewer than 500 workers.
- To be considered small, wholesalers must employ no more than 100 workers.
- Most kinds of retailers and other services can generate up to $6 million in annual sales and still be considered a small business.
- An agricultural business is generally considered small if its sales are no more than $750,000 a year.[7]

The SBA has established size standards for specific industries. These standards, which range from $500,000 to $25 million in sales and from 100 to 1,500 for employees, are available at the SBA's "What Is a Small Business" Web page, http://www.sba.gov/size.

An excellent example of a small business—and its owner—is Barbara Kavovit, founder of New York City–based Barbara K! Enterprises, which sells user-friendly tool kits to women who are inexperienced do-it-yourselfers. Kits come in blue-gray cases that contain easy-to-understand instructions plus all the tools and parts needed for household repairs. Roadside safety and dorm survival kits are also available on the company's Web site or at Home Depot and JCPenney stores.[8] Barbara K!—a $5 million company—has an appropriate motto: "If I can do it, so can you."

Because government agencies offer benefits designed to help small businesses compete with larger firms, small-business owners want to determine whether their companies meet the standards for small-business designation. If it qualifies, a company may be eligible for government loans or for government purchasing programs that encourage proposals from smaller suppliers.

Typical Small-Business Ventures

For decades, small businesses have competed against some of the world's largest organizations, as well as multitudes of other small companies. For example, Shoes for Crews, a 160-employee manufacturer of work shoes in West Palm Beach, Florida, competes against much larger shoe companies, such as Wolverine and Timberland, which have more than 5,000

AP PHOTO/TAMMIE ARROYO

Barbara Kavovit started her first small business as a general contractor in New York City and worked for corporate clients such as IBM, Carnegie Hall, and Polo Ralph Lauren. She started Barbara K! to make power tools and do-it-yourself kits easier for women to use.

employees and sales of $1 billion and $1.5 billion, respectively. How can it compete against these big firms? By offering a serious nonslip guarantee. If a worker slips and falls while wearing its shoes, it pays up to $5,000 per claim. That guarantee is why the Cheesecake Factory, which employs 25,000 employees in 97 restaurants, encourages its workers to buy from Shoes for Crews. Vice President Kurt Leisure said, "The warranty is obviously a big incentive for us to get as many employees as possible into their shoes. It's very shrewd on their part."[9]

The past fifteen years have seen a steady erosion of small businesses in many industries as larger firms have bought out small independent businesses and replaced them with larger operations. For example, the number of independent bookstores and hardware stores has fallen dramatically as Borders Books, Barnes & Noble, Home Depot, and Lowe's have dramatically increased their stores over the last decade. But as Table 5.1 reveals, the businesses least likely to be gobbled up and consolidated into larger firms are those that sell services, not things; rely on consumer trust and proximity; and keep their overhead costs low.

For centuries, most nonfarming small businesses have been concentrated in retailing and the service industries. Recently many entrepreneurs have started successful businesses by providing time-starved homeowners with customized services such as housekeeping, lawn care, and home and computer repair. The small size of such a business allows it to cater to customers in ways that big companies can't. See the accompanying "Business Etiquette" feature for some ideas about how to manage an operation that requires working in other people's homes and on their property.

Table

5.1

David vs. Goliath: Business Sectors Most Dominated and Least Dominated by Small Firms

Most Likely to Be a Small Firm	Fewer Than 20 Workers
Home builders	97%
Florists	97%
Hair salons	96%
Auto repair	96%
Funeral homes	94%

Least Likely to Be a Small Firm	Fewer Than 20 Workers
Paper mills	25%
Nursing homes	27%
Oil pipelines	33%
Electric utilities	42%
Railroad car makers	42%

Source: U.S. Census Bureau, "Number of Firms, Number of Establishments, Employment, and Annual Payroll by Employment Size of the Enterprise for the United States, All Industries," accessed August 31, 2005, http://www.census.gov.

As Figure 5.1 indicates, small businesses provide most jobs in the construction, agricultural services, wholesale trade, services, and retail trade industries. Retailing is another important industry for today's small businessperson. Merchandising giants such as Target and Wal-Mart may be the best-known retailing firms, but small, privately owned retail stores far outnumber them. Small-business retailing includes stores that sell shoes, jewelry, office supplies and stationery, clothing, flowers, drugs, convenience foods, and thousands of other products. People wishing to form their own business have always been attracted to retailing because of the ability to start a firm with limited funds, rent a store rather than build a facility, create a Web site, and use family members to staff the new business.

Powell's Books, based in Portland, Oregon, is one of the most successful retail bookstores in the United States. In contrast to "big box" superstores such as Barnes & Noble and Books-A-Million, which use their huge buying power to secure lower prices for large orders and Amazon.com's well-known high-tech, stock-everything strategy, Powell's competes by specializing in used, sometimes hard-to-find, books. Through its seven bookstores and its Web site (http://www.powells.com), Powell's serves customers who like buying from an independent store instead of one of the larger chains and who don't mind paying extra to find something special to read. Their unique strategies permit Powell's and Amazon to benefit one another. Powell's buys returned books from Amazon.com at a discount and sells them as used books. Amazon

Figure

5.1

Major Industries Dominated by Small Businesses

Industry

Construction 90
Agricultural Services 88
Wholesale Trade 66
Services 56
Retail Trade 51

Percentage of firms with fewer than 500 employees

Source: Office of Advocacy, U.S. Small Business Administration, "Small Business Profile: United States," accessed June 17, 2006, http://www.sba.gov/advo.

fills orders for out-of-print books through Powell's. This strategy will never make Powell's the largest bookseller, but that is just fine with the retailer's founder, Michael Powell.[10]

Small business also plays a significant role in agriculture. Although most farm acreage is in the hands of large corporate farms, most farmers still operate as small businesses. Most U.S. farms are owned by individual farmers or families, not partners or shareholders.[11] The family farm is a classic example of a small-business operation. It is independently owned and operated, with relatively few employees, relying instead on the labor of family members. But today's small farmers must combine savvy business and marketing techniques to thrive, like California-based Earthbound Farm (http://www.ebfarm.com), which grows, packages, and sells organic salads, vegetables, fruits, and dried fruits.

Just over half of small businesses in the United States are **home-based businesses**—firms operated from the residence of the business owner.[12] Between 1960 and 1980, fewer people worked at home, largely because the number of farmers, doctors, and lawyers in home-based practices was declining. But since then, the number of people working at home has more than doubled. A major factor in this growth is the increased availability of personal computers with access to the Internet and other communications devices such as fax machines and cell phones. As computer technology evolves rapidly and more workers prefer the flexibility of working from alternative locations, it is predicted that the number of home-based businesses will grow even faster.[13] Sometimes, however, office space is needed for a meeting or conference or to convey an image of solidity and professionalism. New options for renting such space are springing up in response to the growth of small business, but owners should be wary about projecting an image they can't

live up to, as the "Solving an Ethical Controversy" feature discusses.

Lower costs are one of the main reasons that the number of home-based businesses is growing so quickly. Financing a small business is a difficult challenge, so by not leasing or maintaining separate office or warehouse space, a home-based business owner can pour precious

(b)usiness (e)tiquette

Tips for Your Small Business When Working in Customers' Homes

A growing number of entrepreneurs are starting businesses that operate in other people's homes. Housekeeping, handyman, home improvement, lawn care, computer repair, and other service-based businesses are experiencing rapid growth, and their owners and employees need to be considerate about working in customers' private spaces. Here are some tips for in-home services of all kinds.

1. Wear (or have employees wear) a uniform, not only to establish a sense of professionalism but also to identify yourself and your business to the customer.
2. Be on time. Allow yourself extra time for traffic or other problems, and phone if a delay is unavoidable.
3. Take two steps backward after ringing the doorbell, remove your sunglasses if any, and present your business card when the door is opened.
4. If no adults are at home, wait in your car or truck until a parent arrives.
5. If the homeowner needs to prepare for your work by clearing up toys from the floor or yard, confining a dog, or making sure the yard or pool is not in use, call the night before to remind the customer to expect you.
6. Keep your eyes to yourself; never pry into customers' belongings or areas that are off-limits. As one owner of a handyman franchise suggests, "Pretend everything you see is perfectly normal."
7. Never use foul language while working in the client's home.
8. Be considerate. Always advise the customer before using any machinery that's noisy, use tarps or drop cloths, and contain and remove any waste or debris. Take special care not to leave any tools or equipment behind.
9. Avoid becoming involved in any conversations that might be going on in the home, particularly disagreements.
10. Remember that satisfying the customer is what a service business is all about. If the customer isn't happy, make whatever adjustments are needed to satisfy the promises you've made.

Sources: Gwendolyn Bounds, "Handyman Etiquette: Stay Calm, Avert Eyes," *Wall Street Journal Online*, accessed June 17, 2006, http://www.startupjournal.com; Deborah Crawford, "Great Customer Service," Bella Online, accessed June 17, 2006, http://www.bellaonline.com; "Lawn Care Success Tip of the Week," Lawn Care Success, accessed September 16, 2005, http://www.lawncaresuccess.com.

IS IT ETHICAL TO MAKE YOUR BUSINESS APPEAR LARGER THAN IT IS?

What if clients want to visit your office, but you don't have one? Or what if it's damp and dark because it's your basement? Many shoestring entrepreneurs face this problem. A popular new solution is to rent temporary offices equipped with everything from receptionists and bottled water to computers, fax machines, potted plants and paintings, videoconferencing capability, and voice-mail services.

Some "flex spaces" offer technology support, mail delivery, maintenance, security, and even fellow renters to network with. Convenient leases cost a fraction of what permanent space commands, but while flex space helps start-ups appear large and well established, there are dangers.

"There is a fine line between fraud and puffery," says an ethics professor at UCLA. "When you cross the line is when you have a client with a big project and a lot of money at stake and they're fooled into thinking you're much larger and more capable than you really are."

Tricks that edge entrepreneurs toward that line include filling offices with family members, getting friends to follow up with clients to create the illusion of staff, and printing business cards with different job titles for different occasions.

Should small and entrepreneurial companies try to make themselves seem larger?

PRO

1. Making a business appear larger is a competitive strategy, and no one is lying to the client.
2. If clients think you're on a shoestring budget, they may assume you aren't busy, aren't well established, or have financial difficulties.

CON

1. Clients won't worry about size if you project expertise and reliability. Outsourcing is common these days, so there is nothing to hide or disguise.
2. Pretending you are something you are not is inherently dishonest even if no outright lies are told.

SUMMARY

Partnering with larger companies, attending trade shows, and using promotional tools such as press releases to get mentioned in industry publications are alternate ways to project a big image. As one public-relations CEO says, "You can look bigger; you can use strategies that play on people's perceptions; but if confronted with a question, you'd best tell the truth."

Sources: Kortney Stringer, "Temporary Offices Offer the Best of Both Worlds," *StartupJournal*, accessed June 17, 2006, http://www.startupjournal.com; Geoff Williams, "Creative License," *Entrepreneur*, accessed June 17, 2006, http://www.entrepreneur.com; Nicole Gull, "Move-In Ready," *Inc.*, March 2005, pp. 48, 51.

solving an **ETHICAL** controversy

"They Said It"

"Size certainly matters, and not always in a positive way."
Michael Powell (b. 1941)
Founder and owner, Powell's Books

funds into the business itself. Some home-based business owners have even discovered the benefits of selling their goods through eBay, the online auction site. Ron Jones, who helped his wife Jan start their home-based business, Beads, Creativity, and You, on eBay, said, "If you want to be in business for yourself, it's a great way to do it. It keeps the overhead down—you don't have to have a storefront."[14] The cost of operating from home through eBay is far less than the cost of leasing, staffing, and maintaining a retail store at a high-traffic shopping mall, not to mention the far greater number of consumers eBay reaches.

Other benefits of a home-based business include greater flexibility and freedom from the time and expense of commuting. Drawbacks include isolation and less visibility to customers—except, of course, if your customers visit you online. In that case, they don't care where your office is located.

Many small-business start-ups are more competitive because of the Internet. An estimated three of every five small businesses have an online presence. But the Internet does not automatically guarantee success, as illustrated by the thousands of dot-com failures during the early years of e-commerce. Still, setting up a Web site can be relatively inexpensive and enables a business to reach a huge marketplace.

Tiny Salem Five Cents Savings Bank, a Massachusetts firm with only thirteen branches, has a significant presence on the Internet. It established that presence by acting quickly in the mid-1990s, when Internet banking was still an innovation. Consumers liked the new service and low fees, and before long, Salem Five had attracted thousands of new customers. When bigger banks began adding Internet service, Salem Five honed its focus to New England, where the bank already had a good reputation, and then became the first bank to offer every one of its services, from personal and business banking to mortgages and investing, on the Internet, which earned the company recognition as the Internet Bank of the Year. Today, Salem Five continues to innovate and has opened branches with automated-teller machines and Internet kiosks offering videoconferencing with bank representatives. High technology coupled with concern for customer service keeps Salem Five in business even as the biggest banks spend millions of dollars on advertising.[15]

American business history is filled with inspirational stories of great inventors who launched companies in barns, garages, warehouses, and attics. For young visionaries such as Apple Computer founders Steve Jobs and Steve Wozniak, the logical option for transforming their technical idea into a commercial reality was to begin work in a family garage. The impact of today's entrepreneurs, including home-based businesses, is discussed in more depth in Chapter 6.

COPYRIGHT © 2006, UNITED POSTAL SERVICE OF AMERICA, INC.

Home-based businesses have low costs because their owners aren't spending precious startup funds on office or warehouse space. And as this UPS promotion shows, the only thing that home-based businesses need to ship their products worldwide is an Internet connection, or "About 17 inches."

CONTRIBUTIONS OF SMALL BUSINESS TO THE ECONOMY

Small businesses form the core of the U.S. economy. Businesses with fewer than 500 employees generate 39 percent of total U.S. sales and more than half the nation's gross domestic product. Ninety-two of every 100 U.S. businesses are small businesses. In addition, small businesses employ almost half of the nation's private nonfarm workforce.[16]

Creating New Jobs

Small businesses make tremendous contributions to the U.S. economy and to society as a whole. One impressive contribution is the number of new jobs created each year by small businesses. While it varies from year to year, on average three of every four new jobs are created by companies with fewer than 500 employees.[17] A significant share of these jobs was created by the smallest companies—those with four or fewer employees. Small firms are dominant factors in many of the industries that have added the most jobs: construction trade contractors, wholesale trade, amusement and recreation, service businesses, restaurants, and engineering and management services.[18]

Even if you never plan to start your own business, you will probably work for a small business at some point in your career. Not only do small firms employ about half of all U.S. workers, but they are more likely than large firms to employ the youngest (and oldest) workers. In addition, as detailed in a later section of this chapter, small businesses offer significant opportunities to women and minorities.

Small businesses also contribute to the economy by hiring workers who traditionally have had difficulty finding jobs at larger firms. Compared with large companies, small businesses are more likely to hire former welfare recipients.[19] Driven in part by their limited budgets,

assessment check

1. What characteristics does the SBA use to determine whether a business is a small business?

2. Identify three industries in which small businesses are common.

"They Said It"

"You may not think you're going to make it. You may want to quit. But if you keep your eye on the ball, you can accomplish anything."
Hank Aaron (b. 1934)
American baseball legend

small businesses may be more open to locating in economically depressed areas, where they contribute to rehabilitating neighborhoods and reducing unemployment.

Creating New Industries

The small-business sector also gives entrepreneurs an outlet for developing their ideas and perhaps for creating entirely new industries. Many of today's successful high-tech firms—Microsoft, Dell, Cisco Systems, Yahoo!, and Google—began as small businesses. Most high-tech startups are looking for growth, too, sometimes by moving overseas in creative ways. See the "Hit and Miss" feature for just one example of small business on a global scale.

The growth of new businesses and new industries not only provides new goods and services but also fuels local economies. Tucker Technology provides full-service telecommunications and information technology solutions for *Fortune* 500 companies. Tucker, which is based in Oakland, California, has 132 employees, half of whom live in the local neighborhood. Also, 15 percent of its employees got their jobs when founder Frank Tucker went to community-based organizations that help local people learn new job skills. Tucker said, "I'd see all the human resources on the street corner. Clearly, they had no jobs to go to." So he began hiring them at more than $20 an hour to install network and phone cables in office buildings.[20] For more information on the dramatic effects that small businesses can have on local economies, see http://www.theinnercity100.org.

New industries are sometimes created when small businesses adapt to provide needed services to the larger corporate community. The movement toward corporate downsizing that began in the early 1990s created a demand for other businesses to perform activities previously handled by company employees. Outsourcing such activities as security, maintenance, employee benefits management, and transportation services created opportunities that were often filled by small businesses.

Finally, new industries can be created when small businesses adapt to shifts in consumer interests and preferences. Over the last few years the explosion of wireless Internet access in schools, restaurants, airports, hotels, and cities (some of which are installing wireless access to be used by their entire citizenry) has created tremendous growth opportunities. InterDigital Communications of King of Prussia, Pennsylvania, designs wireless technology chips and devices that are used in mobile phones, personal digital assistants, laptop computers, and other wireless digital devices. With the coming shift to 3G wireless capabilities with speeds up to 2 megabits per second, InterDigital's patents and products will enable consumers to quickly and easily download music, video, and other kinds of digital files and services whenever and wherever they want.[21]

Innovation

Small businesses are much better than large businesses at developing new and better goods and services. Although the DVD rental market was dominated by Blockbuster Video, Reed Hastings knew that there just had to be a better way. Perhaps it was that $40 late fee he had to pay Blockbuster when he forgot to return *Apollo 13*, but Hastings recalls asking himself, "How come movie rentals don't work like a health club, where whether you use it a lot or a little, you get the same charge?" And from that question, Netflix.com, the first successful online DVD rental service, was born.

Today, after just a few years in business, the Californian heads a company with more than 3 million subscribers, a DVD library of 50,000 titles, and revenue approaching $1.2 billion.[22] DVDs are mailed to subscribers and returned in prepaid postage envelopes provided by Netflix. Because they can rent several movies at a time without late fees, Netflix customers rent twice as many movies per month. Netflix is so successful that Wal-Mart discontinued its DVD

HIT & MISS

Tacit Networks Builds a Global Alliance

You've got a hot product or service that you're eager to export overseas. But the problem is that your U.S. operation, while successful, is small—efficient, creative, and experienced, but small. There's no easy way to buy the labor or experience needed to launch overseas operations and deal with differences in language, culture, and legal systems.

That's the problem that faced Tacit Networks, a New Jersey–based technology firm whose software lets networks share files instantly, no matter how far apart they are. With 60 employees and revenue of less than $5 million, Tacit had to come up with a way to build a global business from scratch.

The answer was to find partners first instead of clients. Tacit took its first steps into the European market by contacting technology companies interested in selling just the sort of software Tacit makes. Its first such partner, a London-based tech consulting firm called Solution Centre, agreed to a partnership in which Tacit would sell Solution its software at a 30 to 40 percent discount. Solution sells the software to end users, and Tacit provides tech support. The partnership's first client was the firm that introduced the two partners, and Solution Centre has been helping Tacit look for other business.

Similar partnership deals have since been signed, with tech firms acting as Tacit's resellers in Denmark, Ireland, and Germany. Tacit's overseas partners sign a nondisclosure agreement to protect Tacit's intellectual property. Its latest deal is with a California manufacturer of communications equipment that has a big market in Europe and will sell the file-sharing software preinstalled. "With this kind of partner," says CEO Chuck Foley, "they can't be swayed to the competition as easily."

So how have Tacit's partnerships paid off? Sales have doubled to $10 million as international sales have climbed to 20 percent of Tacit's revenue. Meanwhile, the firm continues to expand; it now has its own offices in England and Australia.

Questions for Critical Thinking

1. Can Tacit's strategy for moving overseas apply to other small-business efforts? Why or why not?
2. Has Tacit done enough to ensure that its intellectual property will remain secure? Why or why not? What makes such precautions necessary?

Sources: Tacit Networks Web site, accessed June 17, 2006, http://www.tacitnetworks .com; Lucas Mearian, "Backing Up the Edge," *Computerworld*, accessed June 17, 2006, http://www.computerworld.com; Laura Kolodny, "Building a Global Alliance," *Inc.*, September 2003, p. 48.

---

rental business, choosing instead to offer Netflix DVD rentals at Wal-Mart.com. Netflix's success has also forced Blockbuster to eliminate the late fees that accounted for most of its profits.[23]

Small businesses are often fertile ground in which to plant innovative ideas for new goods and services. As a chemist in the pharmaceutical industry, Thomas E. D'Ambra saw many exciting ideas neglected because his employer lacked the resources to pursue them. D'Ambra decided that a market existed for a company that would offer research services on a contract basis to firms in the industry. His start-up business, Albany Molecular Research in Albany, New York, focused on obtaining contracts for research and development of new drugs. Today, the company employs 200 chemists and tackles research projects for such industry giants as DuPont Pharmaceuticals and Eli Lilly. With his customers facing a continued shortage of talented chemists, D'Ambra foresees a strong future for Albany Molecular.[24]

In a typical year, small firms develop twice as many product innovations per employee as larger firms. They also obtain more patents per sales dollar than do larger businesses. In addition, the fact that small firms are a richer source of innovations is even more evident than these statistics show because large firms are more likely to patent their discoveries.[25] Key 20th-century innovations that were developed by small businesses include the airplane, the audiotape recorder, double-knit fabrics, the optical scanner, the personal computer, soft contact lenses, and the zipper. One area of innovation that is likely to occupy small businesses

HIT & MISS

Steve Lipscomb, Bluffing His Way to the Top

A lawyer with an entrepreneurial frame of mind, Steve Lipscomb has created a new model of televised poker. After winning a $10,000 prize at a local poker tournament in the World Series of Poker, Lipscomb realized that ESPN, which televised the event, was missing a bet. The broadcasts were "worse than watching paint dry," he says.

The world of high-stakes poker already had several big annual events and tournaments. Lipscomb pulled them all together and created the World Poker Tour (WPT), modeled on the PGA Tour in golf. As Lipscomb says, "I created the only sports league in America where you can come out and play. If you could sell spots for people to suit up and play in the NBA finals for, say, $25,000, many people would do it. But you can't. Here, you can pay your money and compete with the best players in the world. And you can win."

Lipscomb made his dream a debt-free reality by acquiring start-up financing and signing on high-profile casinos that already hosted big events. Next, he created graphics to make viewing exciting. Icons of the cards, the players' names, and the amounts of the bets appear on the TV screen, along with a continual update on each player's odds of winning the game. With everything in place, Lipscomb needed just one more thing—a network partner. He found one in the Travel Channel, an unlikely but happy marriage that has brought the WPT a broad audience. Licensed WPT products completed the picture.

WPT's sponsor-funded prize pools recently passed $10 million, and a celebrity tournament helped bring revenue past $17 million. Although competing shows with similar graphics are springing up on channels such as Bravo and Fox Sports, Lipscomb is confident that "we make the best television." And besides, WPT already has casinos such the Bellagio, Foxwoods, Borgata, Commerce, and the Bicycle Casino on board. Says Lipscomb, "*The New York Times* said that 50 million people were playing poker on a regular basis, and no one had branded it. This became our mission."

Questions for Critical Thinking

1. Which of the steps Lipscomb took to turn an idea into a business would apply to other entrepreneurial ventures? Which were unique to the kind of business he wanted to create?
2. Lipscomb has applied for a patent to protect the graphics he developed for his broadcasts. What else can he do to prevent competitors from adopting too many of his innovations?

Sources: Allyn Jaffrey Shulman, "Steve Lipscomb Changes the Face of Poker," *Card Player*, accessed June 17, 2006, http://www.cardplayer.com; Wendeen Eolis, "Lyle Berman and Steve Lipscomb's Confection: A Poker Tournament Season on National Television," PokerPages.com, accessed September 12, 2005, http://www.pokerpages.com; Larry Olmsted, "How Steve Lipscomb Reinvented Poker and Built the Hottest Business in America," *Inc.*, May 2005, pp. 80–92.

assessment check

1. To what extent do small businesses help create new jobs?
2. In what ways do small businesses contribute to the economy?

during the early years of the 21st century is security—whether it's the protection of information or people. The "Hit & Miss" feature presents another hot business venture—the entrepreneur who designed the World Poker Tour.

WHY SMALL BUSINESSES FAIL

While small businesses benefit the economy by creating new jobs, new industries, and various innovations, small businesses are much more likely to fail than large businesses, especially during economic downturns. Why? Because of management shortcomings, inadequate financing, and difficulty dealing with government regulations. These issues—quality and depth of management, availability of financing, and ability to wade through government rules and requirements—are so important that small businesses with major deficiencies in one or more of these areas may find themselves in bankruptcy proceedings.

As Figure 5.2 shows, almost one new business in three will permanently close within two years of opening, half will close within four years, and 62 percent will fail within the first six years of operation. By the tenth year, 82 of every 100 businesses will have failed. Although highly motivated and well-trained business owner-managers can overcome these potential problems, they should thoroughly analyze whether one or more of these problems may threaten the business before deciding to launch the new company.

Management Shortcomings

Among the most common discoveries at a postmortem examination of a small-business failure is inadequate management. Business founders often possess great strengths in specific areas such as marketing or interpersonal relations, but they may suffer from hopeless deficiencies in others such as finance or order fulfillment. Large firms recruit specialists trained to manage individual functions; small businesses frequently rely on small staffs who must be adept at a variety of skills.

An even worse result occurs when people go into business with little, if any, business training. Some new businesses are begun almost entirely on the basis of what seems like a great idea for a new product. Managers assume that they will acquire needed business expertise on the job. All too often, the result is business bankruptcy.

If you are contemplating starting a new business, heed some words of warning. First, learn the basics of business. Second, recognize your own limitations. Although most small-business owners recognize the need to seek out the specialized skills of accountants and attorneys for financial and legal assistance, they often hesitate to turn to consultants and advisors for assistance in areas such as marketing, where they may lack knowledge or experience.

Founders of new businesses are typically excited about the potential of newly designed products, so they may neglect important details such as marketing research to determine whether potential customers share their excitement. Individuals considering launching a new business should first determine whether the proposed product meets the needs of a large enough market and whether they can convince the public of its superiority over competing offerings.

Inadequate Financing

Another leading cause of small-business problems is inadequate financing. First-time business owners often assume that their firms will generate enough funds from the first month's sales to finance continuing operations. Building a business takes time, though. Employees must be trained, equipment purchased, deposits paid for rent and utilities, and marketing dollars spent to inform potential customers about the new firm and its product offerings. Even a one-person, home-based business has start-up expenses—such as a new computer or additional phone lines. Unless the owner has set aside enough funds to cover cash shortfalls during the first several months while the business is being established, the venture may collapse at an early stage.

Figure 5.2

Rate of Business Failures

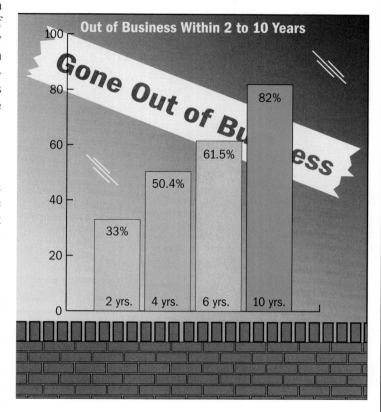

Source: Office of Advocacy, U.S. Small Business Administration, "Frequently Asked Questions: Advocacy Small Business Statistics and Research," accessed June 17, 2006, http://app1.sba.gov/faqs; Amy Knaup, "Survival and Longevity in the Business Employment Dynamics Data," *Monthly Labor Review* (Bureau of Labor Statistics), May 2005, p. 50.

After surviving the cash crunch that often accompanies the first months of operation, a business must confront another major financial problem: uneven cash flows. For most small and large businesses, cash inflows and outflows fluctuate greatly at different times of the year. Small retail outlets generate much of their annual sales revenues during the December holiday period. Florists make most of their deliveries during three holidays: Valentine's Day, Easter, and Mother's Day. Large firms may build sufficient cash reserves to weather periods of below-average sales, or they can turn to banks and other lenders for short-term loans. By contrast, small business start-ups often lack both cash reserves and access to sources of additional funds.

Another reason that small businesses are inadequately financed is that they rely less on debt for financing than large businesses do; 47 percent of small businesses have no outstanding loans at all, and another 25 percent have just one loan to pay off.[26] But when small firms need loans, the most frequent source of funding, as shown in Figure 5.3, is trade credit, that is, buying goods and agreeing to pay for them later, usually within 30 to 60 days. The next most commonly used sources of financing are personal credit cards, loans from commercial banks,

Figure

5.3

Sources of Small-Business Financing

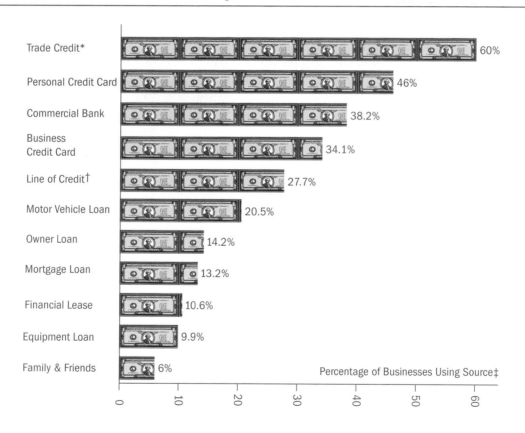

	Percentage of Businesses Using Source‡
Trade Credit*	60%
Personal Credit Card	46%
Commercial Bank	38.2%
Business Credit Card	34.1%
Line of Credit†	27.7%
Motor Vehicle Loan	20.5%
Owner Loan	14.2%
Mortgage Loan	13.2%
Financial Lease	10.6%
Equipment Loan	9.9%
Family & Friends	6%

*Trade credit is purchasing goods or equipment from a supplier who finances the purchase by delaying the date of payment for those goods.

†A line of credit is an agreement between a bank and a borrower, indicating the maximum amount of credit the bank will extend to the borrower.

Note: Total exceeds 100 percent because businesses typically use more than one source of financing.

Source: Small Business Administration, Office of Advocacy, "Financing Patterns of Small Firms," accessed June 17, 2006, http://www.sba.gov/advo; Susan Coleman, "Free and Costly Trade Credit: A Comparison of Small Firms," Academy of Entrepreneurial Finance, accessed June 17, 2006, http://www.aoef.org/papers.

business credit cards, lines of credit from a bank, motor vehicle loans, owner loans in which the owner lends the business money, and then mortgage loans. Figure 5.3 shows that despite their relatively high interest rates, credit cards are an important source of financing for small businesses. The heaviest users of credit cards for business financing are tiny firms with fewer than ten employees. A small-business owner who has a good credit record with a consumer credit card will have relatively easy approval for a corporate credit card. Even a business owner who doesn't have the best credit history will be more apt to win approval on a credit card than on a traditional business loan.[27] As discussed later in this chapter, small-business owners may have other sources of financing as well.

Inadequate financing can compound management shortcomings by making it more difficult for small businesses to attract and keep talented people. Typically, a big company can offer a more attractive benefits package and a higher salary. During the wave of dot-com start-ups, many people decided to take a chance and work for these companies, which often offered stock options—the right to buy stock in a firm at a lower price—in place of higher salaries or better benefits. If a company succeeded, its employees could become rich. If it failed, its workers were left not only without profits but often without jobs.

With less money to spend on employees, successful small companies need to be more creative. Ronald Richey, who runs Precision Plastics, an injection-molding plant in Columbia City, Indiana, watched one-fifth of his employees quit each year. Lacking sufficient employees to operate the factory, he had to keep some of his machinery idle every week. Richey tried better communication and hiring temporary workers, but nothing worked. Then he thought of an innovative arrangement: If employees would work five 6-hour shifts without lunch breaks, he would pay them 40 hours' wages each week for 30 hours of work. Two weeks into the new plan, turnover plummeted—and quality improved. Even with what is effectively a higher pay scale, Precision's profits have grown.[28]

Government Regulation

Small-business owners often complain bitterly about excessive government regulation and red tape. Paperwork costs alone account for billions of small-business dollars each year. A large company can better cope with requirements for forms and reports. Larger firms often find that it makes economic sense to hire or contract with specialists in specific types of regulation, such as employment law and workplace safety regulations. By contrast, small businesses often struggle to absorb the costs of government paperwork because of their more limited staff and budgets. Some small firms close for this reason alone.

Recognizing the burden of regulation on small businesses, Congress sometimes exempts the smallest companies from certain regulations. For example, small businesses with 49 or fewer employees are exempt from the Family and Medical Leave Act, which gives employees up to twelve weeks of unpaid leave each year to take care of a newborn child, adopt a child, or care for a family member who has serious health problems.[29] Most small-business owners comply with employment and other laws, believing that such compliance is ethically correct and fosters better employee relations than trying to determine which regulations don't apply to a small business. To help small businesses obey employment laws, the U.S. Department of Labor provides forms and guidelines at its "elaws Advisors" Web page (http://www .dol.gov/elaws/). Employers can also file these forms online.

Taxes are another burdensome expense for a small business. In addition to local, state, and federal income taxes, employers must pay taxes covering workers' compensation insurance, Social Security payments, and unemployment benefits. Although large companies have similar expenses, they generally have more resources to cover them.

assessment check

1. What percentage of small businesses will still be in business two, four, six, and ten years after starting?

2. How do management shortcomings, inadequate financing, and government regulation make small businesses more likely to fail?

INCREASING THE LIKELIHOOD OF SMALL-BUSINESS SUCCESS

In spite of the challenges just discussed, many small businesses do succeed. How can a prospective owner gain the many advantages of running a smaller firm while also overcoming the disadvantages? Most successful entrepreneurs believe that two recommendations are critical:

- Develop a business plan.
- Use the resources provided by such agencies as the Small Business Administration, local business incubators, and other sources for advice, funding, and networking opportunities.

Creating a Business Plan

Perhaps the most important task a would-be business owner faces is creating a business plan. An effective business plan can mean the difference between a company that succeeds and one that fails. A **business plan** is a written document that provides an orderly statement of a company's goals, the methods by which it intends to achieve these goals, and the standards by which it will measure achievements.

Business plans give the organization a sense of purpose. They provide guidance, influence, and leadership, as well as communicate ideas about goals and the means of achieving them to associates, employees, lenders, and others. In addition, they set standards against which achievements can be measured. Although no single format best suits all situations, a good small-business plan includes the methods and time frames for achieving specific goals (sales, profits, or changes in market share), as well as cash flow projections (both income received by the business and funds disbursed to pay expenses). Because business plans are essential tools for securing funding, the financial section should be thorough, professional, and based on sound assumptions. A business plan also includes the following components:

- An *executive summary* that briefly answers the who, what, why, when, where, and how questions for the business
- An *introduction* that includes a general statement of the concept, purpose, and objectives of the proposed business
- Separate *financial* and *marketing sections* that describe the firm's target market and marketing plan as well as detailed financial forecasts of the need for funds and when the firm is expected to break even—the level of sales at which revenues equal costs
- *Résumés of principals*—especially in plans written to obtain financing

Business plans are discussed in more detail in Appendix C, "Developing a Business Plan," and on the *Contemporary Business* Web site.

Small Business Administration

Small businesses can benefit from using the resources provided by the **Small Business Administration (SBA)**. The SBA is the principal government agency concerned with helping small U.S. firms, and it is the advocate for small businesses within the federal government. Over 3,000 employees staff the SBA's Washington headquarters and its regional and field offices. The primary operating functions of the SBA include providing financial assistance, aiding in government procurement matters, and providing management training and consulting.

Financial Assistance from the SBA   Contrary to popular belief, the SBA seldom provides direct business loans. Its major financing contributions are the guarantees it provides for

business plan written document that provides an orderly statement of a company's goals, the methods by which it intends to achieve those goals, and the standards by which it will measure achievements.

"They Said It"

"Rich people plan for four generations. Poor people plan for Saturday night."
Gloria Steinem (b. 1934) American feminist and journalist

Small Business Administration (SBA) federal agency that aids small businesses by providing management training and consulting, financial assistance, and support in securing government contracts.

small-business loans made by private lenders, including banks and other institutions. Direct SBA loans are available in only a few special situations, such as natural disaster recovery and energy conservation or development programs. For example, after Hurricane Katrina destroyed homes and businesses in New Orleans and the southern coastal regions of Louisiana, Mississippi, and Alabama, the SBA offered small businesses disaster loans up to $1.5 million to repair or replace damaged buildings, equipment, inventory, and supplies.[30] Even in these special instances, a business applicant must contribute a portion of the proposed project's total cost in cash, home equity, or stocks to qualify. However, in the case of Hurricane Katrina, if everything associated with a small business was destroyed, the SBA used the business's real estate as collateral.

The SBA also guarantees **microloans** of up to $35,000 to start-ups and other very small firms.[31] Microloans may be used to buy equipment or operate a business but not to buy real estate or pay off other loans. These loans are available from nonprofit organizations located in most states. Other sources of microloans include the federal Economic Development Administration, some state governments, and certain private lenders, such as credit unions and community development groups.

C. Ray Bergeron salvages his tire inventory as he cleans out the flood-damaged office of his service station in the lakeside area of New Orleans. Bergeron's business was under eight feet of floodwater after Hurricane Katrina hit. Bergeron managed to salvage about $15,000 worth of tires, but the rest of his business was a total loss.

Small-business loans are also available through SBA-licensed organizations called **Small Business Investment Companies (SBICs),** which are run by experienced venture capitalists. SBICs use their own capital, supplemented with government loans, to invest in small businesses. Like banks, SBICs are profit-making enterprises, but they are likely to be more flexible than banks in their lending decisions. Well-known companies that used SBIC financing when they were start-ups include Apple Computer, Callaway Golf, America Online, Federal Express, Intel, Staples, and Outback Steakhouse.

Another financial resource underwritten by the SBA is *Active Capital*, which matches entrepreneurs looking for start-up capital with potential investors willing to exchange their money and advice for partial ownership of the company. Entrepreneurs post information about their businesses on the Active Capital Web site, where potential investors can review it. Interested parties contact the firms. The goal is to help businesses seeking smaller amounts of capital than those typically handled by bigger investment firms. However, small businesses can raise up to $5 million via Active Capital. Why use Active Capital? Because, as a nonprofit organization sanctioned by the SBA, Active Capital charges a small annual fee of $1,000 but no commissions, which makes it a cheap, safe, and secure way for entrepreneurs and investors to exchange information and do business.[32]

Other Specialized Assistance Although government purchases represent a huge market, small companies have difficulty competing for this business with giant firms, which employ specialists to handle the volumes of paperwork involved in preparing proposals and completing bid applications. Today, many government procurement programs set aside portions of government spending for small companies; an additional SBA role is to help small firms secure these contracts. With **set-aside programs** for small businesses, up to 23 percent of certain government contracts are designated for small businesses.[33] Every federal agency with buying authority must maintain an Office of Small and Disadvantaged Business Utilization to ensure that small businesses receive a reasonable portion of government procurement contracts. To help connect small businesses with government agencies, the SBA's Web site offers Central Contractor Registration, which includes a search engine for finding business opportunities as well as a chance for small businesses to provide information about themselves.[34] Set-aside programs are also common in the private sector, particularly among major corporations.

In addition to help with financing and government procurement, the SBA delivers a variety of other services to small businesses. It provides information and advice through toll-free telephone numbers and its Web site, http://www.sba.gov, where you can find detailed information about starting, financing, and managing a small business, along with further information about businesses opportunities and disaster recovery. Finally, through its Small Business Training Network, the SBA offers free online courses; sponsors inexpensive training courses on topics such as taxes, networking, and start-ups in cities and small towns throughout the country; and provides a free online library of more than 200 SBA publications and additional business resources.

Business Incubators

business incubator organization that provides temporary low-cost, shared facilities to small start-up ventures.

Some local community agencies interested in encouraging business development have implemented a concept called a **business incubator** to provide low-cost shared business facilities to small start-up ventures. A typical incubator might section off space in an abandoned plant and rent it to various small firms. Tenants often share clerical staff, computers, and other business services. The objective is that, after a few months or years, the fledgling business will be ready to move out and operate on its own.

Hundreds of business incubator programs operate nationwide. About half are run by not-for-profit organizations, including industrial development authorities. The remainder are divided between college- and university-sponsored incubators and business-run incubators.[35] These facilities offer management support services and valuable management advice from in-house mentors. Operating in an incubator gives entrepreneurs easy access to such basic needs as telephones and human resources experts. They also can trade ideas with one another.

assessment check

1. What components should be part of a good business plan?
2. What are the various ways and methods by which the SBA helps small businesses with financing and getting government contracts?

SMALL-BUSINESS OPPORTUNITIES FOR WOMEN AND MINORITIES

The thousands of new business start-ups each year include growing numbers of women-owned firms as well as new businesses launched by African Americans, Hispanics, and members of other minority groups. The numbers of women-owned and minority-owned businesses are growing much faster than the overall growth in U.S. businesses. The people who start these companies see small-business ownership and operation as an attractive and lucrative alternative to working for someone else.

Women-Owned Businesses

In the United States today, more than 10.6 million women-owned firms provide jobs for almost 19.1 million people. Forty-eight percent of U.S. businesses are owned by women, compared with one-fourth to one-third of businesses worldwide. One of every five of these businesses is owned by minority women.[36]

Women, like men, have a variety of reasons for starting their own companies. Some are driven by an idea that they believe can help others. Some have a unique business idea that they want to bring to life, such as Kimberly See, an African American business woman who founded Arlington, Texas–based kemse & company, which offers a line of multicultural stationery and invitations designed for women of color.[37] Others decide to strike out on their own when they lose their jobs or become frustrated with the bureaucracies in large companies. In other cases, women leave large corporations when they feel blocked from opportunities for advancement. Sometimes this occurs because they hit the so-called glass ceiling, discussed in Chapter 8. Because women are more likely than men to be the primary caregivers in their families, some may seek self-employment as a way to achieve flexible working hours so they can spend more time with their families.

NATALIE CAUDILL/THE DALLAS MORNING NEWS

After being unable to find stationery, invitations, or greeting cards showing people of color, Kim See started her own business, kemse & company. "I decided to take matters into my own hands and create a line of paper products, in particular, invitations, to fill that void." Her products have been featured in the *Dallas Morning News* and *Essence* and *O* magazines.

The fastest growth among women-owned firms is occurring in construction, transportation and communications, and agricultural services.[38] One woman who created a successful manufacturing business is Karen Alvarez of Dublin, California. She got her original product idea when she was grocery shopping with her children and one child fell from the shopping cart. To prevent such accidents, which occur to thousands of children every year, Alvarez developed the Baby Comfort Strap, a simple padded strap that parents use to buckle a small child to a cart or stroller. She consulted experienced retailers and manufacturers for help in developing packaging, pricing, and testing. When the Baby Comfort Strap proved to be a reliable seller, Alvarez began a successful strategy to generate publicity about the frequency of shopping carts' resulting in injuries to small children. This led to widespread awareness of the problem—and about how the Baby Comfort Strap could resolve it. This publicity worked, and Alvarez was able to set up distribution throughout the United States.[39]

As the number of female small-business owners has grown, they have also been able to establish powerful support networks in a relatively short time. Many nationwide business assistance programs serve women exclusively. Among the programs offered by the Small Business Administration are the Contract Assistance for Women Business Owners program, which teaches women how to market to the federal government; the Women's Network for Entrepreneurial Training, which matches experienced female entrepreneurs with women trying to get started; and dozens of Women's Business Centers, which offer training and counseling in operating a business.

Springboard Enterprises is a nonprofit organization based in Washington, D.C., that promotes entrepreneurship and acquisition of capital for women entrepreneurs. Amy Millman, president of Springboard, assesses the small-business environment for women this way: "If you are an entrepreneur, it is always the right time to launch a business. There is great opportunity [if you] focus on the fundamentals. Remember, there is no free lunch."[40] In addition, women can find encouragement, advice, and mentors by joining organizations such as Women Entrepreneurs and the Forum for Women Entrepreneurs and Executives, both of which support women who want to start high-growth companies.[41]

"They Said It"

"Whatever women do, they must do twice as well as men to be thought half as good. Luckily, this is not difficult."
*Charlotte Whitton
(1896–1975)
Mayor of Ottawa*

Minority-Owned Businesses

Business ownership is also an important opportunity for America's racial and ethnic minorities. In recent years, the growth in the number of businesses owned by African Americans, Hispanics, and Asian Americans has far outpaced the growth in the number of U.S. businesses overall. Figure 5.4 shows the percentages of minority ownership in major industries. The relatively strong presence of minorities in the services and retail industries is especially significant because these industries contain the greatest number of businesses.

Hispanics are the nation's largest group of minority business owners, followed by Asian American, African American, and Native American owners.[42] The Small Business Administration attributes some of this pattern to strong population growth among Hispanics, whose disposable income is also growing at twice the rate of non-Hispanics.[43] Even more growth lies ahead for Hispanic-owned businesses during this decade, especially as trade between the United States and Latin America increases under NAFTA and CAFTA (see Chapter 4 for more information on NAFTA and CAFTA).

Historically, large numbers of U.S. immigrants have started businesses. In fact, immigrants own nearly 15 percent of all small businesses.[44] In addition, both male and female immigrants are more likely to own small businesses than are native-born Americans. For example, 8 percent of female immigrants own small businesses compared with 6 percent of women born in

5.4 | Types of Businesses Owned by Racial and Ethnic Minorities

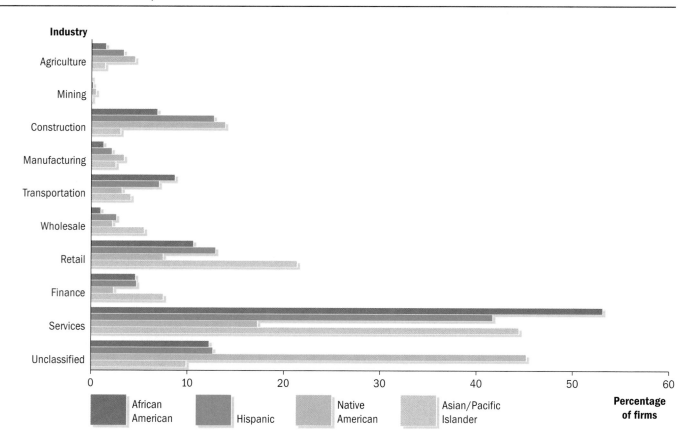

Source: Data from Office of Advocacy, U.S. Small Business Administration, "Minorities in Business," p. 17, accessed June 17, 2006, http://www.sba.gov/advo.

the United States.[45] Susana Cook, originally from Peru, who with her husband owns Cook's Natural Foods and Universal Medical Supply in Little Rock, Arkansas, said, "In our countries owning your own business is a struggle; here it's like a dream come true. Here they do not put so many obstacles or red tape in your way."[46]

Despite their progress, minority business owners still face considerable obstacles. Minority entrepreneurs tend to start businesses on a smaller scale and have more difficulty finding investors than other entrepreneurs. They rely less on bank credit than do other business owners, possibly because they have a harder time getting loans from banks. According to the Federal Reserve, bank loan applications of Hispanic- and African American–owned businesses are rejected at twice the rate of white-owned businesses. Not surprisingly, other research finds that roughly half of minority small-business owners don't even apply for bank loans, presumably because they believe their loan requests will be turned down.[47]

THE FRANCHISING ALTERNATIVE

Franchising is a major factor in the growth of small businesses. **Franchising** is a contractual business arrangement between a manufacturer or another supplier and a dealer. The contract specifies the methods by which the dealer markets the good or service of the supplier. Franchises can involve both goods and services; some well-known franchises are Burger King, KFC, McDonald's, Jiffy Lube, Domino's Pizza, Coldwell Banker Real Estate, and Supercuts.

Starting a small, independent company can be a risky, time-consuming endeavor, but franchising can reduce the amount of time and effort needed to expand. The franchisor has already developed and tested the concept, and the brand may already be familiar to prospective customers.

The Franchising Sector

Franchising started just after the U.S. Civil War, when the Singer Company decided to build its business by franchising retail sewing machine outlets. The concept became increasingly popular after 1900 in the automobile industry. Automobile travel led to demand for local auto sales and service outlets, as well as gasoline, oil, and tire retailers. Auto manufacturers created systems of franchised distributors and then set up local retailers in each retail location—auto dealers, gas stations, tire stores, and auto parts retailers. Dunkin Donuts, Meineke Muffler, and Super 8 Motels also set up their distribution systems through a network of local and regional franchises.

Today, the franchising concept continues its rapid growth. U.S. franchises generate sales of $1.53 trillion annually and employ more than 18 million people.[48] According to *Entrepreneur,* the Number one franchise is Subway, with Curves (exercise centers for women) coming in second. Quizno's Subs, the Jackson Hewitt Tax Service, UPS Stores, Sonic Drive-In, Jani-King (janitorial services), 7-Eleven, Dunkin' Donuts, and RE/MAX real estate complete the rest of *Entrepreneur*'s top ten list.[49] Areas in which strong growth is likely to continue include technology consulting; products for seniors and kids, both of which are growing population segments; and anything having to do with fitness or weight loss. With weight problems at epidemic proportions, Curves, whose slogan is "No men, no mirrors, no makeup," is growing 37 percent per year, has 4 million members and 9,000 centers after ten years in business, and is planning to open another 8,000 centers in Asia and Europe in the near future. Figure 5.5 shows four of the hottest industries in which franchising growth is currently occurring.

Franchising overseas is also a growing trend for franchisors and franchisees who want to expand into foreign markets. It seems that anywhere you go in the world, you can get a

franchising contractual agreement that specifies the methods by which a dealer can produce and market a supplier's good or service.

"They Said It"

"The road to success is dotted with many tempting parking spaces."

Anonymous

Figure

5.5   The Fastest-Growing Franchises by Industry

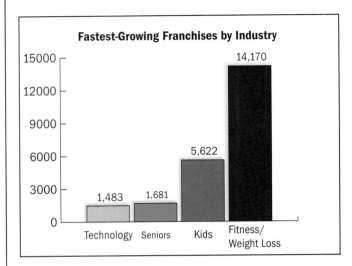

Fastest-Growing Franchises by Industry

Technology: 1,483
Seniors: 1,681
Kids: 5,622
Fitness/Weight Loss: 14,170

Source: Sara Wilson, "All the Rage: Wondering What Everyone Will Be Crazy About in the Coming Year? Take a Sneak Peek at the Hottest Franchising Trends for 2005," *Entrepreneur*, accessed June 17, 2006, http://www.entrepreneur.com.

McDonald's burger. But other international franchises, such as Best Western, Pak Mail, Pizza Hut, KFC, Subway, and 7-Eleven, are almost as common.

Some people get into franchising because they can operate their business from home, another continuing trend. Examples of these franchises include ServiceMaster Clean, Chem-Dry Carpet Drapery & Upholstery Cleaning, Snap-On Tools, and Lawn Doctor.[50]

Franchising Agreements

The two principals in a franchising agreement are the franchisee and the franchisor. The individual or business firm purchasing the franchise is called the **franchisee,** while the small-business owner who contracts to sell the good or service of the supplier is called the **franchisor.** In exchange for some payment (usually a fee plus a percentage of franchise sales) from the franchisee, the franchisor typically provides building plans, site selection help, managerial and accounting systems, and other services to assist the franchisee. Franchisees' total costs can vary over a wide range. The initial fee paid by a franchisee to McDonald's for a new McDonald's franchise is $45,000, but the total start-up costs can run anywhere from $500,000 to $1.6 million. In contrast, the initial fee for a Subway franchise is $12,500, but the total start-up costs range from $70,000 to $220,000.[51] The franchisor also provides name recognition for the small-business owner who becomes a franchisee. This public image is created by their familiarity with the franchise in other geographical areas and by advertising campaigns, all or part of which is paid for by contributions by the franchisees.

Franchise agreements often specify that the franchisee will receive materials, equipment, and training from the franchisor. Charmain and Charles Smith bought a Fruitfull Frozen Fruit Bars franchise from Happy & Healthy Products for $28,000, financing much of the purchase price with an SBA-backed loan. Charmain, with a decade of experience in the food service business, runs the franchise. Her husband, who also has a full-time job as a corporate financial executive, provides accounting and other services. The basic agreement with Happy & Healthy Products provides the franchisees with ten freezers, two pallets of frozen fruit and yogurt bars, and a week of training, which covers sales and the company's products and equipment. The franchisee then sells the product to retailers to be stocked in either Fruitfull freezers or the retailer's own freezers. The Smiths' franchise has accounts in Georgia, including Kroger supermarkets, a chain of health clubs, and school cafeterias.[52]

AP PHOTO/PAT WELLENBACH

Curves, the second-fastest-growing franchise in the United States, uses weightlifting and diet management to help its customers lose weight. For 30 minutes, three times a week, customers build muscles, strengthen joints, and increase flexibility by working their way around a circuit of weight-bearing machines.

Benefits and Problems of Franchising

As with any other business, a franchise purchaser bears the responsibility for researching what he or she is buying. Poorly financed or poorly managed franchise systems offer opportunities no better than those in poorly financed or poorly managed independent businesses. Although franchises are more likely than independent businesses to succeed, many franchises do go out of business. The franchising concept does not eliminate the risks of a potential small-business investment; it simply adds alternatives.

Advantages of franchises include a prior performance record, a recognizable company name, a business model that has proven successful in other locations, a tested management program, and business training for the franchisee. An existing franchise has posted a performance record on which the prospective buyer can base comparisons and judgments. Earlier results can indicate the likelihood of success in a proposed venture. In addition, a widely recognized name gives the franchisee a tremendous advantage; auto dealers, for instance, know that their brand-name products will attract particular segments of the market.

A tested management program usually allows the prospective franchisee to avoid worrying about setting up an accounting system, establishing quality-control standards, or designing employment application forms. In addition, most franchisors offer valuable business training. McDonald's teaches the basics of operating a franchise at its Hamburger University in Oak Brook, Illinois. Franchise operators quickly learn to meet customer expectations by following strict guidelines for how many seconds to cook the french fries and what words to use when serving customers. By following the franchisor's standards and building on an existing brand name, franchise operators typically can generate profits faster than an independent business owner. That was the case for Joe Grimand 25 years ago. After serving as a pilot in the Air Force, he knew he wanted to run his own business, but he had no business experience. So he bought into a Precision Tune Auto Care franchise, worked long hours, followed the company's advice, and adhered to its management system. Today he owns eight Precision stores, which together generate nearly $5 million in annual revenues. Says Grimand, "Looking back, I never thought it would grow to what it is now."[53]

On the negative side, franchise fees and future payments can be very expensive. As with any business, a franchise may well be unprofitable during its first months and at times thereafter. Payments to the franchisor can add to the burden of keeping the business afloat until the owner begins to earn a profit.

Another potential drawback stems from the fact that the franchisee is linked to the reputation and management of the franchise. If customers are unhappy with their experience at one franchised sandwich shop, they might avoid stopping at another one several miles away, even if the second one is owned and operated by someone else. So a strong, effective program of managerial control is essential to maintain a franchise brand's effectiveness. Before signing on with a franchisor, potential franchisees should carefully study its financial performance and reputation and talk with current franchise owners. Sources of information include the franchisor as well as state consumer protection agencies, the Better Business Bureau, and the Federal Trade Commission. The FTC's Web site includes advice for franchisees and reports of complaints against franchisors. Potential franchisees also should study the franchise agreement carefully to make sure they can succeed within the limitations of the agreement. In some instances, franchisors pursue additional sales by establishing new distribution outlets, which may compete directly with established franchisees. In today's online business environment, it is important to ask whether the franchisor retains the right to sell the same products online that the franchisee is trying to sell through a local outlet.

Even well-known, previously successful franchises can suffer from problems. Most people don't realize it, but auto dealers, just like McDonald's and Burger King stores, are franchises with the exclusive right to resell an auto manufacturer's cars. So when a franchisor like GM suffers, its dealers, that is, its franchises, suffer right along with it. And with its U.S. market share at half of what it was 25 years ago, GM has been suffering a lot, and so have its franchises.[54] For example, 20 years ago, Jeff Wooley's Pontiac dealership in Tampa, Florida, was selling 300 cars a month. Today, however, it's about 50 cars a month.[55] By contrast, since his Nissan dealership, which once sold 100 cars a month, now sells twice that many and will likely sell 300 cars a month within a few years, Wooley tore down his large Pontiac showroom, replacing it with a new $4.5 million showroom for Nissans.

Finally, some people are more suited to the demands of operating a franchise than others. Any person who is considering buying a franchise must think first about whether he or she has the right personality for the endeavor. Chapter 6 features an in-depth discussion of the basic characteristics that entrepreneurs should bring to their new endeavors.

assessment check

1. Distinguish between a franchisor and a franchisee.
2. Name some of the largest franchises.
3. What are the benefits and problems of franchising?

ALTERNATIVES FOR ORGANIZING A BUSINESS

Whether small or large, every business fits one of three categories of legal ownership: sole proprietorships, partnerships, and corporations. As Figure 5.6 shows, sole proprietorships are the most common form of business ownership. Although a much smaller percentage of firms are organized as corporations, corporate revenues are nineteen times as large as the revenues earned by all sole proprietorships. After all, a corporate giant such as Wal-Mart, with annual sales of nearly $320 billion, has a huge impact on the nation's economy.

Each form offers unique advantages and disadvantages, as outlined in Table 5.2. To overcome certain limitations of the traditional ownership structures, owners may also use three specialized organizational forms: S corporations, limited-liability partnerships, and limited-liability companies. Along with the basic forms, this section also briefly examines each of these alternatives.

sole proprietorship form of business ownership in which the company is owned and operated by one person.

Sole Proprietorships

The most common form of business ownership, the **sole proprietorship** is also the oldest and the simplest because no legal distinction separates the sole proprietor's status as an individual from his or her status as a business owner. Although sole proprietorships are common in a variety of industries, they are concentrated primarily among small businesses such as repair shops, small retail outlets, and service providers, such as painters, plumbers, and lawn care operations.

Sole proprietorships offer advantages that other business entities cannot. For one, they are easy to form and dissolve. (Partnerships are also easy to form, but difficult to dissolve.) A sole proprietorship offers management flexibility for the owner, along with the right to retain all profits after payment of personal income taxes. Retention of all profits and responsibility for all losses give sole proprietors the incentive to maximize efficiency in their operations.

Minimal legal requirements simplify entering and exiting a sole proprietorship. Usually, the owner must meet only a few legal requirements for starting one, including registering the business or trade name—to guarantee that two firms do not use the same name—and taking out any necessary licenses. Local

Figure

5.6 Forms of Business Ownership

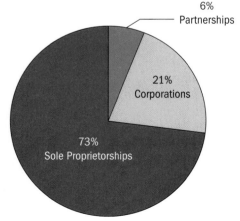

6% Partnerships

21% Corporations

73% Sole Proprietorships

Source: Data from U.S. Census Bureau, "Statistics about Business Size (Including Small Business) from the U.S. Census Bureau," http://www.census.gov.

Table 5.2

Comparing the Three Major Forms of Private Ownership

Form of Ownership	Number of Owners	Liability	Advantages	Disadvantages
Sole proprietorship	One owner	Unlimited personal liability for business debt	1. Owner retains all profits 2. Easy to form and dissolve 3. Owner has flexibility	1. Unlimited financial liability 2. Financing limitations 3. Management deficiencies 4. Lack of continuity
Partnership	Two or more owners	Personal assets of any operating partner at risk from business creditors	1. Easy to form 2. Can benefit from complementary management skills 3. Expanded financial capacity	1. Unlimited financial liability 2. Interpersonal conflicts 3. Lack of continuity 4. Difficult to dissolve
Corporation	Unlimited number of shareholders; up to 75 shareholders for S corporations	Limited	1. Limited financial liability 2. Specialized management skills 3. Expanded financial capacity 4. Economies of large-scale operations	1. Difficult and costly to form and dissolve 2. Tax disadvantages 3. Legal restrictions

governments require that certain kinds of licenses be obtained before opening restaurants, motels, and retail stores. Some occupational licenses require firms to carry specific types of insurance, such as liability coverage.

The ease of dissolving a sole proprietorship is an attractive feature for certain types of enterprises. This advantage is particularly important for temporary businesses set up to handle just a few transactions. Ownership flexibility is another advantage of a sole proprietorship. The owner can make management decisions without consulting others, take prompt action when needed, and keep trade secrets. You've probably heard people say, "I like being my own boss." This flexibility leads many business owners to prefer the sole proprietorship organization form.

A disadvantage of the sole proprietorship form is the owner's personal financial liability for all debts of the business. Also, the business must operate with financial resources limited to the owner's personal funds and money that he or she can borrow. Such financing limitations can keep the business from expanding. Another disadvantage is that the owner must handle a wide range of management and operational tasks; as the firm grows, the owner may not be able to perform all duties with equal effectiveness. Finally, a sole proprietorship lacks long-term continuity, because death, bankruptcy, retirement, or a change in personal interests can terminate it.

These limitations can make potential customers nervous about buying major goods or services from a sole proprietorship. When they know the form of organization being used by their supplier, they may worry that the sole proprietor will not be around long enough or have the resources to fulfill the agreement. Paulette Thomas, who writes the Startup Q&A column for the *Wall Street Journal*, says that because of that risk, "It makes no sense for such behemoths as BellSouth [or any other large corporation] with its $22.6 billion in annual revenue to parcel out that work to solo operators."[56]

Partnerships

partnership form of business ownership in which the company is operated by two or more people who are co-owners by voluntary legal agreement.

Another option for organizing a business is to form a partnership. The Uniform Partnership Act, which regulates this ownership form in most states, defines a **partnership** as an association of two or more persons who operate a business as co-owners by voluntary legal agreement. The partnership was the traditional form of ownership for professionals offering services, such as physicians, lawyers, and dentists. Today, most of these service providers have switched to other organizational forms to limit personal liability.

Like sole proprietorships, partnerships are easy to form. The legal requirements consist of registering the business name and taking out the necessary licenses. Partnerships also offer expanded financial capabilities when each partner invests money. They also usually increase access to borrowed funds compared with sole proprietorships. Another advantage is the opportunity for professionals to combine complementary skills and knowledge. In the earlier example of Charmain and Charles Smith's Fruitfull Frozen Fruit Bars franchise, the two franchise owners each contribute important skills. Charmain has experience as a manager in the food service business, and Charles has a financial background.

Like sole proprietorships, most partnerships have the disadvantage of unlimited financial liability. Each partner bears full responsibility for the debts of the firm, and each is legally liable for the actions of the other partners. Partners must pay the partnership's debts from their personal funds if it ceases operations and its debts exceed its assets. Breaking up a partnership is also a much more complicated undertaking than dissolving a sole proprietorship. Rather than simply withdrawing funds from the bank, the partner who wants out may need to find someone to buy his or her interest in the firm.

In many states, partners can minimize some of these risks by organizing as a limited liability partnership. In many respects, such a partnership resembles a general partnership, but laws limit the liability of the partners to the value of their investments in the company.

The death of a partner also threatens the survival of a partnership. A new partnership must be formed, and the estate of the deceased is entitled to a share of the firm's value. To ease the financial strains of such events, business planners recommend life insurance coverage for each partner, combined with a buy-sell agreement. The insurance proceeds can be used to repay the deceased partner's heirs and allow the surviving partner to retain control of the business.

Because partnerships are vulnerable to personal conflicts that can quickly escalate into business battles, you should carefully choose your business partners. Scott Stewart, whose former business partner spent extravagantly, said, "People told me a business partnership is like a marriage. I didn't understand it until now. You have to go through a dating period to find out if you're compatible."[57] Good communication is the key to resolving conflicts before they damage a partnership's chances for success or even destroy it.

Corporations

corporation business that stands as a legal entity with assets and liabilities separate from those of its owner(s).

A **corporation** is a legal organization with assets and liabilities separate from those of its owner(s). Although even the smallest business can choose the corporate form of organization, most people think of large companies when they hear the term *corporation*. In truth, many corporations are extremely large businesses.

Recently, ExxonMobil, whose annual worldwide sales are nearly $340 billion, passed longtime number one–ranked Wal-Mart to become the largest U.S.-based corporation in terms of sales. ExxonMobil has been ranked third for a number of years, so its move to the number one slot pushed General Motors to number three on the list, ahead of Chevron and Ford Motor Company. The list of the ten largest U.S. corporations contains another manufacturer, General

Electric, as well as banking firm Citigroup, insurance and financial firm AIG, information technology solution provider IBM, and international petroleum giants.[58]

The corporate ownership form offers considerable advantages. First, because a corporation acquires the status of a separate legal entity, its stockholders have only limited financial risk. If the firm fails, they lose only the money they have invested. Protection also applies to legal risk. Class-action suits filed against automakers, cigarette makers, and drug manufacturers are filed against the companies, not the owners of those companies. The limited risk of corporate ownership is clearly reflected in corporate names throughout the world. While many U.S. and Canadian corporations include the designation *Inc.* in their names, British firms use the abbreviation *Ltd.* to identify their limited liability. In Australia, the abbreviation for *proprietary limited*—Pty. Ltd.—is frequently included in corporate names.

Corporations offer other advantages. They can draw on the specialized skills of many employees, unlike the typical sole proprietorship or partnership, for which managerial skills are usually confined to the abilities of their owners and a small number of employees. Corporations gain access to expanded financial capabilities based on the opportunity to offer direct outside investments such as stock sales.

The large-scale operation permitted by corporate ownership also results in a number of advantages for this legal form of organization. Employees can specialize in their most effective tasks. A large firm can generate internal financing for many projects by transferring money from one part of the corporation to another. Long manufacturing runs usually promote efficient production and allow the firm to charge highly competitive prices that attract customers.

One major disadvantage for a corporation is the double taxation of corporate earnings. After a corporation pays federal, state, and local income taxes on its profits, its owners (stockholders) also pay personal taxes on any distributions of those profits they receive from the corporation in the form of dividends. One of the key components of the 2003 U.S. tax cut was the reduction of federal taxes on corporate dividends to 15 percent. Prior to passage of the economic stimulus legislation, people in the highest income bracket would pay more than 38 percent of any dividends received in federal taxes.

Corporate ownership also involves some legal issues that sole proprietorships and partnerships do not encounter. The number of laws and regulations that affect corporations has increased dramatically in recent years.

To avoid double taxation of business income while achieving or retaining limited financial liability for their owners, some firms have modified the traditional corporate and partnership structures. Businesses that meet certain size requirements, including ownership by no more than 75 shareholders, may organize as **S corporations,** also called *subchapter S corporations.* These firms can elect to pay federal income taxes as partnerships while retaining the liability limitations typical of corporations. The tax advantage of S corporations over typical corporations, which incur double taxation, is that S corporations are only taxed once. Unlike regular corporations, S corporations do not pay corporate taxes on their profits. Instead, the untaxed profits of S corporations are paid directly as dividends to shareholders, who then pay the lower 15 percent corporate dividend tax rate. This tax advantage has induced a fivefold increase in the number of S corporations. Consequently, the IRS is closely auditing S corporations for abuse because some businesses that don't meet the legal requirements have formed S corporations to illegally take advantage of the S corporation's lower taxes.[59]

Business owners may also form **limited liability companies (LLCs)** to secure the corporate advantage of limited liability while avoiding the double taxation characteristic of corporations. An LLC is governed by an operating agreement that resembles a partnership agreement, except that it reduces each partner's liability for the actions of the other owners. Professional corporations—such as law offices, accounting firms, and physicians—use a similar approach, with the abbreviation *PC* shown at the end of the name of the business.

Changing Legal Structures to Meet Changing Needs

Before deciding on an appropriate legal form, someone planning to launch a new business must consider dozens of factors, such as these:

- Personal financial situations and the need for additional funds for the business's start-up and continued operation
- Management skills and limitations
- Management styles and capabilities of working with partners and other members of top management
- Concerns about exposure to personal liability

assessment check

1. What are the key differences between sole proprietorships, partnerships, and corporations?

2. What are the advantages and disadvantages of sole proprietorships, partnerships, and corporations?

Although the legal form of organization is a major decision, new business owners need not treat it as a permanent decision. Over time, changing conditions such as business growth may prompt the owner of a sole proprietorship or a group of partners to switch to a more appropriate form. For example, if you have a successful business organized as a limited liability company, but you want to give your children or other family members partial ownership, you can give them shares of the company by switching to a corporation. And you can do this without giving up control of the company or paying a gift tax.[60]

ORGANIZING AND OPERATING A CORPORATION

One of the first decisions in forming a corporation is determining where to locate its headquarters and where it will do business. This section describes the various types of corporations and considers the options and procedures involved in incorporating a business.

Types of Corporations

Corporations fall into three categories: domestic, foreign, or alien. A firm is considered a **domestic corporation** in the state where it is incorporated. When a company does business in states other than the one where it has filed incorporation papers, it is registered as a **foreign corporation** in each of those states. A firm incorporated in one nation that operates in another is known as an **alien corporation** where it operates. Some firms—particularly large corporations with operations scattered around the world—may operate under all three of these designations.

The Incorporation Process

Suppose that you decide to start a business, and you believe that the corporate form offers the best way to organize it. Where should you set up shop? How do you establish a corporate charter? The following paragraphs discuss the procedures for creating a new corporation.

Where to Incorporate Location is one of the most important considerations for any small-business owner. Although most small and medium-sized businesses are incorporated in the states where they do most of their business, a U.S. firm can actually incorporate in any state it chooses. The founders of large corporations, or of those that will do business nationwide, often compare the benefits provided in various states' laws to firms in various industries.

The favorable legal climate in Delaware and the speed and simplicity of incorporating there have prompted more than half of the companies in *Fortune* magazine's list of the top

500 companies to set up operations there. Because of this popularity, incorporation has become a $400 million government-run industry in Delaware.

The Corporate Charter   Each state mandates a specific procedure for incorporating a business. Most states require at least three *incorporators*—the individuals who create the corporation—which opens incorporation possibilities to small businesses. Another requirement demands that a new corporation adopt a name dissimilar from those of other businesses; most states require that the name must end with the word *Company*, *Corporation*, *Incorporated*, or *Limited* to show that the owners have limited liability. Figure 5.7 lists ten elements of the articles of incorporation that most states require for chartering a corporation.

- Name and Address of the Corporation
- Corporate Objectives
- Type and Amount of Stock to Issue
- Expected Life of the Corporation
- Financial Capital at the Time of Incorporation
- Provisions for Transferring Shares of Stock among Owners
- Provisions for Regulating Internal Corporate Affairs
- Address of the Business Office Registered with the State of Incorporation
- Names and Addresses of the Initial Board of Directors
- Names and Addresses of the Incorporators

The information provided in the articles of incorporation forms the basis on which a state grants a **corporate charter**, a legal document that formally establishes a corporation. After securing the charter, the owners prepare the company's bylaws, which describe the rules and procedures for its operation.

Corporate Management

Depending on its size, a corporation has some or all of the ownership and management levels illustrated in Figure 5.8. At the top of the figure are **stockholders.** They acquire shares of stock in the corporation and so become part owners of it. Some companies, such as family businesses, are owned by relatively few stockholders, and the stock is generally unavailable to outsiders. In such a firm, known as a *closed* or *closely held corporation*, the stockholders also control and manage all activities. In contrast, an open corporation, sometimes called a *publicly held corporation*, sells stock to the general public, establishing diversified ownership and often leading to larger operations than those of a closed corporation.

stockholder person or organization who owns shares of stock in a corporation.

Stock Ownership and Stockholder Rights   Publicly held corporations usually hold annual stockholders' meetings. During these meetings, managers report on corporate activities, and stockholders vote on any decisions that require their approval, including elections of officers. Wal-Mart holds the nation's largest stockholder meeting in a university's basketball arena. Approximately 18,000 people attend. In addition to standard shareholder business, the Wal-Mart meeting has featured celebrities and entertainers such as Jessica Simpson, Jimmy Buffett, and Will Smith.[61]

Stockholders' role in the corporation depends on the class of stock they own. Shares are usually classified as common or preferred stock. Although owners of **preferred stock** have limited voting rights, they are entitled to receive dividends before common-stock holders. If the corporation is dissolved, they have first claims on assets, once debtors are repaid. Owners of **common stock** have voting rights but only residual claims on the firm's assets, which means they are last to receive any income distributions. Because one share is typically worth only one vote, small stockholders generally have little influence on corporate management actions.

Board of Directors   Stockholders elect a **board of directors**—the governing body of a corporation. The board sets overall policy, authorizes major transactions involving the corporation, and hires the chief executive officer (CEO). Most boards include both inside directors (corporate executives) and outside directors—people who are not employed by the organization.

board of directors elected governing body of a corporation.

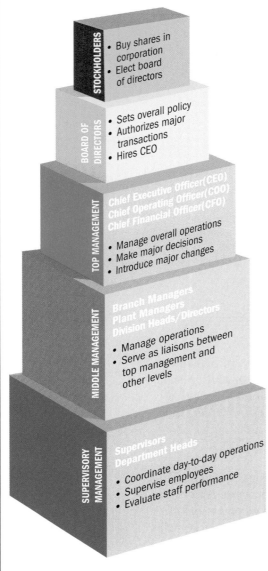

Figure

5.8 Levels of Management in a Corporation

STOCKHOLDERS
- Buy shares in corporation
- Elect board of directors

BOARD OF DIRECTORS
- Sets overall policy
- Authorizes major transactions
- Hires CEO

TOP MANAGEMENT
Chief Executive Officer(CEO)
Chief Operating Officer(COO)
Chief Financial Officer(CFO)
- Manage overall operations
- Make major decisions
- Introduce major changes

MIDDLE MANAGEMENT
Branch Managers
Plant Managers
Division Heads/Directors
- Manage operations
- Serve as liaisons between top management and other levels

SUPERVISORY MANAGEMENT
Supervisors
Department Heads
- Coordinate day-to-day operations
- Supervise employees
- Evaluate staff performance

Sometimes the corporation's top executive also chairs the board. Generally, outside directors are also stockholders.

Corporate Officers and Managers The CEO and other members of top management, such as the chief operating officer (COO) and chief financial officer (CFO), make most major corporate decisions. Managers at the next level down the hierarchy, middle management, handle the ongoing operational functions of the company. At the first tier of management, supervisory personnel coordinate day-to-day operations, assign specific tasks to employees, and evaluate job performance. The activities and responsibilities of managers at various levels in the organization are described in detail in Chapter 8.

In the past, top managers of corporations have had nearly free rein to guide their companies. The firm's CEO has traditionally played a major role in nominating candidates for board membership and often served jointly as board chairperson and CEO. Recent corporate and accounting scandals were traced to a lack of business ethics, coupled with illegal acts of members of top management and failure of the corporate boards to fulfill their obligations to the firm's investors in providing adequate oversight. These failings among a number of large corporations prompted Congress to pass the Sarbanes-Oxley Act of 2002, which tightened requirements of corporate boards and required CEOs and CFOs of major corporations to certify in writing the accuracy of the firm's financial statements. New criminal penalties were established for corporate wrongdoers. This far-reaching legislation, which focuses on improving corporate governance and increasing the accountability of corporate boards, top executives, and accounting firms, was introduced in the appendix titled "A Legal Framework for Business" following Chapter 4. Its impact on business will be also be discussed in the management, accounting, and finance chapters later in the text.

Employee-Owned Corporations

Another alternative in creating a corporation is **employee ownership,** in which workers buy shares of stock in the company that employs them. The corporate organization stays the same, but most stockholders are also employees.

The popularity of this form of corporation is growing. Since the mid-1970s, the number of employee ownership plans has grown sevenfold—to approximately 11,400. But the number of employees participating in such plans today is nearly 34 times as many—nearly 10 million people.[62] Several trends underlie the growth in employee ownership. One is that employees want to share in whatever wealth their company earns. Another is that managers want employees to care deeply about the company's success so that they will contribute their best effort. Because human resources are so essential to the success of a modern business, employers want to build their employees' commitment to the organization. Some of the country's most successful public corporations, including Procter & Gamble, Lowe's, and Southwest Airlines, have embraced employee ownership and watched their stock values hold up better than other companies; sales of employee-owned companies are 2.3 to 2.4 percent larger than nonemployee-owned firms.[63] Employee-owned firms are discussed in more detail in Chapter 9.

assessment check

1. What is the role of stockholders, the board of directors, and corporate officers and management?
2. Identify all the levels of corporate management.

Not-for-Profit Corporations

The same business concepts that apply to organizations whose objectives include earning profits also apply to **not-for-profit corporations**—firms pursuing objectives other than returning profits to owners. About 1.5 million not-for-profits operate in the United States, including charitable groups, social-welfare organizations, and religious congregations. This sector includes museums, libraries, religious and human-service organizations, private secondary schools, healthcare facilities, symphony orchestras, zoos, and thousands of other groups such as government agencies, political parties, and labor unions.

A good example of a not-for-profit corporation is the San Francisco Ballet, which has been at the forefront of dance in America since its founding in 1933 as America's first professional ballet company. It is widely regarded as one of the premier ballet companies in the nation. Visitors to its Web site, http://www.sfballet .org, can learn about upcoming performances, purchase tickets, buy gift certificates, and shop online at the gift shop.[64]

Most states set out separate legal provisions for organizational structures and operations of not-for-profit corporations. These organizations do not issue stock certificates, because they pay no dividends to owners, and ownership rarely changes. They are also exempt from paying income taxes.

The San Francisco Ballet company was founded in 1933 to train dancers to appear in full-length operas. Today, though, the not-for-profit company is the third-largest ballet company in the United States, and it stages more than 100 performances annually. It also trains approximately 325 ballet dancers per year.

WHEN BUSINESSES JOIN FORCES

Today's corporate world features many complex unions of companies, not always in the same industry or even in the same country. Many well-known firms have changed owners, become parts of other corporations, split into smaller units, or experienced financial bankruptcy. Current trends in corporate ownership include mergers and acquisitions, and joint ventures.

Mergers and Acquisitions (M&A)

In recent years, merger mania has hit U.S. corporations. Procter & Gamble paid $54 billion in stock to acquire Gillette. Cingular Wireless paid $41 billion to acquire AT&T Wireless. Sprint paid $35 billion to merge with Nextel Communications. SBC paid $16 billion to acquire AT&T.[65] Typically, 7,000 to 9,000 mergers and acquisitions take place annually.[66]

The terms *merger* and *acquisition* are often used interchangeably, but their meanings differ. In a **merger,** two or more firms combine to form one company; in an **acquisition,** one firm purchases the property and assumes the obligations of another. Acquisitions also occur when one firm buys a division or subsidiary from another firm. Many mergers and acquisitions cross national borders, as managers attempt to enter new markets and improve global competitiveness for their companies. Bermuda-based Bacardi International, one of the world's largest producers of alcoholic beverages, paid $2.29 billion to acquire Grey Goose, a maker of premium vodka ($30+ a bottle) in Cognac, France, from Sidney Frank Importing of New Rochelle, New York. Bacardi not only aims to increase sales of Grey Goose vodka in the United States but wants to double the number of countries around the world in which it is sold.[67]

Mergers can be classified as vertical, horizontal, or conglomerate. A **vertical merger** combines firms operating at different levels in the production and marketing process—the

merger combination of two or more firms to form one company.

acquisition procedure in which one firm purchases the property and assumes the obligations of another.

combination of a manufacturer and a large retailer, for instance. A vertical merger pursues one of two primary goals: (1) to ensure adequate flows of raw materials and supplies needed for a firm's products, or (2) to increase distribution. Software giant Microsoft is well known for acquiring small firms that have developed products with strong market potential, such as Teleo, a provider of voice over Internet protocol (VoIP) software and services that can be used to make phone calls via the Internet.[68] Likewise, large petroleum companies often try to reduce the uncertainty of their future petroleum supplies by acquiring successful oil and gas exploration firms.

A **horizontal merger** joins firms in the same industry that wish to diversify, increase their customer bases, cut costs, or offer expanded product lines. While P&G and Gillette are both in the global consumer goods business, Gillette was strong in shaving, men's grooming, and oral care and toothbrushes, while P&G excelled in beauty care, laundry and household cleaners, baby products, drugs, and pet care. The combined company features 21 brands with annual sales of $1 billion or more.[69]

A **conglomerate merger** combines unrelated firms. The most common reasons for a conglomerate merger are to diversify, spur sales growth, or spend a cash surplus that might otherwise make the firm a tempting target for a takeover effort. Conglomerate mergers may join firms in totally unrelated industries. A company well known for its conglomerate mergers is GE, which owns television broadcaster NBC and cable programmers CNBC and MSNBC, along with its manufacturing businesses such as appliances, aircraft engines, and industrial products. Experts debate whether conglomerate mergers are beneficial. The usual argument in favor of such mergers is that a company can use its management expertise to succeed in a variety of industries. However, the stock of an acquiring company often falls in price when it makes an acquisition, suggesting that investors doubt the value of this strategy.

Joint Ventures: Specialized Partnerships

A **joint venture** is a partnership between companies formed for a specific undertaking. Sometimes a company enters into a joint venture with a local firm or government, sharing the operation's costs, risks, management, and profits with its local partner. A joint venture also may enable companies to solve a mutual problem. Four U.S. pipeline companies entered into a joint venture to provide better service to the oil refineries that use their services. Their venture, called Transport4, created an online resource at which 430 oil companies can schedule use of the pipelines and track the delivery of 4.5 million barrels of petroleum per day, which often must pass through more than one company's pipelines to reach its destination. Transport4 collects orders and schedules petroleum shipments for more than 150,000 oil transactions per day through the four pipeline companies' systems. It frees customers from calling each company to negotiate and renegotiate schedules.[70] As discussed in the previous chapter, joint ventures also offer particularly attractive ways for small firms to conduct international business, because they bring substantial benefits from partners already operating inside the host countries.

assessment check

1. Distinguish between a merger and an acquisition.
2. What are the different kinds of mergers?
3. What is a joint venture?

PUBLIC AND COLLECTIVE OWNERSHIP

Most business organizations are owned privately by individuals or groups of people, but municipal, state, and national governments own some firms. In addition, groups of people collectively own some companies. Public ownership is common in many industries, both in the United States and abroad. In the United States, more than 350 municipalities offer Internet or cable TV services, competing with private firms that offer those same services.[71]

Public Ownership

One alternative to private ownership is some form of **public ownership,** in which a unit or agency of government owns and operates an organization. In the United States, local governments often own parking structures and water systems. The Pennsylvania Turnpike Authority operates a vital highway link across the Keystone State. The federal government operates Hoover Dam in Nevada to provide electricity over a large region.

Government-Owned Corporations

Sometimes public ownership results when private investors are unwilling to invest in a high-risk project. This situation occurred with the rural electrification programs of the 1930s, which expanded utility lines in sparsely populated areas. At other times, public ownership has replaced private ownership of failed organizations. Certain functions, such as municipal water systems, are considered so important to public welfare that government often implements public ownership to protect its citizens from problems. Finally, some nations use public business ownership to foster competition by operating public companies as competitive business enterprises. In Bogota, Colombia, the government runs a TV and radio network, Instituto Nacional de Radio & Television, that broadcasts both educational and commercial programs. Public ownership remains common abroad, despite a general trend toward privatization.

Customer-Owned Businesses: Cooperatives

Another alternative to traditional private business ownership is collective ownership of a production, storage, transportation, or marketing organization. Such collective ownership establishes an organization referred to as a **cooperative** (or **co-op),** whose owners join forces to collectively operate all or part of the functions in their industry.

Cooperatives allow small businesses to obtain quantity discounts on purchases, reducing costs and enabling the co-op to pass on the savings to its members. Marketing and advertising expenses are shared among members, and the co-op's facilities can also serve as a distribution center.

Cooperatives are frequently found in small farming communities, but they also serve large growers of specific crops. For instance, Blue Diamond Growers is a cooperative that represents California almond growers. Retailers have also established co-ops. Ace Hardware is a cooperative of independently owned hardware stores. Financial co-ops, such as credit unions, offer members higher interest rates on deposits and lower interest rates on loans than other profit-seeking institutions could provide.

assessment check

1. What is private ownership? What is public ownership? What is government ownership?
2. Where are cooperatives typically found and what benefits do they provide small businesses?

WHAT'S AHEAD

The next chapter shifts the book's focus to the driving forces behind new-business formation: entrepreneurs. It examines the differences between a small-business owner and an entrepreneur and identifies certain personality traits typical of entrepreneurs. The chapter also details the process of launching a new venture, including identifying opportunities, locating needed financing, and turning good ideas into successful businesses. Finally, the chapter explores a method for infusing the entrepreneurial spirit into established businesses—intrapreneurship.

1 Distinguish between small and large businesses and identify the industries in which most small firms are established.

Small businesses can adopt many profiles, from part-time, home-based businesses to firms with several hundred employees. A small business is a firm that is independently owned and operated, is not dominant in its field, and meets industry-specific size standards for income or number of employees. Small businesses operate in every industry, but retailing, services, and construction feature the highest proportions of small enterprises.

Assessment Check Answers

1.1 What characteristics does the SBA use to determine whether a business is a small business?
The SBA looks at the number of employees, annual sales, and whether a firm is independently owned and not dominant in its field.

1.2 Identify three industries in which small businesses are common.
Construction, wholesale, retail, and service industries are common for small businesses.

2 Discuss the economic and social contributions of small business.

Small businesses create 75 percent of the new jobs in the U.S. economy and employ half of U.S. workers. They provide valuable outlets for entrepreneurial activity and often contribute to the creation of new industries or development of new business processes. Women, minorities, and immigrants find small-business ownership to be an attractive alternative to working in large firms and are starting new companies at a much faster rate than the overall growth in U.S. businesses. Small firms may also offer enhanced lifestyle flexibility and opportunities to gain personal satisfaction.

Assessment Check Answers

2.1 To what extent do small businesses help create new jobs?
On average, three of every four new jobs are created by small businesses.

2.2 In what ways do small businesses contribute to the economy?
Small businesses create new jobs, new industries, and better products and services through innovation.

3 Describe the reasons that small businesses fail.

Because of management shortcomings, inadequate financing, and difficulty dealing with government regulations, small businesses are much more likely to fail than large businesses, especially during economic downturns.

Assessment Check Answers

3.1 What percentage of small businesses will still be in business two, four, six, and ten years after starting?
One-third, 50 percent, 62 percent, and 82 percent of small businesses will have failed within two, four, six, and ten years, respectively.

3.2 How do management shortcomings, inadequate financing, and government regulation make small businesses more likely to fail?
Founders of new businesses often lack the business expertise and experience needed to grow a small business. Inadequate financing prevents small businesses from handling the inevitable cash shortfalls they face and from attracting and keeping talented people. Government regulation burdens small businesses that have limited staff and budgets with expensive, time-consuming red tape and paperwork.

4 Describe how the Small Business Administration assists small-business owners.

The U.S. Small Business Administration helps small-business owners obtain financing through programs that guarantee repayment of their bank loans or match small-business owners with potential investors. The SBA also helps women and minority business owners obtain government purchasing contracts. It offers training and information resources, so business owners can improve their odds of success. Finally, the SBA advocates small-business interests within the federal government.

Assessment Check Answers

4.1 What components should be part of a good business plan?
A good business plan contains an executive summary, an introduction, separate financial and marketing sections, and the résumés of the principals.

4.2 What are the various ways and methods by which the SBA helps small businesses with financing and getting government contracts?
The SBA guarantees business loans, helps small businesses compete for government set-aside programs, and provides business information, advice, and training.

5 Explain how franchising can provide opportunities for both franchisors and franchisees.

A franchisor is a company that sells the rights to use its brand name, operating procedures, and other intellectual property to franchisees. Franchising helps business owners expand their companies' operations with limited financial investments. Franchisees, the individuals who buy the right to operate a business using the franchisor's intellectual property, gain a proven business system, brand recognition, and training and other support from the franchisor.

Assessment Check Answers

5.1 Distinguish between a franchisor and a franchisee.
Franchisors permit franchisees to use their business name and to sell their business's goods and services. Franchisors also provide franchisees a variety of marketing, management, and other services in return for various fees and a percentage of the franchisee's sales.

5.2 Name some of the largest franchises.
McDonald's, Burger King, KFC, Pizza Hut, Taco Bell, Subway, Curves, Quizno's, Jackson Hewitt Tax Services, UPS, Sonic Drive-In, Jani-King, 7-Eleven, Dunkin' Donuts, and RE/MAX are some of the largest franchises.

5.3 What are the benefits and problems of franchising?
Advantages include a prior performance record, a recognizable company name, a business model that has proven successful in other locations, a tested management program, and business training for the franchisee. On the negative side, franchise fee payments can be very expensive, the franchisee is linked to the reputation and management of the franchise, and new franchise outlets may compete directly with established franchises.

6 Summarize the three basic forms of business ownership and the advantages and disadvantages of each form.

A sole proprietorship is owned and operated by one person. While sole proprietorships are easy to set up and offer great operating flexibility, the owner remains personally liable for all of the firm's debts and legal settlements. In a partnership, two or more individuals share responsibility for owning and running the business. Partnerships are relatively easy to set up, but they do not offer protection from liability. Also, partnerships may experience problems by the death of a partner or when partners fail to communicate or establish effective working relationships. When a business is set up as a corporation, it becomes a separate legal entity. Investors receive shares of stock in the firm. Owners have no legal and financial liability beyond their individual investments.

Assessment Check Answers

6.1 What are the key differences between sole proprietorships, partnerships, and corporations?
Sole proprietorships expose their owners to unlimited financial liability from their businesses. Corporations shield business owners from financial liability by separating an organization's assets and liabilities from its business owners' assets and liabilities.

6.2 What are the advantages and disadvantages of sole proprietorships, partnerships, and corporations?
Sole proprietorships are easy to form and dissolve, and they allow owners to retain all business profits. But they lack long-term continuity, and their owners are personally liable for all business debts and must be capable of handling a wide range of business tasks. Partnerships are easy to form and offer expanded financial capabilities and complementary skills and knowledge. But they are difficult to dissolve, are vulnerable to personal conflicts, and make their owners personally liable for all business debts. Corporations shield owners from financial and legal risks, draw on specialized skills of employees, and can expand financial capabilities by selling stock. However, corporations are more difficult to establish, face double taxation of corporate earnings, and are subject to numerous state and federal laws and regulations.

7 Identify the levels of corporate management.

Stockholders, or shareholders, own a corporation. In return for their financial investments, they receive shares of stock in the company. The number of stockholders in a firm can vary widely, depending on whether the firm is privately owned or makes its stock available to the public. Shareholders elect the firm's board of directors, the individuals responsible for overall corporate management. The board has legal

authority to change or create the firm's policies. A company's officers are the top managers who oversee its operating decisions.

Assessment Check Answers

7.1 What is the role of stockholders, the board of directors, and corporate officers and management?
Stockholders acquire shares of stock and become corporate owners. At the annual stockholders' meeting, managers report on corporate activities and stockholders vote on any decisions that require their approval, including elections of officers. The board of directors sets overall policy, authorizes major transactions involving the corporation, and hires the chief executive officer (CEO). The CEO and other members of top management make most major corporate decisions and are accountable to the board and shareholders.

7.2 Identify all the levels of corporate management.
The levels of corporate management include top management, middle management, and supervisory management.

8 Describe recent trends in mergers and acquisitions.
Typically, 7,000 to 9,000 corporate mergers and acquisitions occur each year. U.S. corporations are spending record amounts on mergers and acquisitions. These business combinations occur worldwide, and companies often merge with or acquire other companies to aid their operations across national boundaries. Vertical mergers help a firm ensure access to adequate raw materials and supplies for production or improve its distribution outlets. Horizontal mergers occur when firms in the same industry join to diversify or offer expanded product lines. Conglomerate mergers combine unrelated firms, often to help spend cash surpluses that might otherwise make a firm a takeover target.

Assessment Check Answers

8.1 Distinguish between a merger and an acquisition.
In a merger, two or more firms combine to form one company. In an acquisition, one firm purchases the property and assumes the obligations of another. Acquisitions also occur when one firm buys a division or subsidiary from another firm.

8.2 What are the different kinds of mergers?
Mergers can be classified as vertical, horizontal, or conglomerate.

8.3 What is a joint venture?
A joint venture is a partnership between companies formed for a specific undertaking.

9 Differentiate among private ownership, public ownership, and collective ownership (cooperatives).
Managers or a group of major stockholders sometimes buy all of a firm's stock. The firm then becomes a privately owned company, and its stock is no longer publicly traded. Some firms allow workers to buy large blocks of stock, so the employees gain ownership stakes. Municipal, state, and national governments also own and operate some businesses. This public business ownership has declined, however, through a recent trend toward privatization of publicly run organizations. In a cooperative, individuals or companies band together to collectively operate all or part of an industry's functions. The cooperative's owners control its activities by electing a board of directors from its members. Cooperatives are usually set up to provide for collective ownership of a production, storage, transportation, or marketing organization that is important to an industry.

Assessment Check Answers

9.1 What is private ownership? What is public ownership? What is collective ownership?
Most business organizations are owned privately by individuals or groups of people. Public ownership occurs when a government unit or agency owns and operates an organization. In a cooperative, individuals or companies band together to collectively operate all or part of an industry's functions. The cooperative's owners control its activities by electing a board of directors from their members.

9.2 Where are cooperatives typically found and what benefits do they provide small businesses?
Cooperatives are usually set up to provide for collective ownership of a production, storage, transportation, or marketing organization that is important to an industry.

Business Terms You Need to Know

small business 146
business plan 158
Small Business Administration
   (SBA) 158
business incubator 160

franchising 163
sole proprietorship 166
partnership 168
corporation 168
stockholder 171

board of directors 171
merger 173
acquisition 173

Other Important Business Terms

home-based business 149
microloans 159
Small Business Investment
   Company (SBIC) 159
set-aside program 159
franchisee 164
franchisor 164
S corporation 169

limited liability company
   (LLC) 169
domestic corporation 170
foreign corporation 170
alien corporation 170
corporate charter 171
preferred stock 171
common stock 171

employee ownership 172
not-for-profit corporation 173
vertical merger 173
horizontal merger 174
conglomerate merger 174
joint venture 174
public ownership 175
cooperative (co-op) 175

Review Questions

1. What is meant by the term *small business?* What business sectors are most and least likely to be dominated by small firms?

2. What are the most common industries for small businesses? What opportunities do home-based companies and the Internet provide for small business? How do small businesses contribute to a nation's economy in terms of job creation and new industries and innovation?

3. What percentage of small businesses is likely to fail two, four, six, and ten years after starting? Why are small businesses more likely to fail? Explain how poor management, inadequate financing, and government regulations put small businesses at a disadvantage.

4. What are the benefits of a good business plan? Identify the major components of a business plan.

5. What is the Small Business Administration? How does it assist small companies, financially and in other specialized ways? What are business incubators?

6. To what extent are small businesses creating opportunities for women today? Why have Hispanics become the nation's largest group of minority business owners? To what extent are

other minority groups, including immigrants, taking advantage of opportunities to start and run their own businesses?

7. What are the top franchises and the latest trends in franchising? Describe a typical franchising agreement. What are the advantages and disadvantages of a franchising agreement?

8. What are a sole proprietorship, a partnership, and a corporation? How are they different? What are the advantages and disadvantages of each organizational form?

9. What are the three categories of corporations? What are the steps for creating a new corporation? Why does location matter? What is a corporate charter?

10. What are the levels of management in a corporation? What is the difference between employee-owned and not-for-profit corporations?

11. How are mergers and acquisitions different? What are the three kinds of mergers? What is a joint venture?

12. Distinguish among public ownership, government-owned corporations, and customer-owned businesses (cooperatives).

Projects and Teamwork Applications

1. Go to Entrepreneur.com and look for information on home-based business franchises. Choose three that interest you. Compare their company backgrounds, the costs and fees of becoming a franchisee, the training and support provided by the franchisor, and Entrepreneur.com's ratings for each franchisor. Also, visit the franchisors' Web sites. Which of the three home-based business franchises would represent the best opportunity for you? Why?

2. Read the business page of your local newspaper and choose a small business that has been profiled or mentioned in the paper. What do you think makes this business successful?

3. Propose an idea for a business incubator in an industry that interests you. Describe where the incubator would be located, how it would function, and what it is intended to accomplish.

4. Livewire International, http://www.livewirekiosk .com, a York, Pennsylvania, firm that provides electronic kiosks for ski lift tickets, has made alliances with businesses such as ski resorts and sports retailers. Describe another type of company that Livewire might make an alliance with. How might this alliance benefit Livewire? What precautions should Livewire take in entering into the alliance?

5. Do you think that consumers benefit from public ownership of such functions as municipal water systems and the postal service? Why or why not?

Case 5.1

Armstrong's Supply Rebuilds in the Wake of Hurricane Katrina

Scott Armstrong's family has been in New Orleans since the 1840s, only a generation less than his wife's ancestors. His electrical and lighting supply business, Armstrong's Supply, was founded by a great-uncle there in 1924. So leaving the city after the flooding and other damage wrought by Hurricane Katrina was simply not an option for him.

President and part owner of the electrical services and lighting firm, Armstrong faced numerous problems as New Orleans struggled to dry, clean, and rebuild thousands of ruined homes and businesses. His first priority was to find or account for all of his 32 longtime employees, which included rowing back to the flooded city to check the home of a missing worker. While Armstrong tackled that job, his wife and four other employees raced to every Home Depot and Lowe's in Houston and southern Louisiana to stock up on the electrical service equipment Armstrong's small-business customers and emergency repair crews would soon be asking him for. "I'm trying to make sure that not a single one of my customers has to go to another supplier because we don't

have it," he explained. To ensure he could meet demand, Armstrong also asked his regular wholesale suppliers to rush him shipments of wiring, circuit-breaker panels, and other supplies on credit and to give him six months to pay.

Armstrong then negotiated leases on two buildings, one in a heavily damaged area of the city where he guessed most of the rebuilding would begin. He rented another building near his branch office to take the place of his ruined headquarters, which was inches deep in the flood's toxic mud. Without any means to write a lease, he and the landlord sealed the deal with a handshake. Armstrong had estimated that about 80 percent of his inventory was unsalvageable, along with the company's trucks, computers, and new phone system. So he spent hours on the phone getting the credit limits extended on his personal credit cards to cover necessary business purchases, including $11,000 for new computer equipment.

The next step was rebuilding financial security for the company by taking out short-term loans and wrangling with the insurance company that had protected

Armstrong's business against work stoppages by covering the payroll for up to 90 days. When the insurer explained that his policy didn't cover flooding, Armstrong argued that the government-mandated evacuation had caused the stoppage, along with the city's traumatic power loss and other factors. While waiting for a decision about his insurance settlement, Armstrong struggled to reduce his $25,000 weekly payroll. He contacted suppliers and business acquaintances and asked them to try to give some of his workers jobs. He and two other company executives took an immediate 25 percent pay cut, and workers who returned and whom the firm could still employ were given 10 percent pay cuts. Those who weren't essential for the short term, such as workers in the temporarily defunct retail arm of the business, were being paid half their salaries until further notice. Darren Sixkiller, operations and customer service manager, lost his home in the hurricane and his family was displaced. "Armstrong's Supply is my lifeline right now," he said, "because I have nothing to go back to."

Just days after the storm, Armstrong's Supply had updated its Web site with emergency information for customers and employees and was already selling thousands of devices to connect power lines to individual homes. Because his business computers were down and his records were presumed destroyed, Armstrong asked buyers what they had most recently paid for the same item, and that's what he charged them. Though such sales were encouraging, "It's just not fueling the engine that we have to have fueled," said Armstrong. But on the other hand, he concluded, "If we can survive a month, a month, a month, a month, maybe we will be around."

Questions for Critical Thinking

1. What do you think accounts for Scott Armstrong's dedication to his business in the face of such adversity? List as many factors as you can.
2. No business can truly plan for the kind of emergency Armstrong's Supply faced. What effect do you think its size had on its ability to take the first steps to recovery? Are there other actions it could take?

Sources: Armstrong's SupplyWeb site, accessed June 17, 2006, http://www.armstrongssupply.com; Sarah Rubenstein, "A New Orleans Man Struggles to Rebuild His Small Business," *Wall Street Journal Online*, accessed June 17, 2006, http://online.wsj.com; "Special Report: Katrina Update, Part 3," *Ted Magazine,* accessed September 19, 2005, http://www.tedmag.com.

VIDEO Case 5.2

The UL Mark of Approval

This video case appears on page 612. A recently filmed video, designed to expand and highlight the written case, is available for class use by instructors.

Chapter 6

Starting Your Own Business: The Entrepreneurship Alternative

Learning Goals

1. Define the term *entrepreneur* and distinguish among entrepreneurs, small-business owners, and managers.

2. Identify four different types of entrepreneurs.

3. Explain why people choose to become entrepreneurs.

4. Discuss conditions that encourage opportunities for entrepreneurs.

5. Identify personality traits that typically characterize successful entrepreneurs.

6. Summarize the process of starting a new venture.

7. Explain how organizations promote intrapreneurship.

You need a strong stomach to be an entrepreneur. You have to be willing to ride to the top of the roller coaster, take the plunge to the bottom, and ride to the top again. Bill Gross knows this. No matter what happens to the companies he starts, he is prepared for the ups and downs. He figures it's the only way to get to the top.

Gross began his entrepreneurial career in college—when he founded a business that sold solar-based products during the energy crisis of 1973. The profits from that first company helped him pay his tuition, and he went on to start another company with his brother Larry. In the early 1990s, he established Knowledge Adventure, an educational software firm that grew to a $25-million-a-year business before he moved on to launch CitySearch, the first online metro guide. With his

GETTY IMAGES

Bill Gross: Riding the Entrepreneurial Roller Coaster

string of start-ups, Gross had become a serial entrepreneur, and he'd also caught the attention of celebrity investors such as Steven Spielberg.

But Gross is best known for his firm Idealab, a California-based business incubator for high-tech companies. A decade ago, Idealab appeared to be poised to cash in on the dot-com boom. With 50 start-up companies on its roster, Idealab was on the brink of huge success. But the boom went bust, and with it went many of Idealab's companies. Gross canceled the firm's big plans for an initial public offering (IPO) of stock and closed down its satellite offices in New York, London, and Silicon Valley. Idealab workers lost their jobs, and private investors in the firm counted their financial losses. Company insiders recall this as the "dark time." Company board member Howard Morgan explains, "For all of us, especially Bill, it was a managerial growing up." Gross says, "I never want to be in a position to . . . cut people's jobs again."

Gross is back on the roller coaster again, on his way up. Idealab has cut back on the number of start-ups it funds to about two a year. Each must display true technological

innovation. One such innovation is LaneHawk, vision-recognition software that is being tested at such supermarket chains as Pathmark and Giant Eagle. Internet Brands, which started CarsDirect—an online car-sales firm—is actually making money. And Snap.com enables advertisers such as United Airlines and eBay to pay only when a purchase or transaction takes place because of their ad posting—instead of paying every time someone clicks on the site. Idealab start-ups that survived its early years lend the company credibility as well. Go2.com and Picasa were purchased by Yahoo! and Google, respectively.

Idealab recently completed funding deals with more venture capitalists, indicating that major investors have renewed confidence in Gross. "Bill is starting companies of great promise and of great interest to the venture community," notes Erik Straser, a partner at Mohr Davidow, an investor in the new firm Energy Innovations. "His enthusiasm and passion are still contagious. But now there's a clarity that comes from having to regroup and think about the next wave of companies—and a new ability to take execution to the next level."[1]

Like millions of people, you'd probably love to start and run your own company. Perhaps, just like Idealab's Bill Gross, you've spent time trying to devise a concept for a business you could launch. If you've been bitten by the entrepreneurial bug, you're not alone. More than ever, whether on their own or within an innovative firm, people like you, your classmates, and your friends are choosing the path of entrepreneurship for their careers.

How do you become an entrepreneur? Experts advise aspiring entrepreneurs to learn as much as possible about business by completing academic programs such as the one in which you are currently enrolled and by gaining practical experience by working part or full time for businesses. In addition, you can obtain invaluable insights about the pleasures and pitfalls of entrepreneurship by reading newspaper and magazine articles and biographies of successful entrepreneurs. These sources will help you learn how entrepreneurs handle the challenges of starting their businesses. For advice on how to launch and grow a new venture, turn to magazines such as *Entrepreneur, Success, Black Enterprise, Hispanic,* and *Inc.* Entrepreneurship associations such as the Asso-

ciation of African-American Women Business Owners and the Entrepreneurs' Organization also provide invaluable assistance. Finally, any aspiring entrepreneur should visit these Web sites:

- Center for Entrepreneurial Leadership (http://www.celcee.edu)
- Entrepreneur.com (http://www.entrepreneur.com)
- Kauffman eVenturing (http://www.eventuring.org)
- The Small Business Administration (http://www.sba.gov)
- *Wall Street Journal,* StartupJournal (http://www.startupjournal.com)

In this chapter, we focus on pathways for entering the world of entrepreneurship, describing what entrepreneurs do, the different kinds of entrepreneurs, and why a growing number of people choose to be entrepreneurs. It discusses the business environment in which entrepreneurs work, the characteristics that help entrepreneurs succeed, and the ways they start new ventures. The chapter ends with a discussion of methods by which large companies try to incorporate the entrepreneurial spirit.

WHAT IS AN ENTREPRENEUR?

entrepreneur person who seeks a profitable opportunity and takes the necessary risks to set up and operate a business.

You learned in Chapter 1 that an **entrepreneur** is a risk taker in the private enterprise system, a person who seeks a profitable opportunity and takes the necessary risks to set up and operate a business. Consider Sam Walton, Wal-Mart's founder, who started by franchising a few small Ben Franklin variety stores, and then opened his own Walton Five and Dime stores. Forty-five years later, this small venture has grown into a multibillion-dollar global business that is the largest company on earth.

"They Said It"

"It's just paper. All I own is a pickup truck and a little Wal-Mart stock."
—Sam Walton
(1918–1992)
American entrepreneur

Entrepreneurs differ from many small-business owners. Although many small-business owners possess the same drive, creative energy, and desire to succeed, what makes entrepreneurs different is their overwhelming desire to make their businesses grow. Sam Walton wasn't satisfied with just one successful Ben Franklin franchise, so he purchased others. And when that wasn't enough, he started and grew his own stores. Entrepreneurs combine their ideas and drive with money, employees, and other resources to create a business that fills a market need. That entrepreneurial role can make something significant out of a small beginning. In preparing its annual list of the 500 fastest-growing U.S. companies, *Inc.* magazine found that 29 percent started with less than $20,000 in the bank, that 14 percent started with less than $10,000, and that 15 percent started with less than $1,000. Yet 34 percent of the 500 CEOs on the list estimated their current net worth at more than $5 million.[2]

Entrepreneurs also differ from managers. Managers are employees who direct the efforts of others to achieve an organization's goals. Owners of some small start-up firms serve as owner-managers to implement their plans for their businesses and to offset human resource limitations at their fledgling companies. Entrepreneurs may also perform a managerial role, but their overriding responsibility is to use the resources of their organizations—employees, money, equipment, and facilities—to accomplish their goals. Indeed, their zeal to make their companies successful, particularly in the start-up stage of a new venture, can often turn entrepreneurs into terrible managers. Jim Ansara, founder of Boston-based Shawmut Design and Construction, now a $500 million construction company, said, "There were problems with my management style, and that started to create morale problems. The people I had were very dedicated—it was a cultlike atmosphere in most of the good ways—but they all would have said I was a complete maniac. I was way too intense, I pushed too hard, I didn't listen, I couldn't be reasoned with. Luckily I had a couple of people who were brave enough to tell me that consistently."[3] A key indication of Ansara's success as an entrepreneur was his willingness to recognize his limitations as a manager. When he finally recognized the negative effect he was having on his business, he hired others who were better suited to lead his business than was he.

Entrepreneurs are risk takers and people who have a unique vision of the future. Burt Rutan, already a famous aerospace engineer, brought his dream of commercial spaceflight to reality when his SpaceShipOne took humans to the edge of space and back twice. Rutan's 125-person firm, Scaled Composites, achieved its success without government funding or assistance but with help from private funds from Microsoft co-founder Paul Allen, shown here with Burt.

AP PHOTO/REED SAXON

Studies have identified certain personality traits and behaviors common to entrepreneurs that differ from those required for managerial success. One of these traits is the willingness to assume the risks involved in starting a new venture. Some, like Jim Ansara, the founder of Shawmut Design and Construction, leave their jobs to start their own companies and become successful entrepreneurs. Others find that they lack the characteristics required to start and grow a business. Entrepreneurial characteristics are examined in detail in a later section of this chapter.

assessment check

1. What tools do entrepreneurs use to create a new business?
2. How do entrepreneurs differ from managers?

CATEGORIES OF ENTREPRENEURS

Entrepreneurs apply their talents in different situations. These differences give rise to a set of distinct categories of entrepreneurs. As Figure 6.1 shows, four basic categories exist: classic entrepreneurs, serial entrepreneurs, intrapreneurs, and change agents.

Classic entrepreneurs identify business opportunities and allocate available resources to tap those markets. The story of Ben Serotta exemplifies the actions of a classic entrepreneur. Serotta is the founder of Serotta Competition Bicycles in Saratoga Springs, New York, which sells custom-made bikes that cost from $2,600 to $15,000. Serotta realized that dedicated cyclists would gladly pay big bucks for his company's bikes, as long as they fit their owners—and no one else—like a glove. Serotta's School of Cycling Ergonomics teaches bike shop

classic entrepreneur person who identifies a business opportunity and allocates available resources to tap that market.

6.1 Categories of Entrepreneurs

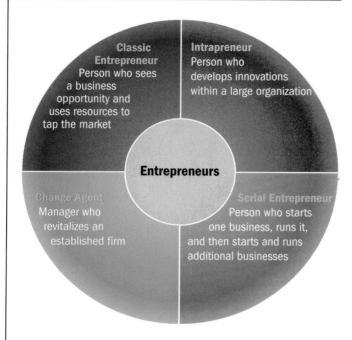

serial entrepreneur person who starts one business, runs it, and then starts and runs additional businesses in succession.

intrapreneur entrepreneurially oriented person who develops innovations within the context of a large organization.

change agent manager who revitalizes an established firm to keep it competitive.

owners how to achieve that custom fit, which usually takes two hours to get right. Kathleen Krumme of Oakley Cycles in Cincinnati, which sells 60 Serotta custom bikes a year, says, "Serotta equips us with the knowledge to sell its products, [and] then trusts us to do it. There isn't another company out there doing that."[4] The "Hit & Miss" feature describes the remarkable story of another classic entrepreneur, John H. Johnson, who created a publishing company and a new industry.

While a classic entrepreneur starts a new company by identifying a business opportunity and allocating resources to tap a new market, **serial entrepreneurs** start one business, run it, and then start and run additional businesses in succession. Stelios Haji-Ioannou, founder of the easyGroup companies, based in London, is a serial entrepreneur. Stelios's first company was easyJet, the low-fare European airline modeled after Southwest Airlines. Four years later, he started easy Internetcafé, which provides low-cost Internet access in high-traffic locations in major cities, such as London, Berlin, and New York, for students, travelers, and anyone else needing high-speed Internet services. Today, in addition to easyJet and easyInternetcafé, Stelios's easyGroup runs easyCar (rentals), easyValue (reviews and price comparisons for online shopping), easyMoney (insurance and credit cards), easyCinema (low-cost movie theaters and online DVD rentals), easyBus, easyHotel, easy4men (toiletries), easyJobs, easyPizza, easyMusic (music downloads by the track), easyCruise, easyMobile (cell phones), and easyWatch (watches for men, women, and children).[5]

Intrapreneurs are entrepreneurially oriented people who develop new products, ideas, and commercial ventures within large organizations. For example, 3M develops innovative products by encouraging intrapreneurship among its personnel. Some of 3M's most successful products began as inspirations of intrapreneurs. Art Frey invented the Post-it note, and intrapreneurs Connie Hubbard and Raymond Heyer invented the Scotch-Brite Never Rust soap pad. Intrapreneurship is discussed later in this chapter.

Change agents, also called *turnaround entrepreneurs*, are managers who revitalize established firms to keep them competitive in today's marketplace. When Bank of America (BofA) paid $47 billion to acquire FleetBoston, the general assessment was that BofA had "grossly overpaid," especially given FleetBoston's weak profits and customer service. But thanks to Liam McGee, BofA's primary change agent and president of BofA's consumer and small-business division, the critics are turning out to be wrong. McGee has worked with managers and employees at the 1,500 branch banks previously run by FleetBoston to change everything from training to the corporate culture. And those changes are beginning to work. For instance, when McGee visited a bank branch in Boston's historic district, he found the branch manager and customer representatives greeting customers as they entered the branch. Said McGee, "If you'd visited here six months ago, you would have seen all these people hidden back in their offices."[6] Also, thanks to new software that approves or rejects mortgage and home equity loans in just 30 minutes, free checking and online bill paying, extensive training on how to interact and greet customers, and a new bonus system that rewards employees only if customers sign up for and use bank services for at least four months, BofA has added 184,000 new checking accounts and 196,000 new savings accounts at Fleet Boston's old bank branches in the first year, all while cutting more than $900 million in costs.

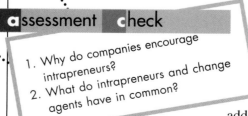

assessment check

1. Why do companies encourage intrapreneurs?
2. What do intrapreneurs and change agents have in common?

HIT & MISS

John H. Johnson Creates a Business—and an Empire

When he died at age 87, John H. Johnson had left a huge imprint on the publishing world. One of the most powerful and influential U.S. entrepreneurs, he was the first to recognize the African American market for media and cosmetics. Johnson founded his magazine *Ebony* in 1945, the first general-interest monthly magazine for African Americans. Today its circulation tops 1.7 million. In 1951, he followed with *Jet*, a weekly newsmagazine written from an African American perspective. *Jet*'s current circulation hovers just under 1 million. And in 1973, Johnson established Fashion Fair Cosmetics—skin care and cosmetics formulated especially for African American women. Fashion Fair also sponsored a large touring fashion show run by Johnson's wife, Eunice.

Johnson Publishing Company—an empire that includes publishing, cosmetics, television production, and fashion—is based in Chicago. With revenues of about $500 million, it is the nation's largest black-owned business. Johnson's daughter, Linda Rice Johnson, now the chief executive officer of the firm, describes her late father as "the greatest salesman and CEO I have ever known." Johnson grew up in poverty but did not let that stop him. "I thought my way out of poverty," he once said. "*Ebony* was my passport."

As an entrepreneur, Johnson insisted on controlling his own companies. He never turned them over to others and tried to keep top positions within the family whenever he could. His daughter, Linda, held several executive positions before becoming CEO upon her father's retirement, and his wife, Eunice, remains secretary-treasurer. Johnson Publishing is a privately held firm. As a visible public figure, Johnson endured criticism from workers who thought he drove them too hard and some African Americans who thought he was too oriented toward the middle class. But Lerone Bennett Jr., executive editor emeritus of *Ebony*, points out, "He virtually invented the black consumer market. He was the first publisher I know of who went to Madison Avenue and persuaded them that they had to address the African American market and use African American models. It paid off."

Questions for Critical Thinking

1. Describe two ways in which you believe John H. Johnson has affected U.S. business in general.
2. Describe ways in which John H. Johnson—and his company—could be considered innovative.

Sources: Johnson Publishing Web site, accessed June 17, 2006, www.johnsonpublishing.com; Tara Burghart, "Hundreds Remember Johnson," *Chicago Sun-Times*, accessed June 17, 2006, http://www.suntimes.com; Cora Daniels, "Pioneers," *Fortune*, August 22, 2005, pp. 72–88; Jason George, "Mourners Reflect on Inspiration," *Chicago Tribune*, August 15, 2005, section 1, pp. 1, 14; Charles Storch and Barbara Sherlock, "A Publishing Pioneer," *Chicago Tribune*, August 9, 2005, section 1, pp. 1, 16.

REASONS TO CHOOSE ENTREPRENEURSHIP AS A CAREER PATH

If you want to run your own business someday, you'll have plenty of company. Studies indicate that more than 11 percent of Americans, about one of every nine people, run their own businesses.[7] Surveys, however, generally indicate that many more people, as many as half of Americans, want to start their own businesses. This interest is even stronger among 14- to 19-year-olds; nearly two-thirds want to start and run their own business.[8] While general interest in entrepreneurship is very high, how many Americans are actually taking steps to start their own businesses at any particular time? In an average month, Americans start approximately 550,000 new businesses![9] And, that number is up substantially in recent years.

The past two decades have witnessed a heightened interest in entrepreneurial careers, spurred in part by publicity celebrating the successes of entrepreneurs such as Pierre Omidyar, who founded eBay; Oprah Winfrey, who has used her immensely popular television program

"They Said It"

"Ignore the stock market, ignore the economy, and buy a business you understand."
—Warren Buffett (b. 1930) CEO, Berkshire Hathaway, and one of America's richest entrepreneurs

ELLICE PEREZ

Warren Brown started baking to relieve the stress of his day job as a federal litigator in Washington, D.C. From hosting dessert parties with his friends, he moved on to open his small bakery, CakeLove. That business became so successful that the small shop was always jammed with customers. The resolution? Brown's Love Café, which opened across the street.

6.2 Why People Become Entrepreneurs

Desire to Be One's Own Boss	Desire to Succeed Financially
Desire for Job Security	Desire for an Improved Quality of Life

as a springboard for ventures into magazine publishing and TV and film production; Michael Dell, who launched what would become personal computer giant Dell following his freshman year at the University of Texas; and Bill Gates, who left Harvard to start Microsoft with friend Paul Allen.

People choose to become entrepreneurs for many different reasons. Some are motivated by dissatisfaction with the organizational work world, citing desires to escape unreasonable bosses or insufficient rewards and recognition. Other people start businesses because they believe their ideas represent opportunities to fulfill customer needs. Luis Espinoza founded a business to meet the unmet demand for Hispanic foods in his new home in northern Indiana. Espinoza had grown up in Texas, where his family enjoyed authentic Mexican foods. Although Espinoza found a significant, growing Hispanic community in Indiana, the local stores didn't know what products to offer these customers. One supermarket chain tried buying foods from a Texas distributor and stocked its shelves with items that appeal to Mexican tastes—in a neighborhood of Puerto Ricans, who prefer less spicy dishes. Espinoza knew he could do better. He learned about local tastes and set up Inca Quality Foods to provide canned goods and spices tailored to stores' local clientele. He convinced a Kroger manager to let him set up a display; when sales increased, he landed a contract to service Kroger stores throughout the area.[10]

As pointed out in Figure 6.2, people become entrepreneurs for one or more of four major reasons: a desire to be their own boss, succeed financially, attain job security, and improve their quality of life. Each of these reasons is described in more detail in the following sections.

Being Your Own Boss

Self-management is the motivation that drives many entrepreneurs. No entrepreneur matches this portrait of the American independent professional as an individual who has control over when, where, and how she works more than Liz Lange, the 30-something founder and CEO of Liz Lange Maternity.

Lange recognized a real need while working as a designer's assistant. Expectant mothers seeking sophisticated maternity wear quickly discovered that they would have to make do with baby-doll dresses or pants with a hole cut in the front—and a Lycra panel to accommodate their unborn child. Lange found herself offended by what was available. "I looked around the market to see what was out there and was frankly horrified. It was all so un-upscale, and much of it was oversized so that a woman could get through nine months in the same outfit. During her early days, a mother-to-be had nothing she could really fit into. It was all frilly—I mean, you are having a baby, not becoming a baby."[11]

Lange left her job to begin work designing a few basic items to show to retail buyers. They stated that pregnant women would not spend money on high-end maternity clothing. Undaunted, she borrowed $50,000 from family and friends and opened a small New York City office where she sold her made-to-order clothes by appointment. Word of the high-fashion maternity clothing spread like wildfire and led to an article in the *New York Times* Style section. Sales exploded after that, and Lange decided to bypass department stores in favor of selected high-fashion boutiques. Soon her slim pants, cashmere sweaters, and fitted slinky dresses were attracting super stylish expectant moms, including such celebrities as Cindy Crawford and Catherine Zeta-Jones.

Today, Lange runs stores in Beverly Hills, on New York's Madison Avenue, and on Long Island, New York, as well as producing an online catalog (http://www.lizlange.com) and a separate, less-expensive line of clothes marketed at more than 1,300 Target stores nationwide. Annual sales exceed $10 million. Both Lange and her satisfied customers agree that her decision to be her own boss was a wise one.

Financial Success

Entrepreneurs are wealth creators. Many start their ventures with the specific goal of creating a profitable business and reaping its financial rewards. Why? Because they believe they won't get rich by working for someone else. And studies indicate they're generally right. While only one in five American workers is self-employed, more than two-thirds of all millionaires are self-employed. Consequently, if you run your own business, you're more likely to become wealthy.[12] The business press, of course, is quick to publish stories about the wealth and "self-made" successes of today's entrepreneurs. For example, it's well known that Google founders Sergey Brin and Larry Page made over $14 billion each when Google sold its shares in an initial public offering, and they are worth much more than that today.[13] Less well known, though, are successful entrepreneurs such as Constantino de Oliveira Jr. and his father, who founded Brazil's third largest airline, Gol Linhas Aéreas Inteligentes (Gol Intelligent Airlines), just five years ago. Gol, or *goal* in English, is the most profitable airline in the world, with an operating margin of 37 percent compared with 20 percent for extremely successful Southwest Airlines. Gol achieves those profits with prices so low that it put its major competitor, Transbrasil, out of business in less than a year. By growing from 38 to 76 planes over the next few years, Gol will likely overtake Varig Airlines and become Brazil's second-largest airline. Today, the value of the Oliveira family's share of Gol is worth more than $2.4 billion.[14]

Although entrepreneurs often mention financial rewards as a motive for starting their businesses, the path to riches can be long and uncertain. As you learned in Chapter 5, one-third of newly started small firms are out of business within two years, more than half within four years, 61 percent within six years, and 82 percent within ten years.[15] So there's clearly no guarantee of success. Furthermore, among the CEOs heading America's fastest-growing private companies (the so-called *Inc.* 500), almost one-fourth took no compensation at all from their business during its first five years of operation. For example, at first, Stephen Culp, founder and CEO of Smart Furniture, a modular-furniture company in Chattanooga, paid everyone in his company *but* himself. Culp reasoned, "If I can survive on cereal and take all the cash that I would have spent on a more extravagant lifestyle and put it back into the company, it increases my chances of success."[16]

Entrepreneurs often work long hours to bring their dreams to life. Mexican immigrants Pablo and Juanita Ceja first worked as grape pickers in the Napa Valley fields from before dawn until after sunset. They scrimped and saved and eventually bought their first fifteen acres of grape fields, which they have added to over the years. Thanks to son Armando, who studied winemaking at UC Davis, the family became prize-winning vintners. Says Armando, "It's the American dream."

© ED KASHI/CORBIS

Job Security

Although the demand for skilled employees remains high in many industries, working for a company, even a *Fortune* 500 firm, is no guarantee of job security. In fact, over the last ten years, large companies sought efficiency by downsizing and actually eliminated more jobs than they created. As a result, a growing number of American workers—both first-time job seekers and laid-off long-term employees—are deciding to create their own job security by starting their own businesses. Why? Because "even if you're the creative director for Disney, Comcast could buy the company, and you could be out of a job," says Mary Furlong, who teaches entrepreneurship at Santa Clara University.[17] While running your own business doesn't guarantee job security, the U.S. Small Business Administration has found that most newly created jobs come from small businesses, with a significant share of those jobs coming from new companies.[18]

The key difference is that an entrepreneur's job depends not on the decisions of employers but instead on the decisions of customers and investors and on the cooperation and commitment of the entrepreneur's own employees. People like Jim Minick, 51, of Smyrna, Georgia, who has been laid off by employers three times in 25 years, would rather work for themselves than for others. Minick, who started his own business, noted, "You don't want to find yourself 55 or 60 with no one wanting to hire you. That's a concern with any 50-year-old."[19] However, many younger workers feel the same way. Twenty-three-year-old pastry chef Sarah Levy quit her high-stress, low-paying restaurant jobs to start her own business, Sarah's Pastries & Candies, in Chicago. Regarding the change, Levy said, "I feel better when I'm working for myself and building a name for myself."[20]

Quality of Life

Entrepreneurship is an attractive career option for people seeking to improve their quality of life. Starting a business gives the founder some choice over when, where, and how to work. Brett Schulte became a **lifestyle entrepreneur,** a person who starts a business to reduce work hours and create a more relaxed lifestyle, after vacationing in Mexico's Baja California. Schulte quit his job at a dot-com company, moved his family to Mexico, and became a Web consultant. Schulte points out how technology has allowed him to be a lifestyle entrepreneur, saying, "Technology is making geography less important. [Internet telephone service] is enabling me to have a U.S. phone number in Mexico."[21] His U.S. clients don't have to know that he's working from his laptop while sitting at the beach.

Despite Brett Schulte's relaxed work environment, most entrepreneurs work long hours and at the whims of their customers. For instance, Eva Rosenberg, who runs a tax accounting business from her home in Irvine, California, began as a lifestyle entrepreneur, working just three days a week. But her business grew so much that she obtained a regular office and began working long hours. Said Rosenberg, "I had so many clients that I was pretty much working almost seven days a week, morning until night. I had an office on Ventura Boulevard, and I was always there. Then somewhere along the way I got married, and I wanted to see my husband."[22] Michelle Tell experienced a similar time crunch when she started her company, Preferred Public Relations & Marketing, in Las Vegas. Tell, who had just left a job with the MGM Grand Hotel and Casino, said, "My goal was to have five clients and take it easy for a while." However, one month after starting her business, she had seven clients. Today, she has 30 clients and seven full-time employees. Says Tell, "Our company took off like a storm, and we find ourselves working seven days a week."[23]

For other lifestyle entrepreneurs, quality of life is not defined by how many hours they work but by their ability to fulfill broader social objectives through their ventures. Darren Patrick founded Rainbow Play Systems in Brookings, South Dakota, when he was 20. Three

lifestyle entrepreneur
person who starts a business to reduce work hours and create a more relaxed lifestyle.

years later, he was a millionaire. Today, Rainbow makes 64 different kinds of redwood and red cedar residential playground equipment and sells it in 250 stores in the United States, Canada, Mexico, Panama, Spain, and South Korea. This year, the company will ring up more than $500 million in sales, making Rainbow one of the nation's largest consumers of redwood.

And that's what worried Patrick from the start. "Since the onset of our business, we have always been concerned about our lumber purchases and the mills that fulfill them," he states. Rainbow buys lumber only from mills participating in sustained-yield programs that protect the redwood population. The firm goes further by educating purchasers about the benefits offered by such programs. As a result, Patrick says, "Today, we have more redwood trees than ever before."[24]

assessment check

1. Are entrepreneurs more likely than employees to achieve financial success?
2. What factors affect the entrepreneur's job security?

THE ENVIRONMENT FOR ENTREPRENEURS

If you are motivated to start your own company, several factors suggest that now may be the right time to begin. First, as discussed earlier in the chapter, the status of entrepreneurship as a career choice has been rising. Entrepreneurship began moving toward the business mainstream in the early 1980s after Steve Jobs of Apple Computer and other high-tech entrepreneurs gained national attention by going public—that is, selling stock in their companies. And, as discussed later in the chapter, today's entrepreneurs are also reaping the benefits of financial interest among investors. In addition to favorable public attitudes toward entrepreneurs and the growing number of financing options, several other factors—identified in Figure 6.3—also support and expand opportunities for entrepreneurs: globalization, education, information technology, and demographic and economic trends. Each of these factors is discussed in the following sections.

Globalization

The rapid globalization of business, described in preceding chapters, has created many opportunities for entrepreneurs. Entrepreneurs market their products abroad and hire international talent. Among the fastest-growing small U.S. companies, almost two of every five have international sales. One entrepreneur who sees international opportunities is Mia Abbruzzese, who, after working for Stride Rite developing shoes to be sold at Target department stores, thought to herself, "If I can do this for Target, what's to say that I can't do it for myself?" So Abbruzzese quit her job at Stride Rite, started her own company, and began working her contacts in China to find a factory that was willing to begin production of her new line of Morgan & Milo shoes. Abbruzzese used freelance designers to develop the look she wanted and then found a maker of shoe parts in China that wanted to move up to producing entire shoes. In her first year, her company made 65,000 shoes and had sales of $800,000. Furthermore, her Morgan & Milo line of shoes now sells at Nordstrom's, Macy's, and Zappos.com, a leading Web shoe retailer.[25]

Growth in entrepreneurship is a worldwide phenomenon. The role of entrepreneurs is growing in most industrialized and newly industrialized nations as well as in the emerging free-market countries in central and eastern Europe. However, as shown in Figure 6.4, the level of entrepreneurship

Figure 6.3

Factors Supporting and Expanding Opportunities for Entrepreneurs

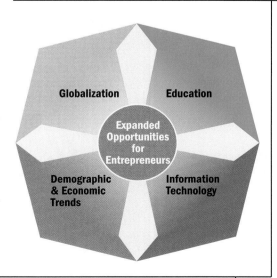

The entrepreneurial spirit thrives in many cultures. Rainsey Ker's family left Cambodia when he was six to flee oppression of the brutal Khmer Rouge government. Ker's Mitpheap Asian Market in Portland, Maine, carries Asian, African, and Hispanic foods. Ker is not content to run his small store, though. He is working part time as a real estate agent and hopes eventually to open his own agency.

© ERIC WEEKS

varies considerably. Worldwide, more than 9 percent of adults are starting or managing a new business. But in Peru, almost four in ten adults are engaged in entrepreneurial activity, followed by Uganda (32 percent), Ecuador (27 percent), Jordan (18 percent), New Zealand (15 percent), and Iceland (14 percent). The United States, with more than 11 percent of adults qualifying as entrepreneurs, is currently in tenth place.[26]

Still, Figure 6.4 also shows that entrepreneurs in many other countries, such as Japan (2 percent), Slovenia and Hong Kong (3 percent each), and Belgium and Sweden (4 percent each), find it much more difficult to start businesses. Obstacles include government regulations, high taxes, and political attitudes that favor big business. In the United Kingdom, which has a below-average rate of entrepreneurship (slightly more than 6 percent), four in ten small-business owners say they would not start a new company because of the heavy burden of government regulations.[27] In addition, cultural values in other countries may differ from those in the United States and other countries, where individualism and risk taking are admired and where high value is placed on seizing a business opportunity.

Figure

6.4 Levels of Entrepreneurial Activity in 34 Countries

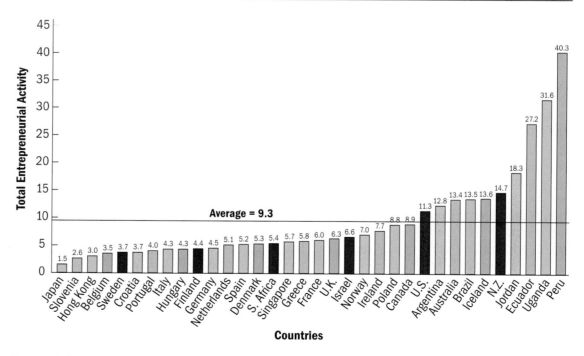

Source: Zoltan Acs, Pia Arenius, Michael Hay, and Maria Minniti, "Global Entrepreneurship Monitor: Executive Report," Global Entrepreneurship Monitor Consortium, accessed June 17, 2006, http://www.gemconsortium.org.

Education

The past two decades have brought tremendous growth in the number of educational opportunities for would-be entrepreneurs. Today, more than 100 U.S. universities offer full-fledged majors in entrepreneurship, another 73 offer an emphasis in entrepreneurship, and hundreds more offer one or two courses in how to start a business.[28] Some schools, including Alfred University, University of St. Thomas, and Miami University of Ohio, offer entrepreneurship courses to nonbusiness students, on the assumption that people in other disciplines will eventually start businesses, too.

Another way business schools are responding to the interest in entrepreneurship is by helping their students start businesses. Babson College has a program in which a few students are permitted to replace several of the usual classes with launching an actual business under coaching from an entrepreneur-turned-professor. At the University of Maryland, entrepreneurship students live together in an exclusive, apartment-style residence hall that, with dedicated meeting rooms, offices, and computer labs, is designed to encourage interaction and ideas. Students are taught by entrepreneurship professors, experienced entrepreneurs, CEOs, and technology specialists from the engineering school and industry. Students in this program are not only expected to start a business but also given responsibility to run the university's business plan competition and technology start-up boot camp.[29]

Besides schools, many organizations have sprouted up in recent years to teach entrepreneurship to young people. The Kauffman Center for Entrepreneurial Leadership offers training programs for learners from kindergarten through community college. The center's Entreprep summer program, which is taught in conjunction with local colleges and universities, teaches high school juniors how to start and manage a company. Students in Free Enterprise (SIFE) is a worldwide not-for-profit organization in which college students, working with faculty advisors, teach grade school and high school students and other community members the value of private enterprise and entrepreneurship.[30] The Association of Collegiate Entrepreneurs has chapters on many college campuses in the United States and Canada.

The question, of course, is whether students who major in entrepreneurship or take entrepreneurship classes are any more likely to successfully start a business. In fact, students who graduate from entrepreneurship programs are three times as likely to be self-employed and three times more likely to help start new companies.[31] Jeffrey Betz, Cecilia Domingos, and Michael Lobsinger started their company, Orca Gear, while in the graduate entrepreneurship program at Rensselaer Polytechnic Institute in Troy, New York. The company designs and manufactures Float Tech outerwear—lightweight all-season jackets with built-in inflatable life jackets; one tug on the rip cord inflates the life jacket. Says Betz, "Our story definitely supports that you can learn entrepreneurship."[32]

Information Technology

The explosion in information technology (IT) has provided one of the biggest boosts for entrepreneurs. As computer and communications technologies have merged and dropped dramatically in cost, entrepreneurs have gained tools that help them compete with large companies. Information technology helps entrepreneurs work quickly and efficiently, provide attentive customer service, increase sales, and project professional images. New technologies helped Kelly Ford's new company, Oriel Wines, which imports and exports 24 handmade wines from 22 wine-producing regions and countries, to sound, act, and look like a large company. Said Ford, "We're a luxury brand, so customers have to think we're bigger than we really are."[33] But with Ford and just five other employees, Oriel Wines is a tiny company that just looks and acts big, thanks to NetSuite software, which manages inventory, accounting, customer orders, newsletters, and marketing, all from one central computer.

Advances in information technology have also created demand for new products, and entrepreneurs have risen to the challenge. Some have started businesses that directly apply information technology. After hearing reports about a missing girl, and "all the talk shows . . . saying, 'If only they'd had better identification information about her,'" Jeremiah Hutchins wondered if the mini-CD business cards that he was producing could enable stressed parents to quickly provide police with the information they needed, such as allergies, scars, birthmarks, blood type, height, weight, and photos to identify and track down lost or abducted children. Today, Safe Kids Cards sells mini CDs, about the size of a credit card, through franchises in the United States, Australia, Canada, Ireland, New Zealand, and South Africa.[34]

Jeremiah Hutchins combined his knowledge of information technology with his desire to help parents and law enforcement officials. The mini-CDs produced by his company, Safe Kids Card, help locate lost or kidnapped children by storing vital statistics and pictures of children.

Yet the Internet is a challenge as well as an opportunity for entrepreneurs. Because customers can go online to check prices and buy from large or small companies anywhere in the world, entrepreneurs need to find a distinctive advantage over big competitors. Raymond Galeotti, president of EvesAddiction.com, which sells jewelry, found that advantage for his small business by pairing with one of the Internet's largest companies, Yahoo! For as little as $30 a month, Yahoo! Small Business Web hosting provides tools to build and maintain his Web site, specialized marketing services that recommend new products to his customers based on their previous purchases, secure purchasing via PayPal and credit cards, and 24-hour toll-free consulting. Most important, though, says Galeotti, "We wanted reliability."[35] And, since he signed on with Yahoo!, his Web site hasn't been down even once.

Demographic and Economic Trends

Demographic trends, such as the aging of the U.S. population, the emergence of Hispanics as the nation's largest ethnic group, and the growth of two-income families, create opportunities for entrepreneurs to market new goods and services. Entrepreneurs take advantage of such trends to offer everything from retirement homes to grocery delivery services. For example, Alere Medical, based in Reno, Nevada, sells equipment that enables nurses to monitor heart-failure patients from their homes. Patients step onto a biometric device the size of a scale, which monitors and reports the patient's weight and physical symptoms. While standing on the monitor, patients use a small interactive display device to respond to yes and no questions about their health. That information is forwarded to Alere's database, where a nurse analyzes the data and immediately notifies physicians and patients when problems are indicated. With 4.6 million Americans already diagnosed with heart failure, and an aging population, Alere's business, which reduces hospital costs and stays and allows patients to recover and monitor their health at home, will continue to grow.[36]

assessment check

1. To what extent is entrepreneurship possible in different countries, and what opportunities does globalization create for today's entrepreneurs?
2. Identify the educational factors that help expand current opportunities for entrepreneurs.
3. Describe current demographic trends that suggest new goods and services for entrepreneurial businesses.

CHARACTERISTICS OF ENTREPRENEURS

The examples of entrepreneurship you've read about so far suggest that people who strike out on their own are a different breed. Well, they are. Successful entrepreneurs are more likely to

Figure

6.5

have had parents who were entrepreneurs. They also tend to possess unique personality traits. Researchers who study successful entrepreneurs report that they are more likely to be inquisitive, passionate, self-motivated, honest, courageous, flexible, intelligent, and reliable people. The eight traits summarized in Figure 6.5 are especially important for people who want to succeed as entrepreneurs.

Characteristics of Entrepreneurs

Entrepreneurial Personality

Vision	Tolerance for Failure
High Energy Level	Creativity
Need to Achieve	Tolerance for Ambiguity
Self-Confidence and Optimism	Internal Locus of Control

Vision

Entrepreneurs begin with a *vision*, an overall idea for how to make their business idea a success, and then they passionately pursue it. Bill Gates and Paul Allen launched Microsoft with the vision of a computer on every desk and in every home, all running Microsoft software. Their vision helped Microsoft become the world's largest marketer of computer software. It guided the company and provided clear direction for employees as Microsoft grew, adapted, and prospered in an industry characterized by tremendous technological change.

Talk about vision, about the ability to think out of the box; talk about the Thomas Edison of the 21st century and you're not talking about Bill Gates, though. No, these descriptions are for wildly successful inventor and entrepreneur Dean Kamen. The tireless and gregarious father of the first portable insulin pump, heart stent, and stair-climbing wheelchair certainly has vision, but he also keeps a close watch on the bottom line of the numerous successful companies that have resulted from his technological breakthroughs.

His latest creation has met with mixed success. The Segway Human Transporter is a two-wheeled self-balancing electric-powered superscooter that allows people to zip along sidewalks and in large business facilities at eight to twelve miles per hour. While Segway sales have been slower than expected, police and security forces, tour companies (you can take guided Segway tours of Atlanta, Budapest, Chicago, Paris, and Washington D.C.), businesses, and people with disabilities are buying Segways.[37] Shane Latham, who was born without a hip, uses a Segway instead of a wheelchair. The Segway allows him to hold hands with his wife while shopping. Moreover, he says, "I am no longer looking at people's belt buckles when I talk to them. I can look them eye to eye."[38]

JONATHAN DRAKE/EPA/LANDOV

The Segway Human Transporter has been a hit for a variety of people—including those with physical handicaps and law enforcement officers. The Segway is just one idea that inventor Dean Kamen has dreamed up and brought to market.

High Energy Level

Entrepreneurs willingly work hard to realize their visions. Starting and building a company require an enormous amount of hard work and long hours. Some entrepreneurs work full time at their regular day jobs and spend weeknights and weekends launching their start-ups. Many devote fourteen-hour days seven days a week to their new ventures. In his ten-year study of entrepreneurs, author Amar Bhidé found that what distinguishes successful entrepreneurs from other business owners is that they "work harder, hustle for customers, and know that the opportunity may not last for more than six or eight months."[39]

A major reason entrepreneurship demands hard work is that start-up companies typically have a small staff and struggle to raise enough capital. Under these resource constraints, the entrepreneur has to make up the difference. When two engineers started Gilat Satellite Networks in Petah Tikva, Israel, to build satellite systems, they had to work extremely hard to compete with giant corporations like EchoStar. They offered to do whatever was necessary to tailor a system to the client's needs. Gilat's first customer was Rite Aid, the drugstore chain. The company won the contract by agreeing to adapt its satellite system in significant ways. The two founders and four other members of the project's development team put in many nights and evenings to achieve their commitment. Co-founder Amiram Levinberg says simply, "In a high-tech start-up such as Gilat . . . it's a given that there will be some 12-hour days."[40]

With studies indicating that the average entrepreneur works between 52 and 56 hours per week, and that one-fifth of all entrepreneurs work seven days a week, the challenge for entrepreneurs is to balance the hard work with the rest, recreation, and family time that are so essential to good health, quality of life, and continued creativity.[41] Serial entrepreneur Peyton Anderson, CEO of North Carolina–based Affinergy, admits that he thinks about business when with his children. "I have three kids 4 and under. And even while I'm singing to them in the bathtub, in the back of my mind, I'm grinding on stuff at work." Still, Anderson creates time for his children by working after they go to bed, not working one day per weekend, and coming into work late once per week. Said Anderson, "I can do a lot of work from 9 P.M. to midnight using my wireless laptop and sending out e-mails. And I try to keep Saturday [open] all day to do things with the kids. I can [also] come in to work at 9:30 one morning, because I know I'll stay late that night."[42]

Need to Achieve

Entrepreneurs work hard because they want to excel. Their strong competitive drive helps them enjoy the challenge of reaching difficult goals and promotes dedication to personal success. Entrepreneurship expert Amar Bhidé says successful entrepreneurs have "an almost maniacal level of ambition. Not just ambition to make a comfortable living, to make a few million dollars, but someone who wants to leave a significant mark on the world."[43]

Maria de Lourdes Sobrino's dream was to find success in the United States. A Mexican immigrant, Sobrino moved with her husband and daughter to Los Angeles, where she opened a travel business concentrating on travel between the United States and Mexico. But economic woes in Mexico ended demand for her services, and personal conflicts ended her marriage. Sobrino needed a new way to support herself, and an idea came to her: selling small cups of flavored gelatin, a common treat in Mexico that had not yet found its way to U.S. stores. Identifying retailers willing to take a chance on the new product required persistence. Store managers didn't understand the product, so Sobrino honed the marketing strategy for her company, LuLu's Dessert Factory. She identified Hispanic communities and visited independent stores. Finally, one allowed her to leave gelatin cups, with payment contingent on sales. When Sobrino returned to her spartan office, a message was waiting for her: "Please come back, Señora. Your gelatins are sold."[44] That was the turning point for LuLu's. When her product became popular in local stores, a food broker began to carry it, and Sobrino borrowed money to expand her facilities. Paying off the loans was difficult and took years, but today LuLu's is a $15 million company with 45 products offered in West Coast stores. And she is working with Wal-Mart to export her products to Mexico. Said Sobrino, "Wal-Mart is a very important company to do business with. It will be very exciting to have LuLu's in Mexico."[45]

Self-Confidence and Optimism

Entrepreneurs believe in their ability to succeed, and they instill their optimism in others. Often their optimism resembles fearlessness in the face of difficult odds. "People thought we were crazy to give up six-figure salaries at investment banking firms to reinvent the earmuff," says Brian LeGette of himself and his business partner Ron Wilson. "They laughed at us." LeGette and Wilson are the founders of 180s LLC, a Baltimore company that got its start with a fleece-covered ear warmer that wraps around the back of the wearer's head. Despite not knowing anything about fabric or sewing, the two business school students put start-up expenses on their credit cards, built a prototype from items they bought at Wal-Mart, and went to work. Within a year, they were a successful start-up, selling their ear warmers for $20 each. Soon they were raising capital to finance growth, hiring additional employees, and adding products. The firm's innovative takes on ordinary products such as sunglasses, beach chairs, and gloves have made 180s into a $50 million firm with 100 employees that sells its products in 18,000 retail stores in 40 countries. One of 180s's latest products is the Quantum Vent, a jacket that allows runners to control their body temperature by pulling cords to lower a vent in the back that draws cool air through a mesh vent. Says LeGette, "We have an inexhaustible desire to question the things that most people think have already been answered. And that's how we succeed in reinventing the wheel."[46]

Sometimes, though, overconfidence can blind entrepreneurs and jeopardize their businesses. This is what happened at 180s. After burning through most of their investors' cash, both LeGette and Wilson have left the company. New investors, who have put $20 million into the company, have now turned the company over to a new CEO with much more experience in the apparel industry.[47]

Tolerance for Failure

Entrepreneurs often succeed by sheer will and the ability to try and try again when others would give up. They also view setbacks and failures as learning experiences and are not easily discouraged or disappointed when things don't go as planned. Howard Schultz, founder and CEO of Starbucks Coffee, said, "I took Starbucks into the magazine business with *Joe*—my idea. Nobody read it. Since *Joe* failed, I've kept a rack of issues in my office so everyone can see the magazine and realize we shouldn't hide behind our mistakes and we should have the courage to keep pushing by not embracing the status quo. I keep that there as a memento. It was an embarrassing defeat, and we lost a fair amount of money, but sometimes you have to have the courage to fail."[48]

Creativity

Entrepreneurs typically conceive new ideas for goods and services, and they devise innovative ways to overcome difficult problems and situations. Kenny Kramm struggled in frustration and despair as he watched his infant daughter try to swallow bitter antiseizure medication four times a day. Often Kramm and his wife had to rush their daughter to the emergency room for treatment for the seizures because she had not been able to take enough of the medicine. Kramm improvised at first, giving his daughter mashed banana to help her stomach her medication. Then inspiration struck: He guessed that he wasn't the only parent who had trouble feeding foul-tasting medications to his child. So Kramm concocted harmless additives in his parents' suburban Washington, D.C., pharmacy, where he worked. The additives sweeten the taste and suppress bitterness without diluting the medicine. From a banana flavor, he branched out to other flavors for liquids, pills, and powders. Today, 30,000 pharmacies in the United

States, Canada, Australia, and New Zealand use FLAVORx to make medicine taste better.[49] And thanks to a contract with Walgreen's and other major drugstore chains, revenues grew from $450,000 to $7.8 million in just six years.[50] Is Kramm finished innovating? Not yet. His flavored pet medications are now used at more than 2,000 vet clinics.

Entrepreneurs like Kenny Kramm often achieve success by making creative improvements, rather than single-handedly revolutionizing an industry. Amar Bhidé's research identified a substantial amount of creativity among entrepreneurs "at the tactical level"—in other words, in the ways entrepreneurs built their businesses, more so than in the product itself.[51]

Tolerance for Ambiguity

Entrepreneurs take in stride the uncertainties associated with launching a venture. Dealing with unexpected events is the norm for most entrepreneurs. Kate and Andy Spade didn't transform their business, Kate Spade, from a small handbag store in New York into a $125 million business by taking unnecessary risks. Kate Spade said, "When we started to have a lot of success with the bags, people said we should expand into this or that category. We knew we had a window of opportunity, but the point was to get into a category that had a growth prospect, and not for growth to simply be the byproduct." In other words, Kate Spade was going to be very careful about which products her company chose to design and sell. Kate's husband, Andy, explains, saying, "If we go into a new category we always ask, 'Do we understand it? Can we design it well?'" And if they don't and can't, they won't design and make those products.[52]

Tolerance for ambiguity is different from the love of risk taking that many people associate with entrepreneurship. Successful entrepreneurship is a far cry from gambling because entrepreneurs look for strategies that they believe have a good chance of success, and they quickly make adjustments when a strategy isn't working. An important way entrepreneurs manage ambiguity is by staying close to customers so that they can adjust their offerings in keeping with customer desires. Amnon Landan, CEO of Mercury, a Mountain View, California–based company that helps banks use information technology to better serve their customers, was named Entrepreneur of the Year by *Forbes* magazine several years ago. Commenting on the importance of being close to customers, Landan says, "It is an overused expression, but the problem is that not too many people are actually exercising it. If you are wise enough to keep close and listen, then you learn about product direction, you learn about the tone of the [customer's] business and where it is moving and shifting." Accordingly, Landan spends 40 percent of his time each year visiting 50 key customers and expects his managers, staff, and especially engineers who design the company's products to spend time with customers, too. Says Landan, "If there is a big deal pending, usually I will not show up to try to close a deal, because you do not learn a lot when you do that. [I go] to our customers to understand how they use the products and what their needs are, and to create communication and trust."[53]

Internal Locus of Control

Entrepreneurs believe that they control their own fates, which means they have an internal locus of control. You won't find entrepreneurs gazing into a crystal ball, calling psychic help lines, or looking for a four-leaf clover; they take personal responsibility for the success or failure of their actions rather than believing in luck or fate. They neither make excuses for their shortcomings nor blame others for their setbacks and failures. Chris Reeve is one entrepreneur who took a hard look at his abilities in light of the needs of his growing business. He took decisive action to get the company on the right track, as described in the "Hit & Miss" feature.

HIT & MISS

Chris Reeve Knives Hunts for a New CEO

Starting a company has been compared to raising a child—at some point, parents must let their grown child enter the world as an independent adult. Entrepreneurs face a similar challenge. Once a business has reached a certain point, its founders may find that their old roles no longer benefit the company, so they struggle to find and fill new ones. They may discover that they enjoy the changes or that they would prefer to move on. The founder of eBay ultimately brought in Meg Whitman to run the company. Yahoo!'s founders tapped Terry Simmel. Chris Reeve, founder of Chris Reeve Knives, finds himself in a similar situation.

Thirty years ago, Chris Reeve established his company in Idaho. His high-end, handmade hunting knives are considered works of art—ranking among the best in the world. Celebrities such as Tom Selleck and Tom Cruise have made purchases. Chris Reeve knives appear in movies and other promotions. But Reeve is no longer sure he's the best person to run his company. "A business like mine that makes something is often started by a very fine craftsman or engineer who is brilliant at what he does," he explains. "That doesn't necessarily translate into being able to run a business and manage and motivate people to do the work properly."

So Reeve is hunting for a new chief. He wants to remain with the firm as its chief designer and inventor—which is how he started out. Several years ago, he tried hiring managers who were friends, or referred by friends—twice. Neither worked out. Reeve understands that the next candidate needs an outside perspective on the company. He also knows that the firm's goals must be made clear. And while he knows he's the best in the world at designing knives, he will have to hire someone who is much better than he is at managing the company—after all, that's the whole point.

Questions for Critical Thinking

1. What entrepreneurial traits does Chris Reeve seem to have?
2. Do you think it will be beneficial for Reeve to step aside as his firm's chief executive? Why or why not?

Sources: Chris Reeve Knives Web site, accessed June 17, 2006, http://www.chrisreeve.com; Perri Capell, "When a Small Company Outgrows Its Founder," *StartupJournal*, accessed June 17, 2006, http://www.startupjournal.com; "Hire People Better Than You," *BusinessWeek*, accessed June 17, 2006, http://www.businessweek.com.

After reading this summary of typical personality traits, maybe you're wondering if you have what it takes to become an entrepreneur. Take the test in Figure 6.6 to find out. Your results may help you determine whether you would succeed in starting your own company.

assessment check

1. What is meant by an entrepreneur's vision?
2. Why is it important for an entrepreneur to have a high energy level and a strong need for achievement?
3. How do entrepreneurs generally feel about the possibility of failure?

STARTING A NEW VENTURE

The examples of entrepreneurs presented so far have introduced many ways to start a business. This section discusses the process of choosing an idea for a new venture and transforming the idea into a working business.

Selecting a Business Idea

In choosing an idea for your business, the two most important considerations are (1) finding something you love to do and are good at doing and (2) determining whether your idea can satisfy a need in the marketplace. People willingly work hard doing something they love, and

Figure

6.6

Testing Your Entrepreneurial Potential

ENTREPRENEUR POTENTIAL ASSESSMENT FORM

Answer each of the following questions:

Yes   No

☐   ☐   1. Are you a first-generation American?

☐   ☐   2. Were you an honor student?

☐   ☐   3. Did you enjoy group functions in school—clubs, team sports, even double dates?

☐   ☐   4. As a youngster, did you frequently prefer to spend time alone?

☐   ☐   5. As a child, did you have a paper route, a lemonade stand, or some other small enterprise?

☐   ☐   6. Were you a stubborn child?

☐   ☐   7. Were you a cautious youngster, the last in the neighborhood to try diving off the high board?

☐   ☐   8. Do you worry about what others think of you?

☐   ☐   9. Are you in a rut, tired of the same routine every day?

☐   ☐   10. Would you be willing to invest your savings—and risk losing all you invested—to go it alone?

☐   ☐   11. If your new business should fail, would you get to work immediately on another?

☐   ☐   12. Are you an optimist?

Add up your total score. A score of 20 or more points indicates strong entrepreneurial tendencies. A score between 0 and 19 points suggests some possibility for success as an entrepreneur. A score between 0 and −10 indicates little chance of successful entrepreneurship. A score below −11 indicates someone who's not the entrepreneurial type.

Answers: 1. Yes = 1, No = −1; 2. Yes = −4, No = 4; 3. Yes = −1, No = 1; 4. Yes = 1, No = −1; 5. Yes = 2, No = −2; 6. Yes = 1, No = −1; 7. Yes = −4, No = 4 (if you were a very daring child, add another 4 points); 8. Yes = −1, No = 1; 9. Yes = 2, No = −2; 10. Yes = 2, No = −2; 11. Yes = 4, No = −4; 12. Yes = 2, No = −2.

Source: Copyright Northwestern Mutual Life Insurance Company. Reprinted with permission.

the experience will bring personal fulfillment. The old adages "Do what makes you happy" and "To thine own self be true" are the best guidelines for deciding on a business idea.

Success also depends on customers, so would-be entrepreneurs must also be sure that the idea they choose has interest in the marketplace. The most successful entrepreneurs tend to operate in industries where a great deal of change is taking place and in which customers have difficulty pinpointing their precise needs. These industries, including advanced technology and consulting, allow entrepreneurs to capitalize on their strengths, such as creativity, hard work, and tolerance of ambiguity, to build customer relationships. Nevertheless, examples of outstanding entrepreneurial success occur in every industry, such as Firefly Mobile, which sells simple five-button mobile phones (Call Mom, Call Dad, Phone Numbers, Hello, and Good-bye) for young children that come with 30 minutes of talking time and let parents restrict incoming and outgoing phone numbers.[54] The following guidelines may help you select an idea that represents a good entrepreneurial opportunity:

- List your interests and abilities. Include your values and beliefs, your goals and dreams, things you like and dislike doing, and your job experiences.
- Make another list of the types of businesses that match your interests and abilities.
- Read newspapers and business and consumer magazines to learn about demographic and economic trends that identify future needs for products that no one yet offers.
- Carefully evaluate existing goods and services, looking for ways you can improve them.
- Decide on a business that matches what you want and offers profit potential.
- Conduct marketing research to determine whether your business idea will attract enough customers to earn a profit.
- Learn as much as you can about the industry in which your new venture will operate, your merchandise or service, and your competitors. Read surveys that project growth in various industries.

Like Kenny Kramm, whose medication-flavoring business was described earlier, many entrepreneurs start businesses to solve problems that they experienced either at work or in their personal lives. When Robert Byerley's $100 dress shirt was ruined at the cleaners, he just wanted his shirt replaced. But when they didn't even apologize, he got the idea for a new business, a premium dry cleaner that stands behind its services. But before he started this business, he did his thinking and his research first. Unable to sleep one night, he created a list of features for the business: "a bank-like drive-through area with curbside delivery; a computerized system that would track clothes all the way through the process and read cleaning preferences off a small bar code; and state-of-the-art, environmentally friendly cleaning processes." Then he spent a week in the library, where he learned that the $16-billion-a-year business is dominated by mom-and-pop businesses. At the Better Business Bureau, he discovered the most common complaint about dry cleaners: not standing behind what they did. Finally, he spent $15,000 to conduct focus groups, asking potential customers to comment on his store's name, features, and advertising and a sample of clothes, which he had taken to the best dry cleaner in town. Today, Byerley's Dallas-based dry cleaning business, Bibbentuckers, has three stores, each of which averages $1 million a year in revenues, four times that of the average dry cleaning store.[55]

While Byerley's Bibbentuckers dry cleaning stores didn't invent a new product or process, many entrepreneurs who start new businesses do. When that happens, the inventor-entrepreneur needs to protect the rights to his or her invention by securing a patent. The U.S. Patent and Trademark Office's Web site (http://www.uspto.gov) provides information about this process, along with forms to apply for a patent. Inventors can also apply for a patent online.

Buying an Existing Business   Some entrepreneurs prefer to buy established businesses rather than assume the risks of starting new ones. Buying an existing business brings many advantages: Employees already in place serve established customers and deal with familiar suppliers, the good or service is known in the marketplace, and the necessary permits and licenses have already been secured. Getting financing for an existing business also is easier than it is for most start-ups. Some sellers may even help the buyers by providing financing and offering to serve as consultants.

To find businesses for sale, contact your local chamber of commerce, brokers who sell businesses, and professionals such as lawyers, accountants, and insurance agents. It is important to analyze the performance of businesses under consideration. Most people want to buy a healthy business so that they can build on its success. When Debra Fine decided to start a business making long-lasting, high-end children's toys to be sold at upscale stores, she bought 40-year-old Small World Toys in Culver City, California, which made high-quality wooden castles and dollhouses. Small World Toys became a division in her new business, Small World Kids. In her first year of business, she increased revenues 13 percent to $29.5 million by selling toys at high-end retailers such as Nordstrom, Neiman Marcus, and Learning Express.[56]

In contrast, turnaround entrepreneurs enjoy the challenge of buying unprofitable firms and making enough improvement in their operations to generate new profits. Hancock & Moore, a leather furniture manufacturer in Hickory, North Carolina, chose this route when it purchased Councill Craftsman, a bankrupt furniture manufacturer. Success with a turnaround strategy requires that the entrepreneur have definite and practical ideas about how to operate the business more profitably. After investing $5.1 million in Councill Craftsman for new production equipment that would raise quality and lower costs, Hancock & Moore focused Councill Craftsman's business from three lines of furniture—office, 18th-century reproductions, and high-end—to just one, custom-made furniture.[57]

Buying a Franchise Like buying an established business, buying a franchise offers a less risky way to begin a business than starting an entirely new firm. But as the previous chapter pointed out, franchising still involves risks. You must do your homework, carefully analyzing the franchisor's fees and capabilities for delivering the support it promises. Energetic preparation helps ensure that your business will earn a profit and grow.

Creating a Business Plan

Traditionally, most entrepreneurs launched their ventures without creating formal business plans. Although planning is an integral part of managing in the world of 21st-century business, entrepreneurs typically seize opportunities as they arise and change course as necessary. Flexibility seems to be the key to business start-ups, especially in rapidly changing markets. Forty-seven percent of the most recent *Inc.* 500 CEOs did not create a formal written plan before launching their companies.[58] Entrepreneurial researcher Amar Bhidé attributes that surprising fact to the types of businesses that today's entrepreneurs start. When businesspeople do not need a large amount of cash to start their businesses, they often do not need financing from outside sources—which usually require plans. Also, the rapid pace of change in some industries reduces the benefit of writing a plan.[59] Still, when an entrepreneur needs additional funds to start or grow a business, a business plan is indispensable.

Although the planning process for entrepreneurs differs from a major company's planning function, today's entrepreneurs are advised to construct business plans following the guidelines presented in Chapter 5 and Appendix C. Careful planning helps the entrepreneur prepare enough resources and stay focused on key objectives, and it provides an important tool for convincing potential investors and employees that the enterprise has the ingredients for success. Entrepreneurial business plans vary depending on the type of start-up, but the basic elements of such a plan—stating company goals, outlining sales and marketing strategies, and determining financial needs and sources of funds—apply to all types of ventures. The Internet also offers a variety of resources for creating business plans. Table 6.1 lists some of these online resources.

Finding Financing

A key issue in any business plan is financing. How much money will you need to start your business and where will you get it? Requirements for **seed capital**, funds used to launch a

seed capital initial funding needed to launch a new venture.

Table

6.1

Online Resources for Preparing a Business Plan

AllBusiness.com http://www.allbusiness.com	The "Business Advice" page provides links to examples, templates, and tips for writing a plan.
Inc. http://www.inc.com	Under "Departments," click "How-To-Guides" and then "Writing a Business Plan," which links to 150+ articles about how to write a business plan.
Kauffman eVenturing http://www.eventuring.org	The "Explore Topics" section has links to information and resources for researching and writing a plan, as well as presenting it to lenders or investors.
MoreBusiness.com http://www.morebusiness.com	To see a sample plan, select "Business & Marketing Plans" from the list of templates.

company, depend on the nature of your business and the type of facilities and equipment you need. On average, CEOs of the fastest-growing small businesses raised $1.5 million in seed capital to start their businesses. This average is highly skewed, though, by a few entrepreneurs who raised tens of millions of dollars for their business. The median amount of seed money, $50,000, was significantly below the average of $1.5 million. In fact, 54 percent of entrepreneurs started their businesses with $50,000 or less.[60]

Most entrepreneurs rely on personal savings, advances on credit cards, and money from partners, family members, and friends to fund their start-ups. When Ben David started his Nurses Now! temporary agency, to provide nurses to local hospitals in the Baltimore, Maryland, area, he used every dollar he had to start the business. David took out a second mortgage on his house, borrowed from his 401(k) retirement account, and maxed out all of his credit cards. Today, he's well on his way to paying off those loans as his business, now in its third year, will have revenues of $5 million this year.[61]

Debt Financing When entrepreneurs like Ben David use **debt financing**, they borrow money that they must repay. Loans from banks, finance companies, credit card companies, and family and friends are all sources of debt financing. Although many entrepreneurs charge business expenses to personal credit cards because they are relatively easy to obtain, high interest rates make this source of funding expensive. Annual interest charges on a credit card can run as high as 20 percent, while rates for a home equity loan (borrowing against the value of a home) currently run between 6 and 8 percent. In exchange for a lower interest rate, borrowers with a home equity loan pledge the value of their home, so a borrower who does not repay the loan risks losing the home.

When a business fails and cannot repay its loans, the owner must often declare bankruptcy. Regardless of legal

debt financing borrowed funds that entrepreneurs must repay.

Roberto Milk found a way to serve society through his company, Novica, which sells handcrafted art from artisans around the world. To obtain the funds to start his business, Milk turned to venture capital firms that invested millions of dollars. His buying teams travel the world in search of unique pieces. And when an item is sold, Novica guarantees artists that they will be paid at least 60 percent of the retail price.

AP PHOTO/RODRIQUE NGOWI

SMALL BUSINESS AND BANKRUPTCY—IS THERE AN ETHICAL RESPONSIBILITY?

When a small business goes bankrupt, its legal obligations to pay creditors are significantly reduced. Most creditors expect to receive pennies on the dollar. But is there an ethical responsibility to reimburse creditors?

The National Hockey League's Pittsburgh Penguins once found itself in this situation. The team suffered from poor performance and declining attendance at its games, and its debt totaled $120 million. So the Penguins finally declared bankruptcy. But in an unusual move—including a comeback from retirement by star player Mario Lemieux—the team made a commitment to pay off 100 percent of its debts.

Does a small business have an ethical responsibility to repay debts, even if it does not have the legal responsibility under bankruptcy protection?

PRO

1. It is more ethical to pay off a debt—even if it takes many months or years—than to negotiate repayments of pennies on the dollar.

2. When a firm goes bankrupt, employees and contract workers, as well as vendors and suppliers, are often hit the hardest. So every effort should be made to compensate them.

CON

1. Bankruptcy law is designed to help companies cut their losses, pay creditors a reasonable amount, and move on to future success. Tying them down with past debt may cost future jobs and interrupt service to new customers.

2. There is no legal requirement to repay the debt, so there should not be an ethical one.

SUMMARY

With the help of Lemieux—who agreed to restructure his salary and who found a group of investors willing to buy the team and keep it in Pittsburgh—the Penguins paid their debts. Even during the NHL strike, which meant no revenues, the team continued to make payments. "That's just the way we do business," explained team president Ken Sawyer. "There's absolutely a sense of pride."

Sources: Helen Huntley, "Bankruptcy Law Ensnares Businesses," *St. Petersburg (FL) Times*, accessed June 17, 2006, http://www.sptimes.com; Judy Newman, "When Companies Go Bankrupt, Employees and Freelancers Often Hit Hardest," *Wisconsin State Journal*, accessed June 17, 2006, http://www.madison.com/wsj; "Penguins Paying Creditors 100 Percent in Rare Bankruptcy Result," Associated Press, August 20, 2005, http://www.ap.org.

solving an ETHICAL controversy

requirements, some entrepreneurs who have been forced to declare bankruptcy still feel obligated to repay their debts. The "Solving an Ethical Controversy" feature debates the ethics of repaying creditors.

Many banks turn down requests for loans to fund start-ups, fearful of the high risk such ventures entail. In fact, Ben David, who relied on credit cards and a second mortgage to start Nurses Now!, said, "Anyone who thinks they can draw up a business plan and walk into a bank and ask for money is crazy. Banks aren't going to give you money for just an idea. You need a track record, and you need backers."[62] Only a small percentage of start-ups raise seed capital through bank loans, although some new firms can get SBA-backed loans, as discussed in Chapter 5.

Applying for a bank loan requires careful preparation. Bank loan officers want to see a business plan and will evaluate the entrepreneur's credit history. Because a start-up has not yet established a business credit history, banks often base lending decisions on evaluations of entrepreneurs' personal credit histories. Banks are more willing to make loans to entrepreneurs who have been in business for a while, show a profit on rising revenues, and need funds to finance expansion. Some entrepreneurs have found that local community banks are more interested in their loan applications than are the major national banks.

Equity Financing   To secure **equity financing,** entrepreneurs exchange a share of ownership in their company for money supplied by one or more investors. Entrepreneurs invest their own money along with funds supplied by other people and firms that become co-owners of the start-ups. An entrepreneur does not have to repay equity funds. Rather, the investors share in the success of the business. Sources of equity financing include family and friends, business partners, venture capital firms, and private investors.

Teaming up with a partner who has funds to invest may benefit an entrepreneur with a good idea and skills but little or no money. Investors may also have business experience, which they will be eager to share because the company's prosperity will benefit them. Like borrowing, however, equity financing has its drawbacks. One is that investment partners may not agree on the future direction of the business, and in the case of partnerships, if they cannot resolve disputes, one partner may have to buy out the other to keep operating. When Joe Strazza founded WinMill Software in New York City, he reduced his ownership stake in the company from 40 to 20 percent by securing $3 million in equity financing from 100 investors, most of whom were family and friends. These funds allowed the company to grow from one office and three workers to four offices in four cities and 180 workers. When the company was doing well, his investors were happy, but when business dropped from $24 million in revenues to $7 million, numerous investors asked to cash out, but they could not because the company lacked funds. Moreover, other investors opposed management decisions—for example, expanding into other lines of business such as installing wireless networks for cities and hospitals. Strazza said, "People say they believe in you and like you. But then when you're down, you learn it was all about the money. That's a very tough lesson to learn as an entrepreneur. You feel like you're losing your friends."[63]

Venture capitalists are business organizations or groups of private individuals that invest in new and growing firms. These investors expect high rates of return, typically more than 30 percent, within short time periods of five years or fewer. Prior to the widespread failures of many dot-coms in the early years of the 21st century, a sizable portion of venture capital flowed into start-up Internet firms. Today, most of the $20 billion that venture capitalists invest annually flows to a very limited number of businesses. Less than one-tenth of firms receiving funds from venture capitalists are start-ups, and most of the remainder are high-tech firms.[64]

Angel investors, wealthy individuals who invest money directly in new ventures in exchange for equity, are a larger source of investment capital for start-up firms. In contrast to venture capitalists, angels focus primarily on new ventures. Many angel investors are successful entrepreneurs who want to help aspiring business owners through the familiar difficulties of launching their businesses. Angel investors back a wide variety of new ventures. Some invest exclusively in certain industries, others invest only in start-ups with socially responsible missions, and still others prefer to back only women entrepreneurs. The "Business Etiquette" feature provides tips on a key strategy that entrepreneurs use to interest investors in their ideas: the business dinner.

Because most entrepreneurs have trouble finding wealthy private investors, angel networks form to match business angels with start-ups in need of capital. As you learned in Chapter 5, the Small Business Administration's Active Capital provides online listings to connect would-be angels with small businesses seeking financing. Similar networks try to expand the old-boy network of venture capitalists to new investors and entrepreneurs as well. Venture capitalists that focus on women include Isabella Capital (http://www.fundisabella.com) and Springboard Enterprises (http://www.springboardenterprises.org). Those interested in minority-owned business include the U.S. Hispanic Chamber of Commerce (http://www.ushcc.com).

equity financing funds invested in new ventures in exchange for part ownership.

venture capitalists business firms or groups of individuals that invest in new and growing firms in exchange for an ownership share.

angel investors wealthy individuals who invest directly in a new venture in exchange for an equity stake.

assessment check

1. What are the two most important considerations in choosing an idea for a new business?
2. What is the purpose of a patent?
3. What is seed capital?

(b)usiness (e)tiquette

Dining for Dollars

Entrepreneurs need money to fund their businesses. Many start with their own savings, but they quickly reach a point at which outside financing is necessary to survive and grow. So being successful means becoming skilled in attracting potential investors. Often the initial courtship occurs over a business meal, which can be a good way to get to know each other in a relaxed setting. But the dinner requires some savvy etiquette. To unravel the mystery of dining for dollars, follow these hints from the experts.

- Before setting up a dinner meeting, think through the mission of the meal. Is it simply to introduce yourself and your business? Are you ready to discuss specific business details? Write down your objectives.
- If possible, choose a restaurant you already know, where you trust the food and the staff. You'll want someplace that is relatively quiet so that you can talk. If you are paying a visit to potential investors outside your own town, research the restaurants ahead of time. You can ask your guests where they would like to eat—but make it clear that you will be the host.
- Arrive at the restaurant ten to fifteen minutes before the reservation time. Let the restaurant host know you are there. Wait in the lobby or near the door for your guests. If the staff prefers to seat you at a table, do not order drinks or food until your guests arrive.
- Greet your guests upon arrival with a smile and a firm handshake. Keep business papers off the table, and turn off your cell phone. Enjoy dinner and follow proper dining etiquette. Limit your alcohol intake, and don't smoke.
- Don't skip dessert and coffee. Key business discussions and decisions often take place during this part of the meal. It is usually acceptable to refer to any documents you may need for discussion at this point.
- When the check arrives, payment is your responsibility. Do so quickly and quietly. Alternatively, if you arrive early enough, you can give the wait staff your credit card so that it is clear you will be paying the bill.
- Escort your guests to the door, shake hands, and thank them for taking the time to join you. Later, you may want to jot down some meeting notes. Send a written note to your guests within a day or two, thanking them again for their time and consideration.

Sources: Naomi Torre Poulson, "Hosting a Formal Dinner," AskMen.com, accessed June 17, 2006, http://www.askmen.com; Scott Reeves, "Hosting a Business Dinner," *Forbes*, accessed June 17, 2006, http://www.forbes.com; Lydia Ramsey, "Sealing the Deal over the Business Meal," *Consulting to Management*, accessed June 17, 2006, http://www.c2m.com.

INTRAPRENEURSHIP

Established companies try to retain the entrepreneurial spirit by encouraging **intrapreneurship,** the process of promoting innovation within their organizational structures. Today's fast-changing business climate compels established firms to innovate continually to maintain their competitive advantages.

At Cambridge Consultants, a 250-person consulting firm in Boston that helps clients create products for five different industries, the entire company is designed around intrapreneurship. Each year, the company uses 10 percent of its revenues to help employees start and run new businesses. All of the firm's five divisions then use that money for a spin-off budget that employees use to develop initial new product ideas. Roughly 15 percent of initial ideas are then approved for more funds, which are used for marketing research and viability—in other words, to determine the likelihood of selling the new products. Finally, the company's top managers review the research studies and typically select one idea per year that is then spun off into its own new product division. Over the last 45 years, Cambridge has launched an average of one new company per year with an average investment of $1 million. When those new businesses are successful, employees and the companies share the profits. But if they fail, employees get their old jobs back, and the company incurs the loss.[65]

Established companies such as 3M support intrapreneurial activity in varied ways. 3M allows its researchers to spend 15 percent of their time working on their own ideas without approval from management. In addition to allowing time for traditional product development, 3M implements two intrapreneurial approaches: skunkworks and pacing programs. A **skunkworks** project is initiated by an employee who conceives an idea and then recruits resources from within 3M to turn it into a commercial product. **Pacing programs** are company-initiated projects that focus on a few products and technologies in which 3M sees potential for rapid marketplace winners. The company provides financing, equipment, and people to support such pacing projects.

Entrepreneurial environments created within companies can help firms retain valuable employees who might otherwise leave to start their own businesses. The Walt Disney Company is an icon of creativity, and many of its creative people leave to start businesses on their own. Among them is Jake Winebaum, formerly president of Walt Disney Magazine Publishing and intrapreneurial founder of Disney Online. While at Disney, he loved the climate of innovation in which he ran Disney.com, ABCNews.com, ESPN.com, and Go.com. He found the process of starting these operations inside Disney very similar to the process of starting a new company. In fact, the experience reminded him how much he loved being an entrepreneur, and he left to start a business incubator called eCompanies, with the goal of helping businesses move from ideas to operating businesses within a few months. Winebaum credits Disney with helping him learn how to identify business ideas with good potential.[66]

intrapreneurship
process of promoting innovation within the structure of an existing organization.

assessment check

1. Why would large companies support intrapreneurship?
2. What is a skunkworks?

WHAT'S AHEAD

The next chapter turns to a realm of business in which many entrepreneurs have been active during the past decade: e-business, or business use of the Internet. The chapter describes the technology behind electronic business. It introduces the challenges and opportunities available to entrepreneurs and other businesspeople who want to communicate with and sell to customers on the Internet. Not many years ago, Internet technology was a novelty except among high-tech firms and tech-savvy individuals. Today it is an integral factor in starting and growing a business.

Summary of Learning Goals

1 Define the term *entrepreneur* and distinguish among entrepreneurs, small-business owners, and managers.
Unlike many small-business owners, entrepreneurs typically own and run their businesses with the goal of building significant firms that create wealth and add jobs. Entrepreneurs are visionaries. They identify opportunities and take the initiative to gather the resources they need to start their businesses quickly. Both managers and entrepreneurs use the resources of their companies to achieve the goals of those organizations.

Assessment Check Answers

1.1 What tools do entrepreneurs use to create a new business?
Entrepreneurs combine their ideas and drive with money, employees, and other resources to create a business that fills a market need.

1.2 How do entrepreneurs differ from managers?
Managers direct the efforts of others to achieve an organization's goals. The drive and impatience that entrepreneurs have to make their companies successful often hurts their ability to manage.

2 Identify four different types of entrepreneurs.
The four categories of entrepreneurs are classic entrepreneurs, serial entrepreneurs, intrapreneurs, and change agents. A classic entrepreneur identifies a business opportunity and allocates available resources to tap that market. A serial entrepreneur starts one business, runs it, and then starts and runs additional businesses in succession. An intrapreneur is an employee who develops a new idea or product within an organizational position. A change agent is a manager who revitalizes an existing firm to make it a competitive success.

Assessment Check Answers

2.1 Why do companies encourage intrapreneurs?
Established companies need intrapreneurs to help develop new products, ideas, and commercial ventures.

2.2 What do intrapreneurs and change agents have in common?
Like intrapreneurs, change agents turn around and revitalize established firms to keep them competitive in today's marketplace.

3 Explain why people choose to become entrepreneurs.
People choose this kind of career for many different reasons. Reasons most frequently cited include desires to be one's own boss, to achieve financial success, to gain job security, and to improve one's quality of life.

Assessment Check Answers

3.1 Are entrepreneurs more likely than employees to achieve financial success?
While only one in five American workers is self-employed, more than two-thirds of all millionaires are self-employed. Consequently, if you run your own business, you're more likely to achieve financial success.

3.2 What factors affect the entrepreneur's job security?
An entrepreneur's job security depends on the decisions of customers and investors and on the cooperation and commitment of the entrepreneur's own employees.

4 Discuss conditions that encourage opportunities for entrepreneurs.
A favorable public perception, availability of financing, the falling cost and widespread availability of information technology, globalization, entrepreneurship education, and changing demographic and economic trends all contribute to a fertile environment for people to start new ventures.

Assessment Check Answers

4.1 To what extent is entrepreneurship possible in different countries, and what opportunities does globalization create for today's entrepreneurs?
More than 9 percent of adults worldwide are starting or managing a new business. As for globalization opportunities, entrepreneurs market their products abroad and hire international talent. Among the fastest-growing small U.S. companies, almost two of every five have international sales.

4.2 Identify the educational factors that help expand current opportunities for entrepreneurs.
More than 100 U.S. universities offer majors in entrepreneurship, another 73 offer an entrepreneurship emphasis, and hundreds more offer courses in how to start a business. Also, organizations such as the Kauffman Center for Entrepreneurial Leadership, Entreprep, and Students in Free Enterprise encourage and teach entrepreneurship.

4.3 Describe current demographic trends that suggest new goods and services for entrepreneurial businesses.
The aging of the U.S. population, the emergence of Hispanics as the nation's largest ethnic group, and the growth of two-income families are creating opportunities for entrepreneurs to market new goods and services.

5 Identify personality traits that typically characterize successful entrepreneurs.
Successful entrepreneurs share several typical traits, including vision, high energy levels, the need to achieve, self-confidence and optimism, tolerance for failure, creativity, tolerance for ambiguity, and an internal locus of control.

Assessment Check Answers

5.1 What is meant by an entrepreneur's vision?
Entrepreneurs begin with a vision, an overall idea for how to make their business idea a success, and then passionately pursue it.

5.2 Why is it important for an entrepreneur to have a high energy level and a strong need for achievement?
Because start-up companies typically have a small staff and struggle to raise enough capital, the entrepreneur has to make up the difference by working long hours. A strong need for achievement helps entrepreneurs enjoy the challenge of reaching difficult goals and promotes dedication to personal success.

5.3 How do entrepreneurs generally feel about the possibility of failure?
They view failure as a learning experience and are not easily discouraged or disappointed when things don't go as planned.

6 Summarize the process of starting a new venture.

Entrepreneurs must select an idea for their business, develop a business plan, obtain financing, and organize the resources they need to operate their start-ups.

Assessment Check Answers

6.1 What are the two most important considerations in choosing an idea for a new business?
Two important considerations are finding something you love to do and are good at doing and determining whether your idea can satisfy a need in the marketplace.

6.2 What is the purpose of a patent?
A patent protects the rights to a new invention, process, or product.

6.3 What is seed capital?
Seed capital is the money that is used to start a company.

7 Explain how organizations promote intrapreneurship.

Organizations encourage intrapreneurial activity within the company in a variety of ways, including hiring practices, dedicated programs such as skunkworks, access to resources, and wide latitude to innovate within established firms.

Assessment Check Answers

7.1 Why would large companies support intrapreneurship?
Large firms support intrapreneurship to retain an entrepreneurial spirit and to promote innovation and change.

7.2 What is a skunkworks?
A skunkworks project is initiated by an employee who conceives an idea and then recruits resources from within the company to turn that idea into a commercial product.

Business Terms You Need to Know

entrepreneur 184	change agent 186	equity financing 205
classic entrepreneur 185	lifestyle entrepreneur 190	venture capitalist 205
serial entrepreneur 186	seed capital 202	angel investor 205
intrapreneur 186	debt financing 203	intrapreneurship 206

Other Important Business Terms

skunkworks 206   **pacing programs 206**

Review Questions

1. What are the similarities and differences among entrepreneurs, small-business owners, and managers? What tools do entrepreneurs use to create a new business?

2. Why do companies encourage intrapreneurs? What do intrapreneurs and change agents have in common?

3. Identify the four categories of entrepreneurs. How are they different from each other?

4. What are the four major reasons for becoming an entrepreneur? Why do you think entrepreneurs are more likely than employees to achieve financial success? What factors affect the entrepreneur's job security?

5. How have globalization and information technology created new opportunities for entrepreneurs? Describe current demographic trends that suggest new goods and services for entrepreneurial businesses.

6. Identify the eight characteristics that are attributed to successful entrepreneurs. Which trait or traits do you believe are the most important for success? Why? Why is it important for an entrepreneur to have a high energy level and a strong need for achievement? How do entrepreneurs generally feel about the possibility of failure?

7. What are the benefits and risks involved in buying an existing business or a franchise?

8. Why is creating a business plan an important step for an entrepreneur?

9. Describe the different types of financing that entrepreneurs may seek for their businesses. What are the risks and benefits involved with each?

10. Why do most entrepreneurs rely on personal savings, credit cards, and money from family and friends? Why is it difficult to obtain bank financing?

11. What is intrapreneurship? How does it differ from entrepreneurship?

Projects and Teamwork Applications

1. Think of an entrepreneur whom you admire or choose one of the following: Bill Gates of Microsoft, Jeff Bezos of Amazon.com, or Oprah Winfrey of Harpo Productions. Explain why you admire this entrepreneur, including ways in which the person has contributed to his or her industry as well as to the economy.

2. Current demographic and economic trends support entrepreneurs who create new businesses. One of these trends is the willingness of Americans to spend more money on certain goods and services, such as pet care. On your own or with a classmate, brainstorm a trend that may be a good idea for a new business. Write one or two paragraphs describing the trend and how it could be applied to a business.

3. Review the eight characteristics of successful entrepreneurs. Which characteristics do you possess? Do you think you would be a good entrepreneur? Why? Write a paragraph or two listing your strengths.

4. Many entrepreneurs are motivated by working in an area they love. Think about something you love to do that you believe could be turned into a business. What aspect of the activity would actually be turned into a business? For example, if you love to play golf or shop at vintage clothing stores for 1970s-style attire, how would you shape this interest into a business?

Case 6.1

Genuine Scooters

Philip McCaleb has always loved riding scooters. When he worked in Europe as a sales manager for a U.S. company, he rode one to his job. It was cheap, maneuverable, and fun. Back home in Chicago a few years later, he began tinkering with the rusty parts of vintage scooters in his basement. He hunted down parts and accessories for old Vespa scooters and painstakingly restored them to life. Before he knew it, he was running a small restoration business called Scooterworks. Although there were a few diehard fans, the two-wheeled vehicles were slow to catch on in the United States. So McCaleb started a Vespa fan club and Internet message board. Today, with more and more consumers taking an interest in vintage scooters, Scooterworks is the largest importer of parts and accessories for the two-wheelers in the United States.

But Scooterworks is now a secondary business for McCaleb. As gas prices have soared, so has interest in alternative forms of travel. Scooters are cheaper than motorcycles, and they don't require a special license. They get anywhere from 50 to 110 miles per gallon, and they can keep up with the flow of general traffic on the road. Consumers who once made fun of scooters—or viewed them as toys—are now taking a second look. Banking on this new interest, McCaleb launched a second company called Genuine Scooter.

In its first three years, Genuine Scooter's popular Stella scooter—designed by McCaleb—has rolled down thousands of driveways. Priced at $2,895, it can reach 55 miles per hour and averages 90 miles per gallon of gas. Customers include urban dwellers, commuters, and even retirees who just want to head into town for lunch or a bag of groceries. But McCaleb emphasizes the fun factor. "A large portion of my market is delayed adolescents, or those looking to return to adolescence," he says with a smile.

As his firm rapidly grows bigger and more successful, McCaleb has a clear understanding of its position in the marketplace. "I always want to grow and compete," he explains, "but there is no way we can compete, or want to compete, with the Hondas or the Yamahas. We carefully look to compete on a scale that focuses on niche, on service, and quality." McCaleb also understands his own role as an entrepreneur. He loves to come up with new ideas, design things, and put them together. But he is not a businessperson. So he hired a consultant to help draw up a formal business plan to achieve the kind of expansion he envisions for Genuine Scooter. "I crave the opportunity to put concepts on the street," says McCaleb. "I'm a horrible bureaucrat and lousy operations guy." With this strategy, McCaleb can focus on what he does best—coming up with ideas for new products and new markets. Recently, Genuine Scooters launched a sidecar that attaches to its scooter and plans to offer a scooter trailer soon. Meanwhile, McCaleb is working on the next generation of scooters, which will be larger and faster. He hopes to win over more consumers who want the ease and flexibility of squeezing through traffic and parking in tight spaces—and who don't mind a little wind in their hair.

Questions for Critical Thinking

1. What conditions do you think opened the door of opportunity for Philip McCaleb's two companies?
2. What type of entrepreneur is Philip McCaleb? What personality traits does he have that could contribute to his success?

Sources: Genuine Scooter Web site, accessed June 17, 2006, http://www.genuine scooters.com; Tara Siegel Bernard, "Scooters' Popularity Offers a Chance for Growth," *Wall Street Journal*, accessed June 17, 2006, http://online.wsj.com; Joe Kafka, "High Prices Pumping Up Scooter Sales," *(Fort Wayne, TX) Journal Gazette*, accessed June 17, 2006, http://www.fortwayne.com/mld/journalgazette; John Schmeltzer, "Sales of Scooters Get in the Fast Lane," *Chicago Tribune*, accessed June 17, 2006, http://www.chicagotribune.com.

VIDEO | Case 6.2

Culver's: Great Food from a Good Business

This video case appears on page 614. A recently filmed video, designed to expand and highlight the written case, is available for class use by instructors.

Chapter 7

E-Business: Doing Business Online

Because teenagers and young adults already spend a lot of time online, it should be easy for marketers to sell them CDs, games, and high-fashion clothing on the Internet, right? After all, they're already at their computers. Why wouldn't they shop there as their parents do?

Selling online to the youth market isn't quite as simple as just offering a Web site. Teens might actually surf fewer hours a week than their parents, because having access at school is limited or focused on specific tasks, which doesn't bring the same freedom to shop that many adults enjoy. And when online, many teens are busy communicating—sending instant messages, writing and reading blogs, and conversing in chat rooms. Further, many teens are price conscious because their earning power is low

Reaching the Elusive Teen Market Online

and few have credit cards. These factors combine to make it easier for teens to window-shop than to actually purchase.

Still, retailers see big potential in capturing the attention of this lucrative—and elusive—market. For one thing, credit cards for many teens are only a year or two away, and the purchasing power of this age group is expected to be high. Within the next few years, roughly 34 million people will be in their teens in the United States, so they are an attractive market. Another motivation for venturing online is the opportunity to build customer loyalty, especially for big retail operations like Macy's Thisit.com, Crate and Barrel's cb2.com, and Pottery Barn's pbteen.com. Young people who begin a relationship online with a department store such as Macy's or a home-and-hearth retailer like Pottery Barn may continue to shop there—online, in person, or by catalog—for many years. So how do retail businesses create Web sites that attract teens and young adults?

Macy's partnered with *Teen Vogue* magazine to develop Thisit.com for girls in the 13- to 17-year-old age range. The home page features a picture of Times Square with numbered billboards and a blimp. Hidden behind the numbers are descriptions of the site's contents—in

place of the typical dull navigation bar. In addition to high-fashion clothes for purchase, the site features flashy graphics, music and video clips to download, and fashion and grooming advice. The manager of Macy's online division says the site is "mostly designed to be about their lifestyle and communicating with them versus a hard sell like 'here's the merchandise, it's on sale.'" The site has no housewares or appliances, for instance, although all items on Thisit.com can be accessed, presumably by parents, from the company's main Web site at Macys.com.

Alloy.com, a specialty-clothing site that caters to female teens, packages polls, contests, sweepstakes, message boards, fashion advice, and horoscopes on its site. The site also features tips and news about trends, books, movies, and music and film celebrities. The polls and message boards help give the company feedback; its buyers can spot emerging trends from posted comments. Hip Web site http://hollisterco.com, owned by Abercrombie & Fitch, has separate pages for "Dudes" and "Bettys" in need of fashionable clothes and accessories, as well as trendy features about pop groups with audio and video clips on its "Club Cali" page. In contrast, eBay doesn't have to dress up its Web site very much to draw teens. In fact, it's hard for other companies to compete with eBay when it comes to entertainment value, and eBay and Amazon are already top destinations for teen shoppers.

But making Web sites entertaining and interactive isn't all retailers need to do. They must also draw teens to visit them, often by linking to popular "social networking" sites such as Facebook.com, Quizilla.com, CollegeBoards.com, and Xanga.com. Even the education site SparkNotes.com is considered a good way to reach teens. One reason is that teens consider social and educational sites safe and tend to trust information they find there. Stores are also experimenting with e-mail promotions and ways to use text messaging to reach teens.

Although many teen sites cater to females, retailers must still grapple with a few gender-related differences of Internet users. First, although teenage girls spend about 22 percent more time online than boys, teen boys buy more items online. The kind of merchandise boys buy—videos, music, games, and high-tech items—doesn't need to be tried on. And, as any parent can attest, teen girls simply like the social aspects of shopping together at the mall. But if Thisit.com brings the customer to the mall, Macy's won't be complaining.[1]

Chapter Overview

Over the past decade few developments in contemporary business have been as monumental as the Internet and its related technologies. The Internet offers businesses and other organizations a source of information, a means of communication, and a channel for buying and selling, all rolled into one. With just a few ticks of the clock and a few clicks of a mouse, the Internet has revolutionized virtually every aspect of business. Consumers use the Internet for a variety of tasks: to pay bills, obtain product information, make purchases, and even consult with their physicians. Businesses use the Internet to exchange information with customers, advertise products, research market trends, and, of course, buy and sell a whole range of goods and services. New words have emerged, such as *blog, RSS, extranet,* and *wiki,* and old words have new meanings: *Web, search marketing, banner, pop-up,* and *online.*

Electronic business (or e-Business) refers to conducting business via the Internet. The size and scope of e-business is difficult to understate. For instance, during a two-week period leading up to Valentine's Day, U.S. consumers spent close to $4 billion online, a 30 percent increase over the previous year.[2] Sigma-Aldrich, a St. Louis–based chemical company that sells products to biologists, has seen its online sales rise fiftyfold—from $4 million to more than $200 million in less than ten years. Office products retailer Staples reports that more than half its orders are placed via the company's Web site. Meanwhile, Ford Motor Credit recently launched an Internet portal for receiving and processing credit applications. Already the portal is processing around half of all the applications that come from Ford dealers, or more than 150,000 per day.[3]

E-business involves much more than just buying and selling. Some surveys suggest that the Web is the number one medium for new-product information, eclipsing catalogs, print ads, and trade shows. The Internet allows retailers and vendors to exchange vital information, improving the overall functioning of inventory and supply, which lowers costs and increases profits. Moreover, an increasing number of Americans now get their news and information from blogs (short for *Web logs,* which are online journals) rather than from traditional media such as television and newspapers. Consequently, a growing number of businesses use blogs to put human faces on their organizations and communicate directly with customers.

Government agencies and not-for-profit organizations have also embraced the Internet. On college and university Web sites, students can obtain academic program information, register for courses, check grades, and even pay their college bills. Many states now allow residents to renew their car registrations online, saving time and trips to the motor vehicle office.

In the past decade, the number of Internet users in the United States and worldwide has grown dramatically. Today an estimated 200 million Americans—more than 63 percent of the U.S. population—access the Internet at home, at school, at work, or at public-access sites. Active at-home Internet users alone exceed 135 million in the United States today. Worldwide, the number of Internet users is close to 900 million.[4] While some of the initial novelty has worn off, the Internet has become a significant presence in the daily lives of a majority of Americans. For instance, according to recent surveys, the average Internet user spends more time online than watching television.[5] Moreover, over half of all Americans accessing the Internet today use broadband connections—such as DSL or cable modems—which vastly increase reaction times and allow nearly seamless graphics and video displays.[6] Experts believe that the continued growth of broadband is one of the keys to the continued growth and development of e-business.

In spite of the past success and future potential of the Internet, issues and concerns relating to e-business remain. Some highly touted e-business applications have proven less than successful, cost savings and profits have occasionally been elusive, and many privacy and security issues still linger. Nevertheless, the benefits and potential of e-business clearly outweigh the concerns and problems.

This chapter examines the current state and potential of e-business. We begin by discussing the capabilities of e-business, the benefits of e-business, and the ways organizations use the Web. Next, we focus on business-to-business (B2B) transactions, which make up the most e-business transactions today. Then we explore business-to-consumer (B2C) e-business—online shopping sites such as Macy's Thisit.com, described in the opening vignette. We also consider some of the challenges of e-business. Next, we explain how organizations use the Web's communication functions to advance their objectives. The chapter concludes with discussions of how to create and maintain an effective Web presence and the global reach of e-business.

WHAT IS E-BUSINESS?

Today the term **e-business** describes a wide range of business activities that take place on the Internet using any of the applications that rely on Internet technology, such as e-mail and virtual shopping carts. E-business can be divided into the following five broad categories:

electronic business (e-business) conducting business via the Internet.

1. e-tailing, or virtual storefronts on Web sites
2. online business-to-business transactions
3. electronic data interchange (EDI), the business-to-business exchange of data using compatible software
4. e-mail, instant messaging, and other Web-enabled communication tools and their use as media for reaching prospective and existing customers
5. the gathering and use of demographic, product, and other information through Web contacts

E-business provides a foundation for launching new businesses, extending the reach of existing companies, and building and retaining customer relationships. A Web presence builds awareness of a company's products and brands, provides the means for one-on-one communication with customers, and permits customers to place orders from anywhere in the world, at any time of day. E-business encompasses all of the following types of activities:

- Legally downloading songs from Apple Computer's iTunes Web site
- Buying a used laptop computer on the online auction site eBay
- Accessing Infotrac (http://www.infotrac.com) through your college's wireless network to find articles to complete a class research assignment
- Researching new-car models on Edmunds.com (http://www.edmunds.com) and getting price quotes from several local dealers

7.1 Services Offered by IBM to Enhance E-Business

Once upon a time,

there was a company with a terrible problem: their servers just kept crashing. So they bought Magic Server Pixie Dust. Simply sprinkle on the Pixie Dust, and crashed servers would suddenly come back to life. Sprinkle it on regularly, and they'd never go down. Servers would run themselves. Repair themselves. On demand. People were staked. They could devote more attention to their other business problems. It seemed almost too good to be true. The truth is, it didn't exist.

AND THAT'S WHEN THEY CALLED IBM.

Right now, IBM servers have the ability to help prevent crashes before they happen. On demand. They also protect and manage themselves in ways never before imagined. This is the kind of autonomic, on demand technology IBM is building for the new "always on" environment. Not Magic Pixie Dust. Visit ibm.com/ondemand

IBM.
@ business on demand

The growth of e-business has attracted an army of specialized software firms and other service suppliers that provide expertise for firms taking their first steps into this competitive arena. Examples include Accenture, IBM, Microsoft, and Oracle. IBM, for instance, offers its business customers both software and services designed to build virtual stores that go far beyond traditional Web sites. Although IBM was originally known as a producer of computer hardware, it now generates more than half its revenue from e-business and other information technology services.[7] IBM even runs e-business systems for companies that want to outsource this activity. The firm's management believes that much of its future lies in providing e-business services. As a result IBM sold its PC manufacturing business. Figure 7.1 illustrates the types of e-business services offered by IBM.

E-business has also had an impact on governments and others in the not-for-profit sector. For instance, MunicipalNet is a growing e-procurement business based in Boston. It focuses on services to states, local governments, and the businesses that supply them. The city of Torrington, Connecticut, recently signed up for the MunicipalNet service. According to Charlene Antonelli, the city's purchasing agent, the service has generated far more bids and had an impact on prices. "We put a request out for a multimedia projector that previously we had a best price of around $3,700. . . . Through the MunicipalNet service, we got a number of bids in at the $2,000 level," noted Antonelli.[8] MunicipalNet can also help governments set up Web sites at which citizens can register cars, pay taxes, or look for government jobs. By one estimate, more than 15 percent of federal, state, and local taxes will be collected online within the next few years.

Capabilities and Benefits of E-Business

The last years of the 20th century and the early years of the 21st century witnessed the change from a manufacturing-based industrial economy to its electronic successor—an economy based on information, the Internet, and other related online technologies. Many people see e-business as a major component of growth for the rest of the 21st century. Since the Web first opened for commercial activity in 1993, e-business has had a major impact on both consumers and businesses. It is estimated that in the United States e-business is currently over 2 percent of GDP. This figure is expected to increase to more than 5 percent within the next three to five years.[9] Some recent successes in e-business are summarized in Table 7.1.

E-business offers a wide variety of capabilities and benefits to contemporary businesspeople.

- *Global reach.* The Net allows goods and services to be sold to customers regardless of geographic location. eBay, for instance, is now the nation's largest used-car dealer.[10] Buyers and sellers throughout the country meet in this virtual used-car marketplace, where more than $7 billion worth of used vehicles are bought and sold annually.
- *Personalization.* Only a handful of Dell computers are waiting for customers at any one time. The production process begins when an order is received and ends a day or two later when the PC is shipped to the customer. Not only does this approach better satisfy customer needs, but it also sharply reduces the amount of inventory Dell has to carry.
- *Interactivity.* Customers and suppliers negotiate prices online in much the same manner as at a local flea market or car dealership. The result is the creation of an ideal product at the right price that satisfies both parties.

Table 7.1

Some E-Business Successes

- More than 70,000 students are taking courses online at the University of Phoenix. The Web has helped the for-profit institution become the largest private college in the United States.

- FreshDirect—an online supermarket—now has annual revenues exceeding $100 million and is the first online supermarket to turn a profit.

- The Boston Symphony Orchestra's Web site attracts thousands of visitors a day, and online ticket sales are approaching $5 million annually. The orchestra credits the Web for a dramatic increase in the number of young concertgoers and season ticket subscribers.

- Americans book more than $62 billion in online travel annually. This figure is expected to reach $91 billion by 2009. By then one out of every three travel dollars will be booked online.

Sources: "About Us," University of Phoenix, accessed July 20, 2006, http://www.uopxonline.com; Erick Schonfeld, "The Big Cheese of Online Grocers," *Business 2.0*, accessed July 20, 2006, http://www.business2.com; Deborah Vence, "Boston Orchestra Tunes Up Net Campaign," *Marketing News*, accessed July 20, 2006, http://www.marketingpower.com; Rob McGann, "U.S. Online Travel Market to Soar," ClickZ Network, accessed June 20, 2006, http://www.clickz.com.

- *Right-time and integrated marketing.* Online retailers, such as Amazon.com and Buy.com, can provide products when and where customers want them. Moreover, the Internet enables the coordination of all promotional activities and communication to create a unified, customer-oriented promotional message.

- *Cost savings.* E-business can markedly reduce the costs associated with operating and starting a business. Ace Hardware says that a Web-based program has reduced inventory costs by around 20 percent.[11]

In addition to the benefits listed here, increasing evidence shows that an effective online presence improves the performance of traditional brick-and-mortar operations. As noted earlier, some surveys suggest that the Web has become the primary source of product information. A study by the Dieringer Group, a marketing and business research firm, found that a significant segment of American consumers—perhaps as many as 83 million—rely on the Internet nearly twice as much for local purchasing information compared with traditional media such as newspaper, local TV, or radio ads. For each dollar these consumers spent online, the study found, they spent $1.60 offline at local stores.[12]

Business Web Sites

Virtually all businesses today have Web sites. They may offer general information, electronic shopping, and promotions such as games, contests, and online coupons. Type in the firm's Internet address, and the Web site's home page appears on your computer screen.

Two types of company Web sites exist. Many firms have established **corporate Web sites** to increase their visibility, promote their offerings, and provide information for other interested parties. Rather than selling goods and services directly, these sites attempt to build customer goodwill and assist retailers and other resellers in their marketing efforts.

assessment check

1. Define e-business.
2. List some benefits of e-business.

corporate Web site Web site designed to increase a firm's visibility, promote its offerings, and provide information to interested parties.

USED WITH PERMISSION FROM FORD MOTOR COMPANY

Ford Motor Company's website is an example of an informational web site as it includes details about Ford's products as well as financial documents, investor relations, and job-related information.

Tips for Using E-Mail

You are probably aware of the general guidelines about using e-mail responsibly, such as following the rules of grammar and spelling, not typing in all caps, and not sending anyone information you wouldn't mind seeing in the daily newspaper. Here are a few tips that should help ensure that your online business correspondence is always effective and appropriate.

1. Choose a professional-looking format; avoid color, fancy type fonts, and emoticons (smiley faces).
2. Keep your message short and to the point.
3. Always include a specific subject line so that your correspondents know what to expect. For instance, write "Revised schedule for McGregor project" instead of "Schedule."
4. If you are replying to an e-mail, respond as promptly as you would to a phone call on the same subject.
5. Write and reply to all the people who need the information you are sending, but only to those people.
6. If you are writing to a large group of people who don't know one another, use the BCC (blind carbon copy) function to ensure that each person's e-mail address remains private from the others.
7. Let recipients know ahead of time if you are sending a very large attachment, because download times can vary. You might want to break large attachments into several smaller ones to make downloading easier.
8. If a disagreement or argument develops during e-mail communications, stop, calm down, and continue the discussion in person or on the phone.
9. Before you send any e-mail, proofread your message and double-check the "To:" line. Make sure you have attached any needed documents and that you've typed your name at the bottom of the message.
10. Remember that e-mails are considered public documents. Avoid writing anything you wouldn't say in person.

Sources: "Email Etiquette," Online Writing Lab at Purdue University, accessed July 20, 2006, http://owl.english.purdue.edu; "Harness E-Mail: E-Mail Etiquette," Learn the Net, accessed July 20, 2006, http://www.learnthenet.com; "Email Etiquette," AllBusiness, accessed July 20, 2006, http://www.allbusiness.com.

For example, the Web site for Levi's jeans offers detailed product information and a chance to view recent commercials. Consumers who want to actually buy jeans, however, can link to the Web sites of retailers such as Kohl's and JCPenney.

In addition to using the Web to communicate product information and build relationships with customers, many companies use their Web sites for a variety of purposes, including disseminating financial information to investors, enabling prospective employees to apply online for jobs, and providing e-mail communication for customers and other interested parties. Some tips for writing and using e-mail in a business setting are listed in the "Business Etiquette" feature.

Although **marketing Web sites** often include information about company history, products, locations, employment opportunities, and financial information, their goal is to increase purchases by site visitors. For instance, the Starbucks Web site contains all of the information traditionally found on a corporate Web site, but it also includes an online store selling everything from coffee to espresso machines. Many marketing Web sites try to engage consumers in interactions that will move them closer to a demonstration, trial visit, purchase, or other marketing outcome. Some marketing Web sites, such as Sony.com, are quite complex. Visitors can go to pages for Sony Pictures Entertainment (with movie trailers and sweepstakes), Sony Music (audio and video clips plus news about recordings), and Sony Online Entertainment (online games plus information about games and gaming systems), among other possibilities.

assessment check

1. Briefly identify the differences between a corporate Web site and a marketing Web site.
2. Visit the Web site for Specialized (http://www.specialized.com). Is this site a corporate Web site or a marketing Web site?

marketing Web site Web site whose main purpose is to increase purchases by visitors.

BUSINESS-TO-BUSINESS (B2B) E-BUSINESS

FedEx's Web site is not designed to be flashy. There are no fancy graphics or streaming video clips, just lots of practical information to assist the firm's customers. The site enables customers to check rates, compare services, schedule package pickups and deliveries, track shipments, and order shipping supplies. This information is vital to FedEx's customers, most of whom are businesses. Customers access the site thousands of times a day.

Business-to-business e-business, known as **B2B,** is the use of the Internet for business transactions between organizations. Although most people are familiar with such consumer-oriented (B2C) online firms as Amazon.com and eBay, B2C transactions are dwarfed by their B2B counterparts. B2B e-business transactions stand at nearly $2.5 trillion. By some estimates, close to 80 percent of all e-commerce activity consists of B2B transactions.[13] In the United Kingdom, more than 30 percent of all businesses purchased goods and services over the Internet in a recent year.[14]

In addition to generating sales revenue, B2B e-business also provides detailed product descriptions whenever they are needed. Payments and other information are transferred on the Web. Moreover, B2B e-business can slash order-processing expenses. Business-to-business transactions, which typically involve more steps than consumer purchases, can be much more efficient on the Internet. Orders placed over the Internet typically contain fewer errors than handwritten ones, and when mistakes occur, the technology can quickly locate them. So the Internet is an attractive option for business buying and selling. In some industries, relying on the Internet to make purchases can reduce costs by almost 25 percent.

B2B e-business activity has become more varied in recent years. In addition to using the Web to conduct one-on-one sales transactions and provide product information, companies use such tools as EDI, extranets, private exchanges, electronic exchanges, and e-procurement.

> **business-to-business (B2B) e-business** electronic business transactions between organizations using the Internet.

Electronic Data Interchanges, Extranets, and Private Exchanges

Electronic Data Interchange One of the oldest applications of technology to business transactions is **electronic data interchange (EDI),** computer-to-computer exchanges of invoices, purchase orders, price quotations, and other sales information between buyers and sellers. EDI requires compatible hardware and software systems to exchange data over a network. Use of EDI cuts paper flow, speeds the order cycle, and reduces errors. In addition, by receiving daily inventory status reports from vendors, companies can set production schedules to match demand.

Wal-Mart was one of the first major corporations to adopt EDI in the early 1990s. In fact, the retailer refuses to do business with distributors and manufacturers that do not use compatible EDI standards. EDI is one of the major reasons Wal-Mart is able to operate with the efficiency that has made it the market leader in retailing. It can buy just the merchandise its customers want and just when it needs to restock its shelves, using a system known as **quick response.** Quick response is the retailing equivalent of *just-in-time inventory,* an inventory management system commonly used in manufacturing. (Just-in-time inventory is discussed in detail in Chapter 11.) Today, most large retailers have adopted variations of Wal-Mart's quick response system.

Early EDI systems were limited due to the requirement that all parties had to use the same computer operating system. So a company using UNIX couldn't easily link up with a company using Windows NT. That changed with the introduction of something called Web

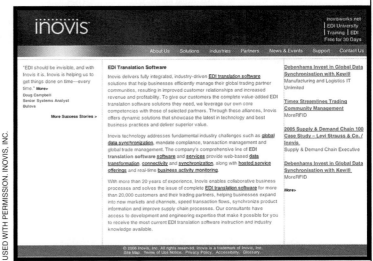

USED WITH PERMISSION. INOVIS, INC.

Inovis is one of many companies that provide a comprehensive line of B2B software and services, including EDI as well as providing Web-based data transformation, real-time business activity monitoring, and exception management capabilities.

services—Internet based systems that allow parties to communicate electronically with one another regardless of the computer operating system used by each individual party. Web services rely on open-source XML (Extensible Markup Language) standards.

Extranets   Internet commerce also offers an efficient way for businesses to collaborate with vendors, partners, and customers through **extranets,** secure networks used for e-business and accessible through the firm's Web site by external customers, suppliers, or other authorized users. Extranets go beyond ordering and fulfillment processes by giving selected outsiders access to internal information. As with other forms of e-business, extranets provide additional benefits such as enhanced relationships with business partners. As noted earlier in the chapter, Ford Motor Credit uses an extranet to process credit applications from Ford dealers. Intelsat, which operates global communications satellites, has an extranet called Intelsat Business Network (IBN). More than 2,500 users of IBN log on from more than 400 organizations to check the availability of satellite capacity, view satellite maps, download corporate documents, and participate in discussion groups. Users can personalize their IBN account so that it shows information about only the services they use.[15]

Security and access authorization remain critical issues, and most companies create virtual private networks that protect information traveling over public communications media. These networks control who uses a company's resources and what users can access. Also, they cost considerably less than leasing dedicated lines.

Private Exchanges   The next generation of extranets is the **private exchange,** a secure Web site at which a company and its suppliers share all types of data related to e-business, from product design through order delivery. A private exchange is more collaborative than a typical extranet, so this type of arrangement has sometimes been called *c-business.* The participants can use it to collaborate on product ideas, production scheduling, distribution, order tracking, and any other functions a business wants to include. Partners in a private exchange often form strategic alliances, similar to those described in Chapter 4. Wal-Mart Stores has a private exchange it calls a *retail link.* The system permits Wal-Mart employees to access detailed sales and inventory information. Suppliers such as Procter & Gamble and Nestlé, in turn, can look up Wal-Mart sales data and forecasts to manage their own inventory and logistics, helping them better meet the needs of the world's largest retailer and its millions of customers worldwide.

Another variant of extranets is an *intranet,* which provides similar capabilities but limits users to an organization's employees. Intranets are discussed in Chapter 15.

Electronic Exchanges and E-Procurement

The earliest types of B2B e-business usually consisted of a company setting up a Web site and offering information, as well as products, to any buyer willing to make online purchases. Then entrepreneurs created **electronic exchanges,** online marketplaces that bring buyers and sellers together and cater to a specific industry's needs. One of the earliest electronic exchanges, FreeMarkets, was set up by a former General Electric executive named Glen Meakem. FreeMarkets allowed suppliers to compete for the business of organizational buyers of anything from gears to printed circuit boards. The idea was to improve the efficiency of the purchase process for hundreds of business products.

Initially, many believed that electronic exchanges would become one of the most popular uses of the Internet. It didn't quite work out that way. Something like 15,000 electronic exchanges were launched within a span of a few years. Today, however, less than 20 percent remain. The others either merged or simply disappeared. (FreeMarkets was acquired recently by the e-business software firm Ariba.) Only electronic exchanges specializing in electronic components and transportation services have proven consistently successful.[16]

Why did many electronic exchanges perform so poorly? Experts believe that many suppliers weren't happy with the pressure to come in with the lowest bid each time a satisfied long-term buyer decided to make a new purchase. Moreover, many buyers preferred to cultivate long-term relationships with their suppliers, even those that charged slightly higher prices occasionally. Purchasing agents simply didn't see enough benefits from electronic exchanges to abandon suppliers they knew.[17]

Evolving from electronic exchanges has been something called **e-procurement,** Web-based systems that enable all types of organizations to improve the efficiency of their procurement processes. Ariba, the company that acquired FreeMarkets, offers a variety of e-procurement software products. Many large corporations, such as Saks and Unilever, use Ariba products such as Buyer for purchasing operating goods and services. Unilever reports that Buyer and other Ariba e-procurement software products have saved the company tens of millions of dollars. Saks believes that Buyer has cut the negotiating cycle time from four months to six weeks and saved the company 10 to 20 percent off regular, published prices.[18]

E-procurement also benefits the public sector. For instance, the State of North Carolina has recently instituted a program called *NC E-Procurement,* which combines Internet technology with traditional procurement practices to streamline the purchasing process and reduce costs. State and local governmental agencies, public schools, and state-supported colleges can use the system to purchase products from state-approved vendors. According to the state, "E-Procurement has reduced prices for goods and services through volume discounts, and also enables administrative and operational cost savings by streamlining processing and interactions with vendors/suppliers." One North Carolina county reported saving more than 30 percent on printer supplies by using E-Procurement.[19]

assessment check

1. What is B2B e-business? How large is it relative to B2C e-business?
2. What is an EDI? An extranet? A private exchange?
3. Briefly explain how e-procurement works.

ONLINE SHOPPING COMES OF AGE

One area of e-business that has consistently grabbed news headlines is Internet shopping. Known as **business-to-consumer e-business,** or **B2C,** it involves selling directly to consumers over the Internet. Driven by convenience and improved security for transmitting credit card numbers and other financial information, online retail sales, sometimes called *e-tailing,* now account for around 8 percent of total retail sales in the United States.[20] During one holiday shopping period, over 10 percent of consumer spending took place online, one-third more than in the prior year.[21] At present, about 30 percent of the population shops online. It is estimated that nearly half of American consumers will soon make purchases online.[22]

Most people generally think of the Web as a giant cybermall of retail stores selling millions of goods online. However, service providers are also important participants in e-business. These firms include providers of financial services. Brick-and-mortar banks, such as Wachovia, and brokerage firms, such as Fidelity Investments, have greatly expanded their online services. In addition, many new online service providers are rapidly attracting customers who want to do more of their own banking and stock trading 24/7. Figure 7.2 illustrates some of the benefits of banking online. Airlines, too, have discovered the power of the Web. For example, Southwest Airlines and JetBlue sell more than half of their tickets online, leading the industry in sales via this low-cost channel.[23] Southwest's Web site is the only airline Web site that regularly makes the top rankings for popularity, ease of use, and revenue generation—more than $3 billion annually in air travel is booked through Southwest.com.[24] The success of Southwest.com is described in more detail in the "Hit & Miss" feature.

business-to-consumer (B2C) e-business selling directly to consumers over the Internet.

7.2 The Benefits of Online Banking

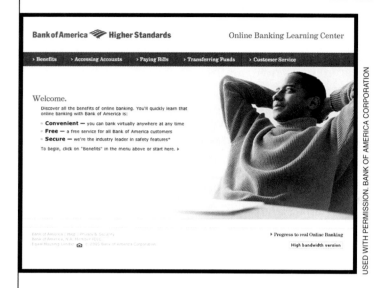

electronic storefront company Web site that sells products to customers.

Another point to remember is that there are basically two types of B2C Web sites: shopping sites and informational sites. Williams-Sonoma has a shopping site (http://www.williams-sonoma.com), where customers can view product information and place orders online. By contrast, Toyota's Web site (http://www.toyota.com) is informational only. Consumers can view detailed product information, compare financing alternatives, and even request a price quote from a local dealer. They *cannot*, however, buy a new car online.

E-Tailing and Electronic Storefronts

Major retailers have staked their claims in cyberspace by setting up **electronic storefronts**, Web sites that sell items to consumers. Wal-Mart received such a positive response to the launch of its electronic storefront a couple of years ago that it expanded online product offerings from 2,500 to more than 40,000 items. Macy's department store has put its bridal registry, personal shopping, and interior-decorating services online. Clothing retailer Lands' End used to generate virtually all of its orders by telephone. A few years ago the company decided to turn to B2C e-business to boost sales and reduce costs. Today, LandsEnd.com is the world's largest apparel Web site and has pioneered several ways to enhance the online shopping experience.[25] Online customers can communicate with customer service representatives in real time, and two customers can even shop on the site simultaneously—just as if they were shopping together in a brick-and-mortar store. Customers can even "try on" clothes using a tool called Virtual Model.

Generally, online retailers—such as L.L. Bean and Barnes & Noble—provide an online catalog where visitors click on items they want to buy. These items are placed in a file called an **electronic shopping cart.** When the shopper indicates that he or she wants to complete the transaction, the items in the electronic shopping cart are listed on the screen, along with the total amount due, so that the customer can review the whole order and make changes before making a payment.

One factor that experts think will have a significant influence on the growth of online shopping is the increased availability of broadband technology. According to data from Nielsen NetRatings, more than 55 percent of American Internet users now have broadband connections. Nielsen projects that 70 percent of all U.S. home Internet users will soon be using broadband. Why is this trend significant for e-tailers? On average, broadband users are online more often for longer periods of time, and, most important, spend more online than narrowband users. Typically, today around 70 percent of all online retail purchases are conducted over broadband connections. Broadband shoppers also spend around 34 percent more online than narrowband shoppers.[26]

Who Are the Online Buyers and Sellers?

The Pew Internet and American Life Project collects and analyzes data about Americans' Internet usage, including online buying behavior. A recent survey they conducted paints a comprehensive demographic picture of online users and buyers. Some of the key findings of the report are summarized in Figure 7.3 on page 224. While the typical Internet user is still

HIT & MISS

Southwest Scores with Its Web Site

Southwest Airlines has solved the problem of communicating great deals to its customers in real time. The company's innovation is no surprise to the travel industry, because Southwest was also the first airline to have its own Web site, now more than ten years old and still one of the most popular Internet sites in any category.

To reach travelers with news about short-term special deals, such as a $33 flight from Chicago to St. Louis that was good for only a three-hour booking window, the innovative carrier created a software program called "DING!," named after the sound some e-mail systems make to announce a new message. Downloading the program from http://www.southwest.com takes a couple of minutes and creates a special icon in the user's system tray at the bottom of the screen. When Southwest has a new rock-bottom special for subscribers a tiny envelope appears on the icon and a "ding" sound is heard. Simply clicking on the icon brings up all the information on the user's computer screen, including a "Book Now" button.

During the registration process, users specify their home city or zip code and receive only information about that destination. Top cities are Baltimore, Chicago, Houston, Los Angeles, Oakland, and Phoenix.

Most offers are available for less than a day and represent savings from $5 to $75 off Southwest's lowest-priced one-way Internet specials. They require fourteen-day advance purchase, and customers have to be near their computers often to take advantage of the short-term offers. But in just the first few months of operation, travelers who like the thrill of getting a great deal booked more than $10 million worth of tickets through DING!, making it a resounding success for the company. "Only Southwest Airlines would dare to offer fares this low," says the publisher of BestFares.com.

Questions for Critical Thinking

1. Why do you think customers are willing to download DING! when the low prices are available for such a short period of time?
2. Can you think of any other uses Southwest might consider for its DING! software?

Sources: "What Is DING!?" Southwest Airlines Web site, accessed July 20, 2006, http://www.southwest.com; "Southwest Airlines Delivers the Heat with Hot Summer Fares," PRWebDirect, accessed July 20, 2006, http://www.prwebdirect.com; Jessica Labrencis, "Southwest's New Ding Fares: Worth the Download?" SmarterTravel.com, accessed July 20, 2006, http://www.smartertravel.com.

---

relatively young, highly educated, urban or suburban, and affluent, the demographics of online buyers are apparently changing. For instance, since 2000, Internet penetration—the percentage of a particular group going online—among older Americans has increased faster than it has among younger Americans. Moreover, today there is much less difference among demographic groups in the percentage of Internet users who purchase products online compared with a few years ago. Women, for example, are today just as likely as men to purchase products online. In 2000, men made up the majority of online shoppers.[27]

Realizing that customers would have little or no opportunity to rely on many of the senses—smelling the freshness of direct-from-the-oven bread, touching the soft fabric of a new cashmere sweater, or squeezing fruit to assess its ripeness—early online sellers focused on offering products that consumers were familiar with and tended to buy frequently, such as books and music. Other popular early online offerings included computer hardware and software, and airline tickets.

Figure 7.4 on page 225 lists the five product categories showing the highest growth in online sales during a recent year. The data illustrate how the B2C market has changed in recent years. A few years ago, books, music, and airline tickets were the most popular items sold online. Today, clothing and apparel, toys and video games, and consumer electronics are tops. In fact, online sales of clothing and apparel are growing at an annual rate of more than 40 percent.[28]

7.3 Demographics of Internet Users

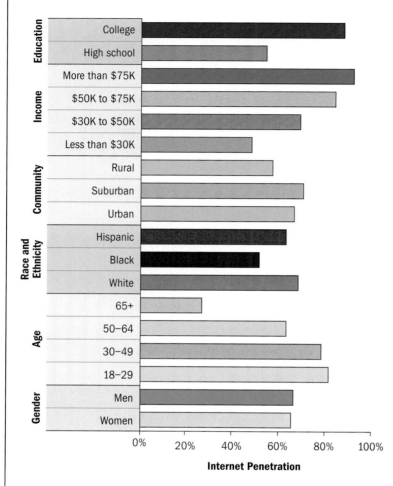

Internet penetration is the percentage of a certain demographic group that accesses the Internet.

Source: Pew Internet and American Life Project, accessed July 20, 2006, http://www.pewinternet.org.

In the coming years online sales of apparel, prescription drugs, and home products will continue to grow rapidly as the demographics of Internet users change. Because women—who spend more money on apparel than men do—will continue to become a larger share of Internet users, online apparel sales are likely to stay hot. Similarly, as the population of online users over age 55 grows, so will the online sales of prescription drugs. Kitchen products, small appliances, and large appliances—which typically are bought more frequently by women and older consumers—will also experience strong growth in the near future.[29]

Benefits of B2C e-Business

Why do consumers shop online? Three main reasons are most often cited in consumer surveys: price, convenience, and personalization.

Lower Prices Many products actually cost less online. Many of the best deals on airfares and hotels, for instance, are found at travel sites on the Internet. If you call Delta Airlines' toll-free number, before you speak to an agent a recorded voice invites you to visit Delta.com, "where lower fares may be available." Visitors to BN.com—the online store of bookseller Barnes & Noble—find that many bestsellers are discounted by up to 40 percent. At the brick-and-mortar stores, bestsellers are marked down only 30 percent. It comes as no surprise to anyone who has ever searched the Web for the best price for software or a newly issued CD that almost 60 percent of Web shoppers cited lower prices as a motivation for shopping online.[30]

The Web is an ideal method for savvy shoppers to compare prices from dozens—even hundreds—of sellers. Online shoppers can compare features and prices at their leisure, without being pressured by a salesperson or having to conform to the company's hours of operation. One of the newer e-commerce tools, **bots,** aid consumers in comparison shopping. Bots—short for *robots*—are search programs that check hundreds of sites, gather information, and bring it back to the sender. Assume you're in the market for a new computer monitor. At Shopping.com, you can specify the type and size of monitor you're looking for, and the Web site displays a list of the highest-ranked monitors, the e-tailer offering the best price on each, and the estimated taxes and shipping expenses. The Web site even ranks the e-tailers by customer experience and tells you whether a particular model is in stock.

Convenience A second important factor in prompting online purchases is shopper convenience. Cybershoppers can order goods and services from around the world at any hour of the day or night. Most e-tailers allow customers to register their credit-card and shipping informa-

Figure

7.4

tion to streamline future purchases. Customer register with a user name and password, which they enter when they place another order. E-tailers typically send an e-mail message confirming an order and the amount charged to the buyer's credit card. Another e-mail is sent once the product is shipped, along with a tracking number that the customer can use to track the order through the delivery process.

Many Web sites offer customized products to match individual customer requirements. Nike (http://nikeid.nike.com) enables online shoppers the opportunity to customize a running shoe, personalizing such features as the outsole, the amount of cushioning, and the width. The personalized shoe costs about $10 more than buying it off the shelves.

Personalization While online shopping often operates with little or no human interaction, successful B2C e-business companies know how important personalization is to the quality of the shopping experience. Customer satisfaction is greatly affected by the firm's ability to offer service tailored to many customers. But each person expects a certain level of customer service. Consequently, most leading online retailers offer customized features on their Web sites.

In the early years of e-commerce, Web marketers cast their nets broadly to land as many buyers as possible. Today, the emphasis has turned toward one-to-one marketing, creating loyal customers who are likely to make repeat purchases. How does personalized marketing work online? Say you buy a book at Amazon.com and register with the site. The site welcomes you back for your next purchase by name. Using software that analyzes your previous purchases, it also suggests other books you might like. You can even choose to receive periodic e-mails from Amazon.com informing you of new products. Many other leading e-tailers have adopted similar types of personalized marketing.

Fastest-Growing Online Retail Categories

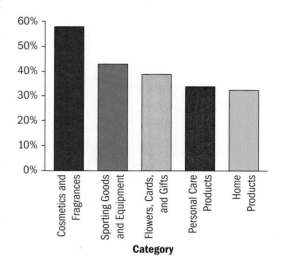

Source: Enid Burns, "Online Retail Growth Robust," ClickZ Network, accessed July 20, 2006, http://www.clickz.com.

Developing Safe Online Payment Systems

In response to consumer concerns about the safety of sending credit card numbers over the Internet, companies have developed secure payment systems for e-business. The most common forms of online payment are electronic cash and electronic wallets. Internet browsers, such as Microsoft Internet Explorer, contain sophisticated encryption systems. **Encryption** is the process of encoding data for security purposes. When such a system is active, users see a special icon indicating that they are at a protected Web site.

To increase consumer security most companies involved in e-business use **Secure Sockets Layer (SSL)** technology to encrypt information and verify the identity of senders and receivers (called *authentication*). SSL consists of a public key and a private key—software that encrypts and decrypts information. The public key is used to encrypt information, and the private key is used to decipher it. When a browser points to a domain with an SSL certificate, the technology authenticates (verifies the identity of) the server and the visitor and establishes an encryption method and a unique session key. Both parties can then begin a secure session that guarantees a message's privacy and integrity. VeriSign is one of the leading providers of SSL technology, which is used by more than 90 percent of *Fortune* 500 companies and the ten largest banks in the United States.[31]

An electronic wallet is another online payment method. An **electronic wallet** is a computer data file at an e-business site's checkout counter that contains not only electronic cash but credit card information, owner identification, and address. With electronic wallets, customers do not have to retype personal information each time they make a purchase at that site. Consumers simply click on the electronic wallet after selecting items, and their credit card payment information, name and address, and preferred mailing method are transmitted instantly.

E-BUSINESS CHALLENGES

Not surprisingly, e-business has had its problems and challenges. Consumers are concerned about protecting their privacy and being victimized by Internet fraud, frustrated with unreliable and hard-to-use Web sites, and annoyed over the inconveniences of scheduling deliveries and returning merchandise. Businesses are concerned about potential conflicts with business partners and difficulty in measuring the effectiveness of Internet-based promotion.

Privacy Issues

Consumers worry that information about them will become available to others without their permission. In fact, research indicates that privacy is one of the top concerns of Internet users and may impede the growth of e-business.[32] As the earlier discussion of Internet payments explained, concern about the privacy of credit card numbers has led to the use of secure payment systems. To add to those security systems, e-business sites require passwords as a form of authentication—that is, to determine that the person using the site is actually the one who is authorized to access the account. More recently, **electronic signatures** have become a way to enter into legal contracts such as home mortgages and insurance policies online. With an e-signature, an individual obtains a form of electronic identification and installs it in his or her Web browser. Signing the contract involves looking up and verifying the buyer's identity with this software.

Thanks to cookies and spyware, which are automatic data collection methods, online companies can track their customers' shopping and viewing habits. The way that companies use these technologies has the potential both to make visits to the Web site more convenient and to invade computer users' privacy. Amazon.com, for instance, has long employed sophisticated data collection systems to track customer habits. While Amazon sees such data gathering as the best way to keep customers happy and loyal, some believe that the company is getting too close to becoming a type of Big Brother—an all-knowing and all-seeing organization, complete with customer's credit card numbers. The "Hit & Miss" feature describes Amazon's latest technologies designed to better know and predict shopping habits—and the concerns these technologies raise.

Most consumers want assurances that any information they provide won't be sold to others without their permission. In response to these concerns, online merchants protect consumer information. For example, many Internet com-

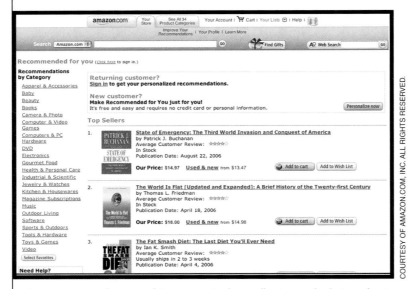

COURTESY OF AMAZON.COM, INC. ALL RIGHTS RESERVED.

Amazon.com makes use of its automatic data collection methods in order to provide personalized recommendation pages based on a user's past purchases and the items they have viewed.

HIT & MISS

Amazon as Big Brother?

Amazon.com, among the biggest and most innovative of online retailers, has been collecting detailed information about its customers' buying habits and preferences for years. Most of that information is crunched by sophisticated software to provide customers with personalized recommendations based on their past searches, browses, and purchases. Amazon recently changed its privacy policies to allow it to share with its suppliers and partners the personal information it collects, and it has launched a new search engine called A9 that can store data on every item a customer has ever searched for.

Amazon, like many other e-tailers, believes its customer-tracking technology is its most important weapon against competition from its rivals—both traditional and Internet retailers. Its storehouse of information about shoppers allows Amazon to suggest new products customers might be interested in, better direct their searches on the site, and even stop them from making duplicate purchases if they're forgetful. All these services come under the heading of "relationship building," according to the company.

But some privacy advocates wish Amazon would ask permission to collect, and share, all the information it gathers. That would allow customers to opt out of these processes if they wished. It might also protect Amazon from charges that it is veering close to the edge of the law, specifically a federal law that limits the gathering of information about children under age 13. Amazon recently received a patent on technology that allows it to track gift-giving habits, including the gift recipient's age. The company says it has not yet used the technology and will not violate any laws.

Questions for Critical Thinking

1. Begun as a book-selling Web site, Amazon has branched into electronics, hardware, software, jewelry, tools, toys, cameras, office products, and more. What effect do you think this expansion of its product offerings has had on its need to protect its competitive position? Why?
2. Do you think Amazon is in danger of violating its customers' privacy? Why or why not?

Sources: Leslie Walker, "Ad Firms Follow Customers around the Web," *Washington Post*, accessed July 20, 2006, http://www.washingtonpost.com; Allison Linn, "Amazon.com Knows, Predicts Shopping Habits," *Yahoo! News*, accessed July 20, 2006, http://news.yahoo.com; Rob Tedeschi, "A Web Site for Gift Seekers," *New York Times*, accessed July 20, 2006, http://www.nytimes.com.

---

panies have signed on with Internet privacy organizations such as TRUSTe, shown in Figure 7.5. By displaying the TRUSTe logo on their Web sites, they indicate that they have promised to disclose how they collect personal data and what they do with the information. Prominently displaying a privacy policy is an effective way to build customers' trust.

A policy is only as good as the company publishing it, though. Consumers have no assurances about what happens if a company is sold or goes out of business. Now-defunct Toysmart .com promised customers that it would never share their personal data with a third party. But when the company landed in bankruptcy court, it considered selling its database, one of its most valuable assets. And Amazon.com has told customers openly that if it or part of its business is purchased at some point, its database would be one of the transferred assets.

Such privacy features may become a necessary feature of Web sites if consumer concerns continue to grow. They also may become legally necessary. Already in the United States, the *Children's Online Privacy Protection Act (COPPA)* requires that Web sites targeting children younger

Figure 7.5

TRUSTe Logo

USED WITH PERMISSION. TRUSTE.

reviewed by
TRUST·e
site privacy statement

enabling customers to check flight schedules and purchase tickets online, Southwest Airlines worked hard to make sure its Web site had the same high service standards the airline is known for. As noted earlier, Southwest.com has proved both very popular and profitable.

Channel Conflicts

Companies spend time and money to nurture relationships with their partners. But when a manufacturer uses the Internet to sell directly to customers, it can compete with its usual partners. Retailers often have their own Web sites. So they don't want their suppliers competing with them for sales. As e-business broadens its reach, producers must decide whether these relationships are more important than the potential of selling directly on the Web. Disputes between producers, wholesalers, and retailers are called **channel conflicts.**

Mattel, well known for producing toys such as Barbie, Cabbage Patch dolls, and Matchbox cars, sells most of its products in toy stores and toy departments of other retailers, such as Target and Wal-Mart. The company wants an Internet presence, but it would cut the retailers out of this important source of revenue if it sold toys online to consumers. Mattel cannot afford to lose the goodwill and purchasing power of giant retailers such as Toys "R" Us and Wal-Mart. So the company sells only specialty products online, including pricey American Girl dolls.

Pricing is another potential area of conflict. In their eagerness to establish themselves as Internet leaders, some companies sell merchandise at discount prices. American Leather sells custom leather furniture through upscale retailers, and each dealer serving a geographic area has an exclusive contract for the collections it offers in its area. But at least one dealer began offering American Leather furniture at a discount to customers outside its market area. Other dealers complained, so American Leather established a policy that dealers were not to advertise the company's products on the Internet. Instead, American Leather offered links to local dealers on its own Web site and made plans to allow buyers to order online, with the sale to be directed to the dealer serving the consumer's geographic area.

assessment check

1. List the major challenges to e-business.
2. Most cases of Internet-related fraud come from what category of online activity?
3. What is a channel conflict?

USING THE WEB'S COMMUNICATION FUNCTION

The Internet has four main functions: e-business, entertainment, information, and communication. Even though e-business is a significant activity and is growing rapidly, communication still remains the most popular Web function. For instance, the volume of e-mail today exceeds regular mail (sometimes called *snail mail*) by an estimated ten to one. It's not surprising, then, that contemporary businesspeople use the communication function of the Internet to advance their organizational objectives.

Companies have long used e-mail to communicate with customers, suppliers, and other partners. Most companies have links on their Web sites that allow outside parties to send e-mails directly to the most appropriate person or division within the company. For instance, if you have a question concerning an online order from Eddie Bauer, you can click on a link on the retailer's Web site and send an e-mail to a customer service representative. Many online retailers have gone even further, offering their customers live help. Using a form of instant messaging, live help provides real-time communication between customers and customer service representatives. Figure 7.6 illustrates how one online retailer uses live help to better meet the needs of its customers.

Firms also use e-mail to inform customers about such company events as new products and special promotions. While using e-mail in this manner can be quite cost effective, companies have to be careful. A growing number of customers consider such e-mails **spam**—the popular name for junk e-mail. In fact, in a recent survey, one of the leading reasons given by consumers for reducing online shopping was "receiving spam after online purchase."[37] Many Internet users use *spam filters* to automatically eliminate junk e-mail from their in boxes.

Online Communities

In addition to e-mail, many firms use Internet forums, newsgroups, electronic bulletin boards, and Web communities that appeal to people who share common interests. All of these sites take advantage of the communication power of the Internet which, as noted earlier in the chapter, is still a main reason people go online. Members congregate online and exchange views and information on topics of interest. These communities may be organized for commercial or noncommercial purposes.

Online communities can take several forms, but all offer specific advantages to users and organizations alike. Online forums, for instance, are Internet discussion groups. Users log in and participate by sending comments and questions or receiving information from other forum members. Forums may operate as electronic bulletin boards, as libraries for storing information, or even as a type of classified ad directory. Firms often use forums to ask questions and exchange information with customers. Adobe, which designs such software as Acrobat and Photoshop, operates a "user-to-user" forum on its Web site as a support community for its customers. Customers who share common personal and professional interests can congregate, exchange industry news and practical product tips, share ideas, and—equally important—create publicity for Adobe products.

Newsgroups are noncommercial Internet versions of forums. Here people post and read messages on specific topics. Tens of thousands of newsgroups exist on the Internet, and the number continues to rise. **Electronic bulletin boards** center on a specific topic or area of interest. For instance, mountain bikers might check online bulletin boards to find out about the latest equipment, new places to ride, or current weather conditions in popular biking locations. While newsgroups resemble two-way conversations, electronic bulletin boards are more like announcements.

Online communities are not limited to consumers. They also facilitate business-to-business marketing. Using the Internet to build communities helps companies find other organizations to benchmark against, including suppliers, distributors, and competitors that may be interested in forming an alliance. Business owners who want to expand internationally frequently seek advice from other members of their online community.

Blogs

Another type of online communication method that is gaining popularity is the **blog.** Short for *Web log*, a blog is a Web page that serves as a publicly accessible personal journal for an individual or organization. Typically updated daily or even more frequently, these hybrid

Online Shopping Site with "Live Help" Function

7.6

USED WITH PERMISSION. CRUTCHFIELD CORPORATION.

spam popular name for junk e-mail.

blog online journal written by a blogger.

diary-guide sites are read on a regular basis by almost 30 percent of American Internet users. Using *RSS (Really Simple Syndication)* software, readers are continually kept up-to-date on new material posted on their favorite blogs whenever they are online. Unlike e-mail and instant messaging, blogs let readers post comments and ask questions aimed at the author (called a *blogger*). Some blogs today also incorporate **wikis.** A wiki is a Web page that anyone can edit, so a reader can, in addition to asking questions or posting comments, actually make changes to the Web page. Video blogs—called **podcasts**—are another emerging technology. Bloggers can prepare a video recording on a PC and then post it to a Web site, from which it can be downloaded to any MP3 player. According to the Web site iPodder.org, more than 3,000 podcasts operate worldwide.[38]

With the growing interest in blogs, many companies incorporate blogs in their e-business strategies. GreenCine—a small online DVD rental company—partially credits its blog for a sharp increase in revenues. Films critiqued by the blog's two writers are often snapped up immediately by renters.[39] Moreover, many believe that corporate blogs, if done properly, can also help build brand trust. An example is iLounge.com, a blog hosted by Apple, which lets users discuss their ideas for the next-generation iPod. David Eastman, managing director of Agency.com, believes that iLounge.com benefits Apple in two ways. First, it helps build the iPod brand; second, it gives Apple ideas to improve the design of Apple's most successful product. On the other hand, Eastman says that companies that try to exploit their audiences using blogs will end up hurting their brands. An example was the blog hosted by Cadbury Schweppes for its Raging Cow milk drink. That site didn't come across as particularly genuine because all it featured were product-endorsing comments from children.[40] In fact, many Internet users view most corporate blogs today as being more public-relations vehicles than anything else, and experts advise companies to use blogs with care. Rebecca Blood, author of *The Weblog Handbook: Practical Advice,* advises companies that "repositioning marketing materials on a blog is a waste of time. . . . Those materials already exist. The blog that is powerful is when it is real."[41]

Some people who write blogs muse about their jobs, including co-workers, bosses, and customers. Sometimes employee blogs make employers very nervous. One blogger who was working for a New York public-relations company described late nights in her cubicle "debating semantics with corporate idiots [clients]." In another posting, the blogger wrote, "I wonder how much longer I can deal with the mediocrity and just plain idiocy of corporate America." Even though the blogger didn't name any names, anyone who knew the blogger personally, or knew where she worked, could have identified the targets of her stinging criticism. The firm's managers discovered the blog and forced the blogger to remove it from the Web before any clients found out about the journal. But an employee blog can also benefit a company. Kevin Dugan works as a public-relations consultant and is a blogger. At the top of Dugan's blog is a disclaimer stating that the opinions expressed are his and are not supported by his firm. Dugan and his employer believe that his blog is more than just a soapbox; it indirectly markets the

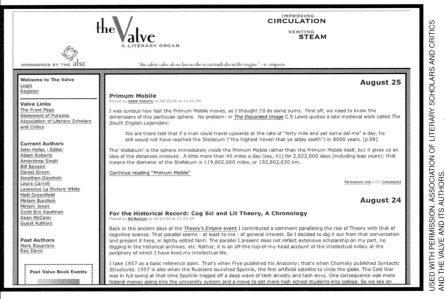

Blogs, web logs or web-based diaries, are a popular feature on the Internet today.

SHOULD COMPANIES MONITOR EMPLOYEE BLOGS?

The explosion of employee blogs (personal Web logs) has unexpectedly brought employers into the spotlight. Mark Jen described his first week at Google, including employee orientation, the cafeteria, and the company's finances. Heather Armstrong wrote colorful anonymous commentary about her boss and co-workers at a California software company. Peter Whitney wrote about his life, his friends, and his work at Wells Fargo. Ellen Simonetti posted revealing photos of herself in her Delta Airlines uniform.

All of these people were fired when their employers discovered their blogs. Whether they intended to harm their employers, thought anonymity would protect them, or complied with a boss's request to remove relevant posts, these and many other bloggers have learned the hard way that few companies are comfortable being the topic of employee comments on the Internet.

Is it ethical for employers to take disciplinary action based on the postings in employees' blogs?

PRO

1. Negative comments on the Internet can circulate worldwide and be preserved in many media without offering the injured party an opportunity to respond.
2. Workers have an ethical responsibility not to harm their employer by criticizing the organization publicly or revealing its trade

secrets and not to use the Internet to launch demoralizing personal attacks against co-workers. Companies should be able to counteract such postings.

CON

1. Employees can talk freely about their jobs and co-workers in public places such as parties, commuter trains, and bars; blogs are no different as a form of free speech.
2. Blogs allow employees to reach out to the public, including customers, clients, and recruits, and firms benefit from the humanizing effect of such frank and personal communication. Positive postings can even boost the company's image.

SUMMARY

A recent study of 526 organizations showed that one in four had

guidelines on blogging, and more firms are sure to follow suit. IBM tells employees to state that they don't speak for the firm; Microsoft actively encourages blogs. "It's great," says a Microsoft group manager. "It's instant feedback. We give a lot of support to blogging and . . . how to be a good blogger." Employee blogging is still a gray area, however, and employment consultants advise that if you must blog, ask first.

Sources: Matt Villano, "Write All about It (at Your Own Risk)", *New York Times*, accessed July 20, 2006, http://www.nytimes.com; Stephanie Armour, "Warning: Your Clever Little Blog Could Get You Fired," *USA Today*, accessed July 20, 2006, http://www.usatoday.com; "Blog-Linked Firings Prompt Calls for Better Policies," CNN.com, accessed July 20, 2006, http://cnn.technology.com.

solving an **ETHICAL** controversy

firm's work and philosophies.[42] The ethics of employee blogs—and what employers should do about them—is debated in more detail in the "Solving an Ethical Controversy" feature.

Web-Based Promotions

Rather than relying completely on their Web sites to attract buyers, companies frequently expand their reach in the marketplace by placing ads on sites their prospective customers are likely to visit. **Banner ads,** the most common form of Internet advertising, are typically small messages placed in high-visibility areas of frequently visited Web sites. **Pop-up ads** are separate windows that contain an advertising message. The effectiveness of pop-up ads, however, is questionable. For one thing, scam artists use pop-ups. For another, many Internet users simply hate pop-up ads—even those from legitimate companies. Consequently, most Internet service providers now offer software that blocks pop-up ads. Google and Microsoft also offer free pop-up ad-blocking software.

search marketing paying search engines, such as Google, a fee to make sure that the company's listing appears toward the top of the search results.

Another type of online advertising gaining popularity is so-called **search marketing.** Firms make sure that they are listed with the major search engines, such as Google. But that is not enough. A single search for an item—say, plastic fasteners—will yield thousands of sites, many of which might not even be relevant. To overcome this problem, companies pay online search engines to have their Web sites or ads pop up after a computer user enters certain words into the search engine, or to make sure that their firm's listing appears toward the top of the search results. Google and other search engines now include "sponsored links" on the right side of the search results page. When a user clicks on one of the sponsored links, he or she is taken to that site and the company pays the search engine a small fee. Many experts consider search marketing the most cost-effective form of Web-based advertising.

Companies also use online coupons to promote their products via the Web. For instance, customers can visit a company's Web site—such as Procter & Gamble's (http://www.pg.com)—to learn about a new product and then print a discount coupon redeemable at participating retailers. Consumers can also search for virtual coupons using such criteria as business name, location, and keyword, and then download and print them. ValPak Marketing Systems, a longtime leader in the paper coupon industry, now offers the online equivalent at its Web site (http://www.valpak.com).

assessment check

1. What are online communities? Explain how online communities can help companies market their products and improve customer service.
2. What is a blog? A wiki? A podcast?
3. Explain the difference between a banner ad, a pop-up ad, and search marketing.

MANAGING A WEB SITE

Business Web sites serve many purposes. They broaden customer bases, provide immediate accessibility to current catalogs, accept and process orders, and offer personalized customer service. As technology becomes increasingly easy to use, anyone with a computer and Internet access can easily design and then publish a site on the Web. How people or organizations use their sites to achieve their goals determines whether their sites will succeed. Figure 7.7 lists some key questions to consider in developing a Web site.

Developing Successful Web Sites

Most Web experts agree that it is easier to build a bad Web site than a good one. When judging Web sites, success means different things to different businesses. One firm might feel satisfied by maintaining a popular site that conveys company information or reinforces name recognition—just as a billboard or magazine ad does—without requiring any immediate sales activity. Web sites like those of the *Los Angeles Times* and *USA Today* draw many visitors who want the latest news, and Yahoo!, Google, and ESPN are successful because they attract heavy traffic. Popular Web sites add to their success by selling advertising space to other businesses.

Internet merchants need to attract customers who transact business on the spot. Some companies host Web sites that offer some value-added service to create goodwill for potential customers. Organizations such as the Mayo Clinic and accounting giant Ernst & Young provide useful information or links to related sites that people frequently visit. But to get people to stay at the site and complete a transaction, the site must also be secure, reliable, and easy to use.

Planning and Preparation   What is the company's goal for its Web site? Answering this question is the first and most important step in the Web site development process. For discount

Figure

7.7

Questions to Consider in Developing a Web Site

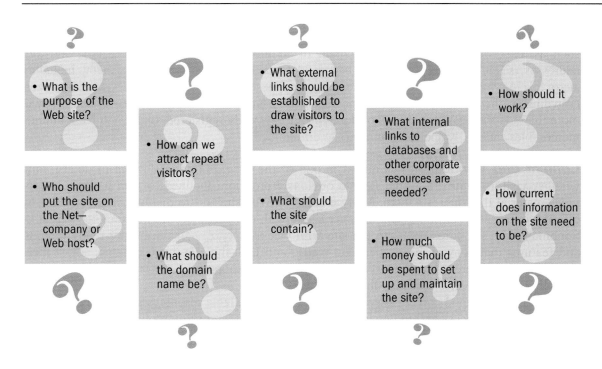

- What is the purpose of the Web site?

- Who should put the site on the Net— company or Web host?

- How can we attract repeat visitors?

- What should the domain name be?

- What external links should be established to draw visitors to the site?

- What should the site contain?

- What internal links to databases and other corporate resources are needed?

- How much money should be spent to set up and maintain the site?

- How should it work?

- How current does information on the site need to be?

brokerage firm Charles Schwab, the primary objective is to sign up new customers. So the Web site designers put a link called "Open an Account" prominently in the upper right-hand corner of the home page. In addition, to reinforce Schwab's image as a respectable investment firm, the site uses a businesslike color scheme.

Objectives for the Web site also determine the scope of the project. If the company's goal is to sell merchandise online, the site must incorporate a way for customers to place orders and ask questions about products, as well as links to the company's databases to track inventory and deliveries. As in this example, the plan includes not only the appearance of the Web site but also the company's behind-the-scenes resources for making the Web site deliver on its promises.

Other key decisions include whether to create and maintain a site in-house or to contract with outside experts. Some companies prefer to retain control over content and design by producing their own sites. However, because acquiring the expertise to develop Web sites can be very time-consuming, hiring specialists may be more cost-effective. Often companies such as Yahoo!, Google, or IBM are enlisted to provide both software and consulting services to clients for their Web sites.

Naming the Web site is another important early step in the planning process. A domain name should reflect the

Yahoo offers many web-related services besides just Internet searches. A successful Web site, such as Yahoo!, requires planning not only for the interest of the site, but also on the business end.

rate has been declining to about 0.5 percent of those viewing an ad. This rate is much lower than the 1.0 to 1.5 percent response rate for direct-mail advertisements. Low click-through rates have made Web advertising less attractive than it was when it was novel and people were clicking on just about anything online. Selling advertising has therefore become a less reliable source of e-business revenues.

conversion rate percentage of visitors to a Web site who make a purchase.

As e-business gains popularity, new models for measuring its effectiveness are being developed. A basic measurement is the **conversion rate,** the percentage of Web site visitors who make purchases. A conversion rate of 3 to 5 percent is average by today's standards. A company can use its advertising cost, site traffic, and conversion rate data to find out the cost to win each customer. E-business companies try to boost their conversion rates by ensuring that their sites download quickly, are easy to use, and deliver on their promises. Many are turning to one of several firms that help companies improve the performance of their Web sites. For instance, CompUSA—a computer and electronics retailer—turned to Web consultants Coremetrics to help it improve the overall performance of its Web site. Using Coremetrics Online Analytics, CompUSA identified the specific online shopping tools that helped create loyal, high-volume customers. By improving these tools and making them more accessible on its Web site, CompUSA increased revenues by more than $2 million.[44]

Besides measuring click-through and conversion rates, companies can study samples of consumers. Research firms such as Media Metrix and RelevantKnowledge recruit panels of computer users to track Internet site performance and evaluate Web activity; this service works in much the same way that television rating firm ACNielsen monitors television audiences. WebTrends provides information on Web site visitors, including where they come from; what they see; and the number of "hits," or visits to the site, during different times of the day. Other surveys of Web users investigate their brand awareness and their attitudes toward Web sites and brands.

assessment check

1. What are the first three questions a company should ask itself when planning a Web site?
2. How does the type of Web site affect measures of effectiveness?
3. Explain the difference between click-through and conversion rates.

THE GLOBAL ENVIRONMENT OF E-BUSINESS

For many companies, future growth is directly linked to a global strategy that incorporates e-business. While the United States still leads the world in technology, communications infrastructure, and ownership of PCs and other consumer technology products, other countries are rapidly catching up. This is also the case when it comes to Internet use. Figure 7.9 shows the top ten nations in terms of number of Internet users and Internet penetration. As the figures show, while the United States leads the world in the number of Internet users—more than 200 million—it ranks only fifth in Internet penetration, at less than 68 percent. Sweden leads the world in Internet penetration, with an estimated 74 percent. Moreover, Internet usage in the United States is growing more slowly than it is in other countries. For instance, in a recent year the average amount of time spent online by U.S. Internet users barely changed. By contrast, average time spent online was up 25 percent in Hong Kong, 19 percent in France, and 12 percent in Japan.[45]

When it comes to e-business, the United States still leads, but the rest of the world is making major strides forward. Forrester Research, an e-business research firm, estimates that online shopping currently accounts for around 5 percent of total retail sales in the United Kingdom, increasing to over 11 percent by 2008. While broadband penetration in Europe and Asia is lower than it is in the United States, the rate of growth in broadband in other countries and regions appears to be accelerating. As we've discussed earlier, people with broadband connections typically spend more online than those with narrowband connections. Moreover, U.S. firms cannot expect that their earlier experience with the Internet and e-business gives

Figure

7.9

World Internet Statistics

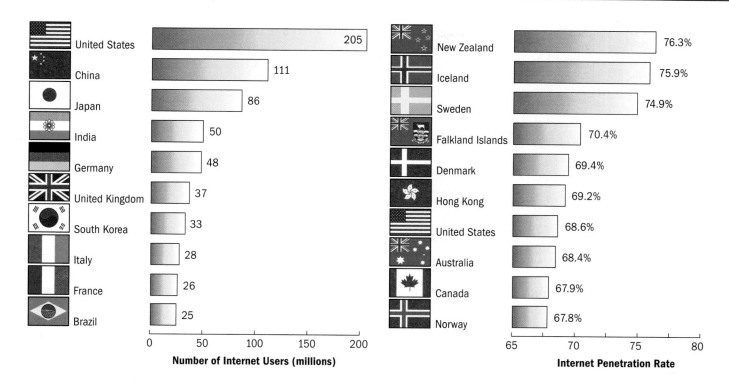

Source: Internet World Stats, accessed July 20, 2006, http://www.internetworldstats.com.

them a natural and permanent edge in foreign markets. According to recent statistics, Web sites run by U.S. firms still make up eight of the ten most popular e-business Web sites in Europe, with eBay and Amazon leading the way. However, Fnac.com—the online subsidiary of giant French retailing group PPR—is now more popular than Amazon in both France and Spain, and it is growing rapidly in other European countries. [46]

With so many users and so much buying power, the Internet creates an enormous pool of potential customers. Companies can market their goods and services internationally and locate distribution sources and trading partners abroad. Customers can search for products at their convenience, browsing through online catalogs that always show current information. Many companies divide their Web sites internationally. For instance, when you visit software company Symantec's Web site, you are first asked your country of origin; after entering the information, you are automatically taken to that country-specific portion of the Web site. A list of the products available for your country are listed, along with local distributors and service centers. And the information on the site is presented in the local language.

One practical implication of this global marketplace is the different languages that buyers and sellers speak. Reflecting the Internet's origins, more than half of users now communicate in English. However, the remainder use other languages, led by Japanese, German, Chinese, Spanish, and French. So far, roughly three of every four Web pages are still in English, slowing the adoption of the Internet in non-English-speaking countries. Other international differences are important, too. Auction site eBay initially goofed in the United Kingdom by launching an auction site with prices stated in U.S. dollars. After realizing that its British audience was offended and confused, the company quickly switched to British pounds.

assessment check

1. How do language differences affect global e-business?
2. How does e-business heighten global competition?

E-business can heighten competition. In the virtual global marketplace, many manufacturers use the Internet to search online catalogs for the lowest-priced parts. No longer can local suppliers assume that they have locked up the business of neighboring firms. Furthermore, the Internet is a valuable way to expand a company's reach, especially for small businesses that would otherwise have difficulty finding customers overseas.

WHAT'S AHEAD

The Internet is revolutionizing the way we communicate, obtain information, seek entertainment, and conduct business. It has created tremendous opportunities for B2B and B2C e-business. So far, B2B transactions are leading the way online. B2C e-business is growing and attracting new buyers every year. Companies are just beginning to harness the communication power of the Web to help achieve higher levels of customer satisfaction and loyalty. In spite of the challenges and roadblocks, the future of e-business looks bright.

In upcoming chapters, we look at other trends that are reshaping the business world of the 21st century. For example, in the next part we explore the critical issues of how companies organize, lead, and manage their work processes; manage and motivate their employees; empower their employees through teamwork and enhanced communication; handle labor and workplace disputes; and create and produce world-class goods and services.

Summary of Learning Goals

1 Define e-business and discuss how it can help achieve business success.

E-business involves targeting customers by collecting and analyzing business information, conducting customer transactions, and maintaining online relationships with customers, suppliers, and other interested parties by means of the Internet. It consists of e-tailing, business-to-business transactions, electronic data interchanges, business-to-business exchange of data, and the use of Web-enabled communication tools such as e-mail. E-business increases a company's global reach, increases personalization, is interactive, offers right-time and integrated marketing, and can reduce costs.

Assessment Check Answers

1.1 Define e-business.
E-business refers to conducting business via the Internet.

1.2 List some benefits of e-business.
Benefits of e-business include global reach, personalization, interactivity, right-time and integrated marketing, and cost savings for both buyers and sellers.

2 Distinguish between a corporate Web site and a marketing Web site.

Virtually all businesses have Web sites. Generally, these sites can be classified as either corporate Web sites or marketing Web sites. Corporate Web sites are designed to increase the firm's visibility, promote their offerings, and provide information to interested parties. Marketing Web sites are also designed to communicate information and build customer relationships, but the main purpose of marketing Web sites is to increase purchases by site visitors.

Assessment Check Answers

2.1 Briefly identify the differences between a corporate Web site and a marketing Web site.
A corporate Web site is designed to increase a firm's visibility, promote its offerings, and provide information for interested parties. A marketing Web site generally includes the same information found on a corporate Web site but is also designed to increase sales to site visitors.

2.2 Visit the Specialized Web site (http://www.specialized.com)**. Is this site a corporate Web site or a marketing Web site?**
Specialized.com is a marketing Web site. It includes an online store where visitors can purchase Specialized products.

3 List the major forms of business-to-business (B2B) e-business.
Electronic data interchange was an early use of technology to conduct business transactions. E-business is the process of selling goods and services through Internet-based exchanges of data. It includes product information; ordering, invoicing, and payment processes; and customer service. In a B2B context, e-business uses Internet technology to conduct transactions between two organizations via extranets, private exchanges, electronic exchanges, and e-procurement.

Assessment Check Answers

3.1 What is B2B e-business? How large is it relative to B2C e-business?
B2B e-business is the use of the Internet for business transactions between organizations. By some estimates, around 80 percent of all e-business activity consists of B2B e-business.

3.2 What is an EDI? An extranet? A private exchange?
An EDI is a computer-to-computer exchange of invoices, purchase orders, price quotations, and other sales information between buyers and sellers. An extra-

net is a secure network accessible through a firm's Web site by authorized users. A private network is a secure Web site at which a company and its suppliers share all types of data from product design to the delivery of orders.

3.3 Briefly explain how e-procurement works.
E-procurement consists of Web-based systems that enable all types of organizations to improve the efficiency of their procurement processes.

4 Explain business-to-consumer (B2C) e-business and identify the products most often sold online.
After a rocky start, business-to-consumer (B2C) e-business is maturing. B2C uses the Internet to connect companies directly with consumers. E-tailing and electronic storefronts are the major forms of online sales to consumers. Online shoppers are young, highly educated, affluent, and urban. However, in the coming years, online consumers will begin to look more like offline shoppers, and the kinds of products sold online will change as well. Benefits of B2C e-business include lower prices, increased convenience, and personalization. Payment methods include electronic cash, electronic wallets, and online transfers of cash.

Assessment Check Answers

4.1 Outline the differences between shopping Web sites and informational sites. Visit the Web site of Cross pens (http://www.cross.com)**. Is this site a shopping or informational B2C Web site?**
An informational site provides product information, technical support, and links to local retailers. A shopping Web site allows visitors to buy a firm's products. The Cross Web site is a shopping site.

4.2 Discuss the characteristics of the typical online buyer, how those characteristics are changing, and the potential impact on the types of products sold online.
While the typical online buyer is still relatively urban, young, and affluent, growing evidence shows that online shoppers are beginning to look more like offline shoppers. As these trends continue, the types of products sold online will likely change. For instance, as online shoppers get older, online sales of pharmaceuticals will likely increase. As the number of

female online shoppers has increased, so too have online sales of shoes, clothing, and kitchen products.

4.3 List some ways online merchants try to ensure secure payment systems.

Online shopping sites use encryption—the process of encoding data for security purposes. Major firms involved in all aspects of e-business use Secure Sockets Layer (SSL) technology, an industry-wide standard for secure Internet payment transactions. Electronic wallets are secure data files at Web sites that contain customer information so customers don't have to retype personal information each time they make a purchase.

5 **Describe some of the challenges associated with e-business.**

The growth of e-business has been hampered by consumer security and privacy concerns, fraud, and system overload. In addition, poor Web design and service, unreliability of delivery and returns, and lack of retail expertise has limited e-business success. The Internet can also generate conflict among buyers and sellers.

Assessment Check Answers

5.1 List the major challenges to e-business.

Challenges to e-business include protecting consumer privacy, fraud, unreliable and hard-to-use Web sites, problems with deliveries and returns, and potential channel conflicts.

5.2 Most cases of Internet-related fraud come from what category of online activity?

The largest number of cases of Internet-related fraud come from online auctions.

5.3 What is a channel conflict?

A channel conflict is a dispute between a producer, wholesaler, and/or retailer.

6 **Discuss how organizations use the communication functions of the Internet to advance their objectives.**

Communication remains the most popular function of the Internet. Companies have long used e-mail to communicate with customers, suppliers, and other partners. Online communities are groups of people who share common interests. Companies use online communities such as forums and electronic bulletin boards to communicate with and obtain feedback from customers and other partners. Blogs are online journals that have gained popularity in recent years. Companies have just begun to explore the potential of blogs. Web-based promotions include advertising on other Web sites, search marketing, and online coupons.

Assessment Check Answers

6.1 What are online communities? Explain how online communities can help companies market their products and improve customer service.

Online communities can take several forms and include Internet discussion groups and electronic bulletin boards. Users log in and participate by sending comments and questions, or receiving information from other forum members. Companies use online communities to ask questions and exchange information with customers.

6.2 What is a blog? A wiki? A podcast?

A blog, short for a *Web log,* and is Web page that serves as a publicly accessible journal for an individual or organization. A wiki is a Web page that anyone can edit, and a podcast is a video blog.

6.3 Explain the difference between a banner ad, a pop-up ad, and search marketing.

Banner ads are small messages placed in high-visibility areas of frequently visited Web sites. A pop-up ad is a separate window that pops up containing an advertising message. Search marketing is an arrangement by which a firm pays a search engine—such as Google—a fee to make sure that the firm's listing appears toward the top of the search results.

7 **List the steps involved in developing successful Web sites and identify methods for measuring Web site effectiveness.**

Businesses establish Web sites to expand their customer bases, increase buyer awareness of their products, improve consumer communications, and provide better service. Before designing a Web site, a company's decision makers must first determine what they want to achieve with the site. Other important decisions include who should create, host, and manage the site; how to promote it; and how much funding to allocate. Successful Web sites contain informative, up-to-date, and visually appealing content. Sites should also download quickly and be easy to use. Finally, management must develop ways to measure how well a site accomplishes its objectives.

Assessment Check Answers

7.1 What are the first three questions a company should ask itself when planning a Web site?
The first question deals with the purpose of the Web site. The second deals with whether the firm should develop the site itself or outsource it to a specialized firm. The third question is determining the name of the site.

7.2 How does the type of Web site affect measures of effectiveness?
For a shopping site, profitability is an important measure of effectiveness, though profitability can be difficult to measure given the presence of so-called Web-to-store shoppers. For company Web sites, online success is measured by increased brand awareness and loyalty, which presumably translates into greater profitability through offline transactions.

7.3 Explain the difference between click-through and conversion rates.
The click-through rate is the percentage of viewers who, when presented with a banner ad, click on it. The conversion rate is the percentage of Web site visitors who actually make purchases.

8 Explain the global scope of e-business.
Technology allows companies to compete in the global market and workplace. Even the smallest firms can sell products and find new vendors in international markets. Through its own Web site, a company can immediately reach customers all over the world. Improved communications among employees in different locations create new ways to collaborate on projects.

Assessment Check Answers

8.1 How do language differences affect global e-business?
Most Web pages, including e-business sites, are still in English, which inhibits the growth of e-business in other countries. Also, online retailers need to be sensitive to cultural differences.

8.2 How does e-business heighten global competition?
In the virtual global marketplace, companies can search online catalogs to find the lowest-priced goods and services. The Internet is also a valuable tool for expanding a company's reach, especially for smaller businesses that would otherwise have difficulty finding overseas customers.

Business Terms You Need to Know

electronic business (e-business) 215
corporate Web site 217
marketing Web site 218
business-to-business (B2B)
   e-business 219

business-to-consumer (B2C)
   e-business 221
electronic storefront 222
phishing 228
spam 231

blog 231
search marketing 234
click-through rate 237
conversion rate 238

Other Important Business Terms

electronic data interchange
   (EDI) 219
quick response 219
extranet 220
private exchange 220
electronic exchange 220
e-procurement 221
electronic shopping cart 222

bot 224
encryption 225
Secure Sockets Layer (SSL) 225
electronic wallet 225
electronic signatures 226
firewall 228
channel conflict 230
electronic bulletin board 231

wiki 232
podcast 232
banner ad 233
pop-up ad 233
Web host 236
Web-to-store 237

1. List the five e-business categories.
2. Explain how a Web presence can improve the performance of traditional brick-and-mortar operations.
3. Describe the type and purpose of information found on a corporate Web site.
4. Which is larger, B2B or B2C e-business?
5. Explain how an electronic data interchange operates. What is rapid response?
6. What is an electronic exchange? Why have they proven to be less successful than many originally projected?
7. What is a bot and how do consumers use it to find the lowest price for a product online?
8. Define encryption and Secure Sockets Layer technology.
9. Describe some of the privacy concerns of online shoppers.
10. What is phishing?
11. Discuss how companies can use blogs.
12. Assume a company spends $100,000 to attract 25,000 visitors to its Web site. If the conversion rate is 5 percent, how much did the company spend to acquire each customer?
13. What are the challenges and benefits of e-commerce in the global business environment?

1. Discuss how the profile of online buyers and sellers is changing. What are some of the implications of these trends for B2C e-business?
2. Communication is still the most popular Web function; team up with a partner and describe how a travel company could take advantage of online communication to market its travel services.
3. Compared with brick-and-mortar retailers, what are the advantages and disadvantages of so-called pure-play e-business companies? Why have so many pure-play e-business companies failed?
4. Assume the role of an online shopper who wishes to purchase a pair of jeans over the Internet. Two leading online clothing retailers are Old Navy (http://www.oldnavy.com) and Eddie Bauer (http://www.eddiebauer.com). Visit both sites and learn enough so that you can describe each to your class, including which of the two you'd be most likely to purchase from and why.
5. Identify a local company that has a significant online presence. Arrange to interview the person in charge of the company's Web site. Ask the following questions:
   a. How was the Web site developed?
   b. Did the company develop the site in-house or did it outsource the task?
   c. How often does the company make changes to the site?
   d. In the opinion of your respondent, what are the advantages and disadvantages of going online?
6. Many consumers are reluctant to purchase online products that are perishable or that consumers typically like to touch, feel, or smell before buying. Working in a small group, suggest ways an e-business company might be able to reduce this reluctance.
7. Identify a local company that operates with little or no online presence. Outline a proposal that explains the benefits to the firm of either going online or significantly expanding its online presence. Sketch out what the firm's Web site should look like and the functions it should perform.
8. Choose one of the following types of companies and describe how it could take advantage of the communication power of the Internet to market its products:
   a. a travel agency that specializes in adventure travel.

b. a real estate firm.

c. a firm that ships gourmet foods—such as lobster, cheeses, or exotic coffees—nationwide.

d. a minor-league hockey team.

9. IBM offers extensive consulting services, software, and hardware (such as servers) for organizations engaged in e-business. Working with a partner, assume you're entrepreneurs and you'd like to expand your presence in the B2B market. Visit the IBM e-business Web site (http://www.ibm .com). Read about the services offered and review some of the case studies in which IBM has assisted firms in their B2B activities. Prepare a report on what you have learned.

10. Using a search engine such as Google (http://www.google.com), identify two or three company-sponsored blogs. Read some of the recent entries and prepare a report summarizing the goals of each blog and your assessment of its effectiveness.

Case 7.1

eBay Backs Off a Price Hike

One of the most popular sites on the Internet, giant auctioneer eBay earns most of its profits by charging sellers modest fees for membership and collecting a small percentage of the final selling price of certain items. The formulas for these fees were usually seen as fair, and sellers prospered. Buyers paid only for their purchases. Then in early 2005 the company announced a new fee structure affecting sellers in the United States, Canada, Australia, and the United Kingdom. The basic monthly subscription fee that sellers would pay to list items on eBay Stores rose from $9.95 to $15.95; the fee for ten-day listings would double to 40 cents; and "Buy It Now" sellers would pay 8 to 16 percent of an item's selling price, instead of a flat fee as before.

"We carefully evaluate the pricing structure and, from time to time, we'll change prices when it's the right thing to do to ensure the vibrancy of the marketplace," an eBay spokesperson told a reporter. "We implement these changes to spur the market in certain categories." Auction industry experts agree that eBay routinely uses its pricing power to draw profit from the features of the site that are most popular every year.

Sellers weren't pleased. To some, the fee hikes—in particular the increase in "Buy It Now" charges—were an attempt to cash in on heavily used site features just to add to the company's coffers at their expense. Loyal sellers bombarded eBay with e-mail protests, threatening to raise their own prices, which would drive buyers away; close their e-stores; or switch to other auction sites such as Overstock.com, which trails eBay in transaction volume by a wide margin. But in a well-timed move, Overstock.com slashed its own fees following eBay's announcement and saw a sharp spike in sales on its site.

One letter-writing campaign was led by a seller of historical costumes and bridal wear, who had never participated in eBay's seller communities before. Others wondered whether it was time for the government to regulate what eBay could charge, especially to protect small sellers who stood to lose the most revenue from the new fees.

EBay responded quickly to its members' unhappiness. "We're listening to everything you have to say," wrote eBay president Bill Cobb in a weekend e-mail sent to all the firm's sellers less than a month later. "I've been taking it all in and thinking hard about how we can make sure eBay remains a fun, safe place to trade, and a prosperous home for our many dedicated sellers."

Putting sentiments into action, the company announced it would issue a credit of $15.95—the price of a one-month subscription—to all its eBay Stores small-business owners of record as of the preceding month. It also reduced the minimum fee for inexpensive auction items and replaced its automated customer service response system with live customer service agents, who would answer questions in real time and for a broader population of sellers than had ever qualified for customer service support before. Some observers called the expanded support an important gesture that would go a long way toward offsetting the effect of price increases for small-business owners. But eBay held firm on the biggest increases.

Many still thought lessons could be learned from the firm's experience. "A price increase is always going to be painful," said one retail analyst. "Companies need to think strategically and communicate to their consumers the value and benefit of what they are getting in exchange for the price increases."

Questions for Critical Thinking

1. Do you think eBay handled its price increase in the best possible way? Why or why not? What, if any-thing, do you think eBay should do differently next time it needs to communicate price changes to its customers? Why?

2. Can improvements in customer service really offset price increases? Would you answer differently for a brick-and-mortar retailer than for an online retailer like eBay? Why or why not?

Sources: "eBay Eats Humble Pie on Fee Hikes," CBS News, accessed July 20, 2006, http://www.cbsnews.com; Jennifer LeClaire, "eBay Responds to Price Hike Outcry," *MacNewsWorld*, accessed July 20, 2006, http://www.macnewsworld.com; Tim Richardson, "eBay Backtracks as It Cuts Some Fees," *The Register*, accessed July 20, 2006, http://www.theregister.co.uk; Rick Aristotle Munarriz, "eBay, Hike, and Other 4-Letter Words," Motley Fool, accessed July 20, 2006, http://www.fool.com; Ryan Naraine, "eBay Flexes Pricing Muscle," eWeek.com, accessed July 20, 2006, http://www.eweek.com.

VIDEO Case 7.2

Manifest Digital: Putting the User First

This video case appears on page 615. A recently filmed video, designed to expand and highlight the written case, is available for class use by instructors.

![The Second City logo]

Second City: An Entrepreneurial Experience from Stage to Strategic Planning

Over the last 50 years, the entrepreneurial spirit of The Second City (SC) has been found in its stock-in-trade: its style of comedy. Its comedic and business philosophy is to *listen and react*. Much like true entrepreneurship, improvisational comedy requires vision, energy, self-confidence, creativity, accountability, a tolerance for ambiguity, and the boldness to plunge ahead in the face of failure.

When a hip group of University of Chicago students began performing comedy shows in 1959, they offered a satirical, uniquely subversive take on society. It was a society beginning to wake from a decade of political docility. Improvisation, an art form based on risk and off-the-cuff reaction, excited audiences of the day. Like the momentum of a good scene, Second City used its innovations in comedy to spawn an amazing variety of related business ventures. Student training centers, corporate training, TV shows, national touring companies, and theaters in Chicago, Toronto, Las Vegas, Detroit, and Denver are all successful extensions of Second City's entrepreneurial character.

The founding of Second City was a collaborative artistic effort. Using improvisation as an entrepreneurial technique, Second City continued to form partnerships on the-

atrical and corporate stages. Notably, SC's first producer, Bernard Sahlins, saw the groundbreaking nature of the SC style and offered the group a needed skill: the ability to balance a checkbook. SC's comedy spoke to a changing cultural climate. Sahlins claimed they "[violated] taboos up to the point of bad taste, without crossing it." Within eight months of opening, Second City grabbed national attention. Second City continued to refine its message and mission. By listening and reacting to public themes and material, their product, Second City comedy, began to take shape as a creative innovation worthy of more expansive entrepreneurial ventures.

Bernie Sahlins took the show to Toronto, where one of Second City's most significant partnerships was formed. After only a short, unsuccessful run in 1973, the Toronto cast arrived at their theater to see the doors padlocked shut. Without the legal ability to sell liquor in the theater, the show had gone bankrupt. The spirit of Second City comedy had, however, unknowingly met the heart of yet another entrepreneur, who faced this supposed "failure" with both confidence and business savvy. Andrew Alexander, a Canadian promoter, bought the Canadian rights to SC from Bernie

Sahlins—a monthly royalty deal was struck between the two men and was signed on a cocktail napkin. This turnaround strategy was risky but in step with the SC personality, and Alexander had prepared practical solutions for improvement. He borrowed money and beckoned a hesitant cast back to Toronto with one such solution—an acquired liquor license. The Toronto branch cultivated and exposed a new generation of talent that continues to be a commodity for SC today. Looking to cast a new sketch TV show, *Saturday Night Live,* Lorne Michaels picked talent right off the Toronto stage—thereby offering SC a new level of fame. In fact, when *Saturday Night Live (SNL)* started, Second City attendance boomed. Alumni such as John Candy, Dan Aykroyd, and Gilda Radner further cemented the Second City legacy.

Second City encountered a series of changes in the entertainment industry that tested its ability to listen and react, just like the comedic timing of its performers. As talent moved into the TV medium, co-owners Sahlins and Alexander felt a need to respond. Concerned that they would continue to lose talent to *SNL,* they decided to give television a try themselves. Andrew Alexander's business partner, Len

Stuart, provided the capital needed to launch SC from the stage to the screen. With only $35,000 for seven episodes, the cast and producers used their underfinanced reality as a backdrop for the program. Self-referenced as a low-budget show, the inexperienced crews and performers became the theme. After an eight-year run, *SCTV* had earned two Emmys for writing, thirteen Emmy nominations, and a place in comedy history. *SCTV* spotlighted more future stars, including Harold Ramis, Rick Moranis, and Martin Short.

The art of improvisation now dominates the comedic world and integrates the artistic and entrepreneurial work of Second City. Its theaters promote innovation within the structure of the business. Second City now boasts training centers in Chicago, Los Angeles, New York, Toronto, and Detroit, offering students of all ages a curriculum based on listening and reacting, team building, communication, and the most subversive of Second City's techniques, humor.

The Second City is a corporation, owned by Andrew Alexander and Len Stuart, who bought SC from Bernie Sahlins in 1984. Today, Second City's senior management team continues to base the company's business ventures on the seemingly undisciplined attitude of improvisational comedy. Vice president Kelly Leonard says that The Second City remains "true to the core" of its lineage. According to

Leonard, "Second City is all about making the new—so entrepreneurship is at the core—both on a creative and business level. You can see that by the expansion of the business into new and lucrative areas of training, touring, education, television, radio, etc." With an abundance of creative proposed ventures to consider, Second City takes professional risks and picks interesting advancements over merely lucrative endeavors. SC's latest undertaking is a deal Leonard brokered with Norwegian Cruise Lines. Second City Theatricals has a select partnership with Norwegian, placing Second City's adventurous style of comedy on the bow of a new performance venue, accessing a new demographic of audience members.

Second City Communications is another branch of the company that other businesses seek out for help in fostering a creative corporate atmosphere. Using improvisational techniques such as confidence, teamwork, and relationship building, Second City Communications trains business professionals and contemporary entrepreneurs in a variety of business practices. SC listens to the needs of its clients and responds accordingly. Mock business encounters are set up in which professionals can learn and experience firsthand how to handle business situations. Corporate events feature customized comedic material. The tried-and-true methods of improvisational comedy

are taught, along with a few other secrets to Second City's charm.

Each of Second City's business and nonprofit ventures appears on its Web site. SC finds the greatest profit return in selling tickets to its theatrical revues. Other creative elements, including blogs and podcasts, are compelling features that routinely increase site traffic. According to Leonard, the trickiest aspect of managing http://www.secondcity.com seems to be making the electronic medium as funny as SC's live comedy.

While the lights come up on future ventures for The Second City, its visionaries will continue to look back on the principals of improv for guidance: *to listen and react.* They teach this method to an impressive variety of interested students from all backgrounds. Anyone can be inspired by the innovative approach of The Second City, but especially talented young actors destined for the footlights and courageous entrepreneurs entering the market.

QUESTIONS

1. What challenges might Second City's entrepreneurial managers face as they continue to field proposals and generate business endeavors?
2. How are a comedic improviser and an entrepreneur similar?
3. How does collaboration and the forming of partnerships benefit the growth of Second City or any business?

In Part 2, "Starting and Growing Your Business," you learned about the many ways that business owners have achieved their dreams of owning their own company and being their own boss. The part's three chapters introduced you to the wide variety of entrepreneurial or small businesses; the forms they can take—sole proprietorship, partnership, corporation, or franchise and the reasons that some new ventures succeed and others fail. You learned that entrepreneurs are visionaries who build firms that create wealth and that they share traits such as vision and creativity, high energy, optimism, a strong need to achieve, and a tolerance for failure. Finally, you learned about the impact of computer technology in making e-business possible and about the importance of the Internet for business operations. By now you might be wondering how you can make all this information work for you. Here are some career ideas and opportunities in the small-business and e-business areas.

First, whatever field attracts you as a future business owner, try to acquire experience by working for someone else in the industry initially. The information and skills you pick up will be invaluable when you start out on your own. Lack of experience is often cited as a leading reason for small-business failure.[1]

Next, look for a good fit between your own skills, abilities, and characteristics and a market need or niche. For instance, the U.S. Department of Labor reports that opportunities in many healthcare fields are rising with the nation's increased demand for health services.[2] As the population of older people rises, and as young families find themselves increasingly pressed for time, the need for child care and elder services will also increase—and so will the opportunities for new businesses in those areas. So keep your eyes on trends to find ideas that you can use or adapt.

Another way to look for market needs is to talk to current customers. Patrick Martucci, founder of United Asset Coverage (UAC), discovered that sometimes the best opportunities for

entrepreneurs are customers whose needs aren't being met. As a sales representative for a firm that maintained only Rolm telephone equipment, Martucci realized that what his client, JCPenney, really needed was a firm to service its entire phone system. The $1.5 million JCPenney contract would have been worth $10 million if Martucci's employer had offered the right service. Shortly after that, Martucci launched UAC, a network of technicians to offer maintenance and repair of any brand of office equipment, at any location. From its first contract covering a single copy machine at a TGI Friday's in St. Louis, UAC has become the largest telecom-maintenance company in the world, with annual earnings of about $40 million.[3]

Are you intrigued by the idea of being your own boss but worried about risking your savings to get a completely new and untried business off the ground? Then owning a franchise, such as Quiznos or Dunkin' Donuts, might be for you. The Small Business Administration advises aspiring entrepreneurs that while franchising can be less risky than starting a new business from scratch, it still requires work and sacrifice. In addition, you need to completely understand both the resources to which you'll be entitled and the responsibilities you'll assume under the franchise agreement. Again, filling a market need is important for success. To find more information about franchising, access the Federal Trade Commission's consumer guide to buying a franchise at http://www.ftc.gov/bcp/conline/pubs/invest/buyfran.htm.

Are you skilled in a particular area of business, technology, or science? The consulting industry will be a rapidly growing area for several years, according to the Bureau of Labor Statistics.[4] Consulting firms offer their expertise to clients in private, government, not-for-profit, and even foreign business operations. Business consultants influence clients' decisions in marketing, finance, manufacturing, information systems, e-commerce, human resources, and many other areas including corporate strategy and organization. Technology consultants support businesses in all fields, with services ranging from setting up a secure Web site or training employees in the use of new software to managing an off-site help desk or planning for disaster recovery. Science consulting firms find plenty of work in the field of environmental consulting, helping businesses deal with pollution cleanup and control, habitat protection, and compliance with government's environmental regulations and standards.

But perhaps none of these areas appeal to you quite so much as tinkering with gears and machinery or with computer graphics and code. If you think you have the insight and creativity to invent something completely new, you need to make sure you're informed about patents, trademarks, and copyright laws to protect your ideas.[5] Each area offers different protections for your work, and none will guarantee success. Here again, hard work, persistence, and a little bit of luck will help you succeed.

Career Assessment Exercises in Entrepreneurship and Business Ownership

1. Find out whether you have what it takes to be an entrepreneur. Review the material on the SBA's Web site http://www.sba.gov/starting_business/startup/basics.html or take the Brigham Young University's Entrepreneurial Test at http://marriottschool.byu.edu/cfe/startingout/test.cfm. Answer the questions there. After you've finished, use the scoring guides to determine how ready you are to strike out on your own. What weak areas did your results disclose? What can you do to strengthen them?

2. Find an independent business or franchise in your area, and make an appointment to talk to the owner about his or her start-up experience. Prepare a list of questions for a ten- to fifteen-minute interview, and remember to ask about details such as the number of hours worked per week, approximate start-up costs, goals of the business, available resources, lessons learned since opening, and rewards of owning the business. How different are the owner's answers from what you expected?

3. Search online for information about how to file for a patent, trademark, or copyright. (A good starting point is http://www.firstgov.gov.) Assume you have an invention you wish to protect. Find out what forms are required; what fees are necessary, if any; how much time is typically needed to complete the legal steps; and what rights and protections you will gain.

Management: Empowering People to Achieve Business Objectives

Part 3

Chapter 8

Management, Leadership, and the Internal Organization

1. Define *management* and the three types of skills necessary for managerial success.

2. Explain the role of vision and ethical standards in business success.

3. Summarize the major benefits of planning and distinguish among strategic planning, tactical planning, and operational planning.

4. Describe the strategic planning process.

5. Contrast the two major types of business decisions and list the steps in the decision-making process.

6. Define *leadership* and compare different leadership styles.

7. Discuss the meaning and importance of corporate culture.

8. Identify the five major forms of departmentalization and the four main types of organization structures.

© DIGITAL VISION/GETTY IMAGES

Microsoft is the world's most profitable technology company, with revenues of nearly $40 billion a year. Its reach is global, employing 60,000 people around the world, and the company receives almost that many job applications every month. Microsoft loses only about 9 percent of its employees a year, lower than the industry average, and of those lucky enough to be offered a job at the software giant, about 90 percent accept.

Yet the company has had its troubles, aside from the long-running legal battles stemming from antitrust charges in the United States and Europe. Its stock price has recently stagnated. And as it has grown, so has its internal bureaucracy, bringing new procedures and more meetings that some workers feel are stifling the creativity

© LOU DEMATTEIS/CORBIS

How Does Bill Gates Plan Microsoft's Future?

that made the company an unbeatable innovator in the past.

A couple of Microsoft researchers recently jotted down "Ten Crazy Ideas to Shake Up Microsoft," a twelve-page memo packed with suggestions to change the company. Some CEOs might not like receiving such advice, but at Microsoft, the memo made its way directly to the desk of founder and chairman Bill Gates.

Twice a year Gates leaves his headquarters office and heads for an undisclosed location in the Pacific Northwest, where he spends one week completely alone to read, think, and plan. His "Think Weeks" are legendary within the firm, and the general manager of the company's MapPoint group says Gates's open call for employee input at those times is "the world's coolest suggestion box." A few weeks before each Think Week, Gates's assistant sorts through papers submitted from every corner of the company and collects those that are priorities for his boss to consider. This year, "Ten Crazy Ideas" was one of them, even though breaking up the company was one of the ideas.

Gates pores over employees' submissions for new products and other input including books, articles, research papers, and industry reports. What began as a

stack of paper when he first started his Think Weeks—at his grandmother's in the 1980s—has now been transformed into a computerized interactive library in which he can enter comments and link entries. Paper versions serve as backup. By the end of the week, Gates has begun firing off e-mails to employees around the world, green-lighting new Microsoft projects, rejecting others, reordering priorities, changing direction, or asking for follow-up or a meeting. The general manager of Microsoft's education group posted Gates's comments on the group's internal Web site to spark further discussion of the team's initiatives. The general manager of MapPoint called a brainstorming meeting to fine-tune plans in response to the chairman's reactions to his group's proposal. The Virtual Earth team was asked to meet with Gates and discuss security issues as a follow-up to its 62-page paper on mapping services.

Planning is, of course, an ongoing activity at Microsoft, as it is in all organizations. But Gates is a firm believer in the value of his Think Weeks for Microsoft. They consist of long days interrupted only by 5-minute breaks to play online bridge or 30-minute walks on the beach. Two meals a day are brought in, and by installing a bathroom and refrigerator in the upstairs office of his hideaway,

Gates can save the time it would have taken him to go up and down the stairs and devote it to thinking and planning.

His technique does seem to produce results. A 1995 Think Week inspired Microsoft's famous decision to overtake Netscape and dominate the Internet with its Web browser, and later sessions led to the creation of the Tablet PC and to strategies designed to improve the security of Microsoft's software, better integrate the company's offerings, and enter the online video game market. Perhaps that's why another of the "Ten Crazy Ideas" submitted by the two researchers was that, like Gates, *every* employee should be given a slice of unscheduled time to think creatively about new ideas and innovations. After all, Google does it.[1]

A management career brings challenges that appeal to many students in introductory business courses. When asked about their professional objectives, many students say, "I want to be a manager." You may think that the role of a manager is basically being the boss. But in today's business world, companies are looking for much more than bosses. They want managers who understand technology, can adapt quickly to change, skillfully motivate subordinates, and realize the importance of satisfying customers. Managers who can master those skills will continue to be in great demand because their performance strongly affects their firms' performance.

This chapter begins by examining how successful organizations use management to turn visions into reality. It describes the levels of management, the skills that managers need, and the functions that managers perform. The chapter explains how the first of these functions, planning, helps managers such as Microsoft's Bill Gates meet the challenges of a rapidly changing business environment and develop strategies that guide a company's future. Other sections of the chapter explore the types of decisions that managers make, the role of managers as leaders, and the importance of corporate culture. The chapter concludes by examining the second function of management—organizing.

WHAT IS MANAGEMENT?

management process of achieving organizational objectives through people and other resources.

Management is the process of achieving organizational objectives through people and other resources. The manager's job is to combine human and technical resources in the best way possible to achieve the company's goals.

Management principles and concepts apply to not-for-profit organizations as well as profit-seeking firms. A city administrator, a Salvation Army major, and the CEO of your local United Way organization all perform the managerial functions described later in this chapter. Managers preside over organizations as diverse as Miami-Dade Community College, the New York Stock Exchange, and the Starbucks coffee shop down the street.

The Management Hierarchy

A local fast-food restaurant such as McDonald's typically works through a very simple organization that consists of an owner-manager and a few assistant managers. By contrast, large organizations develop more complex management structures. Southwest Airlines manages its activities through a chairperson of the board, a vice chairperson and chief executive officer, a president and chief operating officer, three executive vice presidents, a senior vice president, and 23 vice presidents, plus an array of managers and supervisors. All of these people are managers because they combine human and other resources to achieve company objectives. Their jobs differ, however, because they work at different levels of the organization.

A firm's management usually has three levels: top, middle, and supervisory. These levels of management form a management hierarchy, as shown in Figure 8.1. The hierarchy is the traditional structure found in most organizations. Managers at each level perform different activities.

The highest level of management is **top management.** Top managers include such positions as chief executive officer (CEO), chief financial officer (CFO), and executive vice president. Top managers devote most of their time to developing long-range plans for their organizations. They make decisions such as whether to introduce new products, purchase other companies, or enter new geographical markets. Top managers set a direction for their organization and inspire the company's executives and employees to achieve their vision for the company's future.

Michael Bloomberg once headed a media conglomerate—Bloomberg LP—that primarily sells financial data via leased computer terminals. This business made Bloomberg a billionaire. Then he decided to move on to a new CEO position. Today, Michael Bloomberg has what is often called the second toughest job in the United States—mayor of New York City. Instead of building wealth, as mayor he works at building the city's infrastructure, resolving budget problems, and keeping firms from fleeing to the suburbs or elsewhere. Bloomberg still follows the leadership style he used in the corporate world. At Bloomberg LP, he sat in the corner of his TV studio. Now in his second term as mayor, Bloomberg operates out of an open cubicle in a big hall resembling the brokerage trading room where he got his start. The official mayor's office is used only for interviews and similar events. Mayor Bloomberg is providing hands-on direction to his staff—situated in nearby cubicles. The leadership pattern that proved successful at Bloomberg LP is now at work in New York's City Hall.[2]

Middle management, the second tier in the management hierarchy, includes positions such as general managers, plant managers, division managers, and branch managers. Middle managers' attention focuses on specific operations, products, or customer groups within an organization. They are responsible for developing detailed plans and procedures to implement the firm's strategic plans. If top management decided to broaden the distribution of a product, a sales manager would be responsible for determining the number of salespeople required. Middle managers are responsible for targeting the products and customers who are the source of the sales and profit growth expected by their CEOs. To achieve these goals, middle managers might budget money for product development, identify new uses for existing products, and improve the ways they train and motivate salespeople. Middle managers are also responsible for solving unique company problems. After a hurricane destroyed five miles of railroad tracks outside New Orleans, Jeff McCracken of Norfolk Southern managed a team of 100 employees and dozens of engineers who rebuilt the tracks in less than a week. McCracken said, "It was a colossal job that took more than 400 moves with heavy equipment." But McCracken was happiest about "working with people from all parts of the company—and getting the job done without anyone getting hurt."[3]

Figure

8.1

The Management Hierarchy

Top Management	→	Chief Executive Officer, Chief Financial Officer, Governor, Mayor
Middle Management	→	Regional Manager, Division Head, Director, Dean
Supervisory (First-Line) Management	→	Supervisor, Group Leader, Section Chief

Supervisory managers, such as Ozzie Guillen of the Chicago White Sox, are responsible for carrying out the day-to-day activities that help their organizations reach their goals. Guillen needs to assess each player's ability, determine who is available to play, and juggle lineups to compete against each day's opponents.

GETTY IMAGES

Supervisory management, or first-line management, includes positions such as supervisor, section chief, and team leader. These managers are directly responsible for assigning nonmanagerial employees to specific jobs and evaluating their performance. Managers at this first level of the hierarchy work directly with the employees who produce and sell the firm's goods and services. They are responsible for implementing middle managers' plans by motivating workers to accomplish daily, weekly, and monthly goals. For instance, Charles Lee, who is a production supervisor at an American Airlines' maintenance center in Fort Worth, is responsible for motivating employees such as Fred Amato to reduce the cost of replacement parts for planes. Amato did just that when he replaced a $146 part about the size of a quarter with a $5.24 part made in American's machine shop.[4]

Skills Needed for Managerial Success

Managers at every level in the management hierarchy must exercise three basic types of skills: technical, human, and conceptual. All managers must acquire these skills in varying proportions, although the importance of each skill changes at different management levels.

Technical skills are the manager's ability to understand and use the techniques, knowledge, and tools and equipment of a specific discipline or department. Technical skills become less important at higher levels of the management hierarchy, but most top executives started out as technical experts. The résumé of a vice president for information systems probably lists experience as a computer analyst, and that of a vice president for marketing usually shows a background in sales. And, as you read at the beginning of the chapter, Microsoft's founder, Bill Gates, is the company's chairman *and* chief software architect. During his weeklong "Think Weeks," Gates typically reads 100 papers and proposals, nearly all of which deal with technological products or strategies for Microsoft. Not surprisingly, 31 of the 100 papers at his last "Think Week" addressed technological issues related to Internet and computer security.[5]

© KRISTINE LARSEN

David Steinberg, CEO of InPhonic, a company that sells cell phone handsets over the Internet, succeeds in this business by using his human skills. Steinberg began his career as an insurance salesperson, where he mastered the art of give-and-take with clients. Then he moved into the new cell phone industry during its early growth stages, working with company managers to create 350 jobs.

Human skills are interpersonal skills that enable managers to work effectively with and through people. Human skills include the ability to communicate with, motivate, and lead employees to complete assigned activities. Managers need human skills to interact with people both inside and outside the organization. It would be tough for a manager to succeed without such skills, even though they must be adapted to different forms today—for instance, mastering and communicating effectively with staff through e-mail, cell phones, pagers, faxes, and even instant messaging, all of which are widely used in today's offices. And, as you'd expect, all that communication means many interruptions. See the "Business Etiquette" feature for steps managers can take to handle the constant interruptions that are a part of their jobs.

Conceptual skills determine a manager's ability to see the organization as a unified whole and to understand how each part of the overall organization interacts with other parts. These skills involve an ability to see the big picture by acquiring, analyzing, and interpreting information. Conceptual skills are especially important for top-level managers, who must develop long-range plans for the future direction of their organization. For three decades, Microsoft has made its money by building software that was purchased and then installed on people's personal computers. However, facing challenges from Internet companies such as Google and eBay, Microsoft will begin developing a "next-generation Internet services platform" to deliver products, such as Microsoft Office, via the Internet and, perhaps, Internet-based advertising. In terms of Microsoft's need to change its business model, chief technical officer Ray Ozzie said, "It's clear that if we fail to do so, our business as we know it is at risk. We must respond quickly and decisively."[6]

Managerial Functions

In the course of a typical day, managers spend time meeting and talking with people, reading, thinking, and sending e-mail messages. As they perform these activities, managers are carrying out four basic functions: planning, organizing, directing, and controlling. Planning activities lay the groundwork, and the other functions are aimed at carrying out the plans.

planning process of anticipating future events and conditions and determining courses of action for achieving organizational objectives.

Planning   **Planning** is the process of anticipating future events and conditions and determining courses of action for achieving organizational objectives. Effective planning helps businesses crystallize their visions, which are described in the next section, avoid costly mistakes, and seize opportunities. Effective planning requires an evaluation of the business environment and a well-designed road map of the actions needed to lead a firm forward. For example, Alcoa, the world's largest aluminum company, has been hard hit by skyrocketing energy prices, which increased its costs by almost half a billion dollars in less than a year. Consequently, Alcoa is closing aluminum smelting plants in the United States, where energy costs are high. But, it is building plants in Iceland, Trinidad, and Brunei and buying plants in Russia, where energy costs are much cheaper.[7] In a later section of this chapter, we elaborate on the planning process.

Organizing   Once plans have been developed, the next step in the management process typically is **organizing**—the means by which managers blend human and material resources through a formal structure of tasks and authority. This activity involves classifying and dividing work into manageable units by determining specific tasks necessary to accomplish organizational objectives, grouping tasks into a logical pattern or structure, and assigning them to specific personnel. Managers also must staff the organization with competent employees capable of performing the necessary tasks and assigning authority and responsibility to these individuals. Often organizing involves studying a company's existing structure and determining whether to reorganize it so that the company can better meet its objectives. The organizing process is discussed in detail later in this chapter.

Directing   Once plans have been formulated and an organization has been created and staffed, the management task focuses on **directing,** or guiding and motivating employees to accomplish organizational objectives. Directing includes explaining procedures, issuing orders, and seeing that mistakes are corrected. Managers may also direct in other ways, such as getting employees to agree on how they will meet objectives and inspiring them to care about customer satisfaction or their contribution to the company.

The directing function is a vital responsibility of supervisory managers. To fulfill their responsibilities to get things done through people, supervisors must be effective leaders. In addition, middle and top managers must be good leaders and motivators, and they must create an environment that fosters such leadership. A later section of this chapter discusses leadership, and Chapter 9 discusses motivating employees and improving performance.

Controlling   **Controlling** is the function of evaluating an organization's performance to determine whether it is accomplishing its objectives. The basic purpose of controlling is to assess the success of the planning function. Controlling also provides feedback for future rounds of planning.

The four basic steps in controlling are to establish performance standards, monitor actual performance, compare actual performance with established standards, and take corrective action if required. Under the provisions of the Sarbanes-Oxley Act, for example, CEOs and CFOs must monitor the performance of the firm's accounting staff more closely. They must personally attest to the truth of financial reports filed with the Securities and Exchange Commission.

SETTING A VISION AND ETHICAL STANDARDS FOR THE FIRM

As Chapter 1 discusses, business success usually begins with a **vision,** a perception of marketplace needs and the methods an organization can use to satisfy them. Vision serves as the target for a firm's actions, helping direct the company toward opportunities and differentiating it from its competitors. Michael Dell's vision of selling custom-built computers directly to consumers helped distinguish Dell from many other computer industry start-ups. John Schnatter, founder of Papa John's Pizza, keeps his vision—and his menu—focused to satisfy his pizza-loving customers.

A company's vision must be focused and yet flexible enough to adapt to changes in the business environment. The vision for Merck, which develops and manufactures pharmaceuticals, is "to provide society with superior products and services by developing innovations and solutions that improve the quality of life and satisfy customer needs." In the long run, Merck's vision is the same, to develop drugs ("innovations and solutions") that improve people's health. However, it is adaptable to changes as Merck's managers and researchers can accomplish that vision using natural or synthetic chemical compounds or high-tech gene-splicing equipment or low-tech Petri dishes.

Also critical to a firm's long-term success are the ethical standards that top executives set. As we saw in Chapter 2, a company's top managers can take an organization down a slippery slope to bankruptcy—and even criminal—court if they operate unethically. Avoiding that path requires executives to focus on the organization's success, not merely personal gain, like Tyco's former CEO Dennis Kozlowski and Tyco's former chief financial officer, Mark Swartz, who were found guilty of taking at least $150 million for themselves from the company to finance their extravagant lifestyles. Kozlowski and Swartz were sentenced to between $8^1/3$ and 25 years in prison and must pay $240 million in fines and restitution. Both men are awaiting their appeals in jail.[8] Holding the welfare of the company's constituencies—customers, employees, investors, and society in general—as the top priority can build lasting success for a firm. For more on a related issue, see the "Solving an Ethical Controversy" feature, which discusses whether CEOs should get "golden handshakes," that is, lucrative severance packages when they are fired by the company.

The ethical tone that a top management team establishes can also reap nonmonetary rewards. Setting a high ethical standard does not merely restrain employees from doing wrong, but it encourages, motivates, and inspires them to achieve goals they never thought possible. Such satisfaction creates a more productive, stable workforce—one that can create a long-term competitive advantage for the organization.

Still, a leader's vision and ethical conduct are only the first steps along an organization's path to success. Turning a business idea into reality takes careful planning and actions. The next sections take a closer look at the planning and implementation process.

vision perception of marketplace needs and the methods an organization can use to satisfy them.

"They Said It"

"There's no long-term shareholder value if it isn't linked to building long-term values for your people."
—Howard Schultz (b. 1953) Chairman of Starbucks[9]

assessment check

1. What is meant by a vision for the firm?
2. Why is it important for a top executive to set high ethical standards?

IMPORTANCE OF PLANNING

When you think of Wal-Mart, you think of low prices. But in a nod to Target, which is growing twice as fast by selling higher-quality products, Wal-Mart has created a new store prototype with a more attractive layout, with fake wood floors, wider aisles, lower shelves, more

SHOULD CEOS GET GOLDEN HANDSHAKES?

Executive compensation continues to raise eyebrows as departing CEOs walk away with massive financial rewards from companies that may be struggling.

Gary Rodkin, PepsiCo's former North American CEO, received $4.56 million for "consultancy services" on his resignation. Carly Fiorina, deposed CEO of Hewlett-Packard, took home a $21.2 million severance package. Eugene S. Kahn, former CEO of May Department Stores, which is now part of the Federated Department Stores chain, resigned with a payout worth almost $11 million. The average severance package for ex-CEOs is $4.5 million, and surprisingly, those who are dismissed are more likely to receive generous payouts than those who resign.

Should top executives receive multimillion-dollar severance packages when they leave or are fired from their jobs?

PRO

1. Such "golden handshakes" compensate executives for taking risks and encourage visionary leaders to accept these jobs—and the additional risk of losing them.
2. The scarcity of jobs at the top level means it is more difficult for an ex-CEO to find another job, and firings are more likely today than ever before.

CON

1. The size of these payouts is seldom linked to the CEO's actual performance, which means they can be generously rewarded for doing a poor job.
2. Large severance packages cost shareholders money and set unwelcome precedents throughout the corporate world.

Summary

Financial scandals and the passage of the Sarbanes-Oxley Act have focused more attention on internal corporate policies and forced some companies to reexamine their executive compensation practices. More corporate boards have stepped up to fire their CEOs for poor performance, wrongdoing, and even poor ethical decisions. On the other hand, because CEOs often sit on the compensation boards of other corporations, overall executive compensation is still on the rise.

Sources: Marcy Gordon, "SEC Moves for More Exec Pay Disclosure," Associated Press, accessed June 27, 2006, http://news.yahoo.com; Tim McLaughlin, "Golden Parachutes Are Soaring to Platinum Levels," *St. Louis Post-Dispatch,* accessed June 27, 2006, http://www.stltoday.com; Joanne S. Lublin, "CEO Compensation Survey," *Wall Street Journal,* accessed June 27, 2006, http://online.wsj.com; Gary Strauss and Barbara Hansen, "CEO Pay Packages 'Business as Usual'," *USA Today,* accessed June 27, 2006, http://www.usatoday.com.

solving an **ETHICAL** controversy

attractive product displays, and higher-quality goods that appeal to slightly more upscale shoppers. With that in mind, Wal-Mart is now focusing on fashion by spending $12 million to advertise in *Vogue* and opening a strategic planning office for apparel and home furnishings in New York City, not at Wal-Mart's Bentonville, Arkansas, headquarters.[10] Will Wal-Mart's plans work? Shopper Caroline Geppert's comments suggest it will be a challenge: "I've been surprised going to Target and seeing some things that I would buy and wear, whereas in Wal-Mart I usually wouldn't buy anything other than socks or underwear or a basic T-shirt." Let's take a closer look at the various types of planning that businesses do to achieve their goals.

Types of Planning

Planning can be categorized by scope and breadth. Some plans are very broad and long range, while others are short range and very narrow, affecting selected parts of the organization rather than all. Planning can be divided into the following categories: strategic, tactical, operational, and contingency, with each step including more specific information than the last. From the mission statement (described in the next section) to objectives to specific plans, each phase must fit into a comprehensive planning framework. The framework also must include narrow, functional plans aimed at individual employees and work areas relevant to individual

HIT & MISS

When Wal-Mart Was the Only Lifeline

Months and years will pass before the full story of Hurricane Katrina's devastation is told. But in the days immediately following the disaster, one thing was clear: Wal-Mart's emergency plans worked where others failed.

In the wake of the chaos of Hurricane Charlie, which had hit Florida the year before, Wal-Mart decided to prepare for emergencies and specifically for hurricanes in vulnerable states. With its disaster plans in place, the firm was able to act even before the pattern of Katrina's movements became clear. The chain's one-room Emergency Operations Center began moving trucks and supplies into position six days before the storm hit. That action enabled it to respond quickly with basic items that often reached victims before government agencies could and that sometimes made the difference between survival and disaster. Once managers were warned by the company's own meteorologists that the storm had unexpectedly shifted toward New Orleans, the giant retailer started shipping huge quantities of bottled water, packaged food, and other supplies to Louisiana. Fuel, generators, and dry ice were shipped to the stores in the path of the storm. Based on its research into buying patterns in hurricane-vulnerable areas, Wal-Mart's information systems division even knew that in addition to water, food, batteries, flashlights, tarps, chain saws, and mops, customers in stricken areas also bought Pop-Tarts. So employees loaded them up and shipped them with everything else. The company's headquarters also acts as an information clearinghouse in the early stages of emergencies, coordinating store evacuations and passing data among store managers.

When the magnitude of the emergency became clear, many employees made on-the-spot decisions that their communities will long remember. Jessica Lewis, co-manager of a Wal-Mart store in Georgia that was severely damaged by hurricane floodwaters, salvaged shoes, clothing, diapers, food, water, and even medicines from her store and handed them out free to her barefoot and homeless neighbors in the store's parking lot. "This is the right thing to do," she remembers thinking.

Questions for Critical Thinking

1. How effective do you think set plans can be when it comes to natural disasters?
2. What elements of Wal-Mart's plans could not be set ahead of time? How do you think an organization can ensure that on-the-spot decisions are appropriate in emergencies?

Sources: "Wal-Mart Support of the Hurricane Relief Efforts," accessed June 27, 2006, http://www.walmartfacts.com; Thomas Sowell, "Observe Private Businesses' Quick Response to Katrina," *Deseret Morning News,* accessed June 27, 2006, http://deseretnews.com; Devin Leonard, "After Katrina: Crisis Management," *Fortune,* accessed June 27, 2006, http://www.fortune.com; Christopher Leonard, "Katrina Puts Wal-Mart on Alert," *Arkansas Democrat Gazette,* acessed August 30, 2005, http://www.ardemgaz.com.

---

tasks. These plans must fit within the firm's overall planning framework, and help it reach objectives and achieve its mission.

Strategic Planning   The most far-reaching level of planning is **strategic planning**—the process of determining the primary objectives of an organization and then acting and allocating resources to achieve those objectives. At Dell, managers maintain this long-range view. "You may have a great day today and the stock goes down, and you may have a horrible day tomorrow and the stock goes up," says CEO Michael Dell. "But over a long period of time you build a great company."[11]

Tactical Planning   **Tactical planning** involves implementing the activities specified by strategic plans. Tactical plans guide the current and near-term activities required to implement overall strategies. Craig Knouf, CEO of Associated Business Systems, which sells office equipment in Portland, Oregon, examines his company's 30-page business plan every month, with additional semiannual and annual reviews, making tactical changes when needed. After one of

> **"They Said It"**
>
> "If you chase two rabbits, both will escape."
> —*Anonymous*

those reviews, he noticed an unexpected increase in sales of high-volume document scanners. So he changed his business plan to put a greater emphasis on scanners and scanning software. As a result, sales of scanning products have doubled and now account for one-third of all sales. Working without his business plan, says Knouf, "would be like driving a car with no steering wheel."[12]

Operational Planning   **Operational planning** creates the detailed standards that guide implementation of tactical plans. This activity involves choosing specific work targets and assigning employees and teams to carry out plans. Unlike strategic planning, which focuses on the organization as a whole, operational planning deals with developing and implementing tactics in specific functional areas. For example, as part of its larger strategy to sell more expensive, higher-quality goods, the electronics departments in Wal-Mart's new prototype stores are stocking 27-inch to 42-inch plasma HD TVs costing between $1,700 and $2,000. Brent Allen, who manages a new Wal-Mart in McKinney, Texas, is seeing "high-double-digit percentage" sales increases in flat-screen TVs, compared with sales in the old Wal-Mart store he operated across the street.[13]

Contingency Planning   Planning cannot foresee every possibility. Major accidents, natural disasters, and rapid economic downturns can throw even the best-laid plans into chaos. To handle the possibility of business disruption from events of this nature, many firms use **contingency planning,** which allows them to resume operations as quickly and as smoothly as possible after a crisis while openly communicating with the public about what happened. This planning activity involves two components: business continuation and public communication. Many firms have developed management strategies to speed recovery from accidents such as airline crashes, fires and explosions, chemical leaks, package tampering, and product failures.

A contingency plan usually designates a chain of command for crisis management, assigning specific functions to particular managers and employees in an emergency. Contingency planning also involves training workers to respond to emergencies, improving communications systems, and using advanced technology. As discussed in the "Hit & Miss" feature, companies with well-defined disaster recovery plans generally fared better in the aftermath of Hurricane Katrina than those that didn't develop and implement plans.

Planning at Different Organizational Levels

Although managers spend some time on planning virtually every day, the total time spent and the type of planning done differ according to the level of management. As Table 8.1 points

Table 8.1   Planning at Different Management Levels

Primary Type of Planning	Managerial Level	Examples
Strategic	Top management	Organizational objectives, fundamental strategies, long-term plans
Tactical	Middle management	Quarterly and semiannual plans, departmental policies and procedures
Operational	Supervisory management	Daily and weekly plans, rules, and procedures for each department
Contingency	Primarily top management, but all levels contribute	Ongoing plans for actions and communications in an emergency

out, top managers, including a firm's board of directors and CEO, spend a great deal of time on long-range planning, while middle-level managers and supervisors focus on short-term, tactical planning. Employees at all levels can benefit themselves and their company by making plans to meet their own specific goals.

assessment check

1. Outline the planning process.
2. Describe the purpose of tactical planning.
3. Compare the kinds of plans made by top managers and middle managers. How does their focus differ?

THE STRATEGIC PLANNING PROCESS

Strategic planning often makes the difference between an organization's success and failure. Strategic planning has formed the basis of many fundamental management decisions:

- Recognizing the devotion that TiVo-watching consumers had to their personal digital recorders, which record their favorite TV shows to be watched whenever they want at a cost of $10 to $15 a month, cable companies such as Comcast now provide similar on-demand services that let viewers watch TV shows whenever they want—all without purchasing a personal digital recorder.[14]
- With well-established women's beauty products, but a poor selection of men's grooming products, Procter & Gamble paid $54 million to buy Gillette and its market-leading razors and number-two-ranked men's deodorants.[15]

Successful strategic planners typically follow the six steps shown in Figure 8.2: defining a mission, assessing the organization's competitive position, setting organizational objectives, creating strategies for competitive differentiation, implementing the strategy, and evaluating the results and refining the plan.

Defining the Organization's Mission

The first step in strategic planning is to translate the firm's vision into a **mission statement**. A mission statement is a written explanation of an organization's business intentions and aims. It is an enduring statement of a firm's purpose, possibly highlighting the scope of operations, the market it seeks to serve, and the ways it will attempt to set itself apart from competitors. A mission statement guides the actions of people inside the firm and informs customers and

mission statement written explanation of an organization's business intentions and aims.

Steps in the Strategic Planning Process

Define the Organization's Mission → Set Objectives for the Organization → Create Strategies for Competitive Differentiation → Evaluate Results and Refine the Plan

Assess the Organization's Competitive Position

Turn Strategy into Action

Feedback

Figure 8.2

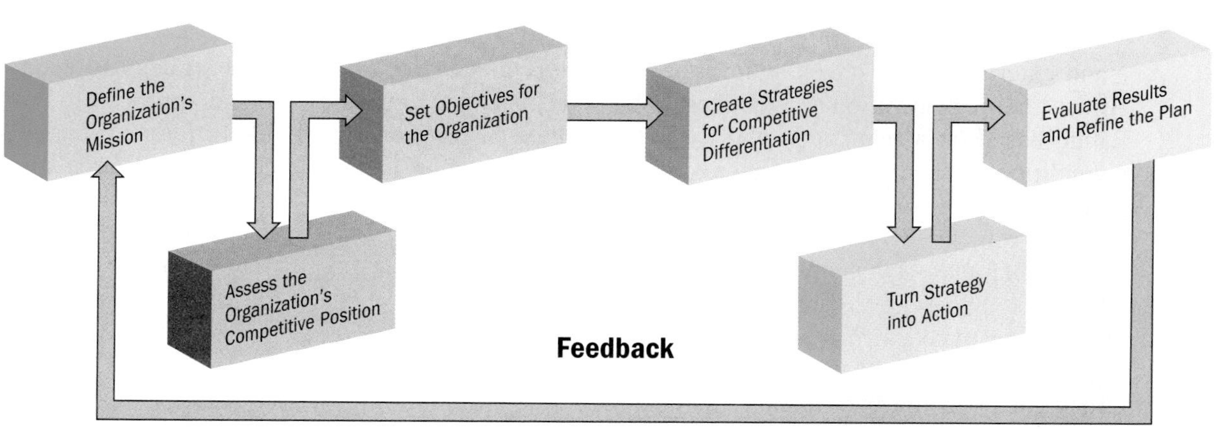

KEVIN P. CASEY/BLOOMBERG NEWS/LANDOV

Starbucks CEO Howard Schultz (above right) is involved in all details of his company's operations, including daily contact with employees and customers. Guiding his actions are his concerns for high ethical standards and for consistent quality in his products. Schultz says he refers to his heart and conscience to ensure that decisions are true to the company's mission and cause.

other stakeholders of the company's underlying reasons for existence. The mission statement should be widely publicized among employees, suppliers, partners, shareholders, customers, and the general public.

Merck's mission statement was outlined earlier in the section on establishing an organization's vision. Mission statements can vary in complexity and length.

- A Birmingham, Alabama, securities firm has a very straightforward mission statement: "The mission of Sterne, Agee, and Leach, Inc. is to build wealth for our clients."
- Google's mission is "to organize the world's information and make it universally accessible and useful."[16]
- German chemical company Bayer's mission statement is "Bayer: Science for a better life." According to Bayer's CEO, "We have set our course for the future. This new mission statement defines our future perspectives, our goals and our values, and guides our strategy at a time of sweeping change. It outlines to our stockholders, our customers, the public and especially our employees how we think and behave as a company."[17]

Developing a mission statement can be one of the most complex and difficult aspects of strategic planning. Completing these statements requires detailed considerations of a company's values and vision. Effective mission statements indicate specific, achievable, inspiring principles. They avoid unrealistic promises and statements.

Assessing Your Competitive Position

Once a mission statement has been created, the next step in the planning process is to assess the firm's current position in the marketplace. This phase also involves examining the factors that may help or hinder the organization in the future. A frequently used tool in this phase of strategic planning is SWOT analysis.

A **SWOT analysis** is an organized approach to assessing a company's internal strengths and weaknesses and its external opportunities and threats. SWOT is an acronym for *strengths, weaknesses, opportunities,* and *threats.* The basic premise of SWOT is that a critical internal and external reality check should lead managers to select the appropriate strategy to accomplish their organization's objectives. SWOT analysis encourages a practical approach to planning based on a realistic view of a firm's situation and scenarios of likely future events and conditions. When gas prices rose to more than $3 a gallon in some areas, sales of large sport-utility vehicles dropped by nearly 10 percent, and automakers immediately began designing family vehicles, which make up more than one-fourth of all car sales, that held five or six people rather than seven or eight and were more fuel efficient.[18] The framework for a SWOT analysis appears in Figure 8.3.

To evaluate a firm's strengths and weaknesses, the planners may examine each functional area such as finance, marketing, information technology, and human resources. Entrepreneurs may focus on the individual skills and experience they bring to a new business. Large firms may also examine strengths and weaknesses of individual decisions and geographical opera-

Figure

8.3

Elements of SWOT Analysis

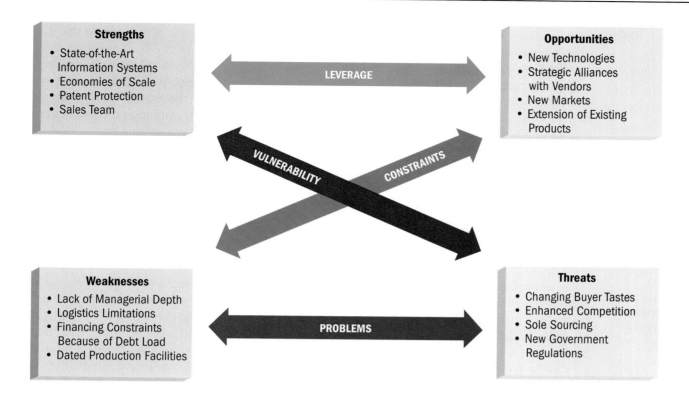

tions. Usually, planners attempt to look at their strengths and weaknesses in relation to those of other firms in the industry.

For Starbucks, a key strength is consumers' positive image of the company's brand, which gets them to stand in line to pay premium prices for coffee. That positive image comes from Starbucks's being one of the best 100 companies to work for in the United States, according to *Fortune*, and from its socially responsible corporate policies. The company's strategic plans have included various ways to build on Starbucks' strong brand loyalty by attaching it to new products expanding into new markets. The expansion efforts have included creating a Web site, selling bottled Frappuccino iced coffee in supermarkets, and opening thousands of Starbucks outlets in Europe, Asia, and the Middle East.

SWOT analysis continues with an attempt to define the major opportunities and threats the firm is likely to face within the time frame of the plan. Possibilities include environmental factors such as market growth, regulatory changes, and increased competition. Starbucks saw an opportunity in the growth of the Internet and the interest in online shopping. Its Web site sells coffee and related accessories. In addition, Starbucks' experience in Japan, where its outlets' average sales top those in the United States, suggested that international expansion presented a solid opportunity. A threat is that consumers could tire of paying $3.50 or so for cappuccinos and lattés and switch to something else. The company has begun addressing that threat with the introduction of gourmet tea products.

Some aspects of Starbucks' strategy have succeeded better than others. Initially, Starbucks tried selling gourmet foods, music, and even furniture on its Web site. Sales were disappointing, and the firm quickly dropped the least successful offerings. Recently, Starbucks has

The final step in the strategic planning process, which ~~~~~~~~~~~~~~ ~~ monitor and adapt plans when actual performance fails to match expectations. Monitoring involves establishing methods of securing feedback about actual performance. Common methods include comparing actual sales and market share data with forecasts, compiling information from supplier and customer surveys, monitoring complaints from the firm's customer hot line, and reviewing reports prepared by production, finance, marketing, and other company units.

Ongoing use of such tools as SWOT analysis and forecasting can help managers adapt objectives and functional plans as changes occur. An increase in the price of a key product component, for instance, could dramatically affect the firm's ability to maintain planned prices and still earn acceptable profits. An unexpected UPS strike may disrupt shipments of products to retail and business customers. In each instance, the original plan may require modification to continue to guide the firm toward achievement of its objectives.

MANAGERS AS DECISION MAKERS

In carrying out planning and the other management functions, executives must make decisions every day. **Decision making** is the process of recognizing a problem or opportunity and then dealing with it. Managers make two basic kinds of decisions, programmed decisions and nonprogrammed decisions.

Programmed and Nonprogrammed Decisions

A **programmed decision** involves simple, common, and frequently occurring problems for which solutions have already been determined. Examples of programmed decisions include assigning a starting salary for the new marketing assistant, reordering raw materials needed in

assessment check

1. What is the purpose of a mission statement?
2. Which of the firm's characteristics does a SWOT analysis compare?
3. How do managers use objectives?

decision making process of recognizing a problem or opportunity, evaluating alternative solutions, selecting and implementing an alternative, and assessing the results.

shifted more of its attention to its retail units, where sales remain strong. Furthermore, Starbucks is now co-branding alcohol products with Jim Beam Brands to sell Starbucks Cream Liqueur and has moved aggressively into selling music, partnering with XM Satellite Radio, Sony BMG, and Virgin Records to sell music in its stores and online at http://www.starbucks.com/hearmusic.[19]

If a firm's strengths and opportunities mesh successfully, as at the Starbucks retail stores, it gains competitive leverage in the marketplace. On the other hand, if internal weaknesses prevent a firm from overcoming external threats, as in the case of the Starbucks Web site, it may face major difficulties. SWOT analysis is useful in the strategic planning process because it forces management to look at factors both inside and outside the organization and determine which steps it must take in the future to minimize external threats and take advantage of strategic opportunities.

Setting Objectives for the Organization

objectives guideposts by which managers define the organization's desired performance in such areas as profitability, customer service, growth, and employee satisfaction.

After defining the company's mission and examining factors that may affect its ability to fulfill that mission, the next step in planning is to develop objectives for the organization. **Objectives** set guideposts by which managers define the organization's desired performance in such areas as profitability, customer service, growth, and employee satisfaction. While the mission statement delineates a company's goals in general terms, objectives are more concrete statements. For instance, Toyota wants to sell 600,000 hybrid gas/electric cars in the United States by 2010. Today, however, out of the 1.1 million cars per year that Toyota sells in the United States, only 80,000, or roughly 7 percent, are hybrids. Because Toyota plans to sell 2 million cars in the United States by 2010, one of every three cars that it sells will have to be a hybrid to reach that goal. Today, while Toyota only offers three hybrid models—the Toyota Prius and Highlander and the Lexus RX400h SUV—it plans to reach its sales goal of 600,000 hybrids a year by eventually offering 50 different hybrid models.[20]

© STACY KRANITZ

Ed Weingartner's firm, Dynamic Restoration, specializes in repairs and reconstruction after disasters, such as the hurricanes that devastated the Gulf Coast. Making quick decisions is crucial so that buildings can be saved, dried out, and restored instead of being demolished. Weingartner must determine whether to hire additional staff to meet expected demand before he has signed contracts, decide where to position teams before storms hit so that they are in place when needed, and estimate the amount of equipment to move or rent for the teams to do their work.

the manufacturing process, and setting a discount schedule for large-volume customers. For these types of decisions, organizations develop rules, policies, and detailed procedures that managers apply to achieve consistent, quick, and inexpensive solutions to common problems. Because such solutions eliminate the time-consuming process of identifying and evaluating alternatives and making new decisions each time a situation occurs, managers can devote their time to the more complex problems associated with nonprogrammed decisions. For example, routine review of the inventory of fresh produce might allow the buyer at Whole Foods Market more time to seek other merchandising opportunities.

A **nonprogrammed decision** involves a complex and unique problem or opportunity with important consequences for the organization. Examples of nonprogrammed decisions include entering a new geographical market, acquiring another company, or introducing a new product. For example, when Microsoft introduced its new Xbox 360 game console, it was the responsibility of Todd Holmdahl, Microsoft's vice president of Xbox manufacturing, to coordinate the flow and manufacture of the Xbox's 1,700 different parts. Approximately 25,000 employees working for 250 suppliers make the parts in China, Japan, Korea, Taiwan, Canada, and La Crosse, Wisconsin, which are assembled in two key plants in China. Says Holmdahl, "With 1,700 components all it takes is one not being there and it's an issue." And not only was the number of parts and the number of suppliers an issue, so was the scale of production, as Microsoft expected to sell 3 million consoles within 90 days and 5.5 million within 8 months. Over time as the bugs were worked out of the production process, Holmdahl switched from making the thousands of unique, nonprogrammed decisions related to the start-up to making the programmed decisions needed to tweak and improve the Xbox manufacturing process. And when those decisions had to be made, said Holmdahl, "Everybody has my phone number here."[23]

How Managers Make Decisions

In a narrow sense, decision making involves choosing among two or more alternatives with the chosen alternative becoming the decision. In a broader sense, decision making involves a systematic, step-by-step process that helps managers make effective choices. This process begins when someone recognizes a problem or opportunity; it proceeds by developing potential courses of action, evaluating the alternatives, selecting and implementing one of them, and assessing the outcome of the decision. The steps in the decision-making process are illustrated in Figure 8.4. This systematic approach can be applied to all decisions, with either programmed or nonprogrammed features.

The decision-making process can be applied in both for-profit and not-for-profit organizations. Consider how Michael Miller built the Portland, Oregon, Goodwill Industries retail business of selling donated items. Miller knew that he had to locate stores where Goodwill's donors and customers meshed. Surveys uncovered that the typical donor was female, age 35 to

Figure

8.4

Steps in the Decision-Making Process

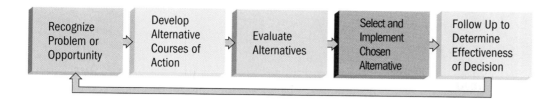

44, with an income of $50,000. In contrast, Miller's customers were women age 25 to 54 with two kids. Their average income was roughly $30,000. Miller then got some help from the locally based Fred Meyer supermarket chain (part of Kroger). Fred Meyer's database contained gender and income demographics by neighborhood. Miller's decision to open stores was then based on where his two target clients intersected. To make customers more comfortable, Miller's 28 stores even feature bookstores and coffee bars.[24]

Making good decisions is never easy, however, because it involves taking risks that can influence a firm's success or failure. Managers' decisions often have complex legal and ethical dimensions. An executive research firm recently tested 1,400 managers to assess their integrity and found that one in eight "believe the rules do not apply to them" and they "rarely possess feelings of guilt."[25]

assessment check

1. Compare and contrast programmed and nonprogrammed decisions.
2. What are the steps in the decision-making process?

MANAGERS AS LEADERS

The most visible component of a manager's responsibilities is **leadership,** directing or inspiring people to attain organizational goals. Leadership is how former CEO Gordon Bethune turned around Continental Airlines and its previously poisonous labor-management relations. Bethune explained it this way: "When I was a mechanic, I knew how much faster I could fix an airplane when I wanted to fix it than when I didn't," he said. "I've tried to make it so our guys want to do it."[26] Because effective leadership is so important to organizational success, a large amount of research has focused on the characteristics of a good leader. Great leaders do not all share the same qualities, but three traits are often mentioned: empathy, which is the ability to imagine yourself in another's position; self-awareness; and objectivity in dealing with others. Many great leaders share other traits, including courage, ability to inspire others, passion, commitment, flexibility, innovation, and willingness to experiment.

Leadership involves the use of influence or power. This influence may come from one or more sources. One source of power is the leader's position in the organization. A national sales manager has the authority to direct the activities of the sales force. Another source of power is a leader's expertise and experience. A first-line supervisor with expert machinist skills will most likely be respected by employees in the machining department. Some leaders derive power from their personalities. Employees may admire a leader because they recognize an exceptionally kind and fair, humorous, energetic, or enthusiastic person.

A well-known example is Herb Kelleher, the retired CEO and now chairman of Southwest Airlines. Kelleher's legendary ability to motivate employees to outperform those at rival airlines came from his dynamic personality, boundless energy, love of fun, and sincere concern for his employees. Kelleher led by example, modeling the behavior he wanted to see in his

leadership ability to direct or inspire people to attain organizational goals.

"They Said It"

"A great leader is not one who does the greatest things. He's the one who gets the people to do the greatest things."
—Ronald Reagan
(1911–2004)
40th president
of the United States

employees. He pitched in to help serve snacks to passengers and load luggage. Employees, inspired by his example, now unload and reload a plane in 20 minutes—one-half of the average time for other airlines.

Leadership Styles

The way a person uses power to lead others determines his or her leadership style. Researchers have identified a continuum of leadership styles based on the amount of employee participation allowed or invited. At one end of the continuum, **autocratic leadership** is centered on the boss. Autocratic leaders make decisions on their own without consulting employees. They reach decisions, communicate them to subordinates, and expect prompt implementation of instructions. An autocratic sales manager might assign quotas to individual salespeople without consulting them.

Democratic leadership involves subordinates in making decisions. Located in the middle of the continuum, this leadership style centers on employees' contributions. Democratic leaders delegate assignments, ask employees for suggestions, and encourage participation. An important trend that has developed in business during the past decade is the concept of **empowerment,** a practice in which managers lead employees by sharing power, responsibility, and decision making with them.

Sometimes the sharing of power is institutionalized, as in a company like Southwest Airlines. Southwest has the highest proportion of union members among all U.S. air carriers and is the only one of the country's top eight airlines to consistently post a profit. Rules governing contract negotiations in unionized firms require labor and management to sit down together and discuss wages, hours, and benefits each time the contract is up for renewal. Typically, such negotiations are contentious, stressful, and difficult. At Southwest Airlines, however, they are much less so because of the positive way in which management treats workers. Colleen Barrett, who started as a legal secretary and is now company president, comments: "Our industry is unionized, and we are too. [Eighty-one percent of Southwest's employees belong to a union.] If you don't have the basic altruistic and caring attitude toward your employees at all times, then, when you have heavy-duty contract negotiations, people won't believe anything that you do if it is out of the norm when there wasn't a contract negotiation. It is so simple to me. We approach labor relations in a totally different way. We approach them as a team. We acknowledge we are going to have strong disagreements. But it is like politicians: We all have our constituents, but there should be common goals and behaviors and expectations that must be met."[27]

At the other end of the continuum from autocratic leadership is **free-rein leadership.** Free-rein leaders believe in minimal supervision. They leave most decisions to their subordinates. Free-rein leaders communicate with employees frequently, as the situation warrants.

Which Leadership Style Is Best?

The most appropriate leadership style depends on the function of the leader, the subordinates, and the situation. Some leaders cannot work comfortably with a high degree of subordinate participation in decision making. Some employees lack the ability or the desire to assume responsibility. In addition, the specific situation helps determine the most effective style of interactions. Sometimes managers must handle problems that require immediate solutions without consulting employees. When time pressure is less acute, participative decision making may work better for the same people.

Democratic leaders often ask for suggestions and advice from their employees but make the final decisions themselves. A manager who prefers the free-rein leadership style may be forced by circumstances to make a particular decision in an autocratic manner. A manager may involve employees in interviewing and hiring decisions but take complete responsibility for firing an employee.

After years of research intended to determine the best types of leaders, experts agree that they cannot identify any single best style of leadership. Instead, they contend that the most effective style depends on the leader's base of power, the difficulty of the tasks involved, and the characteristics of the employees. Both extremely easy and extremely difficult situations are best suited to leaders who emphasize the accomplishment of assigned tasks. Moderately difficult situations are best suited to leaders who emphasize participation and good working relationships with subordinates.

CORPORATE CULTURE

The best leadership style to adopt often depends on the organization's **corporate culture**, its system of principles, beliefs, and values. Managerial philosophies, communications networks, and workplace environments and practices all influence corporate culture. At Home Depot, the corporate culture is based on the belief that employees should fully understand and be enthusiastic about the core business of serving do-it-yourselfers. All newly hired employees, including top managers, must spend their first two weeks working on the sales floor of a Home Depot store. Even CEO Robert Nardelli spends time at an Atlanta-area store helping customers. By working at stores, all employees are exposed to the company's customers and, the company hopes, will soak up some of their can-do spirit. The company also encourages employees to get involved in service projects, such as building homes for Habitat for Humanity, which brings them closer to their community while seeing the stores' products in use. In addition, Home Depot gets employees excited about the business by granting them stock options. This benefit has made millionaires of many Home Depot employees. Stories like that of Franc Gambatse, who started as a sales clerk and less than a decade later was managing a Home Depot store and enjoying prosperity he "never could have imagined," inspire other employees to give their all. The retailer even has a company cheer: "Gimme an H!" and on through the store's name, as the troops reply, ready to support the company's continued growth in stores, sales, and profits.[28]

A corporate culture is typically shaped by the leaders who founded and developed the company and by those who have succeeded them. One generation of employees passes on a corporate culture to newer employees. Sometimes this transfer is part of formal training. New managers who attend sessions at McDonald's Hamburger University may learn skills in management, but they also acquire the basic values of the organization's corporate culture established by McDonald's founder Ray Kroc: quality, service, cleanliness, and value.[29] Employees can absorb corporate culture through informal contacts, as well as by talking with other workers and through their experiences on the job.

Managers use symbols, rituals, ceremonies, and stories to reinforce corporate culture. San Antonio–based Valero Energy Corporation, an oil refining company, has a tough corporate culture—dress codes for managers and regular drug testing to ensure employee safety—but it also puts employees first with its no-layoff policy and by firing managers for cursing at subordinates. When Hurricane Katrina hit, the dedication of Valero's staff shone through—they repaired its severely damaged facilities weeks and months faster than its competitors did. The company had stationed a 50-person "ride-out" crew at its St. Charles refinery, which is near New Orleans. One maintenance supervisor used his personal credit card to stock food for the crew before the storm hit and then stayed up round the clock to cook gumbo for them afterward as

corporate culture organization's system of principles, beliefs, and values.

Chapter 9

Human Resource Management, Motivation, and Labor–Management Relations

PHOTODISC/GETTY IMAGES

Growing economies need raw materials. But there's a critical labor shortage in the world's mines just as demand is rapidly climbing in expanding markets such as China and India. Both of these countries—with populations of more than 1 billion each—are investing heavily in airports, roads, commercial buildings, and communication systems. As they build, their need for iron ore, coal, and other materials produced by mines is increasing at an unprecedented pace. Meanwhile, mining firms such as Virginia-based Massey Energy are scrambling to hire enough employees to fill their customers' needs, both in the United States and overseas.

PHOTODISC/GETTY IMAGES

Recruiting, hiring, training, and managing a world-class workforce is the goal of every company, and Massey Energy is no exception. To meet increased skilled workers. "It's a very high-tech business now with a lot of intellectual challenge and opportunities to do interesting things," says Mike Nelson, an associate professor

Massey Energy: Mining for Employees

demand for its products, the company must attract qualified employees who possess specialized skills—or who can learn them—and who are willing to live in remote areas and face physical danger, such as the Sago Mine explosion in West Virginia that killed a dozen miners. In addition, a generation of well-trained engineers, electricians, and miners is beginning to retire. "In order to replace those who are retiring over the next 10 years, we'll have to triple our production of engineers," predicts Kim McCarter, chairman of the University of Utah's mining department. "That's not assuming any kind of growth. That's just replacing those who are retiring." Currently, only about 100 mining engineers graduate each year from U.S. colleges. Katharine Kenny, vice president at Massey, echoes this concern. "In this industry, it's tough enough just to maintain your [existing] workforce," she says. The shortage of labor is "the most difficult business issue we face."

To boost enrollment, institutions that offer mining programs are providing scholarships and job placement assistance for mining engineers with starting salaries ranging from $50,000 to $60,000. The industry wants students to understand that mining is not an "old" profession; instead, it uses the latest technologies and needs

of mining engineering at the University of Utah. Louis Cononelos of Kennecott Utah Copper emphasizes the career opportunities for recent graduates. "As the industry now has started to pick up, you have fewer candidates to choose from. It's really a great labor market for these recent graduates because now they have the pick of the jobs." In addition to existing college programs, several specialized training academies have opened near the sites of mining companies to help fill the urgent need for workers. Two such academies with programs designed to train coal miners recently opened in West Virginia. "There is an immediate need to train 1,800 to 2,500 miners in the next 18 months," explains Chris Hamilton of the West Virginia Coal Association.

At Massey Energy, recruitment and training efforts are progressing steadily. "We have a workforce in place which is up about 600 [or] 700 persons over where it was," reports chairman and CEO Don Blankenship. "And it's a matter of getting them trained and getting the equipment in place and beginning the mining. We're gaining ground on it in general, although we fell back a little in [one recent] quarter. But we still believe that the numbers we're projecting will be achieved."[1]

The importance of people to the success of any organization is the very definition of **management:** the use of people and other resources to accomplish organizational objectives. In this chapter, we address the critical issues of human resource management and motivation. We begin with a discussion of the ways organizations attract, develop, and retain employees. Then we describe the concepts behind motivation and the way human resource managers apply them to increase employee satisfaction and organizational effectiveness.

We also explore the reasons for labor unions and focus on legislation that affects labor–management relations. The process of collective bargaining is then discussed, along with tools used by unions and management in seeking their objectives.

HUMAN RESOURCE MANAGEMENT IS VITAL TO ALL ORGANIZATIONS

human resource management function of attracting, developing, and retaining enough qualified employees to perform the activities necessary to accomplish organizational objectives.

As you saw with Massey Energy at the opening of the chapter, most organizations devote considerable attention to **human resource management,** the function of attracting, developing, and retaining enough qualified employees to perform the activities necessary to accomplish organizational objectives. Human resource managers are responsible for developing specific programs and activities as well as creating a work environment that generates employee satisfaction and efficiency.

The core responsibilities of human resource management include planning for staffing needs, recruitment and selection, training and evaluating performance, compensation and benefits, and employee separation. In accomplishing these five tasks, shown in Figure 9.1, human resource managers achieve their objectives of (1) providing qualified, well-trained employees for the organization, (2) maximizing employee effectiveness in the organization, and (3) satisfying individual employee needs through monetary compensation, benefits, opportunities to advance, and job satisfaction.

One of the key ways in which human resource managers accomplish those tasks is to develop *human resource plans* based on their organization's competitive strategies. They forecast the number of employees their firm will need and determine the types of skills necessary to implement its plans. Human resource managers are responsible for adjusting their company's workforce to meet the requirements of expanding in new markets; reducing costs, which may require laying off employees; or adapting to new technology. They formulate both long- and short-term plans to provide the right number of qualified employees.

Human resource managers also must plan how to attract and keep good employees with the right combination of pay, benefits, and working conditions. At Trilogy Software, this aspect of human resource planning is at the core of the company's strategy. Trilogy develops software that handles information processing related to sales and marketing, an industry in which only fast-moving, highly sophisticated companies can succeed. So the company has a strategy to expand its staff of software developers. Knowing that it is competing for talent with software giants such as Microsoft and Cisco Systems, Trilogy targets college campuses, recruiting the brightest, most energetic students it can find. As a substitute for work experi-

"They Said It"

"This may sound soft and mushy, but happy people are better for business. They are more creative and productive, they build environments where success is more likely, and you have a much better chance of keeping your best players."
—*Shelly Lazarus (b. 1947) Chairwoman and CEO, Ogilvy & Mather Worldwide*[2]

ence, the company sends these young recruits to an intense three-month orientation program called Trilogy University, where they work on the firm's products as they learn about the software industry and the company culture. Trilogy appeals to recruits by emphasizing that their contribution to the company matters. "By hiring great people and giving them mission-critical responsibilities from the first day on the job, Trilogy ensures our ability to respond to competitive challenges and to achieve the goal of building a high-impact company," states the company Web site.[3]

RECRUITMENT AND SELECTION

In recruiting and selecting employees, human resource managers strive to hire applicants who have skills the organization needs. To ensure that potential employees bring the necessary skills or have the capacity to learn them, most firms implement the recruitment and selection process shown in Figure 9.2.

Finding Qualified Candidates

Finding the right candidate for a job isn't as simple as it sounds. For example, more than eight in ten manufacturers report facing moderate or severe shortages of the highly skilled workers they need to run today's computerized factories.[4] In addition, with 77 million baby boomers in their mid-40s to early 60s beginning to retire in the next five years and with only 46 million so-called Generation X workers, who are age 24 to 40, to take their places, finding talented workers is going to get even more difficult.[5] So human resource managers must be creative in their search for qualified employees. Businesses look to both internal and external sources to find the best candidates for specific jobs. Policies of hiring from within emphasize internal sources, so many employers consider their own employees first for job openings. Internal recruiting is less expensive than external methods, and it helps boost employee morale. But if recruiters cannot find qualified internal candidates, they must look for people outside the organization. Recruitment from external sources involves advertising on the Internet and in newspapers and trade magazines, placing radio and television ads, and working through state and private employment agencies, college recruiting and internship offices, retiree job banks, and job fairs. One of the most effective external sources is employee referrals, in which employers ask current employees to recommend applicants, rewarding them with bonuses or prizes for new hires.

To recruit new workers, firms' Web sites often contain career sections that provide general employment information and list open positions. Applicants may even be able to submit a résumé and apply for an open position online. As the "Launching Your Business Career" feature in the front matter pointed out, some firms also post job openings at employment Web sites, such as Monster.com. Internet recruiting is such a quick, efficient, and inexpensive way to reach a large pool of job seekers that between 82 and 92 percent of companies currently use the Internet to fill job openings. In fact, Internet recruiting is now second to newspaper advertising in terms of the number of applicants it generates. And, with the addition of a new ".jobs" Internet suffix (for example, http://cocacola.jobs/ for jobs at The Coca-Cola Company), more and more companies will now use their Web sites to attract, recruit, and screen job applicants.[6]

Figure 9.1

Human Resource Management Responsibilities

Core Responsibilities of Human Resource Management

Employee Recruitment and Selection

Employee Training and Performance Evaluation

Employee Compensation and Benefits

Employee Separation

Planning for Staffing Needs

assessment check

1. Why do human resource managers need to develop staffing plans?

2. How do human resource managers attract and keep good employees?

to change behavior in an existing one. [These policy changes] would also dissuade unhealthy people from coming to work at Wal-Mart."[21] While many believe that such strategies are illegal or unethical, particularly under the Americans with Disabilities Act, companies such as Union Pacific are already refusing to hire smokers in states where that is legal.

Some benefits are required by law. U.S. firms are required to make Social Security and Medicare contributions, as well as payments to state unemployment insurance and workers' compensation programs, which protect workers in case of job-related injuries or illnesses. The Family and Medical Leave Act of 1993 requires covered employers to offer up to twelve weeks of unpaid, job-protected leave to eligible employees. Firms voluntarily provide other employee benefits, such as child care and health insurance, to help them attract and retain employees. Recently, California became the first state to make paid family leave into law.[22]

Pensions and other retirement plans have been another area of concern for U.S. companies. Some companies have reduced the amount of matching contributions they will make to workers' **401(k) plans,** retirement savings plans to which employees can make pretax contributions to retirement accounts. Some companies have been cutting back on cash contributions to their employees' plans and are contributing company stock instead. Others, such as United Airlines, have gone bankrupt and defaulted on employees' pensions, which originally had guaranteed workers a set monthly payment in retirement. When this occurs, the U.S. government's Pension Benefit Guaranty Corporation pays employees' pensions, but retirement benefits are limited to $45,614 per year, which is sometimes well below the amount promised by their company pension plans.[23] Such defaults are rare so far.

How to Negotiate a Raise

When you are offered your first entry-level job, there isn't much room for negotiation in pay. Your employer is assuming that, although you will bring some natural ability and skills to the job, you will need to be trained. So you will start at the bottom of the salary ladder. Eventually, though, you'll have opportunities for an increase. Some raises occur automatically, according to a specific scale and after a designated period of time. But others don't. In these cases, you'll probably have to do some negotiating. Don't be intimidated; you can learn to negotiate smoothly and successfully. Here are a few tips:

- If salary discussion is not part of your performance review, make an appointment with your supervisor to discuss your salary.
- Before the meeting, review your own salary and benefits package so that you know exactly how much you are being compensated. If possible, ask the human resource

mance," says one training consultant.

- Discuss any other reasons why you deserve a raise. Have you been covering for a colleague who has left or is on leave, doing the job of two people? Are you already handling the responsibilities of the next-level job? In this case, you might be a candidate for a promotion and the raise that comes with it.
- Be realistic in your expectations. Consider the general economic environment and your company's current performance in the marketplace. Keep in mind the salary range for your job. "If you are out of step with reality, at worst you might find yourself in a position where you have to leave and, at best, your boss might question your street smarts," warns one career counselor.
- Discuss your request calmly, intelligently, and politely. If you have done your homework, the meeting shouldn't take more than 20 minutes or so. If your request is

---

If you're wondering how to increase your salary, read the "Business Etiquette" feature on how to negotiate a raise.

Many employers balance rewarding workers with maintaining profits by linking more of their pay to superior performance. They try to motivate employees to excel by offering some type of incentive compensation in addition to salaries or wages. Today, almost one-tenth of the compensation of salaried workers is some form of variable pay. These programs include the following:

- Profit sharing, which awards bonuses based on company profits
- Gain sharing, when companies share the financial value of productivity gains, cost savings, or quality improvements with their workers
- Lump-sum bonuses and stock options, which reward one-time cash payments and the right to purchase stock in the company based on performance
- Pay for knowledge, which distributes wage or salary increases as employees learn new job tasks

Figure 9.3 summarizes the four types of incentive compensation programs.

Employee Benefits

In addition to wages and salaries, firms pro-

Flexible Benefits

In response to the increased diversity of the workplace, human resource managers are developing creative ways to tailor their benefit plans to the varying needs of employees. One approach sets up **flexible benefit plans,** also called *cafeteria plans.* Such a benefit system offers employees a range of options from which they can choose, including different types of medical insurance, dental and vision plans, and life and disability insurance. This flexibility allows one working spouse to choose his or her firm's generous medical coverage for the entire family, and the other spouse can allocate benefit dollars to purchasing other types of coverage. "Employees don't want all the same benefits," explains Jamie Berge, owner of a tax and financial services firm in Anchorage that administers cafeteria plans for small businesses. "With cafeteria plans, you pick and choose."[24] Typically, each employee receives a set allowance (called *flex dollars* or *credits*) to pay for purchases from the benefits menu. A healthy, single employee might choose to allocate fewer flex dollars to health insurance, say, by choosing a higher deductible, and put more flex dollars toward an optional dental or vision plan. By contrast, an older employee might earmark some flex dollars to pay for elder care for aging parents.

Contributions to cafeteria accounts are commonly made by both the employee and employer. Cafeteria plans also offer tax benefits to both employees and employers. Employee contributions are made using so-called *pretax dollars,* meaning that employees don't pay taxes on their contributions. Also, employers don't have to pay unemployment taxes or Social Security and Medicare taxes on the amount deducted from employee paychecks.

When it comes to offering employees benefit choices, many companies now recognize the importance of offering "family-friendly" benefits that help employees care for children, aging parents, or other dependents. Such benefits—ranging from child-care facilities to paid time off and flexible work hours—help employees juggle responsibilities. Almost nine out of ten large U.S. companies offer dependent-care spending accounts to help pay for child care, and almost half offer some form of elder-care program. SAS Institute offers employees an excellent on-site child-care facility for a monthly fee of only $300, a cafeteria with pianists, an on-site health clinic, and a huge fitness center. Men's Wearhouse, which sells men's suits and jackets, offers workers three-week paid sabbaticals every five years, while Starbucks provides domestic partner benefits.[25] For more on how companies are using employee sabbaticals, see the "Hit & Miss" feature on whether corporate sabbaticals pay off.

Another way of increasing the flexibility of employee benefits involves time off from work. Instead of establishing set numbers of holidays, vacation days, and sick days, some employers give each employee a bank of **paid time off (PTO)**. Employees use days from their PTO accounts without having to explain why they need the time. At Republic Bancorp, employees get 35 days of paid time off, or seven weeks per year, to

Timberland is widely known for its community service efforts. Employees can

HIT & MISS

Corporate Sabbaticals: Do They Pay Off?

Imagine having several months or even a year off from your job—paid. This type of time off with pay is known as a *sabbatical,* which stems from a Hebrew word meaning "to rest." Sabbaticals have been around in academic circles for a long time. But increasingly, U.S. companies are recognizing the value of sabbaticals in reducing employee turnover and increasing productivity and loyalty. Firms such as Procter & Gamble, Nike, Intel, *Newsweek,* and Timberland offer sabbaticals to employees. So does publisher Bertelsmann AG's Random House division.

Eligibility requirements for and benefits of the programs vary widely from firm to firm. At Procter & Gamble, employees are eligible for up to 12 weeks of unpaid sabbatical after only 1 year and every 7 years after that. At *Newsweek,* reporters and editors can take 6 months of sabbatical at half their salaries after 15 years. At Random House, full-time employees may take 4 paid weeks off at the end of 10 years; after 20 years, they may take 5 weeks of sabbatical.

Peter Olson, CEO of Random House, admits that the sabbatical plan was "initially met with skepticism by several senior executives." Legitimate concerns included calculating the cost of sabbaticals and figuring out how the work would be accomplished while employees were gone. But Olson believed that sabbaticals would be a simple, low-cost way to motivate and retain his best employees—to encourage them to explore avenues that could result in innovation for the company—so he went ahead with the program. To date, more than 800 Ran-

dom House employees have participated in the sabbatical program. One editor returned to work with an idea for a new list of books, which is now being launched. An unexpected benefit to the program has been the opportunity for lower-level employees to fill in for their supervisors, giving them a chance to broaden their knowledge and skills on the job. "It's become a developmental opportunity," reports Olson.

Human resource experts agree that sabbaticals can motivate employees to return better than ever. Sabbaticals combat a culture "where being overworked is seen as a red badge of courage," reports the Families and Work Institute.

Questions for Critical Thinking

1. Do you think the benefits of a sabbatical outweigh the costs to a firm? Explain.
2. What challenges might a firm face in establishing and maintaining a sabbatical program?

Sources: "Are Employee Sabbaticals Worth the Hassle?" Vault, accessed July 2, 2006, http://www.vault.com; Erin White and Jeffrey A. Trachtenberg, "Sabbaticals Can Be The Pause That Refreshes," *Wall Street Journal,* accessed July 2, 2006, http://online.wsj.com; Kelley M. Butler, "Faced with Worker Burnout, Employers Pay Employees to Get Away," *Employee Benefit News,* accessed July 2, 2006, http://www.benefitnews.com; Alan R. Earls, "Sabbaticals Aren't Just for Academia Anymore," *Boston Globe,* accessed July 2, 2006, http://www.boston.com.

spouses.[27] And 58 percent of companies reward employees who don't use all of their paid time off by "buying back" that time in cash.[28] One recent trend involves giving employees paid time off for volunteer service. Timberland is well known for doing this. The boot and apparel maker gives every employee 40 hours of paid time a year for volunteer work, and its New Hampshire headquarters actually closes one day a year so that Timberland employees can build playgrounds, work at the local SPCA, and assist the elderly. Employees are also eligible for six months of "social service leave" at full pay.[29]

Flexible Work

Another part of the trend toward responsiveness to employee needs is the option of **flexible work plans.** Flexible work plans are benefits that allow employees to adjust their working hours and places of work to accommodate their personal needs. Flexible work plan options

Once the largest corporation in the world, General Motors has fallen on hard times recently. To survive, the company had to lay off 25,000 employees and close plants amongst other actions.

by 70 billion yen, Sanyo Electric of Japan announced that it would cut 14,000 jobs, 8,000 of those within Japan, and close or sell 20 percent of its factories. The reason, said Sanyo's president, Toshimasa Iue, is that "We will no longer conduct operations that don't produce profits."[35]

While some firms report improvements in profits, market share, employee productivity, quality, and customer service after downsizing, studies show that downsizing doesn't guarantee those improvements. Why? A big reason is that eliminating jobs through downsizing can have devastating effects on employee morale. Workers who remain after a downsizing worry about job security and become angry when they have to work harder for the same pay. As commitment to their jobs and their firms weakens, many employees will leave to seek employment offering greater job security. In general, corporate downsizing has encouraged employees to put individual career success before employer loyalty, which has declined in the last two decades.

Employee surveys reveal that many workers are more interested in career security than job security. Specifically, the typical employee may seek training to improve the skills needed for the next job. People are willing to work hard at their current jobs, but they also want to share in the success of their companies in the form of pay-for-performance and stock options. For human resource managers, the new employee-employer relationship requires developing continuous training and learning programs for employees.

Outsourcing

outsourcing contracting with another business to perform tasks or functions previously handled by internal staff members.

In their continuing efforts to remain competitive against domestic and international rivals, a growing number of firms hold down costs by evolving into leaner organizations. Functions that were performed previously by company employees may be contracted to other firms whose employees will perform them in a practice called **outsourcing.** Outsourcing began on a small scale, with firms contracting out services such as maintenance, cleaning, and delivery. Services commonly outsourced today include housekeeping; architectural design; grounds, building, utility, and furniture maintenance; food service; security; and relocation services. Today, outsourcing has expanded to include outside contracting of many tasks once considered fundamental internal functions.

Outsourcing complements today's focus on business competitiveness and flexibility. It allows a firm to continue performing the functions it does best, while hiring other companies to do tasks that they can handle more competently and cost-effectively. Another benefit of outsourcing is the firm's ability to negotiate the best price among competing bidders and the chance to avoid the long-term resource costs associated with in-house operations. Firms that outsource also gain flexibility to change vendors at the end of contract periods if they desire. The key to successful outsourcing is a strong commitment by both parties to form a partnership from which each derives benefits. Having had previous success with outsourcing, Dallas-based Electronic Data Systems (EDS), which provides computer and data services to major companies and has 117,000 employees worldwide, is planning to double the number of jobs that it outsources overseas to lower-wage workers in companies in India and Asia.[36]

assessment check

1. What is the difference between voluntary and involuntary turnover?
2. What is downsizing? How is it different from outsourcing?

MOTIVATING EMPLOYEES

Employee motivation is the key to effective management. And motivation starts with good employee morale. **Morale** is the mental attitude of employees toward their employer and jobs. It involves a sense of common purpose among the members of work groups and throughout the organization as a whole. High morale is a sign of a well-managed organization because workers' attitudes toward their jobs affect the quality of their work. One of the most obvious signs of poor manager-worker relations is poor morale. It lurks behind absenteeism, employee turnover, and strikes. It shows up in falling productivity and rising employee grievances.

In contrast, high employee morale occurs in organizations in which employees feel valued and heard and can contribute what they do best. This climate reinforces a human tendency—that people perform best when they believe they are capable of succeeding. High morale also results from an organization's understanding of human needs and its success at satisfying those needs in ways that reinforce organizational goals.

Each person is motivated to take action designed to satisfy needs. A need is simply a lack of some useful benefit. It reflects a gap between an individual's actual state and his or her desired state. A motive is an inner state that directs a person toward the goal of satisfying a felt need. Once the need—the gap between where a person is now and where he or she wants to be—becomes important enough, it produces tension. The individual is then moved—the root word for *motive*—to reduce the tension and return to a condition of equilibrium. Figure 9.4 depicts the principle behind this process. A need produces a motivation, which leads to goal-directed behavior, resulting in need satisfaction.

Maslow's Hierarchy-of-Needs Theory

The studies of psychologist Abraham H. Maslow suggest how employers can motivate employees. **Maslow's hierarchy of needs** has become a widely accepted list of human needs based on these important assumptions:

- People's needs depend on what they already possess.
- A satisfied need is not a motivator; only needs that remain unsatisfied can influence behavior.
- People's needs are arranged in a hierarchy of importance; once they satisfy one need, at least partially, another emerges and demands satisfaction.

Maslow's hierarchy of needs theory of motivation proposed by Abraham Maslow. According to the theory, people have five levels of needs that they seek to satisfy: physiological, safety, social, esteem, and self-actualization.

The Process of Motivation

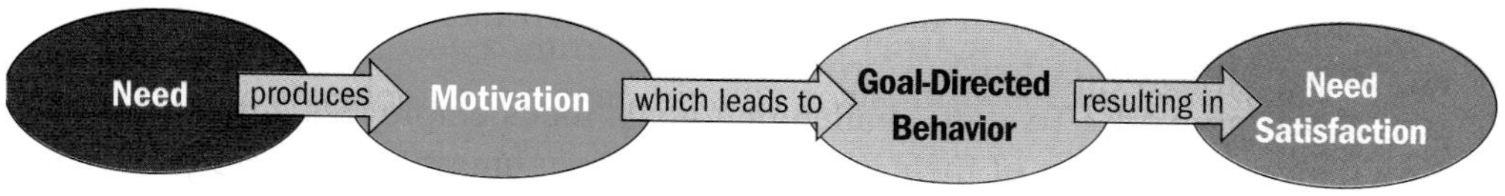

Need → produces → Motivation → which leads to → Goal-Directed Behavior → resulting in → Need Satisfaction

Figure 9.4

tops in the company. Their reward: The VP raised their overall quota by 65% this year, an impossible target. Teams in adjacent areas that did not do nearly as well had their quotas raised 15%. Her whole team is out looking for new jobs and is very discouraged. For my wife,

In his theory, Maslow proposed that all people have basic needs such as hunger and protection that they must satisfy before they can consider higher-order needs such as social rela-

Figure

9.5   Components of Goal-Setting Theory

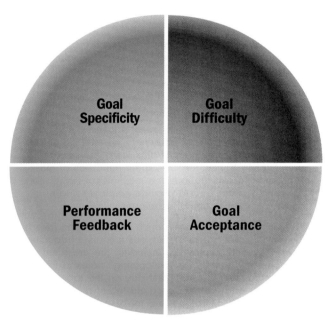

Goal
Specificity

Goal
Difficulty

Performance
Feedback

Goal
Acceptance

job enlargement job design that expands an employee's responsibilities by increasing the number and variety of tasks assigned to the worker.

job enrichment change in job duties to increase employees' authority in planning their work, deciding how it should be done, and learning new skills.

it means she will not make as much this year, and in fact will have a hard time even making quota."[38]

Job Design and Motivation

In their search for ways to improve employee productivity and morale, a growing number of firms are focusing on the motivation inherent in the job itself. Rather than simplifying the tasks involved in a job, employers are broadening tasks to add meaning and satisfaction to employees' work. Two ways employers are applying motivational theories to restructure jobs are job enlargement and job enrichment.

Job enlargement is a job design that expands an employee's responsibilities by increasing the number and variety of tasks they entail. Some firms have successfully applied job enlargement by redesigning the production process. A typical approach is to replace assembly lines on which each worker repeats the same step on each product with modular work areas in which employees perform several tasks on a single item. Similarly, many companies have enlarged administrative assistants' jobs in areas such as communications.

Job enrichment is a change in job duties to increase employees' authority in planning their work, deciding how it should be done, and learning new skills that help them grow. Many companies have developed job enrichment programs that empower employees to take responsibility for their work. The Pampered Chef, a direct seller of kitchen products that is owned by Berkshire Hathaway, gives its managers and consultants the power to make decisions about many aspects of their work. Kitchen consultants, who organize selling and demonstration parties at customers' homes, can choose how much or how little they want to work and receive various incentive rewards for performance. "Over the years, thousands of people from all walks of life have joined our Pampered Chef family. They've found a truly unlimited opportunity and life-changing possibilities," notes founder and chairman Doris Christopher.[39]

Managers' Attitudes and Motivation

The attitudes that managers display toward employees also influence worker motivation. Managers' traditional view of workers as cogs in the production process—much like lathes, drill presses, and other equipment—led them to believe that money was the best way to motivate employees. Maslow's theory has helped managers understand that employees feel needs beyond those satisfied by monetary rewards.

AP PHOTO/RICHARD PATTERSON

To provide more variety and prevent boredom in their jobs, security screeners working for the Transportation Security Administration are rotated to other tasks. These workers are checking bags from a Miami cruise ship for passengers headed to flights home.

Psychologist Douglas McGregor, a student of Maslow, studied motivation from the perspective of how managers view employees. After observing managers' interactions with employees, McGregor coined the terms *Theory X* and *Theory Y* as labels for the assumptions that different managers make about worker behavior and how these assumptions affect management styles.

Theory X assumes that employees dislike work and try to avoid it whenever possible. So managers must coerce or control them or threaten punishment to achieve the organization's goals. Managers who accept this view feel that the average person prefers to receive direction, wishes to avoid responsibility, has relatively little ambition, and can be motivated only by money and job security. Managers who hold these assumptions are likely to keep their subordinates under close and constant observation, hold out the threat of disciplinary action, and demand that they adhere closely to company policies and procedures.

Theory Y assumes that the typical person likes work and learns, under proper conditions, to accept and seek responsibilities to fulfill social, esteem, and self-actualization needs. Theory Y managers consider the expenditure of physical and mental effort in work as an ordinary activity, as natural as play or rest. They assume that most people can think of creative ways to solve work-related problems but that most organizations do not fully utilize the intelligence that most employees bring to their jobs. Unlike the traditional management philosophy that relies on external control and constant supervision, Theory Y emphasizes self-control and self-direction.

Theory Y requires a different management approach that includes worker participation in decisions that Theory X would reserve for management. If people actually behave in the manner described by Theory X, they may do so because the organization satisfies only their lower-order needs. If the organization instead designs ways to satisfy their social, esteem, and self-actualization needs as well, employees may be motivated to behave in different ways.

Another perspective on management proposed by management professor William Ouchi has been labeled **Theory Z**. Organizations structured on Theory Z concepts attempt to blend the best of American and Japanese management practices. This approach views worker involvement as the key to increased productivity for the company and improved quality of work life for employees. Many U.S. firms have adopted the participative management style used in Japanese firms by asking workers for suggestions to improve their jobs and then giving them the authority to implement proposed changes.

"**They Said It**"

"If you perform well, we're going to get along. If you don't, you've got to do push-ups."
—Colin Powell (b. 1937) American military leader and former U.S. Secretary of State, speaking to his staff

assessment check

1. In an organization, what conditions are likely to produce high morale?
2. Explain how goal setting works.
3. Identify two ways that employers structure jobs for motivation.
4. Compare and contrast Theory X, Theory Y, and Theory Z.

LABOR-MANAGEMENT RELATIONS

In nations throughout the world, employees have joined together to increase their power to achieve the goals of improved wages and benefits, fewer working hours, and better working conditions. These efforts have succeeded, especially in the United States; today's workplace is far different from that of a century ago, when child labor, unsafe working conditions, and a 72-hour workweek (six 12-hour days a week) were common. In this section, we review the development of labor unions, labor legislation, the collective bargaining process, settling labor-management disputes, and competitive tactics of unions and management.

Development of Labor Unions

A **labor union** is a group of workers who have banded together to achieve common goals in the areas of wages, hours, and working conditions. Workers gradually learned that bargaining

labor union group of workers who have banded together to achieve common goals in the areas of wages, hours, and working conditions.

as a unified group could bring them improvements in job security, wages, working conditions, and other areas. The organized efforts of Philadelphia printers in 1786 resulted in the first U.S. minimum wage—$1 a day. After 100 more years, New York City streetcar conductors were able to negotiate a reduction in their workday from seventeen to twelve hours.

Labor unions can be found at the local, national, and international levels. A *local union* represents union members in a specific area, such as a single community, while a *national union* is a labor organization consisting of numerous local chapters. An *international union* is a national union with membership outside the United States, usually in Canada. Large national and international unions in the United States include the United Auto Workers, the National Education Association, the Teamsters, the International Brotherhood of Electrical Workers, the International Association of Machinists and Aerospace Workers, the United Steelworkers of America, and the American Federation of Teachers. Over half of U.S. union members belong to one of these giant organizations.

Almost 16 million U.S. workers—close to 13 percent of the nation's full-time work-force—belong to labor unions.[40] Although only about 8 percent of workers in the private sector are unionized, more than one in three government workers belong to unions. The 1.8-million-member Service Employees International Union (SEIU) is the largest union in the United States. In addition to a wide range of service workers—clerical staff, nurses' aides, and janitors—SEIU has also organized such professionals as nurses, doctors, engineers, and librarians. Other large unions include the 1.4 million members of the United Food and Commercial Workers, the 1.4 million members of the International Brotherhood of Teamsters, and the 710,000 members of the United Auto Workers.

Labor Legislation

Government attitudes toward unions have varied considerably over the past century. These shifting attitudes influenced major pieces of legislation enacted during this period. Let's look at the major pieces of labor legislation:

- *National Labor Relations Act of 1935 (Wagner Act):* Legalized collective bargaining and required employers to negotiate with elected representatives of their employees. Established the National Labor Relations Board (NLRB) to supervise union elections and prohibit unfair labor practices such as firing workers for joining unions, refusing to hire union sympathizers, threatening to close if workers unionize, interfering with or dominating the administration of a union, and refusing to bargain with a union.
- *Fair Labor Standards Act of 1938*: Set the initial federal minimum wage (25 cents an hour, with exceptions for farm workers and retail employees) and maximum basic work-week for workers employed in industries engaged in interstate commerce. Outlawed child labor.
- *Taft-Hartley Act of 1947 (Labor-Management Relations Act):* Limited unions' power by prohibiting such practices as coercing employees to join unions; coercing employers to discriminate against employees who are not union members, except for failure to pay union dues under union shop agreements; discrimination against nonunion employees; picketing or conducting secondary boycotts or strikes for illegal purposes; featherbedding; and excessive initiation fees under union shop agreements.
- *Landrum-Griffin Act of 1959 (Labor-Management Reporting and Disclosure Act):* Amended the Taft-Hartley Act to promote honesty and democracy in running unions' internal affairs. Required unions to set up a constitution and bylaws and to hold regularly scheduled elections of union officers by secret ballot. Set forth a bill of rights for members. Required unions to submit certain financial reports to the U.S. secretary of labor.

The Collective Bargaining Process

Labor unions work to increase job security for their members and improvement of wages, hours, and working conditions. These goals are achieved primarily through **collective bargaining**, the process of negotiation between management and union representatives for the purpose of arriving at mutually acceptable wages and working conditions for employees.

Issues covered in collective bargaining include wages, work hours, benefits, union activities and responsibilities, grievance handling and arbitration, layoffs, and employee rights and seniority. As in all types of negotiations, the collective bargaining process involves demands, proposals, and counterproposals that ultimately result in compromise and agreement. The initial demands represent a starting point in negotiations. They are rarely, if ever, accepted by the other party without some compromise. The final agreement depends on the negotiating skills and relative power of management and union representatives.

Union contracts, which typically cover a two- or three-year period, are often the result of weeks or more of discussion, disagreement, compromise, and eventual agreement. Once agreement is reached, union members must vote to accept or reject the contract. If the contract is rejected, union representatives may resume the bargaining process with management representatives, or union members may strike to obtain their demands.

collective bargaining process of negotiation between management and union representatives for the purpose of arriving at mutually acceptable wages and working conditions for employees.

Settling Labor-Management Disputes

Although strikes make newspaper and television headlines, most labor-management negotiations result in a signed agreement without a work stoppage. Approximately 140,000 union contracts are currently in force in the United States. Of these, on average no more than 20 labor-management contract negotiations involve a work stoppage of some kind.[41] The courts are the most visible and familiar vehicle for dispute settlement, but most disputes are settled by negotiations. Dispute resolution mechanisms, such as grievance procedures, mediation, and arbitration, are quicker, cheaper, and less complicated procedurally and receive less publicity.

The union contract serves as a guide to relations between the firm's management and its employees. The rights of each party are stated in the agreement. But no contract, regardless of how detailed, will eliminate the possibility of disagreement. Such differences can be the beginning of a **grievance**, a complaint—by a single employee or by the entire union—that management is violating some provision of the union contract. Almost all union contracts require these complaints to be submitted to a formal grievance procedure similar to the one shown in Figure 9.6.

The procedure typically begins with the employee's supervisor and then moves up the company's chain of command. If the highest company officer cannot settle the grievance, it is submitted to an outside party for mediation or arbitration.

Mediation is the process of settling labor-management disputes through recommendations of an impartial third party. Although the mediator does not serve as a decision maker, union and management representatives can be assisted by the mediator's suggestions, advice, and compromise solutions.

> ## "They Said It"
> "When two teams are interested, you negotiate. When only one team is interested, you beg."
> —Mark Schlereth (b. 1966) Former professional football player, Denver Broncos

Steps in the Grievance Procedure

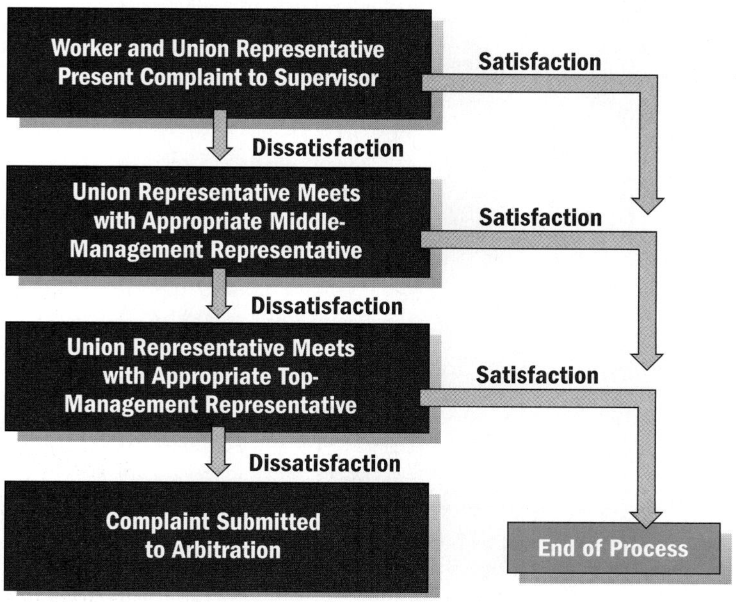

Figure 9.6

Worker and Union Representative Present Complaint to Supervisor → Satisfaction

Dissatisfaction ↓

Union Representative Meets with Appropriate Middle-Management Representative → Satisfaction

Dissatisfaction ↓

Union Representative Meets with Appropriate Top-Management Representative → Satisfaction

Dissatisfaction ↓

Complaint Submitted to Arbitration

End of Process

When disputes cannot be solved voluntarily through mediation, the parties can turn to **arbitration**—bringing in an impartial third party, called an *arbitrator,* who renders a legally binding decision. The arbitrator must be acceptable both to the union and to management, and his or her decision is legally enforceable. In essence, the arbitrator acts as a judge, making a decision after listening to both sides of the argument. Most union contracts call for the use of arbitration if union and management representatives fail to reach an agreement.

Competitive Tactics of Unions and Management

Although most differences between labor and management are settled through the collective bargaining process or through a formal grievance procedure, both unions and management occasionally resort to various tactics to make their demands known.

Union Tactics　The chief tactics of unions are strikes, picketing, and boycotts. The **strike,** or *walkout,* is one of the most effective tools of the labor union. It involves a temporary work stoppage by employees until a dispute has been settled or a contract signed. Although strikes are relatively rare, they do make headlines. In recent years, strikes have involved workers at Supervalu, Ralphs (a supermarket chain owned by Kroger's), home health care agencies in New York City, and hotel and casino employers in Atlantic City.[42]

Although the power to strike represents unions' ultimate tactic, they do not wield it lightly because strikes can do damage in a number of ways, affecting not only one company but an entire industry, as well as related businesses. When 60,000 southern California grocery store workers went on a four-month strike, Safeway, Kroger, and Supervalu lost tens of millions of dollars. However, because profits were weak and the companies were losing business to Wal-Mart, the unions still had to make cost concessions, dropping the pay of new workers from $17.90 to $15.10. Plus, new workers no longer receive free healthcare.[43]

Picketing—workers marching at the entrances of the employer's business as a public protest against some management practice—is another effective form of union pressure. As long as picketing does not involve violence or intimidation, it is protected under the U.S. Constitution as freedom of speech. Picketing may accompany a strike, or it may be a protest against alleged unfair labor practices. When union workers for Boeing, the airplane manufacturer, went on strike and began picketing, it cost the company $70 million a day in lost production. The union and Boeing management eventually agreed on a new contract after a monthlong strike.[44] Because members of other unions often refuse to cross picket lines, the picketed firm may be unable to obtain deliveries and other services. Unions occasionally stage "informational" picketing during contract negotiations to pressure management while still working.

A **boycott** is an organized attempt to keep the public from purchasing the products of a firm. Some unions have been quite successful in organizing boycotts, and some unions even fine members who defy a primary boycott. The United Food and Commercial Workers International Union,

Sometimes strikes cannot be prevented. But when they occur, they are costly to both employees and companies. Shown here are members of the Aircraft Mechanics Fraternal Association picketing against Northwest Airlines.

AP PHOTO/JIM MONE

which would like to unionize Wal-Mart's workers, created a "Wake Up Wal-Mart" campaign in which it encouraged schoolteachers, many of whom are members of teachers' unions, to boycott Wal-Mart for back-to-school purchases.[45]

Management Tactics   Management also has tactics for dealing with organized labor. In the past, it has used the **lockout**—in effect, a management strike to put pressure on union members by closing the firm. However, other than a few high-profile cases, the lockout is not commonly used unless a union strike has partially shut down a plant or engaged in a work slow-down. Firms can easily recruit strikebreakers in high-status fields such as professional sports and in high-paying industries located in areas of high unemployment. Yet even in favorable conditions, management frequently has difficulties securing enough replacement workers with required skills. Some employers get around these difficulties by using supervisors and nonunion replacement employees to continue operations during strikes. When Northwest Airline's 4,400 mechanics went on strike after company management demanded a 25 percent wage cut, Northwest temporarily hired 1,200 replacement workers, employed 300 managers who had been formally trained as mechanics, and relied on 400 mechanics from outside vendors. Northwest's replacement mechanics were so effective that it was able to fly 98 percent of its normal flights during the strike.[46]

The Future of Labor Unions

Union membership and influence grew through most of the 20th century by giving industrial workers a voice in decisions about their wages, benefits, and working conditions. Today, however, union members and influence are declining. As the United States, western Europe, and Japan have shifted from manufacturing economies to information and service economies, the makeup of the workforce has become less favorable for unions. While almost 8 percent of private-sector workers are union members today, that's down from nearly 17 percent in 1983. Likewise, unions have won only 7,224 of the 13,144 union votes (in which employees decide whether they want to be represented by a union) over the last five years.[47] That is a historically low percentage. In fact, unions have been unable to organize any of the Japanese-owned automobile plants in the United States (Toyota, Honda, Nissan) or those of Mercedes Benz, BMW, and Hyundai. Their biggest lack of success has been their inability to organize Wal-Mart's 1.2 million U.S. workers.

How will unions shrinking and why are they having difficulty attracting members? Debbie Moore, who was in a union fourteen years ago when she worked in a manufacturing plant, now works for Wal-Mart in an automotive repair department, where she and her co-workers voted 19–0 to reject union representation. Said Moore, "Right now, in this day and era, I don't think I need a union to pay for anybody to protect me. Years ago, I believe work conditions were bad, and unions had their place of bringing standards up and making jobs safe. Unions are headed downward now. And the government is there to help."[48] Mary Gilleece, director of an information technology school in Somerville, Massachusetts, summarizes the thoughts of many of today's workers when she says, "If it's a decent company, you don't need a union."[49]

At nonunion companies, management often offers a compensation and benefit structure comparable to those of unionized firms in the area. Willingness to offer comparable wages and working conditions, coupled with effective communications, emphasis on promotions from within, employee empowerment, and employee participation in goal setting and grievance handling clearly helps employers avert unionization. Satisfied workers such as Mary Gilleece conclude that they would receive few additional benefits for the union dues they would have to pay.

How will labor unions have to change to maintain their relevance? More than anything else, with manufacturing jobs shrinking from increasing productivity and overseas outsourcing, labor unions are reaching out to nonmanufacturing workers, such as healthcare, high-tech, and service workers. Another possibility is offering affiliate or partial memberships, which offer the same benefits as full memberships except for collective bargaining or grievance issues.[50] Finally, labor unions will have to overcome the widespread belief that they can't succeed unless company management loses. Today, most workers realize that they prosper when their companies prosper, and that it's better for management and workers to work together and to have positive rather than adversarial relationships.

WHAT'S AHEAD

Treating employees well by enriching the work environment will continue to gain importance as a way to recruit and retain a highly motivated workforce. In addition, managers can tap the full potential of their employees by empowering them to make decisions, leading them to work effectively as teams, and fostering clear, positive communication. The next chapter covers these three means of improving performance. By involving employees more fully through empowerment, teamwork, and communication, companies can benefit from their knowledge while employees enjoy a more meaningful role in the company.

Summary of Learning Goals

1 Explain the importance of human resource management, the responsibilities of human resource managers, and the role of human resource planning in an organization's competitive strategy.

Organizations devote considerable attention to attracting, training, and retaining employees to help maintain their competitiveness. Human resource managers are responsible for recruiting, selecting, training, compensating, terminating, and motivating employees. They accomplish these tasks by developing specific programs and creating a work environment that generates employee satisfaction and efficiency. A human resource plan is designed to implement a firm's competitive strategies by providing the right number of employees, training them to meet job requirements, and motivating them to be productive and satisfied workers.

Assessment Check Answers

1.1 Why do human resource managers need to develop staffing plans?

Staffing plans help managers determine how many employees their firms will need and the kinds of skills those employees will need.

1.2 How do human resource managers attract and keep good employees?

Using the right combination of pay, benefits, and working conditions helps managers attract and keep good employees.

2 Describe how recruitment and selection contribute to placing the right person in a job.

Firms use internal and external methods to recruit qualified employees. For needs that the company cannot meet with existing employees, it may find candidates by encouraging employee referrals, advertising, accepting résumés at its Web site, and using job search Web sites. In selecting qualified candidates, human resource managers must follow legal requirements designed to promote equal employment opportunity. Employment tests, such as cognitive ability tests, are often used to assess job candidates' capabilities and help companies hire more qualified workers.

Assessment Check Answers

2.1 What are some of the costs associated with recruitment and selection?

Firms incur costs for advertising job openings, interviewing applicants, and conducting background checks, employment tests, and medical exams. Hiring mistakes increase training costs, can result in lawsuits and unemployment compensation claims, and reduce productivity and employee morale.

2.2 What key federal and state laws apply to recruitment and selection?
Recruitment and selection practices must adhere to Title VII of the Civil Rights Act of 1964, the Americans with Disabilities Act of 1990, the Civil Rights Act of 1991, and other regulations of the Equal Employment Opportunity Commission.

3 Explain how training programs and performance appraisal help companies grow and develop their employees.
Human resource managers use a variety of training techniques, including on-the-job training, computerized training programs, and classroom methods. In addition, management development programs help managers make decisions and improve interpersonal skills. Companies conduct performance appraisals to assess employees' work, as well as their strengths and weaknesses.

Assessment Check Answers

3.1 Describe some aids in on-the-job training.
In on-the-job training, you learn how to perform tasks under the guidance of experienced employees. A variation of on-the-job training is apprenticeship training, in which an employee learns a job by serving for a longer time as an assistant to a trained worker.

3.2 What is a management development program?
A management development program provides training designed to improve the skills and broaden the knowledge of current and potential executives.

3.3 What is the main way an organization provides employees with feedback about their performance?
The main method is a performance appraisal, in which an employee's job performance is compared with desired outcomes. Peer reviews and 360-degree performance reviews are also used to provide feedback.

4 Outline the methods employers use to compensate employees through pay systems and benefit programs.
Firms compensate employees with wages, salaries, and incentive pay systems, such as profit sharing, gain sharing, lump-sum bonuses, stock options, and pay-for-knowledge programs. Benefit programs vary among firms, but most companies offer healthcare programs, insurance, retirement plans, paid time off, and sick leave. A growing number of companies are offering flexible benefit plans and flexible work plans, such as flextime, compressed workweeks, job sharing, and home-based work.

Assessment Check Answers

4.1 Explain the difference between wage and salary.
Wages represent compensation based on an hourly pay rate or the amount of output produced. Salaries represent compensation calculated periodically, such as weekly or monthly.

4.2 What is another name for a *cafeteria plan?*
Cafeteria plans are also called *flexible benefit plans.*

4.3 What types of organizations typically use a compressed workweek?
Hospitals, police and fire departments, airlines, and manufacturing organizations often use compressed workweeks. However, many other kinds of companies are now finding success with compressed workweeks.

5 Discuss employee separation and the impact of downsizing and outsourcing.
Either employers or employees can decide to terminate employment (called *involuntary turnover* and *voluntary turnover,* respectively). Downsizing reduces a company's workforce to reduce labor costs in an effort to improve the firm's competitive position. The company may transfer some responsibilities to contractors, a practice called *outsourcing.* The goals of outsourcing are to reduce costs by giving work to more efficient specialists and to allow the company to focus on the activities it does best.

Assessment Check Answers

5.1 What is the difference between voluntary and involuntary turnover?
Voluntary turnover occurs when employees leave firms to start their own businesses, take jobs with other firms, move to another city, or retire. Involuntary turnover occurs when employers terminate employees because of poor job performance, negative attitudes toward work and co-workers, or misconduct.

5.2 What is downsizing? How is it different from outsourcing?
Downsizing is the process of reducing the number of employees within a firm by eliminating jobs.

Downsizing is done to cut overhead costs and stream-line the organizational structure. With outsourcing, companies contract with other firms to perform non-core jobs or business functions, such as housekeeping, maintenance, or relocation services. This allows companies to focus on what they do best, and can result in a downsized workforce.

6 Explain how Maslow's hierarchy-of-needs theory, goal setting, job design, and managers' attitudes relate to employee motivation.

Employee motivation starts with good employee morale. Maslow's hierarchy-of-needs theory states that all people have basic needs (physiological and safety) that they must satisfy before they can consider higher-order needs (social, esteem, and self-actualization). Goal-setting theory, job enlargement, and job enrichment are three ways in which managers can motivate employees and satisfy various levels of needs. Managers' attitudes can also affect employee motivation. Theory X managers keep their subordinates under close and constant observation. Theory Y managers emphasize workers' self-control and self-direction. Theory Z managers believe that worker involvement is the key to increased productivity for the company and improved quality of work life for employees.

Assessment Check Answers

6.1 In an organization, what conditions are likely to produce high morale?

High employee morale occurs when employees feel valued and heard and can contribute what they do best. High morale also results from an organization's understanding of human needs and its success at satisfying those needs in ways that reinforce organizational goals.

6.2 Explain how goal setting works.

People will be motivated to the extent to which they accept specific, challenging goals and receive feedback that indicates their progress toward goal achievement.

6.3 Identify two ways that employers structure jobs for motivation.

Two ways that employers apply motivational theories to restructure jobs are job enlargement and job enrichment. Job enlargement is a job design that expands an employee's responsibilities by increasing the number and variety of tasks they entail. Job enrichment is a change in job duties to increase employees' authority in planning their work, deciding how it should be done, and learning new skills that help them grow.

6.4 Compare and contrast Theory X, Theory Y, and Theory Z.

Theory X assumes that employees dislike work and try to avoid it whenever possible. Theory Y assumes that the typical person likes work and learns, under proper conditions, to accept and seek responsibilities to fulfill social, esteem, and self-actualization needs. Theory Z views worker involvement as the key to increased productivity for the company and improved quality of work life for employees.

7 Summarize the role of labor unions and the tactics of labor-management conflicts.

A labor union is a group of workers who have banded together to achieve common goals in the key areas of wages, working hours, and working conditions. Labor unions exist at local, national, and international levels. Government attitudes toward unions have varied considerably during the past century and are reflected in the major pieces of labor legislation enacted during this period. Labor unions work to achieve their goals of increased job security and improvements in wages, hours, and working conditions through a process known as *collective bargaining*. Most labor-management negotiations result in a signed agreement without a work stoppage. Even after an agreement is signed, disputes can arise. A grievance is a complaint that management is violating some provision of the union contract. Mediation is the process of settling labor-management disputes through recommendations of an impartial third party. Arbitration is a process in which an impartial third party renders a legally binding decision. Some tactics available to labor unions during disputes include strikes (walkouts), picketing, and boycotts. Tactics available to management include lockouts and hiring replacement workers.

Assessment Check Answers

7.1 How many U.S. workers are represented by labor unions?

Almost 16 million U.S. workers—close to 13 percent of the nation's full-time workforce—belong to labor unions. Although only about 8 percent of workers in the private sector are unionized, more than one in three government workers belong to unions.

7.2 Identify the major issues covered in the collective bargaining process.

The major issues covered in collective bargaining include wages, work hours, benefits, union activities and responsibilities, grievance handling and arbitration, layoffs, and employee rights and seniority.

7.3 Explain picketing, boycotts, and lockouts.

Picketing is when workers march at the entrances of the employer's business to protest against some management practice. A boycott is an organized attempt to keep the public from purchasing the products of a firm. A lockout is a management strike, in which company management pressures labor union members by locking them out of the company and closing the firm.

Business Terms You Need to Know

human resource management 288
performance appraisal 294
wage 295
salary 295
employee benefits 296

downsizing 301
outsourcing 302
Maslow's hierarchy of needs 303
goal 304
goal-setting theory 304

job enlargement 306
job enrichment 306
labor union 307
collective bargaining 309

Other Important Business Terms

management 288
cognitive ability tests 292
on-the-job training 292
management development
   program 293
360-degree performance
   review 295
401(k) plan 297
flexible benefit plan 298

paid time off (PTO) 298
flexible work plan 299
flextime 300
compressed workweek 300
job sharing program 300
telecommuter 300
morale 303
Theory X 307
Theory Y 307

Theory Z 307
grievance 309
mediation 309
arbitration 310
strike 310
picketing 310
boycott 310
lockout 311

Review Questions

1. What are the core responsibilities of human resource management? What are the three main objectives of human resource managers?
2. What methods do companies use to recruit and select employees?
3. What types of training programs are popular today? How does 360-degree feedback work?
4. On what five factors are compensation policies usually based? Name at least three employee benefits that are required by law and three more that are provided voluntarily by many firms.
5. Describe four types of flexible work plans. Identify an industry that would be well suited to each type of plan and explain why.
6. Outline the major reasons for terminating employees. Why do companies downsize? What are some of the difficulties they may encounter in doing so?

Chapter 10

Improving Performance through Empowerment, Teamwork, and Communication

Learning Goals

1. Describe why and how organizations empower employees.

2. Distinguish among the five types of teams in the workplace.

3. Identify the characteristics of an effective team.

4. Summarize the stages of team development.

5. Relate team cohesiveness and norms to effective team performance.

6. Describe the factors that can cause conflict in teams and how to manage conflict.

7. Explain the importance and process of effective communication.

8. Compare the different types of communication.

9. Explain external communication and how to manage a public crisis.

When Diane Davidson accepted a job at W. L. Gore & Associates, she found a corporate structure and culture very different from what she'd experienced in her fifteen years in the apparel industry. Gore makes the famous Gore-Tex fabric and other leading products, which generate about $1.3 billion in sales. Innovation is key to the company's continuing success, and that focus is reflected in its teamwork.

"When I arrived at Gore, I didn't know who did what," Davidson remembers. "I wondered how anything got done here. It was driving me crazy." Struggling with the concept of having a mentor called a "starting sponsor" instead of a manager to report to, Davidson kept asking, "Who's my boss?"

To which her sponsor replied, "Stop using the B-word."

AP PHOTO/ROBERTO BOREA

Associates are free to pursue ideas on their own, to communicate about them with anyone in the firm, to figure out what to do to make the ideas work, and then to attract other associates to

W. L. Gore Frees Its Workers to Perform

Gore's unique combination of self-managed teams, employee empowerment, and employee ownership has kept it on *Fortune*'s list of "100 Best Companies to Work For" every year since the list' debut in 1984, a distinction only seven other companies have ever achieved. Gore is also one of the country's 100 largest companies that are 50 percent or more employee owned. All 7,000 Gore employees own shares in the firm. But the company has no hierarchy, no bosses, and no job titles. As Davidson eventually found out, "Your team is your boss, because you don't want to let them down. Everyone's your boss, and no one's your boss."

Instead of job descriptions, Gore employees—who are called "associates"—have individual sets of "commitments" they make to their teams. Those commitments often allow the person to create a nontraditional work role that bridges several different functions such as sales, marketing, product design, and product sponsorship. It usually takes new team members as much as a year or more to get used to the process, create their roles, and build credibility. During that period, they are also encouraged to spend about 10 percent of their time on developing new ideas.

develop the ideas with them in small teams. Gore believes this practice fosters "natural leadership" and credits it with forming a remarkable environment in which employees work together because of internal motivation, rather than from a sense of duty imposed from the outside. About half the company's employees consider themselves leaders.

Despite the focus on teamwork and independent thinking, not all new initiatives at the company succeed, of course. But those that are axed get a celebratory send-off, the same as is given to ideas that succeed. That endorsement encourages risk taking, as does the pay structure at the firm. Each year, a committee of team members decides the value of an individual's contribution, counting past and present performance as well as future potential.

The company resembles a set of small task forces, with few corporate ranks or titles. In fact, job titles are optional at Gore. Responsibility is "pushed out" to the individual team member, not consolidated in a leader who is defined by a predetermined corporate structure. Some organization, however, is reflected in the company's division into four product areas: (1) fabrics, including the famous breathable waterproof textile;

(2) medical; (3) industrial; and (4) electronic. The firm also has several support functions such as human resources and information technology. Each of these areas has a leader, and CEO Terri Kelly oversees the entire operations as president.

But as Kelly says, "Leaders need to be approachable and real. They can't only fly at 50,000 feet." As for her own job, Kelly says that at Gore, "It's never about the CEO. You're an associate, and you just happen to be the CEO."[1]

Top managers at most firms recognize that teamwork and communication are essential for encouraging employees and helping them improve organizational performance. This chapter focuses on how organizations involve employees by sharing information and empowering them to make critical decisions, allowing them to work in teams, and fostering communication. We begin by discussing the ways managers are expanding their employees' decision-making authority and responsibility. Then we explain why and how a growing number of firms rely on teams of workers rather than individuals to make decisions and carry out assignments. Finally, we discuss how effective communication allows workers to share information that improves decision making.

EMPOWERING EMPLOYEES

empowerment giving employees authority and responsibility to make decisions about their work without traditional managerial approval and control.

An important component of effective management is **empowerment** of employees. Managers promote this goal by giving employees authority and responsibility to make decisions about their work without traditional managerial approval and control. Empowerment seeks to tap the brainpower of all workers to find improved ways of doing their jobs and executing their ideas. Empowerment frees managers from hands-on control of subordinates. It also motivates workers by adding challenges to their jobs and giving them a feeling of ownership. Managers empower employees by sharing company information and decision-making authority and by rewarding them based on company performance.

Sharing Information and Decision-Making Authority

One of the most effective methods of empowering employees is to keep them informed about the company's financial performance. Companies such as Virginia-based Anderson & Associates provide regular reports to their employees on key financial information, such as profit-and-loss statements. Anderson, an engineering firm that designs roads, water and sewer lines, and water treatment facilities, posts financial statements, training schedules, policy documents, and other information on the company's internal Web site.[2] Any employee can visit the site and look up the company's cash flow, design standards, and photos of co-workers in other cities, as well as basic measures of financial performance. Senior vice president Brad Stipes says, "I can open up [CEO] Ken Anderson's time sheet. I'm not just accountable to Ken Anderson. I'm accountable to everybody. We're judged on the numbers, and everyone [in the company] can see those numbers."[3]

HIT & MISS

Hampton Inn Empowers Front-Line Employees

Would you spend a dollar to get $7 back? Hampton Inn, a division of the Hilton hotel group, does it regularly. Each year, the chain of 1,300 hotels refunds about 0.5 percent of its total room revenues to guests who aren't satisfied with their rooms or service. For every dollar refunded, the company estimates it gets back about $7 in new business, either from a new customer or from an unhappy one who was won over when the chain stood by its commitment to service. Hampton Inn guarantees total guest satisfaction in all its hotels throughout the United States, Canada, and Latin America with this statement: "If you're not 100% satisfied, we don't expect you to pay. That's our promise and your guarantee."

What makes the policy so effective is that every employee in the hotel—whether a front desk clerk, a housekeeper, a maintenance worker, or a restaurant hostess—is empowered to offer guests a free stay on the spot if they are unhappy for any reason. Guests don't have to send their complaints to the manager, call an 800 number, answer a lot of questions, or fill out a response card and then wait for a refund. All they need to do is tell someone why they're unhappy, and not only is the problem corrected immediately, but their room is also free.

Recent Hampton Inn guests included Tom Taylor, a Michigan auditor who told the front desk clerk about the incorrect directions on the hotel's Web site, room lights that were left unplugged, and air conditioning that was too cold. Taylor was immediately offered both nights of his stay free, but he was so impressed by the response that one free night was enough to keep him a happy guest; he insisted on paying for the second one himself. Chris Byrd, a pharmaceutical industry consultant from Arizona, found crumbs in a chair and hair in the bathroom of his Hampton Inn room. Even though he left without complaining, the hotel found out about the problems through Byrd's response to the customer satisfaction e-mail it sent him. Offered a free room to apply to his next stay, Byrd, who hadn't planned to use Hampton Inn again, instead became a fan of the chain. "I wouldn't have come back if they didn't come up with an offer," he said.

Questions for Critical Thinking

1. Could Hampton Inn's guarantee work for other service firms? Why or why not?
2. If you managed employees who were empowered as Hampton Inn's are, how would you ensure that they make appropriate decisions on their own about when and how to satisfy customers?

Sources: Hampton Inn Web site, accessed July 2, 2006, http://hamptoninn.hilton.com; Gerri Willis, "Trip from Hell? It's Payback Time," CNN/Money, accessed July 2, 2006, http://money.cnn.com; Gary Stoller, "Companies Give Front-Line Employees More Power," *USA Today,* accessed July 2, 2006, http://www.usatoday.com.

Like other companies that practice this strategy of open-book management, Anderson also trains its employees to interpret financial statements so they can understand how their work contributes to company profits. Using information technology to empower employees does carry some risks. One is that information may reach competitors. Although Anderson & Associates considered this problem, management decided that sharing information was essential to the company's strategy.

The second way in which companies empower employees is to give them broad authority to make workplace decisions that implement a firm's vision and its competitive strategy. Even among nonmanagement staff, empowerment extends to decisions and activities traditionally handled by managers. Employees might be responsible for such tasks as purchasing supplies, making hiring decisions, scheduling production or work hours, overseeing the safety program, and granting pay increases. At Mission Controls Automation, a manufacturing company in Costa Mesa, California, employees not only receive the same financial information as company management but also are responsible for hiring. Every job applicant is reviewed by a team called SNAGs, which stands for Screening New Applicant Groups. No one is hired unless every SNAG member gives his or her approval.[4] For more on employee empowerment, see the "Hit & Miss" feature, which explains how Hampton Inn empowers its employees.

Minding Your Telephone Manners

It's all too easy to forget the importance of the impression we make over the telephone. But that link is as critical for businesses as communicating face-to-face. To ensure that your telephone conversations at work send the right message about you and your firm, check out the following guidelines.

1. Answer your own phone whenever possible, and answer promptly—by the third ring.
2. Say, "Hello, this is [your name] speaking," or a variation that is preferred in your workplace or department.
3. If the caller has the wrong number, be gracious when acknowledging the error and hanging up. If you think you can redirect the call for the person, offer to do so first. Likewise, if you dial a wrong number, apologize briefly and hang up.
4. Reduce background noise when using the phone to avoid distractions and to convey the message that the caller is your first priority.
5. Return all calls within 24 hours. The only exception is urgent calls, which you should return immediately.
6. Speak slowly, clearly, and in a pleasant tone. Smile when you speak—it conveys a positive attitude even if the other person can't see you.
7. If you are taking a call for someone else who is out, give as little detail as possible about where the person is and offer to either take a message or transfer the caller to a voice-mail system. If you take a message, get complete information, including the time of the call; write clearly; and make sure the message is delivered promptly.
8. When you make a call, dial carefully, identify yourself, and ask for the party to whom you wish to speak.
9. Prepare what you need to say ahead of time and get to the point. Be considerate of others' time.
10. Remember that you may be working with people who live in different time zones from yours. Make sure you call during their regular working hours, not yours.

Sources: "Telephone Etiquette," Essortment, accessed July 2, 2006, http://mt.essortment.com; "Telephone Etiquette Guide," California State University, Fullerton: Information Technology, accessed July 2, 2006, http://www.fullerton.edu; Lewena Bayer and Karen Mallett, "Telephone Etiquette," accessed August 15, 2005, Lifewise, http://www.canoe.ca.

Oral Communication Managers spend a great deal of their time engaged in oral communication, both in person and on the phone. Some people prefer to communicate this way, believing that oral channels more accurately convey messages. Face-to-face oral communication allows people to combine words with such cues as facial expressions and tone of voice. Oral communication over the telephone lacks visual cues, but it offers some of the advantages of face-to-face communication, such as opportunities to hear the tone of voice and provide immediate feedback by asking questions about anything the receiver doesn't understand or raising new issues related to the message. For more on oral communication, see the "Business Etiquette" feature on minding your telephone matters.

Procter & Gamble's CEO, A. G. Lafley, believes strongly in the benefits of oral communication. Lafley says, "I'm not a big e-mailer. I prefer face-to-face whenever possible. And usually we're in a cafeteria or an auditorium somewhere, and I talk briefly, and then I spend half to two-thirds of the time on comments and questions and answers, which is when you really get at what's on people's minds."[20]

In any medium, a vital component of oral communication is **listening**—receiving a message and interpreting its genuine meaning by accurately grasping the facts and feeling conveyed. Although listening is the first communication skill that people learn and the one they use most often, it is also the one in which they receive the least formal training.

Listening may seem easy, because the listener makes no obvious effort. This apparent passivity creates a deceptive picture, however. The average person talks at a rate of roughly 150 words per minute, but the brain can handle up to 400 words per minute. This discrepancy can lead to boredom, inattention, and misinterpretation. In fact, immediately after listening to a message, the average person can recall only half of it. After several days, the proportion of a message that a listener can recall falls to 25 percent or less.

Certain types of listening behaviors are common in both business and personal interactions:

- *Cynical listening.* This defensive type of listening occurs when the receiver of a message feels that the sender is trying to gain some advantage from the communication.

listening receiving a message and interpreting its intended meaning by grasping the facts and feelings it conveys.

- *Offensive listening.* In this type of listening, the receiver tries to catch the speaker in a mistake or contradiction.
- *Polite listening.* In this mechanical type of listening, the receiver listens to be polite rather than to communicate. Polite listeners are usually inattentive and spend their time rehearsing what they want to say when the speaker finishes.
- *Active listening.* This form of listening requires involvement with the information and empathy with the speaker's situation. In both business and personal life, active listening is the basis for effective communication.

Learning how to be an active listener is an especially important goal for business leaders, because effective communication is essential to their role.

Written Communication   Channels for written communication include reports, letters, memos, online discussion boards, and e-mail messages. Most of these channels permit only delayed feedback and create a record of the message. So it is important for the sender of a written communication to prepare the message carefully and review it to avoid misunderstandings.

Effective written communication reflects its audience, the channel carrying the message, and the appropriate degree of formality. When writing a formal business document, such as a complex report, a manager must plan in advance and carefully construct the document. The process of writing a formal document involves planning, research, organization, composition and design, and revision. Written communication via e-mail may call for a less-formal writing style, including short sentences, phrases, and lists.

E-mail can be a very effective communication channel, especially for delivering straightforward messages and information. But e-mail's effectiveness also leads to its biggest problem: too much e-mail! Scott McNealy, former CEO of Sun Microsystems, averaged 150 e-mails a day—and that was just from his own employees. Henry McKinnell, Jr., CEO of New York–based Pfizer, the largest pharmaceuticals company in the world, says, "I don't look out the window [when being driven to meetings]. I use my BlackBerry and answer my e-mail." Finally, James Rogers, CEO of Cinergy, a Cincinnati-based provider of gas and electricity, keeps his Black-Berry next to his bed. Before you go to bed, says Rogers, "you don't say your prayers. You check your e-mail."[21]

Another problem with e-mail is security. Because e-mail messages are often informal, senders occasionally forget that they are creating a written record. Also, even if the recipient deletes an e-mail message, other copies exist on company e-mail servers. And if e-mails are available on company servers, they can be used against you and your firm in a lawsuit. Nancy Flynn, executive director of the ePolicy Institute of Columbus, Ohio, says, "You can take it to the bank that your employee e-mail is going to be subpoenaed. If you can't produce the e-mail that the court wants you to produce, then you're going to face court sanctions. And you may even get into a situation where the court gives instructions to the jury to go ahead and draw negative inferences because your organization wasn't able to produce e-mail."[22] So be careful about what you say in your e-mails—someone is probably watching.

To open and improve lines of communication among his staff, Digineer's CEO Michael Lacey held an Iron Chef cook-off. Lacey, who previously had prepared elaborate meals for his staff, had his employees split themselves into teams to create a three-course meal. Lacey judged the results as both fun and delicious.

Formal Communication   A **formal communication channel** carries messages that flow within the chain of command structure defined by an organization. The most familiar channel, downward communication, carries messages from someone who holds a senior position in the organization to subordinates. Managers may communicate downward by sending employees e-mail messages, presiding at department meetings, giving employees policy manuals, posting notices on bulletin boards, and reporting news in company newsletters. The most important factor in formal communication is to be open and honest. "Spinning" bad news to make it look better almost always backfires. Yvonne Hunt, vice president for worldwide internal communications at Hewlett-Packard, said, "When companies spin internally, it is very difficult to build credibility since most news delivered to an internal audience (especially difficult news) is often communicated externally. When there is a disparity between what employees hear from their manager and what they see in the media, it leads to distracted, de-motivated employees who feel a lack of trust caused by a lack of transparency—whether that is real or perceived."[23]

Many firms also define formal channels for upward communications. These channels encourage communication from employees to supervisors and upward to top management levels. Some examples of upward communication channels are employee surveys, suggestion boxes, and systems that allow employees to propose new projects or voice complaints.

Informal Communication   **Informal communication channels** carry messages outside formally authorized channels within an organization's hierarchy. A familiar example of an informal channel is the **grapevine,** an internal channel that passes information from unofficial sources. Research shows that many employees cite the grapevine as their most frequent source of information. Grapevines rapidly disseminate information. A message sent through formal channels may take days to reach its audience, but messages that travel via grapevines can arrive within hours. Grapevines also are surprisingly reliable links. They pass on accurate information 70 to 90 percent of the time.[24] Workplace psychologist Nicholas DiFonzo, who spent months in *Fortune* 500 companies tracking rumors, says, "The main focus of rumor [and the grapevine] is to figure out the truth." When rumors began about downsizing at one of the companies he was studying, "The rumor mill produced a list of people that would be laid off that was 100% accurate."[25] For more on a unique case of information communication, holiday office parties, see the "Solving an Ethical Controversy" feature.

The spontaneity of informal communication may diminish when a company's employees are spread among many locations. Employees who telecommute or travel frequently may miss opportunities to build smooth working relationships or exchange ideas. In those situations, communication technology can help firms promote informal communication. Some companies establish online chat areas for employees, so they can visit each other during breaks. Some also encourage their workers to create home pages that describe their interests and hobbies. In fact, surveys reveal that even among people in the same office, workplace instant messaging is used for personal discussions and work-related gossip. A survey of U.S. and British workers found that 80 percent of workplace instant messages were for gossiping and that nearly two-thirds contained complaints to managers about co-workers.[26]

Verbal and Nonverbal Communication   So far, this section has considered different forms of verbal communication, or communication that conveys meaning through words. Equally important is **nonverbal communication,** which transmits messages through actions and behaviors. Gestures, posture, eye contact, tone of voice, and even clothing choices are all nonverbal actions that become communication cues. Nonverbal cues can strongly influence oral communication by altering or distorting intended meanings.

Nonverbal cues can have a far greater impact on communications than many people realize. One study divided face-to-face conversations into three sources of communication cues: verbal cues (the actual words spoken), vocal cues (pitch or tone of a person's voice), and

"They Said It"

"The difference between the right word and the almost right word is the difference between lightning and lightning bugs."
—Mark Twain (1835–1910) American novelist

SHOULD COMPANIES HOLD HOLIDAY OFFICE PARTIES?

Holidays are times for getting together, renewing relationships, and celebrating with colleagues. Office parties, whether lavish or small, serve all these functions and are a staple of organizational life.

But if inappropriate actions such as excessive drinking or unprofessional behavior occur at office holiday parties, or if nonparticipants feel slighted or left out because they don't observe certain holidays, can such parties really foster better work relationships and improve teamwork? Or will they have the opposite effect?

Should companies hold holiday office parties?

PRO

1. Many people view office parties as a reward for their hard work during the year, and they deserve the chance to gather for social reasons, let down some organizational barriers, and have fun with their co-workers. Parties are also great morale builders.
2. With well-publicized guidelines and safeguards, inappropriate or unsafe behavior can be reduced to a minimum or even eliminated. Holding luncheons is another option to help ensure a safer environment to celebrate. Most people know how to behave and just want to enjoy themselves; most employees are not a problem.

CON

1. It's too difficult to agree on what holidays should be acknowledged and celebrated in the office. It's fairer and less divisive to allow everyone to celebrate their own particular holidays at home with their families and not to single any out at work.
2. Employers may be held legally liable for the actions of drunk drivers or other alcohol-related accidents following an office party where drinks were served. But employees tend to expect alcohol at parties. So it's better to avoid both accidents and liability by not having office parties.

Summary

Some possible solutions for avoiding the drawbacks of holiday parties are to restrict or even ban the flow of liquor. Stopping alcohol service an hour or so before the end of a party and offering coffee, tea, and other nonalcoholic beverages is another option. Companies can also provide transportation home for employees who attend. As for cultural differences, with a little creative effort, businesses can make their parties unique by looking for new themes and traditions that give everyone a reason to celebrate.

Sources: Jessica M. Walker, "Should Auld Acquaintance Forget Themselves at the Office Holiday Party," *New Jersey Law Journal,* accessed July 3, 2006, http://www.law.com/nj; Diane E. Lewis, "Party Like It's Not Quite 9 to 5," *Boston Globe,* accessed July 3, 2006, http://www.boston.com; Mitch Moxley, "Parties No Excuse for Bad Behaviour," *Financial Post,* accessed January 3, 2005, http://www.canada.com/national/nationalpost.

solving an ETHICAL controversy

facial expressions. The researchers found some surprising relative weights of these factors in message interpretation: verbal cues (7 percent), vocal cues (38 percent), and facial expressions (55 percent).[27]

Even personal space—the physical distance between people who are engaging in communication—can convey powerful messages. Figure 10.4 shows a continuum of personal space and social interaction with four zones: intimate, personal, social, and public. In the United States, most business conversations occur within the social zone, roughly between four and twelve feet apart. If one person tries to approach closer than that, the other will likely feel uncomfortable or even threatened.

Interpreting nonverbal cues can be especially challenging for people with different cultural backgrounds. Concepts of appropriate personal space differ dramatically throughout most of the world. Latin Americans conduct business discussions in positions that most Americans and Northern Europeans would find uncomfortably close. Americans often back away to preserve their personal space, a gesture that Latin Americans perceive as a sign of cold and unfriendly relations. To protect their personal space, some Americans separate themselves across desks or tables from their Latin American counterparts—at the risk of challenging their colleagues to maneuver around those obstacles to reduce the uncomfortable distance.

Figure

10.4 | Influence of Personal Space in Nonverbal Communication

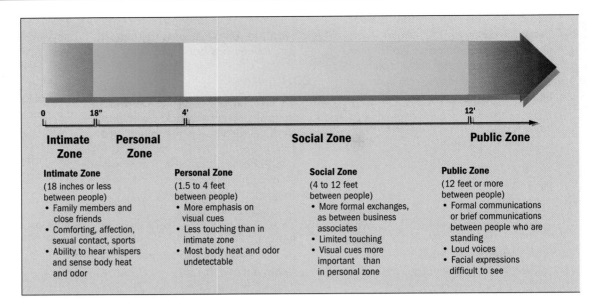

Intimate Zone | **Personal Zone** | **Social Zone** | **Public Zone**

Intimate Zone
(18 inches or less between people)
- Family members and close friends
- Comforting, affection, sexual contact, sports
- Ability to hear whispers and sense body heat and odor

Personal Zone
(1.5 to 4 feet between people)
- More emphasis on visual cues
- Less touching than in intimate zone
- Most body heat and odor undetectable

Social Zone
(4 to 12 feet between people)
- More formal exchanges, as between business associates
- Limited touching
- Visual cues more important than in personal zone

Public Zone
(12 feet or more between people)
- Formal communications or brief communications between people who are standing
- Loud voices
- Facial expressions difficult to see

assessment check

1. What are four common listening behaviors? Characterize each.
2. What are some advantages of e-mail as a communication medium? What are some disadvantages?
3. What are the differences between formal and informal communication?
4. Why do we pay more attention to nonverbal communication cues than to verbal communication cues?

People send nonverbal messages even when they consciously try to avoid doing so. Sometimes nonverbal cues convey a person's true attitudes and thoughts, which may differ from spoken meanings. Generally, when verbal and nonverbal cues conflict, receivers of the communication tend to believe the nonverbal content. This is why Southwest Airlines, which seeks to hire people with good attitudes and a team orientation, closely watches nonverbal behavior during job interviews in which job applicants participate in group sessions with other job candidates applying for the same job. If in those group interviews an applicant frowns or looks discouraged when a competing candidate gives a good answer, Southwest concludes from that nonverbal behavior that this person may not be strongly team oriented.[28]

EXTERNAL COMMUNICATION: CRISIS MANAGEMENT

external communication meaningful exchange of information through messages transmitted between an organization and its major audiences.

External communication is a meaningful exchange of information through messages transmitted between an organization and its major audiences, such as customers, suppliers, other firms, the general public, and government officials. Businesses use external communication to keep their operations functioning, to maintain their positions in the marketplace, and to build customer relationships by supplying information about topics such as product modifications and price changes. Every communication with customers—including sales presentations, customer orders, and advertisements—should create goodwill and contribute to customer satisfaction. However, all of this is threatened when companies experience a public crisis that threatens their reputation or goodwill. For example, Wendy's restaurants saw an immediate decline in sales after reports that a severed finger was found served in a bowl of chili at a Wendy's in San Jose, California. In northern California alone, sales declined by $2.5 million, which resulted in layoffs and reduced working hours. However, one month later, police arrested the woman who "found" the finger, charging her with perpetrating a hoax to win a lawsuit or financial settlement from the company. Joseph Desmond, owner of the Wendy's restaurant in which this all took place, said, "It's been 31 days, and believe me it's been really tough. My thanks also go out to all the little people who were hurt in our stores. They lost a lot of wages because we had to cut back because our business has been down so badly."[29]

So what steps can companies and their managers or spokespersons take when dealing with a public crisis? First, companies must respond quickly when a crisis occurs and with a prepared statement. During the initial news contact, which might be a press conference or simply an interview with a print or TV reporter, prepare by writing a statement—no matter how short—and stick to it. The statement should mention the time, place, initial description of what occurred (not the cause), and the number and status of the people involved.

Second, as soon as possible, put top company management in front of the press. Because the public will hold top management accountable, it's best to have top managers responding to reporters' questions. For instance, after a Southwest Airlines flight ran off the runway in a snowstorm at Chicago's Midway airport, hitting a car and killing a 6-year-old boy, Southwest had CEO Gary Kelly in Chicago the next morning to represent and speak for the company.[30]

Third, when answering reporters' questions, stick to the facts. Don't wing it. If you don't know the details about what happened, then don't speculate. If you speculate and are proven wrong, it will look like you were lying. So tell people only what you know.

Fourth, if you don't know, offer to find out. You don't have to know the answer to each question off the top of your head. When you don't know, say so: "I don't know the answer to that question." When you can find out an answer, say that, too. But then be sure to deliver the answer in a timely manner.

Fifth, never say "no comment." "No comment" is perceived as a statement of guilt. It's better to say, "I don't know."

Sixth, identify and speak to your audience. In the Wendy's case, there were several audiences, among them people who watch TV news and people who like to eat at fast-food restaurants. When speaking to an audience, it's important to recognize that what you say is likely to be only a small part of a TV, print, or radio story. Accordingly, you can speak more effectively to your audience by using visual or word images instead of facts. Most people don't have the time or are reluctant to immerse themselves in the details of a story. Facts are easily forgotten. Images are easily remembered. For instance, when a hypodermic needle was "found" in a can of Pepsi, the company quickly took reporters to their bottling plants where they showed (1) that Pepsi bottles and cans were washed and then dried *upside down* on a high-speed assembly line a split second before being turned right side up and filled with Pepsi, and (2) that the cans were then weighed and any can that didn't correspond to the standard weight was automatically kicked out of the production process.[31]

Finally, acknowledge problems and explain solutions. If a question or factual statement puts your organization in a negative light, acknowledge the problem, and then explain how you're correcting it.

assessment check

1. What is external communication?

2. During a company crisis, why is it dangerous for a spokesperson to say "no comment" when answering reporters' questions?

WHAT'S AHEAD

Today's consumers expect the products they buy to be of the highest value for the price. Firms ensure this value by developing efficient systems for producing goods and services, as well as maintaining high quality. The next chapter examines the ways in which businesses produce world-class goods and services, efficiently organize their production facilities, purchase what they need to produce their goods and services, and manage large inventories to maximize efficiency and reduce costs.

1 **Describe why and how organizations empower employees.**

By empowering employees, a firm finds better ways to perform jobs, motivates people by enhancing the challenges and satisfaction in their work, and frees managers from hands-on control so that they can focus on other tasks. Employers empower workers by sharing information, distributing decision-making authority and responsibility, and linking rewards to company performance through employee stock ownership plans and stock options.

Assessment Check Answers

1.1 What is empowerment?
Empowerment is giving employees authority and responsibility to make decisions about their work without traditional managerial approval and control.

1.2 What kinds of information can companies provide employees to help them share decision-making responsibility?
Sharing information about company performance, particularly financial performance, is one of the best ways to share decision-making responsibility.

1.3 What are some of the risks of sharing this information?
One risk is that proprietary competitive or financial information may reach competitors.

1.4 How do employee stock ownership plans and stock options reward employees and encourage empowerment?
Employee stock ownership plans (ESOPs) benefit employees by giving them ownership stakes in their companies. Employees are motivated to work harder and smarter than they would without ESOPs because they share in their firm's financial success. In contrast to an ESOP, in which the company holds stock for the benefit of employees (when employees leave the company, they cash in their stock), stock options give employees a chance to own the stock themselves if they exercise their options by completing the stock purchase.

2 **Distinguish among the five types of teams in the workplace.**

The five basic types of teams are work teams, problem-solving teams, self-managed teams, cross-functional teams, and virtual teams. Work teams are permanent groups of co-workers who perform the day-to-day tasks necessary to operate the organization. Problem-solving teams are temporary groups of employees who gather to solve specific problems and then disband. Self-managed teams have the authority to make decisions about how their members complete their daily tasks. Cross-functional teams are made up of members from different functions, such as production, marketing, and finance. Virtual teams are groups of geographically or organizationally dispersed co-workers who use a combination of telecommunications and information technologies to accomplish an organizational task.

Assessment Check Answers

2.1 What is a team?
A team is a group of employees who are committed to a common purpose, approach, and set of performance goals.

2.2 What are the five types of teams and how are they different?
Work teams are permanent, while problem-solving teams are temporary. Unlike work teams, self-managed teams have the authority to change how they get their work done. Cross-functional teams are composed of people from different backgrounds, while virtual teams are composed of people from different locations.

3 **Identify the characteristics of an effective team.**

Three important characteristics of a team are its size, team level, and team diversity. Effective teams typically contain between five and twelve members, with about six or seven members being the ideal size. Team level is the average level of ability, experience, personality, or any other factor on a team. For example, a high level of team experience means that members have, on average, particular expertise in some area. Instead of considering similarities, team diversity represents the variances or differences in ability, experience, personality, or any other factor on a team. In other words, strong teams not only have talented members (i.e., team level) but also benefit from the differences in terms of ability, experience, or personality of individual members. Diverse teams tend to display broader ranges of viewpoints and produce more innovative solutions to problems than do homogeneous teams.

Assessment Check Answers

3.1 Teams reach maximum effectiveness, diversity, and communication flow with how many members?
Six or seven members is typically the best size for a team.

3.2 Explain team level and team diversity.
While team level represents the average level or capability on a team, team diversity represents the variances or differences in ability, experience, personality, or any other factor on a team.

④ Summarize the stages of team development.
Teams pass through five stages of development: (1) Forming is an orientation period during which members get to know each other and find out what behaviors are acceptable to the group. (2) Storming is the stage during which individual personalities emerge as members clarify their roles and expectations. (3) Norming is the stage at which differences are resolved, members accept each other, and consensus emerges about the roles of the team leader and other participants. (4) Performing is characterized by problem solving and a focus on task accomplishment. (5) Adjourning is the final stage, with a focus on wrapping up and summarizing the team's experiences and accomplishments.

Assessment Check Answers

4.1 Explain how teams progress through the stages of team development.
Teams pass through five stages of development: forming, storming, norming, performing, and adjourning.

4.2 Explain the difference between the storming and performing stages.
The primary difference is how teams handle conflict in these stages. In the storming stage, people disagree over the team's mission and jockey for position and control of the group. But in the performing stage, those issues have been settled, so team members handle conflicts in constructive ways; in other words, they encourage cognitive conflict to solve problems.

⑤ Relate team cohesiveness and norms to effective team performance.
Team cohesiveness is the extent to which team members feel attracted to the team and motivated to remain on it. Team norms are standards of conduct shared by team members that guide their behavior.

Highly cohesive teams whose members share certain standards of conduct tend to be more productive and effective.

Assessment Check Answers

5.1 How does cohesiveness affect teams?
Members of cohesive teams interact more often, share common attitudes and goals, have higher morale, and are more likely to help each other. Cohesive teams also perform better.

5.2 Explain how team norms positively and negatively affect teams.
Norms are informal standards that identify key values and clarify team members' expectations. But those norms can be positive or negative. Positive norms contribute to constructive work and the accomplishment of team goals. Negative norms can, for example, contribute to reduced work effort, reduced quality, and poor job attendance.

⑥ Describe the factors that can cause conflict in teams and how to manage conflict.
Conflict and disagreement are inevitable in most teams. Conflict can stem from many sources: disagreements about goals and priorities, task-related issues, interpersonal incompatibilities, scarce resources, and simple fatigue. Though most people view conflict negatively, the key to dealing with team conflict is not avoiding it, but making sure that the team experiences the right kind of conflict. Cognitive conflict focuses on problem-related differences of opinion and, when reconciled, strongly improves team performance. By contrast, affective conflict refers to the emotional reactions that can occur when disagreements become personal rather than professional, and these differences strongly decrease team performance. A team leader can limit conflict by focusing team members on broad goals, clarifying participants' respective tasks and areas of authority, acting as mediator, and facilitating effective communication.

Assessment Check Answers

6.1 What is cognitive conflict and how does it affect teams?
With cognitive conflict, team members disagree because their different experiences and expertise lead them to different views of the problem and its solutions. Cognitive conflict is characterized by a willingness to

examine, compare, and reconcile differences to produce the best possible solution.

6.2 Explain affective conflict and its impact on teams.

Because affective conflict often results in hostility, anger, resentment, distrust, cynicism, and apathy, it can make people uncomfortable, cause them to withdraw, decrease their commitment to a team, lower the satisfaction of team members, and decrease team cohesiveness.

7 Explain the importance and process of effective communication.

Managers and employees spend much of their time exchanging information through messages. Communication helps all employees understand the company's goals and values and the parts they play in achieving those goals. Every communication follows a step-by-step process that involves interactions among six elements: sender, message, channel, audience, feedback, and context.

Assessment Check Answers

7.1 What is the difference between communication in low-context and high-context cultures?

Communication in low-context cultures tends to rely on explicit written and verbal messages. By contrast, communication in high-context cultures depends not only on the message itself but also on the conditions that surround it, including nonverbal cues, past and present experiences, and personal relationships between the parties.

7.2 In the context of the communication process, what is noise?

Noise interferes with the transmission of messages and feedback. Noise can result from physical factors such as poor reception of a cell phone message or differences in people's attitudes and perceptions.

8 Compare the different types of communication.

People exchange messages in many ways: oral and written, formal and informal, verbal and nonverbal communication. Effective written communication reflects its audience, its channel, and the appropriate degree of formality. Formal communication channels carry messages within the chain of command. Informal communication channels, such as the grapevine, carry messages outside the formal chain of command.

Nonverbal communication plays a larger role than most people realize. Generally, when verbal and nonverbal cues conflict, the receiver of a message tends to believe the meaning conveyed by nonverbal elements.

Assessment Check Answers

8.1 What are four common listening behaviors? Characterize each.

Cynical listening occurs when the receiver of a message feels that the sender is trying to gain some advantage from the communication. Offensive listening occurs when the receiver tries to catch the speaker in a mistake or contradiction. Polite listening occurs when the receiver acts politely but, rather than listening, is rehearsing what he or she wants to say when the speaker finishes. Active listening requires involvement with the information and empathy with the speaker's situation.

8.2 What are some advantages of e-mail as a communication medium? What are some disadvantages?

E-mail can be a very effective communication channel, especially for delivering straightforward messages and information. But too much e-mail and poor security, meaning that it's easy for people who weren't intended to read a particular e-mail to do so, are some of its disadvantages.

8.3 What are the differences between formal and informal communication?

Formal communication occurs within the formal chain of command defined by an organization, whereas informal communication occurs outside the organization's hierarchy.

8.4 Why do we pay more attention to nonverbal communication cues than to verbal communication cues?

Nonverbal cues can reveal what senders are really thinking or feeling, particularly when nonverbal cues don't match verbal communication.

9 Explain external communication and how to manage a public crisis.

External communication is a meaningful exchange of information through messages transmitted between an organization and its major audiences, such as customers, suppliers, other firms, the general public, and government officials. Every communication with customers should create goodwill and contribute to customer satisfaction. However, all of this is threatened when companies experience a public crisis that threatens their reputations or goodwill. To manage a public crisis, businesses should respond quickly when a crisis occurs with a prepared statement; quickly put top company management in front of the press; answer reporters' questions with facts; offer to find out answers; never say, "No comment"; identify and speak to their audience by using visual or word images instead of facts; and acknowledge problems and explain solutions.

Business Terms You Need to Know

empowerment 320
team 323
work team 323
problem-solving team 324
self-managed team 324
cross-functional team 324

virtual team 324
team level 326
team diversity 326
team cohesiveness 327
team norm 328
conflict 328

communication 329
listening 332
grapevine 334
external communication 336

Other Important Business Terms

employee stock ownership plan (ESOP) 322
stock options 322
cognitive conflict 328
affective conflict 328

low-context culture 330
high-context culture 330
formal communication channel 334

informal communication channel 334
nonverbal communication 334

Review Questions

1. Describe the ways employers can empower their employees. Give a specific example of each.
2. Identify and briefly explain the approaches companies use to provide for worker ownership. What are the main differences between them?
3. How does each of the five team types function? In what instances might a company use each type?
4. How do team level and team diversity affect team performance?
5. What are the characteristics of an effective team? Why are these features so significant?
6. Identify and briefly describe the five stages of team development. At what stages might a team get "stuck" and not be able to move forward?
7. How does affective conflict hinder group effectiveness?
8. What are the major elements in the communication process? Briefly define each element.
9. Outline the two channels for formal communication. Give an example of each.
10. What is the central focus of a company's external communication?

1. Consider your current job or one you have held in the past. Did your employer practice any kind of employee empowerment? If so, what? If not, why not? Or think of your family as a company. Did your parents empower their children? If so, in what ways? In either scenario, what do you think were the consequences of empowerment or nonempowerment?

2. Identify a firm that makes extensive use of teams. Then interview someone from the firm to assess how their teams operate.

3. Do you consider yourself a good listener? First, identify which listening style you think you practice. Then describe the listening styles outlined in this chapter to a friend, family member, or classmate and ask that person what type of listening style he or she thinks you practice. Finally, compare the two responses. Do they agree or dis-

agree? *Note:* You can take this exercise a step further by asking more than one person what type of listening style you practice and then comparing all of the responses.

4. The grapevine is one of the strongest communication links in any organization, from large corporation to college classroom to family. Do you rely on information that travels along the grapevine? Why or why not?

5. Take a seat in the library or dorm lounge, in a mall, in a restaurant, or wherever there is a flow of people whom you can watch unobtrusively. For at least fifteen minutes, observe and jot down the nonverbal cues that you see pass between people. Then try to interpret these cues. How would your interpretation affect any actual communication you might have with one of these people?

Case 10.1

Communicating and Listening at Cabela's

Cabela's, a premier outdoors and sporting-goods supplier founded in 1961, has transformed itself over the last few years from a catalog retailer to a string of a dozen gigantic "destination" stores. And more are on the way. It's not unusual for shoppers to spend two to three hours browsing, testing products, asking questions, and shopping. The stores each hold tens of thousands of products for enthusiasts of fishing, hunting, hiking, and camping. And they feature attractions like gun libraries, shooting galleries, indoor archery ranges, three-dimensional scenes of the African plains, ice-fishing seminars, and exotic sandwiches filled with wild boar, ostrich, bison, and elk meat. Cabela's newest outlet, in Austin, Texas, spans 185,000 square feet on 126 acres and has more stuffed and mounted animals on display than it has employees—571 versus 517.

"People will drive 200 to 300 miles to visit a Cabela's store," says a commercial real estate broker. "It's crazy. But they will."

Unique product offerings, unbeatable entertainment value, and competitive prices have helped the chain grow rapidly in the tough brick-and-mortar world of retail. In a recent year, Cabela's shipped more than 8 million orders through its catalog operation, for sales of more than $970 million, and logged nearly $500 million in revenues from its stores. But with that growth have come new needs: an urgent need for temporary workers to handle the phones at Cabela's five call centers and for salespeople to work in the stores. In one recent busy period, from the fall hunting season through the winter holidays, the number of phone agents doubled to 4,000, and the opening of each new store—six more are in the works—requires the addition of about 500 employees.

"Taking all those people onto staff has become more of a challenge as we've continued to grow," says the company's CFO. "It is hard to manage the people, and it is expensive to continue to retrain them."

How does Cabela's solve the problem of communicating information about its thousands of products to its new recruits? How does it do that successfully enough not only to satisfy its demanding customers but also to avoid costly rehiring and retraining efforts?

One major strategy is Cabela's reliance on a huge and innovative knowledge-sharing system it calls "Item Notes," which puts at their fingertips the product information in-store and call-center employees need to quickly and efficiently answer customers' questions. Do you need to know what to bring on your first hunting trip? Are you worried about whether a camouflage seat cover will fit on your golf cart? Any employee at Cabela's can tell you.

The database of Item Notes has been built up from the experiences of the store's dedicated employees, most of whom are outdoor enthusiasts themselves and who borrow, take home and test, and then report on many of its products. The loans are free, of course, but there is a catch—after returning the item, employees are required to report on its features and benefits, both pros and cons, and explain what they've learned about it to other employees or to customers. The information base grows as other employees learn about the products, even including notes about possible typos in the product's instructions, tips on its use, or unexpected quirks or bugs in its operation. Because there is no rigid format for the information, anything and everything of importance can be included in the database, such as customer feedback.

Select, trusted customers who are outdoor guides or fish and wildlife biologists are also tapped for their contributions to the Item Notes database. They borrow products just as the salespeople do and return them with similar feedback and reports. Customer comments are fed in, whether they come by phone or e-mail, and these reports are also sent to the responsible departments for resolution, if any is needed. Jim Cabela, founder and vice chairman of the firm, reads every e-mail message.

Questions for Critical Thinking

1. Why is it important for Cabela's to collect the kind of information stored in its Item Notes? If the store didn't have this database, what other sources of product information could it tap? Would they be inferior to Item Notes, and if so, why?

2. What are some possible sources of "noise" in a communication system like the Item Notes database? How can they be overcome?

Sources: Michael A. Prospero, "Leading Listener: Cabela's," *Fast Company,* Anthony Lonetree, "Cabela's Makes Rogers a Destination," *Minneapolis–St. Paul Star-Tribune,* accessed July 3, 2006, http://www.startribune.com; Chris Serres, "Big Store for the Big Outdoors," *Minneapolis–St. Paul Star-Tribune,* accessed July 3, 2006, http://www.startribune.com; J. Bonasia, "Managing for Success," *Investor's Business Daily,* accessed July 3, 2006, http://www.investors.com; Patrick Beach, "Cabela's Fans Finally Get to See the Great Indoors," *Austin American-Statesman,* accessed July 3, 2006, http://www.statesman.com.

VIDEO Case 10.2

Meet the People of BP

This video case appears on page 618. A recently filmed video, designed to expand and highlight the written case, is available for class use by instructors.

Chapter 11

Production and Operations Management

CHRIS ZUPPA/EPA/LANDOV

Regardless of where you live, you'll remember the names—Katrina and Rita. They were two of the largest and most devastating hurricanes to ever hit U.S. shores. Lives, homes, and businesses were lost in their floods and high winds.

Offshore in the Gulf of Mexico, the storms pounded oil and natural-gas drilling rigs and platforms, destroying or severely damaging more than 100 of them. Chevron's giant Typhoon platform actually capsized and drifted 70 miles. Two of Global Santa Fe's drilling rigs were found lying in shallow coastal waters, about 80 miles from their original location. About 99 percent of the gulf's daily oil production and 80 percent of its natural-gas production were knocked out during a time when demand was already extremely high. "The impact on the rigs is something that's never been seen by this country before," said

Hurricanes and the U.S. Fuel Industry

Daniel Naatz, director of federal resources for the Independent Petroleum Association of America. On land, damaged refineries lost production of about 1.7 million barrels a day of refined products.

Within days, it became apparent that a lack of workers, helicopters, and equipment would deter efforts to evaluate the damage to oil and natural-gas facilities offshore in the gulf, and a timeline for restarting production was nonexistent. "A lot of dock facilities that boats would leave from are gone. [Air transportation] hangars are messed up. Helicopter availability is tight," said Tony Lentini, a spokesperson for oil exploration company Apache. The longer it took to assess the situation, make repairs, and begin producing again, the higher the prices would rise. "Will it be more difficult to drill? Yes.

Will it be more expensive? Yes. Will the end product cost more? You bet," warned Al Reese Jr., CFO of ATP Oil &

Gas. In addition to lack of workers and equipment, widespread power outages made start-up of the refineries along the coast impossible.

The federal government predicted that average heating-oil and natural-gas bills could climb 50 percent higher than they had the year before. "We think consumers need to know this now so they can take steps to do something about it," noted David Garman, undersecretary of energy. Meanwhile, some experts observed that worldwide demand for oil has grown faster than supply in recent years, thanks in part to developing economies such as China's and consumers' devotion to large cars and trucks. With one-third of the nation's refining capacity located in the Gulf Coast region, all sights are set on finding every drop of liquid gold in the gulf.[1]

ations management can lower a firm's costs of production, boost the quality of its goods and services, allow it to respond dependably to customer demands, and enable it to renew itself by providing new products. Let's look at the differences between mass, flexible, and customer-driven production.

(1912–2002)
American writer and public official

By producing and marketing desired goods and services, businesses satisfy their commitment to society as a whole. They create what economists call *utility*—the

such as fishing, lumber, and mining engage in production, and so do service providers. Services are intangible outputs of production systems. They include outputs as

The Second City

The Second City Theater Continuing Case
Management: Empowering People to Achieve Business Objectives

The most important asset of The Second City is its talent. Well known as the creative launch pad for comedy greats such as John Belushi, Bill Murray, and Mike Myers, the success of The Second City continues to depend on the quality of its performers. Second City managers are adept at finding and cultivating comedians, then producing and presenting that special brand of comedy, which continues to attract and please the paying audience.

In front of the Chicago Second City entrance is a chronological list of names, those of every performer who has opened a new revue on one of Second City's stages. This nondescript list is the first step in Second City's customer-oriented layout. Inside the Second City building, a visitor can see how these names came to life on stage and screen. Large black-and-white pictures capture famous Second City comedians in the costumes and characters that made them famous and the Second City tradition uniquely identifiable. The spirit of creation and off-the-cuff humor are part of the atmosphere in this building. Ascending the spiral staircase, patrons are met with pictures of today's Second City Main Stage cast, the newest generation of comedy mavericks. Once inside the theater, audience members witness a newly created Second City revue

that speeds through both engaging sketch comedy and biting cultural and political satire. The experience is full of energy and based on an intimate relationship between ensemble and audience. Finally, a night at the Second City ends where its tradition began—with a thirty-minute set of completely improvised comedy based on audience suggestions and the momentum of their laughter. The experience has a similar impact at the four other Second City theaters.

The Second City became famous in 1959 with its first cast of characters, called The Compass Players, and has since been able to garner impressive reviews and profitable returns on a regular basis. The Second City comprises a growing comedy dynasty that includes three stages in Chicago, along with stages in Toronto, Las Vegas, Denver, and Detroit. It also has numerous touring companies performing around the world and multiple shows being produced on cruise lines or specifically created for various businesses. In total they have nearly one hundred performers representing the best in comedy. So how does The Second City control the quality of all of its productions? CEO Andrew Alexander, who has produced more than 200 Second City revues since joining the company in 1974, says that SC "looks for individuals that are

intelligent, have a point of a view, and the potential to become a good actor. And a comedic sensibility doesn't hurt." This general welcoming of talent has brought hundreds of performers of all ages to Second City's door. Creating a diverse cast of eight people who can function as a creative team six nights a week, however, calls for a certain kind of vision. This vision and this approach originated with the Compass Players themselves. "SC was founded . . . with the goal to use improvisational techniques developed in the late 1930's by Viola Spolin to create satirical revues for commercial audiences," says Alexander. The Second City ensemble uses improvisational techniques such as risk taking, acceptance, and communication to create comedic material and form a cohesive foundation for the team. Similarly, Second City fosters a relationship with its audience such that new material can be tried out on a nightly basis. Hot topics and sensitive issues are broached by the fearless Second City cast, a collection of scenes, songs, characters, and improvisations that unite the ensemble's creative endeavors under the heading of a new revue. The most successful works are archived for further study and entertainment.

According to Kelly Leonard, vice president of Second City, the corporation's top management continues to advance with the culture of improvisational comedy in mind. "Second City's culture is built upon improvisation. We 'Yes, and . . .' to ideas, we are always creating. We trade ideas, build upon what makes us laugh or think." The concept of affirming an idea ("Yes"), and building on it ("and") has developed a strong cultural infrastructure for the organization. "In the Second City," says Leonard, "authority and the norm are to be disturbed—creativity and originality are to be celebrated."

The Second City actively devotes itself to a variety of endeavors and functions as a markedly departmentalized corporation. The company's initiatives are separated geographically, functionally, and in relation to its customers. It has stages in two countries and touring companies around the world. They function with The Second City Business Company, operating specifically for the corporate community; in regard to its customers, The Second City gains a significant revenue from its box office and its Training Center. External communication, which is usually related to the specific department undertaking, is overseen by management staff working with performers/teachers to build an appropriate business relationship with the client.

The Second City communicates internally through a large e-mail list created for anyone who chooses to be a "Second Citizen" while on the SC website. This list informs patrons and students about news, show openings, reviews, special events, and other interesting happenings in the Second City community. This is the most formal way that management disseminates information to others involved with the theater. With a high number of aspiring actors filling in the Second City environment, an active grapevine enriches the culture with news of upcoming shows and staff openings for performers . . . or cocktail waitresses.

The Second City functions primarily as a comedy club, and most of the employees who staff its bar, box office, and theater house are current or former students of the Training Center. While resident performers are granted Equity Actor Benefits, these lower-level employees are granted flexible, part-time schedules to accommodate their thespian lifestyles and the motivating knowledge that alumni such as Tina Fey, Chris Farley, and Stephen Colbert have all trained at the same institution. A variety of class levels all focus on team-building skills, active listening, and the quick, confident reactions necessary for the Second City brand

of comedy. Exposing its students to the true method of the Second City, the Training Center offers plenty of performance opportunities. Graduates of the Second City Training Program are produced in their own SC style revue, complete with a seasoned Second City director empowering them to use every skill at their disposal.

As new generations of Second City fans come up to the second floor of the concrete building on North Avenue and Wells Street in Chicago, Second City visionaries will cling to its black-and-white photos as the core symbols of success. Meanwhile, the next wave of Second City talent and the newest faces in comedy could be the employees tearing your ticket and serving your beverage.

QUESTIONS

1. How does Second City's management differ from that of a traditional company?
2. How would you summarize the culture of Second City?
3. Why is it important for Second City to maintain its caliber of comedy? How does it do so?
4. How does ensemble play a role in the managerial techniques of Second City?

person make and how do those decisions affect his or her organization?

3. Pick a supervisory management position from the descriptions provided here that interests you. Research the career field. What skills do you possess that would make you a good candidate for a management position in that field? What work and other experience do you need to help you get started? Create a list of both your strengths and weaknesses and formulate a plan to add to your strengths.

Marketing Management

Part 4

STOCKBYTE

Chapter 12

Customer-Driven Marketing

DIGITAL VISION/GETTY IMAGES

The words *natural food* used to conjure up images of bins filled with sprouts, tofu, and cardboard-dry wheat bread. People who actually knew what to do with dried beans purchased in bulk shopped at these markets. Not anymore. Whole Foods Market, which was founded in Austin, Texas, in 1978 by John Mackey and his girlfriend, admittedly had its share of sandal-clad customers driving VW buses. Today, Whole Foods's 168 stores welcome well-heeled customers, along with their Lexuses and Range Rovers, to its parking lots. Whole Foods has figured out what consumers want and how to offer it. "Americans love to eat. And Americans love to shop," says CEO John Mackey. "But we don't like to shop for food. . . . Whole Foods thinks shopping should be fun.

AP PHOTO/HARRY CABLUCK

Whole Foods Market: A Whole New Kind of Grocery Store

With this store, we're pioneering a new lifestyle that synthesizes health and pleasure. We don't see a contradiction."

The Whole Foods experience is better than any spa or theme park. Consumers can stroll along aisles of heirloom tomatoes, wander past the lobster and crab tanks, dip a fresh strawberry into a flowing chocolate fountain, sample any of 350 varieties of cheese, or order a salad while they sip a glass of Chardonnay. They can pick up dinner to go—sushi, goat cheese lasagna, or Indian *aloo mattar*. They can rest assured that it's all offered to promote their good health; Whole Foods specializes in organic foods, those produced without unwanted extras such as pesticides and hormones. Chickens raised for Whole Foods, the firm promises, have never ingested antibiotics or growth hormones. The pasta comes from an Italian farmer who grows acres of organic durum wheat to produce his Montebello brand. Fish is caught fresh every day.

Whole Foods also caters to local and ethnic taste preferences. When the manager of the Whole Foods store in Santa Monica, California, learned that some of his Buddhist customers were unable to eat foods containing onion or garlic, he began posting "No Onion, No Garlic" signs above prepared dishes that did not contain these ingredients. In Glendale, California, customers of

Iranian descent can purchase their pilaf staple by the pound, while Asian customers can pick up gai choy and chicken feet. Hispanic customers have a wide choice of tamale fixings at the same store. Manager Dave Aebersold appreciates the freedom he has to offer selections specific to his customer base. "I'm empowered to run this like it's my own store," he says.

Not surprisingly, all of these delicacies come at a price. A pound of brie that sells for $3.99 at a regular supermarket will cost you $6.23 at Whole Foods, and a half gallon of orange juice that goes for $1.99 elsewhere will set you back $2.69. If you really want to splurge, you can pick up a pound of French aged goat cheese for $25 or a bottle of Villa Manodori balsamic vinegar for $27. That strawberry you dip in the chocolate fountain will cost you $1.59—as much as a pint of strawberries at another store. While some might argue that high prices could drive consumers away, Mackey claims that the quality of his goods attracts shoppers. "If Americans want to eat higher quality, they can pay for it," he remarks. Whole Foods customers are loyal, even if it costs them a little more. "Business is simple," Mackey explains. "Management's job is to take care of employees. The employees' job is to take care of the customers. Happy customers take care of the shareholders. It's a virtuous circle."[1]

Business success in the 21st century is directly tied to a company's ability to identify and serve its target markets. In fact, all organizations—profit-oriented and not-for-profit, manufacturing and retailing—*must* serve customer needs to succeed, just as Whole Foods Market does by providing a wide array of healthful foods tailored to its customers. Marketing is the link between the organization and the people who buy and use its goods and services. It is the way organizations determine buyer needs and inform potential customers that their firms can meet those needs by supplying a quality product at a reasonable price. And it is the path to developing loyal, long-term customers.

Although consumers who purchase goods for their own use and enjoyment or business purchasers seeking products to use in their firm's operation may seem to be huge, undifferentiated masses, marketers see distinct wants and needs for each group. To understand buyers, from huge manufacturers to Web surfers to shoppers in the grocery aisles, companies gather mountains of data on every aspect of consumer lifestyles and buying behaviors. Marketers use the data to understand the needs and wants of both final customers and business buyers so that they can better satisfy them. Satisfying customers goes a long way toward building relationships with them. It's not always easy. To establish links with the buying public, Whole Foods CEO John Mackey invites e-mails from consumers who may—or may not—be customers. After several weeks of electronic debate with an animal welfare activist over Whole Foods's practice of selling duck meat from a particular source, Mackey asked the activist to help rewrite his firm's policies on farm animal treatment. "It made me fall out of my chair," recalls activist Lauren Ornelas. "Now we're working together."[2] This relationship, which developed through direct communication between the CEO and a consumer, has helped Whole Foods cement its relationship with customers who are vegetarian or have other food-source concerns.

This chapter begins with an examination of the marketing concept and the way businesspeople develop a marketing strategy. We then turn to marketing research techniques, leading to an explanation of how businesses apply data to market segmentation and understanding customer behavior. The chapter closes with a detailed look at the important role played by customer relationships in today's highly competitive business world.

WHAT IS MARKETING?

Every organization—from profit-seeking firms such as Costco and Johnson & Johnson to such not-for-profits as the United Way and the M. D. Anderson Cancer Center—must serve customer needs to succeed. Perhaps retail pioneer J. C. Penney best expressed this priority when he told his store managers, "Either you or your replacement will greet the customer within the first 60 seconds."

marketing organizational function and set of processes for creating, communicating, and delivering value to customers and for managing customer relationships in ways that benefit the organization and its stakeholders.

According to the American Marketing Association, **marketing** is "an organizational function and a set of processes for creating, communicating, and delivering value to customers and for managing customer relationships in ways that benefit the organization and its stakeholders."[3] In addition to selling goods and services, marketing techniques help people advocate ideas or viewpoints and educate others. The American Diabetes Association mails out questionnaires that ask, "Are you at risk for diabetes?" The documents help educate the general public about this widespread disease by listing its risk factors and common symptoms and describing the work of the association.

Department store founder Marshall Field explained marketing quite clearly when he advised one employee to "give the lady what she wants." The phrase became the company motto, and it remains a business truism today. The best marketers not only give consumers what they want but even anticipate consumers' needs before those needs surface. Ideally, they can get a jump on the competition by creating a link in consumers' minds between the new need and the fulfillment of that need by the marketers' products. Principal Financial Group markets employee retirement plans to other firms as a strategy for retaining the best employees. NetJets offers fractional jet ownership to executives who want the luxury and flexibility of private ownership at a reduced cost. Samsung offers its next generation of high-definition TV with its trademarked Cinema Smooth Light Engine. "Stop watching TV," says its latest promotion. "Start living it."

As these examples illustrate, marketing is more than just selling. It is a process that begins with discovering unmet customer needs and continues with researching the potential market; producing a good or service capable of satisfying the targeted customers; and promoting, pricing, and distributing that good or service. Throughout the entire marketing process, a successful organization focuses on building customer relationships.

When two or more parties benefit from trading things of value, they have entered into an **exchange process.** When you purchase a cup of coffee, the other party may be a convenience store clerk, a vending machine, or a Starbucks barista. The exchange seems simple—some money changes hands, and you receive your cup of coffee. But the exchange process is more complex than that. It could not occur if you didn't feel the need for a cup of coffee or if the convenience store or vending machine were not available. You wouldn't choose Starbucks unless you were aware of the brand. Because of marketing, your desire for a latte, cappuccino, or plain black coffee is identified, and the coffee manufacturer's business is successful.

Icy cool breath. Now poppin' up everywhere.

Winterfresh

NEW pop 'em out pieces

COURTESY OF WM. WRIGLEY JR. COMPANY

Wrigley's facilitates the exchange process by offering its Winterfresh gum at many outlets, including convenience stores and grocery stores. The bubble packaging keeps each piece fresh until you're ready to share with your friends.

exchange process activity in which two or more parties give something of value to each other to satisfy perceived needs.

How Marketing Creates Utility

Marketing affects many aspects of an organization and its dealings with customers. The ability of a good or service to satisfy the wants and needs of customers is called **utility.** A company's production function creates *form utility* by converting raw materials, component parts, and other inputs into finished goods and services. But the marketing function creates time, place, and ownership utility. **Time utility** is created by making a good or service available when customers want to purchase it. **Place utility** is created by making a product available in a location convenient for customers. **Ownership utility** refers to an orderly transfer of goods and services from the seller to the buyer. Firms may be able to create all three forms of utility. Putting a new spin on the traditional drive-through restaurant, firms such as Applebee's, Outback Steakhouse, and Ruby Tuesday have begun offering curbside service. Customers phone in their orders and then drive to designated spots in the restaurants' parking lots, where employees deliver the food. The service creates time utility by making the food available when customers want to purchase it, place utility by offering a convenient location, and ownership utility by providing the food that customers desire. Industry experts report that this is the fastest-growing trend in casual dining. "It may have started out as a convenience, but it's becoming a complete necessity," says a president of a restaurant consulting firm.[4]

utility want-satisfying power of a good or service.

assessment check

1. What is utility?
2. Identify ways in which marketing creates utility.

EVOLUTION OF THE MARKETING CONCEPT

Marketing has always been a part of business, from the earliest village traders to large 21st-century organizations producing and selling complex goods and services. Over time, however, marketing activities evolved through the four eras shown in Figure 12.1: the production, sales, and marketing eras, and now the relationship era. Note that these eras parallel some of the business eras discussed in Chapter 1.

For centuries, organizations of the *production era* stressed efficiency in producing quality products. Their philosophy could be summed up by the remark, "A good product will sell itself." Although this production orientation continued into the 20th century, it gradually gave way to the *sales era,* in which businesses assumed that consumers would buy as a result of energetic sales efforts. Organizations didn't fully recognize the importance of their customers until the *marketing era* of the 1950s, when they began to adopt a consumer orientation. This focus has intensified in recent years, leading to the emergence of the *relationship era* in the 1990s, which continues to this day. In the relationship era, companies emphasize customer satisfaction and building long-term relationships with customers.

Emergence of the Marketing Concept

marketing concept
company-wide consumer orientation to promote long-run uccess.

The term **marketing concept** refers to a company-wide customer orientation with the objective of achieving long-run success. The basic idea of the marketing concept is that marketplace success begins with the customer. A firm should analyze each customer's needs and then work backward to offer products that fulfill them. The emergence of the marketing concept can be explained best by the shift from a *seller's market,* one with a shortage of goods and services, to a *buyer's market,* one with an abundance of goods and services. During the 1950s, the United States became a strong buyer's market, forcing companies to satisfy customers rather than just producing and selling goods and services. Today, much competition among firms centers on the effort to satisfy customers. Recently, Apple Computer opened an iTunes store in Japan, which has long been considered Sony's domain. But the iPod has already been a hit in

Figure

12.1 Four Eras in the History of Marketing

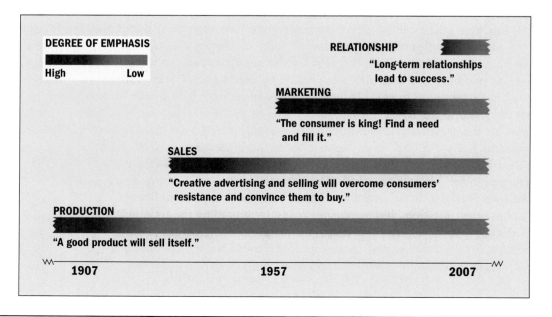

DEGREE OF EMPHASIS

High   Low

RELATIONSHIP
"Long-term relationships lead to success."

MARKETING
"The consumer is king! Find a need and fill it."

SALES
"Creative advertising and selling will overcome consumers' resistance and convince them to buy."

PRODUCTION
"A good product will sell itself."

1907   1957   2007

Japan, despite Sony's alternative MP3 offerings. Apple marketers see the move as a way to reach and satisfy the Japanese market. "We think this is going to change the experience of discovering and buying and enjoying music in Japan," predicts CEO Steve Jobs. "Together with the iPod, we think we are ushering in a new age of digital music."[5]

Delivering Added Value through Customer Satisfaction and Quality

What is the most important sale for a company? Some assume that it's the first, but many marketers argue that the second sale is the most important, because repeat purchases are concrete evidence of **customer satisfaction.** The concept of a good or service pleasing buyers because it has met or exceeded their expectations is crucial to an organization's continued operation. A company that fails to match the customer satisfaction that its competitors provide will not stay in business very long. In contrast, increasing customer loyalty by just 5 percent translates into significant increases in lifetime profits per customer.[6]

The best way to keep a customer is to offer more than just products. Customers today want value, their perception that the quality of goods or services is in balance with the prices charged. When a company exceeds value expectations by adding features, lowering its price, enhancing customer service, or making other improvements that increase customer satisfaction, it provides a **value-added** good or service. As long as customers believe they have received value—good quality for a fair price—they are likely to remain satisfied with the company and continue their relationships. Cereality, the firm described in the "Hit & Miss" feature, offers value to its customers. Providing superior customer service can generate long-term success. FedEx, United Parcel Service, Hewlett-Packard, Nordstrom, and Target are all firms noted for superior customer service. Singapore Airlines is another such firm. Despite service cutbacks in other airlines, Singapore Airlines continues to provide top-notch service to its travelers, winning frequent international awards for doing so. The firm achieves this level of service by sticking to a clear mission and values; requiring continuous training of its employees; and maintaining constant communication with customers.[7]

Quality—the degree of excellence or superiority of an organization's goods and services—is another way firms enhance customer satisfaction. In an intensely competitive industry, Singapore Airlines constantly seeks methods to serve customers better and "get ahead of the pack." The company not only observes its direct competitors but also watches for ways in which hotels, banks, and restaurants improve service and adapts them to its own business.[8]

While a reputation for high quality enhances a firm's competitiveness, a slip in quality can damage a firm's image. Firms such as Ford, Firestone, and even McDonald's have suffered from quality slips and have worked hard to rebuild their reputations. Hyundai used to be viewed by the auto industry—and consumers—as producing a lower-quality vehicle than its competitors did. Now the firm advertises its high quality as well as "America's Best Warranty."

Although quality relates to physical product traits, such as durability and reliability, it also includes customer service. For a firm to be truly successful at providing customer service, the focus must come from the top.

Customer Satisfaction and Feedback

One of the best ways to find out whether customers are satisfied with the goods and services provided by a company is to obtain *customer feedback* through toll-free telephone hotlines, customer satisfaction surveys, Web site message boards, or written correspondence. Some firms find out how well they have satisfied their customers by calling them or making personal visits to their businesses or residences.

customer satisfaction ability of a good or service to meet or exceed a buyer's needs and expectations.

"They Said It"

"In every instance, we found that the best-run companies stay as close to their customers as humanly possible."
—Thomas J. Peters (b. 1942) Coauthor, In Search of Excellence

HIT & MISS

One Company Makes a Cereal Killing

David Roth noticed something about U.S. consumers—they eat a lot of cereal. But they don't just eat it for breakfast; they seem to like it for lunch and dinner, and even snacks in between. "They were eating it everywhere, at different times of day," he recalls of his initial observation. Roth and his friend, designer Rick Bacher, knew they were on to something. Backed by marketing research that told them 95 percent of U.S. consumers like cereal, they decided to figure out a way to make this favorite food available in unusual places.

Roth and Bacher first targeted college students because "they basically live on cereal," says Roth. The two entrepreneurs set up a kiosk at Arizona State University's food court, where students could dish up their favorites—in any combination they wanted. The kiosk was a hit, and Cereality quickly expanded to Philadelphia, Chicago, and other locations near universities.

Here's how a Cereality bar and café works. Customers select from among 30 different types of brand-name cereal and 30 toppings—yes, toppings, including bananas and marshmallows. They can mix and match their Corn Pops and Captain Crunch, then choose what kind of milk they want, such as skim or soy. They can even have Quaker hot cereals made to order. All the cereals are served in individual fold-over boxes by servers wearing pajamas. The boxes even come with long straws to reach milk at the bottom. "You never have a bad bowl of cereal, because you create it," explains Nelson Diaz, a Cereality café manager. In some of the larger cafés, customers can even lounge on couches and use free Internet connections. The experience also fits a college budget—for about $3, a cereal-hungry student can get a meal.

Cereality customers are loyal. The only downside, they say, is that some of the cafés aren't open late enough—when students are pulling all-nighters. "This would be a great study break," says one senior. "It would be smart for them to be open later."

Roth and Bacher are listening. They are also thinking big. Their next targets will be airports, hospitals, and train stations. Roth looks at cereal this way: "[It is] the great equalizer. It crosses all demographics, all races, all ages. People see it as a happy thing."

Questions for Critical Thinking

1. In what ways does Cereality deliver customer satisfaction? How might it improve?
2. Describe two ways in which Cereality could obtain customer feedback.

Sources: April Y. Pennington, "Breakfast of Champions," *Entrepreneur,* accessed July 12, 2006, http://www.entrepreneur.com; "The Loop Gets Ready for Froot Loops Plus 29 Other Cereals," PR Newswire, February 22, 2005, http://biz.yahoo.com; Craig Wilson, "A Whole New Bowl Game," *USA Today,* December 8, 2004, http://www.usatoday.com.

---

assessment check

1. What is the marketing concept?
2. How does customer satisfaction result in a value-added good or service?

Customer complaints are excellent sources of customer feedback, because they present companies with an opportunity to overcome problems and improve their services. Customers often feel greater loyalty after a conflict has been resolved than if they had never complained at all. Complaints can also allow firms to gather innovative ideas for improvement.

EXPANDING MARKETING'S TRADITIONAL BOUNDARIES

The marketing concept has traditionally been associated with products of profit-seeking organizations. Today, however, it is also being applied to not-for-profit sectors and other nontraditional areas ranging from religious organizations to political campaigns.

Not-for-Profit Marketing

Residents of every continent benefit in various ways from the approximately 20 million not-for-profit organizations currently operating around the globe. Some 1.5 million of them are located in the United States, where they employ about 8.6 million workers and benefit from another 7.2 million volunteers. Worldwide, the not-for-profit sector accounts for nearly 5 percent of the gross domestic product.[9] The largest not-for-profit organization in the world is the Red Cross/Red Crescent. Others range from Habitat for Humanity and Save the Children to the National Science Foundation and the World Food Program. These organizations all benefit by applying many of the strategies and business concepts used by profit-seeking firms. They apply marketing tools to reach audiences, secure funding, improve their images, and accomplish their overall missions. Marketing strategies are important for not-for-profit organizations because they are all competing for dollars—from individuals, foundations, and corporations—just as commercial businesses are.

Not-for-profit organizations conduct major marketing campaigns. The Susan G. Komen Breast Cancer Foundation holds races and walks around the country to raise funds for research for a cure.

Not-for-profit organizations operate in both public and private sectors. Public groups include federal, state, and local government units as well as agencies that receive tax funding. A state's department of natural resources, for instance, regulates land conservation and environmental programs; the local animal control officer enforces ordinances protecting people and animals; a city's public health board ensures safe drinking water for its citizens. The private not-for-profit sector comprises many different types of organizations, including California State University–Fullerton's baseball team, the Adirondack Mountain Club, and Portsmouth, New Hampshire–based Cross Roads House for homeless families. Although some private not-for-profits generate surplus revenue, their primary goals are not earning profits. If they earn funds beyond their expenses, they invest the excess in their organizational missions.

In some cases, not-for-profit organizations form a partnership with a profit-seeking company to promote the firm's message or distribute its goods and services. This partnership usually benefits both organizations. Large corporations may form their own not-for-profit charitable organizations. McDonald's is well known for its Ronald McDonald Charities. Designer Ralph Lauren has partnered with the U.S. Tennis Association to market an exclusive line of tennis gear, including tennis balls imprinted with pink polo players on ponies. Sales from the tennis balls help benefit breast cancer research.[10]

In addition, wealthy athletes and other celebrities sometimes form their own not-for-profit organizations to support causes that are personally meaningful to them. Hockey player Mario Lemieux established a foundation that assists hospitals in Pittsburgh and funds neonatal and anticancer research. Tennis star Andre Agassi established an organization to fund an academy for underprivileged children in Las Vegas.[11]

Nontraditional Marketing

Not-for-profit organizations often engage in one or more of five major categories of nontraditional marketing: person marketing, place marketing, event marketing, cause marketing, and organization marketing. Figure 12.2 provides examples of these types of marketing. Through each of these types of marketing, an organization seeks to connect with the audience that is most likely to offer time, money, or other resources. In some cases, the effort may reach the market the organization intends to serve.

12.2 | Categories of Nontraditional Marketing

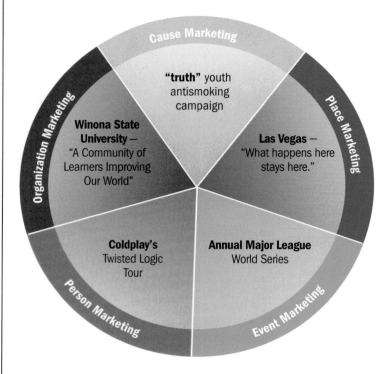

Cause Marketing
"truth" youth antismoking campaign

Organization Marketing
Winona State University —
"A Community of Learners Improving Our World"

Place Marketing
Las Vegas —
"What happens here stays here."

Person Marketing
Coldplay's Twisted Logic Tour

Event Marketing
Annual Major League World Series

THINK THINK THINK THINK THINK THINK THINK THI
FAST FAST FAST FAST FAS T FAST FAST FA

THINK THINK THIN K THIN K THINK THINK TH
FAST F/ ST FAS FAS T FAST FAST FA

THINK THINK THIN INK THINK TH
FAST FAST FAS AST FAST FA

THINK THINK THIN TH THINK THINK TH
FAST FAST FAS AST FAST FA

You probably know that walking is good for your heart. But, here's some news that should really get you moving. New research shows that heart-healthy exercise is also good for your brain.

And it may reduce the risk of Alzheimer's disease. So visit alz.org, and learn more about what you can do to Maintain Your Brain. Thinking ahead now just might make all the difference down the road.

alz.org / 800.272.3900   alzheimer's association

The Alzheimer's Association encourages people to learn more about this crippling and progressive brain disorder. Recent studies show that exercise is good for your brain and may help reduce the risk of Alzheimer's disease, so the association is spreading the word with this promotion.

Person Marketing Efforts designed to attract the attention, interest, and preference of a target market toward a person are called **person marketing.** Campaign managers for a political candidate conduct marketing research, identify groups of voters and financial supporters, and then design advertising campaigns, fund-raising events, and political rallies to reach them. Celebrities such as cyclist Lance Armstrong, who won the *Tour de France* a record seven times, engage in person marketing to expand their audience, attract viewers to events, and enhance their images with the public.

Many successful job seekers apply the tools of person marketing. They research the wants and needs of prospective employers, and they identify ways they can meet them. They seek employers through a variety of channels, sending messages that emphasize how they can benefit the employer.

Place Marketing As the term suggests, **place marketing** attempts to attract people to a particular area, such as a city, state, or nation. It may involve appealing to consumers as a tourist destination or to businesses as a desirable business location. A strategy for place marketing often includes advertising.

Place marketing may be combined with event marketing, such as the Olympics. Beijing, host of the 2008 Summer Olympics, has combined its marketing efforts to attract visitors and businesses to China for more than the athletic events. "For many of China's new brands and leading companies, the Games . . . provide a unique international platform to showcase themselves to the world. For leading global companies, the Games . . . open the gates to the most important market in the world," noted Jacques Rogge, president of the International Olympic Committee.[12]

Event Marketing Marketing or sponsoring short-term events such as athletic competitions and cultural and charitable performances is known as **event marketing.** The No Limits Tour of BMX bike and skateboarding stunts involved event marketing by Skippy peanut butter, *Sports Illustrated Kids,* and Six Flags. Target recently sponsored the first women's junior professional surfing competition.

Event marketing often forges partnerships between not-for-profit and profit-seeking organizations. Many businesses sponsor events such as 10K runs to raise funds for health-related charities. These occasions require a marketing effort to plan the event and attract participants and sponsors. Events may be intended to raise money or awareness, or both.

The United Nations' Food and Agriculture Organization sponsors World Food Day on October 16 each year to raise awareness of worldwide poverty and hunger and to promote sustainable agriculture. More than 150 countries hold national events to observe the day.[13]

Cause Marketing   Marketing that promotes a cause or social issue, such as preventing child abuse, antilittering efforts, and antismoking campaigns, is **cause marketing.** Cause marketing seeks to educate the public and may or may not attempt to directly raise funds. An advertisement often contains a phone number or Web site address through which people can obtain more information.

   Profit-seeking companies look for ways to give back to their communities by joining forces with charities and causes, providing financial, marketing, and human resources. Timberland is well known for its City Year and Bikes for Tikes programs. NBC has underwritten its "The More You Know" public-service announcements for nearly two decades. Celebrities who have participated in the announcements include business mogul Donald Trump and actors Mariska Hargitay and James Caan.

Organization Marketing   The final category of nontraditional marketing, **organization marketing,** influences consumers to accept the goals of, receive the services of, or contribute in some way to an organization. The U.S. Postal Service, the U.S. military, the American Red Cross, and the Tiger Woods Foundation are all examples of organizations that engage in marketing. Organizations such as the American Heart Association and the Disabled American Veterans send out printed return-address labels with donation requests enclosed. These groups hope that consumers will be willing to pay for the customized labels with donations.

assessment check

1. Why do not-for-profit organizations engage in marketing?
2. What are the five types of nontraditional marketing used by not-for-profit organizations?

DEVELOPING A MARKETING STRATEGY

Decision makers in any successful organization, for-profit or not-for-profit, follow a two-step process to develop a *marketing strategy*: First, they study and analyze potential target markets and choose among them. Second, they create a marketing mix to satisfy the chosen market. Figure 12.3 shows the relationship among the target market, the marketing mix variables, and the marketing environment. Later discussions refer back to this figure as they cover each topic. This section describes the development of a marketing strategy.

Target Market and Marketing Mix within the Marketing Environment

Figure

12.3

Chapter 13

Product and Distribution Strategies

AFP/GETTY IMAGES

GETTY IMAGES

Customers can easily determine what makes one toothpaste or detergent better for them. Most of us don't have much trouble choosing a DVD or a new outfit, and we can quickly come up with criteria for choosing a new car. But how does the airline industry decide which jets to buy? Two competitors—Airbus and Boeing—have distinctly different views of what airlines need now and in the future.

Airbus, which is owned by a partnership of French, German, and British companies, and U.S.-based Boeing have been intense rivals for years. While both companies supply planes of all sizes to airlines and freight carriers around the world, their projections for the future of air travel have led them each to create new jets that fill very different needs.

Boeing vs. Airbus: Battle for the Skies

Airbus has invested $13 billion in developing its giant A380, a double-decker superjumbo jet weighing more than 300 tons, with a 262-foot wingspan. The plane is as tall as a seven-story building and carries 555 passengers in three separate cabin classes, about a third more people than one of Boeing's largest planes—the 747—in twice as much space. In fact, the interior of the A380 is roomy enough to include shops, bars, casinos, and nurseries for passengers' use and entertainment.

Airbus thinks that the next 20 years will see air travel become concentrated between big hubs in Asia and other stopover cities, called spokes. The international flights will foster use of jumbo jets for more passenger comfort, and flights will be concentrated among the busiest airports, those that can handle the large number of passengers on each jumbo flight. Some airports, such as Dallas–Fort Worth, are already constructing special hangars and cargo facilities to accommodate the giant craft. The A380 is so large that it can't dock at a regular gate.

The Airbus jet can travel about 5 percent farther than Boeing's longest-range jumbo, a factor projected to reduce operating costs below what buyers of Boeing planes will pay. All these features don't come cheap—the A380 costs $280 million. But before the plane had flown a mile, Air-bus already had orders for 149 units from more than a dozen airline and freight transport customers, most of whom attended the plane's recent grand unveiling in France. That's considered an extraordinary advance sale, and Airbus hopes to move about 600 more planes. Many observers believe the jet heralds a new era in flying, a milestone not surpassed since the dawn of the supersonic Concorde.

Boeing, on the other hand, sees a very different trend in global air travel. Boeing anticipates that airline deregulation will increase competition among airlines, which will opt to entice passengers with more direct flights and invest in smaller, long-range planes to bypass the congested hub-and-spoke cities Airbus hopes to capitalize on. Boeing thinks worldwide demand for planes larger than the 747, like the A380, won't exceed 400 units over the next 20 years. Smaller planes can also be built more quickly than the A380 and will be more fuel-efficient and cheaper for airlines to buy.

As a result, Boeing is producing a new midsize passenger jet it calls the 787 Dreamliner. Boeing already has about 250 advance orders for the 787 and tentative commitments for more than 400 more planes. The new plane is designed to be extremely efficient, using 20 percent less fuel than a traditional airplane of comparable size. With skyrocketing fuel costs, that efficiency could ease airlines' tight budgets. The 787 is also constructed of high-tech composite materials that are lighter than aluminum and stronger than steel. The plane is constructed in large sections through a revolutionary manufacturing process using carbon-fiber reinforced plastics, which are commonly used in military aircraft. These composites can be shaped into huge barrel pieces, avoiding the labor of bolting the typical aluminum plates together. Like the A380, the 787 is expected to be an aviation milestone—if Boeing can succeed in leveraging its revolutionary manufac-

turing process to save the thousands of hours it used to spend stocking and assembling small parts. If it can, then the company will reap billions of dollars in manufacturing savings. That should help Boeing price the 787, which carries 230-some passengers, competitively enough to allow airlines to make money flying it. Boeing is also cutting manufacturing costs by distributing manufacturing operations around the world, making plane parts in Europe and Asia and assembling them in Seattle.

With these two different visions of the aviation future, one question remains: Who will win the battle for the world's airlines?[1]

In this chapter we examine ways in which organizations design and implement marketing strategies that address customers' needs and wants. As the story of Airbus and Boeing illustrates, companies in the same industry can draw very different conclusions about the needs and wants of the same set of customers. Airbus believes commercial airlines will be looking to concentrate passengers in huge planes that fly from hub to hub around the world, and it expects the airlines that buy its A380 to use major airports in Europe and Asia as well as North America. As one industry consultant said, "The economics of the A380 are going to be great as long as you can put a lot of bodies on them. This is not a plane that's going to fly to [smaller airports]."

Boeing, however, with access to the same information about its customers, has drawn very different conclusions about what kind of product they will buy, and it is designing, manufacturing, and pricing its new jet accordingly. Boeing is betting that to serve the needs of their own customers, airlines will want to fly to smaller airports directly, and that requires smaller planes.

The creation of new products, from shampoo to furniture to jumbo jets, is the lifeblood of an organization. Because products do not remain economically viable forever, new ones must be developed to ensure the survival of an organization. If either the 787 Dreamliner or the A380 fails, for instance, airline industry observers predict that their companies will be in serious financial trouble.

This chapter focuses on the first two elements of the marketing mix: product and distribution. Our discussion of product strategy begins by describing the classifications of goods and services, customer service, product lines and the product mix, and the product life cycle. Companies often shape their marketing strategies differently when they are introducing a new product, when the product has established itself in the marketplace, and when it is declining in popularity. We also discuss product identification through brand name and distinctive packaging, and the ways in which companies foster loyalty to their brands to keep customers coming back for more.

Distribution, the second mix variable discussed, focuses on moving goods and services from producer to wholesaler to retailer to buyers. Managing the distribution process includes making decisions such as what kind of wholesaler to use and where to offer products for sale. Retailers can range from specialty stores to factory outlets and everything in between, and they must choose appropriate customer service, pricing, and location strategies in order to succeed. The chapter concludes with a look at logistics, the process of coordinating the flow of information, goods, and services among suppliers and on to final consumers.

PRODUCT STRATEGY

product bundle of physical, service, and symbolic attributes designed to satisfy buyers' wants.

Most people respond to the question "What is a product?" by listing its physical features. By contrast, marketers take a broader view. To them, a **product** is a bundle of physical, service, and symbolic attributes designed to satisfy consumer wants. The chief executive officer of a major tool manufacturer once startled his stockholders with this statement: "Last year our customers bought over 1 million quarter-inch drill bits, and none of them wanted to buy the product. They all wanted quarter-inch holes." Product strategy involves considerably more than just producing a good or service; instead, it focuses on benefits. The marketing conception of a product includes decisions about package design, brand name, trademarks, warranties, product image, new-product development, and customer service. Think, for instance, about your favorite soft drink. Do you like it for its taste alone, or do other attributes, such as clever ads, attractive packaging, ease of purchase from vending machines and other convenient locations, and overall image, also attract you? These other attributes may influence your choice more than you realize.

Classifying Goods and Services

Marketers have found it useful to classify goods and services as either B2C or B2B depending on whether the purchasers of the particular item are consumers or businesses. These classifications can be subdivided further, and each type requires a different competitive strategy.

Classifying Consumer Goods and Services

The classification typically used for ultimate consumers who purchase products for their own use and enjoyment and not for resale is based on consumer buying habits. **Convenience products** are items the consumer seeks to purchase frequently, immediately, and with little effort. Items stocked in 7-Eleven stores, vending machines, and local newsstands are usually convenience products—for example, newspapers, milk, disposable diapers, and bread.

Shopping products are those typically purchased only after the buyer has compared competing products in competing stores. A person intent on buying a new sofa or dining room table may visit many stores, examine perhaps dozens of pieces of furniture, and spend days making the final decision. **Specialty products,** the third category of consumer products, are those that a purchaser is willing to make a special effort to obtain. The purchaser is already familiar with the item and considers it to have no reasonable substitute. The nearest Jaguar dealer may be 75 miles away, but if you have decided you want one—and can afford it—you will make the trip. See the "Solving an Ethical Controversy" feature for a discussion of foie gras, a specialty food product made from goose liver.

Note that a shopping product for one person may be a convenience item for someone else. Each item's product classification is based on buying patterns of the majority of people who purchase it.

The interrelationship of the marketing mix factors is shown in Figure 13.1. By knowing the appropriate classification for a specific product, the marketing decision maker knows much about how the other mix variables will adapt to create a profitable, customer-driven marketing strategy.

Classifying Business Goods

Business products are goods and services such as paycheck services and huge multifunction copying machines used in operating an organization; they

IT'S A GOOD WAY TO FIND THE REDLINE IN YOUR GUT.

THE NEW AMERICAN MOTORCYCLE

The Victory® Vegas." Long, low, stretched style. Custom details. 92 cubic inches of stomach-wrenching American V-twin. Time to discover what's inside. Victory Motorcycles.® A division of Polaris Industries. Visit victorymotorcycles.com

Consumers spend quite a bit of time selecting the perfect motorcycle, so it is a specialty product. But if you've set your mind on a low-slung custom-detailed Victory Vegas cycle, then you'll find the dealer to get one.

COURTESY OF POLARIS INDUSTRIES, INC. PHOTOGRAPHER/MARK LAFAVOR

in Figure 13.1, once a new appliance has been classified as a shopping good, marketers have a better idea of its promotion, pricing, and distribution needs.

industry pioneer

Foie gras is a delicacy usually spread on toast or crackers as a paste, or pâté. In fact, foie gras means "fat liver." It is produced by force-feeding animals, usually geese, in order to artificially fatten their livers to several times their normal size.

Review Questions

1. Classify each of the following business-to-consumer (B2C) and business-to-business (B2B) products:
   a. *Time* or *Newsweek* magazine
   b. six-pack of bottled water
   c. Case forklift truck
   d. Mississippi river barge
   e. lumber
2. What is the relationship between a product line and a product mix?
3. Identify and briefly describe the six stages of new-product development.
4. What are some strategies for extending the product life cycle?
5. What are the three stages of brand loyalty?

6. What are the advantages of direct distribution? When is a producer most likely to use direct distribution?
7. What is the wheel of retailing? How has the Internet affected the wheel of retailing?
8. Identify and briefly describe the four different types of nonstore retailers. Give an example of at least one type of good or service that would be suited to each type of nonstore retailer.
9. What are the three intensity levels of distribution? Give an example of two products for each level.
10. Describe the strengths and weaknesses of each transport mode and explain how companies can improve their competitiveness through effective distribution.

Projects and Teamwork Applications

1. Suggest an appropriate brand name for each of the following goods. Defend your choices.
   a. laundry detergent
   b. sport-utility vehicle
   c. backpack
   d. outdoor boots
   e. fresh-fruit drink
2. As a marketer, review your five-brand list in question 1. What steps you would take to build brand loyalty for three of those products?
3. Which type of distribution intensity would best suit the following products?
   a. Ferrari sports cars
   b. retail shelving units
   c. facial tissue
   d. earth-moving equipment
   e. Altoid flavored mints
4. Think of your favorite store. If it is near where you live or go to school, stop by for a visit. If not, rely on your memory. Describe the store in terms of its atmospherics. What features contribute to your positive experiences and feelings about the store?

5. Suggest the best method for transporting each of the following goods. Explain your choices.
   a. natural gas
   b. oranges and grapefruit
   c. teak furniture from Thailand
   d. redwood lumber from California
   e. industrial machine parts
6. Many products must adhere to a prescribed set of standards. One example is ice hockey equipment. Visit the two Web sites listed and review the basic requirements ice hockey equipment must meet. How do these standards affect manufacturers of ice hockey equipment?
   http://www.usahockey.com
   http://www.iihf.com
7. The International Trademark Association is a worldwide not-for-profit organization of trademark owners and advisors. Visit the association's Web site (http://www.inta.org) and select "Information Center" and then "Learn the Basics." Prepare a brief oral report on the process of selecting and registering a domain name.

Case 13.1

American Eagle Hopes to Soar

American Eagle Outfitters is currently riding a wave of popularity among its teen and young-adult market. With trendy but high-quality clothing in affordable price ranges, the chain of almost 850 stores is a top destination for 15- to 25-year-olds.

American Eagle appeals to teens looking for a casual but preppy look. In price range and style choices, it fills a middle ground in the teen and young adult market.

American Eagle's long-standing partnership with MTV began with the hit show *Road Rules*, for which it provided cast wardrobes. The relationship was recently expanded to include American Eagle's sponsorship of MTV's wildly popular Spring Break promotion, recently held in Cancun. "Spring Break is more than just a vacation for our customers—it is a lifestyle. Memories are made on spring break, and our goal with MTV is to make sure this Spring Break is the best ever and the most memorable," said American Eagle's chief marketing officer of the Cancun bash.

The company is far from taking a vacation, however. After a couple of difficult years when its fickle market shopped elsewhere and sales plunged, American Eagle Outfitters has been beating sales projections in a comeback that brought an increase in sales of nearly 32 percent.

But despite the good news at the mall, with 850 locations management knows the chain is about to run out of room to spread its wings. It is considering expanding the American Eagle brand into Asian mar-

kets and is also expected to soon start testing a new store concept at home for a slightly older market that will provide fresh avenues for continued growth.

Questions for Critical Thinking

1. American Eagle Outfitters has not yet released the name of the new retail clothing chain it plans to test, or any details about the store concept it's considering. What product mix strategies do you think would help ensure the new chain's success? Do you think American Eagle would be wise to try to leverage any brand loyalty among its current customers to win them over to the new stores? Why or why not?

2. Why do retailers in the faddish teen market make their brand names and logos so prominent on many of their T-shirts, polos, jeans, and sweats? Why are customers willing to wear these items? Do you think brand names are the only feature that distinguishes one teen retailer's product line from another's? Why or why not?

Sources: American Eagle Outfitters Web site, accessed July 15, 2006, http://www.ae.com; Teresa F. Lindeman, "'Hot' American Eagle Heats Up Profits, Stock," *Pittsburgh Post-Gazette,* accessed July 15, 2006, http://www.post-gazette.com; Teresa F. Lindeman, "Soaring Eagle Hopes to Avoid Plunging Back to Earth," *Pittsburgh Post-Gazette,* accessed July 15, 2006, http://www.post-gazette.com; "American Eagle Outfitters Makes a Splash at MTV Spring Break," press release, March 3, 2005.

VIDEO Case 13.2

High Sierra Climbs to New Heights

This video case appears on page 622. A recently filmed video, designed to expand and highlight the written case, is available for class use by instructors.

Chapter 14

Promotion and Pricing Strategies

There's nothing cuter than a puppy. But as cuddly and adorable as puppies are, the business of promoting products such as pet food, heartworm medicine, and flea and tick repellent is serious—and highly competitive.

One of the best places to advertise is in veterinary clinics. Pet owners are already a captive audience, and they want to feed and treat their animal companions with the best products. So sales reps for various manufacturers often call on veterinary hospitals to promote their goods. Sometimes they leave free samples; other times they offer discount coupons. Bayer Healthcare, which manufactures K9 Advantix (for dogs) and Advantix (for cats), recently launched a new promotional campaign for its popular flea and tick repellent. The firm introduced three-dimensional promotional cards that sit on counters or tables in 14,000 vets' offices nationwide.

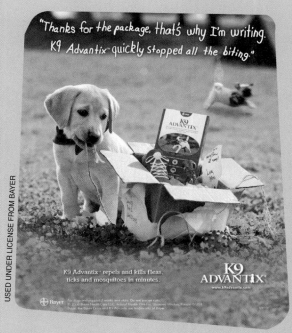

Companies Promoting Pet Products: It's Not Puppy Love

The cards display key images that also appear in Advantix commercials on television. For instance, the card for K9 Advantix shows a puppy asleep in a tent. The tagline reads, "Get rid of fleas, ticks, and mosquitoes and you're left with one happy camper." The cards are easy to ship and simple for veterinary staff to set up. They arrive flat in a box and pop up to create a shadow-box display on the counter. Why put such effort into designing this type of display? "Our number-one goal with this year's program was to have our P-O-P [point-of-purchase] match identically with our visuals," explains marketing manager Drew Mantek. "We wanted to enhance our brand recognition in the clinics, which can be difficult. Even if they don't remember the name of the product, consumers can connect the images from the TV ads to the pieces they see in the clinic."

Pet owners may also watch a K9 Advantix advertising DVD on PetCARE television while they are waiting in the reception area of a vet clinic. PetCARE TV focuses on veterinary healthcare issues and is obtained through a yearly subscription. DVDs like the K9 commercial are shipped to veterinarians monthly.

Sometimes the pet care industry bares its teeth. Recently Meriel, maker of Frontline Plus, which competes directly with Bayer's Advantix, filed a lawsuit against Bayer, alleging unfair competition. The manufacture of flea and tick medicines is part of a multibillion-dollar market—more than $8.5 billion of nonfood pet supplies are sold in one year in the United States. With more than 146 million pets living with U.S. families, the market keeps growing—and every company wants its share. Because pet owners rely heavily on the opinions of their veterinarians, these companies want to create every advantage they can with vets and other animal health professionals. "If a vet tells [an owner] one thing over another, it's the gospel," notes an appointment supervisor for an office of nine vets. The Meriel lawsuit centered on Bayer's use of comparison advertising. As a result, Bayer agreed to withdraw its comparison of Advantix and Frontline in its advertising campaign. But the sleeping puppy remains, and consumers can pick up coupons for free products with another purchase when they read the counter cards at the vet's office. Marketer Drew Mantek says the campaign has been an early success. "The [displays] are appreciated for being appropriately sized for the clinic," he remarks. "And everyone gets a chuckle out of the images."[1]

This chapter focuses on the different types of promotional activities and the way prices are established for goods and services. **Promotion** is the function of informing, persuading, and influencing a purchase decision. This activity is as important to not-for-profit organizations such as the Boys and Girls Clubs and the Huntington's Disease Society of America as it is to profit-seeking companies such as Nationwide Insurance and the Boston Red Sox.

Some promotional strategies try to develop *primary demand,* or consumer desire for a general product category. The objective of such a campaign is to stimulate sales for an entire industry so that individual firms benefit from this market growth. A popular example is the dairy industry's "Got Milk?" campaign. Print and television messages about the nutritional benefits of milk show various celebrities, including Green Bay Packers quarterback Brett Favre and TV host Meredith Vieira. The American Heart Association has also become a part of these ads. Other promotional campaigns aimed at hiking per-capita consumption have been commissioned by the California Strawberry Commission and the National Cattlemen's Beef Association.

Most promotional strategies, in contrast, seek to stimulate *selective demand*—desire for a specific brand. Every driver needs some type of car insurance, and the Geico gecko wants consumers to pick its firm for the best rates.

America's Beef Producers hope to stimulate the overall demand for beef with this advertisement. So it helps increase primary demand.

THERE'S NO SUCH THING AS A CHICKEN KNIFE.

COURTESY OF CATTLEMEN'S BEEF BOARD

promotion the function of informing, persuading, and influencing a purchase decision.

integrated marketing communications (IMC) coordination of all promotional activities—media advertising, direct mail, personal selling, sales promotion, and public relations—to produce a unified customer-focused message.

Sean "P. Diddy" Combs appears in Diet Pepsi commercials, which encourages his fans to choose that brand over competitors. Sales promotions that offer teens a free iTunes song download for trying on a pair of Gap jeans also encourage shoppers to purchase a specific brand.

Marketers choose among many promotional options to communicate with potential customers. Each marketing message a buyer receives—through a television or radio commercial, newspaper or magazine ad, Web site, direct-mail flyer, or sales call—reflects on the product, place, person, cause, or organization promoted in the content. In a process of **integrated marketing communications (IMC)**, marketers coordinate all promotional activities—advertising, sales promotion, personal sales presentations, and public relations—to execute a unified, customer-focused promotional strategy. This coordination is designed to avoid confusing the consumer and to focus positive attention on the promotional message.

This chapter begins by explaining the role of IMC and then discusses the objectives of promotion and the importance of promotional planning. Next, it examines the components of the promotional mix: advertising, sales promotion, personal selling, and public relations. Finally, the chapter addresses pricing strategies for goods and services.

"They Said It"

"Doing business without advertising is like winking at a girl in the dark. You know what you are doing, but nobody else does."

—Steuart Henderson Britt (1907–1979)
American educator

INTEGRATED MARKETING COMMUNICATIONS

An integrated marketing communications strategy focuses on customer needs to create a unified promotional message in the firm's ads, in-store displays, product samples, and presentations by company sales representatives. To gain a competitive advantage, marketers that implement IMC need a broad view of promotion. Media options continue to multiply, and marketers cannot simply rely on traditional broadcast and print media and direct mail. Plans must include all forms of customer contact. Packaging, store displays, sales promotions, sales presentations, and online and interactive media also communicate information about a brand or organization. With IMC, marketers create a unified personality and message for the good, brand, or service they promote. Coordinated activities also enhance the effectiveness of reaching and serving target markets.

Marketing managers set the goals and objectives for the firm's promotional strategy with overall organizational objectives and marketing goals in mind. Based on these objectives, marketers weave the various elements of the strategy—personal selling, advertising, sales promotion, publicity, and public relations—into an integrated communications plan. This document becomes a central part of the firm's total marketing strategy to reach its selected target market. Feedback, including marketing research and sales reports, completes the system by identifying any deviations from the plan and suggesting improvements.

With hundreds of different soft drink brands and flavors lining store shelves around the world, how does Coca-Cola manage to stay on top? When the firm rolled out its new flavored soft drink—Coca-Cola with Lime—it relied on IMC to get the word out to consumers. The company used TV advertising, billboards, and tie-ins to the popular *American Idol* TV show, which has had a long-running partnership with Coke. One of the ads featured an adaptation of the 1971 hit song *Coconut* by Harry Nilsson. The words for the Coke ad sang, "You put the lime in the Coke, you nut." Bottlers also used promotional strategies at the local level—offering free samples at fairs and festivals, sponsoring music or sporting events, and the like.[2]

assessment check

1. What is the objective of an integrated marketing communications program?

2. What types of media are used in integrated marketing communications?

THE PROMOTIONAL MIX

Just as every organization creates a marketing mix combining product, distribution, promotion, and pricing strategies, each also requires a similar mix to blend the many facets of promotion into a cohesive plan. The **promotional mix** consists of two components—personal and nonpersonal selling—that marketers combine to meet the needs of their firm's target customers and effectively and efficiently communicate its message to them. **Personal selling** is the most basic form of promotion: a direct person-to-person promotional presentation to a potential buyer. The buyer-seller communication can occur during a face-to-face meeting or via telephone, videoconference, or interactive computer link.

Nonpersonal selling consists of advertising, sales promotion, direct marketing, and public relations. Advertising is the best-known form of nonpersonal selling, but sales promotion accounts for about half of these marketing expenditures. Spending for sponsorships, which involves marketing messages delivered in association with another activity such as a golf tournament or a benefit concert, is on the rise as well. Marketers need to be careful about the types of promotion they choose or risk alienating the very people they are trying to reach.

Each component in the promotional mix offers its own advantages and disadvantages, as Table 14.1 demonstrates. By selecting the most effective combination of promotional mix elements, a firm may reach its promotional objectives. Spending within the promotional mix varies by industry. Manufacturers of many business-to-business (B2B) products typically spend more on personal selling than on advertising because those products—such as a new telecommunications system—may require a significant investment. Consumer-goods marketers may focus more on advertising and sponsorships. Later sections of this chapter discuss how the parts of the mix contribute to effective promotion.

promotional mix combination of personal and nonpersonal selling techniques designed to achieve promotional objectives.

personal selling interpersonal promotional process involving a seller's face-to-face presentation to a prospective buyer.

Table

14.1   Comparing the Components of the Promotional Mix

Component	Advantages	Disadvantages
Advertising	Reaches large consumer audience at low cost per contact Allows strong control of the message Message can be modified to match different audiences	Difficult to measure effectiveness Limited value for closing sales
Personal selling	Message can be tailored for each customer Produces immediate buyer response Effectiveness is easily measured	High cost per contact High expense and difficulty of attracting and retaining effective salespeople
Sales promotion	Attracts attention and creates awareness Effectiveness is easily measured Produces short-term sales increases	Difficult to differentiate from similar programs of competitors Nonpersonal appeal
Public relations	Enhances product or company credibility Creates a positive attitude about the product or company	Difficult to measure effectiveness Often devoted to nonmarketing activities
Sponsorships	Viewed positively by consumers Enhances brand awareness	Difficult to control message

Figure

14.1   Five Major Promotional Objectives

DIFFERENTIATE PRODUCT
Example: Television ad comparing performance of two leading laundry detergents

PROVIDE INFORMATION
Example: Print ad describing features and availability of a new breakfast cereal

ACCENTUATE PRODUCT VALUE
Example: Warranty programs and guarantees that make a product more attractive than its major competitors

STABILIZE SALES — Example: Even out sales patterns by promoting low weekend rates for hotels, holding contests during slow sales periods, or advertising cold fruit soups during summer months

INCREASE SALES
Example: End-of-aisle grocery displays, or "end caps," to encourage impulse purchases

Objectives of Promotional Strategy

Promotional strategy objectives vary among organizations. Some use promotion to expand their markets, and others use it to defend their current positions. As Figure 14.1 illustrates, common objectives include providing information, differentiating a product, increasing sales, stabilizing sales, and accentuating a product's value.

Marketers often pursue multiple promotional objectives at the same time. To promote its Microsoft Office software, Microsoft has to convince business owners, who buy the software, and their employees, who use the software, that the product is a worthwhile investment.

Marketers need to keep their firm's promotional objectives in mind at all times. Sometimes the objectives are obscured by a fast-paced, creative ad campaign. In this case, the message—or worse, the brand name or image—is lost. One example is a series of ads run by Vonage for its voice-over Internet protocol telephone services. The ads contain segments of home videos showing silly capers that are so distracting it's hard to remember the message—that the service allows consumers to make unlimited phone calls in the United States and Canada for $24.99 a month.[3]

Providing Information A major portion of U.S. advertising is information oriented. Credit card ads provide information about benefits and rates. Ads for hair-care products include information about benefits such as shine and volume. Ads for breakfast cereals often contain nutritional information. Based on new informational guidelines developed by the pharmaceutical industry, drug manufacturer Pfizer has pledged to submit all new TV ads to the U.S. Food and Drug Administration for review and will refrain from advertising new drugs directly to consumers for the first six months. The firm also plans to create more disease-awareness ads that do not mention branded products, along with ads that increase awareness of its discount programs for people without insurance coverage.[4]

REPRINTED WITH PERMISSION FROM MICROSOFT CORPORATION

THE **OOPS I JUST HIT** "REPLY ALL" ERA IS OVER.

Microsoft promotes its latest upgrade to Microsoft Office by showing both companies and workers the benefits of its new features. Mistakes such as sending e-mails to everyone is a practice it considers prehistoric.

Differentiating a Product Promotion can also be used to differentiate a firm's offerings from the competition. Applying a concept called **positioning,** marketers attempt to establish their products in the minds of customers. The idea is to communicate to buyers meaningful distinctions about the attributes, price, quality, or use of a good or service.

When you set out to purchase a car, you have hundreds from which to choose. How do you decide which one to buy? Carmakers do their best to differentiate their vehicles by style, performance, safety features, and price. They must make their vehicles stand out to individual consumers. "Just going out there . . . with a big broad market message can mean a company runs the risk of speaking to everyone and speaking to no one at the same time," warns Rick Wainschel, vice president of marketing research at Kelley Blue Book, the organization that provides pricing information for new and used cars. Recent studies show that fuel efficiency, price, durability, and style are important distinguishing factors for U.S. consumers.[5]

Increasing Sales Increasing sales volume is the most common objective of a promotional strategy. Naturalizer became the third-largest seller of women's dress shoes by appealing to baby boomers. But as these women have grown older, they have bought fewer pairs of shoes each year. Naturalizer wants to keep these customers but also attract the younger generation. So the firm developed a new line of trendy shoes. The promotional strategy included ads in magazines read by younger women—such as *Elle* and *Marie Claire*—featuring young women in beach attire and Naturalizer shoes. The response to this strategy was a substantial increase in Naturalizer's sales through department stores.

Stabilizing Sales Sales stabilization is another goal of promotional strategy. Firms often use sales contests during slack periods, motivating salespeople by offering prizes such as vacations, TVs, camera phones, and cash to those who meet certain goals. Companies distribute sales promotion materials—such as calendars, pens, and notepads—to customers to stimulate sales during the off-season. Jiffy Lube puts that little sticker on your windshield to remind you when to have your car's next oil change—the regular visits help stabilize sales. A stable sales pattern brings several advantages. It evens out the production cycle, reduces some management and production costs, and simplifies financial, purchasing, and marketing planning. An effective promotional strategy can contribute to these goals.

7-Eleven has been advertising its Slurpee to a whole new generation hooked on smoothies and Frappuccinos. The Slurpee is 40 years old but is just as fun as it always was—producing colored tongues and brain freezes. "We've kept it fun with the interesting flavors we've had over the years," says CEO Jim Keyes. "At the heart of it, it's just a fun product that people enjoy." Since 1965, more than 6 billion Slurpees have been sold in seventeen countries. Sales in the United States alone top $170 million each year.[6]

Accentuating the Product's Value Some promotional strategies enhance product values by explaining hidden benefits of ownership. Carmakers offer long-term warranty programs; life insurance companies promote certain policies as investments. The creation of brand awareness and brand loyalty also enhances a product's image and increases its desirability. Advertising with luxurious images supports the reputation of premium brands like Jaguar, Tiffany, and Rolex.

Promotional Planning

Today's marketers can promote their products in many ways, and the lines between the different elements of the promotional mix are blurring. Consider the practice of **product placement.** A growing number of marketers pay placement fees to have their products showcased in various media, ranging from newspapers and magazines to television and movies. Martha Stewart's new syndicated show features General Electric kitchen appliances and food products from Procter & Gamble.[7] The "Hit & Miss" feature describes the leap of product placement from movies into video games. However, television shows and movies account for 90 percent of all product placements.[8]

Another type of promotional planning must be considered by firms with small budgets. **Guerrilla marketing** is innovative, low-cost marketing efforts designed to get consumers' attention in unusual ways. Guerrilla marketing is an increasingly popular tactic for marketers, especially those with limited promotional budgets. Attleboro, Massachusetts–based Willow Tree Poultry Farm hired a well-known chef to develop new recipes and menus featuring its chicken salad and pot pies. Entrepreneur Mark Vinci used guerrilla marketing to launch his own marketing business, K9 Billboards. Vinci lives in New York, and everywhere he takes his Akita puppy, Ling Ling, passersby seem to want to stop to pet her or talk with him. So many people were drawn to his dog it occurred to him that if he could put a brand banner on her, maybe people would be drawn to the brand. He started with a banner for a local ski resort, which was a huge hit with skiers.

Marketers for larger companies have caught on and are using guerrilla approaches as well. Nissan turned six locations in New York and Los Angeles into movie sets with melted props—parking meters, trash cans, and bicycles—near a "hot" Maxima. Called its "Touch" campaign, Nissan wanted passersby to walk past the display and touch the car. "The street scene ties it all together," explained Fred Suckow, director of Nissan marketing.[9]

From this overview of the promotional mix, we now turn to discussions of each of its elements. The following sections detail the major components of advertising, sales promotion, personal selling, and public relations.

assessment check

1. Which component of the promotional mix reaches the largest audience?
2. Why do firms pursue multiple promotional objectives at the same time?
3. What are product placement and guerrilla marketing?

HIT & MISS

Product Placement—A Virtual Success

Product placement has been around for decades. E.T. ate Reese's Pieces simply because Mars turned down the opportunity to have him eat M&M's. Hungry *Survivor* contestants descend on a variety of branded snacks and soft drinks after winning a challenge. Pepsi has been placed in more top films than any other soft drink brand. Product placement has become its own business, so it stands to reason that the practice has taken the next big leap—a virtual one.

Products are now appearing in video games. Electronic Arts, the world's largest video game publisher, made product placements for its Need for Speed Underground 2 game for companies such as Best Buy, Cingular Wireless, Burger King, and even Old Spice. The company reports that its ad revenues have increased 60 percent since it began placing products in its games. In EA's Sims Online, game players use computers that emit familiar Intel tones, and they can buy McDonald's burgers for their hungry Sims characters.

Product placement in video games has become so popular that firms such as Massive are developing software that allows advertisers to update their ads even after a game has been released. If the product comes in a new version or updated package, the advertiser can make the change. In addition, the software allows for customized ads aimed at each player who is using the computer. You might encounter a product placement ad for a CD or a snowboard; your dad might come across one for retirement investments.

Some firms have actually encountered too much of a good thing, though. Vivendi Universal Games found itself turning companies away from product placement opportunities. When alcohol advertisers tried to place their products in Vivendi's Leisure Suit Larry game, the firm said no. Vivendi also denied requests for footwear companies to have the characters wear branded shoes.

Naturally, product placement comes at a price. When determining the fee for product placement, marketers consider such factors as how prominent the product will be, how often a character uses the product, and why the product is being placed in the game or show.

Questions for Critical Thinking

1. Do you think product placement is more effective than traditional advertising? Why or why not?
2. Describe two or three factors—in addition to those already mentioned—that might determine the price of a virtual product placement ad.

Sources: Apryl Duncan, "Product Placement Makes a Virtual Leap," About.com, accessed July 18, 2006, http://advertising.about.com; Abram Sauer, "Brand Channel's 2004 Product Placement Awards," Brandchannel.com, accessed July 18, 2006, http://www.brandchannel.com; Ellen Neuborne, "Ready for Your Product's Close-Up?" *Inc.*, October 2004, pp. 48–50.

ADVERTISING

Consumers receive somewhere between 3,500 and 5,000 marketing messages each day, many of them in the form of advertising.[10] Advertising is the most visible form of nonpersonal promotion—and the most effective for many firms. **Advertising** refers to paid nonpersonal communication usually targeted at large numbers of potential buyers. Although U.S. citizens often think of advertising as a typically American function, it is a global activity. Seven of the top 20 advertisers in the United States are headquartered in other countries: DaimlerChrysler, GlaxoSmithKline, Toyota, Sony, Nissan, L'Oréal, and Unilever. The top five advertisers in the United States are, in order, General Motors, Procter & Gamble, Time Warner, Pfizer, and AT&T.[11]

Advertising expenditures vary among industries, companies, and media. Automotive, retail, and telecommunications take top honors for spending in the United States—carmakers spend a whopping $20 billion per year. Top advertiser General Motors—an auto manufacturer—spends nearly $4 billion a year. Network TV still ranks highest in advertising media

advertising paid nonpersonal communication delivered through various media and designed to inform, persuade, or remind members of a particular audience.

Energy firm Southern Company promotes its commitment to cultivating women's careers through its Supplier Mentor Program, as well as other diversity initiatives. Such a promotion is an example of institutional advertising.

revenues, at $22 billion.[12] Because advertising expenditures are so great, and because consumers are bombarded with so many messages, firms need to be more and more creative and efficient at getting consumers' attention.

Types of Advertising

The two basic types of ads are product and institutional advertisements. **Product advertising** consists of messages designed to sell a particular good or service. Advertisements for Nantucket Nectars, iPods, and Capital One credit cards are examples of product advertising. **Institutional advertising** involves messages that promote concepts, ideas, philosophies, or goodwill for industries, companies, organizations, or government entities. Each year, the Juvenile Diabetes Research Foundation promotes its "Walk for the Cure" fund-raising event, and your college may place advertisements in local papers or news shows to promote its activities.

A form of institutional advertising that is growing in importance, **cause advertising,** promotes a specific viewpoint on a public issue as a way to influence public opinion and the legislative process about issues such as literacy, hunger and poverty, and alternative energy sources. Both not-for-profit organizations and businesses use cause advertising, sometimes called *advocacy advertising.* The massive destruction to Louisiana, Mississippi, and Alabama caused by Hurricane Katrina spawned a slew of cause advertisements to raise funds for aid to victims of the storm. Within days, telethons were announced by major networks and their local affiliates. A special program, "A Concert for Hurricane Relief," was aired on NBC, MSNBC, and CNBC, featuring musicians such as Tim McGraw, Harry Connick Jr., Wynton Marsalis, and Green Day. The concert raised funds for the American Red Cross and other relief organizations.[13]

Advertising and the Product Life Cycle

Both product and institutional advertising fall into one of three categories based on whether the ads are intended to inform, persuade, or remind. A firm uses *informative advertising* to build initial demand for a product in the introductory phase of the product life cycle. Highly publicized new-product entries attract the interest of potential buyers who seek information about the advantages of the new products over existing ones, warranties provided, prices, and places that offer the new products. When Motorola and Apple introduced their Rokr iTunes cell phone, the companies immediately provided the public with the product's details—that it could store up to 100 songs and had a color screen, stereo speakers, stereo headphones, and a camera.[14]

Persuasive advertising attempts to improve the competitive status of a product, institution, or concept, usually in the growth and maturity stages of the product life cycle. One of the most popular types of persuasive product advertising, *comparative advertising,* compares products directly with their competitors—either by name or by inference. Tylenol advertisements mention the possible stomach problems that aspirin could cause, stating that its pain reliever does not irritate the stomach. But advertisers need to be careful when they name competing brands in comparison ads because they might leave themselves open to controversy or even legal action by competitors. Possibly for that reason, Tylenol does not mention a specific aspirin brand in its promotions.

Reminder-oriented advertising often appears in the late maturity or decline stages of the product life cycle to maintain awareness of the importance and usefulness of a product, concept, or institution. Triscuits have been around for a long time, but Nabisco is attempting to mobilize sales with up-to-date advertising that appeals to health and fitness–conscious consumers.

Advertising Media

Marketers must choose how to allocate their advertising budgets among various media. All media offer advantages and disadvantages. Cost is an important consideration in media selection, but marketers must also choose the media best suited for communicating their message. As Figure 14.2 indicates, advertising on television, through direct mail, in newspapers, and in magazines represent the four leading media outlets. However, online interactive advertising is growing fast. Consumers now receive ads when they download news and other information to their handheld wireless devices.

Advertising executives agree that firms need to rethink traditional ad campaigns to incorporate new media as well as updated uses of traditional media. "Today you need a great idea, and you can work out which media types will reflect it," says John Hunt, chief creative officer of international advertising firm TBWA/Chiat/Day. Some ad agencies have developed ways to incorporate adaptive technology with which advertisers can digitally alter television commercials for different markets. Other advertisers are placing more emphasis on the Internet. "The consumer that comes to your Web site is actively looking for you, and that's the best media deal you can make," says Bob Lachky, head of marketing for Anheuser-Busch.[15]

Television Television is still one of America's leading national advertising media. Television advertising can be classified as network, national, local, and cable ads. The four major national networks—ABC, CBS, NBC, and Fox—along with CW, broadcast almost one-fifth of all television ads. Despite a decline in audience share and growing competition from cable, network television remains the easiest way for advertisers to reach large numbers of viewers—10 million to 20 million with a single commercial. Automakers, fast-food restaurants, and food manufacturers are heavy users of network TV advertising.

Nearly two-thirds of U.S. households with TVs now subscribe to cable, drawn to the dozens or even hundreds of channels available through cable or satellite services.[16] As these services broaden their offerings to Internet and interactive programming, their audience is expected to continue growing. The variety of channels on cable and satellite networks lets advertisers target specialized markets and reach selected demographic groups, such as consumers who watch the Outdoor Life Network. BMW, maker of the Mini Cooper, has combined interactive Internet advertising with traditional TV ads that appear on the cable channels E!, History Channel, ESPN, and MTV.[17] Cable companies such as Comcast, Time Warner, Cox, and Charter are launching technologies that send different advertising messages to different neighborhoods.[18] Even TiVo, once famous for making it possible to help consumers skip commercials, is now promoting them. The firm plans to insert symbols that identify advertisers during commercial breaks so that viewers can watch commercials if they choose. "TiVo's proprietary advertising technology presents a real opportunity for advertisers to enhance the effectiveness of traditional television advertising," claims its CFO, David Courtney.[19]

Although television reaches the greatest number of consumers at once, it is the most expensive advertising medium. The price to air a 30-second ad during weeknight prime time

Figure
14.2

Carving up the Advertising Media Pie

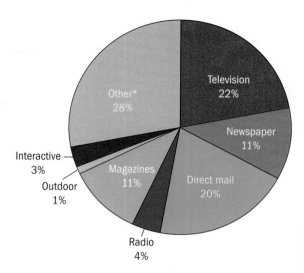

*An additional 28 percent is spent on such miscellaneous media as Yellow Pages listings, Spanish-language media, business papers, transit displays, point-of-purchase displays, cinema advertising, and regional farm papers.

Source: Advertising Age, "Domestic Advertising Spending Totals," *Special Report: Profiles Supplement, 100 Leading National Advertisers,* June 27, 2005, p. 4.

on network television generally ranges from $100,000 to more than $500,000 for the most popular shows. Super Bowl ads have been known to command prices of more than $2 million. So marketers want to be certain that their commercials reach the greatest number of viewers. Because of the high cost, advertisers may demand guarantees of audience size and receive compensation if a show fails to deliver the promised number of viewers.

Newspapers Daily and weekly newspapers continue to dominate local advertising. Marketers can easily tailor newspaper advertising for local tastes and preferences. Advertisers can also coordinate advertisements with other promotional efforts such as discount coupons from supermarkets and one-day sales at department stores. A disadvantage comes from the relatively short life span; people usually discard their newspapers soon after reading. Retailers and automobile dealers rank first among newspaper advertisers. Most newspapers now maintain Web sites, some of which offer separate material and features, to complement their print editions.

Radio Despite the proliferation of other media, the average U.S. household owns five radios—including those in cars—a market penetration that makes radio an important advertising medium. Advertisers like the captive audience of listeners as they commute to and from work. As a result, morning and evening drive-time shows command top ad rates. In major markets, many stations serve different demographic groups with targeted programming. The potential of the Internet to deliver radio programming also offers opportunities for yet more focused targeting. "Many companies have built their businesses on radio advertising," says Hugh Dow, president of media company M2 Universal. "It's a very important medium for many advertisers, particularly many retail advertisers."[20]

Satellite stations have great potential for advertisers. Although Sirius satellite radio—which offers 120 stations to consumers' cars, home, and boats—promises 100 percent commercial-free programming, the station's Web page contains promotions such as sweepstakes and rebates for subscribers. [21]

Magazines Magazines include consumer publications and business trade journals. *Time, Reader's Digest,* and *Sports Illustrated* are consumer magazines, whereas *Advertising Age* and *Oil & Gas Journal* fall into the trade category.

Magazines may customize their publications and target advertising messages to different regions of the country. One method places local advertising in regional editions of the magazine. Other magazines attach wraparounds—half-size covers on top of full-size covers—to highlight articles inside that relate to particular areas; different wraparounds appear in different parts of the country.

Magazines are a natural choice for targeted advertising. Media buyers study demographics of subscribers and select magazines that attract the desired readers. American Express advertises in *Fortune* and *Forbes* to reach businesspeople, while PacSun clothes and Clearasil skin medications are advertised in *teenVogue.*

Direct Mail The average American household receives about 550 pieces of direct mail each year, including 100 catalogs. The huge growth in the variety of direct-mail offerings combined with the convenience they offer to today's busy, time-pressed shoppers has made direct-mail advertising a multibillion-dollar

Etnies Girl Skate Shoes targets fashion-conscious teens with ads in magazines like *teenVogue* and *Seventeen.*

business. Even consumers who like to shop online often page through a catalog before placing an online order. Although direct mail is expensive per person, a small business may be able to spend less on a limited direct-mail campaign than on a television or radio ad. For businesses with a small advertising budget, a carefully targeted direct-mail effort can be highly effective. E-mail is a low-cost form of direct marketing. Marketers can target the most interested Internet users by offering Web site visitors an option to register to receive e-mail. Companies like Amazon.com, Spring Hill Nurseries, and Abercrombie & Fitch routinely send e-mail to regular customers.

Address lists are at the heart of direct-mail advertising. Using data-mining techniques to segment markets, direct-mail marketers create profiles that show the traits of consumers who are likely to buy their products or donate to their organizations. Catalog retailers sometimes experiment by sending direct-mail pieces randomly to people who subscribe to particular magazines. Next, they analyze the orders received from the mailings and develop profiles of purchasers. Finally, they rent lists of additional subscriber names that match the profiles they have developed.

Studies have shown that most U.S. consumers are annoyed by the amount of "junk mail" they receive every day, including catalogs, advertising postcards, and flyers. Among Internet users, a major pet peeve is *spam,* or junk e-mail. Many states have outlawed such practices as sending e-mail promotions without legitimate return addresses, although it is difficult to track down and catch offenders.

The Direct Marketing Association (DMA; http://www.the-dma.org) helps marketers combat negative attitudes by offering its members guidelines on ethical business practices. The DMA also provides consumer information at its Web site, as well as services that enable consumers to opt out of receiving unsolicited offers. In addition, new Federal Trade Commission regulations have taken effect for direct mail in certain industries. Now when you receive that unsolicited, preapproved credit card application in the mail, it must be accompanied by a prominent notice telling you how to get off the bank's mailing list. This law will affect millions of consumers, because 5.8 applications are received by each household every month—or 1.4 billion applications per quarter.[22]

Outdoor Advertising Outdoor advertising accounts for about $3.2 billion in advertising expenditures. The majority of spending on outdoor advertising is for billboards, but spending for other types of outdoor advertising, such as signs in transit stations, stores, airports, and sports stadiums, is growing fast. Advertisers are exploring new forms of outdoor media, many of which involve technology: computerized paintings, video billboards, "trivision" that displays three revolving images on a single billboard, and moving billboards mounted on trucks. Other innovations include displaying ads on the Goodyear blimp, using an electronic system that offers animation and video. And there's the traditional banner flying behind a plane, or skywriting.[23] There's also K9 Billboards, described earlier in the chapter. Outdoor advertising suffers from several disadvantages, however. The medium requires brief messages, and billboards are subject to opposition by preservation and conservation groups.

Online and Interactive Advertising Marketing experts predict that sales from online advertising will double by 2010. Search engine marketing, display ads, and even classified ads are expected to surge.[24]

Online and interactive media have already changed the nature of advertising. Starting with simple banner ads, Internet advertising has become much more complex and sophisticated. Burger King created a media buzz when its Web site featured a Subservient Chicken—a man in a silly chicken suit—who responded to commands typed in by consumers. The ad campaign was such an Internet hit that the company followed it will a boxing match on DirecTV between boxers dressed as chickens—representing different BK chicken sandwiches. Russ

Klein, Burger King's chief marketing officer, is realistic about the future of the nontraditional ad. "In another 10 to 15 years all this stuff will be as normal as talking 30-second ads," he predicts.[25] Before that happens, marketers will be well on their way to coming up with something new.

Subservient Chicken is an example of *viral advertising,* which creates a message that is novel or entertaining enough for consumers to forward it to others, spreading it like a virus. The great advantage is that spreading the word costs the advertiser nothing. Another fast-food restaurant chain, Long John Silver's, recently launched a Web site called ShrimpBuddy.com to promote its Popcorn Shrimp. The site features a two-minute film about a road trip by a guy and his best buddy—who happens to be a shrimp. The ad appealed to young, hip consumers who are Web savvy and have a sense of humor—just the target market that the company hoped to reach.[26]

However, not all online advertising is well received. Like spam, many consumers resent the intrusion of *pop-up ads* that suddenly appear on their computer screen. These ads can be difficult to ignore, remove, or pass by. Some Internet service providers, such as Earthlink, have turned this problem into a marketing advantage by offering service that comes without pop-ups. "You'll never log-on and be greeted by an Earthlink pop-up ad. Your address comes with spam-reducing tools and eight mailboxes," its ads promise.

Sponsorship   One of the hottest trends in promotion offers marketers the ability to integrate several elements of the promotional mix. **Sponsorship** involves providing funds for a sporting or cultural event in exchange for a direct association with the event. Sports sponsorships attract two-thirds of total sponsorship dollars in the U.S. alone. Entertainment, festivals, causes, and the arts divide up the remaining third of sponsorship dollars.

NASCAR, the biggest spectator sport in the United States, thrives on sponsorships. Because it can cost as much as $20 million a year to run a top NASCAR team, drivers depend on sponsorships from companies to keep the wheels turning. Firms may also sponsor charitable or other not-for-profit awards or events. In conjunction with sports network ESPN, Gatorade sponsors its High School Athlete of the Year award, presented to the top male and female high school athletes who "strive for their best on and off the field."

Sponsors benefit in two major ways: exposure to the event's audience and association with the image of the activity. If a celebrity is involved, sponsors usually earn the right to use his or her name along with the name of the event in advertisements. They can set up signs at the event, offer sales promotions, and the like. Sponsorships play an important role in relationship marketing, bringing together the event, its participants, and the sponsoring firms.

Other Media Options   As consumers filter out familiar advertising messages, marketers look for novel ways to catch their attention. In addition to the major media, firms promote through many other vehicles such as infomercials and specialized media. **Infomercials** are a form of broadcast direct marketing, also called *direct response television (DRTV).* These 30-minute programs resemble regular television programs, but are devoted to selling goods or services such as exercise equipment, skin-care products, or kitchenware. The long format allows an advertiser to thoroughly present product benefits,

For two decades, Gatorade has sponsored the High School Athlete of the Year awards. The awards are given to the top male and female who strive to be the best both on and off the field.

increase awareness, and make an impact on consumers. Advertisers also receive immediate responses in the form of sales or inquiries because most infomercials feature toll-free phone numbers. Infomercial stars may become celebrities in their own right, attracting more customers wherever they go. That's what happened to John Carleo, featured in infomercials for the Total Gym. Carleo can be seen demonstrating the exercise machine alongside supermodel Christie Brinkley and actor Chuck Norris. "It got me national recognition," says Carleo. "No matter where I go, someone will come up and say, 'Hey I know you, you're the Total Gym Guy.'" The recognition keeps the Total Gym in the minds of consumers, long after the infomercial is over.[27]

Advertisers use just about any medium they can find. They place messages on subway tickets in New York City and toll receipts on the Massachusetts Turnpike. A more recent development is the use of ATMs for advertising. Some ATMs can play 15-second commercials on their screens, and many can print advertising messages on receipts. An ATM screen has a captive audience because the user must watch the screen to complete a transaction. Directory advertising includes the familiar Yellow Pages listings in telephone books and thousands of other types of directories, most presenting business-related promotions. About 6 percent of total advertising revenue goes to Yellow Pages ads. Besides local and regional directories, publishers also have produced special versions of the Yellow Pages that target ethnic groups.

assessment check

1. What are the two basic types of advertising? Into what three categories do they fall?
2. What is the leading advertising medium in the United States?
3. In what two major ways do firms benefit from sponsorship?

SALES PROMOTION

Traditionally viewed as a supplement to a firm's sales or advertising efforts, sales promotion has emerged as an integral part of the promotional mix. Promotion now accounts for close to half as many marketing dollars as are spent on advertising, and promotion spending is rising faster than ad spending. **Sales promotion** consists of forms of promotion such as coupons, product samples, and rebates that support advertising and personal selling.

Both retailers and manufacturers use sales promotions to offer consumers extra incentives to buy. Beyond the short-term advantage of increased sales, sales promotions can also help marketers build brand equity and enhance customer relationships. Examples include samples, coupons, contests, displays, trade shows, and dealer incentives.

> **sales promotion** nonpersonal marketing activities other than advertising, personal selling, and public relations that stimulate consumer purchasing and dealer effectiveness.

Consumer-Oriented Promotions

The goal of a consumer-oriented sales promotion is to get new and existing customers to try or buy products. In addition, marketers want to encourage repeat purchases by rewarding current users, increase sales of complementary products, and boost impulse purchases. Figure 14.3 shows how marketers allocate their consumer-oriented spending among the categories of promotions.

Premiums, Coupons, Rebates, and Samples
Two of every five sales promotion dollars are spent on *premiums*—items given free or at a reduced price with the purchase of another product. Cosmetics companies such as Clinique offer sample kits with purchases of their products. Fast-food restaurants are also big users of premiums. McDonald's and Burger King include a toy with every children's meal—the toys often tie in with new movies or popular

Figure 14.3

Spending on Consumer-Oriented Promotions

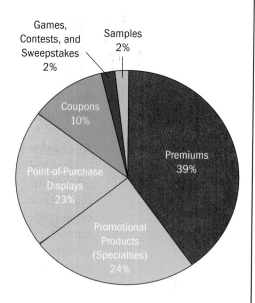

- Games, Contests, and Sweepstakes 2%
- Samples 2%
- Coupons 10%
- Point-of-Purchase Displays 23%
- Premiums 39%
- Promotional Products (Specialties) 24%

DRUG SALES CALLS TO PHYSICIANS: PROVIDING INFORMATION OR SIMPLY SELLING?

Pharmaceutical companies have traditionally employed large numbers of sales representatives—typically called detailers. Their job is to visit physicians' offices to make them aware of new products that could help their patients and to provide special dosage information.

But as the number of drug salespeople tripled to more than 100,000 in a decade and the frequency of visits increased, doctors became increasingly skeptical—and annoyed—with the continual toll on their time schedules. Physicians and the public also wondered whether the purpose of the visits was geared simply toward increasing sales, instead of benefiting patients.

Should the number of direct sales calls to physicians' offices be limited or stopped altogether?

PRO

1. Some drug reps offer free lunches, small tokens such as candies, and free drug samples to physicians who agree to see them. They often befriend office staff to gain entry. Such freebies and behavior can bias a doctor in favor of a product, regardless of its true merits.
2. With the number of drug sales calls expanding, doctors spend more time on calls and less on face time with patients. Such intrusions are burdens to an already stressed healthcare system.

CON

1. Drug company reps can provide doctors with quick, detailed knowledge about a new drug and its uses. Cutting back on this information source limits doctors' awareness of new developments.
2. Pharmaceutical companies deny that their motives are simply to sell more drugs. One company explained that its "longstanding policy is to communicate the benefits and limitations of its products in a fair and balanced manner."

Summary

The American Medical Association offers its member doctors guidelines about limiting the value of the gifts they receive, but it leaves the decision of whether to admit reps to the doctors themselves. Some physicians have become so fed up with the number of calls, they have closed their doors to drug reps or severely limited their access. As part of its ongoing investigation into the pharmaceutical industry, the U.S. Congress is taking a closer look at companies' sales practices to see whether legislation should be passed. Meanwhile, several big pharmaceutical firms, such as Pfizer, Merck, and Wyeth, are already voluntarily limiting their sales calls to physicians. Time will tell whether these efforts will change a well-established sales practice.

Sources: Scott Hensley and Barbara Martinez, "To Sell Their Drugs, Companies Increasingly Rely on Doctors," accessed August 7, 2006, http://www.josmc.org; University of Washington "Drug Sales Pitches Have Little Effect on Physicians, Study Shows," *University Week,* accessed August 7, 2006, http://www.admin.urel.washington.edu; Bruce Japsen, "Drug Sales Calls Wear on Doctors," *Chicago Tribune,* May 8, 2005, section 1, pp. 1, 12; Book review of *Hard Sell: The Evolution of a Viagra Salesman, Fortune,* May 2, 2005, p. 26.

solving an **ETHICAL** controversy

The Sales Process

The sales process typically follows the seven-step sequence shown in Figure 14.4: prospecting and qualifying, the approach, the presentation, the demonstration, handling objections, the closing, and the follow-up. Remember the importance of flexibility, though; a good salesperson is not afraid to vary the sales process based on a customer's responses and needs. The process of selling to a potential customer who is unfamiliar with a company's products differs from the process of serving a longtime customer.

Prospecting, Qualifying, and Approaching At the prospecting stage, salespeople identify potential customers. They may seek leads for prospective sales from such sources as existing customers, friends and family, and business associates. The qualifying process identifies potential customers who have the financial ability and authority to buy.

Figure

14.4

Companies use different tactics to identify and qualify prospects. Some companies rely on business development teams to do this legwork. They use the responses from direct mail to provide leads to sales reps. Other companies believe in personal visits from sales representatives.

Successful salespeople make careful preparations, analyzing available data about a prospective customer's product lines and other pertinent information before making the initial contact. They realize the importance of a first impression in influencing a customer's future attitudes toward the selling company and its products.

Presentation and Demonstration   At the presentation stage, salespeople communicate promotional messages. They may describe the major features of their products, highlight the advantages, and cite examples of satisfied consumers. A demonstration helps reinforce the message that the salesperson has been communicating—a critical step in the sales process. Department-store shoppers can get a free makeover at the cosmetics counter. Anyone looking to buy a car will take it for a test drive before deciding whether to purchase it.

Some products are too large to transport to prospective buyers or require special installation to demonstrate. Using laptop computers and multimedia presentations, sales representatives can demonstrate these products for customers. Others, such as services, are intangible. So a presentation including testimonials from satisfied customers or graphs illustrating results may be helpful.

Seven Steps in the Sales Process

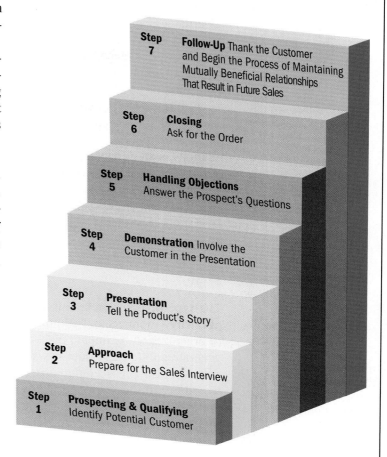

Handling Objections   Some salespeople fear potential customers' objections because they view the questions as criticism. But a good salesperson can use objections as an opportunity to answer questions and explain how the product will benefit the customer. As a general rule, the key is to sell benefits, not features: How will this product help the customer?

Closing   The critical point in the sales process—the time at which the salesperson actually asks the prospect to buy—is the closing. If the presentation effectively matches product benefits to customer needs, the closing should be a natural conclusion. If there are more bumps in the process, the salesperson can try some different techniques, such as offering an alternative product, offering a special incentive for purchase, or restating the product benefits. Closing the sale—and beginning a relationship in which the customer builds loyalty to the brand or product—is the ideal outcome of this interaction. But even if the sale is not made at this time, the salesperson should regard the interaction as the beginning of a potential relationship anyway. The prospect might very well become a customer in the future.

Follow-Up   A salesperson's actions after the sale may determine whether the customer will make another purchase. Follow-up is an important part of building a long-lasting relationship. After closing, the salesperson should process the order efficiently. By calling soon after a purchase, the salesperson provides reassurance about the customer's decision to buy and creates an opportunity to correct any problems.

Public Relations

A final element of the promotional mix, public relations (PR)—including publicity—supports advertising, personal selling, and sales promotion, usually by pursuing broader objectives. Through PR, companies attempt to improve their prestige and image with the public by distributing specific messages or ideas to target audiences. Cause-related promotional activities are often supported by PR and publicity campaigns. In addition, PR helps a firm establish awareness of goods and services, then builds a positive image of them.[33]

public relations organization's communications and relationships with its various audiences.

Public relations refers to an organization's communications with its various public audiences, such as customers, vendors, news media, employees, stockholders, the government, and the general public. Many of these communication efforts serve marketing purposes. Public relations is an efficient, indirect communications channel for promoting products. It can publicize products and help create and maintain a positive image of the company.

The PR department links a firm with the media. It provides the media with news releases and video and audio clips, as well as holding news conferences to announce new products, the formation of strategic alliances, management changes, financial results, and similar developments. Publications issued by the PR department include newsletters, brochures, and reports.

Publicity

publicity stimulation of demand for a good, service, place, idea, person, or organization by disseminating news or obtaining favorable unpaid media presentations.

The type of public relations that is tied most closely to promoting a company's products is **publicity**—nonpersonal stimulation of demand for a good, service, place, idea, event, person, or organization by unpaid placement of information in print or broadcast media. Press releases generate publicity, as does news coverage. Entrepreneur Eric Anderson, CEO of Space Adventures, held a press conference to announce that his firm, along with its Russian partners, would be offering "around the moon" space travel to anyone willing to pay $100 million for the trip. That's $80 million more than the $20 million the group is charging for trips to the International Space Station. Naturally, the announcement generated plenty of buzz in the news media.[34] Not-for-profit organizations benefit from publicity when they receive coverage of events such as the Boston Marathon, in which thousands of runners participate to raise money for sixteen charities, such as the Doug Flutie Foundation for Autism. When a for-profit firm teams up with a not-for-profit firm in a fund-raising effort, the move usually generates good publicity for both organizations.

While good publicity can promote a firm's positive image, negative publicity can cause problems. When home decorating and entertaining expert Martha Stewart was convicted in a stock-trading case, her image as well as that of her company, Martha Stewart Living, suffered. But Stewart took steps to improve her image, even while serving a prison sentence. When she returned to public life, she already had contracts for two television shows.

assessment check

1. Why do retailers and manufacturers use sales promotions?
2. When does a firm use personal selling instead of nonpersonal selling?
3. How does public relations serve a marketing purpose?

PROMOTIONAL STRATEGIES

Many of this chapter's examples demonstrate the considerable overlap among the elements of the promotional mix. Clear boundaries no longer distinguish advertising from sales promotion. By blending advertising, sales promotion, personal selling, and public relations, marketers create an integrated promotional mix that reflects the market, product type, stage in the product life cycle, price, and promotional budget. Then they implement one of two promotional alternatives: pulling or pushing strategies.

Pushing and Pulling Strategies

Marketers can choose between two general promotional strategies: a pushing strategy or a pulling strategy. A **pushing strategy** relies on personal selling to market an item to wholesalers and retailers in a company's distribution channels. So companies promote the product to members of the marketing channel, not to end users. Sales personnel explain to marketing intermediaries why they should carry particular merchandise, usually supported by offers of special discounts and promotional materials. Marketers also provide **cooperative advertising** allowances, in which they share the cost of local advertising of their firm's product or line with channel partners. All of these strategies are designed to motivate wholesalers and retailers to push the good or service to their own customers.

A **pulling strategy** attempts to promote a product by generating consumer demand for it, primarily through advertising and sales promotion appeals. Potential buyers will then request that their suppliers—retailers or local distributors—carry the product, thereby pulling it through the distribution channel. Dove used this strategy when it launched a highly popular advertising campaign—called "Campaign for Real Beauty"—for its products featuring real women instead of professional models. The ads for soap, shampoo, and lotions were placed in magazines, on billboards and buildings, and even along the sides of buses. The strategy was so successful that it also generated good publicity—including a segment on NBC's *Today Show*.[35]

Most marketing situations require combinations of pushing and pulling strategies, although the primary emphasis can vary. Consumer products usually depend more heavily on pulling strategies than do B2B products, which favor pushing strategies.

COURTESY OF UNILEVER USA, INC

☐ grey?
☐ gorgeous?

Why can't more women feel glad to be grey? Join the beauty debate.

campaignforrealbeauty.com ➥ | Dove

Dove's popular ad campaign used a pulling strategy—featuring women with whom consumers could identify—to promote its new line of beauty products.

assessment check

1. Give an example of a pushing strategy.
2. Give an example of a pulling strategy.

ETHICS IN PROMOTION

Of all the elements in a 21st-century business organization, promotion probably raises the most ethical questions. Many people view advertising with a cynical eye, criticizing its influence on consumers, its potential for creating unnecessary needs and wants, its overemphasis on sex and beauty, and its delivery of inappropriate messages to children.

This section examines three controversial issues related to the promotion element of the firm's marketing mix: puffery and deception, promotion to children and teens, and promotion in public schools and on college campuses.

Puffery and Deception

Claims such as "bigger," "best," "most advanced," and "number one" are examples of **puffery.** Puffery is exaggeration about the benefits or superiority of a product. It literally means "puffed up." Puffery is legal because it doesn't guarantee anything, but it certainly raises ethical questions.

Lunesta: The Price of Sleep

Consumers are accustomed to seeing advertisements and other promotions for prescription medications. Television commercials, Internet ads, and magazine promotions with toll-free numbers offering coupons are commonplace. As consumers become increasingly educated about purchasing medications, how do marketers create competitive messages and pricing structures for their products?

Insomnia has been called an epidemic in the United States. Every night, millions of people toss and turn without getting the sleep they need. The market for sleep aids has existed for a long time and has been filled with all kinds of remedies sold by prescription and over the counter. They have a wide range of effectiveness and side effects. Recently, the Food and Drug Administration approved a prescription sleep aid manufactured by Sepracor, called Lunesta. The drug is considered a breakthrough because studies have shown that most patients who take it do not experience drowsiness the next day and its effectiveness does not decrease over time. Because Lunesta is the first such medication to be approved for long-term use, the choices that Sepracor makes for promotion and pricing are critical.

The Lunesta launch was accompanied by a series of ads explaining the benefits of the medication, as well as cautions regarding its correct use. For instance, one ad says, "Lunesta works quickly, so you should only take it right before bed." The ads contain a toll-free number and Web site address so that consumers can learn more about the drug. In the ads, a luminescent butterfly accompanies the image of a sleeping person; that way, consumers will begin to associate the butterfly with the Lunesta brand.

Lunesta comes in different strengths, at different prices. The average price for 30 tablets—a one-month supply of the lowest dose—is $99. The average price for the same number of tablets in the highest dose is $332. The top three nonprescription, natural sleep aids sell for around $30—a large difference in price. Lunesta must compete not only with other prescription medications but also with those that are sold over the counter, so its marketing messages must be strong.

So far, the Lunesta launch has been successful from a business standpoint. "The . . . data suggest that the launch is meeting the already high expectations for the drug," reported investment firm Morgan Stanley just a few months after the drug reached the market. If the drug's track record continues to be positive and doctors continue to provide prescriptions for their patients, then there may be a lot fewer sleepless nights—both for patients and for Sepracor.

Questions for Critical Thinking

1. Identify two or three ethical issues that marketers of prescription drugs such as Lunesta must consider when developing their promotional efforts.

2. How would you describe the pricing objectives of the makers of Lunesta? What do you think would be the best pricing strategy? Why?

Sources: Lunesta Web site, accessed July 18, 2006, http://www.lunesta.ws; "Sepracor Announces Launch Timing for Lunesta Brand Eszopiclone for Treatment of Insomnia," ImmuneSupport.com, accessed July 18, 2006, http://www.immunesupport.com; "Sepracor's Seamless Lunesta Launch," *Forbes,* accessed July 18, 2006, http://www.forbes.com; Cassandra Walters, "Is Lunesta (Eszolpiclone) Right for You?" Consumer Health Digest.com, accessed May 10, 2005, http://consumerhealthdigest.com.

VIDEO Case 14.2

Wild Oats Promotes Local Foods

This video case appears on page 623. A recently filmed video, designed to expand and highlight the written case, is available for class use by instructors.

The Second City Theater Continuing Case
Marketing: This Company Is More Than Just Funny Business

Consider for a moment the various options you might have while visiting Chicago. You may want to go to a Cubs or White Sox game. You could visit Sue, the world's most complete T-Rex at the Field Museum, or perhaps go to the top of Sears Tower and gaze upon one of the largest cities in America. Or . . . you could see why Chicago has been dubbed the comedy capital of the world. The Second City is vastly celebrated in the entertainment industry and continues to attract audiences from around the globe. In fact, since its founding in 1959, SC Chicago has consistently played to sold-out crowds. It first got the term *Second City* from a series of *New Yorker* articles disparaging Chicago. It was a brilliant marketing move, inspired by news and propelled by bold jest.

Tourists coming to the Windy City provide the most significant customer base for Second City. The innovative, fast-paced comedy is a unique experience for travelers who then return home and promote the company by word of mouth. This is Second City's primary form of advertising. With an impressive list of famous performers and the ability to produce quality local shows, Second City has gained extensive brand equity. Because Second City is unparalleled in the comedic theater industry, cable televi-

sion and cinema are the competition. Second City has evolved into a family brand, distributing the company through a variety of channels and thereby capitalizing on its position in the market. Its numerous performance venues, touring companies, training centers, productions on cruise lines, and business communications branch are all marketed as Second City brand endeavors.

Whether you visit Chicago, Detroit, Toronto, Denver, or Las Vegas, the Second City Theater will be decorated with its now famous logo and photos of its famous graduates filling the walls. The cast and everything created before your eyes will be an authentically new experience. Second City's marketing strategies are customized to the character of the locale. In Toronto, the theater deals with a struggling economy by creating a more localized show; in Las Vegas, Second City stands out as a comparatively understated venue in an otherwise overstated city; in Detroit and Denver, the two newer establishments, shows and promotion, are building a core audience in the community; and in Chicago, the theater supplements its flagship Main Stage with additional eclectic shows designed to reattract the local audience. Each theater uses personalized comedy

and marketing to build a relationship with the community.

Kelly Leonard, Second City's vice president, attributes Second City's success in forming long-term relationships with consumers through "our expanded services. We offer kids' classes now, so we have 5-year-olds getting in touch with Second City. We offer workshops and shows in the high schools; we play the colleges; we provide corporate entertainment—basically, we're creating a series of 'ins' that cross over a variety of ages and experiences. The more stuff we can create that is pure to what we do, the better we are positioning ourselves for the future." Across its marketing landscape, The Second City handles their principal product of comedy. For the SC Communications Company, this can foster a limiting perception for a corporate client that may benefit from more than just laughs. Collaborating with clients in the creation process has enriched the relationship. The ability to understand its consumers has provided Second City with various lucrative connections to the business world.

Second City's partnership with Norwegian Cruise Lines illustrates an understanding of its target market. Building on its appeal to tourists, Second City has seized an opportunity to reach a group with similar lifestyles and cultural backgrounds. Naming the group as its exclusive provider of sketch comedy, the exotic cruise line has brought Second City an exciting new platform for product distribution.

Back on land, Second City attracts two primary constituents to its sizable Training Center. The high visibility of the Second City brand throughout the entertainment industry has led aspiring performers from all over the country to learn the art of improvisation. There are also classes intended for the casual humor hobbyist or anyone who would like to relieve stress with what is commonly known as "the best medicine." These students continue to market the institution to their friends and family. The more serious participants find a certain "specialty product" within the unique training. By training with Second City, performers might find themselves graduating from the program and getting hired for one of the touring companies, a cruise ship, or even SC's coveted Main Stage. With the reputation of Second City as the liftoff stage for talent, training at the famous theater can be a key accomplishment. Even

multigenre actors such as Halle Berry and Alan Arkin have benefited from the cherished comedic education.

The Second City touring companies showcase emerging talent in two markets: performing arts centers and colleges. The company performs the signature combination of SC sketch comedy and live improvisation inspired by audience suggestions. A booking agent manages the financial agreements through various conferences and networking. For Kelly Leonard, the touring companies represent the organization's true appeal. "For the performing arts centers we position ourselves as a trusted and respected theatrical brand. For the colleges, we're the cutting-edge comedians," says Leonard. Second City offers a convenient product with the help of these ensembles.

No matter how you might have heard of Second City, its Web site is the most inclusive marketing tool. SecondCity.com includes a full list of alumni, posters, reviews of shows up and running on all its stages, training center information and virtual shorts that market the theatre's services to the corporate industry. The Internet is one place where the family of Second City brands unites.

Now if you wander up to Second City's management offices, you won't find an extensive collection of marketing research studies. They've only recently begun using market research. Second City has distributed its brand by reacting quickly to the ideas fostered in the creative atmosphere that has been with it since the beginning. Its inventive approach to marketing has widely extended its product while preserving its recognizable brand. So if visiting Chicago might not be on your schedule this year, a visit from a Second City touring company might be just around the corner.

QUESTIONS

1. How has Second City been able to maintain its strong brand identity?

2. How does Second City vary its marketing strategies across the company?

3. What is Second City's target market and how is it related to the location of the theater? What are some marketing challenges that Second City faces with its family branding?

Part 4: Launching Your Marketing Career

In Part 4, "Marketing Management," you learned about the goals and functions of marketing. The three chapters in this part emphasized the central role of customer satisfaction in defining value and developing a marketing strategy in traditional and nontraditional marketing settings. You learned about the part played by marketing research and the need for relationship marketing in today's competitive environment. You discovered how new products are developed and how they evolve through the four stages of the product life cycle, from introduction through growth and maturity to decline. You also learned about the role of different channels in creating effective distribution strategies. Finally, you saw the impact of integrated marketing communications on the firm's promotional strategy, the role of advertising, ethical issues in promotion, and the way pricing influences consumer behavior. Perhaps you came across some marketing tasks and functions that sounded especially appealing to you. Here are a few ideas about careers in marketing that you may want to pursue.

The first thing to remember is that, as the chapters in this part made clear, marketing is about a great deal more than personal selling and advertising. For instance, are you curious about why people behave the way they do? Are you good at spotting trends? *Marketing research analysts* seek answers to a wide range of questions about business competition, customer preferences, market trends, and past and future sales. They often design and conduct their own consumer surveys, using the telephone, mail, the Internet, or personal interviews and focus groups. After they analyze the data they've collected, their recommendations form input for managerial decisions about whether to introduce new products, revamp current ones, enter new markets, or abandon products or markets where profitability is low. As members of a new-product development team, marketing researchers often work directly with members of other business departments such as scientists, production and manufacturing personnel, and

finance employees. Also, marketing researchers are increasingly asked to help clients implement their recommendations. With today's highly competitive economy, jobs in this area are expected to grow. Annual earnings for marketing research analysts average $56,000.[1]

Another career path in marketing is sales. Do you work well with others and read their feelings accurately? Are you a self-starter? Being a *sales representative* might be for you. Selling jobs exist in every industry, and because many use a combination of salary and performance-based commissions, they can pay handsomely. Sales jobs are often a first step on the ladder to upper-management positions as well. Sales representatives work for wholesalers and manufacturing companies (and even for publishers such as the one that produces this book). They sell automobiles, computer systems and technology, pharmaceuticals, advertising, insurance, real estate, commodities and financial services, and all kinds of consumer goods and services.

If you're interested in mass communications, note that magazines, newspapers, and broadcast companies such as ESPN and MTV generate most of their revenue from advertising, so sales representatives who sell space and time slots in the media contribute a great deal to the success of these firms.[2] And if you like to travel, consider that travel agents are salespeople, too.

Advertising, marketing management, and public relations are other categories of marketing. In large companies, marketing managers, product managers, promotion managers, and public-relations managers often work long hours under pressure; they may travel frequently or transfer between jobs at headquarters and positions in regional offices. Their responsibilities include directing promotional programs, overseeing advertising campaigns and budgets, and conducting communications such as press releases with the firm's publics. Thousands of new positions are expected to open up in the next several years; the field is expected to grow 22 percent over the next decade.

Growth of the Internet and new media has especially increased demand for advertising and public-relations specialists. [3]

Advertising and public-relations firms employed about 425,000 people in a recent year.[4] About one in five U.S. advertising firms are located in New York or California, and more than a quarter of advertising industry workers live in those two states. Most advertising firms develop specialties; many of the largest are international in scope and earn a major proportion of their revenue abroad. Online advertising is just one area in which new jobs will be opening in the future, as more and more client firms expand their online sales operations.

Career Assessment Exercises in Marketing

1. Select a field that interests you. Use the Internet to research types of sales positions available in that field. Locate a few entry-level job openings and see what career steps that position can lead to. (You might wish to start with a popular job-posting site such as Monster .com.) Note the job requirements, the starting salary, and the form of compensation—straight salary? salary plus commission?—and write a one-page summary of your findings.

2. Use the Internet to identify and investigate two or three of the leading advertising agencies in the United States, such as Young & Rubicam or J. Walter Thompson. What are some of their recent ad campaigns, or who are their best-known clients? Where do the agencies have offices? What job openings do they currently list, and what qualifications should applicants for these positions have? Write a brief report comparing the agencies you selected, decide which one you would prefer to work for, and give your reasons.

3. Test your research skills. Choose an ordinary product, such as toothpaste or soft drinks, and conduct a survey to find out why people chose the brand they most recently purchased. For instance, suppose you wanted to find out how people choose their shampoo. List as many decision criteria as you can think of, such as availability, scent, price, packaging, benefits from use (conditioning, dandruff-reducing, and so on), brand name, and ad campaign. Ask eight to ten friends to rank these decision factors, and note some simple demographics about your research subjects such as their age, gender, and occupation. Tabulate your results. What did you find out about how your subjects made their purchase decision? Did any of your findings surprise you? Can you think of any ways in which you might have improved your survey?

Managing Technology and Information

Part

5

Chapter 15

Using Technology to Manage Information

Learning Goals

1. Distinguish between data and information and explain the role of management information systems in business.

2. Identify and briefly describe the different types of information system programs.

3. Describe the hardware and software used in managing information.

4. Identify how different types of software can help businesspeople.

5. Explain the importance of special network technologies.

6. List the ways that companies can protect themselves from computer crimes.

7. Explain the steps that companies go through in anticipating, planning for, and recovering from information system disasters.

Less than a decade ago, Larry Page and Sergey Brin came up with a brilliant—and ambitious—idea. What if they could organize all the information in the world *and* make it accessible to anyone with a computer? And what if they could somehow turn this idea into a business? With these lofty goals, Google was born.

"Googol" is the mathematical term for a 1 followed by 100 zeros. The term was created by Milton Sirotta, nephew of American mathematician Edward Kasner. Google's use of the term reflects the company's mission to organize the vast amount of information available on the Internet. Founders Page and Brin have been true to their company's name: Google's Internet search engine is so powerful that it has "essentially tamed the Web," writes one industry watcher. And the name is already so pervasive in everyday life and lan-

AP PHOTO/BEN MARGOT

Google pulls in revenues from the text ads that appear next to search results. When a user clicks the ad, the advertiser is charged a fee. These revenues allow the firm to hire engineers and designers to develop new search products. "The number of new [Google] products is related

Google: How to Succeed without Really Selling

guage that it has become a verb. People routinely say, "I'll Google that." Why has Google become this successful this quickly?

First, Google's search products are easy to access and use. Second, they are free. Both consumers and businesses like Google's convenience. Its index now consists of more than 8 billion Web pages. Whether you are looking for information on an obscure artist or a list of Web sites that sell gourmet coffee, you'll find what you need through Google. Specialized Google search products include inboxes (Gmail) and photos (Picasa). If you've forgotten what you searched for in the past, you can click My Search History. Google will hold the data for you until you decide to delete it—an important feature in many people's security-conscious minds. With Google Earth, you can pinpoint just about any location on the planet, including your own home. In fact, the launch of this most recent product has some government officials worried that it could actually provide satellite photos of potential terrorist targets. The governments of India, South Korea, Thailand, and the Netherlands have already expressed concern about Google Earth's capabilities. But Google insists that its software uses only information that is already available to the public.

to the number of engineers—it's a linear function," explains Marissa Mayer, director of the firm's consumer Web products. With more than 4,000 employees, Google is poised to grow much larger. In fact, some industry watchers warn that it is already nipping at the heels of Microsoft, which employs 61,000 workers and holds $38 billion in cash. "When we see a remarkable new company that redefines the technology industry, we either fear it because of all the things it might do or we expect more from it than it can possibly deliver," notes business author John Battelle.

What's next for Google? Engineers are currently working on ways to remove language barriers from the Internet. Currently, Google can automatically translate Web pages from English into German, Spanish, French, Italian, Japanese, Chinese, and several other languages. But Google engineers are developing the technology for all search results to return automatically in a user's native language, regardless of what it is. "The goal is to make the Internet language-independent," explains Alan Eustace, head of Google's research. "In the long term, if you can create technology that can unify information around the world and remove the language barrier, that would be very special."

An Internet free of all language barriers would be very special indeed. Google does not shy away from such challenges. "Google wants to be everywhere that people are," says Danny Sullivan, editor of the newsletter *Search Engine Watch*. It's a simple goal, with far-reaching implications. "The biggest question is whether they can accomplish everything they want before someone else comes along with even better ideas," remarks Battelle. But Google engineers won't stop trying until everyone can say, "I'll Google that."[1]

This chapter explores how businesses manage information as a resource, particularly how they use technology to do so. The chapter begins by differentiating information and data, and describing management information systems. It then looks at ways companies use information systems to organize and use information, including databases and information system programs. Because computers drive information systems, the chapter also discusses computer types and their applications in business settings. Today, specialized networks make information access and transmission function smoothly, so the chapter examines new types of networks to see how businesses are applying them for competitive advantage. Finally, the chapter explores the importance of protecting valuable information and recovering from information system disasters.

---

data raw facts and figures that may or may not be relevant to a business decision.

information knowledge gained from processing data.

management information system (MIS) organized method for providing past, present, and projected information on internal operations as well as external intelligence to support decision making.

"They Said It"

"You can give people responsibility and authority, but without information they are helpless."
—Bill Gates (b. 1955)
Co-founder, Microsoft Corporation

MANAGEMENT INFORMATION SYSTEMS

Every day, businesspeople ask themselves questions such as the following:

- How well is our brand selling in Seattle compared with Charlotte? How has the bird flu epidemic affected sales of poultry products in Asia? In Europe?
- If we raise the price of our products by 2 percent, how will the change affect sales in each city? In each country?
- What impact have higher energy prices had on the cost of raw materials?
- If employees can access the benefits system through our network, will it increase or decrease benefits costs?

An effective information system can help answer these and many other questions. **Data** consist of raw facts and figures that may or may not be relevant to a business decision. **Information** is knowledge gained from processing those facts and figures. So although businesspeople need to gather data about the demographics of a target market or the specifications of a certain product, the data are useless unless they are transformed into relevant information that can be used to make a competitive decision. Technology has advanced so quickly that all businesses, regardless of size or location, now have access to data and information that can make them competitive in a global arena.

A **management information system (MIS)** is an organized method for providing past, present, and projected information on internal operations as well as external intelligence to support decision making. A large organization typically assigns responsibility for directing its MIS and related computer operations to an executive called the **chief information officer (CIO)**. Often the CIO reports directly to the firm's chief executive officer (CEO). But small companies rely just as much on an MIS as do large ones, even if they do not employ a manager assigned to this area on a full-time basis. An effective CIO can understand and harness technology so that the company can communicate internally and externally in one seamless operation.

The role of the CIO is both expanding and changing as the technology to manage information continues to develop. According to one recent survey, around half of all CIOs stated that their job responsibilities have broadened significantly in recent years.[2] CIOs are also well compensated. The Gartner Group, an information technology consulting company, found that annual compensation for CIOs today exceeds $300,000 on average, with many CIOs at larger firms earning more than $1 million per year.[3]

The importance of managing information can also be seen in the growth in demand for college graduates with degrees in information systems. According to the Bureau of Labor Statistics, the number of people employed in information systems and related fields will grow by around 55 percent between now and 2012.[4] Starting salaries for those with undergraduate degrees in information systems average more than $43,000 per year.[5]

Information systems can be tailored to assist many business functions and departments—providing reports for everything from marketing and manufacturing, to finance and accounting. They can manage the overwhelming flood of information by organizing data in a logical and accessible manner. Through the system, a company can monitor all components of its business strategy, identifying problems and opportunities. Information systems gather data from inside and outside the organization; they then process the data to produce information that is relevant to all aspects of the organization. Processing steps could involve storing data for later use, classifying and analyzing it, and retrieving it easily when needed. Computerized location systems are a booming technology that has many applications.

Many companies—and nations—combine high-tech and low-tech solutions to manage the flow of information. E-mail, wireless communications, and videoconferencing haven't totally replaced paper memos, phone conversations, and face-to-face meetings, but they are increasingly common. Information can make the difference between staying in business and going bankrupt. Keeping on top of changing consumer demands, competitors' actions, and the latest government regulations will help a firm fine-tune existing products, develop new winners, and maintain effective marketing.

Databases

The heart of a management information system is its **database,** a centralized integrated collection of data resources. A company designs its databases to meet particular information processing and retrieval requirements that its decision makers encounter. Businesses create databases in many ways. They can hire a staff person to build them on site, hire an outside source to do so, or buy readily available database programs. A database serves as an electronic filing cabinet, capable of storing massive amounts of data and retrieving it within seconds. A database should be continually updated; otherwise, a firm may find itself with data that are outdated and possibly useless. One problem with databases is that they can contribute to information overload—too much data for people to absorb or data that are not relevant to decision making. Because computer processing speed and storage capacity are both increasing rapidly, and as data have become more abundant, businesspeople need to be careful that their databases contain only the facts they need, so they do not waste time wading through unnecessary data.

Decision makers can also look up online data. Online systems give access to enormous amounts of government data, such as economic data from the Bureau of Labor Statistics and the Department of Commerce. One of the largest online databases is that of the U.S. Census Bureau. The census of population, conducted every ten years, attempts to collect data on more than 120 million households across the United States. Selected participants fill out forms containing questions about marital status, place of birth, ethnic background, citizenship, workplaces, commuting time, income, occupation, type of housing, number of telephones and vehicles, even grandparents as caregivers. Households receiving the most recent questionnaire could

database centralized integrated collection of data resources.

The U.S. Census Bureau's Web site is a large, searchable online database with all sorts of information. The "Reference Maps" link in the American Factfinder topic area contains information on states, such as major roads, bodies of water, and other details. Visitors can zoom in and out for different sets of data.

SAS Institute offers business intelligence software to companies to help them analyze their data.

respond in English as well as a variety of other languages including Spanish, Chinese, Vietnamese, and Korean. Not surprisingly, sifting through all the collected data takes time. Although certain restrictions limit how businesspeople can access and use specific census data, the general public may access the data via the American FactFinder on the Census Bureau's Web site (http://www.census.gov), as well as at state data centers and public libraries.

Another source of free information is company Web sites. Interested parties can visit firms' home pages to look for information about customers, suppliers, and competitors. Trade associations and academic institutions also maintain Web sites with information on topics of interest.

Companies also subscribe to commercial online services that provide fee-for-service databases on particular topics. In addition to broad-based online databases available through such services as LexisNexis and Infotrac, firms can also access specialized databases geared to particular industries and functions. Many professional groups and trade associations have set up electronic bulletin board systems on the Internet where data and information are available. For instance, *Bicycle Retailer* maintains an bulletin board on its Web site where bike shop owners and employees can exchange ideas and information. It also provides data to members on bike sales and other industry trends. Businesspeople who gather data online should always try to verify the reliability of their sources, however.

Business Intelligence

Once a company has built a database, its managers need to be able to analyze the data in it. As discussed in Chapter 12, *data mining,* or *business intelligence,* is the task of using computer-based technology to retrieve and evaluate data in a database to identify useful trends. It focuses on identifying relationships that are not obvious to businesspeople—in a sense, answering questions that they may not even have thought to ask. Data mining is an efficient way to sort through huge databases and to make sense of that data. Among other things, data mining can help create customer profiles, pinpoint reasons for customer loyalty, analyze the impact of pricing changes, and forecast sales.

Specialized data mining and business intelligence software is available from a variety of companies such as Oracle and SAP. IBM offers a software product called DB2 Intelligent Miner for Data. Customers use the program to gain new business insights and to harvest valuable business intelligence from all of a company's data, such as high-volume transaction data generated by point-of-sale, ATM, and credit card transactions or call center and e-commerce activities. With Intelligent Miner for Data, executives are better equipped to make insightful decisions, whether the problem is how to develop more precisely targeted marketing campaigns, reduce customer attrition, or increase revenue generated by online shopping.[6]

Some consulting firms, such as Boston-based Data Miners, specialize in data mining for their clients. Recently, Data Miners was asked to investigate transaction-level data from loyalty cardholders of a New England health food supermarket. Data Miners found that 50 percent of the supermarket's customers were meat eaters, and this group was among the store's most valuable customers. Had the supermarket eliminated meat, assuming that its customers were vegetarians, it would have lost a very profitable business segment. The data clearly showed that meat-eating customers were interested in, and willing to pay for, health food.[7] As this example illustrates, successful data mining can help a business discover patterns in the sale of certain goods and services, find new customers, track customer complaints and requests, and evaluate the cost of materials.

assessment check

1. What is the difference between data and information?
2. Define management information system.
3. What is the purpose of business intelligence?

INFORMATION SYSTEMS FOR DECISION MAKING

So much data clogs the Internet, databases, and other data sources that the challenge for businesses has shifted from acquiring data to sorting through it to find the most useful elements, which can then be turned into valuable information. New types of information system software are being developed all the time. These range from tools that help users look up data on various topics to specialized systems that track costs, sales, inventory levels, and other data. Businesses can develop and implement their own systems or hire someone else to do so. Many also hire an outside service to manage data for them.

Decision Support System

A **decision support system (DSS)** is an information system that quickly provides relevant data to help businesspeople make decisions and choose courses of action. It includes software tools that help decision makers generate the type of information they need. These DSS tools may vary from company to company, but they typically include retrieval features that help users obtain needed information from a database, simulation elements that let decision makers create computer models to evaluate future company performance under different conditions, and presentation tools that create graphs and charts.

An information interface is a software program between the user and the underlying information system. Advances in information interfaces have simplified and synthesized data into useful information for a variety of users. For instance, visitors to the *Cooking Light* Web site (http://www.cookinglight.com) can access recipes through an easy-to-use interface. Visitors can search the magazine's vast database by main ingredient, cooking technique, ethnicity, and even special dietary requirements. Comments from users are also available. With a few mouse clicks visitors can create an entire menu, accompanied by a shopping list. Such sophisticated interfaces make information retrieval more efficient.

decision support system (DSS) information system that quickly provides relevant data to help businesspeople make decisions and choose courses of action.

Executive Support Systems Although the trend is increasingly toward employee empowerment and decision making at all levels of an organization, sometimes companies need to create specialized information systems to address the needs of executives. An **executive support system (ESS)** lets top managers access the firm's primary databases, often by touching the computer screen, pointing with a mouse, or even speaking via voice recognition. The typical ESS allows users to choose from many kinds of data, such as the firm's financial statements and sales figures as well as stock market trends for the company and for the industry as a whole. If they wish, managers can start by looking at summaries and then proceed toward more detailed information.

executive support system (ESS) system that allows top managers to access a firm's primary databases.

Expert Systems   An **expert system** is a computer program that imitates human thinking through complicated sets of "if-then" rules. The system applies human knowledge in a specific subject area to solve the problem. Expert systems are used for a variety of business purposes: determining credit limits for credit card applicants, monitoring machinery in a plant to predict potential problems or breakdowns, making mortgage loans, and determining optimal plant layouts. They are typically developed by capturing the knowledge of recognized experts in a field whether within a business itself or outside it.

Trends in Information Systems

New information systems are being developed all the time. Today's computer systems help businesspeople obtain and share information in real time, across departments, across the country, and around the world through networks.

Local Area Networks and Wide Area Networks   Most organizations connect their offices and buildings by creating **local area networks (LANs),** computer networks that connect machines within limited areas, such as a building or several buildings near one another. LANs are useful because they link personal computers and allow them to share printers, documents, and information, as well as provide access to the Internet. Figure 15.1 shows what a small business computer network might look like.

Wide area networks (WANS) tie larger geographical regions together by using telephone lines and microwave and satellite transmission. One familiar WAN is long-distance telephone service. Companies such as AT&T and Verizon provide WAN services to businesses and con-

Figure

15.1 A Local Area Network

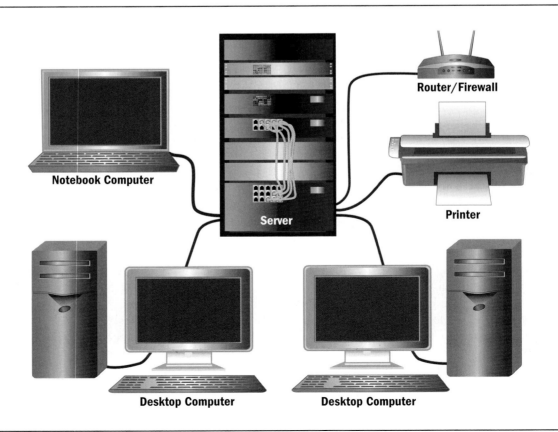

Notebook Computer

Router/Firewall

Server

Printer

Desktop Computer   Desktop Computer

sumers. Firms also use WANs to conduct their own operations. Typically, companies link their own network systems to outside communications equipment and services for transmission across long distances. Later in the chapter, we discuss other specialized networking systems.

Wireless Local Networks   A wireless network allows computers, printers, and other devices to be connected without the hassle of stringing cables in traditional office settings. The current standard for wireless networks is called **Wi-Fi.** Wi-Fi—short for *wireless fidelity*—is a wireless network that connects various devices and allows them to communicate with one another through radio waves. Any PC with a Wi-Fi receptor can connect with the Internet at so-called *hot spots*—locations with a wireless router and a high-speed Internet modem. By one estimate, the number of registered hot spots worldwide now exceeds 70,000.[8] They are found in a variety of places including airports, libraries, and coffee shops. For instance, virtually all Starbucks locations throughout the United States, and in many other countries, are Wi-Fi hot spots. Some hot spots provide free Internet access; others charge fees. AT&T, for example, offers the Freedom Network, a collection of hot spots throughout the nation. Access requires either an annual subscription or the payment of a onetime access fee.

Many believe that the successor to Wi-Fi will be **Wi-Max**, a new wireless standard. Wi-Max recently got a huge boost when Intel announced that it would begin producing computer chips incorporating this new wireless standard.[9] Unlike Wi-Fi's relatively limited geographic coverage area—generally around 300 feet—a single Wi-Max access point can provide coverage over many miles. Hundreds of cities, including San Francisco and Philadelphia, have announced plans to build Wi-Max networks that will, in essence, turn these cities into giant hot spots. Wi-Max also has the potential to bring high-speed Internet access to rural areas where traditional forms of broadband access are too expensive or impractical. For instance, Morrow County, Oregon, has only 11,000 people but covers more than 2,000 square miles. Wi-Max is the only practical and cost-effective way to provide broadband access to this sparsely populated region. So Morrow County became one of the first rural areas in the country to be blanketed by a Wi-Max network. Now onion farmer Bob Hale can open his laptop to check his e-mail, find out the current price of onions, send digital photographs of his crop to restaurant buyers throughout the country, or adjust his irrigation sprinklers. And Hale can accomplish these tasks sitting in the cab of his truck in the middle of his vast onion fields.[10]

Application Service Providers and On-Demand Computing

Because of the increasing cost and complexity of obtaining and maintaining information systems, many firms hire an **application service provider (ASP),** an outside supplier that provides both the computers and the application support for managing an information system. An ASP can simplify complex software for its customers so that it is easier for them to manage and use. When an ASP relationship is successful, the buyer can then devote more time and resources to its core businesses instead of struggling to manage its information systems. Other benefits include stretching the firm's technology dollar farther and giving smaller companies the kind of information power that in the past has been available only to much larger organizations. Even large companies turn to ASPs to manage some or all of their information systems. Recently, the Walt Disney Company decided to outsource much of its IT functions to IBM and Affiliated Computer Services to save money. Around 1,000 Disney employees moved into new jobs with the two vendors.[11]

Another recent trend is **on-demand computing,** also called **utility computing.** Instead of purchasing and maintaining expensive software, firms essentially rent the software time from application providers and pay only for their usage of the software, similar to purchasing

Wi-Fi wireless network that connects various devices and allows them to communicate with one another through radio waves; short for *wireless fidelity*.

application service provider (ASP) specialist in providing both the computers and the application support for managing information systems for clients.

Different types of computers incorporate widely varying memory capacities and processing speeds. As shown in Figure 15.2, these differences define three broad classifications: mainframes, minicomputers, and personal computers. A **mainframe** computer is the largest type of computer system with the most extensive storage capacity and the fastest processing speeds. Especially powerful mainframes called *supercomputers* can handle extremely rapid, complex calculations involving thousands of variables. A **minicomputer** is an intermediate-size computer—more compact and less expensive than a mainframe but also somewhat slower and with less memory. These intermediate computers often toil in universities, factories, and research labs. Minicomputers also appeal to many small businesses that need more power than personal computers can offer to handle specialized tasks. IBM, Sun Microsystems, and Silicon Graphics are major manufacturers of minicomputers.

Personal computers (PCs) are everywhere today—in homes, schools, businesses, nonprofit organizations, and government agencies. For example, an estimated two-thirds of American households have at least one personal computer. They have earned increasing popularity because their ever-expanding capability to handle many of the functions that cumbersome mainframes performed only a few decades ago. These advances were made possible by the development of powerful chips—thin silicon wafers that carry integrated circuits (networks of transistors and electronic circuits). A microprocessor is a fingernail-size chip that contains the PC's entire central processing unit. Intelligent functions of today's new cars, toys, watches, and other household items also rely on microprocessors. Additional chips provide instruction and memory to convert a microprocessor into a PC.

As technology continues to advance, computers have diminished in size. Desktop computers are still the standard PC seen in offices and homes. However, notebook computers are

Figure

15.2 Types of Computers

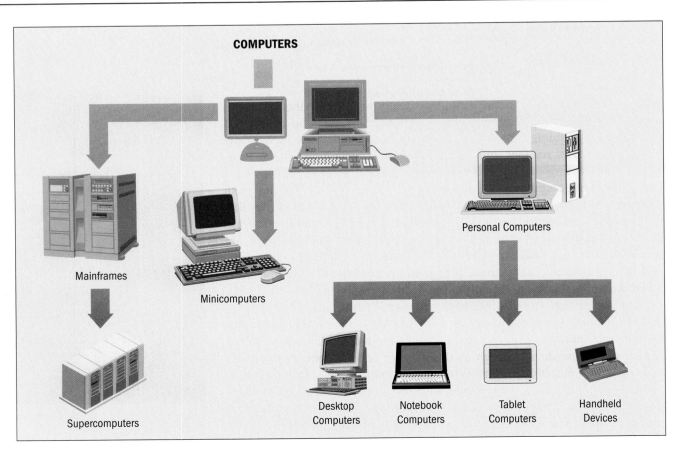

COMPUTERS

Mainframes

Minicomputers

Personal Computers

Supercomputers

Desktop Computers

Notebook Computers

Tablet Computers

Handheld Devices

gaining an increasing share of the PC market each year. While sales of desktop computers have remained relatively flat in recent years, sales of notebook computers are growing at double-digit rates. Recently, for instance, sales of notebook computers exceeded sales of desktop computers for the first time.[13] The increasing popularity of notebook computers is due to many factors, including the increased computing power of notebooks, better displays, expansion in wireless access, and, perhaps most important, a shrinking of the price gap between notebooks and desktops, although notebooks still cost more on average.

A more recent innovation in personal computers is the tablet PC, which looks like a notebook computer but with a difference. The screen is detachable. Users can write on the screen using a special-purpose pen. The handwriting is then digitized and can be converted into a format that can be read by word-processing programs. The pen can also be used to edit existing documents. When tablet PCs were first introduced in 2002, some thought that they would quickly be embraced by a wide variety of users. So far, however, that hasn't happened. Tablet PCs make up less than 5 percent of the notebook computers sold worldwide, although they have taken hold in some markets such as education and healthcare. Experts cite higher prices and the mediocre performance of many handwriting recognition software applications as reasons for slow start to tablet PC sales. However, tablet PC prices are falling, along with notebook prices, and handwriting recognition is improving. So many of these same experts are more optimistic about the future of tablet PCs.[14]

Handheld devices—made by companies such as BlackBerry, Nokia, Palm, HP, Toshiba, and Dell—are even smaller. They fit in a shirt pocket and run on rechargeable batteries. Two kinds of handheld devices are available to most business and consumer users. The original type is the personal digital assistant (PDA). PDAs keep schedules and contact information and have limited software applications such as word processing and spreadsheets. Most PDAs today allow users to access the Internet through wireless networks. The other type of handheld device is the so-called *smart phone*. A smart phone is essentially a device that combines a cell phone with a PDA. Many users like the added features offered by smart phones; consequently, sales of smart phones are growing rapidly. Gartner Research estimates that annual sales of smart phones exceed 20 million units, while the number of PDAs sold per year has declined to less than 13 million units.[15]

DIGITAL VISION/GETTY IMAGES

Notebook computers are gaining a larger share of the PC market.

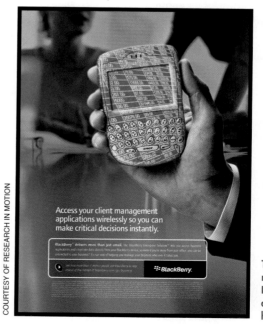

COURTESY OF RESEARCH IN MOTION

Access your client management applications wirelessly so you can make critical decisions instantly.

BlackBerry

The BlackBerry, made by Research In Motion, is one of the most popular handheld devices.

Microsoft Windows runs the majority of PCs.

software set of instructions that tell the computer hardware what to do.

In addition to PDAs and smart phones, specialized handheld devices are used in a variety of businesses for a variety of applications. For instance, DHL, UPS, and FedEx drivers use special handheld devices to track package deliveries. The driver scans each package as it is delivered, and the information is transmitted to the delivery firm's network. Within a few minutes, the sender, using an Internet connection, can obtain the delivery information.

Types of Computer Software

Software includes all of the programs, routines, and computer languages that control a computer and tell it how to operate. The software that controls the basic workings of a computer system is its **operating system.** Moe than 80 percent of personal computers use a version of Microsoft's popular Windows operating system. Personal computers made by Apple use the Mac operating system. Most handheld devices use either the Palm operating system or a special version of Windows called Windows Mobile. Other operating systems include Unix, which runs many minicomputers, and Linux.

A program that performs the specific tasks that the user wants to carry out—such as writing a letter or looking up data—is called **application software.** Examples of application software include Oracle Supply Chain Management Suite, Microsoft Excel, Adobe Acrobat, and QuickBooks. Realtor Trevor Thirsk uses Microsoft Outlook to control his e-mail and organize client paperwork and Microsoft Publisher to create marketing materials. Using these and other software programs helps Thirsk save time—he estimates up to an hour a day—and become one of the top producers at John L. Scott Real Estate, a large residential real estate company in the Pacific Northwest. Even more impressive, Thirsk is one of the youngest, least experienced real estate agents at the firm.[16] The next section discusses the major categories of application software used by business.

assessment check

1. How are computers classified?
2. What are the two major categories of computer software?

HOW COMPUTERS HELP BUSINESSPEOPLE

Computers and their related technologies continue to revolutionize the methods by which businesses manage information. These technologies affect contemporary business in three important ways. First, the enhanced speed and quantity of information available improves the speed and effectiveness of decision making. Second, computers make accurate, unbiased data available to everyone. Third, their information-sharing capabilities support team decision making at low levels of an organization's hierarchy. Every industry has felt at least some impact as computers and information systems have spread.

Consider the Great Harvest Bread Company, headquartered in Dillon, Montana, which operates more than 200 franchised bakeries. Unlike other franchise operations, Great Harvest believes that its franchise operators should be free—after a one-year apprenticeship—to run their stores as they see fit. They aren't required to use the same bread recipe or paint their storefronts the same color. But they are required to share information with each other, which they do via computers. The Great Harvest internal Web site, called the Breadboard, contains announcements of equipment for sale, ongoing electronic charts among franchisees, new recipes, tips for maintaining certain ovens, and archives of other information. Computers help people manage information in an industry that has historically been considered low tech.[17]

Some of the most widely used business applications of computers include enterprise resource planning, word processing, spreadsheets, electronic mail, presentation graphics, and multimedia and interactive media, which are discussed shortly. Users once acquired applications such as these as individual software packages. Today, however, they normally buy integrated software, or *software suites,* which combine several applications into a single package that can share modules for data handling and processing. For personal computer users, the most popular software suite is Microsoft Office, a package that includes word-processing, database management, spreadsheet, presentation, electronic mail, and personal information management software. Businesspeople, for instance, can import data from Access, the database program, into Excel, the spreadsheet program, to create reports and graphs. As another example, you're likely to use PowerPoint—the presentation program—to create dynamic classroom presentations containing text, figures, and even multimedia elements, in many of the classes you take in the coming years.

Some integrated software packages help businesses handle more specific tasks. For example, Palo Alto Software has several software packages that help businesspeople create customized advertising campaigns, marketing plans, and even overall business plans. These programs contain such features as spreadsheet templates designed to evaluate a company's competitiveness in the marketplace.[18]

Today's network technology and software allows multiple users to collaborate on reports and other projects even if they're separated by thousands of miles. Say Ashley and Juan are working on a project. Ashley—who works in the Denver office—writes a preliminary draft using Microsoft Word. She then sends the electronic document to Juan in the Chicago office by e-mail. Juan reviews the document, inserts several figures he created using Microsoft Excel, electronically marks some changes in the Word document, and returns the entire document, including the figures, to Ashley. The process is repeated until they agree on the finished product.

Despite all the advantages of computers, they do have their limitations and should be used to serve the mission of the organization, not just for their own sake. Many businesses have found that their use of computers is actually enhanced by maintaining a human touch—or adding it—to the process. Computers will never replace such face-to-face interactions as phone conversations and meetings.

Enterprise Resource Planning System

As information systems developed in organizations, they were at first contained within functional departments. Soon managers noticed that the data collected about customers during order processing were reentered by inventory control and shipping. The same duplication was found in human resources management systems and finance and accounting. To avoid such rework, eliminate mistakes or inconsistencies in data, and streamline processes, businesses began to demand a system to unify these separate systems. An **enterprise resource planning (ERP) system** is a set of integrated programs designed to collect, process, and provide information about all business operations. Firms such as Microsoft, Oracle, and SAP offer enterprise software programs and suites to help companies run factories, keep track of accounting, manage the human resources function, and assist in marketing efforts.

Oracle, for instance, offers a variety of ERP software suites and programs, each tailored to specific business applications. One is called Oracle Internet Expenses, part of the company's

"They Said It"
"Computers make it easier to do a lot of things, but most of the things they make it easier to do don't need to be done."
—Andy Rooney (b. 1919)
News commentator

enterprise resource planning (ERP) system information system that collects, processes, and provides information about an organization's various functions.

HIT & MISS

Nobody Does It Better: Oracle

Oracle founder Larry Ellison has been described as "a slightly grizzled survivor," having weathered all kinds of storms in the software industry. His reputation for being brash and aggressive hasn't changed, but it has mellowed somewhat as the 60-something entrepreneur continues to run the database company he started in 1977.

In an era when the software industry has become increasingly fragmented, Ellison remains focused—providing his customers with the best business application software in the world and on acquiring the companies he believes he needs in order to do so. Consolidation could be termed Ellison's mantra. "The industry is maturing. It is going to consolidate," maintains Ellison. In fact, Oracle had begun to snap up other companies long before Ellison made the prediction. In a highly publicized takeover, Oracle acquired PeopleSoft, a large human resources ERP software company. Recently, Oracle also acquired Siebel Systems, producer of customer relationship management (CRM) applications. CRM applications collect and navigate through all customer interactions so that businesses can better understand and fulfill their customers' needs. The move was huge for Oracle. "In a single step, Oracle becomes the number one CRM applications company in the world," boasted Ellison.

Even with its acquisitions, Oracle still lags behind Cisco, Google, IBM, Intel, and Microsoft in size. And its largest direct ERP competitor is SAP, a German firm. But some industry experts note that hundreds of small software companies are still out there in the market for Oracle—which has plenty of cash—to purchase. And the point of all this acquisition isn't size alone; its ultimate goal is to allow Oracle to surge ahead as the best in the business of providing software applications to companies. The CRM market alone accounts for nearly $10 billion.

Some analysts give Ellison credit for anticipating the next trend in corporate software as well as the move toward consolidation in the industry. "Larry Ellison is a technology visionary and someone who has taken a long-term perspective," notes one industry analyst. Others warn that it will be years before Ellison's strategy proves itself. Bill McDermott, CEO of SAP America, notes that Oracle is only poising itself for larger battles. "The games begin when Microsoft and Oracle lock horns," he predicts. "That's the big looming battle: Oracle versus Microsoft. You've got IBM in there, too."

Questions for Critical Thinking

1. Oracle seeks to dominate the business software industry. What challenges do you think the firm will face in the next five years?
2. How can a firm like Oracle help its customers improve their own businesses?

Sources: Glen Fest, "Battle of Tech Titans: Oracle vs. SAP: Smoke, but No Fire," *Bank Technology News*, accessed July 21, 2006, http://www.banktechnews.com; Daniel Gross, "The J. P. Morgan of Silicon Valley," *Slate*, accessed July 21, 2006, http://slate.msn.com; Benjamin Pimentel, "Top CEO: Larry Ellison Convinced That the Future in High Tech Depends on Consolidation," *San Francisco Chronicle*, accessed July 21, 2006, http://www.sfgate.com.

E-Business Suite. It is designed to improve the efficiency of travel and entertainment expense reporting and approval. MasterCard International uses Internet Expenses to process the company's own travel and entertainment transactions. The online application quickly validates and approves expense reports while flagging unusual transactions for further investigation. According to MasterCard, since it started using Internet Expenses, productivity increased by 118 percent and reporting costs dropped by more than 50 percent.[19] Through a series of recent acquisitions, Oracle has become one of the world leaders in ERP software. The firm is profiled in the "Hit & Miss" feature.

Word Processing

word processing software that uses a computer to input, store, retrieve, edit, and print various types of documents.

One of the original business applications—and currently one of the most popular—**word processing** uses computers to input, store, retrieve, edit, and print various types of documents.

With word processing, users can revise sentences, check spelling, correct mistakes, and move copy around quickly and cleanly.

Word processing helps a company handle huge volumes of correspondence, process numerous documents, and personalize form letters. Today virtually all companies use general-purpose computers running word-processing software. By far the most popular word-processing software is Microsoft Word, part of the firm's Office suite. Other word-processing programs include Corel's WordPerfect. These programs enable users to include graphics and spreadsheets from other programs in their documents and to create Web sites by translating documents into hypertext markup language (HTML), the language of the World Wide Web.

Many businesses extend word-processing capabilities to create sophisticated documents. **Desktop publishing** employs computer technology to allow users to design and produce attractively formatted printed material themselves rather than hiring professionals. Desktop publishing software combines high-quality type, graphics, and layout tools to create output that can look as attractive as documents produced by professional publishers and printers. Advanced equipment can scan photos and drawings and duplicate them on printed pages. Documents created through desktop publishing can not only be printed on paper but also published on the Web. Two popular desktop publishing programs are Microsoft Publisher and Adobe InDesign.

Many firms use desktop publishing systems to print newsletters, reports, form letters, and Web pages. Advertising and graphic arts departments often use desktop publishing systems to create brochures and marketing materials. A good desktop publishing system can save a company money by allowing staff members to produce such documents, whether they are for internal or external use.

Word processing and desktop publishing can also be used to reduce the amount of paper generated by the typical office. While a true "paperless" office may never become a reality, many businesses realize that cutting down on paper can improve efficiency and save money. For instance, Minnesota-based Farmers Home Mutual Insurance uses the Intelligent Document Platform from Adobe as part of a Web-based system to improve client service and reduce administrative costs. Instead of using a paper application, agents enter client information electronically. Farmers estimates that it saves more than $500,000 per year by eliminating paper application forms. Moreover, the electronic application shortens the time needed to process applications by 70 percent and virtually eliminates errors.[20]

Spreadsheets

An electronic **spreadsheet** is the computerized equivalent of an accountant's worksheet. This software permits businesspeople to manipulate decision variables and determine their impact on such outcomes as profits and sales. With a spreadsheet, a manager can have an accurate answer to a question in seconds and can often glance at the whole financial picture of a company on a single page. Not surprisingly, Microsoft Excel, part of the Office suite, is by far the most popular spreadsheet program. Another popular spreadsheet program is Corel Quattro Pro. Spreadsheet programs can also be used to create graphs and charts, and they have statistical analysis capabilities. Spreadsheets aren't just for accountants or finance professionals; people in other business areas such as marketing, human resources, and production rely on spreadsheet programs as well.

Figure 15.3 demonstrates how a manager uses a spreadsheet to set a price for a proposed product. Note that the manager can analyze alternative decisions using a spreadsheet. For instance, he or she can estimate the impact on sales given a change in the product's price. A more complex spreadsheet may stretch across many more columns and rows and even contain multiple worksheets, but the software still makes new calculations as fast as the manager can change the variables.

spreadsheet software package that creates the computerized equivalent of an accountant's worksheet, allowing the user to manipulate variables and see the impact of alternative decisions on operating results.

Figure

15.3 How a Spreadsheet Works

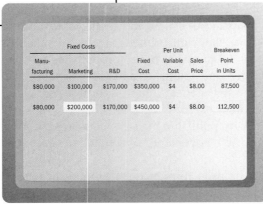

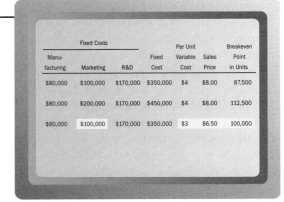

With an $8 selling price, $4 in variable costs for each unit sold, and total fixed costs of $350,000, we have to sell 87,500 units just to break even. Now marketing suggests that we increase marketing expenses another $100,000 to stimulate additional sales. Let's see what the spreadsheet says.

That extra $100,000 had better expand sales! The spreadsheet shows that we now have to sell 112,500 units just to break even. Maybe the second proposal would be better—the one to cut variable costs per unit to $3 and use the savings to shave $1.50 off the retail price. Let's run it through the spreadsheet.

	Fixed Costs		Fixed Cost	Per Unit Variable Cost	Sales Price	Breakeven Point in Units
Manu-facturing	Marketing	R&D				
$80,000	$100,000	$170,000	$350,000	$4	$8.00	87,500
$80,000	$200,000	$170,000	$450,000	$4	$8.00	112,500

	Fixed Costs		Fixed Cost	Per Unit Variable Cost	Sales Price	Breakeven Point in Units
Manu-facturing	Marketing	R&D				
$80,000	$100,000	$170,000	$350,000	$4	$8.00	87,500
$80,000	$200,000	$170,000	$450,000	$4	$8.00	112,500
$80,000	$100,000	$170,000	$350,000	$3	$6.50	100,000

Electronic Mail

Businesspeople need to communicate directly with associates as well as customers, suppliers, and others outside their organization. Increasingly, they turn to their computers for this function, replacing much of their regular mailings (jokingly called *snail mail*) by sending messages via e-mail. Popular e-mail programs include Microsoft Outlook, Outlook Express, and Eudora. While e-mail may be a regular part of your business day, it is important to understand clearly when and how to use it—and the Internet in general—as described in the "Business Etiquette" feature.

As discussed in Chapter 7, a popular adaptation of e-mail is instant messaging. Instant messaging allows users to create private chat rooms with other individuals on their personal lists. The instant messaging system alerts a user whenever somebody on his or her list is online. The user can then initiate a chat session with that individual. There are several different instant messaging systems, including AOL Instant Messenger, Yahoo! Messenger, and Windows Messenger. To communicate, however, all users must use the same instant messaging system.

E-mail and instant messaging are rapid ways to communicate both inside and outside the organization. As a means of internal communication, e-mail is especially useful in organizations with employees located in different parts of the country or in different countries altogether. Employees can typically access their organization's e-mail anytime, anywhere. All it takes is a Web connection.

Certainly e-mail can help companies reduce paperwork, time wasted in playing telephone tag, and similar inefficiencies. But e-mail does have its limitations. It works best for short unemotional messages. Longer documents are best sent as attachments to e-mail or via fax. And e-mail users should be aware that messages are not private; employers may be monitoring messages, so employees should refrain from sending personal messages or jokes to each other. Some messages, such as those containing potentially emotional news or those that may need an explanation, are best transmitted by telephone or in person. Also, as we noted in Chapter 7, some of the benefits of e-mail have been undermined by the proliferation of spam, or junk e-mail.

Presentation Graphics

Analyzing columns of numbers can be a tedious task. But when people see data displayed as charts or graphs, they can often identify patterns and relationships that raw data do not reveal. Businesspeople once had to labor to create charts and graphs or send the data or rough sketches to professional artists and then wait for the finished products. Computer software has greatly simplified the process of creating graphics. As noted earlier, spreadsheet programs can create dozens of types of high-quality graphs. **Presentation software,** the most popular of which is Microsoft PowerPoint, goes one step further. These programs create entire presentations. Users can create bulleted lists, charts, graphs, pictures, audio, and even short video clips. Examples are shown in Figure 15.4. By combining these elements in ways that are easy to read, a user can prepare presentations and handouts for a business meeting. To persuade management to fund a new project, an employee might create a series of graphs and charts to illustrate how the project will benefit the organization over time.

Multimedia and Interactive Media

Today's computers have leaped beyond numbers, text, and graphs to encompass multimedia and interactive media capabilities.

presentation software computer program that includes graphics and tools to produce a variety of charts, graphs, and pictures.

When—and How—to Use Your Computer at Work

Just about anywhere you work, you are bound to have access to a computer. Whether you're in sales, marketing, finance, or human resources, a computer will be nearby—if not actually on your desk. You already know what your computer is for: work. Despite this fact, one recent survey revealed that 93 percent of workers who had a computer at work also used it for personal purposes—e-mailing or accessing the Web. The most popular sites accessed were news, personal e-mail, online banks, travel companies, and shopping. Gaming has also soared in popularity. Microsoft's game site, Zone.com, reports that its busiest time of day is midafternoon Eastern time—when most people are at work.

While this practice may seem harmless, businesses that allow employees to surf the Internet freely may face serious consequences. An employer may be held legally responsible for employees' misuse of e-mail—bullying, threatening, or making sexually explicit comments. A firm is also vulnerable to disclosure of its private information, as well as viruses spread via e-mail. Then there's the lost productivity of employees who are gaming and shopping during work time. So before you log on at work, consider the following:

- Make sure you know your company's policy about computer and Internet use. One firm might allow casual e-mailing or shopping during lunch hours; another might not. If you violate the policy, you could find yourself un-

employed. If your firm doesn't have a formal policy, ask your supervisor for guidelines before you log on. Then use common sense.

- If you may use your computer for some personal messages, be aware that most firms can monitor employee e-mail. "[Employees] should avoid pretty much anything they wouldn't want to print out and hang up on their cubicle walls," warns one technology consultant.

- Be honest about whether you really need to use the Internet during the workday. If you need to make a quick bank deposit online or check the time of your next flight, fine. But if you're surfing the Web for a great pair of shoes to wear next weekend, save it for after work.

Every firm is different, but "the solution lies in balancing employees' needs for personal use of the Web at work without draining overall productivity," advises Geoff Haggart of Internet firm Websense.

Sources: "Monitoring Employees' Use of Company Computers and the Internet," Texas Workforce, accessed July 21, 2006, http://www.twc.state.tx.us; Mimi Ho, "Internet Surfing at the Workplace," CIO, accessed July 21, 2006, http://www2.cio.com; Michele Marrinan, "Beware the Wandering Mouse," Monster.com, accessed July 21, 2006, http://wlb.monster.com; Bureau of Labor Statistics, "Most Common Uses for Computers at Work," U.S. Department of Labor, accessed July 21, 2006, http://www.bls.gov; "Web Surfing as Addictive as Coffee," CNN.com, accessed July 21, 2006, http://edition.cnn.com.

Figure

15.4 | Examples of Presentation Graphics Software

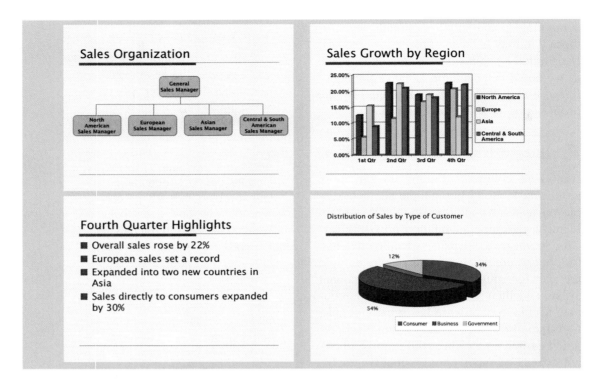

Multimedia computing refers to technologies that integrate two or more types of media, such as text, voice, sound, full-motion video, still video, graphics, and animation into computer-based applications. Many popular business applications have multimedia computing capabilities. For example, as we just noted, Microsoft PowerPoint users can add audio and video clips to their presentations.

One of the growing business applications for multimedia computing is employee business presentations and conferences. The Internet has made transmission of these meetings widely available. Many companies routinely provide multimedia Webcasts of their annual meetings for viewing on their Web sites. Salespeople use their notebook computers to make presentations to customers in the field.

Many applications of multimedia computing use interactive media—programs that allow users to interact with computer displays. Home Depot's Expo Design Centers interactive software allows customers to plan and design home remodeling and building projects either online or at Home Depot stores. Customers can view a variety of 3D products, enter their room dimensions, create orders, and track the installation of their projects on a computer screen.

assessment check

1. What is enterprise resource planning software?

2. Explain the difference between word-processing and desktop publishing software.

3. Briefly discuss how a spreadsheet program might be used to help solve a common business problem.

INTRANETS, VIRTUAL PRIVATE NETWORKS, AND VoIP

A previous section discussed the use of LANs and WANs to allow businesses to communicate, transmit and print documents, and share data. These networks require businesses to install special equipment and connections between office sites. But Internet technology has also been applied to internal company communications and business tasks, tapping a ready-made network. Among these new Internet-based applications are intranets, virtual private networks (VPNs), and voice over Internet protocol (VoIP). Each has contributed to the effectiveness and speed of business processes.

Intranets

A broad approach to sharing information in an organization is to establish a company network patterned after the Internet. Such a network, called an **intranet,** links employees through Internet tools such as e-mail and searches using Web browsers. Intranets are similar to the Internet, but they limit access to employees or other authorized users. An intranet blocks outsiders without valid passwords from entering its network by incorporating software or hardware known as a **firewall.** Firewalls limit data transfers to certain locations and log system use so that managers can identify attempts to log on with invalid passwords and other threats to a system's security. Highly sophisticated packages immediately alert system administrators about suspicious activities and permit authorized personnel to use smart cards to log on from remote terminals.

intranet a computer network that links employees and other authorized users.

Intranets solve the problem of linking different types of computers. Like the Internet, intranets can integrate computers running all kinds of operating systems. In addition, intranets are relatively easy and inexpensive to set up because most businesses already have some of the required hardware and software. For instance, a small business can simply purchase a DSL router and a few cables and create an intranet using phone jacks and internal phone lines. All the business's computers will be linked with each other as well as with the Internet.

Intranets also support teamwork among employees who travel or work from home. Any intranet member with the right identification, a PC, and some sort of Internet access—either dial-up or broadband—can access the intranet and gain access to group calendars, e-mail, documents, and other files. Intranets can also be used for videoconferencing and other forms of virtual meetings.

Global financial services firm Rothschild uses intranet services provided by Interwoven. Interwoven replaced the firm's ad hoc shared network drives and various filing systems with a uniform document management system. The intranet allows access and sharing of financial dealings and client data. Documents, financial models, agreements, reports, and market data can be accessed securely by Rothschild bankers anywhere in the world. This speeds research, facilitates knowledge sharing, and, in the end, provides more consistent client relationships.[21]

Virtual Private Networks

To gain increased security for Internet communications, companies often turn to **virtual private networks (VPNs),** secure connections between two points on the Internet. These VPNs use firewalls and programs that encapsulate data to make them more secure during transit. Loosely defined, a VPN can include a range of networking technologies, from secure Internet connections to private networks from service providers like IBM and AT&T. A VPN is cheaper for a company to use than leasing several of its own lines. It can also take months to install a leased line in some parts of the world, but a new user can be added to a VPN in a day. Because a VPN uses the Internet, it can be wired, wireless, or a combination of the two.

PHOTODISC/GETTY IMAGES

Network management and security are increasing concerns of businesses.

Singapore's Nanyang Technological University (NTU) uses a VPN provided by Juniper Networks. The VPN enables the university's IT staff to remotely manage 85 e-learning servers, which make up the university's e-learning operations center. This eliminates the need for the company's information technology (IT) staff to be physically near the servers, greatly reducing the amount of time and expense needed for server maintenance. Chye Seng of NTU says, "instead of working on the server console in the data center, staff members now have the option to work remotely, saving us time and money, and improving the quality of our e-learning service."[22]

VoIP

VoIP—which stands for *voice over Internet protocol*—is an alternative to traditional telecommunication services provided by companies such as Verizon and Qwest. The VoIP telephone is not connected to a traditional phone jack but rather is connected to a personal computer with any type of broadband connection. Special software transmits phone conversations over the Internet, rather than through telephone lines. A VoIP user dials the phone as usual. Recipients can receive calls made using VoIP through regular telephone connections (land or wireless). Moreover, you can call another person who has VoIP using a regular landline or cell phone.

A growing number of consumers and businesses have embraced VoIP, mainly due to the cost savings and extra features offered by VoIP. For instance, Skype—owned by eBay—has around 6 million users.[23] Home Care Delivered, a Virginia-based healthcare supply firm, decided to go with VoIP when it opened a new facility recently. For CEO Gordy Fox, it made perfect sense because a corporate data network was already in place. Fox believes that the company will save thousands of dollars by bypassing the public phone network. VoIP allows the company to set up an office anywhere there's a fast Internet connection.[24]

In spite of VoIP's apparent advantages, there are several potential drawbacks to replacing traditional telephony with Internet telephony. For one thing, your Internet phone service will be only as reliable as your broadband connection. If your broadband connection goes out, so will your phone service. For another, without extensive safeguards, VoIP can expose a phone system to the havoc affecting the rest of the Internet, such as worms and viruses. Gary Heller, deputy CIO for the Arizona Healthcare Cost Containment System, recently helped install VoIP in system offices throughout the state. Before installing VoIP, Heller focused hard on security and didn't go ahead with VoIP until he thought that all the potential security issues had been resolved. "You'll be sorry if security is an afterthought with VoIP," he says.[25]

assessment check

1. Explain the differences between an intranet and a virtual private network.
2. What are some of the major advantages and disadvantages of VoIP?

PROTECTING INFORMATION SYSTEMS

As information systems become increasingly important business assets, they also become progressively harder to replace. When computers are connected to a network, a problem at any individual computer can affect the entire network. Although many computer security issues go beyond the scope of this book, the following sections discuss three important security threats: computer crime, or e-crime; viruses; and disasters that may damage information systems.

E-Crime

Computers provide efficient ways for employees to share information. But they may also allow people with more malicious intentions to access information. Or they may allow pranksters—who have no motive other than to see whether they can hack into a system—to gain access to classified information. Common e-crimes involve stealing or altering data in several ways:

- Employees or outsiders may change or invent data to produce inaccurate or misleading information.
- Employees or outsiders may modify computer programs to create false information or illegal transactions or to insert viruses.
- Unauthorized people can access computer systems for their own illicit benefit or knowledge or just to see if they can get in.

E-crime is on the rise. According to a recent survey of IT professionals and managers conducted by *CSO* magazine in cooperation with the U.S. Secret Service and Carnegie Mellon University's CERT Coordination Center, 70 percent of respondents reported at least one e-crime and almost half reported an increase in e-crimes compared with the prior year. The typical respondent reported more than 130 e-crimes during the year. The total cost of these crimes was estimated at around $700 million. Of course, the statistics don't include the number of incidents that were not reported, so the total number and cost are probably higher.

Individuals, businesses, and government agencies are all vulnerable to computer crime. Computer hackers—unauthorized users—sometimes work alone and sometimes in groups. Sometimes hackers break into computer systems just to show that they can do it; other times they have more sinister motives. Along a stretch of highway in a shopping area near downtown Miami, hackers obtained credit card information for thousands of customers at four major stores. The thieves identified stores with strong wireless signals and weakly protected data networks. For more than a month, hackers gained access to the stores' computer systems and obtained sensitive financial information from their databases. Security experts and law enforcement officials estimated that more than 1.4 million customer accounts were exposed. The exact dollar amount of losses is not known.[26] In another recent incident, hackers gained access to a LexisNexis database. The security of thousands of Social Security numbers, driver's license data, and other personal information may have been compromised.[27]

Information system administrators implement two basic protections against computer crime: they try to prevent access to their systems by unauthorized users and the viewing of data by unauthorized system users. To prevent access, the simplest method requires authorized users to enter passwords. The company may also install firewalls, described earlier. To prevent system users from reading sensitive information, the company may use encryption software, which encodes, or scrambles, messages. To read encrypted messages, users must use an electronic key to convert them to regular text. But as fast as software developers invent new and more elaborate protective measures, hackers seem to break through their defenses. So security is an ongoing battle. Debate continues over whether stronger laws are needed to protect the sensitive personal information contained in many computer databases. This debate is summarized in the "Solving an Ethical Controversy" feature.

Another form of computer theft is as old as crime itself: theft of equipment. As the size of computer hardware diminishes, it becomes increasingly vulnerable to theft. Handheld devices, for instance, can vanish with a pickpocket or purse snatcher. And because these machines may contain all kinds of important information for a business, employees need to be especially careful not to leave them unattended or out of reach. The recent theft, and subsequent recovery, of a

DOES DATABASE SECURITY EXIST?

Everywhere you go, companies obtain information about you—enough for just about anyone to steal your identity. Firms vow to keep your information secure, but increasingly, those promises are broken by technologically savvy thieves, who in one fell swoop may gain access to a single database containing information about millions of individuals.

Businesses, consumer groups, and the U.S. Congress continue to debate who is ultimately responsible for database security. New legislation and regulations have been proposed.

Are companies doing enough to protect their customer database information?

PRO

1. Companies that engage in financial transactions are already required to establish and enforce information security programs to prevent identify theft. In addition, new legislation strengthens customer notification requirements when security is breached.
2. Companies that make security a top priority have professional support staff who constantly review any possible compromises in the system. This type of vigilance is the best way to maintain security.

CON

1. Experts warn that identity theft is often committed by a company's own workers, vendors, and suppliers, who have access to passcodes, passwords, or key codes. "We're creating this façade that we can protect this information, and in reality we can't," warns Pete Lindstrom of Spire Security LLC. "There are too many people who have legitimate access to this stuff."
2. Although well intentioned, many companies focus too much on outdated methods of security such as encryption. While encryption was once enough protection, experts now advise that it is merely one layer of defense.

Summary

Database security has become increasingly critical as large companies have admitted to massive losses of personal data. ChoicePoint, which collects and sells personal information to government agencies and private firms, announced the potential exposure of information on 35,000 consumers in California. Data provider LexisNexis discovered a security breach of data on more than 310,000 consumers. Organizations as diverse as Bank of America, San Jose Medical Group, and Boston College have also reported security breaches. As a result, financial institutions have agreed to work more closely with the Federal Trade Commission to solve—and ultimately thwart—identity theft crimes.

Sources: Jon Oitsik, "The Truth about Database Security," CNet News.com, accessed July 21, 2006, http://news.com.com; Charles Garry, "Taking a Trip Down Denial," *eWeek*, accessed July 21, 2006, http://www.eweek.com; Lisa Vaas, "Congress Nears Final Identity Theft Legislation," *eWeek*, accessed July 21, 2006, http://www.eweek.com; Karen D. Schwartz, "Financial Institutions to Share Identity-Theft Data," *eWeek*, accessed July 21, 2006, http://www.eweek.com; Judith M. Collins, "Identity Theft: An Inside Job," *eWeek*, accessed July 21, 2006, http://www.eweek.com; Jon Swartz, "Personal Info about 310,000 at Risk," *USA Today*, accessed July 21, 2006, http://www.usatoday.com; Bob Sullivan, "Database Giant Gives Access to Fake Firms," MSNBC, accessed July 21, 2006, http://www.msnbc.com.

solving an **ETHICAL** controversy

notebook computer belonging to an official of the Department of Veterans Affairs, containing sensitive information on millions of veterans and active duty military personnel, illustrates the vulnerability of these devices. Many notebook computers and handheld devices contain special security software that makes it difficult for a thief or any unauthorized person to access the data stored in the computer's memory.

Computer Viruses, Worms, Trojan Horses, and Spyware

Rather than directly tampering with a company's data or computers, computer hackers may create viruses, worms, or Trojan horses to infect computers at random. Attacks by these and other forms of malicious software cost consumers and businesses billions of dollars annually.

Computer *viruses* are programs that secretly attach themselves to other programs (called *hosts*) and change them or destroy data. Viruses can be programmed to become active immediately or to remain dormant for a period of time, after which the infections suddenly activate themselves and cause problems. A virus can reproduce by copying itself onto other programs stored in the same drive. It spreads as users install infected software on their systems or exchange files with others, usually by exchanging e-mail, accessing electronic bulletin boards, trading disks, or downloading programs or data from unknown sources on the Internet.

A *worm* is a small piece of software that exploits a security hole in a network to replicate itself. A copy of the worm scans the network for another machine that has a specific security hole. It copies itself to the new machine using the security hole and then starts replicating from there as well. Unlike viruses, worms don't need host programs to damage computer systems.

A *Trojan horse* is a program that claims to do one thing, but in reality does something else, usually something malicious. For example, a Trojan horse might claim, and even appear, to be a game. When an unsuspecting user clicks the Trojan horse, the program might erase the hard drive or steal any personal data stored on the computer.

Spyware is software that covertly gathers user information through the user's Internet connection without his or her knowledge, usually for advertising purposes. Spyware applications are typically bundled with other programs downloaded from the Internet. Once installed, the spyware monitors user activity on the Internet and transmits that information in the background to someone else.

Attacks by viruses, worms, Trojan horses, and spyware are not limited to computers and computer networks; handheld devices, including cell phones, have been affected as well. Recently, for example, a Trojan horse was discovered that turned Sony's popular PSP (PlayStation Portable) into what one expert referred to as a "brick." The program—which posed as a patch allowing a user to run games not approved by Sony—actually deleted four critical system files, rendering the PSP inoperable. The owner had little choice but to send the infected PSP into Sony for expensive repairs.[28]

As viruses, worms, and Trojan horses become more complex, the technology to fight them must increase in sophistication as well. The simplest way to protect against computer viruses is to install one of the many available antivirus software programs, such as Norton AntiVirus and McAfee VirusScan. These programs, which also protect against worms and some Trojan horses, continuously monitor systems for viruses and automatically eliminate any they spot. Users should regularly update them by downloading the latest virus definitions. In addition, computer users should also install and regularly update antispyware programs because many Trojan horses are forms of spyware.

But management must begin to emphasize security at a deeper level: software design, corporate servers, Web gateways, and Internet service providers. Because more than 80 percent of the world's PCs run on Microsoft operating systems, a single virus, worm, or Trojan horse can spread quickly among them. Individual computer users should carefully choose the files they load onto their systems, scan their systems regularly, make sure their antivirus software is up-to-date, and install software only from known sources. They should also be very careful when opening attachments to e-mails, because many viruses, worms, and Trojan horses are spread that way.

assessment check

1. List some examples of e-crime.
2. Explain the differences between a virus, a worm, and a Trojan horse.

DISASTER RECOVERY AND BACKUP

Natural disasters, power failures, equipment malfunctions, software glitches, human error, and terrorist attacks can disrupt even the most sophisticated computer systems. These disruptions can cost businesses and other organizations billions of dollars.

Recently flooding from the Delaware River damaged a bakery and café owned by Jane and Joel Vitart in New Hope, Pennsylvania. The flood caused about $120,000 in damage and cleanup costs, but the biggest blow was the loss of the business's computer system. As Jane Vitart noted, "I ran my whole business on that computer—all my financial data, inventory, vendor bills, my marketing materials, customer lists, menus." She had backed up some of her financial data, but the backup disk turned out to be defective. The business was closed for six weeks and then reopened only after the couple stretched their credit to the limit and used all their personal savings. Jane Vitart said "I feel like I'm starting from scratch." Now, at the first hint of flooding, she makes sure the computer system is among the first items evacuated.[29]

Software glitches are no less serious. Recently, a software glitch shut down the systems running the New York Stock Exchange. The shutdown halted all trading for about twelve minutes right before the market closed, creating havoc in the financial markets throughout the country. Another recent software glitch at Bank of America resulted in teachers in several California districts not getting paid on time. And a software glitch at a Baltimore Gas and Electric computer caused about 7,000 customers to be overcharged for electricity, some for many years.[30]

Disaster recovery planning—deciding how to prevent system failures and continue operations if computer systems fail—is a critical function of all organizations. Disaster prevention programs can avoid some of these costly problems. The most basic precaution is routinely backing up software and data—at the organizational and individual levels.

Disaster planning helped the Veterans Health Information System get back to normal quickly following Hurricane Katrina. The hurricane affected Veterans Affairs (VA) facilities in New Orleans and in Jackson and Biloxi, Mississippi. However, within a couple of days, the patient database was operating as it did the day before the hurricane. Any patient who was being treated by VA facilities in the affected areas could walk into any VA provider, anywhere in the country, and his or her records could be pulled up on the screen.[31]

Companies can now back up data at such online storage services as Iron Mountain or Network Associates. Technology planners may decide to respond to the possibility of a natural disaster such as an earthquake or flood by paying for extra hardware installation in a secure location that can be accessed during an emergency. PSS/World, a medical equipment distributor based in Jacksonville, uses disaster recovery services from SunGard Availability Services, which cost the company around $500,000 per year. Among other items, PSS/World stores its data in the vendor's Philadelphia facility. As Katrina neared the Gulf Coast, PSS/World decided that its Jackson, Mississippi, call center might be affected. Losing the call center would cost the firm an estimated $3 million a day. The firm alerted SunGard that it was putting its emergency plan into effect. The storm did knock out the Jackson call center for several days, but thanks to its disaster plan and the services provided by SunGard, PSS/World's business wasn't hurt.[32]

assessment check

1. What is a software glitch?
2. Explain disaster recovery planning as it relates to information systems.

WHAT'S AHEAD

This is the first of two chapters devoted to managing technology and information. Chapter 16, "Understanding Accounting and Financial Statements," focuses on the functions of accounting, steps in the accounting process, functions and components of financial statements, and the role of budgets in an organization.

1 **Distinguish between data and information and explain the role of management information systems in business.**

It is important for businesspeople to know the difference between data and information. Data are raw facts and figures that may or may not be relevant to a business decision. Information is knowledge gained from processing those facts and figures. An effective information system can help answer many management questions. A management information system (MIS) is an organized method for providing past, present, and projected information on internal operations as well as external intelligence to support decision making. The heart of an MIS is its database, which serves as an electronic filing cabinet for facts and figures.

Assessment Check Answers

1.1 What is the difference between data and information?
Data consist of raw facts and figures that may or may not be relevant to a business decision. Information is the knowledge gained from processing data.

1.2 Define *management information system.*
A management information system is an organized method for providing past, present, and projected information on internal operations as well as external intelligence to support decision making.

1.3 What is the purpose of business intelligence?
Business intelligence is the task of using computer-based technology to retrieve and evaluate data in a database to identify useful trends.

2 **Identify and briefly describe the different types of information system programs.**

The key to a useful information system is the program that links users to data. Different types of information system programs include decision support systems (DSSs), which provide relevant data to help businesspeople make decisions and choose courses of action; executive support systems, which allow top managers to access the firm's primary databases; and expert systems, which imitate human thinking. Trends in information systems include local area and wide area networks (LANs and WANs); wireless local networks (Wi-Fi and Wi-Max); and application service

providers (ASPs), outside firms that provide both computers and application support for managing an information system.

Assessment Check Answers

2.1 What is a decision support system?
A decision support system is an information system that quickly provides relevant data to help businesspeople make decisions and choose courses of action.

2.2 Why do some organizations use application service providers?
The major advantages of using application service providers are cost and added expertise. Many organizations find it much more cost-effective to outsource information technology than to try to handle it in house.

3 **Describe the hardware and software used in managing information.**

Hardware consists of all tangible elements of a computer system, including input and output devices. Major categories of computers include mainframes, supercomputers, minicomputers, and personal computers (PCs). Newer developments in PCs include notebooks, tablet PCs, and handheld devices. Computer software provides the instructions that tell the hardware what to do. The software that controls the basic workings of the computer is its operating system. Other programs, called *application software,* perform specific tasks that users want to complete.

Assessment Check Answers

3.1 How are computers classified?
Computers are classified as being either mainframes, minicomputers, or personal computers. Personal computers are divided into desktop computers, notebook computers, tablet computers, and handheld devices (PDAs and smart phones).

3.2 What are the two major categories of computer software?
Operating systems control the basic workings of a computer. A program that performs a specific task is called *application software.*

4 Identify how different types of software can help businesspeople.

Individual types of software can help businesses in a variety of ways. Word processing helps a company handle massive volumes of correspondence, reports, and other documents. Desktop publishing allows users to design and produce attractively formatted printed material. Spreadsheets calculate and present information clearly. Electronic mail allows businesspeople to communicate rapidly anywhere in the world. Presentation graphics provide graphs and charts that help businesspeople see patterns in data. Multimedia integrates two or more types of media. Interactive media are programs that allow users to interact with computer displays. Integrated software combines several applications into a single package that can share modules for data handling and processing.

Assessment Check Answers

4.1 What is enterprise resource planning software?
Enterprise resource planning software is a set of integrated programs designed to collect, process, and provide information about all business operations.

4.2 Explain the difference between word-processing and desktop publishing software.
Word-processing software uses computers to input, store, retrieve, edit, and print various types of documents. Desktop publishing takes word processing one step further by combining high-quality type and graphics. Documents can be printed or published on the Web.

4.3 Briefly discuss how a spreadsheet program might be used to help solve a common business problem.
A spreadsheet is a computerized equivalent of an accountant's worksheet. The software helps businesspeople manipulate decision variables and determine their impact on such outcomes as profits and sales. For example, a marketing manager might use a spreadsheet to evaluate the impact of increased promotional expenditures on sales and profits.

5 Explain the importance of special network technologies.

Intranets allow employees to share information on a ready-made company network. Access to an intranet is restricted to authorized users and is protected by a firewall. Virtual private networks (VPNs) help save companies money by providing a secure Internet connection between two or more points. VoIP—voice over Internet protocol—uses a personal computer running special software and a broadband Internet connection to make and receive telephone calls over the Internet rather than over traditional telephone networks. VoIP is usually cheaper than traditional telephony and offers users added flexibility.

Assessment Check Answers

5.1 Explain the differences between an intranet and a virtual private network.
An intranet is a physical network that links an organization's computers, allowing them to share documents, printers, and other devices. A virtual private network links two or more computers over a secure Internet connection.

5.2 What are some of the major advantages and disadvantages of VoIP?
The major advantages of VoIP are lower cost, increased communications flexibility, and additional features. Security and reliability are two drawbacks of VoIP.

6 List the ways that companies can protect themselves from computer crimes.

Companies can protect themselves from computer crime by requiring users to enter passwords, installing firewalls or encryption software, and keeping up to date on new security methods. In addition, managers should install antivirus security programs on all computers and networks.

Assessment Check Answers

6.1 List some examples of e-crime.
Examples of e-crime include the stealing or altering of data and the theft of computer hardware.

6.2 Explain the differences between a virus, a worm, and a Trojan horse.
A virus is a program that secretly attaches itself to other programs and changes the host program or destroys data. A worm is a small piece of software that exploits a security hole in a network and duplicates itself. Worms don't require host programs. A Trojan horse is a program that claims to do one thing but in reality does something else, usually something malicious.

7 Explain the steps that companies go through in anticipating, planning for, and recovering from information system disasters.

Businesses can avoid the results of disaster by routinely backing up software and data, both at an organizational level and at an individual level. They can back up data at online storage services or pay for extra hardware installation in a secure location. They may also want to invest in extra hardware and software sites, which can be accessed during emergencies.

Assessment Check Answers

7.1 What is a software glitch?
A software glitch is an error in a computer program that has an unintended consequence, such as shutting down a system at the wrong time.

7.2 Explain disaster recovery planning as it relates to information systems.
Disaster recovery planning involves deciding how to prevent system failures and to continue operations if computer systems fail because of natural disasters or human error. A basic precaution is routinely backing up data and software and storing the backups in a secure location.

Business Terms You Need to Know

data 484
information 484
management information
  system (MIS) 484
database 485
decision support system (DSS) 487
executive support system (ESS) 487

Wi-Fi 489
application service provider
  (ASP) 489
software 494
enterprise resource planning
  (ERP) system 495
word processing 496

spreadsheet 497
presentation software 499
intranet 501

Other Important Business Terms

chief information officer
  (CIO) 484
expert system 488
local area network (LAN) 488
wide area network (WAN) 488
Wi-Max 489

on-demand (utility)
  computing 489
hardware 491
mainframe 492
minicomputer 492
handheld devices 493

operating system 494
application software 494
desktop publishing 497
firewall 501
virtual private network (VPN) 501
VoIP 502

Review Questions

1. Distinguish between data and information. Why is the distinction important to businesspeople in their management of information?
2. What is business intelligence?
3. Describe three different types of information system programs and give an example of how each might help a particular business.
4. Explain decision support systems, executive support systems, and expert systems.

5. What are the major categories of computers? What is a smart phone?
6. How might a hotel chain use desktop publishing to manage its marketing program?
7. What is enterprise resource planning? How has it streamlined business processes?
8. What is an intranet? Give specific examples of benefits for firms that set up their own intranets.

9. Briefly explain how VoIP works. Why might a business switch from regular telephony to Internet telephony?
10. What steps can organizations and individuals take to prevent computer crime?
11. How does a computer virus work? What can individuals and organizational computer users do to reduce the likelihood of acquiring a computer virus?
12. Why is disaster recovery important for businesses? Relate your answer to a natural disaster such as a hurricane.

Projects and Teamwork Applications

1. Do you believe that information overload is a serious problem in your life? What steps do you (or can you) take to reduce this overload so that you can function more effectively in all areas of your life?

2. Suppose you were chief information officer for Great Harvest Bread Company. Describe the different parts of an integrated software package (in addition to the intranet described in the chapter) that would help your company manage its flow of information. Give an example of how each application you choose would help the company.

3. Working with a partner, research the current status of Wi-Max. Prepare a short report on its growth, its current uses, and its future for business computing.

4. Do you think computer hacking is a serious crime? Defend your answer.

5. What information-related technology lessons do you think businesses learned from Hurricanes Katrina, Rita, and Wilma? How will these lessons help firms respond to other disasters—natural as well as those caused by humans?

6. Assume you're in the market for a new personal computer. First, make a list of your needs. Needs represent the basic configuration that will meet your individual computing requirements. Next, make a list of your wants. Wants represent features you'd like to have in your new PC but don't necessarily need. Finally, decide between a notebook computer and a desktop computer. List the reasons why you chose a desktop or a notebook.
   a. Visit the CNet (http://www.cnet.com) or ZDNet (http://www.zdnet.com) Web site. Research different computer makes and models that meet your specifications. Make a list of the five top-rated systems. What criteria did CNet or ZDNet consider when developing the rankings?
   b. Decide where you will buy your new computer. Will you order it from a direct seller, such as Dell, or will you buy it at a retail store, such as Best Buy? What are the advantages and disadvantages of each option?
   c. Finally, working in a small group, repeat the exercise, assuming you're buying a computer for your job. Explain any differences between a computer purchased for personal and school use and one purchased for business use.

7. Computer viruses and worms pose a major problem for computer users and systems. Software publishers constantly scramble to update their antivirus software programs in response to newly discovered viruses and worms. Searching online, research the current status of worms and viruses and then answer the following questions:
   a. Approximately how many different computer viruses have been discovered?
   b. How many new viruses are discovered each month?
   c. What are the names of the most recently discovered viruses?
   d. What is the best way to protect a computer from viruses?

8. After the terrorist attacks of September 11, 2001, and the more recent string of major hurricanes, interest in data backup and recovery software for critical computer data increased dramatically. Visit the following Web sites and, working with a partner, prepare a report outlining some of the key features of these programs with the goal of convincing the owner of a small business that he or she should invest in critical data backup and recovery software.

   http://www.baymountain.com
   http://www.unitrends.com

Case 15.1

Compaq and Hewlett-Packard: Can They Live Happily Ever After?

Business mergers between companies sometimes seem nearly as common as marriages between people. And like marriages, they may or may not result in happy relationships. The merger between Hewlett-Packard and Compaq—the largest so far in the computer industry—has proved to be rocky. HP's acquisition of Compaq was orchestrated by HP's former CEO, Carly Fiorina. The move met its greatest resistance from HP director Walter Hewlett, son of HP's co-founder William Hewlett. Hewlett argued that the match would dilute HP's profits, trigger layoffs, and not benefit either firm in the long run.

After the first year, HP reported that it had obtained some valuable service contracts, including a $243 million deal to provide help desk and other services to Telecom Italia. Later it announced a contract with Procter & Gamble worth $3 billion over the next decade. But in technological innovation, HP continued to move too slowly, and the acquisition of Compaq failed to satisfy investors. HP's once-healthy market share in printers began to falter because it was devoting resources to its PC business. So far the HP merger with Compaq has yet to produce effective integration between the two organizations and their products—and Fiorina has left the company.

HP is trying to recover its image as a force for innovation and engineering, blend with Compaq, and offer products such as desktop computers at lower prices to consumers and business customers through its HP Compaq division. Industry experts warn that the firm will also have to jump ahead of its competitors—such as Dell—in developing whole new categories of goods and services. It's a task nearly as large as reinventing the wheel.

Questions for Critical Thinking

1. Visit the HP Web site to learn more about HP products and services. Select a new offering that you think will be successful, and explain why.
2. Do you think that eventually the relationship between HP and Compaq will be successful? Why or why not?

Sources: John Gallant, "The Firing of Fiorina: Overdue or Premature?" *Network World,* accessed August 16, 2006, http://www.networkworld.com; John Spooner, "HP Does Desktop PC Price Limbo," *PC Magazine,* accessed July 21, 2006, http://www.PCMagazine.com; "Fallen Star," Online NewsHour, accessed July 21, 2006, http://www.pbs.org/newshour; Robert X. Cringely, "What Carly Will Be Missing," Public Broadcasting Service, accessed July 21, 2006, http://www.pbs.org/cringely; "Hewlett-Packard Top Executive Ousted," MSNBC, accessed July 21, 2006, http://www.msnbc.msn.com.

ⅤⅠⅮⅇⓄ Case 15.2

Peet's Coffee & Tea: Just What the Customer Ordered

This video case appears on page 624. A recently filmed video, designed to expand and highlight the written case, is available for class use by instructors.

Chapter 16

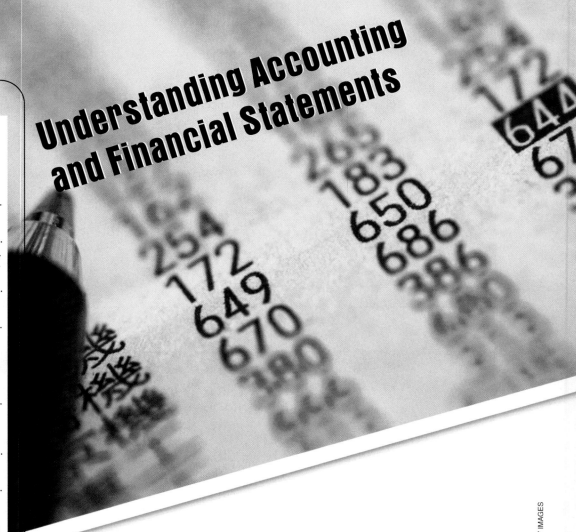

Understanding Accounting and Financial Statements

PHOTODISC/GETTY IMAGES

Keeping the books of large corporations is a complicated task. So most big companies, such as General Motors and Sun Microsystems, have traditionally relied on the giants of the auditing industry, known as the Big Four. These huge accounting firms—Pricewaterhouse Coopers, Ernst & Young, Deloitte & Touche, and KPMG—all have long histories and multinational operations. They are considered the top tier of their industry. But recently, smaller accounting companies have begun to take some of their prestigious, and lucrative, business away. The change came about partly because of a long list of accounting scandals that involved leading audit and consulting firms such as Arthur Andersen, which was virtually destroyed by its association with some law-breaking clients, such as Enron. Other reasons why organizations are giving a second look to relatively small accounting

Who Is Grant Thornton?

practices include their nimbleness in responding to legal and technological changes, their ability to deliver personalized service, their specialization in particular industries, and their stain-free records. The lower fees charged by these "second-tier" firms, such as Grant Thornton, BDO Seidman, McGladrey & Pullen, and Crowe Group, are another big factor.

For instance, Hercules, a Delaware chemicals producer with $2 billion in sales, considered PricewaterhouseCoopers for its audit needs but settled instead on the far smaller firm BDO Seidman. In addition to BDO's speedy decision making and reasonable fees, the firm impressed Hercules with its experience in the chemical industry. And finally, "There was a sense that we would be important to BDO, that there will be top management attention if we have problems," says Hercules's chairman.

Hercules's perception of receiving more personal attention is very real. The Big Four accounting firms are actually giving up some of their clients, sometimes unwillingly, because they often lack the resources to maintain their current client list under the demanding new requirements of the Sarbanes-Oxley Act. These stringent audit reforms lengthen the time required for the typical audit process at a publicly traded company by as much as a

third. That means the bigger firms must work with fewer clients or risk doing an inadequate job for some. A shortage of seasoned auditing professionals has also limited their ability to add staff in the last few years, so all of the Big Four have reduced their number of clients.

As a result of this pressure on the Big Four to reduce their client load, in addition to clients' desire to combine good accounting services with lower professional fees, almost 250 firms earning $100 million a year or more switched auditors in one recent year—away from the top tier. That's about double the number from the year before. BDO was a big winner, netting 71 new clients, while Grant Thornton, McGladrey & Pullen, and Crowe Group added a total of 46.

Some businesses that are required to follow Sarbanes-Oxley guidelines also hire separate accounting services to help them comply. They are performing the act's mandated audits of their own internal controls to prevent financial wrongdoing. Because federal law prohibits a firm from using its own financial auditing staff to assess its accounting controls, the act has created a flood of new work for outside accounting companies at firms of all sizes. Smaller accounting companies are benefiting from the new business, from the new contacts and leads they are getting

Career Assessment Exercises in Information Systems and Accounting

1. The American Institute of Certified Public Accountants is a professional organization dedicated to the enhancement of the public accounting profession. Visit the organization's Web site (http://www.aicpa.org). Review the information on CPA standards and examinations. Write a brief summary on what you learned about how to become a CPA.

2. Assume you're interested in a career as a systems administrator. Go to the following Web site: http://www.sage.org. Prepare a brief report outlining the responsibilities of a systems administrator, who hires for these positions, and what kind of educational background you need to become one.

3. Identify a person working in your local area in the accounting field and arrange an interview with that person (your college career center may be able to help you). Ask that person about his or her job responsibilities, educational background, and the best and worst aspects of his or her job as an accountant.

Managing Financial Resources

Part 6

Chapter 17

Financial Management and Institutions

Learning Goals

1. Identify the functions performed by a firm's financial managers.

2. Describe the characteristics a form of money should have, and list the functions of money.

3. Identify the various measures of the money supply.

4. Explain how a firm uses funds.

5. Compare the two major sources of funds for a business.

6. Identify the likely sources of short- and long-term funds for business operations.

7. Describe the financial system and the major financial institutions.

8. Explain the functions of the Federal Reserve System and the tools it uses to control the supply of money and credit.

9. Describe the global financial system.

© REUTERS/CORBIS

Fannie Mae and Freddie Mac are two of the largest financial institutions in the United States. Their odd names are shortened forms of their official titles, the Federal National Mortgage Association and the Federal Home Loan Mortgage Corporation. Both were created by the federal government and have special charters, even though they are stockholder owned. Their purpose is to increase the supply of mortgage credit available to the public, especially to low- and moderate-income families in all areas of the country and under all economic conditions. Fannie and Freddie, as they are known, buy mortgage loans from banks, mortgage bankers, and other private sources. They finance these purchases by selling bonds and a variety of other types of securities.

Over the years Fannie and Freddie have helped millions of new homeowners and worked to ensure fair

the results were that the validity of its past financial reports was called into question. A report by the Office of Federal Housing Enterprise Oversight found what it called "pervasive misapplication of accounting rules" in the

Reining in Fannie and Freddie

lending practices. They help finance half the home mortgage loans granted in the United States each year and make money from the difference in value between the mortgages they buy and their cost of financing. Thanks to them, says one congressional representative, "we have the strongest, most dynamic housing market in the world."

But recently members of Congress, the Federal Reserve chairman, and some prominent economists have expressed concern that Fannie and Freddie are too loosely regulated. First, Freddie Mac was found to be improperly accounting for its use of certain exotic financial instruments called *derivatives,* and the company was slapped with a $125 million fine. A management shake-up followed.

A few months later, government investigators turned their attention to Fannie Mae. Soon Fannie was criticized too for also using improper accounting methods; among

company's records, some of which allowed Fannie Mae's managers to receive bonuses in a recent year that would not otherwise have been paid. The company was accused of maintaining a corporate culture that encouraged such problems to continue unchecked. Fannie Mae was fined $400 million, one of the largest penalties in an accounting fraud case.

The Senate Banking Committee passed a bill to rein in the two companies with tighter controls as well as by shrinking their investment portfolios, which add up to about $1.5 trillion, by forcing the companies to sell assets that are not related to their mortgage businesses. Passage of the bill in the House remains in doubt, however, and both Fannie Mae and Freddie Mac have criticized its provisions.[1]

Previous chapters discuss two essential functions that a business must perform. First, the company must produce a good or service or contract with suppliers to produce it. Second, the firm must market its good or service to prospective customers. This chapter introduces a third, equally important function: a company's managers must ensure that it has enough money to perform its other tasks successfully, in both the present and the future. Adequate funds must be available to buy materials and equipment, pay bills, purchase additional facilities, and compensate employees. This third business function is **finance**—planning, obtaining, and managing the company's funds in order to accomplish its objectives effectively and efficiently.

An organization's financial objectives include not only meeting expenses but also maximizing its overall worth, often determined by the value of the firm's common stock. Financial managers are responsible for meeting expenses and increasing profits to shareholders.

This chapter focuses on the role of financial managers, the reasons businesses need funds, and the various types and sources of funds. It discusses the role of money and measures of the money supply. The chapter explains the purpose and structure of the financial system, the operations of financial institutions, and the way the Federal Reserve System functions. A discussion of the role of the financial system in the global business environment concludes the chapter.

finance business function of planning, obtaining, and managing a company's funds in order to accomplish its objectives effectively and efficiently.

financial manager executive who develops and implements the firm's financial plan and determines the most appropriate sources and uses of funds.

THE ROLE OF THE FINANCIAL MANAGER

Organizations are placing greater emphasis on measuring and reducing the costs of conducting business as well as increasing revenues and profits. As a result, **financial managers**—executives who develop and implement their firm's financial plan and determine the most appropriate sources and uses of funds—are among the most vital people on the corporate payroll.

The finance organization of a typical company might look like this: at the top is the chief financial officer (CFO). The CFO usually reports directly to the company's chief executive officer (CEO) or chief operating officer (COO), if the firm has one. In some companies, the CFO is also a member of the board of directors. Robert Wayman, for instance, is CFO of Hewlett-Packard and is also a member of the HP board of directors. Reporting directly to the CFO are often three senior managers. While titles can vary, these three executives are commonly called the **vice president for financial management** (or **planning**), the **treasurer,** and the **controller.** The vice president for financial management or planning is responsible for preparing financial forecasts and analyzing major investment decisions. Major investment decisions include new products, new production facilities, and acquisitions. The treasurer is responsible for all of the company's financing activities, including cash management, tax planning and preparation, and shareholder relations. The treasurer also works on the sale of new security issues to investors. The controller is the chief accounting manager. The controller's functions include keeping the company's books, preparing financial statements, and conducting internal audits.

The growing importance of financial professionals is reflected in an expanding number of CEOs promoted from financial positions. By one estimate, around 20 percent of all newly appointed CEOs during a recent year spent time in the finance ranks. A recent example is Louis Raspino. Prior to becoming CEO of oil services firm Pride International, Raspino served as the firm's CFO.[2] The importance of finance professionals is also reflected in how much CFOs earn today. According to a recent survey, annual compensation for CFOs averages around $2.4 million.[3]

In performing their jobs, financial professionals continually seek to balance risks with expected financial returns. Risk is the uncertainty of gain or loss; return is the gain or loss that results from an investment over a specified period of time. Financial managers strive to maximize the wealth of their firm's shareholders by striking the optimal balance between risk and return. This balance is called the **risk-return trade-off.** For example, heavy reliance on borrowed funds may increase the return to shareholders, but the more money a firm borrows, the greater the risks to shareholders. An increase in a firm's cash on hand reduces the risk of meeting unexpected cash needs. However, because cash does not earn any return, failure to invest surplus funds in an income-earning asset—such as in marketable securities—reduces a firm's potential return or profitability.

risk-return trade-off optimal balance between the expected payoff from an investment and the investment's risk.

Every financial manager must perform this risk-return balancing act. For example, in the late 1990s, Airbus wrestled with a major decision: whether to begin development and production of the giant A380 jetliner. The development costs for the aircraft—to be the world's largest jetliner—were initially estimated at more than $10 billion. Before committing to such a huge investment, financial managers had to weigh the potential profits of the A380 with the risk that the profits would not materialize. With its future on the line, Airbus decided to go ahead with the development of the A380. After spending more than $14 billion, Airbus rolled out the first A380 in 2005. Airbus has orders for approximately 150 jetliners at a list price of around $285 million each. It's unclear, however, whether the A380 investment turns out to be a smart, and profitable, decision.[4]

The Financial Plan

Financial managers develop their organization's **financial plan,** a document that specifies the funds needed by a firm for a period of time, the timing of inflows and outflows, and the most appropriate sources and uses of funds. The financial plan is based on forecasts of production costs, purchasing needs, and expected sales activities for the period covered. Financial managers use forecasts to determine the specific amounts and timing of expenditures and receipts. They build a financial plan based on the answers to three questions:

1. What funds will the firm require during the appropriate period of operations?
2. How will it obtain the necessary funds?
3. When will it need more funds?

financial plan document that specifies the funds a firm will need for a period of time, the timing of inflows and outflows, and the most appropriate sources and uses of funds.

Some funds flow into the firm when it sells its goods or services, but funding needs vary. The financial plan must reflect both the amounts and timing of inflows and outflows of funds. Even a profitable firm may well face a financial squeeze as a result of its need for funds when sales lag, when the volume of its credit sales increases, or when customers are slow in making payments.

The cash inflows and outflows of a business are similar to those of a household. The members of a household may depend on weekly or monthly paychecks for funds, but their expenditures vary greatly from one pay period to the next. The financial plan should indicate when the flows of funds entering and leaving the organization will occur and in what amounts.

A good financial plan also involves financial control, a process of checking actual revenues, costs, and expenses and comparing them against forecasts. If this process reveals significant differences between projected and actual figures, it is important to discover them early to take timely corrective action.

Paula Brock, CFO of the Zoological Society of San Diego (which operates the famous San Diego Zoo), credits the zoo's financial plan and planning process with helping it weather a recent outbreak of an exotic bird disease in Southern California. When the disease first appeared, the zoo took immediate action to protect its valuable bird collection. Thanks to these actions, no birds got sick, and the damage to the zoo's finances were minimal, even though the zoo spent more than half a million dollars. The financial plan raised the alarm as resources were redirected to fight the disease, allowing managers to make the necessary adjustments.[5]

"They Said It"

"When I was young, I used to think that money was the most important thing in life; now that I am older, I know it is."
—Oscar Wilde
(1854–1900)
Humorist and playwright

assessment check

1. Define finance and explain the role of the financial manager.
2. What are the three questions on which a financial plan is based?

CHARACTERISTICS AND FUNCTIONS OF MONEY

Playwright George Bernard Shaw once said that the lack of money is the root of all evil. Added comedian Woody Allen, "Money is better than poverty, if only for financial reasons." Most businesspeople would agree, because money is the lubricant of contemporary business.

Characteristics of Money

money anything generally accepted as payment for goods and services.

Money is anything generally accepted as payment for goods and services. Most early forms of money imposed a number of serious disadvantages on users. For example, a cow is a poor form of money for an owner who wants only a loaf of bread and some cheese. Exchanges based on money permit economic specialization and provide a general basis for purchasing power, provided that the form of money used has certain characteristics. Money must be divisible, portable, durable, difficult to counterfeit, and stable in value.

Divisibility A U.S. dollar is divided into cents, nickels, dimes, and quarters. The Canadian dollar is divided similarly, except that Canada has a 20-cent coin and no quarter. Mexico's nuevo peso is broken down into centavos (100 centavos equals one nuevo peso). People can easily exchange these forms of money for products ranging from a cup of coffee to automobiles. Today, most economic activity involves making and spending money.

Portability The light weight of modern paper currency facilitates the exchange process. Portability is an important characteristic, because a typical dollar bill changes hands around 400 times during its lifetime, staying in the average person's pocket or purse fewer than two days.

Durability U.S. dollar bills survive an average of twelve to eighteen months, and they can survive folding some 4,000 times without tearing. Coins, on the other hand, can last 30 years or longer. Most countries have replaced small-denomination paper currency with coins. For instance, there are no one-euro or two-euro bills—only one- and two-euro coins. In the United States there have been several attempts to get Americans to switch to dollar coins, none of which have met with much success. Americans, it appears, are reluctant to give up the dollar bill—the greenback is one of the great icons of American culture. This hasn't stopped the government from trying again. The latest attempt to wean Americans from the paper dollar bill is described in the "Hit & Miss" feature.

Difficulty in Counterfeiting Widespread distribution of counterfeit money undermines a nation's monetary system and economy by ruining the value of legitimate money. For this reason, governments consider counterfeiting a serious crime and take elaborate steps to prevent it. Among counterfeiters, U.S. currency is the most popular. To increase the difficulty of counterfeiting U.S. currency in this age of sophisticated computers and color printers, the U.S. Treasury has redesigned paper bills. The new design adds a letter to each bill's serial number along with the seal of the Federal Reserve, larger portraits that are off-center, and polymer threads that run vertically through the bills and glow under ultraviolet light.

Stability Money should also maintain a relatively stable value. If the value of money fluctuates too much, people hesitate to use it. They begin to abandon it and look for safer means of storing their wealth. Businesses start to demand that bills be paid in other, more stable currencies.

As part of a broad economic reform program, Argentina pegged the value of its currency, the peso, to the U.S. dollar in the early 1990s; one peso equaled one dollar. This policy

Getting Americans to Break the Dollar Habit

Unless you're a coin collector, the first thing that comes to mind about the U.S. dollar coin is probably how you lost 75 cents when you spent it by mistaking it for a quarter. Despite failing twice to get U.S. consumers to adopt the dollar coin as money and not a collectible, starting in 2007 Congress is trying again with a plan to introduce four dollar coins a year, bearing likenesses of the presidents. Like the series of quarters commemorating the states, the new dollars are likely to be hoarded instead of spent. The U.S. Mint isn't worried about that, however; it costs just pennies to mint dollar coins, which last 30 years compared with twelve to eighteen months for a dollar bill. So even if the bid to get them into circulation fails, the new dollars will save money for the government.

Silver dollars were minted from 1794 to the 1930s, and a copper-and-nickel dollar was made in the 1970s. In 1978 the mint unveiled the Susan B. Anthony dollar to great fanfare, but the public rejected it, partly owing to its resemblance to a quarter. A similar fate befell the golden or Sacagawea dollar (named for Lewis and Clark's Shoshone guide) in 2000, despite its more distinctive look.

Critics of the dollar coin say the government has not done a good enough job promoting the new currency—particularly the Sacagawea dollar—and suggest taking paper dollars out of circulation to force consumers to stop hoarding the coins. Canada, for example, stopped printing one- and two-dollar bills after coins were introduced. Mint officials say it takes a year to build awareness of the dollar, and the next step is to get people to use it. The question remaining is, will the third time do the trick?

Questions for Critical Thinking

1. Do consumers really need a dollar coin? Does the government? Why or why not?
2. How do you think the government could do a better job of changing consumers' perception of the dollar coin from curiosity to currency? Would taking the paper dollar out of circulation be a wise move? Why or why not?

Sources: "United States Dollar," Answers.com, accessed July 27, 2006, http://www.answers.com; "The Golden Dollar, One Year Later," About.com, accessed July 27, 2006, http://collectibles.about.com; Gordon T. Anderson, "Congress Tries Again for a Dollar Coin," CNN Money, accessed July 27, 2006; http://money.cnn.com.

worked well for a while as inflation fell sharply and economic growth accelerated. However, a strong U.S. dollar meant a strong peso. This made Argentinean products more expensive and hurt exports. The country's economy started to unravel. The government was forced to close banks and limit cash withdrawals. Finally, it allowed its currency to float independently of the dollar. The peso promptly lost 70 percent of its value relative to the dollar as Argentineans scrambled to convert their pesos into dollars.

Functions of Money

Money performs three basic functions, shown in Figure 17.1. First, it serves primarily as a medium of exchange—a means of facilitating economic transactions and eliminating the need for a barter system. For example, assume you work part time and are paid $10 per hour—money is being used as the medium of exchange: payment for your labor. Second, money functions as a unit of account—a common standard for measuring the value of goods and services. For example, assume the cost of renting an apartment off campus is $500 per month. This standardized unit of account allows you to compare the cost of renting an off-campus apartment to the cost of on-campus housing. Third, money acts as a temporary store of value—a way of keeping accumulated wealth until the owner needs it to make new purchases. Money offers one big advantage as a store of value: its high liquidity allows people to obtain

17.1 Basic Functions of Money

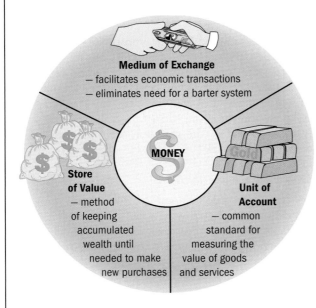

Medium of Exchange
— facilitates economic transactions
— eliminates need for a barter system

MONEY

Store of Value
— method of keeping accumulated wealth until needed to make new purchases

Unit of Account
— common standard for measuring the value of goods and services

it and dispose of it in quick and easy transactions. Money is immediately available for purchasing products or paying debts. You purchase $200 worth of goods from the bookstore. You can pay for your purchases using cash, a credit or debit card, or a check. In each case you're using money as a temporary store of value.

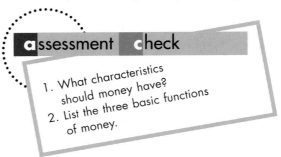

assessment check

1. What characteristics should money have?
2. List the three basic functions of money.

THE MONEY SUPPLY

Ask someone on the street to define the money supply, and he or she might answer that the money supply is the total value of all currency and coins in circulation. That answer, however, is only half right. One measure of the U.S. money supply consists of coins and currency as well as financial assets that also serve as a medium of exchange: traveler's checks, bank checking accounts, and other so-called **demand deposit** accounts (such as NOW accounts and credit union share draft accounts). Government reports and business publications use the term **M1** to refer to the total value of coins, currency, traveler's checks, bank checking account balances, and the balances in other demand deposit accounts. The current breakdown of M1 is shown on the right in Figure 17.2.

Another, broader definition of the money supply is also widely used. Called **M2**, this measure of the money supply includes M1 plus a number of other financial assets that are

17.2 Breakdown of M1 and M2

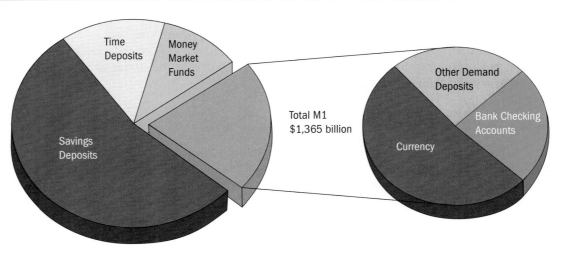

Time Deposits

Money Market Funds

Total M1 $1,365 billion

Other Demand Deposits

Bank Checking Accounts

Savings Deposits

Currency

Total M2 $6,503 billion

Sources: Federal Reserve, accessed August 3, 2006, http://www.federalreserve.gov.

CREDIT CARDS HIT CAMPUS AND DEBTS FOLLOW

Today's college students often graduate with a heavy load of debt, whether they borrowed for tuition expenses or not. More than half have at least one consumer credit card and many are already in debt in their freshman year, carrying an average balance of more than $2,000, often at interest rates up to 15 percent.

This amount may not seem too large, but it can take several years to pay off after graduation. Some students are further burdened by annual fees, by penalties and higher interest rates on delinquent or late monthly payments, or by the even higher fees and rates attached to cash advances.

New college students are bombarded with credit card offers, promoted by "free gifts" such as T-shirts and sunglasses, and many are woefully unprepared for the financial consequences of charging pizza and beer for several years. Parents are not required to cosign the credit applications, and some can't afford to pick up the resulting debt. Debtors age 18 to 24 are among the fastest-growing group of bankruptcy filers. "Abuse of credit cards is a serious problem for young people," said a federal bankruptcy judge in San Diego.

Should the government restrict the marketing of credit cards to college students?

PRO

1. Students can ruin their credit rating in college, making it hard to rent an apartment or even get a job.
2. Credit card companies are taking unfair advantage of students' inexperience with budgeting and managing their money.

CON

1. Most students eventually pay their bills, learning an important lesson from their credit card experience.
2. Many students are responsible about spending, and credit cards offer them a way to pay for necessities without carrying cash.

Summary

Following in the footsteps of hundreds of colleges and universities, Washington State's house of representatives is reviewing a bill to regulate credit companies operating on state campuses. The bill has few teeth—it only requires campuses to set policies, such as limiting the times and places cards can be marketed or forbidding free gift offers. But given the snowballing debt that student cards can create, the bill might be a step in the right direction.

Sources: Amy L. Cooper, "Credit Card Debt: A Survival Guide for College Students," *Young Money,* accessed July 27, 2006, http://www.youngmoney .com; "Senate Approves Bill Restricting Credit Card Marketing to College Students," *News Target,* accessed July 27, 2006, http://www.newstarget.com; Michael Kinsman, "Debt-Loaded Message," *San Diego Union-Tribune,* May 19, 2005, p. C-1.

almost as liquid as cash but do not serve directly as a medium of exchange. These assets include various savings accounts, certificates of deposit, and money market mutual funds. Users must complete some sort of transaction before these assets can fulfill all the functions of money. The current breakdown of M2 is shown on the left in Figure 17.2.

The use of credit cards—often referred to as plastic money—has increased significantly. Over the past 20 years, for instance, the amount of outstanding credit card debt has risen by more than 400 percent.[6] Credit card companies spend billions of dollars each year trying to attract new customers. Recently, many credit card companies have targeted college students in their marketing efforts. Consequently, the percentage of college students with at least one credit card now exceeds 50 percent. Concerns over rising credit card balances among college students have led some states to restrict the marketing of credit cards to college students. The issue of marketing credit cards to college students is debated in the "Solving an Ethical Controversy" feature.

MasterCard and Visa, issued by banks, dominate the credit card market, though the Discover Card has made some inroads. In addition, American Express offers several credit cards. However, its flagship American Express card is not really a credit card but rather a charge

REPRINTED COURTESY OF AMERICAN EXPRESS.

Corporate credit cards are issued to companies. Employees use the cards to pay for business-related expenses.

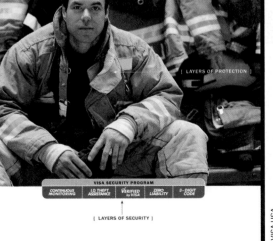

USED WITH PERMISSION, VISA USA

Visa's approach to credit card security to reduce fraud.

card; that is, balances must be paid in full each month. Customers do not have the option of carrying a balance from month to month. American Express, MasterCard, Visa, and Discover card issue credit cards to both individuals as well as businesses. Authorized employees use business, or corporate credit cards to pay for business-related expenses such as travel.

Even though all MasterCard and Visa credit cards are issued by banks, so-called *branded credit cards* have become popular in recent years. Corporations, not-for-profit organizations, and college alumni associations have partnered with banks to issue branded credit cards. The partner receives a payment from the bank based on how much the card is used. Branded cards often provide perks to the cardholder. For instance, holders of an American Express Delta Sky Miles credit card receive Delta Sky Miles for each purchase made with the card.

Another recent trend has been the emergence of prepaid shopping cards. Consumers buy the cards in varying denominations—such as $25, $50, or $100—from retailers such as Barnes & Noble, Best Buy, and Target and then use them to make purchases up to that amount. The cards are reusable, meaning that the consumer can put more money on them anytime. Many cards can also be used to make online purchases. Some cards offer users perks such as special discounts. If you use a Wal-Mart shopping card to buy gas as a station located at a Wal-Mart store, you receive a 3 cent per gallon discount.

Many entrepreneurs rely on credit cards, as mentioned in Chapter 6, to provide seed capital in financing their new ventures. Movie director Spike Lee, for example, reportedly used his American Express card to finance his first film.

Although credit cards are convenient and easy to use, they are a very expensive source of business or consumer credit, with annual interest rates averaging around 15 percent. Another problem with credit cards is fraud. As discussed in Chapter 7, online purchases are especially vulnerable to fraud and cost credit card issuers, merchants, and consumers billions of dollars each year. The credit card industry is experimenting with a variety of ways to improve security and reduce fraud.

assessment check

1. Explain the differences between M1 and M2.
2. Who issues Visa and MasterCard credit cards? Explain the difference between a credit card and a charge card.

WHY ORGANIZATIONS NEED FUNDS

Organizations require funds for many reasons. They need money to run day-to-day operations, compensate employees and hire new ones, pay for inventory, make interest payments on loans, pay dividends to shareholders, and purchase property, facilities, and equipment. A firm's financial plan identifies the amount and time of its specific cash needs.

By comparing these needs with expenditures and expected cash receipts (from sales, payments made by credit purchasers, and other sources), financial managers determine precisely what additional funds they must obtain at any given time. If inflows exceed cash needs, financial managers invest the surplus to earn interest. On the other hand, if inflows do not meet cash needs, they seek additional sources of funds. Figure 17.3 illustrates this process.

Generating Funds from Excess Cash

Many financial managers invest most of their firms' excess cash balances in marketable securities. These financial instruments are very close to cash because they are, by definition, marketable and easy to convert into cash. Four of the most popular marketable securities are U.S. Treasury bills, commercial paper, repurchase agreements, and certificates of deposit.

Treasury bills are short-term securities issued by the U.S. Treasury and backed by the full faith and credit of the U.S. government. Treasury bills are sold with a maturity of either 30, 90, 180, or 360 days and have a minimum denomination of $10,000. They are considered virtually risk-free and easy to resell. Commercial paper is securities sold by corporations, such as General Electric, maturing anywhere from 1 to 270 days from the date of issue. Although slightly riskier than Treasury bills, commercial paper is generally still considered a very low-risk security. Repurchase agreements, or *repos,* are an arrangement in which one party sells a package of U.S. government securities to another party, agreeing to buy back, or repurchase, the securities at a higher price on a later date. Repos are also considered low-risk securities.

A certificate of deposit (CD) is a time deposit at a financial institution, such as a commercial bank, savings bank, or credit union. The sizes and maturity dates of CDs vary considerably and can often be tailored to meet the needs of purchasers. CDs with denominations of $100,000 or less per depositor are federally insured. CDs with larger denominations are not federally insured but can be sold more easily prior to maturity.

Figure 17.3

The Financial Planning Process

EXPENDITURES
- Day-to-Day Activities
- Inventory
- Dividends to Stockholders
- Purchases of Land, Facilities, and Equipment

If the firm has insufficient funds:
- Evaluate alternative sources for additional funds

CASH RECEIPTS
- Product Sales
- Payments from Credit Purchasers
- Sales of Stock
- Additional Funds from Venture Capitalists
- Private Placement Financing

If the firm has excess funds:
- Seek interest-producing investments

assessment check

1. Why do organizations need funds?
2. List several alternatives to holding large cash balances.

SOURCES OF FUNDS

To this point, the discussion has focused on half of the definition of finance—the reasons why organizations need funds and how they use them. A firm's financial plan must give equal importance, however, to the choice of the best sources of needed funds. Sources of funds fall into two categories: debt capital and equity capital.

Debt capital represents funds obtained through borrowing (referred to as *debt financing* in Chapter 6). **Equity capital** consists of funds provided by the firm's owners when they reinvest earnings, make additional contributions, liquidate assets, issue stock to the general public, or raise capital from venture capitalists and other investors (an approach referred to as *equity financing* in Chapter 6). A firm also obtains equity capital whenever it makes a profit.

A company's cash needs vary from one time period to the next, and even an established firm may not generate sufficient funds from operations to cover all costs of a major expansion

"They Said It"

"If you can count your money, you don't have a billion dollars."
—J. Paul Getty (1892–1976)
American oil industrialist

debt capital funds obtained through borrowing.

equity capital funds provided by the firm's owners when they reinvest earnings, make additional contributions, or issue stock to investors.

Characteristics of Debt and Equity Capital

Characteristics	Debt Capital	Equity Capital
1. Payments to security holders	Contractual payment of interest and repayment of principal.	No contractual payments.
2. Maturity	Pays a fixed amount of principal at a set future date.	No maturity.
3. Claim on assets	Lenders have a prior claim on assets in the event of bankruptcy.	In the event of bankruptcy, equity holders receive nothing unless all creditors are repaid.
4. Control	As long as payments are made when due and other terms of the lending contract are followed, debt holders have no control over the company.	Equity holders are owners of the company and usually have the right to vote on major company issues and elect the board of directors.

assessment check

1. What are the two major sources of funds?
2. Do different companies take different approaches to the mix between debt and equity capital?

"They Said It"

"A bank is a place that will lend you money if you can prove that you don't need it."
—Bob Hope (1903–2003)
Actor and comedian

or a significant upgrade of equipment. In these instances, financial managers must evaluate the potential benefits and drawbacks of seeking funds by borrowing. As an alternative to borrowing, the firm may raise new equity capital. A financial manager's job includes determining the most cost-effective balance between equity and borrowed funds and the proper blend of short-term and long-term funds. Table 17.1 compares debt capital and equity capital on the basis of four important criteria.

Different companies can take very different approaches to the mix between debt and equity capital. For instance, Home Depot and Lowe's are both large, profitable, and fast-growing home improvement retailers. Home Depot, however, relies less on debt capital than does Lowe's. For each dollar in debt capital, Home Depot has about $1.64 in equity capital. By contrast, Lowe's has less than $1.19 in equity capital for each dollar in debt capital.[7]

Short-Term Sources of Funds

Many times throughout a year, an organization may discover that its cash needs exceed its available funds. For example, retailers generate surplus cash for most of the year, but they need to build up inventory during the late summer and fall to get ready for the holiday shopping season. Consequently, they often need funds to pay for merchandise until holiday sales generate revenue. Then retailers use the incoming funds to repay the borrowed funds. In these instances, financial managers evaluate short-term sources of funds. By definition, short-term sources of funds are repaid within one year.

Three major sources of short-term funds exist: trade credit, short-term loans, and commercial paper. Trade credit is extended by suppliers when a firm receives goods or services, agreeing to pay for them at a later date. Short-term loans can be either unsecured, meaning the firm does not pledge any assets as collateral, or secured, meaning that specific assets such as inventory are pledged as collateral. A major source of short-term loans is commercial banks such as PNC Bank and Sun Trust. Commercial paper was briefly described earlier in the chapter. The interest cost on commercial paper is typically 1 or 2 percent lower than the interest rate on short-term bank loans, and firms can raise large amounts of money in the commercial paper market. However, only large firms with considerable financial strength and stability can sell commercial paper.

Long-Term Sources of Funds

Funds from short-term sources can help a firm meet current needs for cash or inventory. A larger need, however, such as acquiring another company or making a major investment in real estate or equipment, often requires funds for a much longer period of time. Unlike short-term sources, long-term sources are repaid over many years.

Organizations acquire long-term funds from three sources. One is long-term loans obtained from financial institutions such as commercial banks, life insurance companies, and pension funds. A second source is **bonds**—certificates of indebtedness sold to raise long-term funds for firms and governments. A third source is equity financing acquired by selling stock in the firm or reinvesting company profits (known as *retained earnings*).

bond certificate of indebtedness sold to raise long-term funds for a corporation or government agency.

Public Sale of Stocks and Bonds

Sales of stocks and bonds represent a major source of funds for corporations. Such sales provide cash inflows for the issuing firm and either a share in its ownership (for a stock purchaser) or a specified rate of interest and repayment at a stated time (for a bond purchaser). Because stock and bond issues of many corporations are traded in the securities markets, stockholders and bondholders can easily sell these securities. The decision of whether to issue stock or bonds to finance a firm's plans is an important decision discussed in more detail in Chapter 18.

Private Placements

Some new stock or bond issues may not be sold publicly but rather only to a small group of large investors such as pension funds and insurance companies. These sales are referred to as **private placements.** Most private placements involve corporate debt issues. In a typical year, about one-third of all new corporate debt issues are privately placed. Recent private placements include a $200 million debt issue by SC Johnson and a $300 million debt issue by media company Hearst.[8]

It is often cheaper for a company to sell a security privately than publicly, and there is less government regulation with which to contend. Institutions buy private placements because they typically carry slightly higher interest rates than publicly issued bonds. In addition, the terms of the issue can be tailored to meet the specific needs of both the issuer and the institutional investors. Of course, the institutional investor gives up liquidity. Privately placed securities do not trade in securities markets.

Venture Capitalists

Venture capitalists are an important source of long-term financing, especially to new companies. **Venture capitalists** raise money from wealthy individuals and institutional investors and invest these funds in promising firms. Venture capitalists also provide management consulting advice as well as funds. In exchange for their investment, venture capitalists become part owners of the business. If the business succeeds, venture capitalists can earn substantial profits. US Venture Partners is one of many venture capital firms operating today. Over the past fifteen years, California-based US Venture Partners has invested close to $2 billion in 370 companies, including Sun Microsystems and Check Point Software.[9]

Leverage

Raising needed cash by borrowing allows a firm to benefit from the principle of **leverage,** a technique of increasing the rate of return on funds invested through the use of borrowed funds. The key to managing leverage is ensuring that a company's earnings remain larger than its interest payments, which increases the leverage on the rate of return on shareholders' investment. Of course, if the company earns less than its interest payments, shareholders lose money on their original investments.

leverage technique of increasing the rate of return on an investment by financing it with borrowed funds.

Figure 17.4 shows the relationship between earnings and shareholder returns for two identical hypothetical firms that choose to raise funds in different ways. Leverage Company obtains 50 percent of its funds from lenders who purchase company bonds (Leverage Company pays

17.4 The Impact of Leverage on Risk and Return

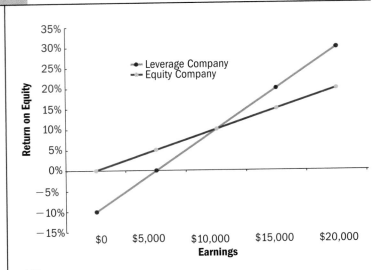

10 percent interest on its bonds). Equity Company raises all of its funds through sales of company stock.

Notice that if earnings double, from say $10,000 to $20,000, returns to shareholders of Equity Company also double (from 10 percent to 20 percent). On the other hand, returns to shareholders of Leverage Company more than double (from 10 percent to 30 percent). However, leverage works in the opposite direction as well. If earnings fall from $10,000 to $5,000, a decline of 50 percent, returns to shareholders of Equity Company also fall by 50 percent (from 10 percent to 5 percent). By contrast, returns to shareholders of Leverage Company fall from 10 percent to zero. Thus, leverage increases potential returns to shareholders but also increases risk. Another problem with borrowing money is that an overreliance on borrowed funds reduces management's flexibility in future financing decisions.

assessment check

1. List the three sources of short-term funds.
2. Define leverage and explain how leverage increases both potential leverage increases both potential returns and potential risks to owners.

financial system system by which funds are transferred from savers to users.

THE FINANCIAL SYSTEM AND FINANCIAL INSTITUTIONS

Households, businesses, government, financial institutions, and financial markets together form what is known as the financial system. The **financial system** is the process by which money flows from savers to users. A simple diagram of the financial system is shown in Figure 17.5.

On the left are savers—those with excess funds. For a variety of reasons, savers choose not to spend all of their current income, so they have a surplus of funds. Users are the opposite of savers; their spending needs exceed their current income so they have a deficit. They need to obtain additional funds to make up the difference. Savings are provided by households, businesses, and government. At the same time, borrowers also consist of households, businesses, and government. Households need money to buy automobiles or homes. Businesses need money to purchase inventory or build new production facilities. Governments need money to build highways and new schools or to fund budget deficits.

Generally, in the United States, households are net savers—meaning that in the aggregate they save more funds than they use—while businesses and governments are net users—meaning that they use more funds than they save. The fact that most of the net savings in the U.S. financial system are provided by households may be a bit of a surprise initially, because Americans do not have the reputation of being thrifty. Yet even though the savings rate of American households is low compared with those of other countries, American households still save hundreds of billions of dollars each year.

Funds can be transferred between savers and users in two ways. One is through the financial markets. For example, whenever a company sells stocks or bonds publicly or privately, funds are transferred between savers and users. Savers expect to receive some sort of return from the firm for the use of their money. The role and functioning of the financial markets will be described in more depth in the next chapter.

The other way in which funds can be transferred is through financial institutions—for example, a commercial bank such as Cincinnati-based Fifth Third or Cleveland-based Key Corporation. For instance, whenever a consumer or business deposits money into a bank account,

Figure

17.5

Overview of the Financial System and Its Components

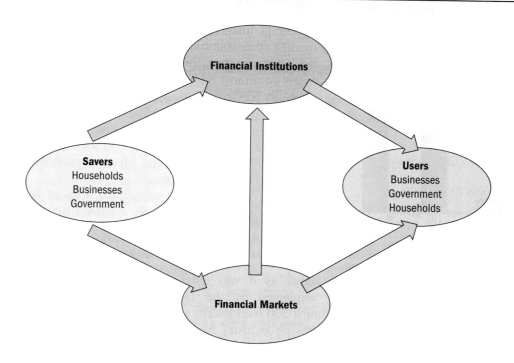

depository institutions
financial institutions that
accept deposits that can
be converted into cash
on demand.

money is transferred indirectly to users. The bank pools customer deposits and uses the funds to make loans to businesses and consumers. These borrowers pay the bank interest, and it, in turn, pays depositors interest for the use of their money.

Financial institutions greatly increase the efficiency and effectiveness of the transfer of funds between savers and users. Because of financial institutions, savers earn more, and users pay less, than they would without financial institutions. Indeed, it is difficult to imagine how any modern economy could function without well-developed financial institutions. Think about how difficult it would be for a businessperson to obtain inventory financing or a consumer to purchase a new home without financial institutions. Prospective borrowers would have to identify and negotiate terms with each saver individually.

Traditionally, financial institutions have been classified into **depository institutions**—institutions that accept deposits that customers can withdraw on demand—and nondepository institutions. Examples of depository institutions include commercial banks (such as Regions and Wells Fargo), savings banks (such as Golden West and Ohio Savings), and credit unions (such as the State Employees Credit Union of North Carolina). Nondepository institutions include life insurance companies (such as Northwestern Mutual), pension funds (such as the Florida state employee pension fund), and the various government-sponsored financial institutions such as Fannie Mae and Freddie Mac (profiled in the chapter's opening vignette). In total, financial institutions have trillions of dollars in assets. Figure 17.6 shows the relative sizes of the major types of financial institutions in the United States.

COURTESY OF KEYBANK N.A.

Commercial banks such as KeyBank offer many services to businesses, such as managing cash, strategic advice, commercial financing, and raising capital.

6. What is the difference between debt capital and equity capital? List several examples of each.
7. Define *leverage.* Construct a simple numerical example to illustrate the effect of leverage.
8. What is the financial system? Why is the direct transfer of funds between savers and users rare?
9. Explain the difference between a depository and a nondepository financial institution. Give several examples of each type of financial institution.
10. Briefly outline how a commercial bank operates. Why is deposit insurance so important?
11. Compare and contrast a commercial bank, a savings bank, and a credit union. Give an example of each.
12. Explain the role of life insurance companies and pension funds in the financial system.
13. How is the Federal Reserve System organized? Discuss the process by which a check clears.
14. Explain how open market operations work.
15. Briefly discuss the global perspective of U.S. financial institutions.

Projects and Teamwork Applications

1. Assume you would like to start a business. Put together a rough financial plan that addresses the three financial planning questions listed in the text.
2. Your business has really grown, but now it needs a substantial infusion of capital. A venture capital firm has agreed to invest the money you need. In return, the venture capital firm will own 75 percent of the business. You will be replaced as board chairman and CEO, but retain the title of company founder and president, and the venture capital firm will provide a new CEO. Would you be willing to take the money but lose control of your business?
3. The owner of your company is trying to decide how to raise an additional $1.5 million, and she has asked for your advice about whether the firm should use debt capital or equity capital. Working in a small group, prepare a brief memo to the owner outlining the advantages and disadvantages of both debt capital and equity capital. Be sure to explain the concept of leverage. Assume your company can borrow $1.5 million at an annual interest rate of 8 percent. It currently has $1.5 million in equity and no debt.
4. As noted in the prior chapter, a company whose stock is publicly traded is required to report financial results on a regular basis. Working with a partner, choose three public companies. Collect recent balance sheets, determine how levered each company is, and decide whether each company has become more or less levered in recent years. Why do some companies appear to rely more heavily on debt financing than other companies? (Note: A good source of financial statements is MSN Money Central, http://moneycentral.msn.com.)
5. Compared with most businesses, is a bank more vulnerable to failure? Why or why not? Why does federal deposit insurance help protect the soundness of the banking system?
6. Working in a small team, identify a large bank. Visit that bank's Web site and obtain its most recent financial statements. Compare the bank's financial statements to those of a nonfinancial company, such as a manufacturer or retailer. Report on your findings.
7. An exchange rate is the rate at which one currency can be exchanged for another. Working with a partner, use the Internet to find the current exchange rate between the U.S. dollar and the following currencies: Australian dollar, euro, British pound, Japanese yen, and Brazilian real. Has the dollar been rising or falling in value relative to these currencies? Assume that there was general agreement that the dollar was "undervalued." Why would an increase in U.S. interest rates help increase the value of the dollar relative to other currencies? Explain how the Federal Reserve could push U.S. interest rates higher.
8. Choose one of the following countries: Canada, the United Kingdom, or Japan. Research that country's central bank. How is the bank organized? Who appoints the members of the central bank? What functions does the central bank perform? How is the central bank similar to the U.S. Federal Reserve? How does it differ from the Fed?

Case 17.1

At Giant Bank of America, Small Businesses Rule

Bank of America is the nation's largest bank in terms of deposits. But small-business lending is still its primary mission, and it maintains a commitment to building local communities with investment and loans.

The Bank of America was recently named Lender of the Year for Oregon and Southwest Washington by the government's Small Business Administration (SBA), for approving 183 loans worth more than $5.5 million. It was also named co-winner of the Minority Lender of the Year award for making loans worth more than $1.2 million to minority-owned small businesses in the area. Such awards are not unusual for the bank, which has also been ranked the number one SBA lender in California, where its average small-business loan is worth $35,000. "The strength of our SBA lending, combined with our conventional lending, is a clear indicator that we intend to be known as 'the' small business bank," says the bank's small-business banking president.

Bank of America is the lender for about 20 percent of the small businesses in the 29 states and the District of Columbia in which it does business. With nearly 3.3 million clients, it is the largest small-business bank in the country.

The bank provides more services than just loans, of course, and among its clients it also counts individual consumers and large corporations, including nearly all the *Fortune* 500 companies. It offers banking, investing, asset management, and risk management services through its roughly 5,800 retail banking offices.

The bank is also broadening its commitment to community development, with an ambitious plan covering the next decade. Working primarily in low- and moderate-income communities, Bank of America plans to focus on lending and investment to support affordable housing, small-business/small-farm loans, con-sumer loans, and economic development. It will lend and invest about $750 billion as its Community Goal, one of the largest in U.S. commercial banking history, unfolds across the country.

Conventional loans and lines of credit will be available for small businesses and small farms, which the bank calls "the economic engines of local communities." Personal, car, and student loans will be available (excluding credit card borrowing), and in fulfillment of its economic development goal, Bank of America will work with government agencies, nonprofit developers, and financial intermediaries to promote neighborhood redevelopment, job creation, and core neighborhoods in rural and urban areas.

To maintain its good record of accountability, Bank of America will report regularly on the results of its plan, both through its Web site (http://www.bankofamerica.com) and directly to shareholders.

Questions for Critical Thinking

1. What kind of image do you think Bank of America conveys to its small-business customers? What is the source of their loyalty to the bank?
2. What are some of the benefits to local areas of the bank's Community Goal? What are the benefits to the bank?

Sources: Kennedy Smith, "SBA Recognizes Lenders of the Year for Oregon and Southwest Washington," *All-Business,* accessed August 16, 2006, http://www.allbusiness.com; "Bank of America Retains Top SBA Lender Status in California," PR Newswire, accessed July 27, 2006, http://www.prnewswire.com; "Bank of America Releases Targets for $750 Billion Community Development Goal," PR Newswire, accessed July 27, 2006, http://www.prnewswire.com.

Video Case 17.2

JPMorganChase Lends a Hand to Small Business

This video case appears on page 627. A recently filmed video, designed to expand and highlight the written case, is available for class use by instructors.

Chapter 18

Financing and Investing through Securities Markets

Every day, companies do exactly what you do as an individual: figure out how much money is needed to cover expenses and still have some left over to invest for the future. Like you, they must determine where and how to obtain any financing to survive and thrive. While you are looking for a job, companies are searching for ways to keep their enterprises operating. One way of finding funds is to take a firm public by selling shares of stock to investors. But recently a number of public corporations have been reversing this trend: they have reverted to private status. Going private has several advantages: the firm no longer has to worry about dips in its stock prices, it no longer has to answer to shareholders or pay out dividends, and it is not required to report financial results.

AP PHOTO/RIC FELD

Cable Companies Leave Public Life

Two cable television companies—Cablevision and Cox Communications—have decided to privatize. By doing so, they can avoid the intense scrutiny of investors and the public eye and exert more internal control. With money borrowed from such sources as Merrill Lynch and Bank of America, Cablevision plans to buy back its stock from shareholders and then spin off two divisions into one smaller public company—Rainbow Media cable and Madison Square Garden. Cox Communications accomplished its move to private status when its controlling shareholder, Cox Enterprises, paid $8.5 billion for the 38 percent of Cox Communications that it didn't already own—effectively taking it off the stock market. Cox Communications is the third-largest cable television provider in the United States, with 6.3 million basic cable subscribers. The firm also offers digital cable, digital telephone, and high-speed Internet services and is now focused on encouraging subscribers to purchase bundled services. Going private cuts the cost of public financial reporting requirements and takes the firm out of the Wall Street spotlight, where investors often focus on short-term performance.

Rumors continue to circulate that cable companies—and Cablevision in particular—are ripe for acquisition. Some industry experts believe that Cablevision, run by the Dolan family, is open to offers. Cablevision, a smaller company than its larger rivals Comcast and Time Warner, is located in the suburbs of New York. But despite its size, the firm has shown an uncanny ability to dominate its market. It also maintains a steady and substantial flow of cash. With its high profile and solid financial standing, Cablevision could be attractive to buyers. But others believe that taking the firm private makes a potential sale more complicated. "Once private, the lack of a public market trading value for [Cablevision] would appear to make an acquisition more complicated," explains one industry analyst, "with the buyer having far less information." It would probably be more expensive, as well. Either way, cable companies are rewriting the script for their industry, and viewers will need to tune in to see what ultimately happens.[1]

The previous chapter discussed two sources of funds for long-term financial needs: debt capital and equity capital. Long-term debt capital takes the form of U.S. government bonds, municipal bonds, and corporate bonds. Equity capital takes the form of common and preferred stock—ownership shares in corporations. Stocks and bonds are commonly called **securities**, because both represent obligations on the part of issuers to provide purchasers with expected or stated returns on the funds invested or loaned.

This chapter examines how securities are bought and sold in two financial markets—the primary market and the secondary market. The primary market involves the initial sale of new securities to investors, and the secondary market consists of the sale of existing securities between investors. As we discussed in Chapter 17, financial markets are an important part of the overall financial system, the system by which funds are transferred from savers to users. Next, we explore the characteristics of stocks, bonds, and money market instruments (short-term debt securities) and the way investors choose specific securities. We then examine the role of organized securities exchanges, such as the New York Stock Exchange, in the financial sector and outline the information included in reports of securities transactions. This section is followed by a discussion of mutual funds—an especially popular option for individual investors. Finally, we review the laws that regulate the securities markets and protect investors.

PRIMARY VERSUS SECONDARY MARKETS

securities financial instruments such as stocks and bonds.

primary market market in which new security issues are first sold to investors; issuers receive the proceeds from the sale.

In the **primary market**, firms and governments issue securities and sell them initially to the public. When a company needs capital to purchase inventory, expand a plant, make major investments, acquire another firm, or pursue other business goals, it may sell a bond or stock issue to the investing public. For example, Wal-Mart Stores recently sold about $800 million in bonds. It used the proceeds to build new stores.[2] Similarly, when Washington State needs capital to build a new highway, to buy a new ferry, or to fulfill other public needs, its leaders may also decide to sell bonds.

A stock offering gives investors the opportunity to purchase ownership shares in a firm such as well-known drug maker Amgen and to participate in its future growth, in exchange for providing current capital. When a company offers stock for sale to the general public for the first time, it is called an **initial public offering (IPO)**. During a recent twelve-month period, around 180 initial public offerings raised a total of more than $30 billion. These companies, on average, had been in existence for seven years prior to going public.[3]

Both profit-seeking corporations and government agencies also rely on primary markets to raise funds by issuing bonds. For example, the federal government sells Treasury bonds to finance part of federal outlays such as interest on outstanding federal debt. State and local governments sell bonds to finance capital projects such as the construction of sewer systems, streets, and fire stations.

Announcements of new stock and bond offerings appear daily in business publications such as the *Wall Street Journal.* These announcements are often in the form of a simple black-and-white ad called a *tombstone.*

Securities are sold to the investment public in two ways: in open auctions and through investment bankers. Virtually all securities sold through open auctions consist of U.S. Treasury securities. A week before an upcoming auction, the Treasury announces the type and number of securities it will be auctioning. Treasury bills are auctioned weekly, whereas longer-term Treasury securities are auctioned once a month or once a quarter. Prospective buyers submit bids to the Treasury. Two types of bids are allowed: competitive and noncompetitive. A competitive bid specifies how much the investor wishes to purchase and the price. The higher the price specified, the lower the return to the investor, and the lower the cost to the

Treasury. In a typical auction the Treasury accepts about half of the competitive bids submitted. An investor submitting a noncompetitive bid only specifies the amount he or she wishes to purchase (up to a limit of $5 million) and agrees to pay a price equal to the average price on accepted competitive bids. Investors may submit bids directly to the Treasury or through banks and investment firms.

Sales of most corporate and municipal securities are made via financial specialists called **investment bankers.** Merrill Lynch, Goldman Sachs, Lehman Brothers, and Crédit Suisse First Boston (CSFB) are examples of well-known investment banking firms. An investment banker is a financial intermediary that purchases the issue from the firm or government and then resells the issue to investors. This process is known as **underwriting.**

Investment bankers underwrite stock and bond issues at a discount, meaning that they pay the issuing firm or government less than the price the investment banker charges investors. This discount is compensation for services rendered, including the risk investment bankers incur whenever they underwrite a new security issue. Although the size of the discount is often negotiable, they usually average around 5 percent for all types of securities. The size of the underwriting discount, however, is generally higher for stock issues than it is for bond issues. For instance, the average underwriting discount for IPOs is close to 7 percent.[4]

Corporations and governments are willing to pay for the services provided by investment bankers because they are financial market experts. In addition to locating buyers for the issue, the underwriter typically advises the issuer on such details as the general characteristics of the issue, its pricing, and the timing of the offering. Several investment bankers commonly participate in the underwriting process. The issuer selects a lead, or primary, investment banker, which in turn forms a syndicate consisting of other investment banking firms. Each member of the syndicate purchases a portion of the security issue, which it resells to investors.

Media reports of stock and bond trading are most likely to refer to trading in the **secondary market,** a collection of financial markets in which previously issued securities are traded among investors. The corporations or governments that originally issued the securities being traded are not directly involved in the secondary market. They neither make any payments when securities are sold nor receive any of the proceeds when securities are purchased. The New York Stock Exchange (NYSE) and the Nasdaq stock market are both secondary markets. In terms of the dollar value of securities bought and sold, the secondary market is four to five times as large as the primary market. During a typical trading day, more than $50 billion worth of stock changes hands on the NYSE alone.[5] We describe secondary markets in more depth later in the chapter.

AP PHOTO/MARK LENNIHAN

Lehman Brothers is one of the world's largest investment banking firms.

secondary market market in which existing security issues are bought and sold by investors.

assessment check

1. Distinguish between the primary and secondary markets for securities. Is the primary market or secondary market larger?

2. Explain the two ways in which securities are sold in the primary market.

TYPES OF SECURITIES

Securities can be classified into three categories: money market instruments, bonds, and stock. Money market instruments and bonds are both debt securities, and stocks are units of ownership in corporations like General Electric, Best Buy, 3M, and PepsiCo.

Money Market Instruments

Money market instruments are short-term debt securities issued by governments, financial institutions, and corporations. By definition, all money market instruments mature within one year from the date of issue. Investors are paid interest by the issuer for the use of their funds. Money market instruments are generally low-risk securities and are purchased by investors when they have surplus cash. As noted in the prior chapter, financial managers often invest surplus cash in money market instruments because they are low risk and are easily convertible into cash. For example, Microsoft has more than $15 billion currently invested in money market instruments.[6] Examples of money market instruments include U.S. Treasury bills, commercial paper, and bank certificates of deposit. These securities were described in the prior chapter.

Bonds

Bondholders are creditors of a corporation. By selling bonds, a firm obtains long-term debt capital. Federal, state, and local governments also acquire funds in this way. Bonds are issued in various denominations (face values), usually between $1,000 and $25,000. Each issue indicates a rate of interest to be paid to the bondholder—stated as a percentage of the bond's face value—as well as a maturity date on which the bondholder is paid the bond's face value. Because bondholders are creditors, they have a claim on the firm's assets that must be satisfied before any claims of stockholders in the event of the firm's bankruptcy, reorganization, or liquidation. For example, when California and Bermuda–based Global Crossing emerged from bankruptcy, existing creditors received about 35 percent of the shares of the newly reorganized company to satisfy their claims. Those who owned shares of Global Crossing at the time of its bankruptcy filing, by contrast, received nothing, losing about $50 billion.[7]

Types of Bonds   A prospective bond investor can choose among a variety of bonds. Major types of bonds are summarized in Table 18.1.

Government bonds are bonds sold by the U.S. Treasury. Because government bonds are backed by the full faith and credit of the U.S. government, they are considered the least risky of all bonds. The Treasury sells bonds that mature in 2, 3, 5, 7, 10, and 30 years from the date of issue. The Treasury stopped selling new 30-year bonds in 2001 but recently reintroduced sales of the so-called *long bond*. The "Hit & Miss" feature on page 580 discusses some of the reasons why the sale of 30-year bonds was resumed.

Municipal bonds are bonds issued by state or local governments. There are two types of municipal bonds. A revenue bond is a bond issue whose proceeds are to be used to pay for a project that will produce revenue—such as a toll road or bridge. The Oklahoma Turnpike Authority has issued such bonds. A general obligation bond is a bond whose proceeds are to be used to pay for a project that will not produce any revenue—such as a new Indiana state police post. General obligation bonds can be sold only by states such as Oregon or local governmental units such as Toledo, Ohio, or Bergen County, New Jersey, that have the power to levy taxes. An important feature of municipal bonds is the exemption of interest payments from federal income tax. Because of this attractive feature, municipal bonds generally carry lower interest rates than either corporate or government bonds.

Corporate bonds are a diverse group and often vary based on the collateral backing the bond. A **secured bond** is backed by a specific pledge of company assets. For example, mortgage bonds are backed by real and personal property owned by the firm, such as machinery or furniture, and collateral trust bonds are backed by stocks and bonds of other companies owned by the firm. In the event of default, bondholders may receive the proceeds from selling these

Table 18.1

Types of Bonds

Issuer	Types of Securities	Risk	Special Features
U.S. Treasury (government bonds)	Notes: Mature in 10 years or fewer from date of issue. Bonds: Mature in 30 years from date of issue	Treasury bonds and notes have virtually no risk.	Interest is exempt from state income taxes.
State and local governments (municipal bonds)	General obligation: Issued by state or local governmental units with taxing authority; backed by the full faith and credit of the state where issued.	Risk varies depending on the financial health of the issuer.	Interest is exempt from federal income taxes and may be exempt from state income taxes.
	Revenue: Issued to pay for projects that generate revenue—such as water systems or toll roads; revenue from project used to pay principal and interest.	Most large municipal bond issues are rated in terms of credit risk (AAA or Aaa is the highest rating).	
Corporations	Secured bonds: Bonds are backed by specific assets.	Risk varies depending on the financial health of the issuer.	A few corporate bonds are convertible into shares of common stock of the issuing company.
	Unsecured bonds (debentures): Backed by the financial health and reputation of the issuer.	Most corporate bond issues are rated in terms of credit risk (AAA or Aaa is the highest rating).	
Financial institutions (such as Fannie Mae and Freddie Mac)	Mortgage pass-through securities	Generally very low risk.	They pay monthly income consisting of both interest and principal.

assets. Because bond purchasers want to balance their financial returns with their risks, bonds backed by pledges of specific assets are less risky than those without such collateral. Consequently, a firm can issue secured bonds at lower interest rates than it would have to pay for comparable unsecured bonds. However, many firms do issue unsecured bonds, called **debentures.** These bonds are backed only by the financial reputation of the issuing corporation.

Another popular type of bond is the **mortgage pass-through security.** Mortgage pass-through securities are sold by Fannie Mae, Freddie Mac, and other financial institutions. The securities are backed by a self-liquidating pool of mortgage loans purchased from lenders such as savings banks. As borrowers make their monthly mortgage payments, these payments are "passed through" to the holders of the pass-through securities. Mortgage pass-through securities are popular because they are relatively safe (mortgages have to be insured) and provide monthly income.

Quality Ratings for Bonds Two factors determine the price of a bond: its risk and its interest rate. Bonds vary considerably in terms of risk. One tool used by bond investors to assess the risk of a bond is its so-called **bond rating.** Two investment firms—Standard & Poor's (S&P) and Moody's—rate most corporate and municipal bonds. The bonds with the least risk are assigned a rating of either AAA (S&P) or Aaa (Moody's). The ratings descend as

HIT & MISS

An Old Investment Makes a Comeback

Treasury bonds aren't glamorous, especially ones with long-range maturity dates. In fact, the U.S. Treasury put a hold on the sale of 30-year bonds for several years because the federal government had a budget surplus and didn't need to borrow the money. But the Treasury recently announced their return to the marketplace. Who's not yawning about the announcement? In the investment industry, it's the fixed-income specialists who are cheering the comeback. "It's like having an old friend back," explains Clifford A. Gladson, a senior vice president for fixed-income investments at USAA Investment Management.

Thirty-year bonds carry with them a reputation for long-term security in the form of guaranteed rates for mutual funds and pension funds, which tend to make long-range investments. But most individuals don't hang onto the same investments for three decades—they can usually do better with shorter-term, slightly riskier investments. And as interest rates in general climb, the value of a long-term bond may diminish even though it pays a higher fixed interest rate than short-term bonds. Still, the 30-year bond has been a benchmark for many investment professionals. "There's a love affair out there for some people," quips one manager of fixed-income portfolios for Vanguard. The 30-year bond provides a guaranteed rate of return and is free of state income taxes, two features that attract investors. It also gives them one more option they did not have for several years.

Anyone interested in making an investment should do the homework before purchasing. Individuals must consider their own needs and goals. An 80-year-old retiree is unlikely to buy a 30-year bond, but a 45-year-old might want this type of investment as part of his or her retirement portfolio. "I think it's good for [investment] portfolios," notes a financial economist at Wachovia Securities. "It adds to the diversification component." So you make the purchase and then hit the snooze button—several times.

Questions for Critical Thinking

1. Would you purchase a 30-year Treasury bond during your career? If so, when and why? If not, why not?
2. If you plan to participate in a firm's pension plan or other investments made on your behalf by your employer, what steps might you take to learn about the types of investments being made?

Sources: Avrum D. Lank, "30-Year Treasury Bonds May Come Up Short for Individual Investors," *Milwaukee Journal Sentinel,* accessed August 16, 2006, http://www.jsonline.com; Elizabeth Harris, "The 30-Year Bond Is Back, and So Is Romance," *New York Times,* accessed July 28, 2006, http://www.nytimes.com; Kathleen Lynn, "Investors, Take Note: The 30-Year Treasury Bond Is Back," *The Record,* accessed August 4, 2005, http://www.recordnet.com; Mike Meyers, "30-Year's Revival May Help Taxpayer," *(Minneapolis) Star Tribune,* accessed August 4, 2005, http://startribune.com.

risk increases. Table 18.2 lists the S&P and Moody's bond ratings. Bonds with ratings of BBB (or Baa) and above are classified as **investment-grade bonds.** Examples of investment-grade bonds include Royal Dutch Shell (rated AA by Standard and Poor's) and the Illinois State Building Authority (rated AAA by Standard & Poor's). By contrast, bonds with ratings of BB (or Ba) and below are classified as speculative, or so-called **junk bonds.** Junk bonds attract investors by offering high interest rates in exchange for greater risk. Today, junk bonds pay about 50 percent more in interest than do investment-grade corporate bonds. An example of speculative-grade bonds is those issued by Ford Motor Company (rated BB by Standard and Poor's).

The second factor affecting the price of a bond is its interest rate. Other things being equal, the higher the interest rate, the higher the price of a bond. However, everything else usually is not equal; the bonds may not be equally risky, or one may have a longer maturity. Investors must evaluate the trade-offs involved.

Another important influence on bond prices is the market interest rate. Because bonds pay fixed rates of interest, as market interest rates rise, bond prices fall, and vice versa. For instance, the price of a ten-year bond, paying 5 percent per year, would fall by about 8 percent if market interest rates rose from 5 percent to 6 percent.

Table
18.2

Bond Ratings

Highest to lowest	Standard & Poor's Rating	Moody's Rating	
	AAA	Aaa	Investment-grade bonds
	AA	Aa	
	A	A	
	BBB	Baa	
	BB	Ba	Speculative-grade bonds (junk bonds)
	B	B	
	CCC	Caa	
	CC	Ca	
	C	C	

Note: Any bond with a rating below is C is currently in default, meaning it is not paying interest or repaying principal.

Retiring Bonds   Because bonds in an issue mature on a specific date, borrowers such as Bed Bath & Beyond or Harris County, Texas, must have the necessary funds available to repay the principal at that time. In some instances, this can create a cash flow problem. To ease the repayment problem, some borrowers issue serial bonds. A serial bond issue consists of bonds that mature on different dates. For example, assume a corporation issues $20 million in serial bonds for a 30-year period. None of the bonds mature during the first 20 years. However, beginning in the 21st year, $2 million in bonds mature each year until all the bonds are repaid at the end of the 30 years.

A variation of the concept of serial bonds is the sinking fund bond, or prerefunded bond. Under this arrangement, the issuer, such as the city of Oakland, California, makes annual deposits to accumulate funds for use in redeeming the bonds when they mature. These deposits are made to the bond's trustee—usually a large bank—who represents bondholders. The deposits must be large enough that their total, plus accrued interest, will be sufficient to redeem the bonds at maturity.

Most corporate and municipal bonds, and some government bonds, are callable. A **call provision** allows the issuer to redeem the bond before its maturity at a prespecified price. Not surprisingly, issuers tend to call bonds when market interest rates are declining. For example, if York County, Pennsylvania, had $50 million in bonds outstanding with a 6 percent annual interest rate, it would pay $3 million annually in interest. If interest rates decline to 4 percent, the county may decide to call the 6 percent bonds, repaying the principal from the proceeds of newly issued 4 percent bonds. Calling the 6 percent bonds, and issuing 4 percent bonds, will save the county $1 million a year in interest payments. The savings in annual interest expense should more than offset the cost of retiring the old bonds and issuing new ones.

Stock

The basic form of corporate ownership is embodied in **common stock.** Purchasers of common stock are the true owners of a corporation. Holders of common stock vote on major company decisions, such as purchasing another company or electing a board of directors. In return for

common stock shares of ownership in a corporation.

the money they invest, they expect to receive some sort of return. This return can come in the form of cash dividend payments and/or expected price appreciation. Dividends vary widely from stock to stock. DuPont, for instance, pays an annual dividend of almost $1.50 per share. By contrast, Starbucks pays no annual dividend to its shareholders. As a general rule, faster-growing companies pay less in dividends because they need more funds to finance their growth. Consequently, investors expect stocks paying little or no cash dividends to show greater price appreciation compared with stocks paying more generous cash dividends.

Common stockholders benefit from company success, and they risk the loss of their investments if the company fails. If a firm dissolves, claims of creditors must be satisfied before stockholders receive anything. Because creditors have a senior claim to assets, holders of common stock are said to have a residual claim on company assets.

Sometimes confusion arises over the difference between the book value and a stock's market value. *Book value* is determined by subtracting the company's liabilities from its assets. When this net figure is divided by the number of shares of common stock outstanding, the book value of each share is known. Recently, Johnson & Johnson had a book value of around $12 per share.

The *market value* of a stock is the price at which the stock is currently selling. Johnson & Johnson had a recent market price of $68 per share. It is easily found by referring to the financial section of daily newspapers or on the Internet and may be more or less than the book value. What determines market value, however, is more complicated. However, while many variables cause stock prices to fluctuate up and down in the short term, in the long run stock prices tend to follow a company's profits. For instance, over the last ten years, both Johnson & Johnson's earnings and stock price have risen by more than 300 percent.

preferred stock stock whose holders have priority over common stockholders in the payment of dividends but usually have no voting rights.

Preferred Stock In addition to common stock, a few companies also issue **preferred stock**—stock whose holders receive preference in the payment of dividends. General Motors and Bank of America are examples of firms with preferred stock outstanding. Also, if a company is dissolved, holders of preferred stock have claims on the firm's assets that are ahead of the claims of common stockholders. On the other hand, preferred stockholders rarely have any voting rights, and the dividend they are paid is fixed, regardless of how profitable the firm becomes. Therefore, although preferred stock is legally equity, many investors consider it to be more like a bond than common stock.

Convertible Securities Companies may issue bonds or preferred stock that contains a conversion feature. This feature gives the bondholder or preferred stockholder the right to exchange the bond or preferred stock for a fixed number of shares of common stock. For example, credit card issuer Providian Financial has a convertible bond outstanding that allows its holder to exchange the bond (which has a face value of $1,000) for around 77 shares of Providian common stock. So if Providian's stock was selling for $20 per share, the convertible bond would be worth at least $1,540 (77 × $20). Convertible bonds pay lower interest rates than those lacking conversion features, helping reduce the interest expense of the issuing firms. Investors are willing to accept these lower interest rates because they value the potential for additional gains if the price of the firm's stock increases.

assessment check

1. Explain the difference between a money market instrument and a bond.
2. What are the two types of bonds issued by state and local governments? Describe the difference between a secured and unsecured bond.
3. Discuss the major investment characteristics of common stock.

SECURITIES PURCHASERS

Two general types of investors buy securities: institutions and individuals. An **institutional investor** is an organization that invests its own funds or those it holds in trust for others. Institutional investors include insurance companies such as New York Life, pension funds such as Alabama's state employee pension fund, T. Rowe Price mutual funds, and not-for-profit organizations such as the American Cancer Society. Many institutional investors are huge. As noted in Chapter 17, pension funds have more than $6.5 trillion in assets, and the total assets of life insurance companies exceed $4.2 trillion.[8] Institutional investors buy and sell large quantities of securities, often in blocks of 10,000 or more shares per transaction. Such block trading represents about half of the total daily volume on the major securities exchanges.[9]

The number of individual investors who own shares through mutual funds or their employer's retirement plans is steadily rising, and the firms that manage their funds control more than half of all U.S. equities.[10] More than half of all Americans now own stocks, either directly or by investing in stock mutual funds. By contrast, 30 years ago, less than one-third of American households owned any stocks at all.[11]

Investment Motivations

Why do individuals and institutions invest? In general, individuals and institutions have five primary motivations for investing: growth in capital, stability of principal, liquidity, current income, and income growth. All investors must rank each motivation in terms of importance, and all investments involve trade-offs. For example, an investment that has the potential for substantial growth in capital may provide no current income. By contrast, an investment that has very stable principal may have little potential for capital growth. The bottom line is this: Some investments are more appropriate for certain investors than for others. Table 18.3 provides a useful guide for evaluating money market instruments, bonds, and stocks.

Growth in Capital   When it comes to potential growth in capital over time, especially over long periods of time, common stocks are the clear winner. For example, over a recent 20-year period, $10,000 invested in common stocks would have grown to more than $64,000. A similar investment in bonds made during the same period would have grown to less than $35,000. This example does not imply, however, that the prices of all common stocks go up all the time, nor do they go up by the same amount. Not surprisingly, stock performance varies considerably. For instance, over the past decade $10,000 invested in Procter & Gamble's common stock would have grown to more than $37,000. By contrast, over the same period, a $10,000 investment in Ford's common stock would have grown to less than $13,500.

Stability of Principal   Treasury bills and other money market instruments are the clear winner when it comes to stability of principal. The odds that the price of a money market

Table 18.3

Comparing Investment Alternatives

Investment Motivation	Money Market Instruments	Bonds	Common Stocks
Growth in capital	*	**	***
Stability of principal	***	**	*
Liquidity	***	**	*
Current income	*	***	**
Growth in income	**	*	***

Note: *** = best or highest.

A key to successful investing is finding a strategy that has an appropriate level of risk. Banks and investment firms such as Wells Fargo often provide investment advice.

investment will fall below the price the investor originally paid are virtually zero. Furthermore, when an investor buys a Treasury bill or other money market instrument, the investor can be pretty sure the original investment will be returned. For example, a 90-day Treasury bill has a face value of $10,000. If you buy the T-bill today, you're virtually ensured that you'll receive $10,000 in three months. With stocks, there is no such guarantee.

Liquidity   Because the prices of stocks, and to a lesser extent bonds, can vary widely, investors cannot count on making profits whenever they decide or need to sell. Liquidity is a measure of the speed at which assets can be converted into cash. Because money market instruments such as a CD issued by Wells Fargo have short maturities and stable prices, they offer investors the highest amount of liquidity.

Current Income   Historically, bonds have provided the highest current income of any security. Interest rates on bonds are usually higher than money market interest rates or the dividends paid on common stocks. For instance, Lowe's has an outstanding bond that pays about 5 percent interest per year. By contrast, the company's common stock has a current dividend yield (annual dividend divided by the stock price) of less than 1 percent. Also, money market interest rates vary, but the interest rate on a bond remains constant. Investors looking for high current income should invest a large portion of their funds in bonds.

Income Growth   When you buy a bond, the interest you receive is fixed for the life of the bond. Interest rates on money market instruments can increase over time, but they can decrease as well. On the other hand, common stock dividends have historically risen at a rate that exceeds the rate of inflation. Over the past 20 years, for instance, Johnson & Johnson's common stock dividend has risen at an average annual rate exceeding 10 percent. There is, however, no guarantee that a company's common stock dividend will *always* increase and can, in fact, decrease. For instance, over the past four years Kodak has cut its common stock dividend by more than 75 percent.[12]

Taxes and Investing

Interest received from government and corporate bonds is considered ordinary income and is taxed at the investor's marginal tax rate. (Interest received from municipal bonds is usually exempt from federal income taxes, although not always from state income taxes.) Dividends received from common and most preferred stocks is taxed at a lower rate than ordinary income. Furthermore, investors who sell securities at a profit owe so-called capital gains taxes on the difference between the selling price and the purchase price.

Taxes can influence investment decisions in a number of ways. Investors in high marginal tax brackets, for instance, are more likely to hold municipal bonds than investors in lower tax brackets. Because capital losses (selling a security for less than the purchase price) offset capital gains, an investor might decide to take a capital loss at the end of the year rather than waiting until the following year.

assessment check

1. Who purchases securities?
2. What are the five motivations for investing? On which of the five motivations for investment do common stocks rank highest?
3. Discuss the tax implications of investing. Are all sources of investment returns taxed equally?

SECURITIES EXCHANGES

Securities exchanges are centralized marketplaces where stocks and bonds are traded. Most of the largest and best-known securities exchanges are commonly called **stock exchanges,** or *stock markets,* because most securities traded are common-stock issues. Stock exchanges are secondary markets. The securities have already been issued by firms, which received proceeds from the issue when it was sold in the primary market. Sales in a securities exchange occur between individual and institutional investors.

Stock exchanges exist throughout the world and most countries today have at least one stock market. The five largest stock exchanges, based on the market value of the stocks traded, are shown in Figure 18.1. As the figure shows, the two largest stock exchanges are located in the United States.

The New York Stock Exchange

The New York Stock Exchange—sometimes referred to as the Big Board—is arguably the most famous and one of the oldest stock markets in the world, having been founded in 1792. Today, more than 3,000 common- and preferred-stock issues are listed on the NYSE. These stocks represent most of the largest, best-known companies in the United States and have a total market value exceeding $13 trillion.[13] In terms of the total value of stock traded, the NYSE is the world's largest stock market.

For a company's stock to be traded on the NYSE, the firm must apply to the exchange for listing and meet certain listing requirements. In addition, the firm must continue to meet requirements each year to remain listed on the NYSE. Corporate bonds are also traded on the NYSE, but bond trading makes up less than 1 percent of the total value of securities traded there during a typical year.

Trading on the NYSE takes place face-to-face on a trading floor. Buy and sell orders are transmitted to a specific post on the floor of the exchange. Buyers and sellers then bid against one another in an open auction. Only investment firms that are members of the NYSE are allowed to trade, meaning that the firm owns at least one of 1,366 "seats." Seats are occasionally bought and sold. Recently a seat on the NYSE sold for $2.8 million.[14]

Each NYSE stock is assigned to a specialist firm. Specialists are unique investment firms that maintain an orderly and liquid market in the stocks assigned to them. Specialists must be willing to buy when there are no other buyers and sell when there are no other sellers. Specialists also act as auctioneers and catalysts, bringing buyers and sellers together.

Some observers portray the NYSE and its trading practices as somewhat old-fashioned, especially in this technological age. Most

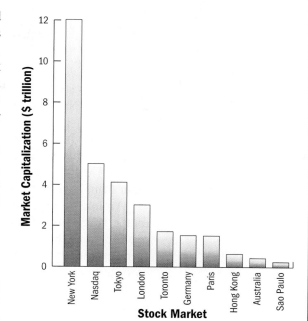

The World's Ten Largest Stock Markets

Figure 18.1

Source: *NYSE Fact Book* (interactive edition), New York Stock Exchange, accessed August 22, 2005, http://www.nyse.com.

stock exchange financial market where stocks are traded.

MONIKA GRAFF/UPI/LANDOV

The New York Stock Exchange is one of the oldest stock exchanges in the world.

markets, they note, have abandoned their trading floors in favor of electronic trading. However, even though the NYSE still retains a trading floor, the exchange has become highly automated in recent years. Its computer systems automatically match and route most orders, which are typically filled within a few seconds.

The Nasdaq Stock Market

The world's second-largest stock market is the Nasdaq Stock Market. It is very different from the NYSE. Nasdaq—which stands for National Association of Securities Dealers Automated Quotations—is actually a computerized communications network that links member investment firms. It is the world's largest intranet.[15] All trading on Nasdaq takes place through its intranet, rather than on a trading floor. Buy and sell orders are entered into the network and executed electronically. All Nasdaq-listed stocks have two or more market makers—investment firms that perform essentially the same functions as NYSE specialists.

Around 5,000 companies have their stocks listed on Nasdaq. Compared with firms listed on the NYSE, Nasdaq-listed corporations tend to be smaller, less well-known firms. Some are relatively new businesses and cannot meet NYSE listing requirements. It is not uncommon for firms eventually to transfer the trading of their stocks from Nasdaq to the NYSE—sixteen did so in a recent year.[16] However, dozens of major companies currently trade on Nasdaq—such as Amgen, Cisco Systems, Dell, Intel, and Microsoft—that would easily meet NYSE listing requirements. For a variety of reasons, these firms have decided to remain listed on Nasdaq.

Other U.S. Stock Markets

In addition to the NYSE and Nasdaq Stock Market, several other stock markets operate in the United States. The American Stock Exchange, or AMEX, is also located in New York. It focuses on the stocks of smaller firms, as well as other financial instruments such as options. In comparison with the NYSE and Nasdaq, the AMEX is tiny. Daily trading volume is only around 60 million shares compared with the one-billion-plus shares on each of the larger two exchanges.[17]

Several regional stock exchanges also operate throughout the United States. They include the Chicago, Pacific (San Francisco), Boston, Cincinnati, and Philadelphia Stock Exchanges. Originally established to trade the shares of small, regional companies, the regional exchanges now list securities of many large corporations as well. In fact, more than half of the companies listed on the NYSE are also listed on one or more regional exchanges.

Foreign Stock Markets

As noted earlier, stock markets exist throughout the world. Virtually all developed countries and many developing countries have stock exchanges. Examples include Bombay, Helsinki, Hong Kong, Mexico City, Paris, and Toronto. One of the largest stock exchanges outside the United States is the London Stock Exchange. Founded in the early 17th century, the London Stock Exchange lists approximately 2,900 stock and bond issues, more than 500 of which are shares of companies located outside the U.K. and Ireland. Trading on the London Stock Exchange takes place using a Nasdaq-type computerized communications network.

ADAM ROUNTREE/BLOOMBERG NEWS/LANDOV

The Nasdaq Stock Exchange, the second-largest exchange in the world, conducts trading through a computerized network.

The London Stock Exchange is very much an international market. Around two-thirds of all cross-border trading in the world—for example, the trading of stocks of American companies outside the United States—takes place in London. It is not uncommon for institutional investors in the United States to trade NYSE- or Nasdaq-listed stocks in London. These investors claim they often get better prices and faster order execution in London than they do in the United States.

ECNs and the Future of Stock Markets

For years a so-called *fourth market* has existed. The fourth market is the direct trading of exchange-listed stocks off the floor of the exchange, in the case of NYSE-listed stocks, or outside the network, in the case of Nasdaq-listed stocks. For the most part, trading in the fourth market was limited to institutional investors buying or selling large blocks of stock.

Now the fourth market has begun to open up to smaller, individual investors through markets called **electronic communications networks (ECNs).** Buyers and sellers meet in a virtual stock market in which they trade directly with one another. No specialist or market maker is involved. ECNs have become a significant force in the stock market in recent years. Around half of all trades involving Nasdaq-listed stocks take place on INET or Archipelago—the two largest ECNs—rather than directly through the Nasdaq system.[18] Some have suggested that ECNs represent the future for stock markets. In fact, INET and Archipelago were recently acquired by Nasdaq and the NYSE, respectively. Industry watchers now speculate that NYSE's acquisition of Archipelago could eventually lead to the exchange's abandoning its centuries-old trading floor and becoming an electronic market.

assessment check

1. Compare and contrast the NYSE and Nasdaq stock markets.
2. Explain the role of specialists and market makers.
3. What is an ECN?

BUYING AND SELLING SECURITIES

Unless an investor is a member of one of the stock exchanges, the investor must use the services of a brokerage firm that is a member of one or more stock exchanges. A **brokerage firm** is a financial intermediary that buys and sells securities for individual and institutional investors. Examples include A. G. Edwards, Raymond James, Morgan Stanley, and Wachovia Securities. Brokerage firms are usually members of most major stock markets. Choosing a brokerage firm, and a specific stockbroker in some cases, is one of the most important decisions investors make. The "Business Etiquette" feature discusses one aspect of developing good business relations—networking.

brokerage firm financial intermediary that buys and sells securities for individual and institutional investors.

Placing an Order

An investor who wants to purchase shares of a stock typically initiates the transaction by contacting his or her brokerage firm. The firm transmits the order to the appropriate market, completes the transaction, and confirms the transaction with the investor, all within a few minutes.

An investor's request to buy or sell stock at the current market price is called a market order. A **market order** instructs the brokerage firm, such as Edward Jones, to obtain the highest price possible, if the investor is selling, or the lowest price possible, if the investor is buying. By contrast, a **limit order** instructs the brokerage firm not to pay more than a specified price for a stock, if the investor is buying, or not to accept less than a specified price, if the investor is selling. If Edward Jones is unable to fill a limit order immediately, it is left with either an NYSE specialist or Nasdaq market maker. If the price reaches the specified price, the order is carried out. Limit orders are often recommended during periods of extreme price volatility.

"They Said It"

"There's always a bull market somewhere."
—Jim Cramer (b. 1955)
Host of Mad Money on CNBC

(b)usiness (e)tiquette

Networking for Successful Business Contacts

Networking is a fact of business life. But there is no need to feel intimidated by it—networking is really a matter of connecting with people and communicating effectively, which is something you do in your life as a student, friend, and family member. Networking helps you reach the right people at the right time to obtain a job, learn more about customers, or close a deal. It involves moving beyond your immediate circle of colleagues and friends. Here are a few suggestions for how to network smoothly and successfully.

1. Be clear about the purpose of your networking. Are you looking for a job in the financial industry? Do you want to develop customers in a certain region? Understanding your purpose will direct your search for the right person or people.
2. When you contact someone, introduce yourself and state your reasons for the contact. Ask for a few minutes of the person's time—a brief phone conversation or e-mail. If you set up a meeting or phone conference, be prompt and respect the person's time.
3. Ask clear questions, and listen carefully to the answers. Give the person an opportunity to give advice or voice an opinion.
4. Build on common ground— you might have attended the same college, grown up in the same region, or cheered for the same sports teams. However, don't stray far off the path of the visit.
5. Thank the person for his or her time and effort, even if the contact was not as helpful as you hoped. The contact may still be helpful at a later date. Offer to reciprocate, if appropriate.
6. When the meeting is over, be sure to respect any confidentiality implied or agreed on. Networking relationships are built on trust.

Sources: Lawrence K. Jones, "Practice Networking Etiquette," Career Key, accessed July 28, 2006, http://www.careerkey.org; Randall S. Hansen, "Online Discussion Group Networking Etiquette Do's and Don'ts," Quintessential Careers, accessed July 28, 2006, http://www.quintcareers.com; "Networking Etiquette," Massachusetts Institute of Technology, accessed July 28, 2006, http://web.mit.edu.

Costs of Trading

When investors buy or sell securities through a brokerage firm, they pay a fee for the related services. Today, these costs vary widely among brokerage firms. A trade that costs less than $20 using E*Trade might cost more than $50 using Smith Barney. Often, the cost depends on what type of brokerage firm the investor uses. A full-service firm—such as NatCity—provides extensive client services and offers considerable investment advice, but charges higher fees. Brokers at full-service firms make recommendations and provide general advice to investors.

By contrast, a discount firm—such as Charles Schwab and Fidelity—charges lower fees but offers less advice and fewer services. However, most discount firms provide a variety of research tools to customers to help them make better decisions, and some offer investment-planning advice for an additional fee. All investors need to weigh the appropriate trade-off between cost, advice, and services when choosing a brokerage firm.

Online brokerage firms—such as Ameritrade—charge among the lowest fees of all brokerage firms. Investors enter buy and sell orders on their PCs or wireless devices. Most online firms also give customers access to a wide range of investment information, although they do not directly provide advice to investors. As online trading increased in popularity, most discount and full-service brokerage firms started offering online trading services. Merrill Lynch, for instance, now offers a wide range of online trading services. In addition, the company's 15,000 brokers—called financial advisors—now offer clients more comprehensive personal financial planning advice.[19]

Reading the Financial News

At least four or five pages of most daily newspapers are devoted to reporting current financial news. This information is also available on countless Web sites. Much of the financial news coverage focuses on the day's securities transactions. Stocks and bonds traded on the various securities markets are listed alphabetically in the newspaper, with separate sections for each of the major markets. Information is provided on the volume of sales and the price of each security.

Today all major stock markets throughout the world quote prices in decimals. In the United States, stock prices are quoted in U.S. dollars and cents per share. In London, stock prices are quoted in pence, and in Japan they are quoted in yen.

Stock Quotations   To understand how to read the stock tables found in newspapers, you need to understand how to interpret the symbols in the various columns. As Figure 18.2 explains, the symbol in column 1 is the 52-week indicator. An arrow pointing up means that a stock hit its 52-week high during the day, and an arrow pointing down means that a stock hit its 52-week low. Column 2 gives the stock's highest and lowest trading prices during the past 52 weeks. Column 3 contains the abbreviation for the company's name, footnotes that provide information about the stock (*pf*, for instance, refers to preferred stock), and the stock's ticker symbol. Column 4 lists the dividend, usually an annual payment based on the last quarterly declaration. Column 5 presents the yield, the annual dividend divided by the stock's closing price.

Column 6 lists the stock's **price-earnings (P/E) ratio,** the current market price divided by the annual earnings per share. The stock's trading volume in 100-share lots is in column 7, and its highest and lowest prices for the day appear in column 8. Column 9 gives the closing price for the day, and column 10 summarizes the stock's net change in price from the close of the previous trading day.

Using online brokerage firms can lower the cost of trading.

How to Read Stock Quote Tables

Figure 18.2

1	2	3		4	5	6	7	8		9	10
52-Weeks					Yld		Vol				Net
High	Low	Stock	Sym	Div	%	PE	(100s)	High	Low	Close	Chg
50^{70}	29^{45}	AAAComp	AAC	1.00	2.00	20	15800	50^{70}	49^{50}	50^{00}	+ 50
30^{00}	14^{00}	AAElec	AAE		...	26	510	22^{00}	19^{45}	21^{06}	−1^{34}
78^{23}	65^{00}	AaronInc.	AAI	.25	.38	17	890	66^{56}	65^{00}	65^{00}	−1^{78}
51^{55}	48^{00}	AaronInc. pf.		3.50	7.00	...	54	50^{10}	49^{75}	50^{00}	+ 05

1 **52-Week Indicators:** ↑ = Hit 52-week high during the day. ↓ = Hit 52-week low.

2 **52-Week High/Low:** Highest and lowest per-share trading prices in the past 52 weeks, adjusted for splits (dollars and cents—78.^{23} means $78.23 per share).

3 **Stock, Sym, and Footnotes:** The company's name abbreviated. A capital letter usually means a new word. AAA-Comp, for example, is AAA Computer. The stock ticker symbol is expressed in capital letters. For AAA Computer, it is AAC. Stock footnotes include the following: **n**—new issue, **pf**—preferred stock, **rt**—rights, **s**—stock split within the past 52 weeks, **wi**—when issued, **wt**—warrant, **x**—ex-dividend.

4 **Div:** Dividends are usually annual payments based on the most recent quarterly declaration.

AAA Computer, for instance, declared a dividend of $0.25 per share in the most recent quarter.

5 **Yld %:** Percentage return from a dividend based on the stock's closing price.

6 **PE:** Price/earnings ratio, calculated by taking the last closing price of the stock and dividing it by the earnings per share for the past fiscal year.

7 **Vol:** Trading volume in 100-share lots. A listing of 510 means that 51,000 traded during the day. A number preceded by **z** is the actual number of shares traded.

8 **High/Low:** The high and low for the day (dollars and cents).

9 **Close:** Closing price (dollars and cents).

10 **Net Chg:** Change in price from the close of the previous trading day.

18.3 How to Read Bond Quote Tables

① Bond: Abbreviation of company name.

② Annual Interest Rate: Annual percentage rate of interest specified on the bond certificate.

③ Maturity Date: Year in which the bond matures and the issuer repays the face value of each bond.

④ Cur Yld: Annual interest payment divided by current price; **cv** means a convertible bond.

⑤ Vol: Number of bonds traded during the day.

① ② ③ Bond	④ Cur Yld	⑤ Vol	⑥ Close	⑦ Net Chg
AAA 9s20	7.8	15	104 3/4	– 1 1/8
ABGasElec 6.5s10	6.6	10	98 1/2	+ 3/4
AlbertoPharm 5s15	cv	20	109 1/2	+ 1/2

⑥ Close: Closing price.

⑦ Net Chg: Change in the price from the close of the previous trading day.

Bond Quotations To learn how to read corporate bond quotations, pick a bond listed in Figure 18.3 and examine the adjacent columns of information. Most corporate bonds are issued in denominations of $1,000, so bond prices must be read a little differently from stock prices. The closing price of the first AAA bond reads 104 3/4, but this does not mean $104.75. Because bond prices are quoted as a percentage of the $1,000 price stated on the face of the bond, the 104 3/4 means $1,047.50.

The notation following the bond name— such as 6.5s10 in the case of AB Gas and Electric—indicates the annual interest rate stated on the bond certificate, 6.5 percent, and the maturity date of 2010. The *s* means that the bonds pays half of its annual interest every six months, so the investor would receive $32.50 every six months. The current yield for the AB Gas and Electric bond is 6.6 percent, slightly more than the 6.5 percent interest rate because the bond is selling for slightly less than $1,000. The price of a bond rises and falls to keep the current yield in line with market interest rates. The *cv* notation means that the bond is convertible.

The next column indicates the total trading volume for the day. The volume of 15 listed for the AAA bond means that $15,000 worth of bonds were traded. The closing bond price is listed next, followed by the change in price since the previous day's closing price.

Stock Indexes

A feature of most financial news reports is the report of current stock indexes or averages. The most familiar is the *Dow Jones Average* (or *Dow*). Two other widely reported indexes on U.S. stocks are the Standard & Poor's 500 and Nasdaq Composite indexes. In addition, there are numerous indexes on foreign stocks, including the DAX (Germany); the FT-100, or "Footsie" (London); and the Nikkei (Tokyo). All of these indexes have been developed to reflect the general activity of specific stock markets.

While several Dow Jones indexes exist, the most widely followed is the so-called *Dow Jones Industrial Average,* consisting of 30 stocks of large, well-known companies. The S&P 500 is made up of 500 stocks, including industrial, financial, utility, and transportation stocks, and is considered a broader measure of overall stock market activity than the Dow. The Nasdaq Composite index consists of all the approximately 5,000 stocks that trade on the Nasdaq Stock Market. Because technology companies—such as Oracle and Intel—make up a substantial portion of the Nasdaq Stock Market, the Nasdaq Composite is considered a bellwether of the "tech" sector of the economy.

The Dow Jones Industrial Average has served as a general measure of changes in overall stock prices and a reflection of the U.S. economy since it was developed by Charles Dow, the original editor of the *Wall Street Journal,* in 1884. The term *industrial* is somewhat of a misnomer today, because the index now combines industrial corporations such as Alcoa, Boeing, General Motors, and United Technologies with such nonindustrial firms as American Express, Citigroup, Home Depot, and Walt Disney.

Periodic changes in the Dow reflect changes in the U.S. economy and composition of the stock market. In fact, General Electric is the only original member of the Dow industrials that remains in the index today. In the most recent changes, American International Group, Pfizer, and Verizon Communications were added and AT&T, Eastman Kodak, and International Paper were dropped from the Dow.

MUTUAL FUNDS AND EXCHANGE-TRADED FUNDS

Many investors choose to invest through mutual funds or exchange-traded funds (ETFs). **Mutual funds** are financial institutions that pool money from purchasers of their shares and use it to acquire diversified portfolios of securities consistent with their stated investment objectives. While mutual funds and exchange-traded funds have similarities, important differences distinguish the two. Let's examine each.

Mutual Funds

Investors who buy shares of a mutual fund become part owners of a large number of securities, thereby lessening their individual risk. Mutual funds also allow investors to purchase part of a diversified portfolio of securities for a relatively small investment, $250 to $3,000 in most cases. Mutual funds are managed by experienced investment professionals whose careers are based on success in analyzing the securities markets and choosing the right mix of securities for their funds. Mutual fund ads often stress performance or highlight the fund's investment philosophy. Most mutual funds are part of mutual families, a number of different funds sponsored by the same organization. The largest mutual fund families in the United States include Dreyfus, Fidelity, Janus, T. Rowe Price, and Vanguard.

Mutual funds have become extremely popular in recent years. Today mutual fund assets exceed $8 trillion. The number of American households owning mutual fund shares has increased from less than 5 million in 1980 to close to 55 million. Mutual funds are not limited to the United States either. Mutual funds in Europe have more than $5 trillion in assets.[20]

Today's mutual fund investors choose among around 8,000 funds in the United States. Some mutual funds invest only in stocks, some invest only in bonds, and others invest in money market instruments. The approximate breakdown of mutual fund assets by stock, bond, and money market funds is shown in Figure 18.4. Most funds pursue more specific goals within these broad categories. Some stock funds concentrate on small companies; others concentrate more on the shares of larger firms. Some bond funds limit their investments to municipal bonds; other bond funds invest in only investment-grade corporate bonds.

Unlike stocks, mutual funds don't trade on stock exchanges. Investors purchase shares directly from the fund. Moreover, an investor who wishes to sell shares of a mutual fund simply sells the shares back to the fund (the technical

mutual fund financial institution that pools money from purchases of its shares and uses the money to acquire diversified portfolios of securities consistent with the fund's investment objectives.

assessment check

1. Explain the difference between a market order and a limit order.
2. Distinguish between full-service and discount brokerage firms.
3. List some of the information contained in stock price quotations.
4. What are the two most closely followed stock market indexes?

Figure 18.4

Distribution of U.S. Mutual Fund Assets by Type of Fund

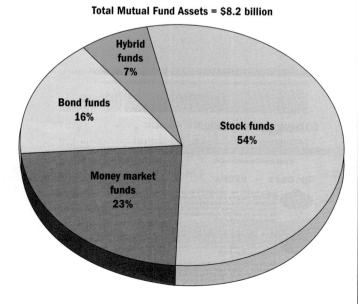

Total Mutual Fund Assets = $8.2 billion

- Hybrid funds 7%
- Bond funds 16%
- Stock funds 54%
- Money market funds 23%

Note: Hybrid funds invest in both stocks and bonds.
Source: "Trends in Mutual Fund Investing," Investment Company Institute, accessed July 3, 2006, http://www.ici.org.

The Future of the New York Stock Exchange

An investment community has existed in New York even before it was New York. When Dutch settlers arrived on the island of Manhattan in the mid-1600s, their purpose was commerce. They named their settlement New Amsterdam and set about building an economic empire. Four hundred years later, New York is a commercial powerhouse of global proportions, and many would claim that the center of this powerhouse is the New York Stock Exchange. With company listings worth $20 trillion, the NYSE has historically banked on its name and the ability of its trading floor specialists to guarantee their investors liquidity. But in the wake of tighter regulations from the Securities and Exchange Commission (SEC) and rapidly evolving technology that threatens to leave the NYSE in the dust, the exchange is poised for change.

When the SEC decided to tighten up the "trade-through" rule that links America's markets, it meant that all investors must have equal access to the best prices available on a given day. The only way to achieve this parity is electronically—something that other stock exchanges had already begun to implement. This put the NYSE—and its customers—at a disadvantage. Nasdaq and the Chicago Mercantile Exchange were already using some form of electronic trading, as were large institutional investors, who often rely on electronic communication networks (ECNs) for rapid trading. NYSE's customers began to complain.

In a radical move, the NYSE acquired Archipelago Holdings, owner of ArcaEx, a large ECN that already handled 25 percent of the trading in Nasdaq-listed shares and had recently acquired the Pacific Stock Exchange, which specializes in high-risk investments called *derivatives*. The merger means some big changes at the NYSE. First, it became a public company—it can raise a huge amount of capital, but it must also answer to shareholders. Second, it now has a way to compete for Nasdaq shares and accept listings from smaller companies that previously did not qualify for listing on the NYSE. Third, the NYSE can now participate more fully in the growing derivatives and ETF markets.

The merger seems to plant the NYSE squarely in the 21st century. But it does have its detractors. Some experts warn that the NYSE and Archipelago are like two different species and that their organizational cultures will not integrate very well. Others worry that the NYSE does not yet know how to use the trading technology used by ArcaEx. Still others point out that Nasdaq has actually acquired a better-fitting company—the electronic trading division of Instinet, which is owned by Reuters. But NYSE's entrance into the electronic trading market should step up competition, which in the long term should decrease costs for investors, speed up transactions, and even encourage more innovation—which is what commerce is all about.

Questions for Critical Thinking

1. Describe at least two regulations that apply to NYSE's acquisition of Archipelago and its future methods of trading.
2. Do you think that the NYSE and Nasdaq will become more similar in the next few years? How might they differentiate themselves?

Sources: "The Cyberbuttonwood Arrives," Economist.com, accessed April 16, 2003, http://www.economist.com; Donna Block, "What NASDAQ Sees in Instinet," *Daily Deal,* accessed August, 2006, http://www.thedeal.com; Jenny Anderson, "Big Changes at the Exchanges Bring Their Self-Regulation into Question," *New York Times,* accessed July 28, 2006, http://www.nytimes.com.

A.G. Edwards: Helping Businesses Grow

This video case appears on page 628. A recently filmed video, designed to expand and highlight the written case, is available for class use by instructors.

The Second City Theater Continuing Case
Managing Financial Resources: Keeping Creativity in the Money

When Second City Communications negotiates a deal with Motorola, or the Chicago Cubs, or Chicago's Steppenwolf Theatre, keeping an eye on the finances is chief financial officer Lou Carbone. Joining the company at its Toronto location in 1998, Carbone became CFO for the entire organization in 2005. He currently operates out of Second City's Chicago office as a strategist, a liaison, a treasurer, and, in his own words, "the father figure who may have to say 'no, you can't play with that toy.'" Behind a desk stacked full of project proposals, Lou Carbone manages Second City's unyielding creation of business ventures. He watches the risk-return trade-offs and designs accurate financial plans to turn concepts into reality. The reality for Lou Carbone is that a company as creative and well recognized as Second City needs a CFO with a practical disposition and an appreciation for the art of acting and the entrepreneurial spirit.

Second City has excelled as a company based on creative mission. As CFO, Lou Carbone approaches the company's lofty ambitions from a pragmatic angle. "My primary function" says Carbone, "is to ensure that there is accurate and timely financial reporting." He does this by developing financial statements with his team and distributing them regu-

larly to top management. Carbone's staff consists of four professionals: a senior accountant, a payroll administrator, a junior accountant, and the building manager. Though a small financial team, they operate as a close-knit crew, well suited for a for-profit business, functioning with a not-for-profit attitude. They have a variety of challenges. For instance, the company is stretched across North America with disparately functioning theaters. Revenue also fluctuates unpredictably throughout the year, and new projects encounter unforeseen costs. Meeting one-on-one with department heads, Lou Carbone has streamlined financial reporting within the organization to improve on past practices in which each department did its own budget. This is just one way in which Lou Carbone has helped Second City evolve financially.

Lou Carbone keeps the Second City stages lit, its actors paid, and its new ideas funded through his relationships with outside agencies. As a liaison for the comedy theater, Carbone meets with Second City's bank, lawyers, and insurance firms to ensure compliance and confirm that there are adequate reserves. Keeping a strong relationship with Second City's bank has been vital for the organization. Amid changes in revenue and struggling project starts

over the last 28 years, Second City has come across times in which bank loans have allowed it to develop as planned. Impressively, Lou Carbone and SC's financial team have maintained a strong alliance with the same bank that it has used since its start.

For all its growth and corresponding challenges, Second City remains a small business choosing to stay private for the foreseeable future. It is owned by three shareholders, two of whom are still closely involved with business operations and maintain a recognizable character throughout the organization.

Second City is clearly an unconventional business. In fact, its five theaters are structured with financial and organizational differences. Second City's Detroit stage is a franchise; Denver has been designed as a limited run to test the market; Las Vegas is a partnership. Chicago and Toronto are the only stages fully owned by the three sole investors, though Toronto operates as a separate legal entity.

Second City's financial management team must oversee all operations while paying close attention to these organizational differences. Overall, Second City's different U.S. bank accounts fuse into a whole that can be used flexibly throughout the organization. This enables Second City to fund start-up operations such as new Theatricals produced in performing arts centers with revenue garnered from mainstage ticket sales. This effort keeps the Second City mission intact across the board.

As the numbers fly around Second City and fall on the desk of Lou Carbone, putting them together to forecast and develop strategic plans is what he finds most interesting. Carbone balances available funds, needed funds, the costs of expansion, and pricing specifics to help inform the top management team about which ventures seem most reasonable. Through this analysis Second City has, for example, determined that new theater expansion should be put on hold. There won't be new Second City Theaters opening any time soon, but finding Second City's style of comedy in the business world is increasingly likely. It has seen its most significant growth in the corporate division over the past five years. Tom Yorton, president of Second City Inc., and Lou Carbone collaborate regularly in negotiations with corporate clients for SC Communications, the division of Second City that provides entertainment, training, and creative and multimedia services to businesses. Companies are looking to foster a more creative atmosphere within the workplace, and SC Communications finds itself increasingly relevant to contemporary business.

Carbone brings financial savvy to a company that is otherwise focused on creating an ideal environment for excellent acting. Yorton says, "Thank God for Lou. The fact is that none of us really have a finance background. He can help educate us to make the place run better. We're an improv theater, so we make it up as we go along. Finance is one area where you really can't make it up as you go along."

The hardest part of Lou Carbone's job isn't finding ways for Second City to increase revenue but to watch where all of it is going. With Detroit operating as a franchise, its status as a locally owned business means less exposure for Second City, and separate accounting practices present less concern for the company's home base. Second City's center, in Chicago, is busy monitoring the other operations around the country. Both Las Vegas and Denver are far enough away that accurate monitoring is a consistent dilemma. Toronto has its own two accountants, and they've been challenged by a struggling economy in their region throughout the last decade. Second City Chicago pulled from reserves and credit lines to back the operation. With so many divisions, Carbone must pay strict attention to monthly reports and annual audits.

At Second City, 40 to 50 percent of all revenue goes toward covering labor costs. Second City's profit fluctuates throughout the fiscal year as demands change, so funds must be carefully managed to meet payroll and cover fixed expenses. For example, the touring companies experience a decrease in sales over the summer, when most schools and colleges are not in full operation. Economic climate and real estate costs present consistent challenges. The company aptly chooses to rent its property, which makes a change of locations easier should its real estate needs change.

Through a small door adjacent to Second City's box office, up a staircase adorned with caricatures of SC alumni and tucked into an office overlooking the famous corner of North and Wells, Lou Carbone can be seen smiling as he wrestles with new project proposals. "I have to be the one to pull in the reins," he says. Carbone sifts through an assortment of inspired business ventures and evaluates the financial and social needs of the project. Inspired and innovative ideas are met with practical evaluation, considering all the costs involved. Perhaps the most innovative use of SC's widely used improv technique "Yes, and," comes from Lou Carbone. In a top management meeting a new idea may come up, to which Carbone must find a way to say "Yes, and . . . then we'd be out of business." Luckily, Second City has listened to its CFO, and the organization can continue to be as creative as possible.

QUESTIONS

1. What are some of the challenges faced by Second City's CFO?
2. If Second City were to create more theaters, would you suggest franchising, partnerships, or another organizational format?
3. Would it be a sound financial decision for Second City to become a public company?
4. What is Lou Carbone's most important function at Second City? Why?

Part 6: Launching Your Finance Career

Part 6, "Managing Financial Resources," describes the finance function in organizations. Finance deals with planning, obtaining, and managing an organization's funds to accomplish its objectives in the most effective way possible. In Chapter 17, we discussed financial plans, sources of funds, and financial institutions, such as commercial banks. In Chapter 18, we examined the structure of the financial, or securities, markets. Throughout both chapters we described the finance functions of a variety of businesses, governments, and not-for-profit organizations. As Part 6 illustrates, finance is a very diverse profession and encompasses many different occupations. According to the U.S. Department of Labor, over the next decade most finance-related occupations are expected to experience employment growth that is at least as fast as the average for all occupations. However, employment in several finance occupations is expected to grow faster than average.[1] Computers and related technology have affected the finance function significantly in recent years.

In most business schools, finance is either the most popular or second most popular major among undergraduates. Combining finance with accounting is a common double major. Those with degrees in finance also enjoy relatively high starting salaries. A recent survey found that the average starting salary for a person with an undergraduate degree in finance was more than $42,000 per year.[2]

All organizations need to obtain and manage funds, so they employ finance professionals. Financial institutions and other financial services firms employ a large percentage of finance graduates. These businesses provide important finance-related services to businesses, governments, and not-for-profit organizations. Some graduates with finance degrees take jobs with financial services firms such as Bank of America and Merrill Lynch, while others begin their careers working in the finance departments of businesses in other indus-tries such as 3M and Boeing, governments, or not-for-profit organizations. You may begin your career evaluating commercial loan applications for a bank, analyzing capital investments for a business, or helping a not-for-profit organization decide how to invest its endowment. Often finance professionals work as members of a team, advising top management. Some individuals spend their entire careers working in finance-related occupations; others use their finance experience to move into other areas of the firm. Today, the chief financial officer—the senior finance executive—holds one of the most critical jobs in any organization. In addition, the number of CEOs who began their careers in finance is growing.

Finance is a diverse, exciting profession. Here are a few of the specific occupations you might find after earning a degree in finance.

Financial managers prepare financial reports, direct investment activities, raise funds, and implement cash management strategies. Computer technology has significantly reduced the time needed to produce financial reports. Many financial managers spend less time preparing reports and more time analyzing financial data. All organizations employ financial managers, although roughly 30 percent of all financial managers work for financial services firms such as commercial banks and insurance companies.[3] Specific responsibilities vary with titles. For instance, credit managers oversee the firm's issuance of credit, establish standards, and monitor the collection of accounts. Cash managers control the flow of cash receipts and disbursements to meet the needs of the organization.

Most *loan officers* work for commercial banks and other financial institutions. They find potential clients and help them apply for loans. Loan officers typically specialize in commercial, consumer, or mortgage loans. In many cases, loan officers act in a sales capacity, contacting individuals and organizations about their need for funds and trying to persuade them to borrow the funds from the loan officer's institution. So loan officers often need marketing as well as finance skills.

Security analysts generally work for financial services firms such as Fidelity or Wachovia. Security analysts review economic data, financial statements, and other information to determine the outlook for securities such as common stocks and bonds. They make investment recommendations to individual and institutional investors. Many senior security analysts hold a CFA (Chartered Financial Analyst) designation. Obtaining a CFA requires a specific educational background, several years of related experience, and a passing grade on a comprehensive, three-stage examination.

Portfolio managers manage money for an individual or institutional client. Many portfolio managers work for pension funds or mutual funds for which they make investment decisions to benefit the funds' beneficiaries. Portfolio managers generally have extensive experience as financial managers or security analysts, and many are CFAs.

Personal financial planners help individuals make decisions in areas such as insurance, investments, and retirement planning. Personal financial planners meet with their clients, assess their needs and goals, and make recommendations. Approximately 40 percent of personal financial planners are self-employed, and many hold CFP (Certified Financial Planner) designations. Like the CFA, obtaining a CFP requires a specific educational background, related experience, and passing a comprehensive examination.

Career Assessment Exercises in Finance

1. Assume you're interested in pursuing a career as a security analyst. You've heard that the CFA is an important designation and can help enhance your career. Visit the CFA's Web site (http://www.cfainstitute.org) to learn more about the CFA. Specifically, what are the requirements to obtain a CFA and what are the professional benefits of having a CFA?

2. Arrange for an interview with a commercial loan officer at a local bank. Ask the loan officer about his or her educational background, what a typical day is like, and what the loan officer likes and doesn't like about his or her job.

3. Ameriprise Financial offers financial planning services to individuals and organizations. Visit the firm's Web site (http://www.ameriprise.com) and click the "Careers" link. Review the material and write a brief summary of what you learned about being a personal financial planner. Does such a career interest you? Why or why not?

Video Case Contents

Peet's Coffee & Tea Brews Good Business

More than 40 years ago, Alfred Peet opened the door to his new shop in Berkeley, California, letting the rich scent of roasting coffee beans waft out to the sidewalk. Passersby were curious. Some couldn't resist. They came in to taste a cup of whatever was being offered. Peet had grown up in his family's coffee business in Holland. Later, he learned the tea trade in Indonesia. By the time he landed in California, he knew the best way to roast and brew both beverages. An entrepreneur at heart, he decided he could offer the very best cup of coffee or tea to customers, so he founded his own business. He chose Berkeley, where a collection of European-style shops and bistros serving fresh cheeses and breads, along with other gourmet delicacies, was beginning to gain popularity with consumers. The original Peet's location—at the corner of Vine and Walnut—is still there, serving up a variety of fresh, deep-roasted coffees, hand-selected teas, and bags of coffee beans ready to be ground and brewed at home.

Today, Peet's operates 111 retail stores in California, Illinois, Massachusetts, Oregon, and Washington. In addition, consumers can find Peet's products at Safeway, Supervalu, Ralphs, and Whole Foods Markets. Loyal fans who don't want to leave their homes in search of Peet's products can visit the firm's Web site. There they can order their favorites through the Home Delivery program, learn how to brew the perfect cup, find out where their coffee beans were grown, and discover how their tea leaves were selected. Customer service representatives are always available to answer questions or help with ordering. Finally, Peet's provides service to offices, restaurants, and food service distributors. "No matter where you buy Peet's, we make sure that all of our coffee [and tea] meets our exceptional standards for quality and freshness," promises the company's Web site.

To control its steady growth, Peet's executives must manage a variety of relationships—with growers who supply coffee beans and tea leaves, with the firm's own employees, with retailers and restaurant owners, with distributors, and with consumers. Peet's works closely with small and cooperative growers in Mexico, Central America, and Africa, where it believes it can obtain the highest-quality beans and leaves. As part of its mission, Peet's also develops programs to improve the lives of people who live in these communities, through education and economic growth. Peet's relationship with its customers is legendary—many have been enjoying Peet's coffees and teas for decades, passing the tradition along to children and grandchildren. The original Peet's fans, who visited the Berkeley shop every morning for their cup of coffee and conversation, were dubbed "Peetniks" (a takeoff on the word *beatnik*) by a Berkeley policeman—and the nickname stuck. Eventually, the nickname evolved to refer to Peet's employees, who are as passionate about their products as the original Peetniks themselves.

Peet's views its workforce as one of its most valuable resources—it is this group of people who roasts the coffee beans, tastes the tea, and packs and ships it to customers across the country. Roasters know exactly what Peet's proprietary blends should taste like—a knowledge base that Peet's believes cannot be duplicated by any other method. "Many coffee companies use computers to roast their coffees," explains the Web site. "But we believe no computer can roast beans like a skilled roaster can." Because it takes skill and experience to achieve this level of expertise, Peet's asks for a ten-year employment commitment from its roasters—an unusual request in an economy in which employers and employees typically part ways after much shorter periods of time. But Peet's believes it takes at least three or four years to learn the craft, and senior master roaster John Weaver points out that "a roaster's education is a continuous, ceaselessly fascinating process."

While nothing replaces the knowledge and experience of a worker, Peet's does rely on technology for some of its operations. Recently, the firm installed a high-speed Flo-Shipper system, which allows Peet's to ship coffee the same day it is roasted. The system sorts and routes verified parcels to the appropriate shipping lane, confirms data on bar code labels, and visually identifies any problems. This system has cut the time to fulfill orders in half—from two work shifts to one. What this means is simple: if you order a pound of Peet's coffee beans, they'll be roasted and shipped to you the same day. You may not hear the delivery truck driving up your street, but you might smell the fresh scent of coffee on its way to your door.

Questions for Critical Thinking

1. In what ways was Alfred Peet an entrepreneur?
2. Peet's was founded during the marketing era. Today it operates in the relationship era. Describe its focus during each era.
3. Describe the employer-employee partnership at Peet's.
4. Would you characterize Peet's as an admired company? Why or why not?

Sources: Peet's Web site, accessed August 8, 2006, http://www.peets.com; "Peet's Coffee & Tea, Inc.," Google Finance Profile, accessed August 8, 2006, http://finance .google.com; Lori Corbin, "Peet's Coffee & Tea Tutorials," KABC-TV Los Angeles, accessed August 8, 2006, http://

abclocal.go.com; "National Coffee Roaster Streamlines B2C Fulfillment System," *FloStor Engineering,* accessed August 8, 2006, http://www.floStor.com; "Peet's Coffee & Tea Celebrates 40 Years of Craftsmanship," *Badgett's Coffee eJournal,* accesssed August 8, 2006, http://www.aboutcoffee.net.

VIDEO Case 2.2

Ford Turns Green with Clean Energy

When the first Ford vehicles rolled off Henry Ford's pioneering assembly line, they were all black. Consumers didn't care—they wouldn't have thought of a car in another color. They also didn't worry about details such as gasoline emissions, as those Model T's and Model A's bounced along dirt roads spewing exhaust. They were more concerned about breakdowns, flat tires, and collisions with horse-drawn wagons.

Today, however, consumers are educated about fuels, pollution, and a responsibility to the environment. And Ford Motor Company is concerned about them, too. Consumers can now buy Ford trucks and cars in all kinds of colors. But perhaps the most innovative—and most important—color isn't the paint chip chosen for the exterior of a vehicle. Instead, it's the "green" that refers to Ford's new clean engines, including the gas-electric hybrid Escape, an SUV designed for consumers who want fuel efficiency without giving up safety, convenience, and style.

The Escape is a full hybrid, meaning that it can run on either its gasoline engine or its electric motor, with a fuel economy of 33 mpg or above in the city and 29 mpg on the highway (depending on the model). In addition, the Escape produces 97 percent less hydrocarbon and nitrogen oxide emissions than other vehicles that meet the current national emissions standards. So far, the new Escape has been a huge success—consumers have been willing to wait months to receive one after placing an order. "When we began work on an Escape Hybrid, we made a commitment to delivering a no-compromise, authentic Ford SUV that's fun to drive, spacious, comfortable and capable, with substantially lower fuel use and emissions," reports Mary Ann Wright, director of Sustainable Mobility Technologies and Hybrid Programs for Ford. "Mission accomplished! It's wonderful to see the vehicle we originally envisioned resonating so strongly with customers."

Ford Motor Company takes its role in protecting the environment and other aspects of social responsibility seriously. While the Escape receives accolades from the public and the industry—it was named "Truck of the Year" at a recent international auto show—Ford continues to design other types of clean engines, including the Ford Focus PZEV (Partial Zero Emissions Vehicle). A PZEV contains a gasoline-powered engine that is "so clean that the exhaust coming [directly] out of the tailpipe is often cleaner than freeway air," says the company. Still, the Focus delivers 130 horsepower—so consumers lose nothing in terms of power and gain by eliminating pollution. Ford doesn't manufacture only clean engines; it also produces a Continuously Variable Transmission (CVT), which allows the engine to operate at its most efficient speed, resulting in greater fuel economy. The CVT also provides a smoother ride than a traditional transmission, because it offers more gear ratios. The Freestyle, Mercury, Five Hundred, and Montego models contain CVTs.

Not much would be accomplished if the manufacturing processes for these new, cleaner engines continued to dump pollutants into the environment. Ford recently redesigned its Dearborn truck plant near Detroit to implement a range of innovations in "green" manufacturing. The plant has a "living" roof that is home to ten acres of plants called sedum, which help prevent stormwater runoff, improve the air quality around the plant by trapping dust and dirt, absorb carbon dioxide and release oxygen, and insulate the building. Sedum also provides a rich habitat for birds, insects, and butterflies; because it insulates the building, Ford uses less energy to heat and cool the manufacturing plant. Inside, Ford scientists have developed a Fumes-to-Fuel technology, which uses fumes from truck paint to power fuel cells, producing electricity. "It's a living laboratory," says Andy Acho, worldwide director of Environmental Outreach

& Strategy for Ford. "As we learn more, we'll find places to apply these technical and environmental initiatives." Consumers are encouraged to visit the plant to view for themselves Ford's environmental innovations.

Ford's environmental initiatives aren't limited to the United States. In Sweden, a Ford dealership is experimenting with the GreenZone project, an alliance with McDonald's and Statoil that encompasses three buildings—a car dealership, a restaurant, and a fuel station. The idea of GreenZone is to reduce energy requirements among the three businesses by installing lantern skylights, redirecting excess heat (say, from the restaurant kitchen to the car showroom), and applying the sedum technology for climate control and water circulation.

Ford continues to establish and take part in a wide range of sustainable energy projects around the world. Once a leader in producing black cars, Ford is now a leader in producing just about anything green.

Questions for Critical Thinking

1. How might Ford's commitment to the environment affect its business ethics?
2. How would you measure Ford's social responsibility?
3. Identify ways in which you think Ford is responsible to its customers, employees, investors, and society.
4. Create an advertisement for a Ford Escape Hybrid, a Ford Focus PZEV, or one of the CVT models that uses green marketing to promote its message.

Sources: Ford Web site, accessed September 8, 2006, http://www.ford.com; "Ford Motor Company Hybrid Sales up 115 Percent," Auto Channel, accessed August 8, 2006, http://www.theautochannel.com; "Ford Escape Hybrid," *Business-Week*, accessed September 8, 2006, http://www.businessweek.com; "Line Up for a Hybrid," *Kiplinger Magazine,* accessed May 19, 2006, http://biz.yahoo.com/Kiplinger; Mark K. Solheim, "Too Many Greenbacks," *Kiplinger Magazine,* accessed May 19, 2006, http://biz.yahoo.com/Kiplinger.

VIDEO Case 3.2

BP Meets Global Energy Challenges Head-On

One industry is headlined in the world news almost every day: oil. Whether in a story on rising or falling prices, a prediction about rates of production, worries about U.S. dependency on foreign oil, or a discussion of alternative energy sources, oil is a daily topic of reporters and broadcasters. London-based BP (British Petroleum) is one of those companies featured in the news. Founded a century ago as the Anglo Persian Oil Company, BP is one of the world's largest energy companies, employing more than 100,000 workers in 100 countries. The firm sells 6.4 million barrels of refined petroleum products every day, serving millions of customers through its retail outlets. Those numbers are astounding, but they also mean that BP faces enormous challenges to serve its global customers, among them a continued search for oil, aggressive development for alternative energies, and the many environmental, political, and economic issues that affect the industry.

Fluctuations in the availability and production of oil have a ripple effect throughout nearly every economy in the world. Changes in political situations in places such as Iraq and Nigeria also affect the flow of oil—and the world economy. Even the free flow of news stories, commentary, and predictions about oil can affect the entire business environment. "Expectations, perceptions often affect the price more than physical changes," notes Manouchehr Takin of the Centre for Global Energy Studies. In an important sign of stability, BP has managed to replace its

oil reserves for more than thirteen years in a row. In addition, the company adds as much as 2 billion new barrels each year, anticipating increased use. Despite the closure of refineries because of natural disasters such as Hurricane Katrina, BP manages to survive from a business standpoint because it engages in a number of cost-efficiency programs and continues to invest profits in the business.

BP executives know that fossil fuels such as oil are not renewable—eventually, they will run out. In addition, more and more evidence points to damage to the environment, including climate change, from overuse of these fuels. BP is at the center of a global challenge of the greatest magnitude: how to provide the world's businesses and consumers with the fuel they need, at a profit, without causing further changes to the natural environment. So through its various divisions devoted to exploration, research, and development, BP is pursuing alternative forms of energy. In India, BP has funded a $9.4 million project led by The Energy and Resources Institute (TERI) to research and demonstrate the feasibility of producing a biodiesel fuel from a nonedible oil-bearing crop called *Jatropha curcas* The plant can be easily grown in India, which has spare land to devote to such projects. "In some parts of the world there is only limited availability of land to produce food crops and therefore no surplus which can be used for energy crops," explains Phil New, senior vice president of BP's fuel management group. Both organizations will be keeping a sharp eye on the bottom line of this project.

"Recent developments have made green fuels economically attractive," says TERI director general R. K. Pachauri.

Closer to home, BP is developing the world's first industrial-scale capacity to generate electricity using hydrogen power. By creating this decarbonized fuel, BP could reduce carbon dioxide emissions by as much as 90 percent. The technologies involved already exist, but BP is the first to combine them to create decarbonized fuel. The process converts natural gas from wells beneath the North Sea into hydrogen and carbon dioxide, then "captures" the carbon dioxide separately and uses the hydrogen as a power source. Hydrogen is a clean fuel that produces only water—not pollutants—as a byproduct when burned.

The success of these and other energy projects depends on the health of economies—globally and locally. It also depends to some degree on the support of governments. While many agree that worldwide consumption of oil must be reduced, few agree on how to achieve this objective. The Rocky Mountain Institute in the United States recommends encouraging consumers to buy hybrid cars and trucks such as those made by Toyota, Honda, and Ford. The institute also suggests levying special fees on consumers who continue driving gasoline-only vehicles, with tax breaks for those who buy hybrids. While no single answer exists, BP continues to pursue many possibilities.

Meanwhile, the firm is tapping new markets. Already a huge investor in China, BP has entered into a joint venture with Sinopec, an arm of China Petroleum Chemical Corporation. Conducting business in China can be a complicated but ultimately profitable process. China represents an enormous market. Currently, there is now one car per 1,000 Chinese. Experts predict that number will grow to one car per 25 people within 25 years. With China's huge population, that represents a massive market opportunity. And BP isn't waiting around for others to grab it.

Questions for Critical Thinking

1. Describe several supply and demand factors that could affect BP specifically and the oil industry as a whole.
2. What macroeconomic factors might affect a firm such as BP?
3. What challenges and opportunities does BP face as it enters a market such as China with a planned economy?
4. Why is it economically important for BP to research alternative energies?

Sources: British Petroleum Web site, accessed September 8, 2006, http://www.bp.com; Kevin G. Hall, "The Struggle to Quit Oil," *Philadelphia Inquirer*, accessed September 8, 2006, http://www.philly.com; Nick Mathiason, "China Paves Way for £14bn BP Oil Stake," *The Observer*, accessed September 8, 2006, http://observer.guardian.co.uk; Ben Richardson, "Oil Looms Large over a World Stage," BBC News, accessed September 8, 2006, http://news.bbc.co.uk; Timothy Gardner, "US Hopes to Reverse Oil Decline by Burying CO_2," Reuters, accessed March 13, 2006, http://news.yahoo.com.

VIDEO Case 4.2

Cold Stone Creamery Cools Off Consumers around the World

On a steamy summer day, there's nothing like a cold, creamy dish of ice cream. Perhaps you are one of those ice cream connoisseurs who has favorite mix-ins or toppings—candy, nuts, fresh fruit, or good old-fashioned sprinkles. Maybe you prefer the clean taste of frozen yogurt or sorbet to help you chill. Cold Stone Creamery has it all, plus the most important ingredient: top-quality ice cream. Cold Stone uses fresh ingredients and churns its ice cream with very low air content, which makes it dense and creamy. Kids and adults love it, flocking to the nearly 1,000 stores (company-owned and franchises) across the country to order their favorites—whether it's Birthday Cake Remix, a blend of cake batter ice cream, rainbow sprinkles, brownies, and fudge, or Paradise Found, white chocolate ice cream with coconut, pineapples, and bananas mixed in.

Cold Stone Creamery was founded in 1988 in Tempe, Arizona, by Don and Susan Sutherland. It's *hot* in Arizona, especially in the summer, and people there like ice cream to cool off, too. Cold Stone serves 12 flavors of its own super-premium ice cream, waffle cones, and brownies—all made fresh daily at its stores. Its employees—called crew members—learn exactly how to scoop the ice cream onto a stone-cold slab and add any of the 38 mix-ins to create a custom confection for each customer. Some stores even feature singing crew members who entertain customers while they wait. A Cold Stone cone doesn't come cheap—it can cost $5 or more. And lines may snake around the block. But consumers don't seem to mind. "Consumers are willing to pay more and wait a little longer perceiving they're getting more of an upscale experience along with more 'made for me,'" explains industry analyst Ron Paul.

Cold Stone is not content to stop at U.S. shores. Instead, the firm's leaders have taken their passion for ice cream overseas, starting with the Caribbean and Guam,

Case 11.2

Washburn Guitars: Sound Since 1883

Well-run businesses tend to stay sound for a long time. They grow, they change, they add and delete products, they open and close manufacturing plants, they streamline and expand their operations. But their basic business foundation remains strong, no matter what happens.

Washburn Guitars has been making beautiful sounds since it was founded in Chicago in 1883. Location has always been a key component of the company's overall strategy; when the firm became Washburn International nearly 100 years later, it wasn't long before its manufacturing, office headquarters, and warehouse divisions were consolidated into a single 130,000-square-foot facility outside Mundelein, Illinois. This allowed the firm to incorporate its SoundTech speaker division, which had been operating elsewhere, into the same facility. Perhaps the most important reason for the move, however, was the availability of a skilled workforce nearby. Company president Rudy Schlacher explained that moving to the new location allowed the firm to "tap into an exceptional local workforce." About three years after the move, Washburn International morphed again—into U.S. Music Corporation—which now includes even more divisions, such as Randall Amplifiers, Vinci Strings and Accessories, SoundTech Professional Audio, and Oscar Schmidt folk instruments. The organizational change "gives us the opportunity to clearly separate the parent corporation [U.S. Music] from the name of its producing division, Washburn Guitars," explained Schlacher.

Building fine musical instruments is an art in itself, and the production crew at Washburn takes its job seriously. "Every guitar that is shipped from the Chicago area factory is constructed with passion only a musician can feel," says the Washburn Web site. Each acoustic guitar is built by one craftsperson—called a luthier—from start to finish. "These guitars are crafted with the hard-working spirit and quality standards of the luthiers that have crafted Washburn guitars since the late 1800s for musicians and songwriters around the world."

"I like working with wood, taking it from raw lumber to an actual musical instrument with its own voice," says luthier John Stover. Stover has built acoustic guitars for such musical stars as Dolly Parton and Dan Donegan of Chicago-based metal band Disturbed.

Even though the guitars are built by hand, Washburn uses computer-aided design and manufacturing (CAD/CAM) technologies in its manufacturing process. A CAD/CAM engineer helps design and draw new guitar models. The electric models that are built on an assembly line are still guided by expert craftspeople whose jobs may be assembly lead or neck lead (the worker in charge of building and assembling guitar necks).

Building only 2,500 guitars a year for the general public while maintaining Washburn's high quality standards is expensive. But Washburn finds ways to save in production costs so that it can charge customers reasonable prices for its products; many of its models retail for between $500 and $1,000. Some models are manufactured in Indonesia, where labor is less expensive. Also, although Washburn accepts customized requests through dealers on its current line of guitars and basses made in the United States, the firm does not offer individual custom designs. So a customer could ask for a different paint finish or a left-handed conversion—but not an entirely different design. This system means that customers generally get what they want—without paying exorbitant prices. And it allows Washburn to carefully control its inventory of raw materials and components.

Occasionally Washburn creates an alliance with a musician such as Dan Donegan for a particular series of instruments. Together with Washburn's luthiers and production team, Donegan designed a new series of guitars called Maya (after Donegan's daughter). "Washburn really went above and beyond to make sure my guitars are to my exact specification. I really wanted to create a guitar that is somewhat unique but appeals to artists of all musical genres," said Donegan of his experience with Washburn. The Maya standard and Maya Pro guitars are both built in the United States and come with a range of components. The Maya standard is made of poplar and retails at about $1,500, while the Pro is made of mahogany and retails for just under $2,700. Washburn is also producing a limited customized edition of the Maya line that will be available through select dealers.

Building a guitar is clearly a labor of love for those who work at Washburn. These craftspeople understand the needs of their customers because most of them are musicians themselves. So working with someone like Dan Donegan is as smooth a process as strumming an old tune. Production manager Gil Vasquez explains his job at Washburn this way: "My knowledge of guitars is vast, and I am constantly searching for the ultimate tone, whether it is in the way the guitar is constructed or in the electronics that are being used." Vasquez knows what he is talking about; his customers include Lenny Kravitz, Eric Clapton, Jimmy Page—and Dan Donegan.

1. How do production and operations management contribute to the long-term success of Washburn Guitars?
2. Describe the manufacturing technique(s) you think are applicable to Washburn. Also, explain how CAD and CAM contribute to the design and production processes at Washburn.
3. Describe the physical variables and human factors involved in Washburn's choice of location for its headquarters and production facility in Mundelein, Illinois.
4. What are the benefits of quality control at Washburn? What methods might the firm use for controlling quality?

Sources: Washburn Web site, accessed September 8, 2006, http://www.washburn.com; Dan Moran, "U.S. Music Corp.'s Washburn Guitars No Strangers to Fame," *Suburban Chicago News,* accessed September 8, 2006, http://www.suburban chicagonews.com; "Washburn Guitars," Answers.com, accessed September 8, 2006, http://www.answers.com; "Disturbed's Dan Donegan Signature Series Washburn Guitar at Winter NAMM," All About Jazz, September 8, 2006, http://www.allaboutjazz.com; Washburn's 2006 Winter Catalog.

VIDEO Case 12.2

Harley-Davidson: An American Icon Cruises into Its Second Century

Freedom. Adventure. Fun. These three words best describe the experience of riding a Harley-Davidson motorcycle, and the Milwaukee-based company wants to keep it that way. Harley-Davidson has been manufacturing its heavyweight motorcycles for more than a century—so long, in fact, that they are woven into America's automotive heritage. From the telltale pop and roar of their engines to their signature teardrop-shaped gas tanks, Harley "hogs" have been a key part of America's motorcycle racing and touring culture. Elvis Presley even appeared on the cover of the company's *Enthusiast* magazine. So how did Harley-Davidson become so popular with its riders? By treating them as part of a family—one they can choose to join.

Through market segmentation, Harley-Davidson researched who its customers are. The company knows that the largest customer segment of Harley owners—its target market—is a 40-something male with a median income of a little more than $80,000 who probably owned a Harley-Davidson motorcycle previously. The company's Web site lists the statistical breakdown of its purchasers as 89 percent male and 11 percent female. Approximately 43 percent have already owned a Harley, 29 percent have owned a competitor's motorcycle, and 28 percent have not owned a motorcycle before. Marketers at the company use this information to help them design their products and programs.

To make sure that customers can find exactly the type of bike they want, the company manufactures 36 Harley-Davidson models and 8 Buell sport motorcycle models. And it makes sure that the bikes are ready where and when customers are ready to purchase them, committing its manufacturing plants to producing a record of roughly 350,000 motorcycles in a recent year. With such production rates, company finances have been roaring ahead. In fact, over the past decade Harley-Davidson's annual growth rates for revenues and earnings have been climbing steadily. To make purchasing its motorcycles even more convenient, the company offers its Harley-Davidson Financial Services program, which provides financing and insurance programs for both its dealers and customers.

A key part of developing long-term relationships with customers is the Harley Owners Group (HOGs), with more than 1 million members worldwide. A one-year full membership is automatically given to anyone who purchases a new, unregistered Harley-Davidson motorcycle. Full HOG memberships cost $45 a year, with discounts for two- or three-year memberships. The company also offers associate memberships for HOG family members and passengers and life memberships for those die-hard Harley owners. What do members get for enrolling? Entry into the members-only portion of the HOG Web site, three to four issues of *Enthusiast* magazine a year, a subscription to the company's *Hogtales* member publication, a membership manual, access to a toll-free number with customer-service representatives available during daytime hours, and a touring handbook for trip planning. In addition, Harley-Davidson sponsors local chapters in the United States, Canada, Europe, Australia, New Zealand, and Japan. The company also sponsors events such as touring rallies, Pin Stops at which members can receive commemorative pins, Pit Stops where members can relax and socialize with other Harley owners at motorcycle races, open houses, parades and charity functions, and a HOG Hospitality area at Daytona Bike Week and the Sturgis Rally and Races.

For those wanting to take extended bike trips to faraway places, the company provides a travel service through its Web site, where members can schedule a Fly & Ride vacation. With a three-week advance reservation and payment of a deposit, full HOG members can fly to 41 locations throughout the United States, Canada, Europe, and Australia and pick up a Harley-Davidson motorcycle from a local dealership to tour in style. Or members can simply rent cycles through selected dealerships. And because the company wants riders for life, it also sponsors a safe rider skills program, through which it reimburses HOG members with a $50 coupon for successfully completing an accredited Motorcycle Safety Foundation training program.

Once customers have purchased a Harley-Davidson motorcycle, they may need some gear to go with it—a black leather jacket, T-shirt, or other equipment emblazoned with the familiar orange-and-black bar-and-shield logo. In addition to the more than 1,300 dealerships in 60 countries worldwide, satellite stores in shopping malls and other retail areas can outfit customers from head to toe. The company also offers collectible patches and pins for special events throughout the calendar year.

Harley-Davidson says its mission is to fulfill dreams through motorcycling experiences. Many HOGs across the globe would agree that it is succeeding.

Questions for Critical Thinking

1. How does Harley-Davidson provide customers with form, time, place, and ownership utility for its motorcycles?

2. Would you say that Harley-Davidson creates customer satisfaction with its products? Support your answer.

3. What are the characteristics of Harley-Davidson's target market? Should the company's marketers focus solely on that market segment?

4. In what ways does Harley-Davidson practice relationship marketing?

Sources: Harley-Davidson Web site, accessed September 8, 2006, http://www.harley-davidson.com; Harley Owners Group Web site, accessed September 8, 2006, http://www.hog.com; Harley-Davidson Motor Company brochure, downloaded from the company Web site; Library of Congress "Hog Heaven: Celebrating 100 Years of the Harley-Davidson," accessed September 8, 2006, http://www.loc.gov.

VIDEO Case 13.2

High Sierra Climbs to New Heights

Long gone are the days when only hikers carried backpacks into the mountains or stuffed duffels with climbing gear and lashed them to the back of a mule or llama. Today, these bags are the gear of choice for students and savvy travelers of all types. They are lightweight and durable and can be stowed easily under an airplane seat, on a bus, or in the back of an SUV. High Sierra Sport Company is one of the premier manufacturers of adventure bags—regardless of how you define *adventure*—and in less than 30 years has become the tenth largest outdoor company in the United States.

High Sierra manufactures an impressive array of day packs, backpacks, and duffels. But the firm also makes book bags specifically for students, business and computer cases, bike messenger bags, yoga bags, hydration packs (packs with water reservoirs), lumbar packs, and ski and snowboard packs. Many of these items also come in wheeled models for easy transport. In short, whatever activity you do, High Sierra probably has a pack or bag made specifically for it. The firm even has a "Build-a-Bag" service for customers who can't find exactly what they want.

High Sierra distributes its goods through more than 1,500 retailers—both online and in brick-and-mortar stores—including such outlets as MC Sports, Modell's, Bag'n Baggage, eBags, TravelGizmos.com, Kittery Trading Post, and Fogdog Sports. You can't buy your bag directly from the company, but you can visit the site to view every single bag they make, read about the features, and even get some tips on how to get the perfect fit. In addition to retailers, High Sierra also has corporate accounts, providing bags and packs to companies. And the firm has a strong presence at the Travel Goods Association (TGA) convention, where travel industry experts eagerly examine more than 2,000 new product lines every year.

High Sierra is always innovating with its designs and construction techniques. Its executives—including top officer Hank Bernbaum—and employees are travelers who use the products they make, and they constantly look for ideas to create new products and improve existing ones. New colors, lighter and more durable fabrics, additional security features, multiuse bags, and trendy accessories are often on the list of improvements. "Consumers are driving this continuing surge of innovation," explains TGA president

Michele Marini Pittenger. "They want to travel more safely and securely, with greater comfort. And manufacturers and retailers have learned just how fast they can adapt to those changing needs. Rather than a year to get a new product to market, they're realizing they can do it in months."

High Sierra added to its reputation for quality and cutting-edge design a few years ago, when it became the official supplier of bags to the U.S. Olympic Ski Team and U.S. Olympic Snowboarding Team. The firm manufactures customized backpacks, boot bags, ski and board bags, and duffels for these teams. In addition, High Sierra makes a limited number of these models available for sale to consumers—with the official team logos—including the Loop Pack, the Jackknife Pack, the Mia Messenger Bag, and the Kahuna 70 Hydration Pack. So a few lucky skiers and snowboarders can own the same bags the U.S. Olympians carry. All of these models and more are available through the U.S. Ski Team and Snowboarding Team Web sites. High Sierra has also won various awards for design and for customer service.

High Sierra continues to reach new heights in supplying goods to travelers, students, skiers and boarders, hikers, and everyone else who wants durable, fashionable packs and bags. "You provide the adventure, we provide the gear," says the company slogan. Whether you're standing on a mountain summit or a street corner, High Sierra's got a bag for you.

Questions for Critical Thinking

1. How would you classify High Sierra's products? Explain your choice.
2. Visit High Sierra's Web site at http//www.highsierrasport.com to view the firm's products. Briefly describe High Sierra's overall product mix. Then choose a product line and outline the features that make it unique as well as those that make it fit the mix.
3. Describe the factors that contribute to High Sierra's brand equity.
4. High Sierra sells its products through retailers and through the U.S. Ski and Snowboarding Teams. Do you view this as an effective distribution strategy? Why or why not?

Sources: U.S. Ski Team Web site, accessed September 8, 2006, http://www.ussa.org; High Sierra Web site, accessed September 8, 2006, http://www.highsierrasport.com; "Great Gifts for Grads," *USA Shopping News,* accessed September 8, 2006, http://www.usa101.com; "High Sierra Sport Company," Google Finance, accessed September 8, 2006, http://www .google.com/finance; Gear Trends, accessed September 8, 2006, http://www.geartrends.com; "Cyber Sidebar/Leader of the Pack," *Hemispheres,* accessed September 8, 2006, http:// www.zipitgear.com; "About High Sierra," Luggage.com, accessed September 8, 2006, http://www.luggage.com; "High Sierra Sport Company Wins Microsoft Pinnacle Award," Sikich Worldwide, September 8, 2006, http://www.icsadvantage.com.

VIDEO   Case 14.2

Wild Oats Promotes Local Foods

Whether or not you shop at organic food stores, by now you have seen entire sections of organic foods in even the biggest supermarket chains. Organic foods range from the more typical fresh produce to packaged goods such as corn chips and macaroni and cheese. Although organic and natural foods still make up only 8 percent of the grocery market, they are the fastest-growing food segment in the United States. According to the U.S. Department of Agriculture, the number of farmers' markets has increased 79 percent in just over a decade, and 75 percent of consumers surveyed want to know more about what is in—and on—the food they buy.

Wild Oats Markets is part of this trend. Founded in 1987 with a single store, the Boulder, Colorado–based firm now operates more than 110 stores in 25 states and Canada. Wild Oats sells only natural, organic, premium, and gourmet foods. Its fruit and vegetables are grown without syn-

thetic pesticides, herbicides, or fertilizers. Its seafood is chemical free, not soaked or dipped to increase its weight or alter its appearance. Its candy is naturally sweetened without refined sugar. Its meat and poultry are raised without antibiotics, artificial hormones, or other growth-promoting drugs. Its breads are baked fresh daily with all-natural ingredients. All of this means healthful foods for consumers—and a brand identity for Wild Oats. "Because we are a specialty retailer, we think of ourselves as a brand, not as a grocery store," says company spokesperson Laura Copeland. "The sort of items we offer are not available in many stores." Copeland observes that Wild Oats promotes to a specific market. "Our customers tend to be more educated, with a higher income," she observes. "Education is the biggest driver for the consumption of natural and organic foods."

Knowing who its customers are is the basis for Wild Oats's promotional strategy. Instead of spending a lot of time and money on television advertising, Wild Oats focuses much of its mass media promotion on print advertising—because its customers tend to be readers. "Our print ads have vibrant food images, but they tend to be text heavy," says Copeland. "We provide a lot of information about the products and services we offer. Generally we'll run a recipe, and we might feature one of our employees." In addition, Wild Oats publishes a monthly magazine insert distributed in newspapers. The magazine has full-color photographs, recipes, information about products, and a calendar of store events. It also lists sale items.

Wild Oats reaches out to the communities in which it operates—or where its products are grown—building good public relations. One of its community programs is called "Choose Local," which features fresh, organic produce from local growers, farmers, and artisans in each of its stores during the month of July. "We believe strongly in supporting the local communities where we do business, and we're dedicated to providing high-quality, local products whenever possible," says Perry Odak, president and CEO. "This local focus boosts area economies, reduces negative environmental impacts, and supports sustainable agriculture. Our commitment to these efforts is long term; it's part of our mission."

Each Wild Oats store has its own marketing person and budget, so many of the promotional efforts are local and rely on grassroots marketing. The local marketer attends community events, helping build awareness of Wild Oats and its products. Wild Oats also takes a visible stance on food issues, which generates publicity. "We have a high profile, so we get a lot of exposure in that area," notes Laura Copeland. "Public relations is very important. The power of the written word is most effective when it is not purchased." Wild Oats was recently praised for donating $55,000 to the Sierra Club in recognition of Earth Day and for announcing that it would begin sales of eggs from hens that are certified as humanely raised.

Having an in-store marketer means that store promotions can be tailored to meet the needs of each location and its customers. Education is the main focus of many of the promotional materials—the company reasons that customers

who know and understand the products will buy them. "We have a lot of in-store signage," says Copeland, "but it's more about information than price. There are a lot of informational and educational posters and signs and shelf takers—giant signs that attach to the front of the shelf. Instead of featuring coupons, they feature information." Savvy customers find store coupons at the Wild Oats Web site. The staff is trained to provide more information and suggestions to customers, who often act on those suggestions by making purchases. Wild Oats also does a lot of in-store sampling—if customers try a specialty cheese or take a bite of grilled, marinated chicken, they are more likely to buy it.

All of this effort comes at a price—Wild Oats products may cost a bit more, but loyal customers are evidence that the expense is worthwhile. A bowl of fresh blueberries, a warm loaf of crusty bread, and a decadent chocolate cake all speak for themselves. They're all good food.

Questions for Critical Thinking

1. How does Wild Oats use integrated marketing communications to create a unified promotional strategy?
2. Describe the components of the Wild Oats promotional mix and the way they contribute to the firm's objectives of promotion.
3. Why are personal selling and public relations such an important part of Wild Oats's promotional strategy?
4. What ethical issues might arise for Wild Oats in its promotional activities?

Sources: Wild Oats Web site, accessed September 8, 2006, http://www.wildoats.com; "Wild Oats Markets Redefines Green Grocer," The marketing info, accessed September 8, 2006, http://the-marketing.info; "Wild Oats Urges Customers to Choose Local," IDFA Smart Brief, accessed September 8, 2006, http://smartbrief.com/news; "Food Fest at Wild Oats," *Saugus Advertiser,* accessed September 8, 2006, http://www.townonline.com; "Wild Oats to Sell Eggs Certified as Humanely Raised," *New Mexico Business Weekly,* accessed September 8, 2006, http://www.bizjournals.com; "Wild Oats Donates $55K-Plus to Sierra Club for Earth Day," *Progressive Grocer,* accessed September 8, 2006, http://www.progressivegrocer.com.

 Case 15.2

Peet's Coffee & Tea: Just What the Customer Ordered

A freshly brewed cup of coffee is one of life's simple pleasures; there's nothing high-tech about it. Or is there? California-based Peet's Coffee & Tea has specialized in offering consumers the richest, freshest coffee beans and select teas

for more than 40 years. Although Peet's roasts its coffee beans in small batches by hand—every day—technology is still involved in the way the firm handles customer orders, processes information, and sends out shipments.

Peet's sells 32 different kinds of coffee—single bean, blends, and decaffeinated. It also sells a variety of teas. The coffee beans are roasted daily, and some are then ground to order in a variety of styles. Each order, large or small, is packaged and shipped the same day for freshness. Managing information in order to accomplish these tasks quickly and sell through five different channels—the company's 100-plus retail stores, mail order, the Internet, grocery stores, and corporate food services—requires the right technology. An individual customer may place an order through Peets.com, while grocery stores use an extranet at Peets.net. Or a customer may phone the call center, which transfers the order to the company's intranet. The firm also offers the Peetniks program, which automatically generates reorders for customers. Online customers have until midnight Pacific Standard Time to place an order for the next day.

Peet's relies on an order-fulfillment system designed by software producer Great Plains and modified over the years to meet the changing needs of the firm as it has grown. The system creates a roasting spreadsheet, which shows the roasters how many pounds of each kind of coffee to roast on a given day. The system also generates reports that show how big the order size of each type of coffee is and where it is going, which determines which roasting machine will be used. Once the coffee has finished the roasting process, the system indicates how much of each type of coffee will go to each channel. Because each channel uses different packaging, the system diverts the right amount of each coffee to the correct order-fulfillment department for packaging. A spreadsheet tells workers how much coffee goes into grocery packaging, how much goes into 5-pound "pillow packs" for Peet's retail stores, and how much goes into 1-pound bags for mail-order and Internet customers.

Finally, the system produces labels for the packages and shipping labels. The labels designate the type of coffee and the roasting date, so groceries and Peet's stores can monitor their inventory for freshness. This ordering process takes place continually throughout the day, with the system sorting information and directing the right coffee to the right place. "Before we had this system, the roasting staff just estimated what they needed to roast each day," recalls Mike Cloutier of Peet's. "This system is far more efficient."

Computer software can't physically transport a package of coffee from one location to another. So Peet's uses the FloShipper system, an automated conveyor system that boxes and tapes each packaged order of coffee, weighs it, and slots it into the appropriate shipping lane. The system is designed specially to handle individual orders from consumers. The hand-roasted coffee then gets to customers more quickly. Before Peet's adopted this system, Peet's workers took two shifts to complete an order manually; now the time is down to one shift. "We could not meet our same day roast-and-ship standards without the FloShipper system," says Peet's director of plant operations.

Throughout the Peet's organization, technology meets craftsmanship every day. Without the order-fulfillment software and automated shipping systems, customers would not receive the freshest coffee—which is still roasted by hand every day, the way it was 40 years ago.

Questions for Critical Thinking

1. What are some of the data that Peet's order-fulfillment system gathers? What kind of information does it provide to workers?

2. How does technology help Peet's devote more time and resources to its core business?

3. How might Peet's use an enterprise resource planning (ERP) system?

4. How might Peet's use desktop publishing systems to communicate with consumers and business customers?

Sources: Peet's Web site, accessed September 8, 2006, http://www.peets.com; "National Coffee Roaster Streamlines B2C Fulfillment System," FloStor, accessed September 8, 2006, http://www.flostor.com; "Peet's Coffee & Tea, Inc.," Google Finance, accessed September 8, 2006, http://finance.google.com; "Peet's Coffee & Tea Celebrates 40 Years of Craftsmanship," *Badgett's Coffee Journal,* accessed September 8, 2006, http://www.aboutcoffee.net.

VIDEO | **Case 16.2**

Taking Account: The Little Guys

Accounting is a vital part of every business, large and small. The Little Guys—an independent retailer based in the Chicago suburbs that specializes in selling and installing home theater equipment—is no exception. How does The Little Guys stay ahead of big guys such as Best Buy and Circuit City? By focusing carefully on what its customers want and purchasing and stocking merchandise wisely. The firm has made a name for itself through customer service, including hiring a friendly, knowledgeable staff that is eager to educate customers on the latest high-tech equipment. And it has adapted to changes in the market. "The biggest change in the industry is that five years ago brands drove people to our store," observes co-founder David Wexler. "Today, the manufacturers' brands are everywhere, so the brand is now us. It's 'The Little Guys' name that's most important." In fact, industry surveys confirm that consumers now care more about customer service and financial incentives than they do about big brand names in consumer electronics.

Making decisions about such issues as merchandise and staff payroll is all part of accounting—both short term and long term. Co-founder Evie Wexler handles most of the day-to-day accounting for The Little Guys with the help of the software program QuickBooks. Many small-business owners use such commercially available programs to help run their firms. Wexler reports that QuickBooks simplifies many accounting tasks, automatically placing data in the correct category. "[QuickBooks] writes all the checks, so that when you balance the checkbook, it's all there," she says. "When we started, we were small enough that someone could have kept the books by hand. What we've grown into—the amount of things we receive each day, the amount that goes out, the number of employees we have—it's too complex. The program gives us a better picture of what goes on in the business every day."

For more complex accounting issues, the Wexlers turn to an outside accountant, whom they view as a business consultant—not just someone who fills out forms and reports. They have relied on their accountant's expertise from the beginning. "When we first opened the store, we worked with the accountant as a consultant," recalls David. "He helped us understand some of the technicalities of opening a business. We wrote out a business plan." The business plan specified how much they would spend on advertising, rent, utilities, payroll, and other expenses.

Operating expenses such as payroll and overhead must be tracked carefully. Payroll in particular is a complicated accounting task for The Little Guys. The sales staff is paid based on a percentage of sales, providing an incentive for each salesperson to perform. "Because we pay on a percentage, payroll is difficult," explains Evie Wexler. "There are percentages and base pay. There are lots of idiosyncracies—401k, federal tax, [state] tax, Social Security, and Medicare. You have to track all of this." Overhead expenses such as warehousing and truck maintenance are another part of the accounting puzzle. And the retail store also needs to be insured. "When you look at your profit/loss statement, you can see how much it costs you to do business every day," says Evie.

The Wexlers and their business partner meet to review financial statements for each quarter. They evaluate each expense category to determine whether they are spending too much or not enough to get the results they want. David focuses on the sales figures for each month and compares them with the same month of the previous year. He notes that when they started their business, he tried to look at the sales figures for every day. But he learned that "you can't

do that—you'll drive yourself crazy. Now I'll look every week or ten days. You need a bigger slice of time." He points out that variables such as snowstorms, five Saturdays in a month, or a major sale can all skew the numbers. But he explains that they examine overall trends to make decisions. Perhaps surprisingly, Evie says, "We don't set financial goals. We look at how we did for the year. Then we'll decide how much better we're doing this year."

The Little Guys prides itself on offering customers the latest, highest-quality home theater products. With those high-end products come high prices. But the firm's customers don't pay the ticket price. Instead, they negotiate a deal for a full home theater system, including installation. This customization affects the firm's cash flow. "Sometimes we find ourselves in hot water, and then we react," says Evie. During one season, customers were placing special orders for items that The Little Guys had to pay the manufacturers for up front. Meanwhile, in-stock items were sitting on the shelves. So the Wexlers instructed the sales staff to concentrate on selling those in-stock items in order to improve the store's cash flow.

Because The Little Guys is—yes—little, it can be more flexible in the way it handles buying decisions than larger firms can. "Most businesses are more structured," says Evie. "Because we own the business, we don't buy new things without talking to each other. We have to be a little bit risky in order to be flexible and offer our customers the best products." As a result, the business doesn't have a rigid budget for the products it purchases. But the Wexlers wouldn't operate any other way. Evie admits that worrying about bills sometimes keeps her up at night. But years of experience have taught these business owners that they can compete successfully against the big guys.

Questions for Critical Thinking

1. What role does an outside accountant play for a small firm like The Little Guys?

2. How might accounting help The Little Guys grow as a business?

3. For The Little Guys, create a table with three columns and list the major classifications of data in the accounting equation—assets, liabilities, and owners' equity—that could be used later in the firm's balance sheet.

4. Evie Wexler says that her firm does not have a rigid budget for purchasing items to sell in the store. But what role does a budget play in planning and providing standards by which The Little Guys can measure its performance?

Sources: The Little Guys Web site, accessed September 8, 2006, http://www.thelittleguys.com; Alan Wolf, "Consumers Cutting Back on CE Purchases This Summer," *This Week in Consumer Electronics,* accessed September 8, 2006, http://www.twice.com; Lisa Johnston, "Study: Brand-Name Importance Drops for CE Shoppers," *This Week in Consumer Electronics,* accessed September 8, 2006, http://www.twice.com; Alan Wolf, "Glikes to HTSA: Stay Ahead of the Curve," *This Week in Consumer Electronics,* accessed September 8, 2006, http://www.twice.com.

JPMorganChase Lends a Hand to Small Business

If you own a small business or are thinking of starting one, you can get help from a big name in banking: JPMorgan-Chase. Ranked seventeenth on a recent *Fortune* 500 list, the bank is the third-largest in the United States in terms of revenues. JPMorganChase has assets of $1.3 trillion and operates in more than 50 countries worldwide. In short, the bank has considerable clout in the financial world. So you might think that it would concentrate only on serving huge corporations and the very wealthy. Not true: through its U.S. consumer and commercial banking subsidiary, Chicago-based Chase, the company reaches out to small businesses—those with revenues up to $10 million—with a variety of financial services and the latest technology.

Noting the importance of service to individual customers, CEO James Dimon says, "Huge companies operating in . . . fiercely competitive industries like ours can only achieve and sustain their success by competing where 'the rubber hits the road'—at the level of the store, the product, and the banker—not at corporate headquarters." So Chase works hard to offer small businesses both service and convenience. The firm's Chase Online for Small Business site allows companies to manage their checking and savings accounts, review their account history, make payments such as employee payroll via direct deposit, pay certain federal taxes, download account transactions into their business accounting software, reorder checks, stop payments, and even change their address—all with security protection. Chase also offers ATM/ debit cards, which companies can use to access ATM terminals or to make payments without writing checks. Customers who have personal as well as business accounts can manage them online through their personal account linkage. For those doing business globally, Chase also offers a foreign exchange transfer service. All of these services are available to clients using personal computers or Macs and standard browsers with security features called 128-bit encryption. You can even check your browser's encryption capability at the Chase Web site.

To fund daily expenses or major expansions, a small-business owner can obtain credit and loans from Chase. Through its Business Line of Credit, Business Overdraft Line of Credit, and Business Credit Card services, Chase allows firms to meet short-term cash needs. The line of credit service allows firms to borrow $10,000 or more through a revolving account, by which borrowers repay principal and interest on the funds used. Credit lines can be accessed by writing checks, using a company card, or telephoning a personal banker, and customers repay the borrowed funds via monthly installments. The overdraft line of credit covers a firm's checking account, protecting it if the account is overdrawn. But if a business owner never overdraws the account, he or she pays nothing, and there is no annual fee. The Chase Business Credit Card services offer a variety of products; some have low introductory rates and no annual fees, while others give cash back for purchases or travel rewards.

Long-term loans can be obtained to purchase major equipment or expand the business in other ways. Loans range upward from $5,000 and carry either fixed or variable rates. Payments can be deducted automatically from the company's business checking account. Chase also provides real estate loans starting at $50,000 and, if firms qualify, Small Business Administration Loans, which have longer repayment terms and higher borrowing limits. If the company wants to lease capital equipment, it can set up a True Lease or Motor Vehicle Lease for large transportation, manufacturing, and construction equipment or furniture, fixtures, and computers. At the end of the lease term, the firm has the option to purchase the equipment or return it to the owner.

When a business earns profits, it can turn to Chase to invest those funds to generate additional revenue or even to set up a retirement plan. Chase also provides Merchant Services that allow retail companies to accept payments 24/7 in many forms.

If you're just starting out and need assistance in writing a business plan or completing financial statements, Chase can help through its Business Resource Center. That link on the Web site explains financial terms used in the industry, details what a business plan should contain, and provides sample calculations for key financial statements.

Of course, offering all of these technical services to small businesses does not mean that Chase isn't interested in the owners themselves. The bank has spent hundreds of millions of dollars to open 150 new branches in a recent year, added more retail loan officers, and hired additional personal bankers. So if you feel like strolling into a Chase bank and getting to know your banker face to face, someone will be close by, ready to give you a handshake and discuss your financial needs.

Questions for Critical Thinking

1. If you were a small-business owner, how might Chase help you organize and track day-to-day income and expenses? Why is it important to track these items?

2. What types of short-term funds does Chase offer to small businesses? What types of long-term funds?
3. As a financial institution, how would you classify JPMorganChase? Explain your reasoning.
4. What types of electronic banking services does Chase offer? How could they help a small-business owner?

Sources: JPMorganChase Web site, accessed September 8, 2006, http://www.jpmorganchase.com; Chase Web site, accessed September 8, 2006, http://www.chase.com; "J.P. Morgan Chase & Co.," *Fortune* 500 2006, http://money.cnn.com, accessed September 8, 2006; JPMorganChase, Annual Report 2005, accessed September 8, 2006, http://www.jpmorganchase.com.

VIDEO   Case 18.2

A.G. Edwards: Helping Businesses Grow

Your first experience with money undoubtedly was a piggy bank. By now, you may have tried your hand at investing in a few securities. Businesses also save and invest their funds. To grow, they invest some of their profits in a variety of financial instruments. A.G. Edwards is a full-service brokerage firm that helps businesses—and individuals—select and manage their investments. A member of the New York Stock Exchange (NYSE), A.G. Edwards employs nearly 7,000 consultants in more than 700 offices in the U.S. and abroad. As the firm reaches its 120th year in business, it continues to focus on its mission to "furnish financial services of value to our clients."

A.G. Edwards was founded by General Albert Gallatin Edwards upon his retirement from the post of assistant secretary of the treasury in St. Louis, to which he was appointed by President Abraham Lincoln. His founding partner was his son, Benjamin Franklin Edwards. Later, the small firm helped middle-class investors purchase Liberty Bonds, and unlike other firms, it suffered only minor losses in the stock crash of 1929. In the 1970s, A.G. Edwards became one of the first publicly held brokerage firms. By the 21st century, Edwards had been on *Fortune*'s list of "100 Best Companies to Work For" many times.

Edwards conducts business in a couple of ways. Although the firm usually acts as a broker-dealer in the purchasing and selling of securities, it also takes the role of investment advisor for certain designated accounts. Edwards's financial consultants do not have instructions to sell their company's products and do not fulfill sales quotas for those products. Investors—large or small—are not required to maintain a minimum balance in their accounts.

Technology has transformed the financial industry—instead of emptying your piggy bank to make an investment, you can make your purchase online. Clients can buy and sell securities at any time of the day, seven days a week. To accomplish these transactions and all of its other services—reporting and tracking tasks, and manipulation of data required to run an investment business—A.G. Edwards must have state-of-the-art information technology (IT) systems. In the last few years, Chief Technology Officer John Parker has revamped the firm's entire IT department, including the software and methodologies it uses to complete new projects. Parker credits the success of this technology update to top management's commitment to innovation. "If you try to fix [IT] project management without fixing the top first, you're not going to have much success," he explains. But upper management gave him the go-ahead to make the necessary changes. The IT department now boasts an 88 percent success rate in completing systems projects on time and on budget—a remarkable track record.

These new information systems translate to greater efficiency—and personalization—for clients. Clients who are new to A.G. Edwards receive their own home page at the firm's Web site. Brokers can post customized information on their clients' home pages, while the clients can access detailed spreadsheets showing activity on all their accounts. The A.G. Edwards site provides research information and analysis such as its Market Monitor column and real-time market quotes, with online stock and option trading on the near horizon. Tech support is always available. Business clients may use customized financial systems to implement employee benefit plans, invest cash for the short term, provide insurance for the business and employees, and research financing.

Do you think you want to be a financial consultant? A.G. Edwards emphasizes the importance of discipline, perseverance, accountability, and a positive attitude. The firm recognizes that it is handling people's life savings and businesses' opportunities to soar or crash. So Edwards searches carefully for people who are organized and focused, who don't mind working long hours for clients, who take responsibility for their own decisions, and whose positive outlook attracts clients.

Edwards has survived economic upswings and downturns for more than a century. Visitors to the Web site learn quickly that the firm expects to be in the business for the long term, helping individual and institutional investors achieve the most they can with their money. Says the firm, "We've been making sure we put our clients' needs first for more than 118 years, and we plan to continue this mission for another 118."

Questions for Critical Thinking

1. Describe the goals of an individual investor that A.G. Edwards might serve. Describe the goals of an institutional investor that A.G. Edwards might serve.
2. A.G. Edwards is a full-service brokerage firm. How would its services differ from those of a discount firm?
3. Why is it important for potential employees of A.G. Edwards to possess the qualities of discipline, perseverance, accountability, and a positive attitude described in the case?
4. Suppose you had started your own business in the last year. How might A.G. Edwards help your firm grow?

Sources: A.G. Edwards Web site, accessed September 8, 2006, http://www.agedwards.com; "A.G. Edwards, *Fortune* 100 Best Companies to Work For 2006," CNN Money.com, accessed September 8, 2006, http://money.cnn.com; Jocelyn Drake, "Financials Find Their Footing," *Forbes,* accessed September 8, 2006, http://www.forbes.com; Meredith Levinson, "When Failure Is Not an Option," *CIO Magazine,* accessed September 8, 2006, http://www.cio.com.

Risk Management and Insurance

NEED INSURANCE? AISLE 4, ON THE RIGHT

Consumers have long been accustomed to buying everything from disposable razors to caviar and kayaks at "big box" stores such as Sam's Club and Costco. So these retailers have decided that insurance is another good product to offer for one-stop shoppers.

Costco, which has more than 400 warehouse-style stores in 36 states, has been offering its small-business customers PacifiCare Health System's health insurance coverage for a few years now. The company's assistant vice president of insurance services says that the discount retailer's recent decision to sell individual policies as well grew naturally out of the success of the small-business offering. "A lot of our business members have very small businesses, including sole proprietorships and husband-and-wife teams," she explains. "It's a logical extension of that program."

The individual coverage is being offered on a trial basis in the greater Los Angeles area. Costco hasn't set a date for a national rollout, which would require new partnerships with all the other insurers it works with outside California. Further complicating the possibility of expansion beyond California is the fact that health insurance regulations vary from state to state. But Costco hopes that the response in California will be big. To enroll in the individual plan, a shopper must have an executive membership card at Costco, which costs $100 a year and already includes such extras as long-distance phone service and auto financing. Almost half the company's 3.4 million executive members live in California.

Individual health insurance customers will be able to choose one of two plans: One has a deductible—the amount you must pay out of pocket for medical fees before your benefits kick in—of $1,500 a year, and the other has a deductible of $3,000. Each allows patients to see their doctors of choice for $35 per office visit.

The cost of the premiums—what people pay to sign up for the insurance—are in the neighborhood of 5 to 20 percent cheaper than comparable plans, depending on the buyer's age, location, number of dependents, and health history. The discount reflects lower commissions for sales agents and lower administrative costs because there are only two plans from which to choose. Costco and PacifiCare are hoping the plan's low cost may attract not only people interested in a cheaper plan than what they already have but also some of the country's 43 million people who have no insurance at all to cover their risk of high medical bills. With healthcare costs rising faster than most families' incomes, Costco just might be on to something.[1]

APPENDIX OVERVIEW

Risk is a daily fact of life for both individuals and businesses. Sometimes it appears in the form of a serious illness or premature death. In other instances, it takes the form of property loss, such as the extensive damage to homes and businesses due to forest fires in Idaho or hurricanes in Louisiana. Risk can also occur as the result of the actions of others—such as a pizza delivery driver running a red light and striking another vehicle. In still other cases, risk may occur as a result of our own actions—we may not eat as many healthful foods as we should or decline an extended service warranty on a new computer.

Businesspeople must understand the types of risk they face and develop methods for dealing with them. One approach to risk is to shift it to specialized firms called *insurance companies.* This appendix discusses the concept of insurance in a business setting. It begins with a definition of risk. We then describe the various ways in which risk can be managed. Next, we list some of the major insurance concepts, such as what constitutes an insurable risk. The appendix concludes with an overview of the major types of insurance.

THE CONCEPT OF RISK

risk uncertainty about loss or injury

Risk is uncertainty about loss or injury. Consider the risks faced by a typical business. A factory or warehouse faces the risk of fire, burglary, water damage, and physical deterioration. Accidents, judgments due to lawsuits, and natural disasters are just some of the risks faced by businesses. Risks can be divided into two major categories: speculative risk and pure risk.

Speculative risk gives the firm or individual the chance of either a profit or a loss. Purchasing shares of stock on the basis of the latest hot tip from an acquaintance at the local health club can result in profits or losses. Expanding operations into a new market may result in higher profits or the loss of invested funds.

Pure risk, on the other hand, involves only the chance of loss. Motorists, for example, always face the risk of accidents. If they occur, both financial and physical losses may result. If they do not occur, however, drivers do not profit. Insurance often helps individuals and businesses protect against financial loss resulting from pure risk.

RISK MANAGEMENT

Because risk is an unavoidable part of business, managers must find ways to deal with it. The first step in any risk management plan is to recognize what's at risk and why it's at risk. After that, the manager must decide how to handle the risk. In general, businesses have four alternatives in handling risk: avoid it, minimize it, assume it, or transfer it.

Executives must consider many factors when evaluating the risks, both at home and abroad. These factors include a nation's economic stability; social and cultural factors, such as language; available technologies; distribution systems; and government regulations. International businesses are typically exposed to less risk in countries with stable economic, social and cultural, and political and legal environments.

Avoiding Risk

Some of the pure risks facing individuals can be avoided by taking a healthy approach to life. Abstaining from smoking, getting regular exercise and staying physically fit, and not driving during blizzards and other hazardous conditions are three ways of avoiding personal risk. By the same token, businesses can also avoid some of the pure risks they face. For example, a manufacturer can locate a new production facility away from a flood-prone area.

Reducing Risk

Managers can reduce or even eliminate many types of risk by removing hazards or taking preventive measures. Many companies develop safety programs to educate employees about potential hazards and the proper methods of performing certain dangerous tasks. For instance, any employee who works at a hazardous waste site is required to have training and medical monitoring that meet the federal Occupational Safety and Health Administration (OSHA) standards. The training and monitoring not only reduce risk but pay off on the bottom line. Aside from the human tragedy, accidents cost companies time and money.

Employees working at a hazardous waste site are required to have proper training and medical monitoring. This helps companies reduce risk.

Although many actions can reduce the risk involved in business operations, they cannot eliminate risk entirely. Most major business insurers help their clients avoid or minimize risk by offering the services of loss-prevention experts to conduct thorough reviews of their operations. These health and safety professionals evaluate customers' work environments and recommend procedures and equipment to help firms minimize worker injuries and property losses.

Self-Insuring against Risk

Instead of purchasing insurance against certain types of pure risk, some companies accumulate funds to cover potential losses. So-called *self-insurance funds* are special funds created by periodically setting aside cash reserves that the firm can draw on in the event of a financial loss resulting from a pure risk. A firm makes regular payments to the fund, and it charges losses to the fund. Such a fund typically accompanies a risk-reduction program aimed at minimizing losses.

One of the most common forms of self-insurance is employee health insurance. Most companies provide health insurance coverage to employees as a component of their fringe benefit programs. Some firms, especially large ones, find it more economical to create a self-insurance fund covering employee healthcare expenses, as opposed to purchasing a health insurance policy from an insurance provider.

Shifting Risk to an Insurance Company

Although a business or not-for-profit organization can take steps to avoid or reduce risk, the most common method of dealing with it is to shift it to others in the form of **insurance**—a contract by which an insurer, for a fee, agrees to reimburse another firm or individual a sum of money if a loss occurs. The insured party's fee to the insurance company for coverage against losses is called a **premium.** Insurance substitutes a small, known loss—the insurance premium—for a larger, unknown loss that may or may not occur. In the case of life insurance, the loss—death—is a certainty; the main uncertainty is the date when it will occur.

It is important for the insurer to understand the customer's business, risk exposure, and insurance needs. Firms that operate in several countries usually do business with insurance companies that maintain global networks of offices.

insurance contract by which the insurer, for a fee (the premium), agrees to reimburse another firm or individual a sum of money if a loss occurs

premium amount paid by the insured to the insurance company in exchange for insurance coverage

BASIC INSURANCE CONCEPTS

Figure A.1 illustrates how an insurance company operates. The insurer collects premiums from policyholders in exchange for insurance coverage. The insurance company uses some of these funds to pay current claims and operating expenses. What's left over is held in the form of reserves, which are in turn invested. Reserves can be used to pay for unexpected losses. The returns from insurance company reserves may allow the insurer to reduce premiums, generate profits, or both. By investing reserves, the insurance industry represents a major source of long-term financing for other businesses.

An insurance company is a professional risk taker. For a fee, it accepts risks of loss or damage to businesses and individuals. Three basic principles underlie insurance: the concept of insurable interest, the concept of insurable risk, and the law of large numbers.

Insurable Interest

insurable interest demonstration that a direct financial loss will result if some event occurs

insurable risk requirement that a pure risk must meet for the insurer to agree to provide protection

underwriting process used by an insurance company to determine who, or what, to insure and how much to charge for an insurance policy

To purchase insurance, an applicant must demonstrate an **insurable interest** in the property or life of the insured. In other words, the policyholder must stand to suffer a loss, financial or otherwise, due to fire, storm damage, accident, theft, illness, death, or lawsuit. A homeowner, for example, has an insurable interest in his or her home and its contents. In the case of life insurance coverage purchased for someone providing the bulk of a household's income, the policyholder's spouse and minor children have a clear insurable interest.

A firm can purchase property and liability insurance on physical assets—such as offices and factories—to cover losses due to such hazards as fire and theft because the company can demonstrate an obvious insurable interest. Similarly, because top managers are important assets to a company, a business often purchases key person life insurance, which compensates the business should an important manager die. By contrast, a businessperson cannot collect on insurance to cover damage to property of competitors because that person cannot demonstrate an insurable interest.

Figure

A.1 How an Insurance Company Operates

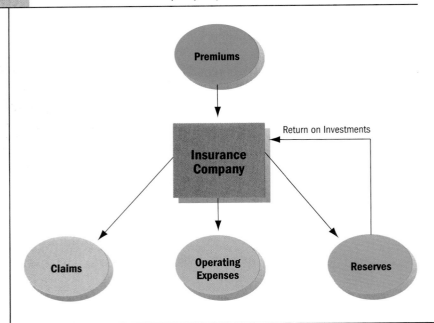

Insurable Risk

Insurable risk refers to the requirements that a risk must meet in order for the insurer to provide protection. Only some pure risks, and no speculative ones, are insurable. Insurance companies impose five basic requirements for a pure risk to be considered an insurable risk:

1. The likelihood of loss should be reasonably predictable. If an insurance company cannot reasonably predict losses, it has no way of setting affordable premiums.
2. The loss should be financially measurable.
3. The loss should be accidental, or fortuitous.
4. The risk should be spread over a wide geographic area.
5. The insurance company has the right to set standards for accepting risk. This process of setting these standards is known as **underwriting.**

The Law of Large Numbers

Insurance is based on the law of averages, or statistical probability. Insurance companies simply cannot afford to sell insurance policies unless they can reasonably predict losses. As a result, insurance companies have studied the chances of occurrences of deaths, injuries, property damage, lawsuits, and other types of hazards. Table A.1 is an example of the kind of data insurance companies examine. It shows the number of automobile accidents, by the age of the driver, for a recent year. From their investigations, insurance companies have developed **actuarial tables,** which predict the number of fires, automobile accidents, or deaths that will occur in a given year. Premiums charged for insurance coverage are based on these tables. Actuarial tables are based on the **law of large numbers.** In essence, the law of large numbers states that seemingly random events will follow a predictable pattern if enough events are observed.

actuarial table probability calculation of the number of specific events—such as deaths, injuries, fire, or windstorm losses—expected to occur within a given year

law of large numbers concept that seemingly random events will follow a predictable pattern if enough events are observed

An example can demonstrate how insurers use the law of large numbers to calculate premiums. Previously collected statistical data on a city with 50,000 homes indicates that the city will experience an average of 500 fires a year, with damages averaging $30,000 per occurrence. What is the minimum annual premium an insurance company would charge to insure a house against fire?

To simplify the calculations, assume that the premiums would not produce profits or cover any of the insurance company's operating expenses—they would just produce enough income to pay policyholders for their losses. In total, fires in the city would generate claims of $15 million (500 homes damaged × $30,000). If these losses were spread over all 50,000 homes, each homeowner would be charged an annual premium of $300 ($15 million divided by 50,000 homes). In reality, though, the insurance company would set the premium at a higher figure to cover operating expenses, build reserves, and earn a reasonable profit.

Some losses are easier for insurance companies to predict than others. Life insurance companies, for example, can pretty accurately predict the number of policyholders who will die within a specified period of time. Losses from such hazards as automobile accidents and weather events are much more difficult to predict. Insured losses resulting from a major hurricane—such as Katrina—can easily exceed $15 to $20 billion, but hurricanes are notoriously unpredictable.

Table A.1

Relationship between the Age of Driver and the Number of Motor Vehicle Accidents

Age of Driver	Accidents per 100 Drivers
Under 19	46
Between 20 and 24	22
Between 25 and 34	11
Between 35 and 44	8
Between 45 and 54	6
Between 55 and 64	5
Between 65 and 74	5
75 and older	5

Source: *Statistical Abstract of the United States (2006 edition),* accessed July 19, 2006, http://www.census.gov.

SOURCES OF INSURANCE COVERAGE

The insurance industry includes both for-profit companies, such as Prudential, State Farm, and GEICO (part of famed investor Warren Buffett's Berkshire Hathaway), and a number of public agencies that provide insurance coverage for business firms, not-for-profit organizations, and individuals. Let's look at the primary features of this array of insurers.

Public Insurance Agencies

A **public insurance agency** is a state or federal government unit established to provide specialized insurance protection for individuals and organizations. It provides protection in such areas as job loss (unemployment insurance) and work-related injuries (workers' compensation). Public insurance agencies also sponsor specialized programs, such as deposit, flood, and crop insurance.

Unemployment Insurance Every state has an unemployment insurance program that assists unemployed workers by providing financial benefits, job counseling, and placement services. Compensation amounts vary depending on workers' previous incomes and the states in which they file claims. These insurance programs are funded by payroll taxes paid by employers.

Workers' Compensation Under state laws, employers must provide workers' compensation insurance to guarantee payment of wages and salaries, medical care costs, and such rehabilitation services as retraining, job placement, and vocational rehabilitation to employees who are injured on the job. In addition, workers' compensation provides benefits in the form of weekly payments or single, lump-sum payments to survivors of workers who die as a result of work-related injuries. Premiums are based on the company's payroll, the on-the-job hazards to which it exposes workers, and its safety record.

Social Security The federal government is the nation's largest insurer. The Social Security program, established in 1935, provides retirement, survivor, and disability benefits to millions of Americans. **Medicare** was added to the Social Security program in 1965 to provide health insurance for people age 65 and older and certain other Social Security recipients. More than nine out of ten workers in the United States and their dependents are eligible for Social Security program benefits. The program is funded through a payroll tax, half of which is paid by employers and half by workers. Self-employed people pay the full tax.

Private Insurance Companies

Much of the insurance in force is provided by private firms. These companies provide protection in exchange for the payment of premiums. Some private insurance companies are stockholder owned, and therefore are run like any other business, and others are so-called *mutual associations*. Most, though not all, mutual insurance companies specialize in life insurance. Technically, mutual insurance companies are owned by their policyholders, who may receive premium rebates in the form of dividends. In spite of this, however, there is no evidence that an insurance policy from a mutual company costs any less than a comparable policy from a stockholder-owned insurer. In recent years some mutual insurance companies have reorganized as stockholder-owned companies, including Prudential, one of the nation's largest insurers.

TYPES OF INSURANCE

property and liability insurance general category of insurance that protects against financial losses due to a number of perils

Individuals and businesses spend hundreds of billions of dollars each year on insurance coverage. All too often, however, both business firms and individual households make poor decisions when buying insurance. Several commonsense tips for buying insurance are offered in Table A.2. Although insurers offer hundreds of different policies, they all fall into three broad categories: property and liability insurance, health and disability insurance, and life insurance.

Property and Liability Insurance

Insurance that protects against fire, accident, theft, or other destructive events is called **property and liability insurance.** Examples of this insurance category include homeowners' insurance, auto insurance, business or commercial insurance, and liability insurance.

Homeowners' Insurance Homeowners' insurance protects homeowners from damage to their homes due to various perils. If a home is destroyed by fire, for example, the homeowners' policy will pay to replace the home and its contents. Although standard policies cover a wide range of perils, most do not cover damage from widespread catastrophes such as floods and earthquakes. The federal government, through the National Flood Insurance Program, offers flood insurance as a supplement to a standard homeowners' policy. At an average cost of around $350 a year, flood insurance is often a wise purchase. Many of the homes in Florida, Louisiana, and Mississippi were damaged or destroyed by floods—not wind—as a result of Hurricane Katrina.

Homeowners in earthquake-prone areas can purchase earthquake insurance from a private insurer as an add-on to their homeowners' policy. However, earthquake coverage is expensive—the annual

COURTESY OF LIBERTY MUTUAL INSURANCE COMPANY.

Homeowners' insurance protects people from the loss of what is usually their largest asset.

Table A.2

Some Commonsense Tips When Buying Insurance

- *Insure against big losses, not small ones.* Buy insurance to protect against big potential losses, but don't buy insurance to protect against small losses. A good example of this tip in action is to select the highest deductible you can afford on your property and liability insurance policies.

- *Buy insurance with broad coverage, not narrow coverage.* For example, it is much more cost-effective to buy a comprehensive health insurance policy, one that covers a wide range of illnesses and accidents, rather than several policies that cover only specific illnesses and accidents. It is extremely expensive to buy insurance coverage one disease at a time.

- *Shop around.* Insurance premiums for the same coverage can vary substantially. Insurance premiums also change frequently, so make sure to compare rates before renewing a policy.

- *Buy insurance only from financially strong companies.* Insurance companies occasionally go bankrupt. If this happens, you'll be left with no coverage and little chance of getting your premiums back. Several organizations—such as A.M. Best and Standard & Poor's—rate the financial strength of insurance companies.

Source: Louis E. Boone, David L. Kurtz, and Douglas Hearth, *Planning Your Financial Future*, 4th ed. (Mason, OH: Thomson South-Western, 2006), pp. 256–259.

premium often exceeds $1,000 with a $5,000 deductible—and not always available. States in earthquake-prone areas, such as California, are working with the insurance industry to make earthquake coverage more widely available and more affordable.

Auto Insurance With more than $130 billion in annual premiums, automobile insurance is the country's largest single type of property and liability insurance. Automobile insurance policies cover losses due to automobile accidents, including personal and property claims that result from accidents, fire, or theft. Virtually all states require drivers to have a minimum amount of auto insurance.

Commercial and Business Insurance Commercial and business insurance protects firms from financial losses resulting from the interruption of business operations (**business interruption insurance**) or physical damage to property as a result of fires, accidents, thefts, or other destructive events. Commercial and business insurance policies may also protect employers from employee dishonesty or losses resulting from nonperformance of contracts.

Liability Insurance **Liability insurance** protects an individual or business against financial losses to others for which the individual or business was responsible. If a driver runs a red light and hits another car, his or her liability insurance would pay to repair the damage to the other car. If a business sells a defective product, the firm's liability insurance would pay for financial losses sustained by customers. A standard amount of liability coverage is usually attached to auto, homeowners', and commercial insurance policies. Additional amounts of liability insurance can be purchased if needed. Adequate liability insurance is critically important today for both businesses and individuals. Wal-Mart, for example, requires all of its suppliers to have at least $2 million in liability coverage for their products.

business interruption insurance insurance that protects firms from financial losses resulting from the interruption of business operations

health insurance insurance that covers losses due to illness or accidents

Providing health insurance is a major decision for employers.

COURTESY OF UNITED HEALTHCARE AND PUBLICIS ADVERTISING AGENCY. PHOTOGRAPH/GETTY IMAGES

Health and Disability Insurance

Each of us faces the risk of getting sick or being injured in some way. Even a relatively minor illness can result in substantial healthcare bills. To guard against this risk, most Americans have some form of **health insurance**—insurance that provides coverage for losses due to sickness or accidents. With soaring costs in healthcare, this type of insurance has become an important consideration for both businesses and individuals.

Sources of health insurance include private individual policies, private group policies, and the federal government, through Medicare and Medicaid (health insurance for lower-income people). More than 60 percent of Americans are covered by private group health insurance provided by their employer as an employee benefit. Four of every five U.S. employees work for businesses and not-for-profits that offer some form of group health insurance. Group policies resemble individual health insurance policies but are offered at lower premiums. Individual health insurance policies are simply too expensive for most people. Of every ten dollars spent by employers on employee compensation (wages, salaries, and employee benefits), more than one dollar goes to cover the cost of health insurance. As noted in the opening vignette, health insurance costs have soared in recent years and employers have responded by cutting back on benefits, requiring employees to pay more of the premium, or even dropping coverage altogether.

Private health insurance plans fall into one of two general categories: fee-for-service plans and managed care plans. In a **fee-for-service plan,** the insured picks his or her doctor and has almost unlimited access to specialists. Fee-for-service plans charge an annual deductible and copayments. By contrast, a **managed care plan** pays most of the insured's healthcare bills. In return, the program has a great deal of say over the conditions of healthcare provided for the insured. Most managed care plans, for example, restrict the use of specialists and may specify which hospitals and pharmacies can be used. Some employers offer employees a choice between a fee-for-service and a managed care plan. (Some even offer multiple managed care plans.) Table A.3 compares the pros and cons of both types of healthcare plans.

Managed care plans have become extremely popular in recent years. More than 150 million Americans are enrolled in some form of managed care plan, and many fee-for-service plans have adopted some elements of managed care. A primary reason for the popularity of managed care is simply cost: managed care plans generally cost employers and employees less than fee-for-service plans. Managed care, however, is not without its critics. The effort to control costs has caused a backlash because of restrictions placed on doctors and patients. Legislation at both the federal and state level has forced managed care plans to give patients and physicians more control over medical decisions.

Types of Managed Care Plans Two types of managed care plans can be found in the United States: health maintenance organizations and preferred provider organizations. Although both manage healthcare, important differences exist between the two.

Health maintenance organizations (HMOs) do not provide health insurance, they provide healthcare. An HMO supplies all of the individual's healthcare needs, including prescription drugs and hospitalization. The individual must use the HMO's own doctors and approved treatment facilities in order to receive benefits. Doctors and other healthcare professionals are actually employees of the HMO. Individuals pick a primary care physician and cannot see a specialist without a referral. An HMO charges no deductibles and only a low, fixed-dollar copayment.

Table A.3

Comparing Fee-for-Service Plans and Managed Care Health Plans

	Fee-for-Service Plan	Managed-Care Plan
Pros	• Almost unlimited choice of healthcare providers	• Little or no paperwork
	• Easy access to medical specialists	• Lower out-of-pocket expenses
	• Fewer limits on tests and diagnostic procedures	• No wait in getting reimbursed
		• Pays for routine physicals and immunizations
Cons	• Higher out-of-pocket expenses (deductible and copayment)	• Choice of healthcare providers limited
	• Some plans involve more paperwork and delays in getting reimbursed	• More difficult to change doctors
	• Potentially more disputes with insurance company over charges	• Access to specialists restricted
	• Some plans do not pay for routine physicals and immunizations	• Limits on tests and diagnostic procedures

Source: Louis E. Boone, David L. Kurtz, and Douglas Hearth, *Planning Your Financial Future,* 4th ed. (Mason, OH: Thomson South-Western, 2006), p. 289.

The second type of managed care plan is the **preferred provider organization (PPO).** Although PPOs may get less publicity than HMOs, they actually cover more people. A PPO is an arrangement in which an employer negotiates a contract between local healthcare providers (physicians, hospitals, and pharmacies) to provide medical care to its employees at a discount. These plans have low fixed-dollar copayments. They are generally much more flexible than HMOs. Members can choose their primary care physician from a list of doctors. If a referral is given or hospitalization is required, the member again chooses from a list of approved healthcare providers. A member who obtains treatment from a healthcare provider outside the PPO network will likely be reimbursed for part of the cost.

Disability Income Insurance   Not only is disability income insurance one of the most overlooked forms of insurance, but many workers don't have enough coverage. The odds of a person developing a disability are considerably higher than most people realize. Take a group of five randomly selected 45-year-olds. There is approximately a 95 percent chance that one of the five will develop some form of a disability during the next 20 years. **Disability income insurance** is designed to replace lost income when a wage earner cannot work due to an accident or illness.

Two sources of disability income insurance exist: Social Security and private disability insurance policies. Social Security disability benefits are available to virtually all workers, but they have very strict requirements. Private disability insurance is available on either an individual or group basis. As with health insurance, a group policy is much cheaper than an individual policy. Many employers provide at least some disability coverage as an employee benefit. Employees often have the option of obtaining additional coverage by paying more.

Life Insurance

Life insurance protects people against the financial losses that occur with premature death. Three of every four Americans have some form of life insurance. The main reason people buy life insurance is to provide financial security for their families in the event of their death. With assets totaling more than $4 trillion, the life insurance industry is one of the nation's largest businesses.

Types of Life Insurance   As with health and disability insurance, both individual and group life insurance policies are available. Many employers offer life insurance to employees as a component of the firm's benefit program. However, unlike health and disability insurance, an individual life insurance policy is usually cheaper than a group policy for younger people.

The different types of life insurance fall neatly into two categories: **term policies** and so-called **cash value policies.** Term policies provide a death benefit if the policyholder dies within a specified period of time. It has no value at the end of that period. Cash value policies—such as whole and universal life—combine life insurance protection with a savings or investment feature. The cash value represents the savings or investment portion of the life insurance policy. Although there are arguments in favor of cash value policies, many

COURTESY OF PRUDENTIAL FINANCIAL INC.

Life insurance helps protect families against the loss of premature death. With the advent of two-income families and the soaring cost of child care, more and more women are obtaining life insurance policies.

experts believe that term life insurance is a better choice for most consumers. For one thing, a term policy is much cheaper than a cash value policy, especially for younger people.

How Much Life Insurance Should You Have?   People can purchase life insurance policies for almost any amount. Life insurance purchases are limited only by the amount of premiums people can afford and their ability to meet medical qualifications. The amount of life insurance a person needs, however, is a very personal decision. The general rule of thumb is that a person needs life insurance if he or she has family members who financially depend on that individual. A young parent with three small children could easily need $500,000 or more of life insurance. A single person with no dependents would reasonably see little or no need for a life insurance policy.

Businesses, as well as individuals, buy life insurance. The death of a partner or a key executive is likely to result in a financial loss to an organization. Key person insurance reimburses the organization for the loss of the services of an essential senior manager and to cover the executive search expenses needed to find a replacement. In addition, life insurance policies may be purchased for each member of a partnership to be able to repay the deceased partner's survivors for his or her share of the firm and permit the business to continue.

Business Terms You Need to Know

risk A-2
insurance A-3
premium A-3
insurable interest A-4

insurable risk A-4
underwriting A-4
actuarial table A-5
law of large numbers A-5

property and liability insurance A-7
business interruption insurance A-8
health insurance A-8
life insurance A-10

Other Important Business Terms

speculative risk A-2
pure risk A-2
public insurance agency A-6
Medicare A-6
liability insurance A-8
fee-for-service plan A-9

managed care plan A-9
health maintenance organization
  (HMO) A-9
preferred provider organization
  (PPO) A-10

disability income insurance A-10
term policy A-10
cash value policy A-10

Projects and Teamwork Applications

1. Assume you're the owner of a small manufacturing facility. Working with a partner, list some of some of the major risks your business faces. How should each risk be handled (avoided, reduced, assumed, or transferred)? What types of insurance will your business likely have to have, including those types of insurance required by law?

2. For many people one frustrating aspect of insurance is deciphering insurance terminology. The following Web site provides a lexicon of insurance terms: http://www.insweb.com/learningcenter/glossary/general-a.htm. Visit the Web site and look up the following terms:

> accommodation line
> fortuitous
> housekeeping
> earned premium
> tickler

3. Many companies currently sell insurance online. Two prominent companies that sell auto insurance policies online are GEICO (http://www.geico.com) and Progressive (http://www.progressive.com). Visit both Web sites and write a brief report on your experience. Would you consider buying insurance online? What are the advantages and disadvantages?

4. Several insurance-oriented Web sites have interactive worksheets to help you determine whether you need life insurance and, if so, how much you need. Visit the MSN Money Web site (http://moneycentral.msn.com/investor/calcs/n_life/main.asp). Complete the interactive worksheet. If you need life insurance, what kind of policy should you buy? How much will it cost?

5. If you own a car, you know how expensive auto insurance is. There are several commonsense ways to reduce your auto insurance bill. Visit http://www.pueblo.gsa.gov/cic_text/cars/autoinsu/autoinsu.htm and prepare a brief report on reducing the cost of auto insurance.

Personal Financial Planning

PILOTING YOUR OWN FINANCIAL SHIP

Gone are the days when employees started work after receiving their education, stayed with a firm for 30 years, and then retired with a gold watch and a company-funded pension plan. From businesses' current perspective, large pension set-asides are a drag on their profitability, especially when they are competing against newer start-ups that do not carry such obligations. For instance, United Airlines recently defaulted on $6.6 billion in pension payments it was to make to retired employees, which the court allowed because its pension debt would hinder United's recovery from bankruptcy. Meanwhile, the government's backup fund—the Pension Benefit Guaranty Corporation, which assumes the pensions of private companies that default—is stretched to its limits. So, lacking the means to pay their future obligations, other firms are freezing or terminating traditional defined-benefit pension plans more frequently. Defined-benefit plans promise a specific monthly payment to retirees.

From employees' perspective, few workers want to remain with an employer for their entire lifetime. They change jobs and even career paths more frequently to gain skills, seek fulfillment, and accept new challenges. And with the current frantic pace of mergers and acquisitions, they may not want to link their future success too closely with one firm's fortunes. So they want their pension plans to be portable and flexible, not tied to a specific employer. Increasingly, workers are planning ahead, taking control, and saving money to ensure a comfortable retirement.

As a result of this fundamental shift in the workplace, businesses now typically offer defined-contribution plans, such as 401k savings programs. Under these plans, employees set aside certain percentages of their annual wages, and employers often match funds up to a set level. Those funds are then invested and accumulate during a worker's lifetime. Getting an early start in these programs is key so that the investment can be compounded and grow over many years.

Still, nine out of ten Americans worry about saving enough for retirement, according to a recent study by banking and securities giant Wachovia. So what can today's workers do to ensure a secure retirement? In short, save—and start now. The saving habit can be acquired, and the sooner it is started, the easier and the more profitable it will be. Some financial planners suggest that young workers start saving at least 10 percent of their income. Others recommend as much as 20 to 25 percent. Although those numbers may seem high, they advise that workers will never look back and wish they had saved less. And the savings vehicles people use in this new do-it-yourself retirement environment range from the 401k plans mentioned earlier to individual retirement accounts (IRAs), which employees set up on their own and contribute to yearly. But those plans may soon be just the tip of the iceberg as flexible new retirement savings plans are developed to encourage employees to take their financial future into their own hands. With a little advance planning and periodic reassessment and fine-tuning, creating and managing your own retirement fund need not become a burden. You just need to plan and start early.[1]

APPENDIX OVERVIEW

You are studying business, but much of what you learn in this course will also apply to your personal life. For instance, you learn about each of the important functions of a business—from accounting to marketing, from finance to management. Learning about each business function will help you choose a career, and a career choice is one of the most important personal financial decisions you will make. You will learn why firms prepare budgets and financial statements. But budgets and financial statements are also important tools for individuals.

Everyone, regardless of age or income, can probably do a better job of managing his or her finances. As a group, Americans are much better at making money than they are at managing money. This appendix introduces you to personal financial management. **Personal financial management** deals with a variety of issues and decisions that affect a person's financial well-being. It includes basic money management, credit, tax planning, major consumer purchases, insurance, investing, and retirement planning.

The appendix will draw from many of the topics you will learn while studying business, but it introduces you to some new concepts as well. It is hoped that after completing the appendix, you will be a better-informed financial consumer and personal money manager and that you will be motivated to learn more about personal finance. The rewards, in both monetary and nonmonetary terms, can be tremendous.

THE MEANING AND IMPORTANCE OF PERSONAL FINANCE

Personal finance is the study of the economic factors and personal decisions that affect a person's financial well-being. Personal finance affects, and is affected by, many things we do and many decisions we make throughout our lives.

On one level, personal finance involves money know-how. It is essential to know how to earn money, as well as how to save, spend, invest, and control it in order to achieve goals. The reward of sound money management is an improvement in one's **standard of living.** Standard of living consists of the necessities, comforts, or luxuries an individual seeks to attain or maintain.

On another level, personal finance is intertwined with each person's **lifestyle**—the way we live our daily lives. Our choice of careers, friends, hobbies, communities, and possessions is determined by personal finances, and yet our personal finances can also be determined by our lifestyles. If, for example, you're a college student living independently on a shoestring budget, you will probably have to make many financial sacrifices to achieve your educational goals. Where you live is determined by what school you attend and how much you can afford to pay for rent; your vacation is set by your academic schedule and your checkbook balance; your clothing depends on the climate and your budget. All these lifestyle decisions are partially determined by your personal finances.

The Importance of Personal Finance Today

Good money management has always been important, but major changes in the external environment over the past couple of decades have made personal finance even more important today. And this is true whether you're a 20-year-old college student, a 40-year-old parent with a mortgage, or a 60-year-old thinking about retirement. Let's look at three reasons why personal financial planning is so important in today's environment.

Sluggish Growth in Personal Income Personal income in the United States has grown very slowly in recent years. For instance, over the last ten years, wages and salaries, by far the largest component of personal income, have increased at an average annual rate that has barely exceeded the annual rate of inflation. In other words, when measured in so-called *real terms,* the wages and salaries of the average American worker have remained virtually unchanged. Will this trend continue? Perhaps. Many economists forecast that annual increases in wages and salaries will barely keep pace with the rate of inflation in the coming years.

The sluggish growth in personal income makes sound money management very important. You cannot count on rising personal income to improve your standard of living. Rather, you need to save and invest more money, stick to a budget, and make major purchases wisely.

Financial planning advice is available from life insurance companies and other financial service firms.

Changes in the Labor Market Job security and the notion of work have changed in recent years. The traditional model of working for the same company for one's entire career is very rare today. Many people entering the workforce today will change jobs and employers several times during their working lives. Some will end up working part time or on a contract basis, with little job security and fewer benefits. Others will take time off to care for small children or elderly parents. And a goal many people have today is to start their own business and work for themselves.

Furthermore, it is estimated that one in four workers today will be unemployed at some point during their working lives. Frankly, you never know when your employer will "downsize," taking your job with it, or "outsource" your job to someone else. Just review today's headlines, and you will see that announcements of prominent companies downsizing and outsourcing are common.

These changes make sound personal financial management even more important. You have to keep your career skills up-to-date and accumulate sufficient financial resources to weather an unexpected crisis.

More Options The number of choices today in such areas as banking, credit, investments, and retirement planning can be bewildering. Today you can do most of your banking with a brokerage firm and then buy mutual fund shares at a bank. Even the simple checking account has become more complicated. The typical bank offers several different types of checking accounts, each with its own features and fees. Choosing the wrong account could easily cost you a hundred dollars or more in unnecessary fees each year.

Fifteen years ago, few college students carried credit cards, and those who did typically carried cards tied to their parents' accounts. The situation is much different today. Most college students have their own credit card accounts; many have multiple accounts. Approximately half of all college students carry a balance from month to month, and credit problems are a major reason why some students drop out of college. Today, you can choose whether to use credit properly.

One of the first things you'll do when you start a new job is make decisions concerning employee benefits. The typical employer may offer lots of choices in such areas as health

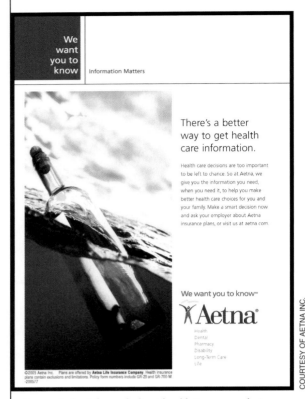

It pays to be informed about health insurance choices.

insurance, disability insurance, group life insurance, and retirement plans. Select the wrong health insurance plan, for example, and you could end up paying thousands of dollars more in out-of-pocket costs. Making the wrong decisions concerning retirement, even if you're still in your 20s, could make it difficult to achieve a financially secure retirement.

Most people believe that choice is a good thing, and having more choices in the personal finance arena means the consumer is likely to find what he or she seeks. At the same time, however, a longer menu of choices means it's easier to make mistakes. The more informed you are, the better choices and fewer costly mistakes you are likely to make.

Personal Financial Planning— A Lifelong Activity

Personal financial planning is as important an activity whether you're 20, 40, or 60; whether you're single or married with children; and whether your annual income is $20,000 or $200,000. Many experts say that if you can't stick to a budget and control your spending when you're making $25,000 a year, you'll find it difficult to live within your means even if your income doubles or triples.

The fact that sound planning is a lifelong activity, of course, doesn't mean your financial goals and plans remain constant throughout your life—they won't. The major goal when you're young may be to buy your first home or pay off your college loans. For older people, the major goal is probably making their retirement funds last for the rest of their lives.

Also, the importance of personal finance goals will change as you go through life. Although we should all begin planning for retirement as soon as we begin our careers, the relative importance of retirement and estate planning increases as retirement nears. Choosing the right life insurance policy is a major decision for a 30-year-old father of two, but not for a 65-year-old grandfather. On the other hand, estate planning may be far more important for the 65-year-old than it is for the 30-year-old.

For many people, getting started toward a better financial future is one of the hardest tasks of all. Table B.1 lists, in rough order, what the experts believe your financial priorities should be. As always, the first step is to figure out exactly where you currently stand financially.

Getting Professional Help

Many people believe they need professional help when it comes to managing their finances. The world is full of people and organizations who are willing to give you advice on everything from preparing a budget to estate planning. More than a few colleges and universities, for instance, offer credit counseling and other basic financial services to students who find themselves in financial trouble. When you are older, you may find it prudent to use the services of a certified public accountant (CPA) when preparing your tax returns or a professional investment advisor when choosing the right investments to fund your retirement. Dozens of financial self-help books are published annually. A great deal of financial information and advice is also available online. Two of the better personal finance Web sites are Quicken.com (http://www.quicken.com) and MSN Money (http://moneycentral.msn.com).

Getting Started: Your Financial Priorities

Okay, let's assume you're in your early 20s, recently graduated from college, and just got your first "real" job. Congratulations; you're probably making more money than you ever have before. However, you're also likely spending more money than ever, and probably came out of college with some debts—student loans, credit cards, an auto loan, and so forth. You know you need to start managing your money, but where do you start? You start by establishing some financial priorities. According to the experts, those in their 20s should do the following (in rough order):

- Figure out where you currently stand financially.
- Put yourself on a budget.
- Insure yourself against financial ruin.
- Get your debts under control.
- Start saving for retirement.
- Set up a regular savings program.

You may not be able to do everything immediately, but you do need to get started. Take it one step at a time. The worst mistake you can make is to procrastinate.

Source: Adapted from Louis Boone, David Kurtz, and Douglas Hearth, *Planning Your Financial Future*, 4th ed. (Mason, OH: Thomson South-Western, 2006), p. 6.

One thing you must recognize is that almost anyone can call himself or herself a financial planner, regardless of background or training. While financial planners must have certain federal and state licenses to sell many financial products, there are almost no standards governing financial planners. However, a professional organization—called the Certified Financial Planner Board—certifies financial planners. Anyone who obtains the Certified Financial Planner (CFP) designation has met a set of educational and professional requirements and passed a comprehensive examination.

A PERSONAL FINANCIAL MANAGEMENT MODEL

A **financial plan** is a guide to help you reach targeted goals in the future. These goals could include buying a home, starting your own business, sending children to college, or retiring early. Developing a personal financial plan consists of several steps, as illustrated in Figure B.1.

The first step in the financial planning process is to develop a series of short- and long-term goals. These goals should be influenced by your values, as well as an assessment of your current financial situation. The next step is to establish a set of financial strategies—in each of the personal planning areas—designed to help close the gap between where you are now and where you want to be in the future. Next, put your plan into action and closely monitor its performance. Periodically evaluate the effectiveness of your financial plan and make adjustments when necessary.

Financial plans cannot be developed in a vacuum. They should reflect your available resources—especially salary and fringe benefits, such as health insurance and retirement

USED WITH PERMISSION. CITIBANK, N.A. PHOTOGRAPH/GETTY IMAGES

The stock market doesn't lie awake at night wondering what kind of day you had.

Tired of counting sheep? Bulls? And bears?

Come in, sit down and we'll help you set up a free financial game plan. [Getting organized is great for insomnia.]

Sweet dreams.

Live richly.

citi.com

Banks offer a wide range of financial products and advice today.

financial plan guide to help a person reach desired goals

B.1 The Financial Planning Process

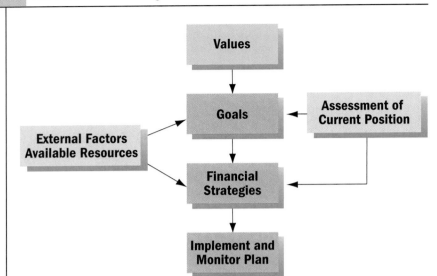

Source: Adapted from Louis Boone, David Kurtz, and Douglas Hearth, *Planning Your Financial Future,* 4th ed. (Mason, OH: Thomson South-Western, 2006), p. 7.

plans. For example, your goals and financial strategies must be based on a realistic estimate of your future income. If you cannot reach your financial goals through your present career path, you will have to scale back your goals or consider switching careers.

In addition, external factors—such as economic conditions and government policy—will influence your financial plan and decisions. For instance, assume you're in the market for a new car, much of which you will have to finance. Obviously, interest rates affect the size of your monthly payment and how much car you can afford. So you will need to keep track of interest rates. If interest rates appear to be falling, a smart financial decision may be to postpone the purchase in order to get a better rate on a new-car loan.

General Themes Common to All Financial Plans

Regardless of the specifics, all financial plans revolve around three general themes: (1) maximizing income and wealth, (2) using money more effectively, and (3) monitoring expenditures.

Maximizing Income and Wealth Maximizing your income and wealth means getting more money. Work smarter; seek retraining for a better, higher-paying job; take career risks that may pay off in the long run; make sound investment decisions—all these are examples of the implementation of the first step. The amount of money you earn is a vital part of any financial plan, and it is up to you to make the most of your opportunities.

Using Money More Effectively Money has two basic uses: consumption and savings. Even if you are a regular saver, you'll still spend most of your income, probably more than 90 percent. You must try to spend every dollar wisely and make every major buying decision part of your overall financial plan. Avoid impulsive spending or giving in to the hard sell.

And it's not just big expenditures you need to watch. Cutting back your spending on small items can make a difference. Little purchases do add up. For example, taking your lunch a couple of times a week rather than eating out could save about $15 a week. Invest that savings at 6 percent interest (per year) and you'll have more than $65,000 in 30 years.

Monitoring Expenditures Budgeting is the key to controlling expenditures. A budget focuses on where the money is going and whether a person's goals are being met. It also suggests appropriate times for reevaluating priorities. If your budget doesn't reflect what you want from life both now and in the future, change it.

Information also helps you keep your expenditures under control. The more you know about real estate, consumer loans, insurance, taxes, and major purchases, the more likely you are to spend the least money to purchase the greatest value.

"They Said It"

"Money was never a big motivation for me, except as a way to keep score. The real excitement is playing the game."

—Donald Trump (b. 1946)
Businessperson and entrepreneur

The Pitfalls of Poor Financial Planning

Unfortunately, too many people fail to effectively plan their financial future. Not only do many of these people find it difficult to improve their standard of living, but quite a few also find themselves with mounting debts and a general inability to make ends meet. In a recent year, more than 1.5 million Americans filed for bankruptcy. What happens to people when they cannot meet their debt obligations?

Creditors will not ignore missed or consistently late payments. First, they will send written inquiries concerning your failure to make required payments on time. Unless you make the payment or contact them about making other arrangements, your creditors are likely to take further actions. Examples of actions creditors can take include repossessing your property, garnishing your wages, or even sending you into personal bankruptcy. At the very least, your ability to obtain credit will be seriously damaged.

SETTING PERSONAL GOALS

Whatever your personal financial goals, they should reflect your values. Values are a set of fundamental beliefs of what is important, desirable, and worthwhile in your life. Your values will influence how you spend your money and, therefore, should be the foundation of your financial plan. Each person's financial goals will be determined by the individual's values because every individual considers some things more desirable or important than others. Start by asking yourself some questions about your values, the things that are most important to you, and what you would like to accomplish in your life.

Your goals are also influenced by your current financial situation. Prepare a set of current financial statements for yourself. An income statement is a statement of income and expenditures. A balance sheet is a statement of what you own (assets) and what you owe (liabilities). For an individual or household, the difference between assets and liabilities is called **net worth.**

Figure B.2 shows a set of financial statements for a hypothetical couple, Brian and Michelle. Notice that on their income statement, which reflected income and expenditures for an entire year, Brian and Michelle divided their expenses into several major categories (such as housing, transportation, and child care). Because they spent less than they made, Brian and Michelle added money to their savings during the year.

Their balance sheet was prepared at the end of the year. Note that Brian and Michelle divided their assets into current financial assets, long-term financial assets, and nonfinancial or real assets. Likewise, they divided their liabilities into those that are due within a short amount of time and those that are not.

After reviewing your current financial statements, you should prepare a budget. Most households prepare budgets on a monthly basis. A budget is an excellent tool for monitoring your expenditures and cash flow and permits you to track past and current expenditures and plan future ones.

A sample budget is shown in Figure B.3. Expenses are divided into fixed expenses (those that vary little from month to month) and variable expenses (those that vary from month to month).

Next, establish a series of financial goals based on your values and current financial situation. Separate your goals into short-term goals (those you would like to accomplish within the next year or so) and long-term goals (those you would like to accomplish within the next several years). An example of a short-term goal is "pay off the outstanding balance on my Visa

"They Said It"

"My problem lies in reconciling my gross habits with my net income."
—Errol Flynn (1909–1959) Actor

Financial
Statements for Brian
and Michelle

Balance Sheet

Assets		Liabilities & Net Worth	
Current financial assets		**Current liabilities**	
Checking account	$2,500	Utilities	$200
Savings account	5,000	Insurance	250
Money market funds	4,500	Credit card	500
Total	$12,000	Other	0
Long-term financial assets		Total	$950
Mutual funds	$12,000	**Long-term liabilities**	
Stocks and bonds	$0	Auto loan	$8,000
Pension	$0	Student loans	3,500
401k	30,000	Mortgage	130,000
IRAs	2,500	Other	0
Other	1,500	Total	$141,500
Total	$46,000		
Fixed assets		**Total Liabilities**	142,450
Home	$165,000		
Auto 1:	13,000	**Net Worth**	**$127,050**
Auto 2:	8,500		
Furniture	15,000		
Personal property	5,000		
Other	5,000		
Total fixed	$211,500		
Total Assets	**$269,500**		

Income Statement

Wages earned	
Brian	38,500
Michelle	43,000
Other income	
Bonuses	2,500
Interest & dividends	1,000
Tax refunds	500
Other	0
Total income	$85,500
Income and FICA taxes	$16,000
Net income	**$69,500**
Expenditures	
Housing	
House payment	12,000
Utilities	3,500
Property taxes	1,800
Maintenance	2,500
Insurance	500
Other housing	3,500
Total housing	$23,800
Transportation	
Car payments	3,600
Gas & repairs	1,500
Insurance	1,000
Registration	200
Other transportation	300
Total transportation	$6,600
Food & clothing	8,000
Medical & dental expenses	1,500
Child care	5,000
Vacation & entertainment	3,500
Student loan payments	2,000
Credit card interest	0
Life insurance premiums	1,500
Cash allowances	5,000
Other expenses	2,500
Total expenditures	**$59,400**
Amount available for savings	**$10,100**

Josh and Ellie's Monthly Budget

	July			August		
	Budget	Actual	Difference	Budget	Actual	Difference
Cash Inflows						
Net salary (Josh)	2,800	2,800	—	2,800	2,800	—
Net salary (Ellie)	2,300	2,300	—	2,300	2,300	—
Dividends and interest	100	125	25	100	100	—
Bonus	—	—	—	1,500	2,000	500
Other	—	—	—	—	—	—
Total inflows	**5,200**	**5,225**	**25**	**6,700**	**7,200**	**500**
Cash Outflows						
Fixed expenses						
Mortgage/rent	1,100	1,100	—	1,100	1,100	—
Auto loan	350	350	—	350	350	—
Student loan	300	300	—	300	300	—
Credit card payments	—	—	—	—	—	—
Automatic savings transfer	500	500	—	500	500	—
Variable expenses						
Utilities	325	375	50	300	250	(50)
Food	500	550	50	400	400	—
Medical and dental	100	200	100	100	—	(100)
Clothing and personal care	250	325	75	150	100	(50)
Entertainment and recreation	200	125	(75)	1,200	1,500	300
Transportation expenses	200	200	—	150	100	(50)
Gifts and contributions	100	175	75	100	150	50
Personal spending money	400	475	75	400	350	(50)
Life insurance	50	50	—	—	—	—
Auto insurance	350	325	(25)	—	—	—
Homeowners' insurance	—	—	—	450	475	25
Other expenses	—	—	—	800	600	(200)
Total cash outflows	**4,725**	**5,050**	**325**	**6,300**	**6,175**	**(125)**
Net cash flow	**475**	**175**	**(300)**	**400**	**1,025**	**625**

card by this time next year." A long-term goal might be to buy a house by age 30. It is important, of course, that your short-term goals support your long-term goals. For instance, if your long-term goal is to buy a house, short-term goals should include starting a regular savings program and paying off credit card debt.

In addition, some of your goals will be monetary in nature—meaning you can put a price tag on them—while other goals will be nonmonetary. If you want to pay off the outstanding balance on your Visa card by this time next year, and the current balance is $1,000, that is an example of a monetary goal. A goal of constructing and following a monthly budget is an example of a nonmonetary goal.

Whether short-term or long-term, monetary or nonmonetary, your financial goals should be defined as specifically as possible and focus on results. Goals should also be realistic and attainable. Paying off the $1,000 balance on your Visa card within the next twelve months may be realistic; paying it off in the next two months may not be. If your monthly take-home pay is $3,000, and your fixed monthly expenses—such as rent, utilities, transportation, and loan payments—amount to $2,000, setting a goal of saving $750 per month is probably not very realistic. On the other hand, setting a monthly savings goal of $250 may be reasonable.

Financial goals change throughout a person's lifetime, and for this reason they should be written down and reviewed periodically. To be effective, goals should reflect changes in

B.4 Personal Goals Worksheet

Short-Term Financial Goals

Description	Actions	Target Date	Estimated Cost	Priority
Example: Establish regular savings program.	Set up automatic monthly transfer between checking and savings accounts.	Immediate	$250 per month	High

Long-Term Financial Goals

Description	Actions	Target Date	Estimated Cost	Priority
Example: Pay off credit card balance.	1. Pay $250 more than minimum payment each month. 2. Use card only in emergencies.	2008 or 2009	$250 per month	High

Nonfinancial Goals

Description	Actions	Target Date
Example: Create a monthly budget.	Categorize expenses; estimate income and expenses; compare estimate to current income and spending levels.	One month

circumstances, such as education, family, career, the economic environment, and even your emotional and physical well-being. The worksheet shown in Figure B.4 is one way of formulating and tracking your personal financial goals. Notice that it separates short-term from long-term goals and monetary from nonmonetary goals. It also divides goals into major categories—such as saving, spending, and credit. The worksheet also asks you to estimate the cost of each goal, if monetary, and establish each goal's priority. Your worksheet should be updated regularly as you achieve short-term goals or your life situation changes.

YOUR PERSONAL FINANCIAL DECISIONS

An individual's economic future is charted via financial strategies in such personal planning areas as career choice, credit management, and tax planning. These strategies should reflect your goals and be designed to close the gap between where you are and where you want to be.

Career Choice

No factor exerts as strong an influence on an individual's personal finances as does a career choice. Virtually all of your income, especially when you're just starting out, will come from wages and salaries. It is through work that all of us acquire the income needed to build a lifestyle; to buy goods and services, including insurance protection; to save and invest; and to plan for retirement. Your job is also the source of many important fringe benefits, such as health insurance and retirement savings plans, that are important components of your financial future. Throughout *Contemporary Business,* we've discussed ways to select a career that fits your skills and interests, find a job, and perform in that job.

Basic Money Management

Basic money management involves managing checking and savings accounts. Properly managing these relatively simple financial assets is an important first step toward proper management of more complicated financial assets such as investment and retirement accounts. You must choose a bank or other financial institution and then select the right checking account. Banks today offer several different types of checking accounts, each with its own set of features and fees. Table B.2 lists several tips for selecting and managing a checking account. Managing a savings account involves understanding the importance of savings, setting savings goals, and picking the best savings option.

Credit Management

Not surprisingly, credit is the area of personal finance that gets more people into financial difficulties than any other area. **Credit** allows a person to purchase goods and services by borrowing the necessary funds from a lender, such as a bank. The borrower agrees to repay the loan over a specified period of time, paying a specified rate of interest. Credit is available from many sources today, but rates vary, so it pays to shop around.

There are two broad types of consumer credit: revolving (or open-end) credit and installment credit. Revolving credit is a type of credit arrangement that enables consumers to make a number of different purchases up to a credit limit, specified by the lender. The consumer has the option of repaying some or all of the outstanding balance each month. If the consumer carries a balance from month to month, finance charges (interest) are levied. An example of revolving credit is a credit card, such as Visa or MasterCard. An installment loan is a credit arrangement in which the borrower takes out a loan for a specified amount, agreeing to repay the loan in regular installments over a specified period of time. The installments include the finance charge. Student loans, auto loans, and home mortgage loans are examples of installment loans.

credit receiving money, goods, or services on the basis of an agreement between the lender and the borrower that the loan is for a specified period of time with a specified rate of interest

Keeping a Lid on Bank Fees

Table

B.2

Banks today charge customers fees for a variety of services, but the amount can vary substantially. If you are not careful, you can end up paying a couple of hundred dollars a year, or more, in unnecessary fees. Here are some tips for keeping bank fees under control.

* Choose the right checking account.
* Shop around.
* Regularly balance your checkbook.
* Watch how you use your ATM card.
* Sign up for overdraft protection.
* Understand how your bank computes the minimum balance.
* Consider using your personal computer to pay bills electronically.
* Read the fine print in your monthly statement.

Source: Adapted from Louis Boone, David Kurtz, and Douglas Hearth, *Planning Your Financial Future,* 4th ed. (Mason, OH: Thomson South-Western, 2006), p. 96.

People have good reasons for borrowing money. They include purchasing large, important goods and services (cars, homes, or a college education), dealing with financial emergencies, taking advantage of opportunities or of convenience, and establishing or improving your credit rating. All of these reasons are appropriate uses of credit *if* you can repay the loans in a timely manner.

However, a wrong reason for borrowing money is using credit to live beyond your means. For instance, you may want to go to Cancun for vacation but really cannot afford to, so you charge the trip. Using credit to live beyond your means often leads to credit problems. Watch for these warning signs:

- You use credit to meet basic living expenses.
- You use credit to make impulse purchases.
- You take a cash advance on one credit card to repay another, and the unpaid balance increases month after month.

Consumers who think of credit purchases as a series of small monthly payments are fooling themselves. Today most college students have credit cards, and most carry balances from month to month averaging more than $2,000.[2] How long would it take someone with the average balance to become debt free, assuming he or she made only the minimum payment each month (the minimum payment is typically $25 or 2.5 percent of the outstanding balance, whichever is greater) and is charged the average rate of interest (around 16 percent)? The answer is almost *11 years* (129 months to be exact), during which time the borrower would pay almost $2,000 in interest. What's more, the preceding example assumes that the person does not charge anything else while paying off the balance.

If you feel as though you have a problem with credit, or may be developing one, you should seek help as soon as possible. Your college or university may offer credit counseling services. If not, contact a local not-for-profit credit counseling service or the National Federation for Credit Counseling (800-388-2227 or http://www.nfcc.org). According to the experts, one of the keys to the wise use of credit is education. Learning about the pros and cons of borrowing money, as well as learning about responsible spending, can help people avoid future problems with credit.

Tax Planning

Everyone pays a variety of taxes to federal, state, and local governments. The major taxes paid by individuals include federal and state income taxes, FICA (Social Security and Medicare) taxes, property taxes, and sales taxes. The median-income family paid almost 38 percent of its income in taxes during a recent year. Think about your own situation and the taxes you pay. If you work, you have federal income taxes withheld from each paycheck. In addition, if you live in one of the 41 states with a state income tax, you have state income tax withheld also. Social Security and Medicare taxes amount to 15.3 percent of your wages split between you and your employer (you pay the entire amount if you're self-employed). If you rent an apartment, part of your monthly rent goes to pay the landlord's property tax bill. Every time you buy something, you likely pay sales tax to your state and local governments.

Unfortunately, there is very little you can do to reduce some of the taxes you pay. The only tax over which you have some control is the federal income tax. But even with the federal income tax, people have only a handful of ways to legally reduce their tax bill. Still, you need to understand the federal income tax system and know what kinds of tax records to keep. Even though millions of Americans pay someone else to do their taxes, many people have relatively simple returns. Preparing a tax return is one of the best ways of learning more about your personal finances. The Internal Revenue Service (IRS) has several excellent publications to help you prepare a federal income tax return. One of the best is IRS Publication #17 (*You and Your Federal Income Tax*). This and all other IRS publications are available free of charge from local IRS offices or the IRS Web site (http://www.irs.gov). We also strongly suggest that you use one of the tax preparation software programs (TurboTax or TaxCut) and your personal computer to prepare your federal and state income tax returns.

Major Purchases

Even if you are a great budgeter and saver, you will still spend most of your income each year. Effective buying is an important part of your financial plan. Within personal budget limits, an individual exercises his or her rights as a consumer to select or reject the wide range of goods and services that are available. As you purchase an automobile, a home, or any other major item, you need to carefully evaluate alternatives, separate needs from wants, and determine how you are going to finance the purchase. Your goal is to make every dollar you spend count.

Americans spend more than $500 billion annually on transportation, most of which goes to purchasing and maintaining automobiles. Given that new vehicles average more than $20,000 today, and even good used cars can cost in excess of $12,000, buying an automobile is a substantial purchase. On top of that, most car purchases are financed. Buying a car involves weighing many factors, including whether you want a new or used car, what makes and models appeal to you, and how much you can afford to pay.

For most people, housing consumes the largest share of their monthly budgets. Most Americans—more than 70 percent—own their own homes, and home ownership is a goal of most people. Owning a home has a number of advantages, both financial and nonfinancial. Some of the financial benefits include tax savings (home mortgage interest and property taxes are both tax deductible) and the potential increase in the home's value. Nonfinancial benefits include pride of ownership. For those who don't own homes, the major barrier to home ownership is the down payment required to get a mortgage loan, along with other so-called *closing costs*. Even a modestly priced home will require that the buyer have around $20,000 in cash.

The other major housing option is renting. Renting also offers a number of advantages, including cost savings (the landlord takes care of maintenance and repairs) and mobility. It is much easier to move if you rent than if you own a home. People who plan on staying in a area for a short period of time are usually better off renting. The choice between buying and renting is obviously a major financial decision that needs to be approached rationally, not emotionally—especially true for first-time home buyers.

Insurance

Another important personal planning area is insurance. Insurance is an admittedly expensive—Americans spend more than $125 billion each year on auto insurance alone—but necessary purchase. Some of the basic principles and the various types of insurance are described in Appendix A of *Contemporary Business*. Although the focus of that appendix is business insurance, much of what is discussed applies to your personal insurance needs as well.

Your goal is to have adequate and appropriate coverage in each of the major insurance types—life, health, disability, and property and liability. Insurance needs can vary substantially from individual to individual. For instance, what are the insurance needs of Karen (a single 25-year-old who rents an apartment) and Bill (a divorced 40-year-old with custody of young children who owns a home)? Their individual insurance needs are listed in Figure B.5. Notice that they both need health, disability, and auto coverage, but only Bill needs life insurance. Bill's children are financially dependent on him, but Karen has no financial dependents. Karen should have renters' insurance, while Bill needs homeowners' insurance.

Personal Characteristics	Bill	Karen
Age	43	26
Annual income	$75,000	$40,000
Marital status	Divorced	Single
Number of dependent children	2 (has custody)	0
Own automobile (yes/no)	Yes	Yes
Homeowner (yes/no)	Yes	No

Type of Insurance	Bill's Needs	Karen's Needs
Life	Needs life insurance amounting to several times his annual salary; perhaps $500,000 or more.	Needs no life insurance.
Health	Major medical plan that covers Bill and his children is required. Obtain from employer.	Karen should be covered by a major medical plan. Obtain from employer.
Disability	Should have a policy that pays an annual benefit of between $45,000 and $50,000. Obtain from employer.	Should have a policy that provides an annual benefit of between $30,000 and $33,000 per year. Obtain from employer.
Auto	Should have substantial liability coverage and, depending on the age and value of his car, collision and comprehensive as well. Uninsured driver coverage is strongly recommended.	Should have as much liability coverage as she can afford. Collision and comprehensive are recommended, depending on the age and value of her car. Uninsured driver coverage is strongly recommended.
Homeowners'	Should have comprehensive, full replacement coverage on both the structure and contents of his home.	Should have a renters' policy covering her personal property.
Personal liability	Liability portions of auto and homeowner's policies probably sufficient.	Liability portions of auto and renters' policies probably sufficient.

As noted earlier in *Contemporary Business,* some types of insurance are provided to employees as fringe benefits. They typically include health insurance, disability insurance, and life insurance. In the standard arrangement, the premium is split between the employee and employer. A few employers contract with insurance companies to offer employees auto and homeowners' insurance at discounts.

Investment Planning

Investing is a process by which money acquired through work, inheritance, or other sources is preserved and increased. Sound investment management is an important component of the financial plan and can make it easier to attain other personal goals, such as buying a home, sending children to college, starting a business, or retiring comfortably. Furthermore, it is very difficult today to substantially increase wealth without investing. And, given the changes to the external environment—such as employer-sponsored retirement plans—it is likely that everyone will have to make investment decisions at some point during his or her life.

The investment process consists of four steps. The first step is to complete some preliminary tasks, including setting overall personal goals, having a regular savings program, and managing credit properly. The second step is to establish a set of investment goals—why you want to invest, what you want to accomplish, and what kind of time frame you have. Obviously, your investment goals should be closely related to your overall personal goals. Next, you need to assess risk and return. You invest because you expect to earn some future rate of return. At the same time, however, all investing exposes you to a variety of risks. You need to find the proper balance between risk and return because investments offering the highest potential returns also expose you to more risk. Your age, income, and short- or long-term investment time frames all have an impact on the risk/return trade-off.

The final step is to select the appropriate investments. As discussed in Chapter 18 of *Contemporary Business,* there are three general types of investments: money market instruments, bonds, and common stock. The proper mix of these three investments depends on such factors as your investment goals and investment time horizon. For instance, a 25-year-old investing for retirement should have close to 100 percent of his or her funds invested in common stocks because growth in capital is the overriding investment objective. Over longer periods of time, stocks tend to outperform money market instruments and bonds. On the other hand, if the 25-year-old is investing to have sufficient funds for a down payment on a house within the next couple of years, the investor should have most of his or her funds invested in money market instruments and bonds. Liquidity, current income, and stability of principal are the most important investment objectives. Even after selecting the appropriate investments, the investor must monitor their performance and be prepared to make changes when necessary.

Financial Planning for Tomorrow

The last major personal planning area deals with future financial issues, such as sending children to college and retirement and estate planning. As you know, college is expensive and is likely to become even more expensive in the coming years. By beginning a college savings program early, parents can ensure that they will have sufficient financial resources to send their children to college when the time comes. Today a variety of college savings programs exist, some of which provide parents with tax benefits.

Most people want to eventually retire with sufficient funds to ensure a degree of financial security. Social Security will provide only a fraction of what you will need; you will be responsible for the rest. According to the experts, you will need to have a savings nest egg of at least $1.5 million by the time you retire. Four important principles apply when it comes to saving for retirement: start early, save as much as you can each month, take advantage of all tax-deferred retirement savings plans to which you are entitled, and invest your retirement savings appropriately.

Aside from Social Security, two other major sources of retirement income exist: employer-sponsored retirement plans and individual retirement plans. Most employers offer their workers a retirement plan; many offer more than one plan. For most people, employer-sponsored retirement plans will likely provide the bulk of their retirement income. Essentially, two types of employer-sponsored retirement plans exist. A

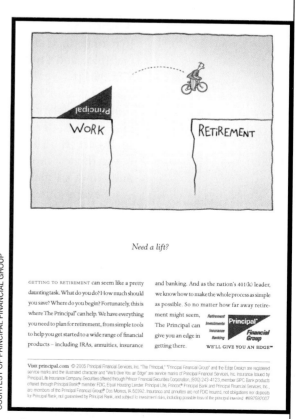

Retirement is a major personal goal.

defined benefit plan guarantees a worker a certain retirement benefit each year. The size depends on a number of factors, including the worker's income and the length of time he or she worked for the employer. Pension plans are classified as defined benefit plans.

The other type of employer-sponsored retirement plan is the *defined contribution plan*. In this type of retirement plan, you contribute to your retirement account and so does your employer. You are given some choice of where your retirement funds can be invested. Often you are given a list of mutual funds in which to invest your money. A 401k is an example of a defined contribution plan. Defined contribution plans are becoming more common and, as the opening vignette notes, are in many cases replacing defined benefit plans.

Millions of Americans have some sort of individual retirement plan, which they often set up and administer and are not tied to any employer. These workers may be self-employed or may merely want to supplement their retirement savings. Examples of individual retirement plans include regular IRAs (individual retirement accounts), Roth IRAs, Keogh plans, and SEP plans. To set up one of these retirement plans, you must meet certain eligibility requirements.

Another element of financial planning for tomorrow is estate planning. Of all the personal planning areas, estate planning is probably the least relevant for you, although your parents and grandparents probably face some estate-planning issues. However, *all* adults, regardless of age, need to have two documents: a valid will (naming a guardian if you have any minor children) and a durable power of attorney (the name varies from state to state, but it is a document that gives someone else the power to make financial and medical decisions if you are incapacitated).

AN EXAMPLE OF A FINANCIAL PLAN

Alberto and Anita Mendoza are a married couple in their late 20s. They have one child and live outside Cincinnati, Ohio. Alberto works as an assistant brand manager at Procter & Gamble, and Anita works for Fifth Third Bank. Their combined annual income is around $95,000 per year, and they own their own home. Sam and Anita put together their first financial plan shortly before they were married. They review it at least once a year, or after a major change in their lives. For example, Alberto and Anita substantially revised their financial plan shortly after their daughter was born. Parts of their current financial plan are shown in Figure B.6. Notice that all three general themes of a financial plan—increasing wealth, using money more effectively, and monitoring expenditures—are present throughout Alberto and Anita's financial plan.

Several other noteworthy items appear in Alberto and Anita's financial plan. First, they've divided it into several categories—spending, credit, investments, insurance, and other personal goals. This makes the plan easier to follow and generally more organized. Second, notice how they have established a time frame for each of their goals and how short-term goals support long-term goals. Third, Alberto and Anita have put a dollar value on each goal, if possible. Reducing nonmortgage debt to zero, for instance, will cost around $20,000. Finally, a strategy (or strategies) is attached to each goal. For example, paying off their nonmortgage debt by 2008 will require that they double up on their car and student-loan payments. Doing so requires that the couple cut back on nonessential spending.

Alberto and Anita's financial plans also reflects the couple's dreams. They want to have another child within the next couple of years. Anita would like to be able to cut back on her work schedule and begin working from home. They'd also like to remodel their kitchen, and Alberto would like to start working on his MBA. Without sound planning today, these and other dreams will be more difficult to achieve.

Financial Plan for Alberto and Anita Mendoza

Goal	Time Frame	Estimated Cost or Dollar Goal	Strategy
A. Spending			
1. Cut nonessential spending by 5%	Ongoing	$2,000 to $3,000 annually	Review budget quarterly; keep better track of cash.
2. Buy new bedroom set	2009	$3,000	Wait for sale; use money from savings.
3. Buy a new car	2009 or 2010	$25,000	Save $200 a month toward down payment; save bonuses.
B. Debt			
1. Reduce nonmortgage debt to zero	2009	$20,000	Double up on loan payments.
2. Refinance mortgage	Ongoing	$1,500 (estimated closing costs)	Refinance once fixed-rate loans decrease to 6%; use savings to pay refinancing costs.
C. Investments and Savings			
1. Build emergency fund	Ongoing	$15,000 by 2008	Cut spending by 5%.
2. Build nonretirement savings	Ongoing	$65,000 by 2009	Cut spending by 5%; try to save/invest all pay increases.
3. Build retirement savings	Ongoing	$150,000 by 2010	Maximum contribution to retirement accounts; invest appropriately.
4. Build college fund	Ongoing	$75,000 by 2025	Cut spending by 5%; try to save/invest all pay increases.
D. Insurance			
1. Life	Ongoing	Depends	Regularly review coverage; increase if necessary.
2. Health and disability	Ongoing	Depends	Regularly review coverage.
3. Property and liability	Ongoing	Depends	Regularly review coverage; drop unnecessary coverage; raise deductibles.
E. Other goals			
1. Have second child	2009 or 2011	$20,000 in lost income; $5,000 in additional expenses per year.	Build financial cushion; budget for additional expenses.
2. Pursue MBA	2011 or 2012	$5,000 per year	Keep spending under control; invest regularly and wisely.

WHAT'S AHEAD

This appendix has just scratched the surface of personal financial planning. We hope it has encouraged you to learn more. Dozens of helpful books, Web sites, and other resources are available. If you can fit it into your class schedule, consider taking a class in personal financial planning. Your college or university probably offers one. Taking such a class may be one of the smartest decisions you make while you're in college.

Business Terms You Need to Know

personal financial management B-2
standard of living B-2

financial plan B-5
credit B-11

Other Important Business Terms

lifestyle B-2
net worth B-7

Projects and Teamwork Applications

1. Prepare a current set of financial statements for yourself using a format similar to the one shown in Figure 2. What do you think your financial statements will look like a year from now? Five years from now?

2. One of the most important tools for managing your personal finances is a budget. The earlier you learn to prepare and follow a budget, the better off you will be. If Figure 3 looks a bit intimidating, there are a variety of interactive budget forms available on the Internet. Go to http://www .nelliemae.com/calc/calc10.asp and fill out the budget worksheet. Compare your entries with the guidelines listed. Remember, a budget has to be realistic and support your overall goals. How difficult will it be for you to follow the budget you prepared?

3. You have probably heard of credit files (or reports). In fact, if you have a credit card, a student loan, or some other form of credit, you already have a credit file. Working with a partner, visit the Federal Trade Commission's website (http://ftc.gov/), searching under the "consumer" category, and the TransUnion Bank website (http://truecredit.com/), searching under the "Credit Learning Center." Review the materials that these websites provide on credit files and credit reporting.
   a. What is a credit file?
   b. What information is contained in a credit file?
   c. Who compiles the information contained in a credit file?
   d. Who has access to a credit file?
   e. Regarding your credit file, what rights do you have?

4. Even though you are still in college, you face a number of important financial issues, everything from paying college expenses to dealing with credit cards. Visit http://www.nhheaf.org/pdfs/ 10steps.pdf listed here and click "10 Steps to Financial Fitness." What are the ten steps? Which of these will be easiest for you to complete? Which will be the most difficult?

5. Analyze your current credit situation. What are your existing debts? How much are you paying each month? Did you borrow for the right reasons? List some steps you think you should start taking to improve your management of credit. Compare your findings with those of a classmate.

Developing a Business Plan

DRAPER FISHER JURVETSON SEARCHES FOR BILLION-DOLLAR IDEAS—MAYBE YOURS?

Every would-be entrepreneur dreams of hatching the next hot business idea, one that changes the world as we know it forever. And every venture capitalist's wish is to find that upcoming entrepreneur first, before competitors. That's what venture capitalists do—take risks, invest in new firms, and help get them off the ground and soaring to new heights for a hoped-for big payoff. Tim Draper of Silicon Valley–based Draper Fisher Jurvetson (DFJ) has had uncanny success in backing high-tech start-ups that go on to revolutionize business. Heard of Hotmail? That was one of Draper's early investments. The company was eventually purchased for $400 million by none other than Microsoft.

More recent successes have included Internet telephony company Skype, which eBay purchased for $2.6 billion, and Chinese search engine Baidu, whose shares skyrocketed more than 350 percent in its first day of trading. DFJ had a 10 percent share in Skype and a 28 percent share in Baidu, which together are worth nearly $1.5 billion for the VC firm. Of course, not all investments pay off, and that's where the risk part of the equation comes into play. But Draper prefers not to dwell on the failures.

So how does DFJ learn about new companies and decide whether they are worth their investment? By talking with entrepreneurs and studying their business plans. Draper says he does a lot of reading—including technical journals, philosophy, science fiction, and history—to help him understand the world and the way it works. But, he adds, "The overwhelming amount of reading I do is business plans and e-mails." He also searches the world through affiliate companies in developing markets such as Ukraine, China, and India for the best new ideas. To cast its net even wider, DFJ put a blog on the Internet encouraging businesspeople to "pitch Tim Draper on your billion-dollar idea." The company narrowed the responses it received to eleven ideas, and those entrepreneurs discussed their plans with Draper via a video conference. One was eventually funded. DFJ has held several of these conferences.

Other areas of interest for the company are memory devices, nanotechnology and life sciences, and alternative, clean energies. The firm aims to be on the cutting edge of the high-tech world because Draper believes that business fuels many more of the solutions to society's problems than government does. He maintains, "The next big energy breakthrough will happen through a business. . . . Medicine has been advanced through business. It turns out that it's the businesspeople that tend to be the ones who solve all this stuff."

Such enthusiasm got Draper's own business off the ground. He got his start with a $6 million loan from the U.S. Small Business Administration. The first three years were rocky, and Draper thought his company might fail. But in 1990, "We had a series of about five IPOs [initial public offerings]. It went from near disaster to the best-performing fund of its ilk. Now there's a picture of me in the lobby of the SBA."

Do you have a great idea for a high-tech start-up—one that can dominate its market? Draper would love to hear about it. The company's Web site features a "Submit Business Plan" link to make it simple. So do your research, go to your computer, and get busy. This appendix can help you plan for your new business adventure, whatever it may be.[1]

APPENDIX OVERVIEW

Many entrepreneurs and small-business owners have written business plans to help them organize their businesses, get them up and running, and raise money for expansion. In this appendix, we cover the basics of business planning: what business plans are, why they're important, and who needs them. We also explain the steps involved in writing a good plan and the major elements it should contain. Finally, we cover additional resources to get you started with your own business plan—to help you bring your unique ideas to reality with a business of your own.

WHAT IS A BUSINESS PLAN?

You may wonder how the millions of different businesses operating in the United States and throughout the world today got their start. Often it is with a formal business plan. A business plan is a written document that articulates what a company's objectives are, how these objectives will be achieved, how the business will be financed, and how much money the company expects to bring in. In short, it describes where a company is, where it wants to go, and how it intends to get there. Elizabeth Wasserman, writing in the magazine MBA Jungle, states that a business plan has to be "a compelling story with drama (a demonstrated need), hope (how your product can fill that need), heroes (the management team), and a happy ending (return on investment)."[2]

Why a Business Plan Is So Important

A well-written business plan can be used for many purposes, but it serves two key functions:

1. It organizes the business and validates its central idea.
2. It summarizes the business and its strategy to obtain funding from lenders and investors.

First, a business plan gives a business formal direction, whether it is just starting, going through a phase of growth, or struggling. The business plan forces the principals—the owners—through rigorous planning, to think through the realities of running and financing a business. In their planning, they consider many details. How will inventory be stored, shipped, and stocked? Where should the business be located? How will the business use the Internet? And most important, how will the business make enough money to make it all worthwhile?

A business plan also gives the owners a well-reasoned blueprint to refer to when daily challenges arise, and it acts as a benchmark by which successes and disappointments can be measured. Additionally, a solid business plan will sell the potential owner on the validity of the idea. In some cases, the by-product of developing the plan is demonstrating to a starry-eyed person that he or she is trying to start a bad business. In other words, the process of writing a plan benefits a would-be businessperson as much as the final plan benefits potential investors.

Finally, a business plan articulates the business's strategy to financiers who can fund the business, and it is usually required to obtain a bank loan. Lenders and venture capitalists need to see that the business owner has thought through the critical issues and presented a promising idea before they will consider investing in it. They are, after all, interested in whether it will bring them significant returns.

Who Needs a Business Plan?

Some people mistakenly believe that they need a business plan only if it will land on the desk of a venture capitalist or the loan committee of the company's bank. Others think that writing a plan is unnecessary if their bank or lending institution doesn't require it. Such assumptions miss the point of planning, because a business plan acts as a map to guide the way through the often tangled roads of running a business. The answer to the question of who needs a plan is anyone who is serious abut being successful. Every small-business owner should develop a business plan because it empowers that person to take control.

HOW DO I WRITE A BUSINESS PLAN?

Developing a business plan should mean something different to everyone. Think of a business plan as a clear statement of a business's identity. A travel agency has a different identity from a newly launched magazine, which has yet a different identity from a restaurant hoping to expand its share of the market. Each business has unique objectives and processes, and each faces different obstacles.

At the same time, good business plans contain some similar elements no matter who the business owner is, what he or she sells, or how far the owner is into the venture. A savvy business owner molds the elements of a business plan into a professional and personal representation of the firm's needs and goals. The plan should also realistically assess the risks and obstacles specific to the business and present solutions for overcoming them.

Because the document is important, it takes time to collect needed information and organize it. Don't be misled into believing that you will simply sit down and begin writing. Before any writing begins, the business owner must become an expert in his or her field. Readying important information about the company and the market will make the writing easier and faster. Some critical pieces of information to have on hand are the following items:

- The company's name, legal form of organization, location, financial highlights, and owners or shareholders (if any).
- Organization charts, list of top managers, consultants or directors, and employee agreements.
- Marketing research, customer surveys, and information about the company's major competitors.
- Product information, including goods and services offered; brochures; patents, licenses, and trademarks; and research and development plans.
- Marketing plans and materials.
- Financial statements (both current and forecasted).

The business owner also must do a lot of soul searching and brainstorming to answer important questions necessary to build the backbone of a healthy business. Figure C.1 lists some critical questions to ask yourself.

Once equipped with these answers, you can begin writing the document, which can be anywhere between 10 and 50 pages long. The length of the plan depends on the complexity of the company, whether the company is a start-up (established companies have longer histories to detail), and what the plan will be used for. Regardless of size, the document should be well organized and easy to use, especially if the business plan is intended for external uses, such as

> **"They Said It"**
>
> "Good plans shape good decisions. That's why good planning helps to make elusive dreams come true."
> —Lester R. Bittel (b. 1918)
> In The Nine Master Keys of Management

Figure

C.1 Self-Evaluation Questions

Take a few minutes to read and answer these questions.
Don't worry about answering in too much detail at this point.
The questions are preliminary and
intended to help you think through your venture.

1. In general terms, how would you explain your idea to a friend?

2. What is the purpose or objective of your venture?

3. What service are you going to provide, or what goods are you going to manufacture?

4. Is there any significant difference between what you are planning and what already exists?

5. How will the quality of your product compare with competitive offerings?

6. What is the overview of the industry or service sector you are going to enter? Write it out.

7. What is the history, current status, and future of the industry?

8. Who is your customer or client base?

9. Where and by whom will your good or service be marketed?

10. How much will you charge for the product you are planning?

11. Where is the financing going to come from to initiate your venture?

12. What training and experience do you have that qualifies you for this venture?

13. Does such training or experience give you a significant edge?

14. If you lack specific experience, how do you plan to gain it?

to secure financing. Number all pages, include a table of contents, and make sure the format is attractive and professional. Include two or three illustrative charts or graphs and highlight the sections and important points with headings and bulleted lists. Figure C.2 outlines the major sections of a business plan.

The following paragraphs discuss the most common elements of an effective business plan. When you need additional instruction or information as you write, refer to the "Resources" section at the end of the appendix.

Executive Summary

The primary purpose of an executive summary is to entice readers sufficiently to read more about the business. An **executive summary** is a one- to two-page snapshot of what the overall business plan explains in detail. Consider it a business plan within a business plan. Through its enthusiasm and quick momentum, the summary should capture the reader's imagination.

Figure

C.2

Outline of a Business Plan

Describe your strategy for succeeding in a positive, intriguing, and realistic way and briefly yet thoroughly answer the first questions anyone would have about your business: who, what, why, when, where, and how. Financiers always turn to the executive summary first. If it isn't well presented or lacks the proper information, they will quickly move on to the next business plan in the stack. The executive summary is just as important to people funding the business with personal resources, however, because it channels their motivations into an articulate mission statement. It is a good idea to write the summary last, because it will inevitably be revised once the business plan takes final shape.

To write an effective executive summary, focus on the issues that are most important to your business's success and save the supporting matters for the body. The executive summary should describe the business's strategy and goals, the good or service it is selling, and the advantages it has over the competition. It should also give a snapshot of how much money will be required to launch the business, how it will be used, and how the lenders or investors will recoup their funds.

Introduction

The **introduction** follows the executive summary. After the executive summary has offered an attractive synopsis, the introduction should begin to discuss the fine details of the business. It should be crafted to include any material the upcoming marketing and financing sections do not cover. The introduction should describe the company, the management team, and the product in detail. If one of these topics is particularly noteworthy for your business, you may want to present that topic as its own section. Listen to what you write and respond as the plan takes shape.

Include basic information about the company—its past, present, and future. What are the company's roots, what is its current status, and what actions need to be taken to achieve its goals? If you are starting a company, include a description of the evolution of the concept. Be sure to tie all of the business's goals and plans to the industry in which it will operate, and describe the industry itself.

A business doesn't run itself, of course. People are the heart of a business, so write an appealing picture of the business's management team. Who are the key players and how does their experience resonate with the company's goals? Describe their—or your, if you are a sole proprietor—education, training, and experience, and highlight and refer to their résumés included later in the plan. Be honest, however—not all businesses are started by experts. If you lack demonstrated experience in a certain area, explain how you plan to get it.

Also describe the product, the driving force behind the venture. What are you offering, and why is it special? What are the costs of the service or price tag on the good? Analyze the features of the offering and the effect these features have on the overall cost.

The Business Plan

I. Executive Summary
- Who, what, when, where, why, and how?

II. Table of Contents

III. Introduction
- The concept and the company
- The management team
- The product

IV. Marketing Strategy
- Demographics
- Trends
- Market penetration
- Potential sales revenue

V. Financing the Business
- Cash flow analysis
- Pro forma balance sheet
- Income statement

VI. Résumés of Principals

Web Sites

- *Entrepreneur* and *Inc.* magazines offer knowledgeable guides to writing a business plan. *Entrepreneur*'s Web site also contains sample business plans.

  http://www.entrepreneur.com
  http://www.inc.com

- Deloitte & Touche offers a useful document called "Writing an Effective Business Plan." It can be found on the firm's Web site.

  http://www.deloitte.com

- American Express offers several business planning tools on its Web site.

  http://www.americanexpress.com/open

- If you are hoping to obtain funding with your business plan, you should familiarize yourself with what venture capitalists are looking for in a business plan. An example can be found at the following site:

  http://cpvp.com/submit/businessplan.html

- New Enterprise Associates has a useful Web site.

  http://www.nea.com

Software

Business-planning software can give an initial shape to your business plan. However, a word of caution is in order if you write a business plan using the software's template. Bankers and potential investors, such as venture capitalists, read so many business plans that those based on templates may sink to the bottom of the pile. Also, if you aren't looking for funding, using software can undercut a chief purpose of writing a plan—learning about your unique idea. So think twice before you deprive yourself of that experience. Remember, software is a tool. It can help you get started, stay organized, and build a professional-looking business plan, but it can't actually write the plan for you.

Associations and Organizations

Many government and professional organizations provide assistance to would-be business owners. Here is a partial list:

- The U.S. Small Business Administration offers planning materials, along with other resources.

  http://www.sba.gov/starting_business

The SBA also has a center specifically designed for female entrepreneurs.

  http://www.onlinewbc.gov

- One of the missions of the Ewing Marion Kauffman Foundation is to encourage entrepreneurship across the U.S. The foundation's Web site offers an online resource center for new and growing businesses.

  http://entreworld.com

Glossary

360-degree performance review employee performance review that gathers feedback from co-workers, supervisors, managers, and sometimes customers.

401(k) plan retirement savings plan to which employees can make pretax contributions; sometimes employers make additional contributions to the plan.

accounting process of measuring, interpreting, and communicating financial information to support internal and external business decision making.

accounting process set of activities involved in converting information about individual transactions into financial statements.

accrual accounting accounting method that records revenue and expenses when they occur, not necessarily when cash actually changes hands.

acquisition procedure in which one firm purchases the property and assumes the obligations of another.

activity ratios measures of how efficiently a firm utilizes its assets.

actuarial table probability calculation of the number of specific events—such as deaths, injuries, fire, or windstorm losses—expected to occur within a given year.

advertising paid nonpersonal communication delivered through various media and designed to inform, persuade, or remind members of a particular audience.

affective conflict disagreement that focuses on individuals or personal issues.

affinity program marketing effort sponsored by an organization that solicits involvement by individuals who share common interests and activities.

agency legal relationship whereby one party, called a principal, appoints another party, called an agent, to enter into contracts with third parties on the principal's behalf.

alien corporation firm incorporated in one nation and operating in another nation.

angel investors wealthy individuals who invest directly in a new venture in exchange for an equity stake.

appellate courts courts that hear appeals of decisions made at the general trial court level; both the federal and state systems have appellate courts.

application service provider (ASP) specialist in providing both the computers and the application support for managing information systems for clients.

application software programs that carry out a specific task such as word processing.

arbitration bringing in an impartial third party called an arbitrator to render a binding decision in a dispute.

assembly line manufacturing technique that carries the product on a conveyor system past several workstations where workers perform specialized tasks.

asset anything of value owned or leased by a business.

autocratic leadership management approach whereby leaders make decisions on their own without consulting employees.

balance of payments overall money flows into and out of a country.

balance of trade difference between a nation's exports and imports.

balance sheet statement of a firm's financial position—what it owns and the claims against its assets—at a particular point in time.

balanced budget situation in which total revenues raised by taxes and fees equal total proposed government spending for the year.

bankruptcy legal nonpayment of financial obligations.

banner ad ad placed by an organization on another organization's Web site; interested parties click the ad for more information.

basic accounting equation relationship that states that assets equal liabilities plus owners' equity.

benchmarking process of determining other companies' standards and best practices.

blog online journal written by a blogger.

board of directors elected governing body of a corporation.

bond rating tool used by investors to assess the credit risk of municipal and corporate bonds.

bond certificate of indebtedness sold to raise long-term funds for a corporation or government agency.

bot software program that allows online shoppers to compare the price of a particular product offered by several online retailers.

bottom line another term for net income or profits after taxes.

boycott effort to prevent people from purchasing a firm's goods or services.

brand equity added value that a respected and successful name gives to a product.

brand name part of a brand consisting of words or letters that form a name that identifies and distinguishes an offering from those of competitors.

brand name, term, sign, symbol, design, or some combination that identifies the products of one firm and differentiates them from competitors' offerings.

branding process of creating an identity in consumers' minds for a good, service, or company; a major marketing tool in contemporary business.

breach of contract violation of a valid contract.

breakeven analysis pricing technique used to determine the minimum sales volume a product must generate at a certain price level to cover all costs.

brokerage firm financial intermediary that buys and sells securities for individual and institutional investors.

budget organization's plan for how it will raise and spend money during a given period of time.

budget deficit funding shortfall in which government spends more than the amount of funds raised through taxes and fees.

budget surplus excess funding that occurs when government spends less than the amount of funds raised through taxes and fees.

business all profit-seeking activities and enterprises that provide goods and services necessary to an economic system.

business (B2B) product good or service purchased to be used, either directly or indirectly, in the production of other goods for resale.

business ethics standards of conduct and moral values involving right and wrong actions arising in the work environment.

business incubator organization that provides temporary low-cost, shared facilities to small start-up ventures.

business interruption insurance insurance that protects firms from financial losses resulting from the interruption of business operations.

business law aspects of law that most directly influence and regulate the management of business activity.

business plan written document that provides an orderly statement of a company's goals, the methods by which it intends to achieve those goals, and the standards by which it will measure achievements.

business-to-business (B2B) e-business electronic business transactions between organizations using the Internet.

business-to-consumer (B2C) e-business selling directly to consumers over the Internet.

call provision provision that allows a bond issuer to buy the bond back from investors before maturity.

capital production inputs consisting of technology, tools, information, and physical facilities.

capitalism economic system that rewards firms for their ability to perceive and serve the needs and demands of consumers; also called the private enterprise system.

cash budget accounting report that tracks the firm's cash inflows and outflows; usually prepared monthly.

cash flow sources of cash minus uses of cash during a specified period of time.

cash value policy type of life insurance that combines a death benefit with some sort of savings feature.

category advisor vendor that is designated by the business customer as the major supplier to deal with all other suppliers for a special purchase and to present the entire package to the business buyer.

category manager person who oversees an entire group of products and assumes profit responsibility for the product group.

cause advertising form of institutional advertising that promotes a specific viewpoint on a public issue as a way to influence public opinion and the legislative process.

cause marketing marketing that promotes a cause or social issue, such as preventing child abuse, antilittering efforts, and anti-smoking campaigns.

Central American Free Trade Agreement (CAFTA) agreement among the United States, Costa Rica, the Dominican Republic, El Salvador, Guatemala, Honduras, and Nicaragua to reduce tariffs and trade restrictions.

centralization decision making based at the top of the management hierarchy.

certified public accountant (CPA) accountant who meets specified educational and experiential requirements and has passed a comprehensive examination on accounting theory and practice.

chain of command set of relationships that indicates who directs which activities and who reports to whom.

change agent manager who revitalizes an established firm to keep it competitive.

channel conflict conflict between two or more members of a supply chain, such as manufacturers, wholesalers, and retailers.

chief information officer (CIO) executive responsible for managing a firm's information technology.

Class-Action Fairness Act of 2005 law that moves most large, multistate class-action lawsuits to federal courts, ensures judicial oversight of plaintiffs' compensation, bases lawyers' compensation on awards actually distributed or actual time spent, and ensures that plaintiffs' interests are protected equally with their lawyers'.

classic entrepreneur person who identifies a business opportunity and allocates available resources to tap that market.

click-through rate percentage of people presented with a Web banner ad who click on it.

cobranding cooperative arrangement in which two or more businesses team up to closely link their names on a single product.

code of conduct formal statement that defines how the organization expects employees to resolve ethical issues.

cognitive ability tests tests that measure job candidates' abilities in perceptual speed, verbal comprehension, numerical aptitude, general reasoning, and spatial aptitude.

cognitive conflict disagreement that focuses on problem- and issue-related differences of opinion.

collective bargaining process of negotiation between management and union representatives for the purpose of arriving at mutually acceptable wages and working conditions for employees.

comarketing cooperative arrangement in which two businesses jointly market each other's products.

committee organization organizational structure that places authority and responsibility jointly in the hands of a group of individuals rather than a single manager.

common law body of law arising out of judicial decisions, some of which can be traced back to early England.

common stock shares of ownership in a corporation.

communication meaningful exchange of information through messages.

communism planned economic system in which private property is eliminated, goods are owned in common, and factors of production and production decisions are controlled by the state.

competition battle among businesses for consumer acceptance.

competitive differentiation unique combination of organizational abilities, products, and approaches that sets a company apart from competitors in the minds of customers.

competitive pricing pricing strategy that tries to reduce the emphasis on price competition by matching other firms' prices and concentrating marketing efforts on the product, distribution, and promotional elements of the marketing mix.

compressed workweek scheduling option that allows employees to work the regular number of hours per week in fewer than the typical five days.

computer-aided design (CAD) system for interactions between a designer and a computer to create a product, facility, or part that meets predetermined specifications.

computer-aided manufacturing (CAM) electronic tools to analyze CAD output and determine necessary steps to implement the design, followed by electronic transmission of instructions to guide the activities of production equipment.

computer-integrated manufacturing (CIM) production system that integrates computer tools and human workers to design products, control machines, handle materials, and control production.

conceptual skills ability to see the organization as a unified whole and to understand how each part interacts with others.

conflict of interest situation in which an employee must make a decision about a business's welfare versus personal gain.

conflict antagonistic interaction in which one party attempts to thwart the intentions or goals of another.

conglomerate merger combination of two or more unrelated firms, usually with the goal of diversification, spurring sales growth, or spending a cash surplus that might otherwise make the firm a tempting target for a takeover attempt.

consumer (B2C) product good or service that is purchased by end users.

consumer behavior actions of ultimate consumers directly involved in obtaining, consuming, and disposing of products and the decision processes that precede and follow these actions.

consumer orientation business philosophy that focuses first on determining unmet consumer needs and then designing products to satisfy those needs.

Consumer Price Index (CPI) monthly measure of changes in retail price levels by comparisons of changes in the prices of a "market basket" of goods and services most commonly purchased by urban consumers.

consumerism public demand that a business consider the wants and needs of its customers in making decisions.

contingency planning plans that allow a firm to resume operations as quickly and as smoothly as possible after a crisis while openly communicating with the public about what happened.

contract legally enforceable agreement between two or more parties regarding a specified act or thing.

controller chief accounting manager; the person who keeps the company's books, prepares financial statements, and conducts internal audits.

controlling function of evaluating an organization's performance to determine whether it is accomplishing its objectives.

convenience product item the consumer seeks to purchase frequently, immediately, and with little effort.

conversion rate percentage of visitors to a Web site who make a purchase.

cooperative advertising allowances provided by marketers in which they share the cost of local advertising of their firm's product or product line with channel partners.

cooperative organization whose owners join forces to collectively operate all or part of the functions in their business.

copyright protection of written material such as books, designs, cartoon illustrations, photos, and computer software.

core inflation rate the underlying inflation rate of the economy after energy and food prices are removed.

corporate charter legal document that formally establishes a corporation.

corporate culture organization's system of principles, beliefs, and values.

corporate philanthropy act of an organization giving something back to the communities in which it earns profits.

corporate Web site Web site designed to increase a firm's visibility, promote its offerings, and provide information to interested parties.

corporation business that stands as a legal entity with assets and liabilities separate from those of its owner(s).

cost-based pricing adding a percentage (markup) to the base cost of a product to cover overhead costs and generate profits.

countertrade barter agreement whereby trade between two or more nations involves payment made in the form of local products instead of currency.

creative selling personal selling that involves skillful proposals of solutions for the customer's needs.

creativity capacity to develop novel solutions to perceived organizational problems.

credit receiving money, goods, or services on the basis of an agreement between the lender and the borrower that the loan is for a specified period of time with a specified rate of interest.

critical path sequence of operations that requires the longest time for completion.

critical thinking ability to analyze and assess information to pinpoint problems or opportunities.

cross-functional team team made up of members from different functions, such as production, marketing, and finance.

customer satisfaction ability of a good or service to meet or exceed a buyer's needs and expectations.

damages financial payments to compensate for a loss and related suffering.

data raw facts and figures that may or may not be relevant to a business decision.

data mining computer searches of customer data to detect patterns and relationships.

data warehouse customer database that allows managers to combine data from several different organizational functions.

database centralized integrated collection of data resources.

debenture bond backed by the reputation of the issuer rather than by a specific pledge of a company's assets.

debt capital funds obtained through borrowing.

debt financing borrowed funds that entrepreneurs must repay.

decentralization decision making based at lower levels of the organization.

decision making process of recognizing a problem or opportunity, evaluating alternative solutions, selecting and implementing an alternative, and assessing the results.

decision support system (DSS) information system that quickly provides relevant data to help businesspeople make decisions and choose courses of action.

deflation falling prices caused by a combination of reduced consumer demand and decreases in the costs of raw materials, component parts, human resources, and other factors of production.

delegation act of assigning work activities to subordinates.

demand willingness and ability of buyers to purchase goods and services.

demand curve graph of the amount of a product that buyers will purchase at different prices; generally slopes downward to reflect larger quantities likely to be purchased as prices decline.

demand deposits deposits held in banks and other financial institutions that are payable on demand, such as checking accounts.

democratic leadership management approach whereby leaders delegate assignments, ask employees for suggestions, and encourage their participation.

demographic segmentation dividing markets on the basis of various demographic or socioeconomic characteristics such as gender, age, income, occupation, household size, stage in family life cycle, education, or ethnic group.

demographics statistical characteristics of the segment of the market that might purchase a product.

departmentalization process of dividing work activities into units within the organization.

depository institutions financial institutions that accept deposits that can be converted into cash on demand.

deregulation regulatory trend toward elimination of legal restraints on competition in industries previously served by a single firm in an attempt to improve customer service and lower prices through increased competition.

desktop publishing computer technology that allows users to design and produce attractively formatted documents.

devaluation reduction in a currency's value relative to other currencies or to a fixed standard.

direct distribution channel marketing channel that moves goods directly from producer to ultimate user.

directing guiding and motivating employees to accomplish organizational objectives.

disability income insurance insurance that pays benefits to those who cannot work due to some sort of a disability.

discount rate rate the Federal Reserve charges member banks for loans.

dispatching phase of production control in which the manager instructs each department on what work to do and the time allowed for its completion.

distribution channel path through which products—and legal ownership of them—flow from producer to consumers or business users.

distribution strategy planning that ensures that customers find their products in the proper quantities at the right times and places.

diversity blending individuals of different genders, ethnic backgrounds, cultures, religions, ages, and physical and mental abilities to enhance a firm's chances of success.

domestic corporation firm that operates in the state where it is incorporated.

double-entry bookkeeping process by which accounting transactions are entered; each individual transaction always has an offsetting transaction.

downsizing process of reducing the number of employees within a firm by eliminating jobs.

dumping selling products abroad at prices below production costs or below typical prices in the home market to capture market share from domestic competitors.

economics social science that analyzes the choices people and governments make in allocating scarce resources.

electronic bulletin board Internet chat room that allows users to post and read messages on a specific topic.

electronic business (e-business) conducting business via the Internet.

electronic communications network (ECN) computerized market that directly matches buyers and sellers.

electronic data interchange (EDI) computer-to-computer exchanges of invoices, purchase orders, price quotations, and other information between buyers and sellers.

electronic exchange online marketplace that caters to a specific industry's needs.

electronic funds transfer systems computerized systems for conducting financial transactions over electronic links.

electronic shopping cart file that holds items that the online shopper has chosen to buy.

electronic signatures form of electronic identification.

electronic storefront company Web site that sells products to customers.

electronic wallet computer data file set up by an online shopper at an e-business site's checkout counter that contains not only electronic cash but credit card information and owner identification.

embargo total ban on importing specific products or a total halt to trading with a particular country.

employee benefits rewards such as retirement plans, health insurance, vacation, and tuition reimbursement provided for employees either entirely or in part at the company's expense.

employee ownership business in which workers purchase shares of stock in the firm that employs them.

employee stock ownership plan (ESOP) plan that benefits employees by giving them ownership stakes in the companies for which they work.

empowerment giving employees authority and responsibility to make decisions about their work without traditional managerial approval and control.

encryption process of encoding data for security purposes, using software that encodes or scrambles messages.

end-use segmentation marketing strategy that focuses on the precise way a B2B purchaser will use a product.

enterprise resource planning (ERP) system information system that collects, processes, and provides information about an organization's various functions.

entrepreneur person who seeks a profitable opportunity and takes the necessary risks to set up and operate a business.

entrepreneurship willingness to take risks to create and operate a business.

environmental impact study study that analyzes how a proposed plant would affect the quality of life in the surrounding area.

e-procurement use of the Internet by businesses and government agencies to solicit bids and purchase goods and services from suppliers.

Equal Employment Opportunity Commission (EEOC) government agency created to increase job opportunities for women and minorities and to help end discrimination based on race, color, religion, disability, gender, or national origin in any personnel action.

equilibrium price prevailing market price; the point at which the quantity demanded of a product equals the quantity supplied.

equity capital funds provided by the firm's owners when they reinvest earnings, make additional contributions, or issue stock to investors.

equity financing funds invested in new ventures in exchange for part ownership.

European Union (EU) 25-nation European economic alliance.

event marketing marketing or sponsoring short-term events such as athletic competitions and cultural and charitable performances.

everyday low pricing (EDLP) pricing strategy devoted to maintaining continuous low prices rather than relying on short-term price cuts such as cents-off coupons, rebates, and special sales.

exchange control restriction on importation of certain products or against certain companies to reduce trade and expenditures of foreign currency.

exchange process activity in which two or more parties give something of value to each other to satisfy perceived needs.

exchange rate value of one nation's currency relative to the currencies of other countries.

exchange-traded fund (ETF) fund with a fixed number of shares outstanding that trades on a stock market; generally invests in the securities that make up a well-known index.

exclusive distribution distribution strategy involving limited market coverage by a single retailer or wholesaler in a specific geographical territory.

executive summary one- to two-page snapshot of what the overall business plan explains in detail.

executive support system (ESS) system that allows top managers to access a firm's primary databases.

expert system computer program that imitates human thinking through complicated sets of "if-then" rules.

exports domestically produced goods and services sold in other countries.

external communication meaningful exchange of information through messages transmitted between an organization and its major audiences.

extranet secure networks accessible from outside a firm, but only by authorized third parties.

factors of production four basic inputs for effective operation: natural resources, capital, human resources, and entrepreneurship.

family brand brand name used to identify several different, but related, products.

family leave granting up to 12 weeks of unpaid leave annually for employees who have or adopt a child, are becoming foster parents, are caring for a seriously ill relative or spouse, or are themselves seriously ill.

Federal Reserve System U.S. central bank.

fee-for-service plan traditional form of health insurance in which the insured chooses his or her healthcare provider, pays for treatment, and is reimbursed by

the insurance company; also called an indemnity plan.

finance business function of planning, obtaining, and managing a company's funds in order to accomplish its objectives effectively and efficiently.

Financial Accounting Standards Board (FASB) organization that interprets and modifies GAAP in the United States.

financial manager executive who develops and implements the firm's financial plan and determines the most appropriate sources and uses of funds.

financial plan document that specifies the funds a firm will need for a period of time, the timing of inflows and outflows, and the most appropriate sources and uses of funds.

financial system system by which funds are transferred from savers to users.

financing section section of a business plan that demonstrates the cost of the product, operating expenses, expected sales revenue and profit, and the amount of the business owner's own funds that will be invested to get the business up and running.

firewall electronic barrier between a company's internal network and the Internet that limits access into and out of the network.

fiscal policy government spending and taxation decisions designed to control inflation, reduce unemployment, improve the general welfare of citizens, and encourage economic growth.

flexible benefit plan benefit system that offers employees a range of options from which they may choose the types of benefits they receive.

flexible manufacturing system (FMS) facility that workers can quickly modify to manufacture different products.

flexible work plan employment that allows personnel to adjust their working hours and places of work to accommodate their personal needs.

flextime scheduling system that allows employees to set their own work hours within constraints specified by the firm.

follow-up phase of production control in which employees and their supervisors spot problems in the production process and determine needed adjustments.

foreign corporation firm that operates in states where it is not incorporated.

foreign licensing agreement international agreement in which one firm allows another to produce or sell its product, or use its trade-

mark, patent, or manufacturing processes, in a specific geographical area in return for royalties or other compensation.

formal communication channel messages that flow within the chain of command defined by an organization.

franchise contractual agreement in which a franchisee gains the right to produce and/or sell the franchisor's products under that company's brand name if they agree to certain operating requirements.

franchisee small-business owner who contracts to sell the good or service of a supplier (the franchisor) in exchange for a payment (usually a flat fee plus a percentage of sales).

franchising contractual agreement that specifies the methods by which a dealer can produce and market a supplier's good or service.

franchisor business owner who permits the franchisee to sell its products and use its name, as well as providing a variety of marketing, management, and other services in return for the payment of various fees and a percentage of sales.

free-rein leadership management style of leaders who believe in minimal supervision and leave most decisions to their subordinates.

frequency marketing marketing initiative that rewards frequent purchases with cash, rebates, merchandise, or other premiums.

full and fair disclosure requirement that investors should be told all relevant information by stock or bond issuers so they can make informed decisions.

General Agreement on Tariffs and Trade (GATT) international trade accord that substantially reduced worldwide tariffs and other trade barriers.

generally accepted accounting principles (GAAP) principles that encompass the conventions, rules, and procedures for determining acceptable accounting practices at a particular time.

geographical segmentation dividing an overall market into homogeneous groups on the basis of their locations.

global business strategy offering a standardized, worldwide product and selling it in essentially the same manner throughout a firm's domestic and foreign markets.

goal target, objective, or result that someone tries to accomplish.

goal-setting theory theory that people will be motivated to the extent to which they accept specific, challenging goals and receive feedback that indicates their progress toward goal achievement.

government accountant accountant who performs professional services similar to those of management accountants and determines how efficiently government agencies accomplish their objectives.

government bond bond issued by the U.S. Treasury.

grapevine internal information channel that transmits information from unofficial sources.

green marketing marketing strategy that promotes environmentally safe products and production methods.

grievance formal complaint filed by an employee or a union that management is violating some provision of a union contract.

gross domestic product (GDP) sum of all goods and services produced within a country's boundaries during a specific time period, such as a year.

guerrilla marketing innovative, low-cost marketing schemes designed to get consumers' attention in unusual ways.

handheld devices small computerized devices that operate on rechargeable batteries; includes personal digital assistants and smart phones.

hardware all tangible elements of a computer system.

health insurance insurance that covers losses due to illness or accidents.

health maintenance organization (HMO) organization that, in return for a monthly fee, provides all of the insured's healthcare.

high-context culture a society in which communication depends not only on the message itself but also on nonverbal cues, past and present experiences, and personal relationships between the parties.

home-based business company operated from the residence of the business owner.

horizontal merger combination of two or more firms in the same industry that wish to diversify, increase their customer bases, cut costs, or offer expanded product lines.

human resource management function of attracting, developing, and retaining enough qualified employees to perform the

activities necessary to accomplish organizational objectives.

human resources production inputs consisting of anyone who works, including both the physical labor and the intellectual inputs contributed by workers.

human skills interpersonal skills that enable a manager to work effectively with and through people; the ability to communicate with, motivate, and lead employees to accomplish assigned activities.

imports foreign goods and services purchased by domestic customers.

income statement financial record of a company's revenues, expenses, and profits over a period of time.

individual brand different brand names given to each product within a line.

inflation rising prices caused by a combination of excess consumer demand and increases in the costs of raw materials, component parts, human resources, and other factors of production.

infomercial form of broadcast direct marketing; 30-minute programs that resemble regular TV programs, but are devoted to selling goods or services.

informal communication channel messages outside formally authorized channels within an organization's hierarchy.

information knowledge gained from processing data.

infrastructure basic systems of communication, transportation, and energy facilities in a country.

initial public offering (IPO) first sale of a firm's stock to the investing public.

insider trading use of material, nonpublic information to make investor profits.

institutional advertising promotion of concepts, ideas, philosophies, or goodwill for industries, companies, organizations, or government entities.

institutional investors large investors such as pension funds and life insurance companies that invest for the benefit of others.

insurable interest demonstration that a direct financial loss will result if some event occurs.

insurable risk requirement that a pure risk must meet for the insurer to agree to provide protection.

insurance contract by which the insurer, for a fee (the premium), agrees to reimburse

another firm or individual a sum of money if a loss occurs.

integrated marketing communications (IMC) coordination of all promotional activities—media advertising, direct mail, personal selling, sales promotion, and public relations—to produce a unified customer-focused message.

integrity adhering to deeply felt ethical principles in business situations.

intensive distribution distribution strategy that involves placing a firm's products in nearly every available outlet.

international law regulations that govern international commerce.

International Monetary Fund (IMF) organization created to promote trade, eliminate barriers, and make short-term loans to member nations that are unable to meet their budgets.

International Organization for Standardization (ISO) organization whose mission is to promote the development of standardized products to facilitate trade and cooperation across national borders.

intranet a computer network that links employees and other authorized users.

intrapreneur entrepreneurially oriented person who develops innovations within a large organization.

intrapreneurship process of promoting innovation within the structure of an existing organization.

introduction section of a business plan that describes the company, the management team, and the product in detail.

inventory control management effort to balance the priority of limiting inventory costs with that of meeting customer demand.

investment banker financial intermediary that purchases an issue or securities from the firm or government and then resells the issue to investors.

investment-grade bond corporate or municipal bond with a rating of BBB or above.

job enlargement job design that expands an employee's responsibilities by increasing the number and variety of tasks assigned to the worker.

job enrichment change in job duties to increase employees' authority in planning their work, deciding how it should be done, and learning new skills.

job sharing program management decision that allows two or more employees to divide the tasks of one job.

joint venture partnership between companies formed for a specific undertaking.

judiciary branch of the government charged with deciding disputes among parties through the application of laws.

junk bond corporate or municipal bond with a rating of BB or below.

just-in-time (JIT) system management philosophy aimed at improving profits and return on investment by minimizing costs and eliminating waste through cutting inventory on hand.

labor union group of workers who have banded together to achieve common goals in the areas of wages, hours, and working conditions.

law of large numbers concept that seemingly random events will follow a predictable pattern if enough events are observed.

law standards set by government and society in the form of either legislation or custom.

leadership ability to direct or inspire people to attain organizational goals.

leverage technique of increasing the rate of return on an investment by financing it with borrowed funds.

leverage ratios measures of the extent to which a company relies on borrowed funds.

liability claim against a firm's assets by a creditor.

liability insurance insurance that protects against financial losses to others for acts for which the insured was responsible.

life insurance insurance that protects people against the financial losses that occur with premature death.

lifestyle expression of how one lives one's daily life.

lifestyle entrepreneur person who starts a business to reduce work hours and create a more relaxed lifestyle.

lifetime value of a customer revenues and intangible benefits (referrals and customer feedback) from a customer over the life of the relationship, minus the amount the company must spend to acquire and serve that customer.

limit order investor's request to buy or sell a security but specifying a maximum price (if buying) or a minimum price (if selling).

limited liability company (LLC) legal form of organization allowing business owners to secure the corporate advantage of limited liability while avoiding the double taxation characteristic of corporations.

line manager executive involved with the functions of production, financing, or marketing.

line organization organizational structure that establishes a direct flow of authority from the chief executive to subordinates.

line-and-staff organization structure that combines the direct flow of authority of a line organization with staff departments that support the line departments.

liquidity ratios measures of a firm's ability to meet its short-term obligations.

listening receiving a message and interpreting its intended meaning by grasping the facts and feelings it conveys.

local area network (LAN) computer network that connects machines within limited areas, such as one building or several buildings near each other; allows personal computers to share printers, documents, and information.

lockout management decision to put pressure on union members by closing the firm.

logistics activities involved in controlling the flow of goods, services, and information among members of the supply chain.

low-context culture a society in which communication tends to rely on explicit written and verbal messages.

M1 measure of the money supply that equals the total of coins and currency in circulation plus checking and other demand deposit account balances.

M2 a measure of the money supply that equals M1 plus savings account and money market mutual fund balances.

macroeconomics study of a nation's overall economic issues, such as how an economy maintains and allocates resources and how a government's policies affect the standards of living of its citizens.

mainframe computer system containing the most extensive storage capacity and the fastest processing speeds.

make, buy, or lease decision choosing whether to manufacture a needed product or component in house, purchase it from an outside supplier, or lease it.

managed care plan healthcare plan in which most, if not all, of the insured's healthcare bills are paid by the insurance company; in exchange, the insured has much less say over his or her treatment.

management process of achieving organizational objectives through people and other resources.

management accountant accountant who works for a company other than a public accounting firm.

management development program training designed to improve the skills and broaden the knowledge of current and potential executives.

management information system (MIS) organized method for providing past, present, and projected information on internal operations as well as external intelligence to support decision making.

manufacturer's (national) brand brand offered and promoted by a manufacturer or producer.

market order investor's request to buy or sell a security at the current market price.

market penetration percentage of the market that has purchased your product.

market segmentation process of dividing a total market into several relatively homogeneous groups.

marketing organizational function and set of processes for creating, communicating, and delivering value to customers and for managing customer relationships in ways that benefit the organization and its stakeholders.

marketing concept company-wide consumer orientation to promote long-run success.

marketing mix blending the four elements of marketing strategy—product, distribution, promotion, and pricing—to satisfy chosen customer segments.

marketing research collecting and evaluating information to support marketing decision making.

marketing strategy section of a business plan that presents information describing the market's need for a product and how the business will satisfy it.

marketing Web site Web site whose main purpose is to increase purchases by visitors.

Maslow's hierarchy of needs theory of motivation proposed by Abraham Maslow. According to the theory, people have five levels of needs that they seek to satisfy: physiological, safety, social, esteem, and self-actualization.

mass production system for manufacturing products in large amounts through effective combinations of specialized labor, mechanization, and standardization.

materials requirement planning (MRP) computer-based production planning system by which a firm can ensure that it has needed parts and materials available at the right time and place in the correct amounts.

matrix structure project management structure that links employees from different parts of the organization to work together on specific projects.

mediation dispute resolution process that uses a third party, called a mediator, to make recommendations for settling labor-management differences.

Medicare health insurance program for those age 65 and older.

merger combination of two or more firms to form one company.

microeconomics study of small economic units, such as individual consumers, families, and businesses.

microloans Small Business Administration-guaranteed loans of up to $35,000 made to start-ups and other very small firms.

middle management second tier in the management pyramid that focuses on specific operations within the organizations.

minicomputer intermediate-size computer—more compact and less expensive than a mainframe but more powerful and expensive than a personal computer.

mission statement written explanation of an organization's business intentions and aims.

missionary selling indirect selling in which specialized salespeople promote the firm's goodwill among customers, often by assisting them in product use.

mixed market economy economic system that combines characteristics of both planned and market economies in varying degrees, including the presence of both government ownership and private enterprise.

monetary policy using interest rates and other tools to control the supply of money and credit in the economy.

money anything generally accepted as payment for goods and services.

money market instruments short-term debt securities issued by corporations, financial institutions, and governments.

monopolistic competition market structure, like that for retailing, in which large numbers of buyers and sellers exchange relatively well-differentiated (heterogeneous) products, so each participant has some control over price.

monopoly market structure in which a single seller dominates trade in a good or service for which buyers can find no close substitutes.

morale mental attitude of employees toward their employer and jobs.

mortgage pass-through security security backed by a self-liquidating pool of mortgage loans.

multidomestic business strategy developing and marketing products to serve different needs and tastes of separate national markets.

multinational corporation (MNC) firm with significant operations and marketing activities outside its home country.

municipal bond bond issued by a state or local government.

mutual fund financial institution that pools money from purchases of its shares and uses the money to acquire diversified portfolios of securities consistent with the fund's investment objectives.

national debt money owed by government to individuals, businesses, and government agencies who purchase Treasury bills, Treasury notes, and Treasury bonds sold as a result of trade deficits and other expenditures.

natural resources all production inputs that are useful in their natural states, including agricultural land, building sites, forests, and mineral deposits.

nearshoring outsourcing production or services to locations near a firm's home base.

negotiable instrument commercial paper that is transferable among individuals and businesses.

net worth difference between what a person owns (assets) and what the person owes (liabilities).

nonpersonal selling promotion that includes advertising, sales promotion, direct marketing, public relations, and sponsorships—all conducted without face-to-face contact with the buyer.

nonprogrammed decision complex and unique problem or opportunity with important consequences for the organization.

nonverbal communication transmission of messages through actions and behaviors.

North American Free Trade Agreement (NAFTA) agreement among the United States, Canada, and Mexico to break down tariffs and trade restrictions.

not-for-profit corporation businesslike organization such as a charitable group, social welfare group, or religious congregation that pursues objectives other than returning profit to its owners.

not-for-profit organization organization that has primary objectives such as public service rather than returning a profit to its owners.

objectives guideposts by which managers define the organization's desired performance in such areas as profitability, customer service, growth, and employee satisfaction.

odd pricing pricing method using uneven amounts, which appear less than they really are to consumers.

offshoring the relocation of business processes to lower-cost locations overseas.

oligopoly market structure, like those in the airline and steel industries, in which relatively few sellers compete and high start-up costs form barriers that keep out most new competitors.

on-demand (utility) computing renting software time from an application provider rather than purchasing and maintaining the software.

on-the-job training training method that teaches an employee to complete new tasks by performing them under the guidance of an experienced employee.

open market operations buying and selling of government securities by the Federal Reserve to affect the money supply.

open-book management policy of giving all employees access to important financial information.

operating system software that controls a computer's basic functions.

operational planning detailed standards that guide implementation of tactical plans.

order processing form of selling, mostly at the wholesale and retail levels, that involves identifying customer needs, pointing them out to customers, and completing orders.

organization structured grouping of people working together to achieve common goals.

organization chart visual representation of a firm's structure that illustrates job positions and functions.

organization marketing marketing strategy that influences consumers to accept the goals of, receive the services of, or contribute in some way to an organization.

organizing process of blending human and material resources through a formal structure of tasks and authority; arranging work, dividing tasks among employees, and coordinating them to ensure implementation of plans and accomplishment of objectives.

outsourcing using outside vendors to produce goods or fulfill services and functions that were previously handled in-country or in-house.

owners' equity all claims of the proprietor, partners, or stockholders against the assets of a firm, equal to the excess of assets over liabilities.

ownership utility orderly transfer of goods and services from the seller to the buyer; also called possession utility.

pacing program company-initiated and -financed program to develop new products.

paid time off (PTO) bank of time that employees can use for holidays, vacation, and sick days.

partnership form of business ownership in which the company is operated by two or more people who are co-owners by voluntary legal agreement.

patent guarantee to an inventor exclusive rights to an invention for seventeen years.

penetration pricing pricing strategy that sets a low price as a major marketing tactic.

performance appraisal evaluation of an employee's job performance that compares actual results with desired outcomes.

perpetual inventory system that continuously monitors the amounts and locations of a company's stocks.

person marketing use of efforts designed to attract the attention, interest, and preference of a target market toward a person.

personal financial management study of the economic factors and personal decisions that affect a person's financial well-being.

personal selling interpersonal promotional process involving a seller's face-to-face presentation to a prospective buyer.

PERT (Program Evaluation and Review Technique) chart that seeks to minimize delays by coordinating all aspects of the production process.

phishing high-tech scam that uses authentic looking e-mail or pop-up ads to get unsuspecting victims to reveal personal information.

physical distribution actual movement of products from producer to consumers or business users.

picketing workers marching at a plant entrance to protest some management practice.

place marketing attempt to attract people to a particular area, such as a city, state, or nation.

place utility availability of a product in a location convenient for customers.

planned economy economic system in which strict government controls determine business ownership, profits, and resource allocation to accomplish government goals rather than those set by individual businesses.

planning process of anticipating future events and conditions and determining courses of action for achieving organizational objectives.

podcast online video blog.

point-of-purchase (POP) advertising displays or demonstrations that promote products when and where consumers buy them, such as in retail stores.

pollution environmental damage caused by a company's products or operating processes.

pop-up ad online ad that "pops up" as a separate window; interested parties click the ad for more information.

positioning concept in which marketers attempt to establish their own places in the minds of customers by communicating to prospective purchasers meaningful distinctions about the attributes, price, quality, or use of a good or service.

potential sales revenue amount of revenue the business would collect if its market penetration were 100 percent.

preferred provider organization (PPO) contract between local healthcare providers and employers to provide employee medical care at a discount.

preferred stock stock whose holders have priority over common stockholders in the payment of dividends but usually have no voting rights.

premium amount paid by the insured to the insurance company in exchange for insurance coverage.

presentation software computer program that includes graphics and tools to produce a variety of charts, graphs, and pictures.

prestige pricing establishing a relatively high price to develop and maintain an image of quality and exclusiveness.

price exchange value of a good or service.

price-earnings (P/E) ratio a stock's current price divided by its current earnings.

primary market market in which new security issues are first sold to investors; issuers receive the proceeds from the sale.

private (store) brand product that is not linked to the manufacturer, but instead carries the label of a retailer or wholesaler.

private enterprise system economic system that rewards firms for their ability to identify and serve the needs and demands of customers.

private exchange secure Web site at which a company and its suppliers share all types of data related to e-business, from product design through order delivery.

private placements private sale of securities to large institutional investors.

private property most basic freedom under the private enterprise system; the right to own, use, buy, sell, and bequeath land, buildings, machinery, equipment, patents, and various intangible kinds of property.

privatization recent international trend to convert government-owned and -operated companies into privately held businesses.

problem-solving team temporary combination of workers who gather to solve a specific problem and then disband.

product bundle of physical, service, and symbolic attributes designed to satisfy buyers' wants.

product advertising nonpersonal selling of a particular good or service.

product liability responsibility of manufacturers for injuries and damages caused by their products.

product life cycle four basic stages—introduction, growth, maturity, and decline—through which a successful product progresses.

product line group of related products that are physically similar or are intended for the same market.

product mix company's assortment of product lines and individual offerings.

product placement form of promotion in which marketers pay fees to have their products showcased in movies and television shows.

production application of resources such as people and machinery to convert materials into finished goods and services.

production and operations management managing people and machinery in converting materials and resources into finished goods and services.

production control process that creates a well-defined set of procedures for coordinating people, materials, and machinery to provide maximum production efficiency.

production planning phase of production control that determines the amount of resources (including raw materials and other components) a firm needs in order to produce a certain output.

productivity relationship between the number of units produced and the number of human and other production inputs necessary to produce them.

product-related segmentation dividing consumer markets into groups based on benefits sought by buyers and usage rates.

profitability objectives firm's goal to generate enough money (its revenues) through its pricing policies to cover its expenses.

profitability ratios measures of a company's overall financial performance by evaluating its ability to generate revenues in excess of expenses.

profits rewards for business-people who take the risks involved to offer goods and services to customers.

programmed decision simple, common, and frequently occurring problem for which a solution has already been determined.

promotion the function of informing, persuading, and influencing a purchase decision.

promotional mix combination of personal and nonpersonal selling techniques designed to achieve promotional objectives.

property and liability insurance general category of insurance that protects against financial losses due to a number of perils.

psychographic segmentation dividing consumer markets into groups with similar attitudes, values, and lifestyles.

public accountant accountant who works for an independent accounting firm.

public insurance agency government agency that provides certain types of insurance protection.

public ownership organization owned and operated by a unit or agency of government.

public relations organization's communications and relationships with its various audiences.

publicity stimulation of demand for a good, service, place, idea, person, or organization by disseminating news or obtaining favorable unpaid media presentations.

puffery exaggerated claims of a product's superiority or the use of subjective or vague statements that may not be literally true.

pulling strategy promotional effort by a seller to stimulate demand among final users, who will then exert pressure on the distribution channel to carry the good or service, pulling it through the distribution channel.

pure competition market structure, like that of small-scale agriculture, in which large numbers of buyers and sellers exchange homogeneous products and no single participant has a significant influence on price.

pure risk risk where there is no chance of gain, only a chance of loss.

pushing strategy promotional effort by a seller to members of the distribution channel intended to stimulate personal selling of the good or service, thereby pushing it through the channel.

quality control measuring goods and services against established quality standards.

quick response system that allows a retailer to buy just the merchandise from suppliers that its customers want and just when it needs to restock its shelves; the retailing equivalent of just-in-time inventory systems.

quota limit set on the amounts of particular products that can be imported.

ratio analysis commonly used tool for measuring the financial strength of a firm.

recession cyclical economic contraction that lasts for six months or longer.

recycling reprocessing used materials for reuse.

Regulation FD provision requiring that firms disclose information to all investors at the same time.

relationship era the business era in which firms seek ways to build long-term relationships with customers by managing every interaction.

relationship management collection of activities that build and maintain ongoing, mutually beneficial ties between a business and its customers and other parties.

relationship marketing developing and maintaining long-term, cost-effective exchange relationships with partners.

retailer channel member that sells goods and services to individuals for their own use rather than for resale.

risk uncertainty about loss or injury.

risk-return trade-off optimal balance between the expected payoff from an investment and the investment's risk.

robot reprogrammable machine capable of performing numerous tasks that require manipulation of materials and tools.

routing phase of production control that determines the sequence of work throughout the facility and specifies who will perform each aspect of production at what location.

S corporation modified form of the traditional corporate structure often used by firms with fewer than 75 shareholders; such businesses can elect to pay federal income taxes as partnerships while retaining the liability limitations typical of corporations.

salary compensation calculated on a periodic basis, such as weekly or monthly.

sales law law governing the sale of goods or services for money or on credit.

sales promotion nonpersonal marketing activities other than advertising, personal selling, and public relations that stimulate consumer purchasing and dealer effectiveness.

Sarbanes-Oxley Act of 2002 federal legislation designed to deter and punish corporate and accounting fraud and corruption and to protect the interests of workers and shareholders through enhanced financial disclosures, criminal penalties on CEOs and CFOs who defraud investors, safeguards for whistle-blowers, and establishment of a new regulatory body for public accounting firms.

scheduling development of timetables that specify how long each operation in the production process takes and when workers should perform it.

search marketing paying search engines, such as Google, a fee to make sure that the company's listing appears toward the top of the search results.

secondary market market in which existing security issues are bought and sold by investors.

Secure Sockets Layer (SSL) technology that secures a Web site by encrypting information and providing authentication.

secured bond bond that is backed by specific assets as collateral.

securities financial instruments such as stocks and bonds.

seed capital initial funding needed to launch a new venture.

selective distribution distribution strategy in which a manufacturer selects only a limited number of retailers to distribute its product lines.

self-managed team work team that has the authority to decide how its members complete their daily tasks.

serial entrepreneur person who starts one business, runs it, and then starts and runs additional businesses in succession.

set-aside program component of a government contract specifying that certain government contracts (or portions of those contracts) are restricted to small businesses and/or to women- or minority-owned companies.

sexism discrimination against members of either sex, but primarily affecting women.

sexual harassment inappropriate actions of a sexual nature in the workplace.

shopping product item typically purchased only after the buyer has compared competing products in competing stores.

skimming pricing pricing strategy that sets an intentionally high price relative to the prices of competing products.

skunkworks project initiated by a company employee who conceives the idea, convinces top management of its potential, and then recruits human and other resources from within the firm to turn it into a commercial project.

small business firm that is independently owned and operated, is not dominant in its field, and meets industry-specific size standards for income or number of employees.

Small Business Administration (SBA) federal agency that aids small businesses by providing management training and consulting, financial assitance, and support in securing government contracts.

Small Business Investment Company (SBIC) business licensed by the Small Business Administration to provide loans to small businesses.

social audit formal procedure that identifies and evaluates all company activities that relate to social issues such as conservation, employment practices, environmental protection, and philanthropy.

social responsibility business's consideration of society's well-being and consumer satisfaction in addition to profits.

socialism planned economic system characterized by government ownership and operation of major industries.

software set of instructions that tell the computer hardware what to do.

sole proprietorship form of business ownership in which the company is owned and operated by one person.

spam popular name for junk e-mail.

span of management number of subordinates a manager can supervise effectively.

specialty advertising promotional items that prominently display a firm's name, logo, or business slogan.

specialty product item that a purchaser is willing to make a special effort to obtain.

speculative risk risk where there is a chance of gain as well as a chance of loss.

sponsorship funding a sporting or cultural event in exchange for a direct association with the event.

spreadsheet software package that creates the computerized equivalent of an accountant's worksheet, allowing the user to manipulate variables and see the impact of alternative decisions on operating results.

staff manager executive who provides information, advice, or technical assistance to aid line managers; does not have the authority to give orders outside his or her own department or to compel line managers to take action.

standard of living necessities, comforts, and luxuries one seeks to obtain or to maintain.

statement of cash flows statement of a firm's cash receipts and cash payments that presents information on its sources and uses of cash.

statutory law written law, including state and federal constitutions, legislative enactments, treaties of the federal government, and ordinances of local governments.

stock exchange financial market where stocks are traded.

stock options rights to buy a specified amount of company stock at a given price within a given time period.

stockholder person or organization who owns shares of stock in a corporation.

strategic alliance partnership formed to create a competitive advantage for the businesses involved; in international business, a business strategy in which a company finds a partner in the country where it wants to do business.

strategic planning process of determining the primary objectives of an organization and then acting and allocating resources to achieve those objectives.

strike temporary work stoppage by employees until a dispute is settled or a contract signed.

subcontracting international agreement that involves hiring local companies to produce, distribute, or sell goods or services in a specific country or geographical region.

supervisory management first-line management; includes positions such as supervisor, line manager, and group leader; responsible for assigning nonmanagerial employees to specific jobs and evaluating their performance every day.

supply willingness and ability of sellers to provide goods and services.

supply chain complete sequence of suppliers that contribute to creating a good or service and delivering it to business users and final consumers.

supply curve graph of the amount of a product that suppliers will offer for sale at different prices; generally slopes upward to reflect larger quantities likely to be offered for sale as prices increase.

SWOT analysis method of assessing a company's internal strengths and weaknesses and its external opportunities and threats.

tactical planning implementing the activities specified by strategic plans.

target market group of people toward whom an organization markets its goods, services, or ideas with a strategy designed to satisfy their specific needs and preferences.

tariff tax imposed on imported goods.

tax assessment by a governmental unit.

team group of employees who are committed to a common purpose, approach, and set of performance goals.

team cohesiveness extent to which team members feel attracted to the team and motivated to remain part of it.

team diversity variances or differences in ability, experience, personality, or any other factor on a team.

team level average level of ability, experience, personality, or any other factor on a team.

team norm informal standard of conduct shared by team members that guides their behavior.

technical skills manager's ability to understand and use techniques, knowledge, and tools and equipment of a specific discipline or department.

technology business application of knowledge based on scientific discoveries, inventions, and innovations.

telecommuter home-based employee.

telemarketing personal selling conducted entirely by telephone, which provides a firm's marketers with a high return on their expenditures, an immediate response, and an opportunity for personalized two-way conversation.

term policy pure type of life insurance providing only a death benefit.

test marketing introduction of a new product supported by a complete marketing campaign to a selected city or TV coverage area to examine both consumer responses to the new offering and the marketing effort used to support it.

Theory X assumption that employees dislike work and will try to avoid it.

Theory Y assumption that employees enjoy work and seek social, esteem, and self-actualization fulfillment.

Theory Z assumption that employee involvement is key to productivity and quality of work life.

time utility availability of a good or service when customers want to purchase it.

top management managers at the highest level of the management pyramid who devote most of their time to developing long-range plans for their organizations.

tort civil wrong inflicted on another person or the person's property.

trade promotion sales promotion geared to marketing intermediaries rather than to final consumers.

trademark brand with legal protection against another company's use, not only of the brand name but also of pictorial designs, slogans, packaging elements, and product features such as color and shape.

transaction management building and promoting products in the hope that enough customers will buy them to cover costs and earn profits.

treasurer executive responsible for all of the company's financing activities, including cash management, tax planning and preparation, and shareholder relations.

trends consumer and business tendencies or patterns that firms can exploit to gain market share in an industry.

trial courts federal and state courts of general jurisdiction.

underwriting the process insurance companies use to determine whom to insure and what to charge.

unemployment insurance benefits paid to workers who are currently unemployed.

unemployment rate indicator of a nation's economic health, typically expressed as a percentage of the total workforce who are actively seeking work but are currently unemployed.

Uniform Commercial Code the basis of U.S. business law; referred to as the UCC.

utility want-satisfying power of a good or service.

value-added describes a good or service that exceeds value expectation because the company has added features, lowered its price, enhanced customer service, or made other improvements that increase customer satisfaction.

vendor-managed inventory company's decision to hand over its inventory control functions to suppliers.

venture capitalist firm or group of individuals that invests in new and growing firms in exchange for an ownership share.

vertical merger combination of two or more firms operating at different levels in the production and marketing process.

vice president for financial management executive who prepares financial forecasts and analyzes major investment decisions.

virtual private network (VPN) linking of two or more computers over secure Internet connections.

virtual team group of geographically and/or organizationally dispersed co-workers who use a combination of telecommunications and information technologies to accomplish an organizational task.

vision perception of marketplace needs and the methods an organization can use to satisfy them.

VoIP technology that uses a personal computer, special software, and a broadband network connection to make and receive telephone calls over the Internet.

volume objectives pricing decisions based on market share—the percentage of a market controlled by a certain company or product.

wage compensation based on an hourly pay rate or the amount of output produced.

Web host company that provides server space to other commercial Web sites for a fee.

Web-to-store use of the Internet to aid shoppers at brick-and-mortar retailers.

wheel of retailing theory of retailing in which new retailers gain a competitive foothold by offering low prices and limited services and then add services and raise prices, creating opportunities for new low-price competitors.

whistle-blowing employee's disclosure to company officials, government authorities, or the media of illegal, immoral, or unethical practices committed by an organization.

wholesaler distribution channel member that sells primarily to retailers, other wholesalers, or business users.

wide area network (WAN) computer network that ties larger geographical regions together by using telephone lines and microwave and satellite transmission.

Wi-Fi wireless network that connects various devices and allows them to communicate with one another through radio waves; short for *wireless fidelity.*

wiki Web page that anyone can edit.

Wi-Max a new wireless standard that provides coverage over much larger geographic areas.

word processing software that uses a computer to input, store, retrieve, edit, and print various types of documents.

work team relatively permanent group of employees with complementary skills who perform the day-to-day work of organizations.

worker's compensation insurance benefits paid to workers who are injured on the job.

World Bank organization established by industrialized nations to lend money to less developed countries.

World Trade Organization (WTO) 149-member international institution that monitors GATT agreements and mediates international trade disputes.

Notes

Prologue

1. Penelope Wang, "Four Myths about College Costs," *Money,* February 2005, p. 49.

2. Virginia Gewin, "Making It in the Biotech Business," *Nature,* accessed August 2006, http://www.nature.com.

3. Elizabeth Levin, "Getting Hired Full Time after an Internship," *College Journal,* accessed August 2006, http://www.collegejournal.com.

4. Silpada Web site, accessed August 2006, http://www.silpada.com.

5. "Prepare Your Resume for E-Mailing or Posting on the Internet," *Riley Guide,* accessed August 2006, http://www.rileyguide.com.

6. Liz Ryan, "The Elephant in Your Résumé," *BusinessWeek,* accessed August 2006, http://www.businessweek.com.

7. Marshall Loeb, "Six Tips for Writing a Winning Cover Letter," *College Journal,* accessed August 2006, http://www.collegejournal.com.

8. "Prepare Your Résumé for E-Mailing or Posting on the Internet."

9. Olivia Barker and Sarah Bailey, "Going Toe-to-Toe on Office Etiquette," *USA Today,* August 15, 2005, p. D1.

10. "Fifty Standard Interview Questions," CollegeGrad.com, accessed August 2006, http://www.collegegrad.com.

11. "Tomorrow's Jobs," *Occupational Outlook Handbook,* Bureau of Labor Statistics, accessed August 2006, http://www.bls.gov.

12. "Tomorrow's Jobs."

13. Anne Fisher, "Hot Careers for the Next 10 Years," *Fortune,* March 21, 2005, p. 131.

14. "Tomorrow's Jobs."

Chapter 1

1. Procter & Gamble Web site, accessed August 2006, http://www.pg.com; Jerry Useem, "America's Most Admired Companies," *Fortune,* March 7, 2005, pp. 67–68; "It Was a No-Brainer," *Fortune,* February 21, 2005, pp. 97–102; Nanette Byrnes et al., "Branding: Five New Lessons," *BusinessWeek,* February 14, 2005, pp. 26–28; Robert Berner, Nanette Byrnes, and Wendy Zellner, "P&G Has Rivals in a Wringer," *BusinessWeek,* October 4, 2004, p. 74.

2. "U.S. Hospitality Industry Sees Boom through 2007," *Hotel Marketing,* accessed August 2006, http://www.hotelmarketing.com; "Fitch: Travel Rebound Fuels U.S. Lodging Sector 2005 Outlook," *Hospitality Net,* accessed August 2006, http://www.hospitality.org.

3. "Corp. Travel Rebound Contributes to Record Amex Quarter," *Business Travel News,* accessed August 2006, http://www.btnmag.com.

4. Ross Kerber, "Industry Invests in Students—Its Future Workers," *Boston Globe,* accessed August 2006, http://www.boston.com.

5. "Homeland Security and Traveler Safety Information," American Hotel & Lodging Association, accessed August 2006, http://www.ahla.com.

6. "Number of Nonprofit Organizations in the United States 1996–2004," National Center for Charitable Statistics at the Urban Institute, accessed August 2006, http://nccsdataweb.urban.org.

7. Stephen Kaufman, "Former Presidents' Visit to Tsunami-Affected Countries a Success," International Information Programs, August 2006, http://usinfo.state.gov.

8. Lance Armstrong Foundation, accessed August 2006, http://www.livestrong.org.

9. Peter Lewis, "The Keys to Happiness," *Fortune,* September 20, 2004, pp. 74–75.

10. "Get Ready for WiMax," *eWeek,* accessed August 2006, http://www.eweek.com.

11. David Neeleman, "Turn Managers into Leaders," *Business 2.0,* September 2004, p. 70.

12. Kathy Ireland Worldwide Web site, accessed August 2006, http://www.kathyireland.com; Elyssa Lee and Rob Turner, "Celebrity Entrepreneurs," *Inc.,* December 2004, p. 74.

13. "Carlos Gutierrez Biography," U.S. Department of Commerce Web site, accessed August 2006, http://www.commerce.gov; Matthew Boyle, "The Man Who Fixed Kellogg," *Fortune,* September 6, 2004, pp. 218–226.

14. Carrie Johnson, "Fifteen NYSE Traders Indicted," *Washington Post,* April 13, 2005, p. A1; Julie Creswell, "The Exchange Faces Change," *Fortune,* August 9, 2004, pp. 108–114.

15. U.S. Census Bureau, accessed August 2006, http://www.census.gov.

16. Blitz Web site, accessed August 2006, http://www.timetoblitz.com; Jeffrey Ressner, "Fighting for Fitness," *Time,* November 8, 2004, p.113.

17. Thorlo Web site, accessed August 2006, http://www.thorlo.com.

18. Granite Rock Web site, accessed August 2006, http://www.graniterock.com.

19. Lauren Gard, "Online Extra: Stonyfield Farm's Blog Culture," *BusinessWeek Online,* accessed August 2006, http://www.businessweek.com.

20. eBay Web site, accessed August 2006, http://www.ebay.com.

21. "Apple Eyes Fizz in Pepsi iTunes Giveaway," C/Net, accessed August 2006, http://www.news.com.com.

22. Barbara Rose, "Retirees Preparing to Step Back, Not Away," *Chicago Tribune,* January 16, 2005, section 1, pp. 1, 19.

23. Haya el Nasser, "Youthquakes Shake Up Gray-Haired States," *USA Today,* March 10, 2005, p. 3A.

24. Rose, "Retirees Preparing to Step Back, Not Away."

25. "The Immigrant Policy Project," National Conference of State Legislatures, accessed August 2006, http://www.ncsl.org.

26. "The Immigrant Policy Project."

27. "Diversity at UPS," UPS Web site, accessed August 2006, http://www.ups.com.

28. Jim Hopkins, "To Start Up Here, Companies Hire Over There," *USA Today,* accessed August 2006, http://www.usatoday.com.

29. John W. Miller, "Eastern Europe Becomes Hub for 'Nearshoring' Call-Center Jobs," *The Wall Street Journal*'s Career Journal Europe,

accessed August 2006, http://www.careerjournaleurope.com;
Andy Reinhardt, "Forget India, Let's Go to Bulgaria," *Business-Week*, March 1, 2004, p. 93.

30. "How to Exploit Innovation," *Business 2.0*, December 2004, p. 104.

31. "Bose's Sound Strategy," *Chief Executive*, accessed August 2006, http://www.chiefexecutive.net; Brian Dumaine, "I'd Rather Be Inventing," in "14 Innovators," *Fortune*, November 15, 2004, p. 194.

32. "The Story," Kate Spade Web site, accessed August 2006, http://www.katespade.com; Julie Creswell, "You Can't Say, 'The Customer Doesn't Get It,'" in "14 Innovators," p. 196.

33. Abraham Lustgarten, "A Hot, Steaming Cup of Customer Awareness," in "14 Innovators," p. 192.

34. Andrew Martin, "What's Next for Fast Food? McTofu?" *Chicago Tribune*, accessed August 2006, http://www.chicagotribune.com; Matthew Boyle, "Can You Really Make Fast Food Healthy?" *Fortune*, August 9, 2004, pp. 134–140.

35. Jerry Useem, "America's Most Admired Companies," *Fortune*, March 7, 2005, pp. 67–70.

36. Useem, "America's Most Admired Companies."

Chapter 2

1. Green Mountain Coffee Roasters Web site, accessed August 2006, http://www.greenmountaincoffee.com; "Green Mountain Coffee Roasters Brews an Optimized Workforce with Human Resources, Payroll and Time and Labor Solutions from Kronos," press release, May 2, 2005; Mark Pendergrast, "Green Mountain Coffee Roasters: Doing Well by Doing Good," *Tea & Coffee Trade Journal*, April 20, 2004, pp. 100ff.

2. "National Business Ethics Survey," Ethics Research Center, accessed August 2006, http://www.ethics.org.

3. Johnson & Johnson Web site, accessed August 2006, http://www.jnj.com.

4. David Teather, "GE Doubles Research on Clean Technology," *The Guardian*, accessed August 2006, http://www.guardian.co.uk; Marc Gunther, "Money and Morals at GE," *Fortune*, November 15, 2004, pp. 176–182.

5. "Where Americans and Business Leaders Agree/Disagree on Business Ethics," Public Agenda, accessed August 2006, http://www.publicagenda.org.

6. "Coors Ethics Program among Best in Nation," accessed August 2006, http://accounting.smartpros.com.

7. "Deskside Skiving Adds Up to Seven Days Holiday a Year," *Personnel Today*, accessed August 2006, http://www.personneltoday.com.

8. Scott Kirsner, "Reebok Offers Help Fighting Overseas Abuse," *Boston Globe*, accessed August 2006, http://www.boston.com; "Fair Factories Clearinghouse Created to Support Compliance with Workplace Conditions in Factories," FFC press release, January 13, 2005.

9. Paul Fireman, "What We Can Do about Burma," *Wall Street Journal Online*, accessed August 2006, http://online.wsj.com.

10. George Cahlink, "Ex-Pentagon Procurement Executive Gets Jail Time," *Government Executive*, accessed August 2006, http://www.govexec.com.

11. Peter Saalfield, "Internet Misuse Costs Businesses $178 Billion Annually," *Info World*, accessed August 2006, http://www.infoworld.com; Tim Higgins, "Workplaces Frown If Sex Pops up on a Computer," *Des Moines Register*, accessed August 2006, http://desmoinesregister.com.

12. Robin L. Wakefield, "Employee Monitoring and Surveillance: The Growing Trend," Information Systems Audit and Control Association, accessed August 2006, http://www.isaca.org.

13. Neil Weinberg, "The Dark Side of Whistleblowing," *Forbes*, accessed August 2006, http://www.forbes.com.

14. Nortel Networks Web site, accessed August 2006, http://www.nortel.com

15. Ronald J. Alsop, "B-Schools Still Seeking Ways to Stress Ethics," *CollegeJournal*, accessed August 2006, http://www.collegejournal.com.

16. Kavaljit Singh, "Citi Never Sleeps," Asia-Europe Dialogue, accessed February 6, 2005, http://www.ased.org; Mark Train, "Citigroup Embroiled in Bond Selling Scandal," *The Guardian*, accessed August 2006, http://www.guardian.co.uk.

17. Nortel Networks Web site, accessed August 2006, http://www.nortel.com

18. "100 Best Corporate Citizens: 2004," *Business Ethics*, accessed August 2006, http://www.business-ethics.com.

19. Council on Economic Priorities Web site, accessed August 2006, http://www.web.ca/~robrien/papers/sri/players/cep.html and http://www.geocites.com/CapitolHill/Senate/1777/cep.htm.

20. Center for Science in the Public Interest Web site, accessed August 2006, http://www.cspinet.org.

21. Judy Silber, "Chiron to Produce Less Vaccine," *(San Jose, CA) Mercury News*, accessed June 15, 2005, http://www.mercurynews.com; "U.S. Government Outlines Flu Vaccine Guidelines," MSNBC, accessed August 2006, http://www.msnbc.msn.com.

22. Michael E. Hochman, "New Drug Tests Try to Keep Up with Athletes," *Boston Globe*, accessed August 2006, http://www.boston.com; Mark Sappenfield, "States Taking on Teen Steroid Use," *Christian Science Monitor*, accessed August 2006, http://www.csmonitor.com; Nicholas Thompson, "Bud Selig," Slate, accessed August 2006, http://slate.com; Mark Madden, "Baseball's War on Steroids Probably Can't Be Won," *(Pittsburgh, PA) Post-Gazette*, accessed August 2006, http://www.post-gazette.com.

23. Lara Jill Rosenblith, "The Hidden Harm of the Technological Revolution," *Fact Sheet—Electronics Waste (E-Waste)*, http://environment.about.com; Ellen Simon, "'E-Junk' Recycling Still in Its Infancy," Yahoo! News, accessed December 6, 2004, http://www.yahoo.com.

24. Juliet Eilperin, "Dead Electronics Going to Waste," *Washington Post*, accessed August 2006, http://www.washingtonpost.com.

25. Dee-Ann Durbin, "Hybrid Car Sales Soar in U.S. in 2004," Yahoo! News, accessed April 25, 2005, http://www.yahoo.com.

26. "Scientists Make Phone that Turns into a Sunflower," Yahoo! News, accessed December 6, 2004, http://www.yahoo.com.

27. Ellen Simon, "'E-Junk' Recycling Still in Its Infancy."

28. Juliet Elperin, "Dead Electronics Going to Waste."

29. Leonard Anderson and Timothy Gardner, "U.S. Cities Eye Ocean Waves for Power Supplies," Yahoo! News, accessed February 14, 2005, http://www.yahoo.com.

30. "The Gift of a College Degree Lasts a Lifetime," *Princeton Review*, accessed August 2006, http://www.princetonreview.com; U.S. Department of Labor Web site, accessed August 2006, http://www.dol.gov.

31. Target Web site, accessed August 2006, http://www.target.com.

32. "Community Action," General Mills Web site, accessed August 2006, http://www.generalmills.com; Ellen P. Gabler, "Strategic Giving Provides Win-Win for Corporations," *Business Journal,* accessed August 2006, http://www.bizjournals.com/twincities.

33. David Henderson, "The Role of Business in the World of Today," *Journal of Corporate Citizenship,* accessed August 2006, http://www.greenleaf-publishing.com; Jessi Hempel and Lauren Gard, "The Corporate Givers," *BusinessWeek,* accessed August 2006, http://www.businessweek.com.

34. "GM Recalls 300,000 Vehicles to Repair Turn-Signal Problems," *The Wall Street Journal,* May 11, 2005, p. D5.

35. "Security and Resolution Center," eBay Web site, accessed August 2006, http://pages.ebay.com/securitycenter/buying_tips.html.

36. Jewel-Osco Web site, accessed August 2006, http://www.jewelosco.com.

37. Tatsha Robertson, "Between Work and Life There's Balance," *Boston Globe,* accessed August 2006, http://www.boston.com; Diane Brady, "Hopping aboard the Daddy Track," *BusinessWeek,* November 8, 2004, pp. 100–101.

38. Christine Larson, "Family Balance," *U.S. News & World Report,* March 21, 2005, pp. 44–46.

39. Hope Yen, "Court Issues Age Discrimination Ruling," Yahoo! News, accessed March 30, 2005, http://www.yahoo.com.

40. "Hands off the employees," *St. Louis Post-Dispatch,* accessed August 2006, http://www.stltoday.com.

41. Bureau of Labor Statistics, "Women in the Labor Force: A Databook," accessed August 2006, http://www.bls.gov.cps/wlf-databook2005.htm; Jenny Strasburg, "Equity: Losing Ground," *San Francisco Chronicle,* accessed August 2006, http://www.sfgate.com.

42. Jenny Strasburg, "Equity: Losing Ground."

Chapter 3

1. "Chrysler Rolls Out New Dodge Charger Police Car," ConsumerAffairs.com, accessed August 2006, http://www.consumeraffairs.com; Sharon Silke Carty, "Crown Vic Challenged in Police Vehicle Arena," *USA Today,* March 28, 2005, p. 4B; "Arkansas Presses Ford Police Car Suit," ConsumerAffairs.com, accessed August 2006, http://www.consumeraffairs.com.

2. Shannon Dininny, "Apple Growers Happy about McDonald's Shift," Yahoo! News, accessed May 1, 2005, http://www.yahoo.com.

3. Steven Levy and Brad Stone, "Grand Theft Identity," *Newsweek,* July 4, 2005, pp. 38–47.

4. "Oil Prices Rise, with Focus on Hurricane Emily, Chinese Demand Concerns," Yahoo! News, accessed July 15, 2005, http://www.yahoo.com.

5. Christopher Calnan, "Summer Travel Not Expected to Cool," *(Jacksonville) Florida Times-Union,* accessed May 28, 2005, http://www.jacksonville.com.

6. Alexandra Marks and Robert Tuttle, "Oil Prices Spread to Grapes, TVs, Pizza," *Christian Science Monitor,* accessed August 2006, http://www.csmonitor.com.

7. "Oil Prices Rise, with Focus on Hurricane Emily, Chinese Demand Concerns."

8. Shannon Dininny, "Apple Growers Happy about McDonald's Shift."

9. "GM Announces Employee Pricing for Everyone," advertising section, *Sports Illustrated,* June 20, 2005.

10. Cemex Web site, accessed August 2006, http://www.cemex.com.

11. Anick Jesdanun, "Microsoft's Share of Browser Market Slips," Yahoo! News, accessed May 12, 2005, http://www.yahoo.com.

12. Air Canada Web site, accessed August 2006, http://www.aircanada.com.

13. David Wyss, "Productivity Won't Always Save the Day," *BusinessWeek,* accessed August 2006, http://www.businessweek.com.

14. Michael Mandel, "The Case of the Missing Trillion," *BusinessWeek,* accessed August 2006, http://www.businessweek.com.

15. Ron Scherer, "Inflation Flickers Again on Horizon," *Christian Science Monitor,* accessed August 2006, http://www.csmonitor.com.

16. Martin Crutsinger, "Greenspan Signals Further Rate Increases," Yahoo! News, accessed July 20, 2005, http://www.yahoo.com.

17. Steve Forbes, "Why Forgive Kleptocracy and Economic Incompetence?" *Forbes,* April 11, 2005, pp. 31–32.

18. Mortimer B. Zuckerman, "The Case of the 12 Zeros," *U.S. News & World Report,* March 21, 2005, p. 68.

19. Rama Lakshmi, "Indian Call Centers Cursed," *Morning News,* March 4, 2005, p. 3B.

Chapter 4

1. Red Wing Web site, accessed August 2006, http://www.redwingshoe.com; Scott A. Briggs, "Change Is Afoot," *Twin Cities Business Monthly,* accessed May 2005, http://www.redwingshoe.com; Timothy Aeppel, "Red Wing Digs In Its Heels," *Wall Street Journal,* September 28, 2004, pp. B1, B6.

2. U.S. Census Bureau, "Foreign Trade Statistics: Annual Trade Highlights," accessed February 10, 2005, http://www.census.gov/foreign-trade; U.S. Census Bureau, "Foreign Trade Statistics: U.S. International Trade in Goods and Services Highlights," accessed May 11, 2005, http://www.census.gov/indicator/www/ustrade.html.

3. Anthony Faiola, "A Baby Bust Empties Out Japan's Schools," *Washington Post,* accessed August 2006, http://www.washingtonpost.com; Phillip Longman, "The Global Baby Bust," *Foreign Affairs,* accessed August 2006, http://www.foreignaffairs.org; "Lower Birth Rate, AIDS Deaths Help Slow World Population Growth," *San Francisco Chronicle,* accessed March 23, 2004, http://www.sfgate.com.

4. Data from Central Intelligence Agency, *World Factbook,* accessed August 9, 2005, http://www.cia.gov.

5. Associated Press, "Wal-Mart to Nearly Double Stores in China," accessed July 25, 2005, Yahoo! News, http://www.yahoo.com.

6. U.S. Census Bureau, "Top Ten Countries with Which the U.S. Trades," accessed April 2005, http://www.census.gov/foreign'trade/top/dst/current/balance.html.

7. TradeStats Express, "State Export Data," accessed August 2006, http://tse.export.gov.

8. "Saffron," Spice Advice Encyclopedia, accessed August 2006, http://www.spiceadvice.com.

9. Ron Scherer, "Imports Increasingly Burden U.S. Economy," *Christian Science Monitor,* accessed August 2006, http://www.csmonitor.com.

10. Chester Dawson, "Why the Dollar Is Blooming Again," *BusinessWeek,* accessed August 2006, http://www.businessweek.com.

11. Patrick O'Gilfoil Healy, "For Muslims, Loans for the Conscience," *New York Times,* accessed August 2006, http://www.nytimes.com;

Feisal Abdul Rauf, "Bringing Muslim Nations into the Global Century," *Fortune*, October 18, 2004, pp. 80–81.

12. George Obulutsa, "Kenyans Text Messaging Their Way to Jobs," Reuters Limited, accessed April 13, 2005, http://www.yahoo.com.

13. "News Analysis: Kids' TV Confronts Junk-food Fear," *PRWeek*, accessed May 5, 2005, http://www.prweek.com.

14. Organization for Economic Cooperation and Development, "The OECD Anti-Bribery Convention: How it Works," accessed August 2006, http://www.oecd.org.

15. En-Lai Yeoh, "Report: Software Piracy Cost $8B in Asia," Yahoo! News, accessed May 18, 2005, http://www.yahoo.com; Roy Mark, "U.S. Ups Pressure on China over IP Rights," Internet News.com, accessed August 2006, http://www.internetnews.com.

16. "How to Hurt American Business," *New York Times*, editorial, accessed August 2006, http://www.nytimes.com.

17. Martin Crutsinger, "White House Re-Imposes Quotas on China," Yahoo! News, accessed May 13, 2005, http://www.yahoo.com.

18. Elizabeth Wasserman, "Happy Birthday, WTO?" *Inc.*, January 2005, pp. 21–23

19. United States Mission to the European Union, "G8 Summit Ends with Commitment to Finalize World Trade Talks," accessed August 2006, http://www.useu.be.

20. Dana Bash and Robin Oakley, "Bush, Blair Push African Debt Relief," CNN.com, accessed August 2006, http://www.cnn.com.

21. Central Intelligence Agency, "Canadian, Mexican, and U.S. populations" and GDP data, *World Factbook*, http://www.cia.gov/cia/publications/factbook.

22. Central Intelligence Agency, "Canada," *World Factbook*, http://www.cia.gov/cia/publications/factbook.

23. Central Intelligence Agency, "Mexico," *World Factbook*, http://www.cia.gov/cia/publications/factbook.

24. Geri Smith, "A Border Transformed," *BusinessWeek*, accessed August 2006, http://www.businessweek.com.

25. Robert Manor, "CAFTA Called an Export Builder," *Chicago Tribune*, accessed August 2006, http://www.chicagotribune.com; "CAFTA Could Help Agri Companies," *Northwest Arkansas Business Journal*, July 18, 2005, p. 4.

26. Economic Research Service, "Briefing Room: European Union," U.S. Dept. of Agriculture, accessed August 2006, http://www.ers.usda.gov/Briefing/EuropeanUnion/basicinfo.htm.

27. John Chalmers, "Wounded EU Limps On after Double 'No' to Treaty," Yahoo! News, accessed June 2, 2005, http://www.yahoo.com.

28. Roots Canada Web site, accessed August 2006, http://www.roots.com; "Roots Canada Ltd.," accessed August 2006, www.hoovers.com; "Roots Canada Ltd.," Yahoo! Finance, accessed August 2006, http://finance.yahoo.com.

29. "Delivering at Domino's Pizza," *Fortune*, February 7, 2005, p. 28.

30. Michael Kanellos, "Hello Kitty's Guide to Business Success," CNet News.com, accessed August 2006, http://news.com.com.

31. Pacific Bridge Medical Web site, accessed August 2006, http://www.pacificbridgemedical.com.

32. Whirlpool Corporation Web site, accessed August 2006, http://www.whirlpoolcorp.com; Keith Bradsher, "Made in India vs. Made in China," *New York Times*, accessed August 2006, http://www.nytimes.com.

33. "Outsourcing: 100 U.S. Bills Target India," *Economic Times*, accessed August 2006, http://economictimes.indiatimes.com; Ed Frauenheim and Mike Yamamoto, "Reforms, Not Rhetoric, Needed to Keep Jobs on U.S. Soil," CNet News.com, accessed August 2006, http://news.com.com.

34. Rachel Konrad, "U.S. Interminable Workday," *Arizona Republic*, accessed May 15, 2005, http://www.azcentral.com.

35. "Lenovo's Long March," *BusinessWeek*, accessed August 2006, http://www.businessweek.com; Richard J. Newman, "Big Blue Goes Red," *U.S. News & World Report*, December 20, 2004, pp. 38–40.

36. "Heinz Acquires Majority Stake in Leading Russian Maker of Ketchup, Condiments, and Sauces," press release, accessed May 3, 2005, http://biz.yahoo.com.

37. Panasonic Web site, accessed August 2006, http://www.panasonic.com.

38. General Electric Web site, accessed August 2006, http://www.ge.com.

39. Toyota Web site, accessed August 2006, http://www.toyota.com.

40. Randall Frost, "Local Success on a Global Scale," *Brandchannel.com*, accessed August 2006, http://www.brandchannel.com; Geoffrey A. Fowler and Ramin Setoodeh, "Outsiders Get Smarter about China's Tastes," *Wall Street Journal*, August 5, 2004, p. B1.

Part 1 Appendix

1. Mike France, "How to Fix the Tort System," *BusinessWeek*, March 14, 2005, pp. 70–78; Dan Zegart, "Tort Reform Triumphs," *The Nation*, accessed August 2006, http://www.thenation.com; "Bush Signs So-Called Class-Action Fairness Act of 2005," Legal News Watch, accessed August 2006, http://www.legalnewswatch.com; "President Signs Class-Action Fairness Act of 2005," The White House, accessed August 2006, http://www.whitehouse.gov.

2. Dan Ackman, "Bernie Ebbers Guilty," *Forbes*, accessed August 2006, http://www.forbes.com.

3. Tom Cole, "Frivolous Litigation, a Tax on Americans," press release, accessed August 2006, http://www.house.gov.

4. Howard Witt, "Much a Doodle-Doo about Nothing," *Chicago Tribune*, May 22, 2005, pp. 1, 10.

5. "U.S. Federal Laws," FindLaw, accessed August 2006, http://findlaw.com/casecode.

6. "Supreme Court of the United States," Encarta, accessed August 2006, http://www.encarta.msn.com.

7. Cain Burdeau, "Canada to Slap Surtax on American Oysters," *Seafood News*, accessed August 2006, http://www.seafood-norway.com.

8. Jeannine Aversa, "Pension Bailout Posed to Fed Boss," *The Cincinnati Enquirer*, accessed July 22, 2005, http://news.enquirer.com.

9. Glen Johnson, "House Votes to Extend Patriot Act," Yahoo! News, accessed July 22, 2005, http://www.yahoo.com.

10. Katie Merx and Kortney Stringer, "Drug Ad Changes Looming," *Detroit Free Press*, accessed June 20, 2005, http://www.freep.com; "Prescription Drug Advertising Will Get More Scrutiny, FDA Promises," News Target, accessed August 2006, http://www.newstarget.com.

11. Albert B. Crenshaw, "Retiree Benefits Can't Be Cut at 65, Judge Says," *Washington Post*, accessed August 2006, http://www.washingtonpost.com.

12. Hope Yen, "Court: File-Sharing Services May Be Sued," Yahoo! News, accessed June 27, 2005, http://www.yahoo.com.

13. "Uniform Commercial Code (UCC)," accessed August 2006, http://www.smartagreements.com.

14. "Uniform Commercial Code (UCC)."

15. *Kelo v. New London*, U.S Supreme Court Database, accessed August 2006, http://www.usscplus.com; Adam Karlin, "Property Seizure Backlash," *Christian Science Monitor*, accessed August 2006, http://www.csmonitor.com.

16. R. Subramanyam, "Wipro Accused of Infringement by German Company," *Economic Times*, accessed August 2006, http://economictimes.indiatimes.com.

17. Ben Mutzabaugh, "Today in the Sky," *USA Today*, accessed June 8, 2005, http://www.usatoday.com.

18. Michelle Kessler, "Pressure Mounts for Reform of Patent System," *USA Today*, accessed August 2006, http://www.usatoday.com.

19. Steven Musil, "This Week in Copyright Infringement," CNet News.com, accessed August 2006, http://news.com.com.

20. Hope Yen, "Court: File-Sharing Services May Be Sued."

21. Steven Musil, "This Week in Copyright Infringement."

22. Steven Musil, "This Week in Copyright Infringement."

23. Laura Parker, "When Pets Die at the Vet, Grieving Owners Call Lawyers," *USA Today*, March 15, 2005, pp. 1A, 2A.

24. Sandra Block, "Filing Chapter 7 Bankruptcy Will Get Tougher Soon," *USA Today*, April 21, 2005, p. 4B.

25. James Vicini, "Court Overturns Andersen Enron Conviction," Yahoo! News, accessed May 31, 2005, http://www.yahoo.com.

26. Gregory M. Lamb, "Creative Work Makes for Slippery Private Property Online," *Christian Science Monitor*, accessed August 2006, http://www.csmonitor.com; Emily Bazelon, "Grok around the Clock," *Slate*, accessed August 2006, http://slate.com.

Part 1: Launching Your Global Business and Economics Career

1. U.S. Department of Labor, "Tomorrow's Jobs," *Occupational Outlook Handbook*, 2006–2007 edition, U.S. Bureau of Labor Statistics, accessed August 2006, http://www.bls.gov.

2. U.S. Department of Labor, "Economists," *Occupational Outlook Handbook*, 2006–2007 edition, U.S. Bureau of Labor Statistics, accessed August 2006, http://www.bls.gov.

3. Adapted from Michael R. Czinkota, Ilkka A. Ronkainen, and Michael H. Moffett, "Criteria for Selecting Managers for Overseas Assignments," in *International Business*, 7th ed. (Mason, OH: South-Western, 2005), Table 19.2, p. 634.

4. Del Jones, "New MBAs Finding Education Pays Off Big Time," *USA Today*, accessed August 2006, http://www.usatoday.com.

5. Erin White, "For M.B.A. Students, a Good Career Move Means a Job in Asia," *Wall Street Journal*, accessed August 2006, http://online.wsj.com.

6. Carol Hymowitz, "Diversity in a Global Economy—Ways Some Firms Get It Right," Career Journal, accessed August 2006, http://www.careerjournal.com.

Chapter 5

1. Sherri Daye Scott, "The Phenomenon," *QSR Magazine*, accessed August 2006, http://www.qsrmagazine.com; Oscar Avila, "Nostalgia Served Piping Hot," *Chicago Tribune*, accessed August 2006,
http://www.chicagotribune.com; Rebecca Flass, "Guatemalan Restaurant Chain Plays Chicken with Big Brands," *Los Angeles Business Journal*, accessed August 2006, http://www.findarticles.com; "Mayor Michael R. Bloomberg Cuts Ribbon for the First Pollo Campero Restaurant in New York City," New York City press release, accessed August 2006, http://www.nyc.gov; "Pollo Campero," Ahorre.com, accessed August 2006, http://www.hispanicmarket.net.

2. U.S. Census Bureau, "Statistics about Business Size," accessed August 2006, http://www.census.gov.

3. Ibid.

4. Office of Advocacy, U.S. Small Business Administration, "Frequently Asked Questions: Advocacy Small Business Statistics and Research," accessed August 2006, http://app1.sba.gov/faqs.

5. Office of Advocacy, U.S. Small Business Administration, "Women-owned Business Economic Research," accessed August 2006, http://www.sba.gov/advo.

6. Office of Advocacy, U.S. Small Business Administration, "Frequently Asked Questions."

7. Small Business Administration, "Frequently Asked Questions (FAQs) about Small Business Size Standards," accessed August 2006, http://www.sba.gov/size.

8. Allen Roberts, Jr., "How I Did It: Barbara K," *Inc.*, May 2005, p. 112.

9. Dee Gill, ". . . Or Your Money Back," *Inc.*, September 2005, p. 46.

10. Powell's Web site, accessed August 2006, http://www.powells.com; "They Said It" quotation from "Michael Powell," *Inc.*, accessed September 1, 2005, http://www.inc.com.

11. U.S. Department of Agriculture, Agriculture Fact Book, pp. 20, 23, accessed August 2006, http://www.usda.gov/factbook.

12. Office of Advocacy, U.S. Small Business Administration, "The Small Business Economy: A Report to the President," accessed August 2006, http://www.sba.gov/advo.

13. Gerald Oettinger, "The Growth in Home-Based Wage and Salary Employment in the United States, 1980-2000: How Much and Why?" University of Chicago Graduate School of Business, accessed September 3, 2005, http://gsb.uchicago.edu.

14. Allison Bruce, "Bead Business Booming for eBay-Using Camarillo Couple," *Ventura County (CA) Star*, June 5, 2005.

15. Salem Five Web site, accessed August 2006, http://www.salemfive.com.

16. Office of Advocacy, U.S. Small Business Administration, "Frequently Asked Questions."

17. Small Business Administration, "Small Business Statistics," accessed August 2006, http://www.sba.gov/advo.

18. Office of Advocacy, U.S. Small Business Administration, "U.S. Receipt Size of Firm by Major Industry Group," accessed August 2006, http://www.sba.gov/advo.

19. Small Business Administration, "Welfare to Work Program," accessed September 3, 2005, http://www.sba.gov.

20. Christopher Caggiano, "Insider Training," *Inc.*, accessed August 2006, http://www.inc.com; Tucker Technology Web site, accessed August 2006, http://www.tuckertech.com.

21. InterDigital Communications, "Profile," accessed August 2006, http://www.interdigital.com.

22. Netflix, "Fact Sheet," accessed August 2006, http://www.ir.netflix.com.

23. Daniel McGinn & Ramin Setoodeh, "Rewinding a Video Giant," *Newsweek,* June 27, 2005, p. 38; Wal-Mart, "What to Know about Wal-Mart DVD Rentals," accessed September 3, 2005, http://www.walmart.com.

24. "Interview with Thomas D'Ambra," accessed August 2006, https://secure.twst.com.

25. Chi Research, "Small Serial Innovators: The Small Firm Contribution to Technical Change," Small Business Administration, accessed August 2006, http://www.sba.gov/advo; "They Said It" quotation from "Zach Nelson," *Inc.,* February 2005, p. 71.

26. Small Business Administration, Office of Advocacy, "Financing Patterns of Small Firms," accessed August 2006, http://www.sba.gov/advo.

27. C. J. Prince, "Plastic Rap," *Entrepreneur,* accessed August 2006, http://www.entrepreneur.com.

28. "Precision Plastics: An Employee-Owned Company," accessed August 2006, http://www.pplastic.com.

29. U.S. Department of Labor, "As an Employer, Are You Engaged in Commerce or in an Industry or Activity Affecting Commerce?" elaws—Family and Medical Leave Act Advisor, accessed August 2006, http://www.dol.gov.

30. Small Business Administration, Office of Disaster Assistance, "Fact Sheet about U.S. Small Business Administration Disaster Loans," accessed August 2006, http://www.sba.gov.

31. Small Business Administration, "The Microloan Program for Entrepreneurs," accessed August 2006, http://www.sba.gov.

32. Active Capital, "Frequently Asked Questions," accessed August 2006, http://activecapital.org.

33. Small Business Administration, "Government Contracting: What We Do," accessed August 2006, http://www.sba.gov.

34. Small Business Administration, "SBA, OMB, GSA and DOD Work Together to Integrate PRO-Net and CCR Database and Simplify Contracting Process for Small Businesses," accessed August 2006, http://www.pro-net.sba.gov.

35. National Business Incubator Association, accessed August 2006, http://www.nbia.org.

36. National Foundation for Women Business Owners, "Top Facts about Women-Owned Businesses," accessed September 4, 2005, http://www.nfwbo.org; National Foundation for Women Business Owners, "Businesses Owned by Women of Color in the United States: A Fact Sheet," accessed September 4, 2005, http://www.nfwbo.org.

37. kemse & company, "About Us," accessed August 2006, http://www.kemseandcompany.com.

38. National Foundation for Women Business Owners, "Privately-Held, 50% or More Women-Owned Businesses in the United States: A Fact Sheet," accessed September 4, 2005, http://www.nfwbo.org.

39. Bridget McCrea, "Doing Her Part to Ensure the Safety of Children," AdvancingChildren Network, accessed August 2006, http://www.advancingwomen.com/_business/entpr_8.html.

40. Aliza Sherman, "The Opposite Sex: Women in Search of Money Still Face a Man's World," *Entrepreneur,* accessed August 2006, http://www.entrepreneur.com.

41. Forum for Women Entrepreneurs and Executives, accessed August 2006, http://www.fwe.org; Women Entrepreneurs, "Information . . . Action . . . Results," accessed August 2006, http://www.we-inc.org.

42. Robert Fairlie, "Self-Employed Business Ownership Rates in the United States: 1979–2003," Small Business Administration, accessed August 2006, http://www.sba.gov/advo.

43. Hispanic Trends, "Economic Clout," accessed August 2006, http://www.hispaniconline.com.

44. Robert Fairlie, "Self-Employed Business Ownership Rates in the United States."

45. Stephanie Clifford, "Business Ownership among Immigrant Women on the Rise," *Inc.,* accessed August 2006, http://www.inc.com.

46. Associated Press, "Arkansas Hispanics See Success in Business," July 30, 2005.

47. Cora Daniels, "Minority Entrepreneurs: Minority Rule," *Fortune,* accessed August 2006, http://www.money.cnn.com; Robert Lussier, Gregory Greenberg, and Joel Corman, "Bank Financing Discrimination against African-American Owned Small Business," Small Business Advancement National Center, University of Central Arkansas, accessed August 2006, http://www.sbaer.uca.edu; Karlyn Mitchell and Douglas K. Pearce, "Availability of Financing to Small Firms Using the Survey of Small Business Finances," Small Business Administration, accessed August 2006, http://www.sba.gov/advo.

48. "Testimony of Matthew R. Shay, President, International Franchise Association" Subcommittee on Economic Opportunity of the Committee on Veterans Affairs, U.S. House of Representatives, accessed September 5, 2005, http://www.franchise.org.

49. "Entrepreneur's 26th Annual Franchise 500," *Entrepreneur,* accessed August 2006, http://www.entrepreneur.com.

50. "Top Homebased Franchises 2005 Rankings," *Entrepreneur,* accessed August 2006, http://www.entrepreneur.com.

51. McDonald's, "New Restaurants," accessed August 2006, http://www.mcdonalds.com/corp; "McDonald's Franchise for Sale and McDonald's Franchise Information—Franchise Zone," *Entrepreneur,* accessed August 2006, http://www.entrepreneur.com; "Subway Franchise for Sale and Subway Franchise Information—Franchise Zone," *Entrepreneur,* accessed August 2006, http://www.entrepreneur.com.

52. "Welcome from Happy & Healthy Products Inc. and Our Fantastic Fruitfulls Franchisees!" Happy & Healthy Products Web site, accessed August 2006, http://www.fruitfull.com.

53. Gene Koprowski, "Successful Franchisees Embrace 'The System,'" *StartupJournal,* accessed August 2006, http://www.startupjournal.com.

54. David Welch, Dan Beucke, Kathleen Kerwin, Michael Arndt, Brian Hindo, Emily Thornton, and David Kiley, "Why GM's Plan Won't Work," *BusinessWeek Online,* accessed August 2006, http://www.businessweek.com.

55. Norihiko Shirouzu, "Dealers' Dilemma—Popular Asian Autos Seek More Space in Showrooms as U.S. Makers Try to Reduce," *Wall Street Journal,* 17 June 2005, p. B1.

56. Paulette Thomas, "Startup Q&A, Corporate Giants are Unlikely First Customers," *StartupJournal,* accessed August 2006, http://www.startupjournal.com.

57. Perri Capell, "Many Partnerships Form for the Wrong Reasons," *StartupJournal,* accessed August 2006, http://www.startupjournal.com.

58. "The 2005 *Fortune* 500: Full List," *Fortune,* accessed August 2006, http://www.money.cnn.com.

59. Internal Revenue Service, "IRS Launches Study of S Corporation Reporting Compliance," accessed August 2006, http://www.irs.gov.

60. Nolo Press, "Corporations FAQ: Who Should Form a Corporation?" accessed August 2006, http://www.nolo.com.

61. David Teather, "'Gimme a W, Gimme an A, Gimme an L . . . It's the Best Firm in the World': Retail Rocks at Annual Wal-Mart Rally," *The Guardian,* June 4, 2005, p. 27.

62. National Center for Employee Ownership, "Research and Statistics: A Statistical Profile of Employee Ownership," accessed August 2006, http://www.nceo.org.

63. National Center for Employee Ownership, "Largest Study Yet Shows ESOPs Improve Performance and Employee Benefits," accessed August 2006, http://www.nceo.org.

64. Information from San Francisco Ballet Web site, accessed August 2006, http://www.sfballet.org; Jesse Drucker and Almar Latour, "Verizon Wins Bidding for MCI; Qwest Drops Out," *Wall Street Journal,* May 3, 2005, p. A1.

65. Nikhil Deogun, Charles Forelle, Dennis K. Berman, and Emily Nelson, "Razor's Edge: P&G to Buy Gillette for $54 Billion," *Wall Street Journal,* January 28, 2005, p. A1.

66. Robert Weisman, "Merger Activity at Full Tilt, Even before Gillette: Number of Deals Up 8 Percent, in Part on Dollar's Weakness," *Boston Globe,* accessed August 2006, http://www.boston.com.

67. Christina Passariello, "Bacardi's Spirited Campaign—It Aims to Keep Grey Goose Vodka Flying above Rival Brands," *Wall Street Journal,* September 5, 2005, p. A4.

68. "Microsoft Acquires Teleo, Innovative VoIP Technology Company," Microsoft PressPass-Information for Journalists, accessed August 2006, http://www.microsoft.com.

69. Nikhil Deogun, Charles Forelle, Dennis K. Berman, and Emily Nelson, "Razor's Edge: P&G to Buy Gillette for $54 Billion."

70. "Transport4: What We Do," Transport 4 Web site, accessed August 2006, http://www.transport4.com.

71. David Fish, "Survey: Government-Owned Telecom Up 54 Percent," IT&T News, accessed August 2006, http://www.heartland.org.

Chapter 6

1. Idealab Web site, accessed August 2006, http://www.idealab.com; Nadira A. Hira, "Idealab Reloaded: Surprise! Ex-Dot-Com-Wizard Bill Gross Is Back," *Fortune,* accessed August 2006, http://www.money.cnn.com; Michael Liedtke, "Search Engine Pioneer Raises $10 Million for Latest Quest," Associated Press, accessed July 19, 2005, http://www.ap.com; "Planned Online Ad System to Charge Only If Purchase Made," Dow Jones International News, accessed July 18, 2005, http://www.dowjones.com.

2. "Crunching the Numbers: Highlights From the *Inc.* 500 CEO Survey," *Inc. 500 Special Issue,* Fall 2005, p. 109.

3. Burt Helm, "How I Did It: Hall of Fame Profile, Jim Ansara—On the Importance of Growing with Your Company," *Inc. 500 Special Issue,* p. 10, accessed August 2006, http://www.inc.com.

4. Nadine Heintz, "Training Wheels," *Inc.,* October 2005, p. 51.

5. "The Portal Site for All easyGroup Companies," easyGroup, accessed August 2006, http://www.easy.com.

6. Dean Foust, "BofA's Happy Surprise," *BusinessWeek,* February 27, 2005, p. 68.

7. Zoltan Acs, Pia Arenius, Michael Hay, and Maria Minniti, "Global Entrepreneurship Monitor: Executive Report," Global Entrepreneurship Monitor Consortium, accessed August 2006, http://www.gemconsortium.org.

8. "America's Young Entrepreneurs: Trend Data at-a-Glance," National Association for the Self-Employed, accessed August 2006, http://www.nase.org.

9. Robert W. Fairlie, "Table 4, Kauffman Index of Entrepreneurial Activity by Age," Kauffman Index of Entrepreneurial Activity, Ewing Marion Kauffman Foundation, accessed August 2006, http://www.kauffman.org.

10. Nancy J. Lyons, "Moonlight over Indiana," Inc.com, accessed August 2006, http://www.inc.com/magazine.

11. Pallavi Gogoi, "Liz Lange's Labor of Love," *BusinessWeek Online,* accessed August 2006, http://www.businessweek.com.

12. Thomas Stanley and William Danko, "Chapter One: Meet the Millionaire Next Door," in *The Millionaire Next Door: The Surprising Secrets of America's Wealthy,* accessed August 2006, http://www.nytimes.com.

13. Luisa Kroll and Allison Fass, "Billionaires Rush to Riches," October 26, 2005, News.com.au via Forbes.com, accessed, http://www.finance.news.com.au.

14. Kerry Dolan, "From Buses to Planes; How to Build an Airline from Scratch: First, Steal Ideas from JetBlue and Southwest?" *Forbes,* October 21, 2005, p. 118.

15. Office of Advocacy, U.S. Small Business Administration, "Frequently Asked Questions: Advocacy Small Business Statistics and Research," accessed August 2006, http://app1.sba.gov/faqs; Amy Knaup, "Survival and Longevity in the Business Employment Dynamics Data," *Monthly Labor Review* (Bureau of Labor Statistics), May 2005, p. 50.

16. Alison Stein, "Are You Paying Yourself Enough?" *Inc.,* accessed August 2006, http://www.inc.com.

17. *Kiplinger's Personal Finance,* May, p. 21, accessed August 2006, http://www.kiplinger.com/magazine.

18. Office of Advocacy, U.S. Small Business Administration, "The Facts about Small Business," accessed November 2, 2005, http://www.sba.gov/advo.

19. Jim Hopkins, "The New Entrepreneurs: Americans over 50," *USA Today,* January 18, 2005, p. A1.

20. Martha Irvine, "Young and Self-Employed," *Associated Press Newswires,* November 10, 2004.

21. Joshua Kurlantzick, "About Face," *Entrepreneur,* accessed August 2006, http://www.entrepreneur.com.

22. Mark Henricks, "Some Entrepreneurs Can't Find the Slow Lane," *StartupJournal,* accessed August 2006, http://www.startupjournal.com.

23. Ibid.

24. Rainbow Play Systems Web site, accessed August 2006, http://www.rainbowplay.com; Joseph Conlin, "Natural Order," Entrepreneur, accessed August 2006, http://www.entrepreneur.com.

25. Paulette Thomas, "Now What . . . Make It: In a Global Economy, It Isn't Easy to Transform an Idea into a Product," *Wall Street Journal,* May 9, 2005, p. R6.

26. Zoltan Acs, Pia Arenius, Michael Hay, and Maria Minniti, "Global Entrepreneurship Monitor: Executive Report."

27. Michelle Henery, "Four out of Ten Business Owners Say 'Never Again in the UK,'" *The Times,* June 16, 2005, p. 61.

28. "Top 100 Entrepreneurial Colleges for 2005," *Entrepreneur,* accessed August 2006, http://www.entrepreneur.com.

29. "Hinman CEOs Overview," Hinman Campus Entrepreneurship Opportunities Program, accessed August 2006, http://www.hinmanceos.umd.edu.

30. "Students in Free Enterprise," SIFE, accessed August 2006, http://www.sife.org.

31. Mark Henricks, "Honor Roll," *Entrepreneur,* accessed August 2006, http://www.entrepreneur.com.

32. Mark Henricks, "Honor Roll"; "About Us," Float Tech, accessed August 2006, http://www.floattech.com.

33. Amy Chozick, "Managing Technology—Appearances Are Deceiving," *Wall Street Journal,* September 19, 2005, p. R7.

34. Gwendolyn Bounds, "You Have a Great Idea; Now What?" *Wall Street Journal,* May 9, 2005, p. R1.

35. David Kesmodel, "Beyond eBay: Small E-Tailers Discover Life Outside The Big Online Marketplaces," *Wall Street Journal,* July 18, 2005, p. R8.

36. "About Alere," Alere Medical, accessed August 2006, http://www.alere.com.

37. "Segway Tours by City Segway Tours," City Segway Tours, accessed August 2006, http://www.citysegwaytours.com.

38. Cynthia Yeldell, "Segway Finds Niche among People with Disabilities," *Pittsburgh Post-Gazette,* October 12, 2005, p. E-2.

39. George Gendron, "The Origin of the Entrepreneurial Species," *Inc.,* February 2000, p. 106.

40. Gilat Satellite Network Web site, accessed August 2006, http://www.gilat.com.

41. Rosie Del Campo, "It's Important to Strike Right Work-Life Mix," *Toronto Star,* 13 October 2005, p. J07; Eric Beauchesne, "Entrepreneurs Generally Enjoy Happier Work Life," Small Business Centre, accessed August 2006, http://www.canada.com.

42. Mark Henricks, "Parent Trap?" *Entrepreneur,* accessed August 2006, http://www.entrepreneur.com.

43. George Gendron, "The Origin of the Entrepreneurial Species," p. 110.

44. LuLu's Dessert Factory Web site, accessed August 2006, http://www.lulusdessert.com; Michele Prather, "Gettin' Jiggly with It," *Entrepreneur,* accessed August 2006, http://www.entrepreneur.com.

45. Sherri Cruz, "LuLu's Back in OC, Battling with Costs," *Orange County Business Journal,* March 7, 2005, p. 3.

46. Mike Hofman, "Inside Innovative Minds," *Inc.,* accessed August 2006, http://www.inc.com/magazine; Bill Atkinson, "CEO Finds Taking Risks Is Fast Track to Success," *Baltimore Sun,* accessed August 2006, http://www.baltimoresun.com.

47. John Anderson, "The Company That Grew Too Fast," *Inc.,* November 2005, p. 104.

48. Abrahm Lustgarten, Brian Dumaine, Julie Creswell, Christopher Tkaczyk, Matthew Boyle, Nadira A. Hira, Kate Bonamici, Fred Vogelstein, and Julia Boorstin, "14 Innovators," *Fortune,* accessed August 2006, http://www.money.cnn.com.

49. "A Scientist, as Humanitarian," FLAVORx, accessed November 6, 2005, http://www.flavorx.com.

50. Neil Adler, "A Conversation with Kenny Kramm," *Washington Business Journal,* accessed November 6, 2005, http://washington.bizjournals.com.

51. George Gendron, "The Origin of the Entrepreneurial Species," pp. 109–110.

52. Abrahm Lustgarten et al., "14 Innovators."

53. Brad Howarth, "Motivation Factor," *Business Review Weekly,* January 27, 2005, p. 64.

54. "Firefly Phone," Firefly Web site, accessed August 2006, http://www.fireflymobile.com.

55. Ann Zimmerman, "Do the Research: To Understand the Market—and the Competition—for Your Idea, You'll Have to Delve beyond the Obvious," *Wall Street Journal,* May 9, 2005, p. R3.

56. Ibid.

57. Richard Craver, "Made in the USA; Furniture-Maker Bucks Trend toward Imports by Retooling and Hiring Back Former Workers," *Winston-Salem (NC) Journal,* September 11, 2005, p. 1.

58. "In Good Company: CEO Survey, Part II," *Inc.,* November 2005, p. 140.

59. Sarah Bartlett, "Seat of the Pants," *Inc.,* accessed August 2006, http://www.inc.com/magazine.

60. Darren Dahl, "Start-up Capital: CEO Survey, Part II," *Inc.,* November 2005, p. 140.

61. Neil Young, "Commentary: Eye on the Entrepreneur: Baltimore Entrepreneur Delivers Nurses Now," *(Baltimore, MD) Daily Record,* October 14, 2005.

62. Ibid.

63. Diya Gullapalli, "What You Need to Know Before Selling Off Equity," *StartupJournal,* accessed August 2006, http://www.startupjournal.com.

64. Darren Dahl, "Start-Up Capital."

65. Larry Olmsted, "Nonstop Innovation," *Inc.,* July 2005, p. 34.

66. "About Us" and "Management Team," eCompanies and Business.com Web sites, accessed August 2006, http://www.ecompanies.com and http://www.business.com.

Chapter 7

1. Lauri Giesen, "What Teens Want," *Internet Retailer,* accessed August 2006, http://internetretailer.com; Bob Tedeschi, "E-Commerce Report: Teenagers Are among Online Retailers' Most Sought-After Customers," *New York Times,* February 28, 2005, p. C3; Mark Albright, "Macy's Targets Young Women with Hip Web Site, Hot Fashions," *St. Petersburg (FL) Times,* accessed August 2006, www.sptimes.com; "Macy's to Launch New Website for Juniors," *Apparel Search,* accessed August 2006, http://www.apparelsearch.com.

2. "VeriSign Announces Valentine's Day-Related Online Shopping Activity," PR Newswire, LexisNexis Web site, accessed May 29, 2006, http://www.lexis-nexis.com.

3. "Web Integration: Then and Now," *Network World,* InfoTrac Web site, accessed March 16, 2005, http://www.infotrac.com.

4. Internet World Statistics, accessed August 2006, http://www.internetworldstats.com; Rob McGann, "Web Usage Growth Flatlines in U.S., Other Mature Markets," ClickZ Network, accessed August 2006, http://www.clickz.com.

5. Rob McGann, "Internet Edges Out Family Time More Than TV Time," ClickZ Network, accessed August 2006, http://www.clickz.com.

6. Rob McGann, "Broadband: High Speed, High Spend," ClickZ Network, accessed August 2006, http://www.clickz.com.

7. 2004 IBM Annual Report, accessed August 2006, http://www.ibm.com.

8. "Giving E-Procurement a Civic Twist," FCW.com, accessed March 23, 2005, http://www.fcw.com.

9. Laura Rush, "E-Commerce Growth Spurred by Maturation," ClickZ Network, accessed August 2006, http://www.clickz.com.

10. Betsey Streisand, "Make New Sales, But Keep the Old," *U.S. News & World Report,* accessed August 2006, http://www.usnews.com.

11. Amy Tsao, "Where Retailers Shop for Savings," BusinessWeek, accessed August 2006, http://www.businessweek.com.

12. Rob McGann, "Web-to-Store Consumers Spend, Shop More at Local Stores," ClickZ Network, accessed August 2006, http://www.clickz.com.

13. Timothy Mullaney, "The E Biz Surprise." *Business Week,* accessed August 2006, http://www.bwonline.com.

14. "More Businesses are Buying over the Internet," M2 Presswire, accessed May 29, 2006, http://www.lexis-nexis.com.

15. "About Us," Intelsat Business Network, accessed May 29, 2006, http://www.intelsat.com/aboutus/.

16. David Hannon, "Exchanges are Dead, but Collaboration Is Not," *Purchasing,* accessed August 2006, http://www.purchasing.com; Cara Cannella, "Why Online Exchanges Died," *Inc.,* accessed August 2006, http://www.inc.com; Arundhati Parmar, "A Focus on Services Helped Revive B2B E-Exchanges," *Marketing News,* accessed May 1, 2006, http://www.marketingpower.com.

17. "The Role of E-Marketplaces in Relationship-Based Supply Chains: A Survey," *IBM Systems Journal,* accessed May 29, 2006, http://www.infotrac.com.

18. "Ariba at Work: Customer Spotlight," Ariba, accessed May 29, 2006, http://www.ariba.com.

19. "General Information" and "Benefits," State of North Carolina E-Procurement Program, accessed August 2006, http://www.ncgov.com.

20. Estimate by Dr. Gene Huang, *Business Forecast 2005,* Sam M. Walton College of Business, University of Arkansas, January 28, 2005.

21. David Kaplan, "Internet Retailers Score Big," *Houston Chronicle,* accessed May 29, 2006, http://www.lexis-nexis.com.

22. Laura Rush, "E-Commerce Growth Spurred by Maturation," ClickZ Network, accessed August 2006, http://www.clickz.com.

23. Dan Reed, "Southwest Counters Cost Pressures with Longer Routes, Revved Growth," *USA Today,* accessed August 2006, http://www.usatoday.com.

24. "Southwest Airlines Sends Hottest Fares Directly to Customers' Computer Desktops," Southwest Airlines press release, accessed May 29, 2006, http://www.southwest.com.

25. "About Lands' End," Lands' End, accessed August 2006, http://www.landsend.com.

26. Rob McGann, "Broadband: High Speed, High Spend."

27. "Trends," Pew Internet and American Life Project, August 2006, http://www.pewinternet.org.

28. Laura Rush, "Women, Comparison Shopping Help Boost E-Commerce Holiday Revenues," ClickZ Network, accessed August 2006, http://www.clickz.com.

29. "Irrelevance through Constant Consumer Analysis," Jupiter Media Metrix, accessed March 6, 2005, http://www.jmm.com.

30. Robyn Greenspan, "E-Tailers Will See Green." ClickZ Network, accessed August 2006, http://www.clickz.com.

31. "About VeriSign," accessed August 2006, http://www.verisign.com.

32. Rob McGann, "Concerns over Online Threats this Holiday Season," ClickZ Network, accessed August 2006, http://www.clickz.com.

33. "Personal Data of 59,000 People Stolen," Associated Press, accessed March 22, 2005, http://www.yahoo.com.

34. Internet Crime Complaint Center, *Internet Fraud Crime Report,* Federal Bureau of Investigation, accessed August 2006, http://www.ic3.gov.

35. "How Not to Get Hooked by a Phishing Scam," FTC Consumer Alert, accessed August 2006, http://www.ftc.gov.

36. Bob Tedeschi, "Holiday Slowdowns and Crashes at Kmart.com, Amazon.com and Others Highlight the Web's Persistent Growing Pains," *New York Times,* accessed August 2006, http://www.nytimes.com.

37. Rob McGann, "Concerns over Online Threats This Holiday Season."

38. Kate Zernike, "Tired of TiVo? Beyond Blogs? Podcasts Are Here," *New York Times,* accessed August 2006, http://www.nytimes.com.

39. Riva Richmond, "Blogs Keep Internet Customers Coming Back," *Wall Street Journal,* March 1, 2005, p. B8.

40. "News Analysis: How Blogs Help Brands Build Trust Online," *Revolution,* accessed May 29, 2006, http://www.infotrac.com.

41. Amy Joyce, "More PR Than No-Holds-Barred on Bosses' Corporate Blogs," *Washington Post,* accessed August 2006, http://www.washingtonpost.com.

42. "Employee Blogs Can Be Good for Business," *PRWeek,* accessed March 3, 2005, http://www.infotrac.com.

43. Rob McGann, "Web-to-Store Consumers Spend, Shop More at Local Stores."

44. "Success Stories," Coremetrics, accessed August 2006, http://www.coremetrics.com.

45. Rob McGann, "Web Usage Growth Flatlines in U.S., Other Mature Markets," ClickZ Network, accessed August 2006, http://www.clickz.com.

46. Lucy Aitken, "E-Commerce: Survey of Surveys," *Management Today,* accessed August 29, 2006, http://www.infotrac.com.

Part 2 Launching Your Entrepreneurial Career

1. Michael Ames in *Small Business Management,* cited in "Are You Ready?" Small Business Administration, accessed August 2006, http://www.sba.gov.

2. U.S. Department of Labor, *Occupational Outlook Handbook,* 2006–2007 edition, Bureau of Labor Statistics, accessed August 2006, http://www.bls.gov.

3. Paulette Thomas, "How One Employee Became an Entrepreneur," *CollegeJournal,* accessed August 2006, http://www.collegejournal.com.

4. U.S. Department of Labor, "Career Guide to Industries," Bureau of Labor Statistics, accessed August 2006, http://www.bls.gov.

5. U.S. Small Business Administration, "Protecting Your Ideas," accessed August 2006, http://www.sba.gov.

Chapter 8

1. Ina Fried and Michael Kanellos, "Microsoft: We're in Fighting Shape," CNet News.com, accessed August 2006, http://news.com.com; Jay Greene, Steve Hamm, Diane Brady, and Mara Der Hovanesian, "Troubling Exits at Microsoft," *BusinessWeek,* accessed August 2006, http://www.businessweek.com; Robert A. Guth, "Think Pad: In Secret Hideaway, Bill Gates Ponders

Microsoft's Future," *Wall Street Journal,* accessed August 2006, http://online.wsj.com; Ina Fried, "Microsoft Gets Outside the Box with Software," CNet News.com, accessed August 2006, http://news.com.com.

2. Jared Sandberg, "The CEO in the Next Cube—Bosses Who Abandon Offices Win Kudos for Collegiality, But Make Neighbors Nervous," *Wall Street Journal,* June 22, 2005, p. B1.

3. Carol Hymowitz, "Middle Managers Are Unsung Heroes on Corporate Stage," *Wall Street Journal,* September 19, 2005, p. B1.

4. Melanie Trottman, "Nuts-and-Bolts Savings—To Cut Costs, Airlines Make More of Their Own Parts; Jettisoning a $719 Toilet Seat," *Wall Street Journal,* May 3, 2005, p. B1.

5. Robert A. Guth, "Think Pad."

6. Robert Guth, "Microsoft Revamp for Online Push Gains Urgency," *Wall Street Journal,* November 9, 2005, p. A3.

7. P. Glader, "Aluminum Foil: As Alcoa Struggles, O'Neill's Successor Tries New Direction," *Wall Street Journal,* October 12, 2005, p. A1.

8. Mark Maremont, "Tyco Figures Will Be Jailed at Least 7 Years—Judge Orders Kozlowski, Swartz to Also Pay Back $240 Million; CEO's 'Kleptocratic Management,'" *Wall Street Journal,* September 20, 2005, p. C1.

9. Quoted in "Conscience in a Cup of Coffee," U.S. News & World Report, October 31, 2005, p. 48.

10. Ann Zimmerman and Kris Hudson, "Target Practice: Looking Upscale, Wal-Mart Begins a Big Makeover," *Wall Street Journal,* September 17, 2005, p. A1.

11. Del Jones, "Dell: Take Time to Build," *USA Today,* August 2006, http://www.usatoday.com.

12. Nicole Gull, "Plan B (and C and D and . . .)," *Inc.,* accessed August 2006, http://www.inc.com.

13. Ann Zimmerman and Kris Hudson, "Target Practice."

14. Peter Grant and Dionne Searcey, "How to Watch TV," *Wall Street Journal,* November 9, 2005, p. D1.

15. Nikhil Deogun, Charles Forelle, Dennis Berman, and Emily Nelson, "Razor's Edge: P&G to Buy Gillette for $54 Billion," *Wall Street Journal,* January 28, 2005, p. A1.

16. "Corporate Information: Company Overview," Google, accessed August 2006, http://www.google.com.

17. "Bayer: Science for a Better Life," Bayer Annual Report 2004, accessed January 17, 2006.

18. Jennifer Saranow, "Smaller Models; 43 Crossovers to Choose From," *Wall Street Journal,* October 27, 2005, p. D1.

19. Starbucks Corporation Annual Report, accessed August 2006, http://www.starbucks.com; press releases, Starbucks Web site, accessed August 2006, http://www.starbucks.com.

20. Jack Speer, "Automakers Unveil New Hybrids at Detroit Show," National Public Radio, accessed August 2006, http://www.npr.org; Neal Boudette and Ann Keeton, "Toyota Expects Surge in Sales of Hybrid Vehicles," *Wall Street Journal,* August 4, 2005, p. D3.

21. David Bauder, "Profits Are Big, but Ratings Slip as Its Unique Niche among Networks Appears to Fade," *Houston Chronicle,* June 20, 2005, p. 3.

22. Business Writers, "Hibernia to Boost Credit Card Business; Capitol One's Muscle to Grow with Merger," *Times-Picayune,* May 22, 2005, p.1.

23. Robert Guth, "Getting Xbox 360 to Market—Microsoft Must Coordinate Game Player's 1,700 Parts to Ensure Big Enough Supply," *Wall Street Journal,* November 18, 2005, p. B1.

24. Thomas Kellner, "One Man's Trash . . . , " *Forbes,* accessed August 2006, http://www.forbes.com.

25. Louis Lavelle, "Another Crop of Sleazy CEOs?" *BusinessWeek,* accessed August 2006, http://www.businessweek.com.

26. J. Helyar, "Why Is This Man Smiling?" *Fortune,* accessed August 2006, http://www.money.cnn.com.

27. Kim Clark, "Flying High after Disaster," *U.S. News & World Report,* accessed August 2006, http://www.usnews.com.

28. "Living Our Values," Home Depot Web site, accessed January 17, 2006, http://careers.homedepot.com; Lorrie Grant, "Home Depot's Chief Builds on Big Dreams," *USA Today,* accessed August 2006, http://www.usatoday.com; Daintry Duffy, "Cultural Evolution," *CIO Enterprise,* CIO Web site, August 2006, http://www.cio.com.

29. "Hamburger University," McDonald's Web site, accessed August 2006, http://www.mcdonalds.com.

30. Janet Guyon, "The Soul of a Moneymaking Machine," *Fortune,* October 3, 2005, p. 113.

31. Jill Nash, "A Comprehensive Campaign Helps Gap Employees Embrace Cultural Change," *Communication World,* November 1, 2005, p. 42.

32. "The State of the Church," *Time,* accessed August 2006, http://www.time.com.

33. "Products & Services," 3M, accessed August 2006, http://www.3M.com.

34. Scott Hensley, "Christine Poon: Women to Watch (A Special Report)—In Line to Lead," *Wall Street Journal,* October 31, 2005, p. R6.

35. Jared Sandberg, "Office Democracies: How Many Bosses Can One Person Have?" *Wall Street Journal,* November 22, 2005, p. B1.

Chapter 9

1. Breakdown at Sago Mine: Trouble and Tragedy Two Miles In," *Pittsburgh Post-Gazette,* accessed August 2006, http://www.post-gazette.com; Ted David, "Massey Energy—Chairman & CEO Interview," CNBC/Dow Jones Business Video, accessed September 9, 2005, http://www.cnbc.com; Dave Anderson, "Few Graduates Dig Mining," *Deseret Morning News,* accessed August 26, 2005, http://deseretnews.com; Patrick Barta, "Lack of Qualified Workers Strains Mining Companies," *Wall Street Journal,* accessed August 2006, http://online.wsj.com; "Mining Schools Set to Open, Legislators Told," Associated Press, accessed August 9, 2005, http://www.ap.org.

2. Quoted in "My Golden Rule," *Business 2.0,* December 2005, p. 110.

3. Trilogy Web site, accessed August 2006, http://www.trilogy.com.

4. Timothy Aeppel, "Firms' New Grail: Skilled Workers—U.S. Manufacturers Report Shortages Are Widespread; Critics Cite Training Cuts," *Wall Street Journal,* November 22, 2005, p. A2.

5. Nanette Byrnes and Amy Barrett, "Star Search: How to Recruit, Train, and Hold On to Great People. What Works, What Doesn't," *BusinessWeek,* October 10, 2005, p. 68.

6. "New .jobs Suffix Approved for Worldwide Recruiting/Hiring," *Human Resource Department Management Report,* May 2005, p. 9.

7. D. Lewis, "EEOC: Damage Awards; Reach $420m in 2004," *Boston Globe,* February 20, 2005, p. D2.

8. Sam Walker, "The NFL's Smartest Team," *Wall Street Journal,* September 30, 2005, p. W1.

9. Robert Levering, Milton Moskowitz, Ann Harrington, Nadira Hira, and Christopher Tkaczyk, "The 100 Best Companies to Work For," *Fortune,* January 24, 2005, p. 72.

10. Matthew Boyler and Ellen Kratz, "The Wegmans Way," *Fortune,* January 24, 2005, p. 62.

11. M. Totty, "Better Training through Gaming," *CareerJournal,* April 25, 2005, p. R6.

12. J. Borzo, "Almost Human: Using Avatars for Corporate Training, Advocates Say, Can Combine the Best Parts of Face-to-Face Interaction and Computer-based Learning," *Wall Street Journal,* May 24, 2004, p. R4.

13. J. Borzo, "Almost Human."

14. Nanette Byrnes and Amy Barrett, "Star Search."

15. Kathleen Gallagher, "GE Investing in Future Leaders; Executive's Program Challenges a Select Few," *Milwaukee Journal Sentinel,* October 24, 2005, p. D1.

16. "Halogen eAppraisal Case Studies," Halogen Software, accessed August 2006, http://www.halogensoftware.com.

17. Michael Kinsman, "Coach for Executives," *San Diego Union-Tribune,* October 11, 2005, p. C-1.

18. "Employer Costs for Employee Compensation Summary," Bureau of Labor Statistics, accessed August 2006, http://www.bls.gov.

19. Lee Hawkins Jr., "As GM Battles Surging Costs, Workers' Health Becomes Issue," *Wall Street Journal,* April 7, 2005, p. A1.

20. Ann Zimmerman, Robert Matthews, and Kris Hudson, "Can Employers Alter Hiring Policies to Cut Health Costs?" *Wall Street Journal,* October 27, 2005, p. B1.

21. Ibid.

22. "Paid Family Leave Insurance," Employee Development Department, accessed August 2006, http://www.edd.ca.gov.

23. Jeff Opdyke and Kelly Greene, "Is Your Retirement Money Safe? UAL's Move to Default Highlights Range of Risks and Protections for Different Types of Plans," *Wall Street Journal,* May 12, 2005, p. D1.

24. Deborah Myers, "Cafeteria Plans Offer Flexible Insurance Options," *Alaska Business Monthly,* accessed December 4, 2005, http://akbizmag.com.

25. Robert Levering and Milton Moskowitz, "The 100 Best Companies to Work For," *Fortune,* January 24, 2005, p. 72.

26. Ibid.

27. Jill Carlson, "Employers Can Help Employee Caregivers Win on Two Fronts," *Capital Region Business Journal,* December 1, 2005, p. 36.

28. Knight Ridder/Tribune Business News, "Staffing Survey Reveals Rise in Employees' Personal Days Off," *Daily Oklahoman,* November 20, 2005.

29. Shirley Won, "Doing Good Helps You Do Well at Work; Corporate Volunteerism Grows as Companies Realize Host of Benefits for Staff and Themselves," *Globe and Mail,* January 19, 2005, p. C1.

30. Joyce Gannon, "Study Says Flex Time Boosts Morale While Reducing Turnover," *Pittsburgh Post-Gazette,* November 8, 2005.

31. Katherine Lewis, "This Time-Share Involves Working," *Grand Rapids (MI) Press,* November 27, 2005, p, H1.

32. Ibid.

33. "Annual Survey Shows Americans Are Working from Many Different Locations Outside Their Employer's Office," International Telework Association and Council, accessed August 2006, http://www.workingfromanywhere.org.

34. Nanette Byrnes and Amy Barrett, "Star Search."

35. Kazuhiro Shimamura, Arran Scott, and Ginny Parker, "Sanyo to Cut Staff 15%, Shut Factories," *Wall Street Journal,* July 6, 2005, p. A3.

36. Frank Byrt, "EDS to Double Jobs Outsourced to Low-Wage Regions in 2 Years," *Wall Street Journal,* December 1, 2005, p. B2.

37. Quoted in "How I Got There," *Newsweek,* October 24, 2005, p. 59.

38. Carol Hymowitz, "Readers Share Tales of Jobs Where Strategy Became Meeting Target," *Wall Street Journal,* March 22, 2005, p. B1.

39. Pampered Chef Web site, accessed August 2006, http://www.pamperedchef.com.

40. "Union Members in 2004," Bureau of Labor Statistics, accessed December 5, 2005, http://www.bls.gov.

41. "Major Work Stoppages in 2004," Bureau of Labor Statistics, accessed August 2006, http://www.bls.gov.

42. Ibid.

43. Gary Fields, Timothy Aeppel, Kris Maher, and Janet Adam, "Can the New Economy Be Organized?" *Wall Street Journal,* July 27, 2005, p. B1.

44. J. Lynn Lunsford, "Boeing, Idled for a Month, Agrees to Meet Most of Union's Demands," *Wall Street Journal,* September 26, 2005, p. A3.

45. Kris Maher, "Labor Leaders Say Multination Effort Targets Wal-Mart," *Wall Street Journal,* August 23, 2005, p. B2.

46. Amy Merrick and Kris Maher, "Using Temps Proves Potent at Northwest," *Wall Street Journal,* August 29, 2005, p. B1.

47. Robert Matthews and Kris Maher, "Labor's PR Problem—As More Workers Find Unions Weak and Irrelevant, Leaders Seek to Restore Positive Image," *Wall Street Journal,* August 15, 2005, p. B1.

48. Ibid.

49. Ibid.

50. Gary Fields, et al., "Can the New Economy Be Organized?"

Chapter 10

1. Alan Deutschman, "The Un-CEO," *Fast Company,* accessed August 2006, http://www.fastcompany.com; Richard Donkin, "New Angle on the Search for Workplace Flexibility," *Financial Times,* accessed August 2006, http://www.ft.com; Sara J. Welch, "The Fabric of Success," *Successful Meetings,* August 2006, http://www.mimegasite.com; Chris Markham, "Full Bore at Gore," accessed August 2006, *Arizona Daily Sun,* http://www.azdaily-sun.com; Alan Deutschman, "The Fabric of Creativity," *Fast Company,* accessed August 2006, http://www.fastcompany.com.

2. "About A&A," Anderson & Associates, accessed August 2006, http://www.andassoc.com.

3. Paul Dellinger, "Workers Buy Anderson & Associates," *Roanoke Times & World News,* May 8, 2005, p. 16.

4. Jan Norman, "People Power: A Costa Mesa Engineering Firm Empowers Its Workers with Financial Information to Build Business and Avoid Layoffs," *Orange County Register,* March 23, 2005, p. 1.

5. "A Statistical Profile of Employee Ownership," National Center for Employee Ownership, accessed August 2006, http://www.nceo.org.

6. Andrew Blackman, "You're the Boss: New Accounting Rules May Reduce the Number of Employee-Owned Firms; But Anson Industries Sees the Benefits Far Outweighing the Costs," *Wall Street Journal,* April 11, 2005, p. R5.

7. "A Statistical Profile of Employee Ownership."

8. Andrew Blackman, "You're the Boss."

9. "How to Choose an Employee Stock Plan for Your Company," National Center for Employee Ownership, accessed August 2006, http://www.nceo.org.

10. "Our Core Values," Whole Foods Market, accessed August 2006, http://www.wholefoodsmarket.com.

11. S. Thurm, "Teamwork Raises Everyone's Game—Having Employees Bond Benefits Companies More than Promoting 'Stars,'" *Wall Street Journal,* November 7, 2005, p. B8.

12. Jack Gordon, "Do Your Virtual Teams Deliver Only Virtual Performance?" *Training,* June 1, 2005, p. 20.

13. Mallory Stark, "The Five Keys to Successful Teams," Working Knowledge from Harvard Business School, PricewaterhouseCoopers, accessed August 2006, http://hbswk.hbs.edu.

14. Lingling Wei, "Brokers Increasingly Use Teamwork," *Wall Street Journal,* February 23, 2005.

15. Laura Landro, "The Informed Patient: Bringing Surgeons Down to Earth—New Programs Aim to Curb Fear that Prevents Nurses from Flagging Problems," *Wall Street Journal,* November 16, 2005, p. D1.

16. Ibid.

17. Jessica Mintz, "Career Journal: The Jungle," *Wall Street Journal,* August 30, 2005, p. B6.

18. Vanessa Fuhrmans, "Oops! As Health Plans Become More Complicated, They're Also Subject to a Lot More Costly Mistakes," *Wall Street Journal,* January 24, 2005, p. R4.

19. Christopher Tkaczyk and Matthew Boyle, "Follow These Leaders," *Fortune,* December 12, 2005, p. 125.

20. Ibid.

21. Joann Lublin, "The 'Open Inbox'—Some CEOs Stay Up Late Reading Employee E-Mails; Replies Can Be Brief: 'Thanks,'" *Wall Street Journal,* October 10, 2005, p. B1.

22. Peter Loftus, "Send and Save: Regulations on Storing Old E-Mails Can Be a Huge Burden for Small Firms," *Wall Street Journal,* September 19, 2005, p. R7.

23. Gretchen Hoover, "Maintaining Employee Engagement when Communicating Difficult Issues: An IABC Survey Shows That Companies That Take a Strong Position and Answer Questions as Forthrightly as Possible Reap the Benefits," *Communication World,* November 1, 2005, p. 25.

24. Sheri Rosen, "Carry on the Conversation: Helping Employees Make Sense of What Happens at Work," *Communication World,* March 1, 2005, p. 24.

25. Kevin Voigt, "Making the Rumor Mill Work for You," *Asian Wall Street Journal,* January 21, 2005, p. P1.

26. Ibid.

27. Albert Mehrabian, *Silent Messages* (Belmont, CA: Wadsworth, 1971); Albert Mehrabian, "Communication without Words," *Psychology Today,* September 1968, pp. 53–55.

28. Marilyn Much, "Stopping Workplace Incivility; More Companies Realize that On-the-Job Rudeness Can Mean Lower Revenue," *Investor's Business Daily,* February 28, 2005, p. A7.

29. Associated Press, "Wendy's Hopes Arrest Will Bring Back Customers: Investigators Call Finger Incident a Hoax," MSNBC, accessed August 2006, http://www.msnbc.msn.com.

30. Trebor Banstetter, "Crash Tests Southwest's Disaster Response," *Fort Worth Star-Telegram,* December 10, 2005, p. 1A.

31. "A 1993 Instance of Product Tampering Resulted in Syringes Being Found in Cans of Pepsi," Urban Legends Reference Pages, accessed August 2006, http://www.snopes.com.

Chapter 11

1. Russell Gold and Michael M. Phillips, "Gulf Energy Facilities Get Off to a Slow Restart after Storms," *Wall Street Journal,* accessed August 2006, http://online.wsj.com; Chip Cummins, Bhushan Bahree, and Jeffrey Ball, "Gulf Coast: Why the World Is One Storm Away from Energy Crisis," *Wall Street Journal,* accessed August 2006, http://online.wsj.com; Jessica Resnick-Ault, Beth Heinsohn and Bhushan Bahree, "Gulf Coast Refineries Hunker Down," *Wall Street Journal,* accessed August 2006, http://online.wsj.com.

2. Neal Boudette and Norihiko Shirouzu, "Amid Price War, Chrysler to Revamp Manufacturing—Move to 'Flexible' Plants Aims to Improve Efficiency in Fragmented Auto Market," *Wall Street Journal,* August 2, 2005, p. A1.

3. William Hoffman, "Dell Beats the Clock," *Traffic World,* October 24, 2005.

4. Jennifer Yario, "2005 Top Fab: IBM," *Semiconductor International,* December 1, 2005, p. 55.

5. "Robotic Palletizing Leads to 55 Percent Productivity Gain at JTM Products," *Robotics World,* September 1, 2005, p. 14.

6. Allan Madrid, "Gang Run; VistaPrint Produces Thousands of Short-Run Jobs Daily on 400 Presses by Automating Combo Runs," *Graphic Arts Monthly,* August 1, 2005, p. 52.

7. James Salzer, "'Growing Jobs' No Snap: Perdue Finds Task Easier Said Than Done," *Atlanta Journal-Constitution,* August 10, 2005, p. C1.

8. Ed Anderson, "Workers Key to Luring Businesses; Executives Rank Work Force Issues as Most Important," *(New Orleans, LA) Times-Picayune,* January 27, 2005, p. 1.

9. Neal Boudette and Norihiko Shirouzu, "Amid Price War, Chrysler to Revamp Manufacturing."

10. Gary S. Vasilash, "Honda's Hat Trick," Automotive Manufacturing and Production, accessed August 2006, http://www.autofieldguide.com.

11. Ford Motor Company press releases, accessed August 2006, http://media.ford.com.

12. Daniel Michaels and J. Lynn Lunsford, "Streamlined Plane Making: Boeing, Airbus Look to Car Companies' Methods to Speed Up Jetliner Production," *Wall Street Journal,* April 1, 2005, p. B1.

13. Stephanie Fitch, "The Progress of Change—Inch by Inch," *Forbes,* accessed August 2006, http://www.forbes.com; Allison Linn, "Boeing Moving Right Along," *The Morning News,* April 12, 2002, p. 7C.

14. "Spend Management Overview," Ariba, accessed August 2006, http://www.ariba.com.

15. Ed Christman, "Retail Track: Best Buy to Rely on Vendor-Managed Pipeline," *Billboard,* January 29, 2005.

16. J. Bonasia, "Just-in-Time Cuts Costs, But Has Risks, as Dock Lockout Shows System Increases Rate of Deliveries," *Investor's Business Daily,* accessed December 16, 2005, http://www.investors.com.

17. Jeff Sabatini, "Turning Japanese," Automotive Manufacturing and Production, accessed August 2006, http://www.autofieldguide.com.

18. Nicholas Enticknapp, "Getting the Best Measure of the Business," *Computer Weekly,* November 15, 2005, p. 44.

19. J. Bonasia, "GE Black Belts to the Rescue; Consultants from Firm's Financial Arm Help Borrowers Improve Processes," *Investor's Business Daily,* April 25, 2005, p. A10.

20. J. Briscoe, S. Fawcett, and R. Todd, "The Implementation and Impact of ISO 9000 among Small Manufacturing Enterprises," *Journal of Small Business Management,* July 2005, p. 309.

Part 3 Launching Your Management Career

1. U.S. Department of Labor, "Tomorrow's Jobs," *Occupational Outlook Handbook,* 2006–2007 edition, Bureau of Labor Statistics, accessed August 2006, http://www.bls.gov.

2. U.S. Department of Labor, "Administrative Services Managers," *Occupational Outlook Handbook,* 2006–2007 edition, Bureau of Labor Statistics, accessed August 2006, http://www.bls.gov.

3. U.S. Department of Labor, "Construction Managers," *Occupational Outlook Handbook,* 2006–2007 edition, Bureau of Labor Statistics, accessed August 2006, http://www.bls.gov.

4. U.S. Department of Labor, "Food Service Managers," *Occupational Outlook Handbook,* 2006–2007 edition, Bureau of Labor Statistics, accessed August 2006, http://www.bls.gov.

5. U.S. Department of Labor, "Human Resources, Training, and Labor Relations Managers and Specialists," *Occupational Outlook Handbook,* 2006–2007 edition, Bureau of Labor Statistics, accessed August 2006, http://www.bls.gov.

6. U.S. Department of Labor, "Lodging Managers," *Occupational Outlook Handbook,* 2006–2007 edition, Bureau of Labor Statistics, accessed August 2006, http://www.bls.gov.

7. U.S. Department of Labor, "Purchasing Managers, Buyers, and Purchasing Agents," *Occupational Outlook Handbook,* 2006–2007 edition, Bureau of Labor Statistics, accessed August 2006, http://www.bls.gov.

8. U.S. Department of Labor, "Medical and Health Services Managers," *Occupational Outlook Handbook,* 2006–2007 edition, Bureau of Labor Statistics, accessed January 25, 2006, http://www.bls.gov.

9. U.S. Department of Labor, "Industrial Production Managers," *Occupational Outlook Handbook,* 2006–2007 edition, Bureau of Labor Statistics, accessed August 2006, http://www.bls.gov.

Chapter 12

1. Whole Foods Web site, accessed August 2006, http://www.wholefoodsmarket.com; Daniel McGinn, "The Green Machine," *Newsweek,* March 21, 2005, pp. E8–E12; Bruce Horovitz, "A Whole New Ballgame in Grocery Shopping," *USA Today,* March 9, 2005, pp. B1–B2; Seth Lubove, "Food Porn," *Forbes,* February 14, 2005, pp. 102–12.

2. Daniel McGinn, "The Green Machine."

3. American Marketing Association, "AMA Adopts New Definition of Marketing," MarketingPower.com, accessed August 2006, http://www.marketingpower.com.

4. "Crazy about Curbside," About.com, accessed August 16, 2005, http://houston.about.com; Bruce Horovitz, "Casual Dining Puts Spin on Drive-Thru," *USA Today,* September 20, 2004, p. B1.

5. Yuri Kageyama, "Apple Opens iTunes Music Store in Japan," Yahoo! News, accessed August 4, 2005, http://www.yahoo.com.

6. Andrew Mennie, "The Value of Customer Satisfaction," CRM Today, accessed August 2006, http://www.crm2day.com.

7. Ron Kaufman, "How Does Singapore Airlines Fly So High?" CRM Today, accessed July 11, 2005, http://www.crm2day.com.

8. Ibid.

9. "Social Enterprise," Harvard Business School, accessed August 2006, http://www.hbs.edu.

10. Betsy Kroll, "Fashion Statements," *Time,* August 8, 2005, p. 75.

11. Jonah Freedman, "The Fortunate 50," *Sports Illustrated,* July 4, 2005, pp. 65–69.

12. "Beijing 2008 Marketing Plan Officially Launched," PR Newswire, accessed August 8, 2005, http://www.news.com.com.

13. United Nations Food and Agriculture Organization, "About World Food Day," accessed August 2006, http://www.fao.org.

14. Barbara K! Web site, accessed August 2006, http://www.barbarak.com; Allen P. Roberts, "How I Did It: Barbara K," *Inc.,* May 2005, pp. 112–14; Penelope Green, "Home Improvement, Self-Improvement," *New York Times,* May 8, 2005, pp. 11-1, 11-4.

15. "KFC Hits Home Run in China," Fox News, accessed August 2006, http://www.foxnews.com.

16. John Gartner, "Smart Car Seeks Small Niche," Wired News, accessed August 2006, http://www.wired.com.

17. Teenage Research Unlimited, accessed August 2006, http://www.teenresearch.com.

18. Michael Barbaro, "Wal-Mart Trend Office Seeks Out What's Hip," *The Morning News,* August 14, 2005, pp. 1D, 3D.

19. Teenage Research Unlimited.

20. Melanie Wells, "Have It Your Way," *Forbes,* February 14, 2005, pp. 78–86.

21. Daniel McGinn, "From Harvard to Las Vegas," *Newsweek,* April 18, 2005, pp. E8–E14.

22. Emily Fredrix, "What's Brown and White and Bread All Over?" Yahoo! News, accessed August 9, 2005, http://www.yahoo.com.

23. David Welch, "GM Goes Gunning for the Coasts," *BusinessWeek,* June 27, 2005, p. 14.

24. Bath and Body Works Web site, accessed August 2006, http://www.bathandbodyworks.com.

25. "Miss Independent Steps Up to the D-I-Y Plate," Lowe's, accessed August 2006, http://www.lowes.mediaroom.com.

26. Nicholas Varchaver, "Pitchman for the Gray Revolution," *Fortune,* July 11, 2005, pp. 63–72.

27. Ibid.; statistics based on a Merrill Lynch survey of 3,448 Americans born between 1946 and 1964.

28. Jeremy Caplan, "Gotta Have It," *Time,* August 8, 2005, pp. 46–47.

Box."